Aging as a Social Process

Canadian Perspectives

Fourth Edition

Barry D. McPherson

OXFORD

UNIVERSITY PRESS

1904 ♦ 2004

100 YEARS OF
CANADIAN PUBLISHING

OXFORD
UNIVERSITY PRESS

70 Wynford Drive, Don Mills, Ontario M3C 1J9
www.oup.com/ca

Oxford University Press is a department of the University of Oxford.
It furthers the University's objective of excellence in research, scholarship,
and education by publishing worldwide in

Oxford New York
Auckland Cape Town Dar es Salaam Hong Kong Karachi
Kuala Lumpur Madrid Melbourne Mexico City Nairobi
New Delhi Shanghai Taipei Toronto

Oxford is a trade mark of Oxford University Press
in the UK and in certain other countries

Published in Canada
by Oxford University Press

National Library of Canada Cataloguing in Publication

McPherson, Barry D.
Aging as a social process: Canadian perspectives / Barry D. McPherson. — 4th ed.

Includes bibliographical references and index.
ISBN-10: 0-19-541902-2   ISBN-13: 978-0-19-541902-3

1. Aging—Social aspects. 2. Older people—Social conditions.
3. Aging—Social aspects—Canada. 4. Older people—Canada–Social conditions. I. Title.

HQ1061.M38 2004   305.26   C2004-902269-5

Cover design: Brett Miller
Cover image: Denis Felix / Getty Images

3 4 - 07 06
This book is printed on permanent (acid-free) paper ∞.
Printed in Canada

CONTENTS

Note: each chapter ends with Notes and References

To be able to learn is to be young, and whoever keeps the joy of learning in him or her remains forever young.

J.G. Bennett (1897–1974)

Dedication

To my father, David (1911–2002) who, early in my life, emphasized the importance of grammar, spelling, proofreading, and editing, never knowing then how many words would flow over my life course because of his insistence on writing carefully, thoroughly, and critically.

In earlier editions of this book I reported how he and my mother exemplified, into their late 80s, active and healthy aging with travels to China, New Zealand, and Africa, and a tour of Scotland with me as the designated driver; and how he invested actively and wisely in the stock market and in his extended family. That was the good side of aging. Prior to writing this edition, we acquired first-hand experience with the less pleasant side of later life as he and I spent the last four months of his life struggling with access to, and the quality of, acute care and home care; and with my mother's eventual, but very difficult, adaptation to living in a retirement home. Some of these personal experiences are reflected in this edition.

To Ellen Gee (1950–2002), scholar, friend, colleague, and mentor par excellence to many across Canada. Her varied and significant contributions to basic and applied knowledge and to policy development are cited in almost every chapter of this book. All Canadians, whether scholars or aging citizens, are impoverished by the loss of her creative, critical, and analytical contributions to knowledge, practice, and policy.

PREFACE

This book was written while I was on administrative leave after serving as a Dean of Graduate Studies and Research for 15 consecutive years. It was a time of reflection and interpretation, and hopefully, these elements are present to a greater extent in this fourth edition. Throughout, the objective has been to present a synthesis and interpretation of social science research and census data concerning individual and population aging in Canada. The emphasis is on identifying, describing, and explaining patterns, processes, and current issues associated with individual and population aging, rather than on describing programs or providing prescriptions for older Canadians. This approach enables students and practitioners to acquire basic knowledge about older people and to develop an understanding of aging processes and issues that you, your parents, and your grandparents may experience across the life course. The book includes more than just information to be mastered for a mid-term or a final examination. As you read, personalize the information so that you are better informed and are prepared to move through life with reflection and understanding, to help family members as they age, to participate in an aging society as an employee or as a volunteer serving older adults, and to function as a concerned global citizen who can lobby or vote with valid knowledge about aging-related issues confronting your community, region, province, or the world.

The 1983 edition of this book was the first textbook on aging in Canada, and was written at a time when few scholarly resources about aging were available in Canada. The second and third (1990 and 1998) editions reflected the growth of Canadian research about aging in Canada. This edition includes even more 'made-in-Canada'

knowledge about aging. That is why, for the first time, the book is subtitled 'Canadian Perspectives'.

Each chapter has been rewritten and updated, although some of the classic research studies from the earlier editions are retained. Moreover, the structure has been revised in response to suggestions from students and faculty who have used previous editions, and new chapters on individual aging, and health and aging, have been added. As well, new or expanded sections are included on such topics as home care, homelessness, gay and lesbian relationships, being childless in later life, the impact of physical and cognitive aging on daily living in later life, sexuality and later life relationships, ethics for an aging population, human rights in later life, and dying with dignity. A glossary defines concepts that appear in boldface in the text, and an appendix lists study resources (handbooks, journals, monographs, encyclopedias, and Internet websites). And, as of January 2004, when this book went to press, all available data from the 2001 Canadian census that pertain to older persons have been included. Additional 2001 census data and analyses will continue to appear until data from the 2006 mini-census are released, sometime after 2007 or 2008. For the most recent census data, visit the Statistics Canada website (www.statcan.ca).

Each chapter opens with 'Focal Points', a list of questions about the issues and/or ideas discussed in the chapter. To encourage debate and reflection and to develop critical thinking and observational skills, each chapter concludes with a section entitled 'For Reflection, Debate or Action'. Hopefully, the focal points and the stimuli for reflection, debate, or action will enable you to become a more critical thinker who questions commonly held assumptions, myths, and erroneous beliefs about aging and older people, both in your family and your community. Critical thinking and reflection are essential skills to acquire since uncertainty, differing opinions and interpretations, and even controversy concerning issues, processes, programs, or policies for aging adults or an aging society are prevalent in contemporary Canadian society. In each chapter references are cited in the text or in a note. These serve a twofold purpose. First, they provide theoretical or research support for the ideas. Second, they are a resource to help you locate and use primary sources in the basic literature. These sources will be useful if you are required to write a term paper on a specific topic, or if you wish to acquire additional information about a particular subject.

Before social policies and programs for older Canadians can be initiated, we must identify and verify that a problem or a situation exists. We must understand *why* and *how* the problem or issue evolved, and then find alternative solutions. Guesswork, hunches, or past practices are not sufficient. Nor will programs and policies implemented in another community or country work in every context. Rather, new information must be produced through research and then applied if effective policies and programs are to be implemented. Moreover, research can refute prevailing myths about older persons, thereby changing or eliminating some of the negative stereotypes that we may hold about aging and about the later stages of life.

This book uses a variety of theoretical and methodological orientations to describe and explain aging processes. Although it might be desirable to write a book from a single theoretical perspective, this is impossible at present since the social science literature about aging and later life requires a number of perspectives from a variety of disciplines if a more complete understanding of social phenomena is to be realized. However, throughout this edition, the life-course perspective is employed as an overriding framework since events, actions, decisions, constraints, and

opportunities at earlier stages in life often have cumulative effects at later stages, both for aging individuals (namely, you) and aging birth cohorts (for example, the baby boomers). Moreover, unlike in previous editions, more content is based on knowledge generated by the interpretive perspective and by qualitative research, which reflects the increasing use of these approaches by the Canadian research community.

The material in this book is based on the premise that aging, as a social process, involves multi-level and complex interactions between individuals and various social structures; within changing social, economic, political, and physical environments; and across diverse cultural contexts, all of which vary at specific periods in history. Thus, aging as a social process is considered from an interacting micro- (individual) perspective and a macro- (societal) perspective. This book has three general objectives:

1. To provide you with basic concepts, theories, and methodologies that can be used to understand social phenomena related to individual and population aging; and to develop critical thinking, as well as observational and interpretive skills. Where possible, alternative explanations for aging processes are emphasized more than a single description or interpretation of a process or problem.

2. To sensitize you to the fact that aging is not just a biological process, but an equally complex social process. In fact, you may be left with the impression that relatively little is known about aging as a social process. Herein lies a challenge to the curious, innovative reader who may wish to pursue a career in this field.

3. To make you aware of the dynamic interplay between your individual life course and the local, national, and global historical and cultural forces that shape your life experiences and opportunities. Aging, as a lifelong

process, must be of interest and concern to people of all ages and in all communities and countries.

In conclusion, despite the growth in knowledge about aging in Canada, the sociology of aging is still in its infancy. Thus, you should become a critical reader and thinker, question carefully, and discuss with others the validity and applicability of research findings presented in any single study. One published article on a particular subject does not represent the absolute truth. Indeed, even many research studies on a topic may not provide a complete and valid explanation of a particular process, pattern, or problem. This is especially true where attributes such as gender, ethnicity, education, place and type of residence, health status, income, or occupation have a profound impact on aging processes and on the everyday life of older adults. To illustrate, many studies describe only one slice of a particu-

lar social setting or community (often white, middle-class, Anglo-Saxon older men) at one point in time (for example, 2003). Other relevant social, individual, cultural, structural, or historical factors may not be considered in the analysis and interpretation of the results. Therefore, I encourage you to search for, and debate the merits of, alternative explanations, and to be cautious in what you accept as fact—including what you read in this book.

Finally, the test of how well a book serves as a learning resource is whether students find the material useful, interesting, clearly written, and comprehensive. Please provide feedback about this book to your instructor and to the author (bmcphers@wlu.ca).

Barry D. McPherson, Ph.D.
Waterloo, Ontario
January 2004

ACKNOWLEDGEMENTS

Writing a book is a lonely and formidable task that cannot be completed without the support and assistance of friends and colleagues. First, thanks are due to the many professors, students, and practitioners across Canada who submitted constructive criticisms about the content and structure of previous editions, especially Norah Keating, Sherry Anne Chapman, and Andrew Wister. I am especially indebted to Ingrid Connidis, who in the fall of 2002, as I was writing this fourth edition, provided a chapter-by-chapter critique each week as she and her students used the third edition.

At various times during the research and writing stage, substantive input, critical feedback, and support were provided by such close colleagues and friends as Victor Marshall, Anne Martin Matthews, Mark Rosenberg, and Carolyn Rosenthal. At Health Canada, Susan Fletcher and her colleagues provided important resources about Aboriginal people. My good friend Bill Herzog spent his early retirement days filling my mail and e-mail box with a weekly supply of articles about aging and older adults. These were neatly scissored from the many magazines and newspapers he consumes daily. Some of these clippings appear as Highlights. Bill, never stop reading, clipping, or sharing. I also wish to acknowledge the continuing informal support of my former administrative assistant, Janet Bannister, and my successor as Dean, Adele Reinhartz, for making the resources of my former office available during the writing and production of this book.

Behind every author is an efficient and diligent research assistant. For this edition, I was fortunate to work with Joanna Jacobs, a Ph.D. candidate in sociology at the University of Waterloo. Throughout the writing and editing stage, Joanna was a critical and involved colleague who not only completed the necessary clerical work, but also added substance to the text by providing new references, statistics, and sources for the Highlights. Throughout the writing and editing stage she provided a critical eye for typos and often questioned meanings and interpretations as she read the numerous drafts. Joanna, thank you for your interest and input, and all the best for a successful academic career. Hopefully, this experience has not discouraged you from writing a book in the future.

On the production side at Oxford, I am indebted to the following for their support and many contributions: Megan Mueller, Phyllis Wilson, David Stover, and Lisa Meschino. Freya Godard improved the manuscript with her copy editing.

Finally, deserving a special paragraph of recognition is Mrs Helen Paret, who sacrificed many evenings and weekends over a 10-month period to produce many drafts. While entering or revising over 300,000 words, she thought about the content and offered valuable feedback not only about grammar, spelling, and style, but also about the meaning of the words and sentences. Helen, sincere thanks for your time, dedication, substantive input, support, and friendship. And please express my appreciation to your family (Pat, Taylor, and Katie), who sacrificed time with you so that you could spend your leisure time working on this manuscript.

PART 1

An Introduction to Individual and Population Aging

For centuries, humans have sought ways to prolong life and to be healthier in later life. Throughout this search for a magic elixir—drugs, healthy lifestyles, surgery, the fountain of youth—they have also tried to understand the aging process, primarily from a biological or medical perspective. Increasingly, however, it has been recognized that historical, socio-cultural and environmental factors, as well as biological factors and disease states, influence both individual and population aging, and the situation of older people in any society or community.

The journey you are about to begin by reading this book will, like the life course, be different for each person. The subject matter will present different challenges, degrees of interest, success and opportunities for personal reflection. By acquiring knowledge, separating facts from myths, and applying this information, you can enrich your own life course, that of older age cohorts, and society in general. Whether as a concerned citizen, as a practitioner working with older adults, as a policy-maker, or as a researcher, knowledge about individual and population aging is a life-long pursuit and investment. Part 1 consists of four chapters that introduce facts, trends, and ways of thinking about aging and about growing older in a global society.

Chapter 1 introduces the concept of aging as a social process; distinguishes between individual and population aging; defines four types of aging; and identifies some major issues and challenges, as well as images and myths, about aging in Canada. In addition, arguments are introduced as to why it is important to understand aging phenomena throughout the life course from a number of disciplinary and theoretical perspectives (see also Chapter 5). This chapter stresses that we do not age in a vacuum, but rather in a highly interactive and ever-changing social world as we move through our individual life courses.

Chapter 2 illustrates the diversity in the process of aging and in the status of older people across time, because of cultural differences and historical events. Aging and being labelled as 'old', 'elderly', or a 'senior', varies across time, both within and across countries. A major change in the status of older people is alleged to have occurred as societies moved from pre-industrial to industrial to post-modern states, especially after the onset of modernization. Within a multicultural society such as Canada, the process of aging varies within indigenous, language, ethnic, rural, and religious subcultures.

Chapter 3 briefly describes how the various physical and cognitive systems of the human organism change and adapt through the life course. The focus is on how physical and cognitive changes, which may or may not occur in all aging individuals at the same rate or to the same degree, influence the nature and frequency of social relations throughout the life course, but more so in later life. Some of these natural and inevitable changes lead, in later life, to a loss of independence, a lower quality of life, and a need for informal and formal support from others to complete everday activities of daily living like dressing, eating, and bathing.

Chapter 4 presents an overview of demographic processes and indicators that describe the size, composition, and distribution of the population by age. Demographic facts from both developed and developing countries are introduced to place the Canadian situation in a global context. Demographic processes are dynamic, and the implications of demographic changes over time are discussed, especially with respect to fertility, mortality, and immigration rates. The final section examines the geographic distribution of populations by age across provincial and rural-urban boundaries, and illustrates how immigration contributes to the diversity of Canada's older population. Population aging is a universal phenomenon which has created fear among some members of the media and government. They argue that 'demography is destiny' and that population aging will lead to the bankruptcy of public pension systems and to the destruction, through over-use, of the health care system. Whether this view is myth or fact is discussed in this chapter.

CHAPTER 1

Aging as a Social Process

Focal Points

- To what extent, and why, does population aging influence life chances and lifestyles throughout the life course?
- Is old age a disease or an outcome of the interaction of normal biological, psychological, and social processes?
- Why and how do age and aging matter in our everyday lives, and does the meaning of age and aging change across the life course?
- In what way, and why, is aging a social process?
- Are older people a burden to society or an untapped resource?
- How do media images about being old influence the aging process?
- How do the culture and social structure of a society influence individual aging?
- Why and how are individual aging and population aging universally linked?
- Why and how should the human rights of older people be protected?

Introduction

The world is growing older as the number and proportion of older people in each country increases. In developed countries like Canada, this growth has occurred over the past 40 years as fertility rates declined after the baby boom of 1946–66. This growth is expected to level off in about 30 years when the oldest members of the baby boom cohort begin to die. In developing countries much of the increase in population aging will occur in the next 30–40 years as fertility rates decline, and sanitation and public health improve. That is, with fewer births, older people begin to comprise a larger proportion of the total population; and with improved sanitation and

public health, people live longer and that again increases the proportion of the population that is older. This global phenomenon, known as population aging, is illustrated by the following facts or projections (United Nations, 2000).

- One out of ten persons is 60 years of age or older; by 2050, one out of five will be 60 and older.
- In developed or modernized countries, one in five persons is 60 or over. In some countries the proportion is projected to reach one in four, one in three, or even one in two in the next 30 years as the baby boom cohort ages.

- The number of older people in developing countries is projected to quadruple in the next 50 years.

- In most developed countries, people over 80 years of age comprise the fastest growing segment of the older population. They represented 11 per cent of the 60-plus age group at present and are projected to represent 19 per cent by mid-century.

We live not only in an aging world where people live longer and older people are more visible than previously, but in a society where older citizens are healthier and more active. As individuals and as a society, we cannot ignore the challenges of population aging and the needs of older adults. Understanding and developing a society for all ages is essential, today, and in the future when you and members of your family grow older. More than you can imagine, we all interact with, and are influenced by, aging individuals and an aging society, both within the family and as a citizen. The effects of population aging permeate all spheres of social life—work, the family, leisure, transportation, politics, public policy, the economy, housing, and health care. Consequently, both challenges and opportunities are created for aging individuals; as well as for family members, politicians, employers and employees, health and social services personnel, and public-policy-makers. Indeed, aging issues are linked to many of the well-known challenges facing societies, including gender inequality; intergenerational family relations, retirement and economic security, universal access to health care, and social assistance in later life, to name but a few issues where age and aging matter.

Throughout the book, aging as a social process and the social world of older adults are introduced and explained. We do not age in a vacuum. Rather, individually and collectively (as a family, community or society), we live in a social world. In this lifelong journey we interact with other individuals and age cohorts across time and within a unique culture, social structure, and community. Just as individuals change as they grow older, so too do social institutions—such as the family, the labour force, the economy, and the educational system. This evolution creates both challenges and opportunities for aging individuals and our society. In short, we do not age alone, nor do we have total freedom in selecting our lifestyle or life course. There is constant two-way interaction between individuals and various social processes and social structures across the life course (Ryff and Marshall, 1999; Heinz and Marshall, 2003). To illustrate, mandatory retirement at age 65, or its elimination, has positive and/or negative implications for both the individual who attains 65 years of age and for the broader society. Similarly, the state of our health and needs at any stage in life are linked to personal decisions about diet and lifestyle, and the quality of care provided by the health-care system. It was C. Wright Mills (1959), a well-known sociologist, who first stressed that we must understand and appreciate how, and why, the 'private troubles', or personal responsibilities, of individuals interact with the 'public issues', or public responsibilities, of a society—at the local, regional, national, and global level. This dialectical private-public debate and process pervades the study of individual and population aging, and it should be on the agenda whenever policies or programs for older adults are being considered. Highlight 1.1 summarizes why the study of aging processes and the social world of older adults is important.

Population Aging: Adding Years to Life

Throughout history, humans have been preoccupied with searching for a fountain of youth, for ways to look younger in later life and to prolong life (Gruman, 2003). However, it was not until the twentieth century that enormous gains in longevity were achieved, as evidenced by an

Highlight 1.1 Why Study Aging and Older Adults?

- To challenge, refute, and eliminate myths about aging and older people
- To question popular, taken-for-granted assumptions about aging
- To know thyself, and others, by examining personal journeys across the life course
- To assist and support older family members as they move through the later stages of life
- To prepare for a job or career (as a practitioner, policy-maker, or researcher) where the mandate is to address aging issues or to serve an older population
- To understand inter-generational relations and the status of older adults in a multicultural society
- To evaluate policies and practices for an aging population, and to identify gaps where the needs of older adults are not being met
- To understand aging and older people from an interdisciplinary perspective—their potential, their competencies, their history, and their changing physical, social, and cognitive needs
- To enhance the quality and quantity of interaction with older people in your personal and professional life

increase in the average and maximum **life span** of humans, in the average **life expectancy** at birth, and in the number who attain the age of 100 or more—**centenarians**. The 2001 Census of Canada counted 3,795 Canadians aged 100 or older (a 21 per cent increase from the previous census), with women centenarians outnumbering men four to one. While each centenarian has a different life history, their longevity, in general, can be attributed to some combination of genetics, environmental factors, and lifestyle choices.

Life span is the fixed, finite maximum limit of survival for a species (about 20 years for dogs, about 85 for elephants, and about 120 for humans). The longest-living human with a verified birth certificate was Madame Jeanne Calment, who was born in 1875 in Arles, France—before films, cars, or airplanes were invented. She died at the age of 122 in 1997. More people would survive closer to the maximum life span if all forms of disease were eliminated and if accidents, wars, and environmental hazards could be prevented. The maximum life

span for humans is unlikely to increase to any great extent in the immediate future unless the major cancers, cardiovascular, cardiopulmonary, and dementia diseases are eradicated.

Life expectancy is the average number of years a person is projected to live at birth or at a specific age (such as 65). Average life expectancy has increased in the past 50 years and will continue to increase, although more in the developing nations, where it is still quite low because of high infant mortality rates, AIDS, and poor living conditions. In the early 1800s, average life expectancy in Canada was about 40 years; by the late 1800s it had reached about 50 to 55; and by the late 1900s it was 75 to 80. Put another way, in 1900 a 20-year-old had only about a 52 per cent chance of surviving to age 65. Today a 20 year old has an 83 per cent chance of reaching age 65. These dramatic increases are part of an evolving 'health transition' (Riley, 2001) in which there are fewer deaths at birth and in infancy, and both **morbidity** and **mortality** rates have declined owing to health promotion, disease prevention, advances in medicine for treating acute and chronic diseases, and healthier living conditions thanks to public sanitation, fewer accidents, and less pollution. Not surprisingly, these gains in life expectancy have stimulated dreams of even longer lives but without all the physical changes that occur with age. To satisfy these wishes, entrepreneurs market anti-aging products which claim to slow, stop, or reverse the physical process of aging. However, there is little or no scientific evidence for such claims, and indeed, some of the products or treatments (such as drugs or cosmetic surgery) may be harmful (Olshansky et al., 2002).

Life expectancy varies by culture, geographic region, gender, ethnicity, race, education, personal habits (such as diet, exercise, smoking, and drinking), and birth cohort. In Canada, for example, the average life expectancy at birth for women is 82 years, and for men, 76. But among Aboriginal people, life expectancy is lower—77 years for women, and 69 for men. And because of

the diversity of genetic, environmental, and lifestyle factors, some Canadians will die before reaching the average life expectancy for their region, ethnic group, or gender, and few will ever approach the theoretical maximum life span. Nevertheless, more Canadians are living longer, and those 80 or older constitute the fastest-growing segment of the 65 and older age group in Canada. The number of centenarians is also increasing.

Increased life expectancy is only part of the reason why the proportion of older people in a society increases. The most important factor is a significant decline in the fertility rate. In 2002, Canada's birth rate was about 10.6 infants per 1,000 population, down from a high of 26.9 per 1,000 in 1946, when the baby boom started. This ratio of 10.6 per 1,000 represents the fewest number of annual births over the 56-year period.

Figure 1.1 shows that, as of the 2001 census, there were about 4 million Canadians 65 and

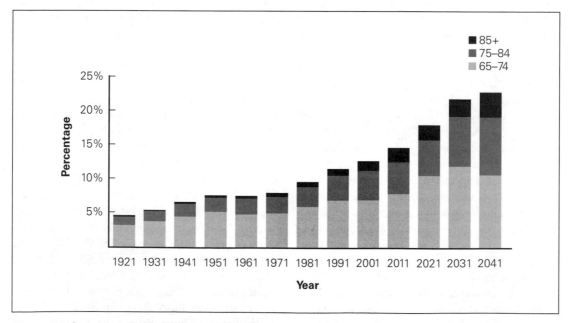

Figure 1.1 Canada's Aging Population, 1921–2041

Source: Health Canada (2002). *Canada's Aging Population*. Ottawa: Minister of Public Works and Government Services Canada.

older (1 in 8 Canadians), an increase of 66 per cent since 1981. As the baby boomers age, the population of those 65 and older is projected to reach about 7 million in 2021 and 9 million in 2041 (almost 1 in 4 Canadians). In 2001, those 65 and over comprised 13 per cent of the population, but by 2041 they will comprise almost 25 per cent; with 1.6 million (4 per cent of the total population) being 80 years of age or more in 2041, an increase from about 900,000 in 2001.

The process whereby there is an increase in the proportion of the population that is over 65 years of age is known as **population aging**. The process began in Canada after the end of the baby boom period, when a 'baby bust' period (from about 1966–80) began. During this period women had fewer than two children on average, and the first pregnancy was often delayed until a woman was in her mid- to late 30s (McDaniel, 1986: 96). This 'baby bust' period was followed by a small 'baby boom echo' from about 1980 until the mid-1990s. However, the number of 'echo' births was only about 30 per cent of the number in the original baby boom. Since the mid-1990s, fertility rates have fallen further to about 1.5 children per woman. This low fertility rate is below the 'replacement rate' of at least two children per woman that is needed to replenish the population when normal fertility and mortality rates prevail.

Some politicians and media personnel claim that this rapid aging of the population will weaken the viability of the Canada Pension Plan, the Canadian economy, and the health-care system; will cause an enormous demand for long-term care and social support of older adults; and may lead to intergenerational inequities or conflict. In Quebec, these issues are accompanied by additional concerns about the linguistic future of the province (Cheal, 2003a). Indeed, some consider population aging to be an impending crisis for our society. Such fears can interfere with rational policy making (Cheal, 2003a). Those with this view argue that older people are, or will become, a burden to society. Highlight 1.2 illustrates newspaper headlines and comments from the

mid- to late 1990s, when such views were most prevalent in Canada, although they tend to reappear whenever new statistics indicate an increase in population aging, an increase in public debt, or a crisis in the health-care system.

More rational thinkers, including an active research community in Canada, have demonstrated that with health promotion and health-care improvements, increased savings and private investments, higher levels of education, and creative and timely policy planning, older people, as a group, will not be a drain on societal resources. Indeed, healthier, better-educated, and more active older people are an untapped human resource for society that can serve as volunteers or as paid workers when the labour force shrinks (Phillipson, 1998; Gee, 2000; Mérette, 2002; Cheal, 2003b).

This labelling of older people as a burden to society has been called 'apocalyptic', 'catastrophic', or 'voodoo' demography. That is, population aging is seen as the root cause of many societal problems. Gee (2000: 5) described apocalyptic demography as 'an ideology . . . a set of beliefs that justifies (or rationalizes) action . . . wherein the beliefs converge on the idea that an aging population has negative implications for societal resources—which get funnelled to the sick, the old, and the retired at the expense of the healthy, the young, and the working'. This way of thinking has been influenced by a governing system where public policies are designed for hypothetical average or typical people, and by projections of the number of people who must be supported by public funds in the future. The media, and policy-makers, faced with an increasing number of older people, ask such questions as:

- Will there be sufficient funds in the public pension system when future birth cohorts reach 65, or will the C/QPP (Canada/Quebec Pension Plan) become bankrupt while supporting the large baby boom cohort which will retire from about 2011 to 2031?

- Will hospitals disproportionately serve frail older people and make it difficult for those in

Highlight 1.2 Journalistic Views of Population Aging

Raise Seniors' Taxes

Ottawa should hit older people and their estates with new taxes to pay down the national debt, says a top tax lawyer. Seniors have benefitted from a lifetime of economic growth boosted by government spending and it is now time for them to pay the country back. . . . The $500 billion federal debt 'belongs' to older Canadians, but younger generations are being asked to pay for it.

Toronto Star, 11 Nov. 1994

Letter to the Editor

The old women lugging their pension-laden purses from store to store aren't suffering. It's the people who are too young for the pension who are hard up.

Toronto Star, 5 Dec. 1994

Painful Decisions Must Be Made to Ensure Future of Social Programs

If you think we are having a hard time affording our social programs today, just wait a few years. What is little understood is how the demographic clock is working against us and how fast it is ticking.

Peter Hadekel, *Montreal Gazette*, 10 Dec. 1994

Grandma! Grandpa! Get Back to Work!

Retirement isn't a birthright. Those who enjoy it haven't earned it. Canadians enjoy retirement, and why not? Most retirees are having the time of their lives: long, lazy summers at the cottage, gambling jaunts to Vegas in the winter, golf all year round.

Peter Shawn Taylor, *Saturday Night*, June 1995

Paying for the Boomers

Blame it on the baby boomers. Last week, Finance Minister Paul Martin announced that Canada Pension Plan contributions will increase to 9.9 per cent of pensionable earnings.

Maclean's, 24 Feb. 1997

Pension Plan Pins Prospects on Market

Faced with the daunting demographic challenges of an aging baby-boom . . . Canadians—younger ones in particular—are skeptical . . . will the CPP be around for their retirement. And they have every reason to worry.

Shawn McCarthy and Rob Carrick, *Globe and Mail*, 11 Apr. 1998

Reprinted with permission from Gee and Gutman (2000: 6–7)

other age groups to receive hospital treatment?

- Will the decreasing number of younger workers in the labour force be less able and

willing to pay higher taxes to support social services and a pension plan that will be supporting more and more older people?

- Who will provide home care and social

support to the large number of aging people, especially when more middle-aged daughters and daughters-in-law are employed full-time in the labour force?

• Will conflict emerge between younger and older generations over what are perceived to be intergenerational inequities favouring older people in the receipt of public services?

Some of these apocalyptic fears were enhanced in the late 1980s and throughout the 1990s by the onset of a global economic recession and high government debt. These economic conditions, combined with projections of exponential increases in per capita costs for economic, health, and social support services, encouraged governments to propose reducing economic or social support for older people. They also employed these arguments as they attempted to download more of the costs to lower levels of government or to families. To illustrate, in the past decade when governments were faced with an increasing public debt, they built fewer long-term care facilities and reduced the operating budgets of existing facilities, thereby forcing families to be involved, at a greater personal and financial cost, in the long-term care of aging parents. Governments argued that instead of living in a hospital or a publicly funded nursing home, elderly people should remain at home, live in the home of a child, or move into a privately funded retirement or nursing home. Seldom were new, alternative, and more economical types of care proposed (see Chapter 11). This issue of public support for older Canadians is a classic example of the debate proposed by Mills (1959) as to whether support in a welfare state should be a 'public responsibility' of the state, or a 'personal responsibility' for the individual and the family.

Despite questions about the sustainability of Canada's universal pension and health-care systems, there is increasing evidence that the significant growth in population aging over the next 30 to 40 years will not bankrupt the pension system, will not be a major contributor to escalating health-care

costs, and will not cause intergenerational conflict (Denton and Spencer, 2000; Gee, 2000; Evans et al., 2001; Hébert, 2002; Myles, 2002; Cheal, 2003a, 2003b). However, some elements of the apocalyptic scenario might occur in the United States or in the United Kingdom, where the state, traditionally, is less responsible for the economic, social, and health support of its citizens (Phillipson, 1998). Denton and Spencer (2000) argue that, in Canada, the highest dependency on the state by any age cohort was actually in the 1950s and 1960s when the baby boom cohort, during their childhood and adolescent years, needed greatly expanded educational facilities and teachers.

In the health-care domain, Hébert (2002) states that the disproportionate use of health services by older adults in the future will not be a problem. He argues that the demand for services will not be as high as projected, that there will be improved efficiencies in the health-care system, and that there will be more use of home care services to offset the need for costly hospital and residential care. Similarly, Evans et al. (2001: 188) conclude that 'the actual evidence is absolutely clear. Whatever the trends in health-care expenditures, and whatever the 'sustainability' of particular financing arrangements (public or private), we have nothing to fear from the aging of the population, only from those who continue to promulgate the fiction of a doomsday scenario'.

Consequently, despite periodic fear-mongering by politicians and the media, we should not fear population aging, nor view it as a crisis. Instead, population aging should be viewed as a significant, but manageable, challenge. This will be especially true when the large baby boom cohort retires. This aging cohort will spend their retirement years in better health, with more education and economic resources, and they will be more physically and socially active than previous cohorts of older adults. Moreover, as they have done for most of their adult lives, they will continue to spend their wealth on leisure, travel, and health-care products. As Gee (2000) and others (Friedland and Summer, 1999) have concluded, 'demography is not destiny'. Changes in the age structure can be managed by policies, programs and changes within social institutions. More will be said about these institutional changes and public policies in later chapters.

Individual Aging: Adding Life to Years

Scholars and policy-makers at one time focused on the biomedical aspects of aging that caused illness, frailty, dependence, and death in later life. Today, **individual aging** is viewed as a multi-dimensional process of growth and development which involves physical, social, behavioural, and cognitive changes throughout the **life course**. Yes, we all experience biological aging at different rates, and with varying degrees of disease states which intervene to negatively influence and perhaps shorten our individual lives. These changes, whether social, cognitive, or medical, and the rate of change, influence our **life chances** and **lifestyle**, including our degree of independence. In short, biological aging occurs in an ever-changing social world that is unique to individuals or age cohorts in different societies, in different regions of a country, or with different life chances and lifestyles across the life course. Our place in historical time, our culture, and our social structure present different barriers, opportunities, and challenges across the life course. Depending on when we were born and where we live out our lives, our health, lifestyle choices, and life chances as we age are shaped by social conditions and social change. Historical events such as economic depressions, wars, baby booms, technological revolutions, or social movements shape the life trajectories or pathways of individuals or age cohorts. The impact of these events on a given individual or age cohort usually depends on the chronological age or stage in life when the event occurred.

To understand aging individuals and older age cohorts, a historical and a developmental perspective is required. These criteria are met by the **life course perspective**, which examines the interplay among individual life stories, our social structures and environments, and the effect of specific historical events at particular times in the life of individuals or age cohorts. Through this approach we understand how the problems, advantages, disadvantages, needs, and lifestyles of later life are shaped by earlier life transitions, decisions, opportunities, and experiences within specific historical or cultural contexts (Dannefer and Uhlenberg, 1999; Hagestad and Dannefer, 2001; Harevan, 2001; Dannefer, 2003; Heinz and Marshall, 2003). The life course perspective links the individual and society as we study age-related transitions that begin with birth and entry into the school system, and conclude with retirement, widowhood, and death in later life.

The life course, for an individual or an age cohort, is a social construct involving the interaction of personal, historical, or societal events from birth to death. This construct enables us to observe and analyze how different individual or societal events influence variations in the aging process within and between cohorts and individuals. Some events (a war, an economic depression, a flu epidemic) will have an impact on some age cohorts but not on others, or only on specific individuals within an age cohort, perhaps because of their position in the social structure. For example, the feminist movement that started in the 1970s has had a profound influence on the life course of women born just before and after the 1970s. But, in general, the feminist movement has had little influence on women who are now in the later stages of life (70 and older). Statistics Canada has created an interesting life-course micro-simulation model of individual and family lives from birth to death (www.statcan.ca/english/spsd/LifePaths.htm). This model, entitled LifePaths, enables us to answer such questions as these:

- What is the economic benefit, if any, of post-secondary education?

- Do people plan for their retirement?

- How long do we need to work and save to ensure economic security in retirement?

The model can also assist in developing effective policies by employing integrated life-course data (Rowe, 2003).

Figure 1.2 illustrates the cohort effects of being at a particular stage in life at a particular time in history. For example, during the late 1990s, a period of economic restructuring and high unemployment in Canada, members of cohort A, born in the early 1940s, were probably at the 'empty-nest' stage and within five to ten years of retirement. Many were probably coping well with the prevailing social and economic conditions, assuming they did not lose their job to downsizing by their employer. In contrast, some members of cohort B, born in the early 1970s, experienced unemployment or underemployment in early adulthood, and many delayed

getting married and buying a house. Cohort C, born in the early 1990s, were school-age children in the late 1990s and were less likely to be affected directly by the economic climate, unless one or both their parents were unemployed. Thus, past and current social conditions, as well as life histories, have a different impact on age cohorts. Some of these factors have an influence on most members of an age cohort throughout their lives (for example, cohort B); others are affected at only certain periods of their lives. Or an event may have an effect only on some segments of a birth cohort (according to social class, gender, race, or ethnicity).

Your life course will be different from that of earlier and later age cohorts and from others of about the same age in other countries and perhaps even in other parts of Canada. Such differences result from cultural, regional, or political variations in opportunities, lifestyles, values, or beliefs. The events a person experiences through-

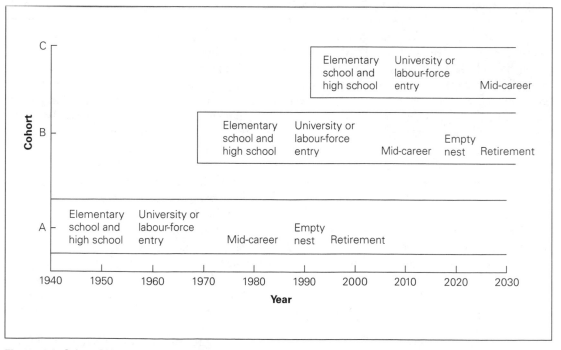

Figure 1.2 Cohort Differences and the Aging Process

out the life course will vary, as well, because of particular social or political events that affect some, but not all, age cohorts. One's experience will also differ from that of others in the same birth cohort because of social inequality in life chances and lifestyles.

Personal biographies interact with structural, cultural, and historical factors to influence how we age across the life course. Thus, we need to understand why there is diversity in aging among individuals in the same birth cohort (all those born in the same year) and in different birth cohorts (those born at different points in history—you, your parents, your grandparents). Much of this diversity arises because of where an individual or cohort is located in the **social structure.**

A social structure, whether based on class, age, gender, or ethnicity involves established ways of behaving and acting (Giddens, 1984). The structural elements provide a set of guidelines or expectations concerning behaviour, and they may establish limits on life chances and lifestyles. People's everyday actions reinforce and reproduce a set of expectations—the social forces and social structures which guide our daily lives. These elements, or rules of social order, can be changed, and are changed when people ignore them, replace them, or reproduce them in different forms. Gender, age, ethnicity, race and social class, as major components of the social structure, influence our life chances and create opportunities or barriers for individuals across the life course. These structural factors interact and become cumulative across the life course, often leading to extreme differences in the quality of life for older adults (O'Rand, 1996).

While living within a social structure, we are not merely reactive puppets. Our social life is more than random, controlled individual acts, and social interaction is not determined solely by social forces. Individuals in similar situations can act in different ways and make different decisions (Smith et al., 2000; Connidis, 2001: 15–16). This process, known as **human agency**, enables individuals to make choices and decisions, and to take advantage of opportunities, and to act within the constraints and boundaries of our personal history and social structures. Personal agency is the ability and willingness to act on one's own behalf, although our position in the social structure or in an institution, such as the workplace or family, influences the extent to which we are able to act or make decisions.

Agency is most often evident in family, work, and leisure interactions. Through agency we create unique identities, develop personal meanings, and decide which social groups are significant in our lives. Glen Elder, a pioneer in the study of the life course, argues that agency is a 'principle', one of five defining principles of the life course (Elder and Johnson, 2003: 57–71). These principles are described in Chapter 5. Elder defined agency as a process by which individuals construct their life course by making choices and taking actions. These intentional choices and actions are strongly influenced by the constraints and opportunities of social structures, by personal history and past experiences, and by significant others in our daily lives. Dannefer (1999: 73) argues that 'human behavior is purposeful; it is not guided by instincts but by intentions'. Similarly, Marshall (2000: 11) argues that agency refers to the human capacity 'to act intentionally, planfully and reflexively, and in a temporal or biographical mode throughout the life course'. Marshall (2000: 9–10) also stresses the personal responsibility that we inherit to invoke agency:

> Agency has been seen as the production of a life. The agent is the producer; human development, the lived life, the narrative, is produced by agency . . . people not only react but act and, in acting, produce their biographical selves . . . agency refers to a culturally legitimated responsibility to act—on behalf of others, of organizations or ideas, or of one's own self.

One outcome of the dialectical interaction between agency and social structure is that older people represent a very heterogeneous cohort. Considerable variations in lifestyles, experiences, and quality of life evolve within different age cohorts in the older population. No other age cohort or category includes people who differ in chronological age and age-related experiences by as much as 30 years (i.e., 60–90). Consequently, Canada's population of older adults is a diverse, heterogeneous group that varies by wealth, type and place of residence, education, gender, chronological age, health status, ethnicity, social status, and living arrangements. Treating them as a homogeneous group with common needs, interests, and experiences is a mistake that can lead to ineffective policies and programs. Some older adults are poor and some are wealthy; some live alone and some live with a partner; some live in urban areas and some in rural or remote communities; some are active, mobile, and independent, and some are sedentary, disabled, frail, and dependent; and most fall somewhere in between these extremes. This diversity must be recognized in policies and programs for older Canadians. Chapter 6 elaborates further on the relationship between the social structure and individual aging, Chapter 7 explores the relationship between the individual and his or her lived environment (the search for person-environment 'fit'); while Chapters 11 and 12 address policy issues for a diverse aging population.

Aging Processes

Although there are a number of separate aging processes, they do interact. For example, a decline in vision (a biological change) may lead to an inability to read or drive a car, thereby restricting a person's mobility and independence. Similarly, mandatory retirement (a social act) may have positive or negative psychological or social outcomes for individuals and for a society. Furthermore, there is variation within and between individuals in the onset and speed of aging among the various processes.

Chronological Aging

The passage of calendar time from one birthday to the next represents chronological aging. Our age in years determines our rights (often through legislation) and influences the way we live. Chronological age serves as an approximate indicator of physical growth and decline, social and emotional development, and expected patterns of social interaction. However, chronological age can be deceiving. A 30-year-old with facial features more like a 40-year-old may behave and dress more like a 20-year-old. Some may consider this person to be 'old' for his or her age, while others may consider him or her to be 'immature'. Similarly, a person who appears 'elderly' from his or her physical appearance may exhibit social, cognitive, or physical behaviour that is similar to that of a much younger adult.

The social meaning or value attached to a specific chronological age, as defined within a particular social context, is often more important than actual chronological age in determining social or cognitive behaviour. (For example, people are told to 'act their age'.) However, such age-based norms are increasingly less influential if we live in an age-integrated, rather than an age-segregated society. Consequently, actions or decisions pertaining to education, work, leisure, family, and health are less tied to chronological age than previously.

Chronological age defines 'legal' age and thereby provides some social order and control in a society. However, legal definitions based on years since birth often constrain individual rights and freedoms. For example, mandatory retirement at age 65 implies that all citizens are no longer able to contribute to the labour force at that age! While some are not able to perform tasks as effectively, or may not wish to continue working, others have the capacity, experience, and desire to continue as contributing members of the labour force.

Laws or regulations based on a specific chronological age—for example, the age we enter school or are eligible to drive a car, vote, or retire—are established according to what was considered the best, or 'normal', chronological age for the specific event at the time the law was passed. Age is used in law to assign advantages and benefits, or to impose obligations or restrictions (Law Commission of Canada, 2004). Sometimes legal age is based on the best available knowledge about capacity or potential at a specific age, or on **chronological age norms**—how most individuals behave in a given situation or perform a particular task at a specific age. Or legal age may be influenced by *functional age*—how well an individual performs specific physical, cognitive, or social tasks (driving a car past 80 years of age). Or a law based on age may be established according to what is considered best for the society (e.g., mandatory retirement).

Functional age is often a more useful guideline than chronological age. It is based on the fact that aging is a multi-faceted, diverse process in which individuals at a specific chronological age are either 'older' or 'younger' than age peers in terms of some relevant skill or experience. For example, where mandatory retirement is not required, the right to continue working might be based on a person's ability to work effectively and efficiently. But how we objectively measure physical and cognitive abilities is a difficult and, so far, unsolvable problem. Hence, functional age, as fair as it seems, has not received much support in the labour or political domains.

Some have argued that the traditional marker for 'old age', 65 years, should be revised upwards because of gains in life expectancy (Denton and Spencer, 2002). This has occurred in the United States, where the eligibility for full social security pension benefits is being increased gradually (by 2027) from 65 to 67 years of age for those born after 1966. In Sweden, eligibility for pension benefits is indexed to gains in life expectancy. Denton and Spencer (2002), as economists, argue that with reduced mortality and morbidity, improvements in health, and increases in life expectancy,

Canada could redefine 'old' to mean 70, and 'very old' or 'oldest old' to mean 90. This, of course, would not prevent the population from aging, but it would reduce the number who fall into each category, thereby delaying or reducing pension benefits at a great cost saving to society.

Biological Aging

Internal and external biological changes influence behaviour, longevity, and one's quality of life. These genetic and environmentally induced changes take place in the muscular, skeletal, reproductive, neural, and sensory systems. The rate and incidence of biological changes influence the number of years a person is likely to survive and the extent to which he or she is likely to experience illness or disability. These changes and their accompanying adaptations interact with the social and psychological processes of aging. For example, visible changes, such as greying of the hair and wrinkling of the skin, influence whether we are thought by others to be young, middle-aged, or elderly. Similarly, our lifestyle, including the amount of stress or depression we experience, can slow down or accelerate the biological processes of aging. Although a further discussion of biological aging is beyond the scope of this book (Schneider and Rowe, 1996), we should not ignore the effect of such changes when studying aging as a social process. Chapter 3 returns to this theme as we examine the influence of physical and cognitive changes on social behaviour and social interactions.

Psychological Aging

Changes in learning ability, memory, and creativity occur across the life course (Birren and Schaie, 2001). Psychological aging involves the interaction of individual cognitive and behavioural changes with social and environmental factors, such as the loss of a spouse or a change in housing location, that affect our psychological state. A decline in memory or attention span can reduce or eliminate a lifelong interest in reading or learning. This, in turn, changes an individual's leisure habits and may lead to boredom, depression, and a deteriorating quality of life. Similarly, a stressful life event such as divorce, the death of a spouse, or unemployment alters the emotional, behavioural, and cognitive processes of an individual at any chronological age. Adapting to stresses often depends not only on personal psychological capacities, but also on the amount and type of social support and assistance received from the family and others in the community. Psychological aging is influenced, as well, by cultural differences, such as whether or not older people are valued. Chapter 3 describes cognitive and personality changes associated with aging.

Social Aging

Biological aging and, to some extent, psychological aging are somewhat similar in all cultures. Social aging, however, varies within and across societies and across time, depending on the interactions between aging individuals and others in a particular family, society, or subculture at a specific period in history. Thus, an identical twin separated at birth from a sibling and raised in a different family and community would exhibit behaviour, values, and beliefs that are more similar to age peers in his or her own social world than to those of the sibling.

Patterns of social interaction across the life course are learned within a social structure, whether it be the nuclear family, the workplace, the local community, or Canada. The age structure of a society is stratified like a ladder. While earlier societies included only a few strata (childhood, adulthood, and old age), modern societies involve many age strata—infancy, early childhood, preadolescence, adolescence, young adulthood, middle age, early late life, and very late life. The behaviour and status of the members of each stratum are influenced, at least partially, by the rights and responsibilities assigned on the basis of age or age group, and by attitudes toward specific age groups as defined by that society. In some societies, for example, older people are highly valued; in others, they are considered less attractive and less valued than younger people. In the latter society, being defined as 'old' means that one is marginalized and stigmatized.

Within each culture, social timetables define the approximate or ideal chronological age when we 'should' or 'must' enter or leave various social positions. Some of these transitions involve institutionalized rites of passage, such as a bar mitzvah, a twenty-first birthday party, convocation at university, a wedding, or a retirement party. Within an age cohort the meaning and significance attached to a rite of passage or to a particular age status varies, as well, by social status. For example, for a woman without much formal education, marriage early in her 20s may be considered more important than for a woman with a university degree because of class-based norms or values about the right age for women to marry. Similarly, age-related norms or expectations about childbearing have more significance for women according to their level of education, career goals, or class background. The meanings attached to membership in an age stratum or to specific events change as a society changes. For example, some people in your grandparents' generation may have believed that a woman who was not married by her mid-20s was, or would become, an 'old maid'. Today, a single woman in her early or mid-30s may be viewed as independent, 'liberated', and modern. She may be praised for not rushing into an early marriage and for pursuing a career.

These variations in social values illustrate why chronological age is a poor indicator of the needs, capabilities, and interests of adults across the life course. Increasingly, the time when major life events take place is no longer dictated by chronological age. For example, women give birth for the first time in their teens or in their early 40s; parents become grandparents as early as age 30 or as late as 70; and marriages are occurring at all chronological ages, including a first marriage or a remarriage for those in their 60s, 70s, and 80s.

Social aging is influenced, as well, by the composition of the age structure, which comprises many different birth or age cohorts. Even people born at the same period in history exhibit considerable diversity because of variations in gender, health, race, ethnicity, class, education, and place of residence. As the life course evolves for each cohort, social inequality on one or more of these dimensions accounts for different patterns of aging within the cohort. For example, two women born in the same year in the same community might follow different life trajectories depending on their education and their views about marriage, childbearing, and careers. Similarly, a child in an upper-class family where both parents earn an income will have different life experiences than a child born in the same year to a single mother who drops out of school to work and support her child.

No cohort ages alone. Aging involves interaction among cohorts and cohort succession. Each cohort is linked to others through social interaction in family, work, or leisure settings. These inter-cohort relations have the potential to create both co-operation and conflict between generations. This is especially true if social differences in a society create age strata with higher or lower status, and therefore greater or lesser power. In societies where older people are highly valued, intergenerational relations are generally positive and each cohort moves from one age stratum to the next with little or no conflict. In contrast, in societies where youth is valued more highly than old age, or where elderly people are marginalized, inter-generational rivalry and conflict are more likely. In such societies, elderly people often resent the loss of status and power they once held. It was this resentment and concern that launched the 'grey power' movement in the 1970s (Pratt, 1976) and an awareness of growing generational inequities in the 1980s (Bengtson et al., 1985).

Aging as a Social Process

The Social World and Aging: History, Culture, and Structure

Aging and the status of older people in everyday life are linked to the period of history in which we live and to the culture and social structure of the society or communities where we are born and live out our lives. Our place in history and our culture influence the type and quality of life we experience, as Chapter 2 illustrates in more detail. For now, think of the differences in how one might age or spend later life if one lived at a time when one *either* did or did not experience or have access to drugs (for cancer, heart disease, or AIDS) or such medical devices as pacemakers and artificial hips; mandatory retirement and a universal pension system; nursing and retirement homes; technological devices such as home and personal alarm systems, microwaves, or e-mail; and subsidies to older adults for transportation, home care, or leisure.

As you consider aging issues, think about history and culture to understand fully the circumstances in which older adults in a particular society and as a member of a specific cohort spent their earlier and later years. On a personal note, my grandparents were labourers; they never completed education beyond high school; one set never owned a car; and they did not have a television, a microwave, or a private pension. Nor did they travel far beyond their home town. My father, but not my mother(!), completed university; they both worked and they owned two cars, travelled throughout the world until their mid-80s; reluctantly, but very late in life, used a microwave and a portable (but not a cellular) phone; and both retired with large government and private pensions.

Culture, the way of life passed from generation to generation, varies within societies and changes across time in a society. Our culture creates ideas, beliefs, norms, values, and attitudes that shape our thinking and behaviour about aging and about being old. Thus, to understand the lifestyles of individuals as they age, and the views of a society about aging, one needs to consider the cultural elements prevailing at a particular period in history and the changes that occur in cultural values and meanings across generations.

Diversity in aging experiences and the considerable heterogeneity among those in older age cohorts occur because of both cultural and social differentiation in the social structure of a community or society. **Social stratification** is a process by which social attributes (age, gender, religion, social class, race, and ethnicity) are evaluated differentially according to their value in the eyes of the society. These attributes create a structure in which some people are considered superior to others. In North America, for example, individuals are generally evaluated more highly if they are young rather than elderly, male rather than female, and white rather than a member of a visible-minority group. These evaluations of social attributes influence our identity, life chances, and lifestyle all through our lives and foster social inequalities.

Each stratification system interacts within a complex social structure. Consequently, every age cohort is a heterogeneous mix of individuals who vary along inter-connecting gender, racial, economic, ethnic, educational, religious, and marital dimensions. Age, as a social construct and a continuum from birth to death and from infancy to old age, interacts with other stratification systems across the life course to influence the degree of social integration and social support and the quality of life experienced by older adults. To illustrate, we live in a 'gendered' society. Gender distinctions are socially constructed so that women generally have a lower position in everyday social and work life. Consequently, their situation and interpretation of growing old is different. There are many gender inequities in the aging process, as noted first by Susan Sontag (1972), who spoke of the 'double standard of

aging' (Sontag, 1972; Gee and Kimball, 1987; Kimmel, 2000). Gender and aging are strongly connected across the life course, and as we will see in more detail in Chapter 6, some consider aging to be primarily a 'women's issue' (Arber and Ginn, 1995; Moen, 1995, 2001).

Place of residence, while not generally considered a stratification system, is an important factor when one is discussing diversity in aging lifestyles and in the situation of older adults. There is considerable diversity in the lifestyles and backgrounds of rural versus urban residents, as well as diversity within rural communities. Some older people have lived in a rural community their entire life; others are more recent, and often more affluent, migrants to the community (Highlight 1.3).

The Social Construction of Old Age: Images and Labels

There are many myths and misconceptions about growing older and about being elderly. Before reading this section, readers can assess their knowledge about aging by answering the questions[1] in Highlight 1.4.

Whereas chronological age is a precise measure of how many years someone has lived, it is seldom an accurate representation or definition of being 'old' or of being at a specific stage in life. The reality of aging is clouded if chronological age is employed as the way to assign meanings to a specific age or stage in life—if, for example, 65+ means to be retired, dependent, and perhaps poor and frail. Such labelling creates and perpetuates stereotypes and fosters prejudices about, and discrimination toward, members of specific age groups; in short, it constitutes **ageism**. Such views discourage older adults from participating in the labour force, or in some social, leisure, or volunteer activities. Ageism can also influence how young adults are treated by others. To illustrate, students are refused apartments because of stereotypes about the risk of renting to young adults, especially students.

Highlight 1.3 Aging in Rural Environments

In-Migrants

Mr and Mrs P moved from Ottawa to the small town of Annapolis Royal, Nova Scotia to enjoy an active outdoor life in retirement. Many older adults live in this scenic area, which enjoys a fairly mild winter climate. Some, like the P's, were 'new' transplants from the city with no family nearby; some are people who grew up here and chose to return after retirement; and many have always lived in the area, working in farming, fishing, or the lumber industry. Since her husband's death, Mrs P finds it difficult to maintain a three-bedroom house and large yard alone. Although she drives, has many friends, and is involved in several community and church groups, she feels somewhat isolated from her children and grandchildren in Ontario and Alberta. Moving back to a large city would be difficult; she would miss the friendliness and close community ties of Annapolis Royal, the view of the river and mountains, and the many varieties of birds that come to her feeder.

Life-Long Residents

Mr and Mrs A have lived on the family farm for over 50 years since inheriting the land from Mr A's father. Both were born in the local village, attended school together, and married at the age of 20. Now in their 70s, with three children living in three different metropolitan areas in other provinces, Mr and Mrs A depend on the assistance of neighbours to harvest grain crops, and for farm main-tenance and animal care. Two years ago Mr A was hospitalized for two months in an urban centre over 100 km from the farm. Mrs A found this period stressful, and they are now searching for a way to sell the farm and move to an apartment in a nearby town. Their major concerns are whether the sale will generate sufficient income, if it can be sold, and if they will have sufficient income for Mrs A to survive on her own should Mr A die in the next few years.

Source: National Advisory Council on Aging (1993b: 2). Reproduced with permission.

'Old' age, being 'elderly', or becoming a 'senior' does not happen overnight when, on a given day, a person turns 65. Rather, the meaning of being 'old', 'elderly', or a 'senior' is socially constructed and reinforced when cultural values and misconceptions define those who are 65 or over as 'elderly', 'old', or a 'senior'. These labels are not based on the abilities or health of an individual, but rather are assigned to everyone on the basis of stereotypes about those who reach a particular chronological age.[2] In an analysis of 4,200 jokes appearing in three books of 'adult' jokes, a rigid, simplistic, and erroneous stereotype of elderly persons was found in 102 of the jokes (Bowd, 2003). Eight stereotypes emerged: the impotent male; the vain and virile male; the insatiable sex-ual appetite of females; the female uninterested in sex; the unattractive female body; the forgetful older person; the infirm older person; and the innocence associated with a second childhood. Note the contrasting images of some of these stereotypes, which, in reality, reflect diversity among the older population concerning their interest or participation in sex.

This process of labelling is reinforced and institutionalized in a society when social policies require all citizens to meet some requirement based on age, such as mandatory retirement at age 65. In addition, cultural elements produce verbal and visual images about aging or elderly people through literature,[3] art, films,[4] song lyrics, photographs, television shows, jokes, and greeting cards. Often these images express the view, with or without humour, that later life is equated with illness, losses, loneliness, asexuality, and poverty. Many images of older people presented on television are created to generate humour, through references to asexuality, deafness, or forgetfulness, but in so doing they reinforce common (usually erroneous) stereotypes. Similarly, newspapers focus either on the horrors or tragedies of aging or the marvels of truly unique, but atypical long-lived `people who have accomplished feats unusual for their age, or have celebrated birthdays beyond 90 years of age. Seldom, however, is the current reality of aging or of being old, as experienced by the majority of older

people in their 70s or 80s, reflected in the media.

The negative or atypical images, when accepted as fact by the media, the public, and policy-makers, can shape public opinion about aging, influence which public programs are funded (should community recreational facilities be built for youth, older adults, or both?), and undermine the potential of adults as they move into the later years. In short, these labels and images foster a self-fulfilling prophecy whereby some older adults believe they should think and behave like the stereotypes perpetuated by the media. This, in turn, leads to a loss of self-esteem, isolation, and the labelling of oneself as 'old'.

Highlight 1.4 Some Facts about Aging: True or False?

Palmore (1997, 1980, 1981, 1988, 1990), Miller and Dodder (1980), Martin Matthews et al. (1984), and Harris and Changas (1994) all developed versions of a true-or-false 'Facts on Aging' quiz. The items in the test are based on documented research, and the following ten questions represent the type of questions included in the various versions.

T   F   1.   Older people tend to become more religious as they age.

T   F   2.   Most old people are set in their ways and unable to change.

T   F   3.   The majority of old people are seldom bored.

T   F   4.   The health and socioeconomic status of older people (compared with younger people) in the future will probably be about the same as it is now.

T   F   5.   Older people have more acute (short-term) illnesses than people under 65.

T   F   6.   The majority of old people are seldom irritated or angry.

T   F   7.   Older workers have less absenteeism than younger workers.

T   F   8.   The elderly have higher rates of criminal victimization than people under 65.

T   F   9.   The majority of older people live alone.

T   F   10.   Older people who reduce their activity tend to be happier than those who remain active.

This quiz reflects knowledge of facts, and cannot be regarded as a direct measure of attitudes. In reality, where misconceptions are found—and they have been found in all age groups—they often reflect lack of personal experience with older adults, inaccurate conclusions based on personal observations of elderly people from a distance rather than through direct interaction with a friend or family member, or the unquestioned acceptance of myths and images presented by the mass media.

Source: Palmore (1977: 315–20; 1981: 431–7). Reprinted by permission of The Gerontological Society of America.

One example of a socially constructed label applied to some older adults late in the life course is the term 'frailty'. In fact, however, frailty, which is a severe biomedical condition, is not experienced by most older people. Indeed, the conditions implied by this label may never appear, or may only apply to those who, through a natural progression of aging, lose strength, endurance, weight, and perhaps some degree of cognitive functioning (see Chapter 3).

We must be careful in the selection and use of labels about older people and later life. The language we use directly affects the behaviour of older persons or influences the behaviour of others, who may avoid or ignore older persons or apply the stereotypes as they interact with older persons. Such erroneous beliefs and inaccurate labels or myths can misguide those responsible for developing policies and programs for older Canadians. Moreover, such labels or images mask the considerable heterogeneity among older people. In short, there is no 'typical' older person who can be depicted or defined by one image. Similarly, it is impossible to discuss 'successful' aging, or to develop a model of 'successful' aging that could be used for developing policies for the entire older population. Given the heterogeneity of the older population, one recipe, model, formula, or policy will not lead to 'successful' aging in a rapidly changing and diverse social world.

Impact of Ageist Images

Stereotypes

Images of aging and of being old are created and perpetuated in a variety of cultural artifacts, in advertising (where older people rarely appear unless they are the target market) and in everyday language. Many of these images are based on the changing appearance of the aging body (wrinkles, changing body shapes, baldness for men, or greying colour, etc.), or on reported or observed changes in the social, physical, or cognitive behaviour of some older persons. These images vary across history, and usually vary among different ethnic, racial, or religious groups in a society. In some cultures, wrinkles are a sign of high status and wisdom; in others, they are a sign of decay and a symbol of being less attractive, valued, and useful. Similarly, paintings in some earlier eras show that short, plump women were admired, whereas today, photographs and paintings idealize women who are tall and very thin. This latter example illustrates how images are socially constructed and how they can change (de Beauvoir,[5] 1970; Featherstone and Hepworth, 1995, Phillipson, 1998).

Misleading stereotypes of older adults can also be found in elementary-school texts, children's literature, and adult fiction, where older people are seldom, if ever, portrayed in illustrations. Older people are usually peripheral to the plot, have limited abilities, and play passive rather than active roles. Furthermore, they are usually under-represented in relation to their proportion in the real world. And older women are under-represented even more, although they comprise a higher proportion of the older population than men. Not surprisingly, elderly members of minority groups are seldom included in books, except in literature written by and about members of specific ethnic or racial groups. Thus, there is a constant need for education to eliminate false images and to eradicate stereotypes. To achieve this goal, gerontology is taught in some elementary and high schools (Krout and Wasyliw, 2002).

We must be careful, however, not to assume that a misleading and stereotypical view of aging and older adults is acquired solely by reading or watching television. There is no proof of a direct causal relationship between the reading of books in which older people are ignored, under-represented, or misrepresented and the adoption of negative attitudes toward older people. Furthermore, since school textbooks are interpreted by teachers, elementary-school students could be more sensitized to the realities of aging issues, depending on the supplementary material presented by a particular teacher. Certainly children's literature and the mass media contain stereotypical views of older people, but whether this leads directly to stereotypes or negative attitudes about aging has yet to be demonstrated. Nevertheless, critical thinking and media literacy skills are necessary so that television images, especially those concerning older women, can be criticized and, hopefully, eliminated.

Myths can, with time and research, be refuted. For example, in recent years older people are being portrayed in a wider variety of occupations and social roles that more closely coincide with reality. They are depicted as active, independent, influential citizens and family members, and as having skills and experiences of value to society. The presentation of a more positive view of aging and older people is due, partly, to a recognition by the mass media of the changing demographic profile of society in general and of television viewers in particular. The change is also due to the recognition by entrepreneurs that a large, wealthy 'senior market' is emerging. By some estimates, people over 50 control more than 80 per cent of the savings in Canada, making them the most economically advantaged age group. As of 2001, there were about 9 million Canadians over the age of 50, and by 2021 it is projected this group will contain 14 million, or 40 per cent of the population.

Negative and ageist images of older adults are being challenged and eliminated, as well, by increasingly politically active and age-conscious older people. This pressure can lead to a deconstruction and reconstruction of the images and discourse about aging and later life. Negative and inaccurate social images and words are replaced with more accurate, modern pictures and descriptions of active, vibrant and independent older adults. By challenging the current discourse and images, we refute the apocalyptic view of population aging and its hypothesized dreaded outcomes for a society.

The more realistic and current images of aging and of the meaning of being older are developed through interviews with, and reflections by,

older adults. Much of the credit for the emergence of more accurate images belongs to anthropologists and sociologists who employ a qualitative approach to understanding social behaviour, to humanists who employ biographical narratives to identify the meaning of later life (Kenyon et al., 2001), and to poets and authors who provide evocative portrayals of older people in real-life situations. Fiction, drama, poetry, autobiographies, and biographies sensitize and inform us about aging issues, now or in the past. These literary contributions depict the philosophy of life and the trials, tribulations, and achievements of older adults; and they provide insight into intergenerational relations. Many present the voices of women and of people from diverse ethnic groups, social classes, or regional environments (Auger and Tedford-Litle, 2002).

Older adults, by telling their life stories, and by sharing their thoughts and feelings, enable us to understand later life as it is experienced by those living that life. This method of study, narrative gerontology, focuses on the lived experience of an aging person (Kenyon et al., 1999: 54). This method often helps older adults, through such a life review, to reinforce their sense of identity. It builds on the storytelling of earlier eras where some of this knowledge was passed on when elderly people told stories to their grandchildren. Highlight 1.5 describes aging in the words of older people.

Age Identity

Age identity is a subjective measure of age that represents the psychological and social meaning of aging rather than chronological age. This concept illustrates how aging and age are symbolically or socially constructed. People of the same chronological age (e.g., 65) may report a wide range of age identities. Some may feel younger and report feeling like 55; others may feel older and identify with 75-year-olds, although this 'age as older' identification seldom happens except on days or during periods when health and energy are low. Age identity, as a subjective experience, is shaped

Highlight 1.5 Voices of Older Adults

People Living in the Community

- I think it's quite normal to be anxious about aging. For all of us it means entering unknown territory, with its attendant fears. The reality for me is that growing older has meant a time of much greater freedom. My children are grown and increasingly independent. I am free to develop my own person, in a way that I never had the courage to do when I was younger. I am discovering strengths and recognizing weaknesses. I don't need to apologize and explain as much as I used to. I wish I'd known ten years ago that getting older would be this interesting, because I have spent too much time in the past worrying about it.[1]

- I would hate to be moved into a strange surrounding and have to make friends and establish new trusts in people. I guess I'm not normal because I'm happy in Oakville. My roots are deep in this community . . . A major reason for my happy attitude and satisfaction with life is the contribution made by my wife of over 41 years. In that span of togetherness we have never had a serious disagreement. Her support has kept me in a sphere of contentment.[2]

- My life has been more happy than sad, much more good than bad. Still, for the past several years, I learned about the troubles of aging as my strong and vigorous husband gradually became weaker and more ill. When he was young, I thought he was like a great oak tree and that nothing could ever bring him down. Yet he is gone, and I, never particularly strong or robust, remain well and active and learning to manage on my own . . . I drive my car, baby-sit grandchildren, and make plans to travel and visit around the country. I spend a great deal of time just being thankful for many things younger people take for granted. I am thankful to still have so many people to love and share my life—children, sisters and their families, many other relatives and good friends, and the many nice people around this city[2].

Residents of Long-Term-Care Facilities:

- When my wife had her stroke, she spent almost a year in a hospital. I lived alone and was terribly depressed. When we both got accepted here I was really glad to be with her again. I have to admit that living like this with her is sometimes depressing for me. We only have one room and the children can't come very often. But I've adapted. At least I'm not lonely for her anymore[3].

- My eyesight and ability to walk are very bad. I have a hard time getting around. But I am feeling alright because I have enough money, thanks to my pension, and I am in a home where people look after me. I don't have any family so I like being here because everyone is a friend[3].

- They take care of me here but they don't do it the same as I would myself. I can't take care of myself because I'm all 'crippled up'. Sometimes I think this place is run more for the convenience of the staff than for the residents. I resent having to go to bed so early just to suit them . . . I only have $90 a month to get by on. That is not very much. It is very hard for me to take a bus to go anywhere.[3]

Source:
[1]Rodriguez (1992: 26). Reprinted by permission.
[2]Adapted from *Are you Listening? Essays by Ontario Senior Citizens on What It Means to Be a Senior* (Toronto: Office for Seniors' Issues, Ministry of Citizenship, 1989). Reprinted by permission.
[3]*The NACA Position on Canada's Oldest Seniors: Maintaining the Quality of Their Lives*, p. 54–5 (1922). Ottawa: National Advisory Council on Aging. Reproduced with the consent of the National Advisory Council on Aging (NACA) and the Minister of Public Works and Government Services Canada, 2004.

by social experiences—how an individual views the self, and how an individual thinks that others view and react to them. Increasingly, this author is addressed as 'sir', although no one has yet offered him a seat on a bus or volunteered to help him cross the street! Kaufman and Elder (2003), in a study of grandparenting and age identity, found that those who become grandparents in their 30s and 40s feel older than those who acquire this role 'on time', i.e, later in life. Older people who enjoyed being grandparents felt younger, believed that people become 'old' at older ages, and hoped to live longer than those who reported they did not enjoy being grandparents.

Some older people deny they are aging and, when asked, represent themselves to others and to themselves as younger than they are. Or they accept the social label of 'old' and then either change their identity to be 'old', or they disengage from social life and become isolated. The identification of the self as younger than one's actual chronological age is more likely among those who are in good health and physically active and among those who are employed. Individuals from lower socio-economic strata often experience an earlier onset of health limitations and a faster rate of decline in functional ability. Consequently, it has been found that they tend to hold 'older' identities (Barrett, 2003). For some older people, negative societal attitudes about aging are a threat to self-esteem. For others, however, old-age stereotypes are functional in that the individuals may, in comparison with the stereotypes, see that they are better off than most elderly people.

This inner subjective view of the self, sometimes referred to as 'subjective age', is influenced by societal images, by interaction with others, and by interpretations of health status and activity level compared to age peers. In reality, many older people do not think of themselves as old, and often report feeling and acting younger than their chronological age. In an examination of five dimensions of age identity in later life, Kaufman and Elder (2002) found that as people age their subjective and desired ages become further removed from their actual chronological age. That is, personal age identity changes as we age, but these personal perceptions and definitions lag behind our real age and are different from the public images of older adults. As you interact with older people, notice whether some say they are younger than they are; or whether some attempt to disguise their age with clothing, a new lifestyle, cosmetics, or surgery. Others will report feeling 'young on the inside and old on the outside' (Dionigi, 2002).

Older people often define themselves as being different than others of the same age by presenting themselves as active and healthy. For example, a 91-year-old women in Finland (Jolanki et al., 2000), in response to questions about how she interprets old age and views herself, talked about 'dancing', 'racing around', and 'walking up stairs and around the yard'. She concluded the interview by stating, 'I haven't taken to a walking stick yet. And there are others here who go around with a stick and a walker' (Jolanki et al., 2000: 366). This respondent defines herself as being more active and more independent than those who are younger or of the same age in her retirement home. Similarly, Hurd (1999), in a study of older women who attended a senior centre in central Canada, found that older women distance themselves from those they consider old, and that they actively work at presenting an alternative image of what it means to age. The demonstration of 'active aging' is a form of identity management designed to present and interpret oneself as separate from, and different than, 'older' people. Highlight 1.6 illustrates the attitude and philosophy of an older person who values and practises autonomy and personal choice.

Ageism: A Form of Discrimination

In 1968, the public housing authority in Chevy Chase, Maryland, applied to convert a building in a white, middle-class suburb into housing for older citizens. The public hearings degenerated into a riot as residents of the area fought to keep 'all those old people' out of their community. As a

Highlight 1.6 Autonomy and Choice in Later Life

She is 92 years old, petite, well poised, and proud. She is fully dressed each morning by eight o'clock, with her hair fashionably coifed, and her makeup perfectly applied, in spite of the fact she is legally blind.

Today she has moved to a nursing home. Her husband of 70 years recently passed away, making this move necessary. After many hours of waiting patiently in the lobby of the nursing home where I am employed, she smiled sweetly when told her room was ready. As she manoeuvred her walker to the elevator, I provided a visual description of her tiny room, including the eyelet curtains that had been hung on her window.

'I love it,' she stated with the enthusiasm of an eight-year-old having just been presented with a new puppy. 'Mrs Jones, you haven't seen the room . . . just wait,' I said. Then she spoke these words that I will never forget: 'That does not have anything to do with it,' she gently replied.

'Happiness is something you decide on ahead of time. Whether I like my room or not, does not depend on how the furniture is arranged. It is how I arrange my mind. I have already decided to love it. It is a decision I make every morning when I wake up. I have a choice. I can spend the day in bed recounting the difficulty I have with the parts of my body that no longer work, or I can get out of bed and be thankful for the ones that do work. Each day is a gift, and as long as my eyes open, I will focus on the new day and all of the happy memories I have stored away . . . just for this time in my life.

Old age is like a bank account. You withdraw from what you have already put in. I believe that our background and circumstances may have influenced who we are, but we are responsible for who we become.'

Source: 'The Friday Morning Story, 4 October 2002', *52 Best*, www.52best.com/gracious.asp

result of this incident, Butler (1969) coined the term **ageism**. He considered ageism to be similar to racism and sexism in that inherent biological factors are used to define personality or character traits. Butler defined ageism as a process of systematic stereotyping of, and discrimination against, people because they are old. Ageism can be expressed, fostered, and perpetuated by the media, by public policies, in the workplace, and in casual daily interactions with older people. Indeed, even those who work with or study older people may employ unintentional, insensitive ageist language (Palmore, 2000, 2001).

A large body of literature has examined the attitudes of various age groups toward aging and older people, as well as the effects of those attitudes on the older person. These studies indicate that many children, adolescents, college students, and young adults express negative attitudes about growing old. Highlight 1.7 illustrates some positive and negative views about older people held by children.

Attitudes toward aging are influenced by a number of factors, including the age, ethnicity, level of education, gender, and socio-economic status of the respondents. Those with more education consistently show more positive attitudes toward aging, perhaps because they have more knowledge and perhaps because they have more contact with older adults. Similarly, those who have frequent and meaningful interaction with older people, especially in a family, have more positive attitudes. This occurs primarily because the frequent contact provides factual, personal knowledge which refutes the myths and stereotypes about aging that are encountered elsewhere in society.

Highlight 1.7 Children's Views of Older People

In response to a question posed by their teacher, 'What does it mean to be old?' elementary-school children wrote the following comments. There is diversity in the extent to which positive and negative elements are included, and different perceptions are held by those in Grades 4 and 5 compared to those in Grade 8.

Grade 4

- 'To have wrinkles, having glasses, getting shorter, sometimes getting a hearing aid, being retired and having hobbies.'
- 'What being old means to me is getting ready to die. You need help most of the time. It is harder to see. You don't go to work anymore.'
- 'If you are 67 to 110 you are old. Sometimes all you do is sit around your house. If you are 60 you are semi-old, and if you are 65 you are almost old, but if you are 67 you are old.'

Grade 5

- 'Old people are funny and kind when you go to see them. They like to bake things. When old people see young kids they feel they should kiss and hug you all the time.'
- 'Old people are sometimes nice. But they can be mean too. Old people usually like to be left alone. Most don't like to go anywhere. If you make any noise they can be very mean.'
- 'Old people are sometimes cranky and sometimes nice. Sometimes they give you candy and sometimes they give you heck. Some like plants and some like men.'
- 'I think old is when you get wrinkles and pimples for the rest of your life. People are not the only ones who get old, animals and food get old too.'

Grade 8

- 'Everywhere you go you run into an elderly man or woman. Elderly people are kind, considerate, neat, easy going, lovable, great at sewing or knitting, understanding and most of all great at making delicious apple pies. If you are in a tight spot or in trouble you can turn to elderly people because they have the answers. They might not be as active as us but they are a lot wiser and more understanding than you think. They are great.'
- 'When I think of old people I think of an elderly person with greying hair, wrinkles and very wise. Most old people are more active than a lot of people think. While we are at work or school they are busy doing their own thing such as walking, writing, painting, knitting, working with wood, crafts, and doing volunteer work. I think elderly people should be well respected like any other human being. I have six grandparents and they are all active.'
- 'Personally I think older people are great! Some of them may not be able to move around very well, but if you are willing to listen they always have an interesting story to tell. The problem is people aren't always willing to listen and I think they are missing out.'
- 'In my opinion an old person is a person who thinks that they are old. Physically a person can look old but mentally they can be going one hundred miles an hour.'

Ageism is a socially constructed way of thinking about, and behaving toward older people. It is based on negative attitudes and stereotypes about aging and older people, and involves an assumption that the passing of time represents decay and is therefore grounds for discrimination or marginalization. Where negative attitudes and stereotypes become pervasive and institutionalized in legal (mandatory retirement) or moral codes, they represent a form of discrimination on the basis of actual or perceived chronological age. These stereotypes are used, in turn, to justify prejudicial and discriminatory social acts, such as mandatory retirement at a specific chronological age. Or, on the basis of age, people are excluded from social interaction or denied equal access to services in the public and private sectors. Where ageism exists, older people are devalued and their human rights are limited or denied.

With the onset of population aging and increasing awareness of the changing age structure, age has been used to 'explain' the limitations, rights, abilities, and characteristics of people of a certain chronological age. Age is also used to 'explain' withdrawal from the labour force, or the onset of illness, disability, or dependency. Two types of ageism emerged: 'self-directed' and 'other-directed', in which one's own, or other people's limitations or abilities were attributed, respectively, to attaining a specific chronological age (Bodily, 1991). For example, an elderly woman responded to a questionnaire by stating, 'I have no opinions, I'm 73 years old' (Bodily, 1991). It is ageism that partially accounts for why someone with 73 years of life experience would suggest that she has no opinions, or at least opinions that others would be interested in hearing. Bodily (1991: 258) argued that ageism should be defined as 'the attribution of characteristics, abilities, limitations or events to the mere passing of time.'

The importance of age in trying to explain attitudes, beliefs, or behaviours is vividly illustrated in a study of 1,546 unemployed nurses over 50 years of age (Bodily, 1991). Over 1,200

self- or other-directed ageist statements were identified as the nurses tried to explain why they were out of work, why they were experiencing health problems, or why they were engaged in volunteer work ('I'm too old to work'). Moreover, a number of nurses returned unanswered questionnaires, saying they were 'too old' to offer useful information. Some of the questionnaires were returned by a friend or relative who reported the potential respondent's age ('she is now 75'), implying that she was too old to respond, or there was no merit in hearing from that person because of her age. In short, chronological age in later life is a commonly accepted explanation for events, thoughts, and behaviour, and its use in everyday language reproduces ageist assumptions (Coupland and Coupland, 1993).

As in most forms of discrimination, it is difficult to obtain reliable research evidence to explain the extent of ageism or why it exists (Cohen, 2001; Nelson, 2002). It may be that the occurrence and degree of ageism is closely linked to demographic and economic factors in a society. For example, with a declining birth rate and increasing longevity, when the aging baby boom reaches retirement age after 2010, the skills of older people may be needed in order to meet the demands of the labour force. In that case, ageism would ebb or disappear, and incentives to continue working beyond the normal or mandatory retirement age might be introduced. In another 20 to 30 years, older people will be a near-majority group in the social structure, and ageism may be much less common, especially if older people are perceived as necessary and useful contributors to the labour force.

Regardless of what social changes the future may bring, 'age' should not be employed as a convenient benchmark for behaviour or rights, or as an explanation for processes or outcomes in later life. As Cooper (1984: 4) stated:

> Most would agree that ageism is not the total
> experience of age . . . But only if we learn to

recognize ageism—name it, resist it, refine our understanding of it, stop participating in it—only then can we separate growing old from the fog of ageism which diminishes us. Then, and only then, are true acceptance and celebration of age possible.

Similarly, Bodily (1991: 260) argued that the study of 'age effects' should be abandoned, and that 'age differences' are not synonymous with 'differences due to age'. He concluded:

> Gerontologists do not study the effects of age; rather, they study processes, the effects of which tend to surface among older populations, not because these people are older, but because the processes themselves take time or depend on other processes which take time. This distinction is crucial because it preempts the possibility of casting 'age' as a cause, thereby making room not only for variations 'between' different age groups, but variation 'among' the same age group. People age differently both because they are subject to different events and processes and because the same events and processes affect them differently.

As members of a society become better informed about aging, chronological age as the defining marker of being old will be eroded. Increased research, a longer life expectancy, and visible, more active, and independent older people are revising the definition of later life. However, some researchers and politicians are still enamoured with the use of chronological age as a marker for labels or rights. To illustrate, Denton and Spencer (2002) argue, as researchers, that, with the gains in life expectancy and the reduction in mortality and morbidity, the marker for defining 'old age' should be raised from 65 to 70 for mandatory retirement and pension eligibility if mandatory retirement itself cannot be eliminated. Equally disturbing is the political decree, based on impressions of chronological age, that was made by the President of Turkmenistan in 2002. He ruled that adolescence would, henceforth, be extended until the age of 25, and he 'postponed' the onset of 'old' age until 85, which is well beyond the life expectancy of the average Turkmenian. Referring to chronological age, he divided the later life into three periods with descriptive labels invoking traditional views of being old: the prophetic, the inspirational, and the wise periods of life.

The Study of Aging Phenomena

Gerontology, a multidisciplinary field of study, is the study of aging processes and aging individuals, as well as of the practices and policies that are designed to assist older adults. It includes research conducted in the biological and health sciences, clinical medicine, the behavioural and social sciences, and the humanities; as well as analyses of policies and practices developed at the global, federal, provincial, regional, or local level. The latest information in the field can be found in the proceedings of conferences; in articles in newspapers, magazines, and research journals; in government documents; and on the Internet.[6] Geriatrics, not to be confused with gerontology, is a sub-specialty of medicine which focuses on the physical and mental diseases of later life, and on the treatment and care of elderly patients.

Social gerontology, a sub-set of gerontology, studies the social processes, issues, practices, and policies associated with aging and older people. It was not until the 1960s that scholars in Canada began to study aging processes and individuals in later life. This early research was concerned with developing, evaluating, or critiquing welfare programs or social policies for older people, and describing and explaining aging processes and the status and behaviour of older adults. The researchers in this latter group were affiliated with a traditional discipline such as sociology, psychology, political science, geography, history, or economics. Since the 1980s, aging phenomena and issues have been studied, as well, by practitioners and scholars in professions such as social work, nursing, dentistry, education, architecture, pharmacy, law, criminology, urban and regional planning, recreation and leisure studies, and kinesiology and physical education. More recently, scholars in disciplines such as philosophy, literature, fine arts, communication and film studies, women's studies, and cultural studies have been offering critiques of the way that old age and older people are depicted in the arts, the media, and scholarly publications.

Gerontology can be further divided into two general components: the *academic community*, which produces research, theory, and critiques about the aging process and the situation of older people; and the *professions*, which apply research knowledge and theory in the development and implementation of policies and programs to enhance the quality of life for older adults. The Canadian Association on Gerontology (www.cagacg.ca), which welcomes student members, is composed of researchers, graduate students, government policy-makers, and practitioners in the public or private sector who are employed in a variety of positions that serve older adults. Annually, this diverse group of members meet to share information which will advance knowledge and improve the life of older Canadians.

In Canada, research about aging began in the 1960s, and courses on the sociology of aging and social gerontology have been taught since the early 1970s. The first Canadian reader and textbook with a focus on social aging were published in the early 1980s (Marshall, 1980; McPherson, 1983). In 1971 the Canadian Association on Gerontology was founded, and in 1982 the Association launched the *Canadian Journal on Aging*, a quarterly research journal (Martin Matthews and Béland, 2001). In June 2000, a

national Institute on Aging was established at the University of Sherbrooke under the Scientific Directorship of Dr Réjean Hébert. This Institute expects to begin the first Canadian Longitudinal Study of Aging by 2006, although a provincial longitudinal study on aging was conducted in Manitoba in 1971 under the leadership of Professor Betty Havens. Other notable developments that have increased our knowledge and awareness about aging in Canada include the formation of Centres on Aging at universities or colleges, some with federal support in the 1980s from the Social Sciences and Humanities Research Council; the development of diploma, undergraduate, and graduate programs in some universities and colleges since the 1980s; the creation of provincial gerontology associations; the funding of the Canadian Aging Research Network (CARNET) from 1990 to 1995 by the federal Centres of Excellence program; the creation of the National Advisory Council on Aging (NACA), the Division of Aging and Seniors in Health Canada, and various departments or ministries concerned with aging issues in the federal, provincial, regional, or local levels of government; and many research grants and contracts funded by provincial and federal agencies since the 1980s (see Martin Matthews and Béland, 2001: 25–81; 205–11).

Today, the study of aging from a variety of perspectives is thriving in Canada (Chappell and Penning, 2001). New research knowledge is published quarterly in the *Canadian Journal on Aging* and is presented at annual meetings of the Canadian Association on Gerontology, the provincial gerontology associations, and discipline-based scientific meetings. As well, many government agencies produce regular reports about aging issues and older adults (Statistics Canada, Health Canada, the National Advisory Council on Aging, Veterans Affairs). With the aging of the population expected to reach new heights in the next 30 years, jobs or careers in aging-related fields should present good opportunities.[7]

The Study of Aging Phenomena: Levels of Analysis

Many methods can be used in the study of aging phenomena. Depending on the research question or problem or on the researcher's theoretical perspective, different, but interacting levels of analysis could be selected. Three important levels of analysis are described below: personal troubles and public issues; agency and social structure; and the micro (individual) and macro (structural) elements of daily life.

The levels of analysis do not represent bipolar, independent, and opposing forces. Rather, while they refer to different aspects of social life, they are inextricably interrelated and interdependent, but are separated, conceptually, to enable us to understand an extremely complex social world more completely. The three dimensions interact and overlap with each other in a complementary way: personal troubles of an individual, human agency, and micro levels of analysis are similar, but different level, concepts; as are public issues, the social structure, and the macro-level of analysis.

Similarly, as we will learn in Chapter 5, there are interacting bi-polar dimensions in research methods (quantitative-qualitative) and theoretical perspectives (normative-interpretive). The *normative* theoretical perspective assumes that social order is maintained by well-established norms and status levels to which individuals conform, thereby enabling a society to survive and remain stable—this represents the society/social structure/macro view of the social world. In contrast, the *interpretive* perspective views individuals as social actors who, through negotiation, define, construct, deconstruct, reconstruct, interpret, and control their place in society, thereby creating and changing the social order—this represents the individual/agency/micro view of the social world.

Finally, in terms of research methods, scholars employ a 'quantitative' and/or a 'qualitative' approach to building knowledge, although increasingly both approaches are used in the same research study. *Quantitative* researchers primarily use survey research and large-scale data sets, and most of their interpretations and conclusions are based on numerical data. *Qualitative* scholars base their interpretations and conclusions on personal observations and conversations with people in a social group or situation. Here analyses are based on interpretations of what respondents say and do and of the meanings that the respondents express about their interactions and behaviour in a given setting (such as living in a retirement home), or at a given stage in life (being a widow).

Personal Troubles and Public Issues

To understand our social world, we need to consider relationships and links between individuals and their society. This dialectic focuses on how social order and change are created out of the disparate needs and motivations of many diverse individuals who make up a society, group, or organization. Often this view of the relationship between personal troubles (of individuals) and public issues (responsibilities of society) assumes that individuals are mere puppets influenced by structural forces which control and guide our life depending on where we are located in the social structure. Unfortunately, this erroneous view ignores the presence of human agency and how it interacts with social structures.

Agency and Social Structure

Agency involves individual or group action, based on the ability and willingness to make decisions that affect social relationships. We develop individual or group identities as we interact with others and form social relations across the life course as a result of human agency or individual action within the constraints and opportunities of our social world. We have the potential, as individuals or groups, to construct and change our social world, at least within the boundaries of the social structures and social contexts in which we live. Or, as Giddens (1984) noted, 'agency' refers to the ability of human beings to make a difference in the world. The individual or group can act, with varying degrees of freedom, within a social context (structures, institutions, cultural artifacts) that shapes, defines and limits social interaction.

Social structures provide the social context or conditions under which people act and form social relationships. Most components of this structure—race, gender, ethnicity, and class—are present from birth and endure across the life course. To summarize, 'the agency-structure issue focuses on the way in which human beings both create social life at the same time as they are influenced and shaped by existing social arrangements' (Layder 1994: 5) .

Micro- and Macro-analyses

A third bi-polar dimension influencing our analysis of social life across the life course is the micro-macro distinction. This dialectic analyzes the interaction of those elements that focus on personal face-to-face social interactions in the daily life of individuals or small groups (a micro-analysis), and on those that focus on the larger, impersonal structural components of a society—organizations, institutions, culture and their sub-elements of power, class and resources (a macro-analysis).

Issues and Challenges for an Aging Society

As you begin your journey toward increased understanding of, and sensitivity toward, aging processes and growing older, a number of issues and challenges should be at the forefront of your thinking and acting. These will be addressed in more detail throughout the book. Specifically, note that:

- Aging is not an illness or a disease state— avoid the medicalization of aging and old age view; and the view that aging can be 'cured'

through anti-aging medicines and modalities (Fisher and Morley, 2002; Binstock, 2003). Be wary of e-mail spam and advertising that claims to remove wrinkles and cellulite; to prevent biological aging; and to reverse a range of aging signs, including loss of energy, declining sexual performance, memory loss, etc. Often marketed as HGH (human growth hormone), or an 'anti-aging agent', the drug is either injected (in some cases at a cost of more than $1000 per month) or it is sold as an oral spray. To date, there is no consistent or strong evidence that HGH, in whatever form or dosage, can add 'years to life' or 'life to years'.

- Aging, as a social process, occurs in a changing social world with diverse structural opportunities and barriers—there is inequality in the aging process and in later life, due to lifelong variations in gender, race, ethnicity, education, economic status and place of residence.

- Individual and population aging are inevitably linked and constitute an evolving dialectic wherein aging issues (retirement, pensions, health care, social support) impinge on both the individual and society. Similarly, social, political and economic structures influence the personal experience of aging.

- As birth cohorts grow older, there is increasing diversity among members of the cohort—in health status, lifestyles, income, attitudes, mobility, and independence, to name only a few dimensions.

- We live in, and are connected to, an aging world. Much of the growth in population aging in the 21st century will occur in developing countries, and we can not ignore the social, economic and political implications of this changing global age structure.

- Aging is primarily a women's issue—women live longer, often alone, and face more challenges in later life, especially if divorced, widowed or never married.

- Aging issues and trends may be due to either age changes across the life course, within individuals (aging effects), or to differences among cohorts born at different periods of history (cohort effects).

- Social institutions change across time and present different opportunities and challenges to emerging age cohorts—note the shift over time in the family from the traditional, ever-married couple with 2–4 children, to families characterized by divorce, remarriage, never-married people, common-law or serial relationships, childless marriages, and gay and lesbian relationships.

- Policies and practices for an aging society must reflect the social reality of the present and the future, not the past, and must evolve to avoid perpetuating inequities or inadequate service. For example, we have seen the emphasis in public-policy debates shift from a concern about pension funds to a concern about labour shortages and the need to keep older workers in the labour force through delayed or partial retirement.

- Population aging will not weaken or destroy a society as proponents of apocalyptic demography would have us believe. But, population aging will present us with challenging policy and political issues to resolve.

- The attention paid to 'seniors'' issues by governments at all levels, as expressed in policies, programs, and financial support, varies across time and in different places. Currently, there appears to be a lack of attention to unmet needs for home care and long-term care (NAC, 2003).

- The baby boom cohort will retire and die in your lifetime; at which time the population will become younger again.

To meet the needs of an ever-changing, increasingly diverse older population, a balance of collective versus individual responsibility must evolve; especially with respect to economic security, health care, and social support and personal care. This will require a change in view from believing that population aging is a threat, to one where it is viewed as an opportunity—to make social and economic gains for society, and to enhance the quality of life for longer living older Canadians. Population aging is a life course, society-wide, issue as much as an older person's issue. As the United Nations has argued with respect to global population aging, we need to build 'a society for all ages'. This will require a transformation of national and international thinking (Hicks, 2003). Two essential steps in this direction involve ensuring the ethical treatment of older people, especially those who are vulnerable; and ensuring that human rights in later life are protected.

Ethics for an Aging Population

Ethics is embedded in everyday living, including in later life. Ethics represents an objective and reflective way of thinking about how one should act in a specific situation by taking into account the best interests of everyone involved in the situation—the individual, family members, professional workers, society. Thus, ethical caregiving provides care for an older person based on concern for the self and for others (Voyer, 1998). For both individuals and the state, ethics involves:

- 'should' questions (for example, should life-sustaining technology be used for those with a terminal illness?);

- ethical issues (such as how to prevent elder abuse by caregivers) and ethical dilemmas (for example, does a physician prevent or delay death or initiate death through physician-assisted suicide?); and

- decisions about what is right, good, or appropriate for an individual or for society (for example, who should make, and when, decisions about ceasing treatment, extending life, or employing costly surgery?).

Ethics, as a discipline, does not provide a set of rules for decision-making or behaving, nor a set of easy answers or solutions. Rather, a set of culturally induced principles and values (fairness, privacy, autonomy, freedom, honesty) are employed when debating and resolving moral, religious, or social issues; or, when solving ethical dilemmas facing an older person, his or her family, legal advocates, care workers, and society. Ethics involves a *theoretical* dimension (should individualism or collectivism guide public policy, and in what proportion?), a *practice* dimension (should an 85 year old receive a heart transplant, a hip replacement, or kidney dialysis?), and a *professionalism* dimension (adherence to the Hippocratic oath taken by physicians; the development of standards of care for home care aides; a bill of rights for those in a long-term care facility).

The onset of population aging, along with bio-medical technological developments that foster new ways of thinking and acting, raise legal, moral, philosophical, and ethical questions about aging and older adults.[8] Some of these issues operate at the level of the individual, others at the level of society. Discussions and debates concerning ethics should recognize that there will be individual differences of opinion within and among age cohorts; and by gender, religion, class, ethnicity, and race. Among the questions that will be the subject of such debates are the following:

- Should age or need be a criterion for entitlement to scarce resources like economic security or expensive elective surgery?

- Should economic and health resources be rationed and priority given to young people?

- Should families be responsible for the care of their dependent parents?

- Should older people have the right to die a 'good death' with dignity and at a time of their choosing? Can they decide as autonomous individuals, or should a third party be involved? Who can make a decision if an older person is not competent to decide?

- Should an older person's driver's licence be renewed?

- Should an older person who cannot carry out the necessary activities of daily living be removed from his or her home?

- Who should make decisions about living wills, power of attorney, the use of protective restraints and drugs in nursing homes, and euthanasia?

- Should frail or demented older people be subjects in biomedical experiments and other research projects where they cannot give informed consent?

- Should medical technology be used to extend a person's life if the quality of life deteriorates significantly or below an acceptable level because of a terminal illness or a severe dementia?

- How should autonomy, privacy and the rights of institutionalized and cognitively impaired older people be protected?

In all debates and decision-making around ethical issues, we must ask whose best interest is being served by the decision—that of the older person, a caregiver, an organization, or society? And we must decide what is best at this time, in this situation, and for a specific dependent person. As much as possible, the older person, a family member, or both should be a partner in decisions about personal matters, while older adults, in general, must participate in public debates about ethical issues pertaining to later life, such as whether euthanasia should be legalized. Many decisions about home or health care in later life involve competing or conflicting values, beliefs, or opinions. Often laypeople and professionals disagree on issues with an ethics dimension. They may disagree about what treatment or outcomes would best serve a dependent older person, the family, or society. Yet many decisions are made, or influential advice given, about an elderly person by medical or social services personnel, or by family or friends on behalf of the older adult, who is not consulted, even if he or she is able to make personal decisions.

Ethical issues and dilemmas emerge and evolve over time as values, beliefs, and knowledge change and evolve. Therefore, they need to be debated frequently, and resolved, because of the possible implications of an unethical decision or situation for an individual or for society. Throughout the book, specific ethical issues are discussed with respect to conducting research with older adults (Chapter 5); driving in later life and living in a long-term care facility (Chapter 7); ensuring economic security for an aging population (Chapter 8); elder care and elder abuse (Chapter 11); and end-of-life decisions such as assisted suicide, euthanasia, and the use of technology to sustain life (Chapter 12).

Protecting Human Rights in Later Life

Respect, autonomy, and dignity must be assured as rights for older adults, especially if they are likely to experience discrimination[9], ageism, neglect, abuse, poverty, homelessness, or malnutrition. Increasingly, some 'seniors' issues are being addressed as an integral component of a rights-based society which seeks to improve the standard of living and the quality of life for all older adults (Morgan and David, 2002). Human rights should be permanent, consistent, and universal across the life course; not devalued or lost as one ages and becomes more vulnerable or at risk in later life.

To protect human rights in later life, a Declaration of the Rights of Older Persons (Highlight 1.8) was presented to the second United Nations World Assembly on Aging in April, 2002 (Butler, 2002). This Declaration, which pertains to societies as well as individuals, concludes with a call for action to improve the quality of life of older adults throughout the world.

Highlight 1.8 United Nations Declaration of the Rights of Older Persons[1]

Preamble

At the first United Nations World Assembly on Ageing in 1982, some consideration was given to human rights issues, and in 2000, Mary Robinson, United Nations Commissioner on Human Rights, emphasized the importance of protecting the human rights of older people. However, no official United Nations document has ever identified and specified what these rights are and why they are important. At the second United Nations World Assembly on Ageing in April, 2002, the International Longevity Center-USA, in collaboration with its sister centers in Japan, France, the United Kingdom, and the Dominican Republic, proposed that the following Declaration of the Rights of Older Persons become the basis of action as well as discussion at the Assembly and beyond.

Declaration of the Rights of Older Persons

Whereas the recognition of the inherent dignity and of the equal and inalienable rights of all members of the human family is the foundation of freedom, justice, and peace in the world,

Whereas human progress has increased longevity and enabled the human family to encompass several generations within one lifetime, and whereas the older generations have historically served as the creators, elders, guides, and mentors of the generations that followed,

continued

Hightlight 1.8 continued

Whereas the older members of society are subject to exploitation that takes the form of physical, sexual, emotional, and financial abuse, occurring in their homes as well as in institutions such as nursing homes, and are often treated in cruel and inaccurate ways in language, images, and actions,

Whereas the older members of society are not provided the same rich opportunities for social, cultural, and productive roles and are subject to selective discrimination in the delivery of services otherwise available to other members of the society,

Whereas the older members of society are subject to selective discrimination in the attainment of credit and insurance available to other members of the society and are subject to selective job discrimination in hiring, promotion, and discharge,

Whereas older women live longer than men and experience more poverty, abuse, chronic diseases, institutionalization, and isolation,

Whereas disregard for the basic human rights of any group results in prejudice, marginalization, and abuse, recourse must be sought from all appropriate venues, including the civil, government, and corporate worlds, as well as by advocacy of individuals, families, and older persons,

Whereas older people were once young and the young will one day be old and exist in the context of the unity and continuity of life,

Whereas the United Nations Universal Declaration of Human Rights and other United Nations documents attesting to the inalienable rights of all humankind do not identify and specify older persons as a protected group,

Therefore new laws must be created, and laws that are already in affect must be enforced to combat all forms of discrimination against older people,

Further, the cultural and economic roles of older persons must be expanded to utilize the experience and wisdom that come with age,

Further, to expand the cultural and economic roles of older persons, an official declaration of the rights of older persons must be established, in conjunction with the adoption by nongovernment organizations of a manifesto which advocates that the world's nations commit themselves to protecting the human rights and freedoms of older persons at home, in the workplace, and in institutions and offers affirmatively the rights to work, a decent retirement, protective services when vulnerable, and end-of-life care with dignity.

[1]Reprinted with permission from Butler (2002).

Summary

The older population consists of a heterogeneous group of individuals with a variety of personal characteristics, social attributes, and life experiences. An appreciation of this diversity is essential as you study aging processes, work directly with older adults, or design and implement policies or programs for middle-aged and older adults.

The aging process is influenced by the social, economic, and age structures of a society; by a variety of social processes; by social, political, and economic change within a given culture or subculture; and by major historical events. These factors influence both individual and population aging, and they interact with biological and psychological factors to influence social opportunities and social behaviour throughout the life course. As you study aging processes and elderly persons, question the validity of images of aging that you confront (are they myths and stereotypes?), and search for cross-cultural or subcultural variations in the aging process, particularly with respect to the treatment and status of older adults in different segments of Canadian society (from homeless older persons, to elderly Aboriginal people living in remote northern communities, to recent immigrants, to upper-class, wealthy Canadians living in the most affluent neighbourhoods in metropolitan areas).

Above all, remember that we are not puppets acting and behaving according to formal roles and rigid social structures as we proceed through the life course. We do not all age in a similar way, but we are not totally autonomous either. We act with agency and play out our individual life course as part of an age cohort which interacts with, and is influenced by, other individuals and age cohorts. Our life course evolves within social structures that foster equity or inequity across the life course. Our life chances and lifestyles are influenced by the cultural, historical, and structural factors that pervade our particular social world. This social world involves living in different neighbourhoods and communities, and being a social actor in a variety of ever-changing social institutions, of which the family, the labour force, and the educational, political, and economic systems are the most influential. We do not age in a vacuum, but rather in a highly interactive and changing social world where our life course is inter-dependent with other individuals, groups, and social institutions, both within Canada, and globally.

As you reflect on the various topics and issues introduced in this text and in other sources, you will find that a number of common themes pervade serious discussions and examinations of aging as a social process. Some of these themes include:

- Aging occurs across the life course—it is not just an event in later life.

- Extreme diversity or heterogeneity, on a number of social, cultural, cognitive, and physical dimensions, is common among older populations.

- Aging is a gendered experience which tends to favour men, except with respect to longevity.

- Individual aging and population aging are linked processes.

- Human agency interacts with social structures to influence the nature and quality of the aging experience.

- Demography is not destiny—population aging will not destroy society.

- Aging, especially in the public-policy domain, is either, or both, a private trouble (for the individual and family) or a public issue (for society or an institution).

- Older people seek dignity and respect, and strive to remain independent and function as autonomous beings.

- Aging involves continuity *and* change across the life course.

- Aging is a holistic process involving the interaction of biological, cultural, environmental, economic, social and psychological processes that interact to influence life chances and lifestyles across the life course.

For Reflection, Debate, or Action

1. Interview members of your extended family to identify historical and cultural factors that may have influenced the process of aging for earlier generations. Identify some problem or issue they have experienced while aging, and try to determine why the problem arose, and how or if it was resolved.

2. Identify some factors in your life course, to date, which may or may not have an impact on your journey across the life course.

3. Identify the living generations in your family, and define and contrast the characteristics and life situation of the oldest woman (the matriarch) and man (the patriarch).

4. Ask your oldest living relative(s) to tell stories about their parents and grandparents, and about the everyday life and challenges of earlier generations in your family.

5. Meet with an older person who is not a member of your extended family, and who has lived in a different neighbourhood or community than your parents and grandparents. Ask the person to tell you a story about his or her life, in general, or ask them to reconstruct a few significant events that may have changed their life course, or that have given special meaning to aging or to being elderly at the present time. Contrast their life with that of someone about the same age in your family.

6. Develop an argument to support or refute one of the ideas or concerns expressed in Highlight 1.2.

7. Select one or two television shows and watch them over a 3–4 week period. Observe, record and interpret if, and how, older characters are portrayed, including what they say about themselves, how they dress and behave, how others view them, or whether they are a major or minor character in their social world.

8. Administer the Facts on Aging Quiz (Highlight 1.4) to four or five friends and four or five family members. Note any differences in the responses, in general, or to specific questions, by chronological age. For erroneous responses, inform the person why their response is incorrect.

9. Interview older adults living in the community and in institutionalized settings about what aging and becoming older 'means' to them in their everyday lives.

10. Interview a number of your friends, and ask them to define 'old' and 'old age'; then interview friends of your parents and grandparents, asking the same question. If there are differences in perceptions and definitions, what are they and why do they occur?

Notes

1. The correct responses are: 1-F; 2-F; 3-T; 4-F; 5-F; 6-T; 7-T; 8-F; 9-F; 10-F.

2. When we study aging and later life there is no commonly agreed terminology to refer to older adults–seniors, elders, agers, golden agers, the old, the oldest old, the old old, the frail elderly, etc. And preferred terms vary in usage across time, and in different domains. For example, government personnel use 'seniors' in much of their written and oral communications; scholars use 'older persons' or 'older adults' to generically describe people in later life. The perfect term, and a commonly accepted term, has yet to be derived.

3. Some excellent fiction and non-fiction books about aging include: S. de Beauvoir, *The Coming of Age* (1970); M. Laurence, *The Stone Angel* (1964); W. Booth, *The Art of Growing Older* (1992); Yahnke and Eastman (1995); M. Albom, *Tuesdays with Morrie* (1997).

4. The 'Audiovisual Reviews' section of *The Gerontologist* includes reviews of both educational and feature-length films with aging themes (see *The Gerontologist* 39(4): 504–10 for a review of many feature-length films that were produced before 1999).

5. Simone de Beauvoir (1970), in an early study and critique of aging, presented a history of thought about aging from early Egypt to the modern era, and examined aging as a subjective experience.

6. The endnotes to each chapter and Appendix B, Study Resources', list many websites, as well as a number of books, periodicals, and government reports.

7. For job or career ideas, scan www.cagacg.ca; www.aghe.org; www.geron.org; and contact representatives of provincial gerontology associations, as well as faculty working in colleges and univer-

sities. Local social service agencies, retirement and nursing homes, and hospitals may provide volunteer opportunities to work with older adults.

8. For a discussion of ethical questions and dilemmas, see NACA (1993a); Cole and Holstein (1996); Moody (1996); Morgan (1996); Smith (1996); Johnson (1999); Clements (2002); Ross et al. (2002); and current and past issues of the *Journal*

of *Ethics, Law and Aging*, the *Journal of Medical Ethics*, and *Ethics and Values in Health Care*.

9. In June 2002, the Ontario Human Rights Commission released a *Policy on Discrimination Against Older Persons Because of Age*. The policy emphasizes issues pertaining to the older worker, housing issues and special needs in services and facilities in health care and transit services (http://www.ohrc.on.ca).

References

Albom, M. 1997. *Tuesdays with Morrie: An Old Man, a Young Man and Life's Greatest Lesson.* New York: Doubleday.

Arber, S., and J. Ginn (eds). 1995. *Connecting Gender and Aging: A Sociological Approach.* Philadelphia, Penn.: Open University Press.

Auger, J., and D. Tedford-Litle. 2002. *From the Inside Looking Out: Competing Ideas about Growing Old.* Halifax: Fernwood.

Barrett, A. 2003. 'Socioeconomic Status and Age Identity: The Role of Dimensions of Health in the Subjective Construction of Age', *Journal of Gerontology: Social Sciences*, 58B(2), S101–9.

Bengtson, V., et al. 1985. 'Generations, Cohorts and Relations between Age Groups'. Pp. 304–38 in R. Binstock and E. Shanas (eds), *Handbook of Aging and the Social Sciences.* New York: Van Nostrand Reinhold.

Binstock, R. 2003. 'The War on Anti-Aging Medicine', *The Gerontologist*, 43(1), 4–14.

Birren, J., and K.W. Schaie (eds). 2001. *Handbook of the Psychology of Aging.* New York: Academic Press.

Bodily, C. 1991. 'I Have No Opinions, I'm 73 Years Old— Rethinking Ageism', *Journal of Aging Studies*, 5(3), 245–64.

Booth, W. (ed.). 1992. *The Art of Growing Older: Writers on Living and Aging.* Toronto: Poseidon Press.

Bowd, A. 2003. 'Stereotypes of Elderly Persons in Narrative Jokes', *Research on Aging*, 25(1), 22–35.

Butler, R. 1969. 'Ageism: Another Form of Bigotry', *The Gerontologist*, 9(3), 243–6.

———. 2002. 'Declaration of the Rights of Older Persons', *The Gerontologist*, 42(2), 152–3.

Chappell, N., and M. Penning 2001. 'Sociology of Aging in Canada: Issues for the Millenium', *Canadian Journal on Aging*, 20 (Supp. 1), 82–110.

Cheal, D. 2003a. 'Aging and Demographic Change in Canadian Context', *Horizons* 6(2), 21–3.

———. (ed.). 2003b. *Aging and Demographic Change in Canadian Context.* Toronto: University of Toronto Press.

Clements, G. 2002. 'Ethical and Legal Issues: A Legal Perspective'. Pp. 333–60 in M. Stephenson and E. Sawyer (eds), *Continuing the Care: The Issues and Challenges for Long-Term Care.* Ottawa: CHA Press.

Cohen, E. 2001. 'The Complex Nature of Ageism: What Is It? Who Does It? Who Perceives It?', *The Gerontologist*, 41(5), 576–7.

Cole, T., and M. Holstein. 1996. 'Ethics and Aging'. Pp. 480–97 in R. Binstock and L. George (eds), *Handbook of Aging and the Social Sciences.* San Diego, Calif.: Academic Press.

Connidis, I. 2001. *Family Ties and Aging.* Thousand Oaks, Calif.: Sage.

———. 2003. 'The Impact of Demographic and Social Trends on Informal Support for Older Persons'. Pp. 105–32 in D. Cheal (ed.), *Aging and Demographic Change in Canadian Context.* Toronto: University of Toronto Press.

Cooper, B. 1984. *Over the Hill.* Freedom, Calif.: The Crossing Press.

Coupland, N., and J. Coupland. 1993. 'Discourses of Ageism and Anti-Ageism', *Journal of Aging Studies*, 7(3), 279–301.

Dannefer, D. 1999. 'Neoteny, Naturalization and Other Constituents of Human Development'. Pp. 67–93 in C. Ryff and V. Marshall (eds), *The Self and Society in Aging Processes.* New York: Springer.

———. 2003. 'Cumulative Advantage/Disadvantage and the Life Course: Cross-Fertilizing Age and Social Science Theory', *Journal of Gerontology: Social Sciences*, 58B(6), S327–37.

————., and P. Uhlenberg. 1999. 'Paths of the Life Course: A Typology'. Pp. 306–26 in V. Bengtson and W. Schaie (eds), *Handbook of Theories of Aging*. New York: Springer.

De Beauvoir, S. 1970. *The Coming of Age*. New York: W.W. Norton.

Denton, F., and B. Spencer. 2000. 'Population Aging and its Economic Costs: A Survey of the Issues and Evidence', *Canadian Journal on Aging*, 19(1), 1–31.

————. 2002. 'Some Demographic Consequences of Revising the Definition of "Old Age" to Reflect Future Changes in Life Table Probabilities', *Canadian Journal on Aging*, 21(3), 349–56.

Dionigi, R. 2002. 'Leisure and Identity Management in Later Life: Understanding Competitive Sport Participation Among Older Adults', *World Leisure*, 44(3), 4–15.

Elder, G., and M. Johnson. 2003. 'The Life Course and Aging: Challenges, Lessons and New Directions'. Pp. 49–81 in R. Settersten (ed.), *Invitation to the Life Course: Toward a New Understanding of Later Life*. New York: Baywood.

Evans, R., et al, 2001. 'Apocalypse No: Population Aging and the Future of Health Care Systems', *Canadian Journal on Aging*, 20 (Supp. 1), 160–91.

Featherstone, M., and M. Hepworth (eds). 1995. *Images of Aging: Cultural Representations of Later Life*. London: Routledge.

Fisher, A., and J. Morley 2002. 'Antiaging Medicine: The Good, the Bad and the Ugly', *Journal of Gerontology: Medical Sciences*, 57A(10), M636–9.

Friedland, R., and L. Summer. 1999. *Demography is Not Destiny*. Washington, DC: National Academy on an Aging Society.

FTP 1999. *Rapport sur la santé des canadiens et des canadiennes*. Ottawa: Préparé par le Comité consultatif fédéral, provincial territorial sur la santé de la population, Canada.

Gee, E. 2000. 'Population and Politics: Voodoo Demography, Population Aging, and Canadian Social Policy'. Pp. 5–25 in E. Gee and G. Gutman (eds), *The Overselling of Population Aging: Apocalyptic Demography, Intergenerational Challenges and Social Policy*. Don Mills, Ont.: Oxford University Press.

————, and G. Gutman (eds). 2000. *The Overselling of Population Aging: Apocalyptic Demography, Intergenerational Challenges and Social Policy*. Don Mills, Ont.: Oxford University Press.

————, and M. Kimball 1987. *Women and Aging*. Toronto: Butterworths.

Giddens, A. 1984. *The Constitution of Society*. Cambridge, UK: Polity Press.

Gruman, G. 2003. *A History of Ideas about the Prolongation of Life*. New York: Springer.

Hagestad, G., and D. Dannefer 2001. 'Concepts and Theories of Aging: Beyond Microfication in Social Science Approaches'. Pp. 3–21 in R. Binstock and L. George (eds), *Handbook of Aging and the Social Sciences*. New York: Academic Press.

Hareven, T. 2001. 'Historical Perspectives on Aging and Family Relations'. Pp. 141–59 in R. Binstock and L. George (eds), *Handbook of Aging and the Social Sciences*. New York: Academic Press.

Harris, D., and P. Changas. 1994. 'Revision of Palmore's Facts on Aging Quiz from a True-False to a Multiple-Choice Format', *Educational Gerontology*, 20(6), 741–54.

Health Canada. 2002. *Canada's Aging Population*. Division of Aging and Seniors. Ottawa: Minister of Public Works and Government Services Canada.

Hébert, R. 2002. 'Research on Aging: Providing Evidence for Rescuing the Canadian Health Care System', *Canadian Journal on Aging*, 21(3), 343–7.

Heinz, W., and V. Marshall (eds). 2003. *Social Dynamics of the Life Course: Transitions, Institutions and Interrelations*. Hawthorne, NY: Aldine de Gruyter.

Hicks, P. 2003. 'The Policy Implications of Aging: A Transformation of National and International Thinking', *Horizons*, 6(2), 12–16.

Hurd, L. 1999. '"We're Not Old!": Older Women's Negotiation of Aging and Oldness', *Journal of Aging Studies*, 13(4), 419–39.

Johnson, T. (ed.). 1999. *Handbook on Ethical Issues in Aging*. Westport, Conn.: Greenwood Press.

Jolanki, O., et al. 2000. 'Old Age As a Choice and As a Necessity: Two Interpretive Repertoires', *Journal of Aging Studies*, 14(4), 359–72.

Kaufman, G., and G. Elder 2002. 'Revisiting Age Identity: A Research Note', *Journal of Aging Studies*, 16(2), 169–176.

————. 2003. 'Grandparenting and Age Identity', *Journal of Aging Studies*, 17(3), 269–82.

Kenyon, G., et al. 1999. 'Elements of a Narrative Gerontology'. Pp. 40–58 in V. Bengtson and W. Schaie (eds), *Handbook of Theories of Aging*. New York: Springer.

————. 2001. *Narrative Gerontology: Theory, Research and Practice*. New York: Springer.

Krout, J., and Z. Wasyliw. 2002. 'Infusing Gerontology Into Grades 7–12 Social Studies Curricula', *The Gerontologist*, 42(3), 387–91.

Layder, D. 1994. *Understanding Social Theory*. Thousand Oaks, Calif.: Sage Publications.

Kimmel, M. 2000. *The Gendered Society*. New York: Oxford University Press.

Laurence, M. 1964. *The Stone Angel*. Toronto: McClelland and Stewart-Bantam

Law Commission of Canada. 2004. *Does Age Matter? Law and Relationships Between Generations*. Ottawa: Law Commission of Canada.

McDaniel, S. 1986. *Canada's Aging Population*. Toronto: Butterworths.

McPherson, B. 1983. *Aging As a Social Process: An Introduction to Individual and Population Aging*. Toronto: Butterworths.

Marshall, V. 1980. *Aging in Canada: Social Perspectives*. Don Mills, Ont.: Fitzhenry and Whiteside.

———. 2000. 'Agency, Structure, and the Life Course in the Era of Reflexive Modernization'. Paper presented at the American Sociological Association Annual Meeting, August 2000, Washington, DC.

Martin Matthews, A., and F. Béland (eds). 2001. *Canadian Journal on Aging*, 20 (Supp. 1), 2001.

Martin Matthews, A., et al . 1984. 'The Facts on Aging Quiz: A Canadian Validation and Cross-Cultural Comparison', *Canadian Journal on Aging*, 3(4), 165–74.

Mills, C.W. 1959. *The Sociological Imagination*. Oxford: Oxford University Press.

Mérette, M. 2002. 'The Bright Side: A Positive View on the Economics of Aging', *Choices*, 8(1), 1–28.

Miller, R., and R. Dodder. 1980. 'A Revision of Palmore's Facts on Aging Quiz', *The Gerontologist*, 20(6), 673–9.

Moen, P. 1995. 'Gender, Age and the Life Course'. Pp. 171–87 in R. Binstock and L. George (eds), *Handbook of Aging and the Social Sciences*. San Diego, Calif.: Academic Press.

———. 2001. 'The Gendered Life Course'. Pp. 179–96 in R. Binstock and L. George (eds), *Handbook of Aging and the Social Sciences*. New York: Academic Press.

Moody, H. 1996. *Ethics in an Aging Society*. Baltimore, Md.: Johns Hopkins University Press.

Morgan, J. 1996. *Ethical Issues in the Care of the Dying and Bereaved Aged*. Amityville, NY: Baywood.

Morgan, R., and S. David. 2002. 'Human Rights: A New Language for Aging Advocacy', *The Gerontologist*, 42(4), 436–42.

Myles, J. 2002. 'Back to Bismarck? The Public Policy Implications of Living Longer', *Canadian Journal on Aging*, 21(3), 325–9.

NACA (National Advisory Council on Aging). 1993a. *Ethics and Aging*. Ottawa: NACA.

———. 1993b. *Expression*, 9(1), 2.

——— 2001. 'Storytelling', *Expression*, 14(4). Ottawa: NACA.

———. 2003. *Interim Report Card—Seniors in Canada, 2003*. Ottawa: NACA.

Nelson, T. (ed.). 2002. *Ageism: Stereotyping and Prejudice against Older Persons*. Cambridge, Mass.: MIT Press.

Olshansky, S.J., et al. 2002. 'Position Statement on Human Aging', *Journal of Gerontology: Biological Sciences*, 57A(8), B292–7.

O'Rand, A. 1996. 'The Cumulative Stratification of the Life Course'. Pp. 188–207 in R. Binstock and L. George (eds), *Handbook of Aging and the Social Sciences*. San Diego, Calif.: Academic Press.

Palmore, E. 1977. 'Facts on Aging: A Short Quiz', *The Gerontologist*, 17(4), 315–20.

———. 1980. 'The Facts on Aging Quiz: A Review of Findings', *The Gerontologist*, 20(6), 669–72.

———. 1981. *The Facts on Aging Quiz: A Handbook of Uses and Results*. New York: Springer.

———. 1988. *The Facts on Aging Quiz: A Handbook of Uses and Results*. New York: Springer.

———. 1990. *Ageism: Negative and Positive*. New York: Springer.

———. 2000. 'Ageism in Gerontological Language', *The Gerontologist*, 40(6), 645.

———. 2001. 'The Ageism Survey: First Findings', *The Gerontologist*, 41(5), 572–5.

Phillipson, C. 1998. *Reconstructing Old Age*. Thousand Oaks, Calif.: Sage.

Pratt, H. 1976. *The Gray Lobby*. Chicago, Ill.: University of Chicago Press.

Riley, J. 2001. *Rising Life Expectancy: A Global History*. New York: Cambridge University Press.

Rodriguez, L. 1992. 'Susanna Re-Membered', *Canadian Woman Studies*, 12(2), 24–30.

Ross, M., et al. 2002. 'End of Life Care: The Experience of Seniors and Informal Caregivers', *Canadian Journal on Aging*, 21(1), 137–46.

Rowe, G. 2003. 'Fragments of Lives: Enabling New Policy Directions through Integrated Life-Course Data', *Horizons*, 6(2), 7–11.

Ryff, C., and V. Marshall (eds). 1999. *The Self and Society in Aging Processes*. New Yorker: Springer.

Schneider, E. and J. Rowe (eds). 1996. *Handbook of the Biology of Aging*. San Diego, Calif.: Academic Press.

Smith, G. 1996. *Legal and Healthcare Ethics for the Elderly*. Washington, DC: Taylor and Francis.

————, et al. 2000. 'The Effects of Interpersonal and Personal Agency on Perceived Control and Psychological Well-Being in Adulthood', *The Gerontologist*, 40(4), 458–68.

Sontag, S. 1972. 'The Double Standard of Aging', *The Saturday Review of the Society*, 1(1), 29–38.

United Nations. 2000. www.un.org/esa/socdev/ageing/agewpop.htm. Accessed May 2000.

Voyer, G. 1998. 'What Is Ethical Care?' *Canadian Journal on Aging*, 17(1), i–vii.

Yahnke, R., and R. Eastman 1995. *Literature and Gerontology: A Research Guide*. Westport, Conn.: Greenwood Press.

CHAPTER 2

Historical and Cultural Perspectives on Aging

Focal Points

- In what way is our life course influenced by the period of history in which we live?

- How does culture shape the meaning of being older in a society, and how does culture influence the challenges, experiences, and outcomes of the aging process?

- In what way have modernization and other technological advances changed the status of elderly people in different cultures and at different times?

- What can the study of other cultures, past and present, teach us about growing older in our society?

- Does being a member of a subculture influence how older members are viewed and supported in later life?

- To what extent, and why, are aging Aboriginal people disadvantaged in Canadian society?

Introduction

Individual and population aging are universal phenomena, but the processes may vary at different periods of history and in different cultures. There are differences within and across cultures in how 'old age' is defined; in the extent to which older people are valued, supported, and cared for in later life; and in the cultural stereotypes of aging and of being elderly. A sensitivity to cultural differences and similarities is essential for the development of effective policies and service programs, for meeting the unique needs of older people with different cultural roots, for refuting myths about aging, and for understanding the future of aging societies, and within a given society. This chapter examines diversity in aging experiences and in the status of older persons in selected cultures throughout history, as well as in a few Canadian subcultures.

At one time anthropologists and historians interviewed the 'elders' of a society primarily to learn about the customs and history of that society. Seldom did they study the elders themselves, the meaning of aging, or aging processes in the society. Today, the meaning of age and aging and the place of older people in their communities, is studied in many cultural and ethnic groups.[1] This research activity has increased because, whereas biological aging is a universal experience, different patterns of social aging are found in different cultures throughout the world and in different historical periods. Our culture, and the period of history we pass through, influences how we age and the extent to which we are valued and supported in our later years. For example, the words used to describe older people in some cultures, at some periods in history ('hag', 'old geezer', 'old maid'), reveals their low status in that culture (Fry, 1996).

To understand the cultural basis of aging in a global context, four common research approaches have been used: (1) a historical comparison of early and later societies (from preliterate to postmodern); (2) a comparison of two or more somewhat similar societies at the same point in time, such as Japan, Canada, and Sweden); (3) a comparison of eastern with western societies, such as Japan and Canada; and (4) a comparison of developed with developing regions or countries, such as Canada compared to Somalia. An example of one of these approaches is a comparison of the responsibility of families and the state for supporting and caring for elderly persons in eastern and western societies (Bengtson et al., 2000). The following were some of the findings:

Cultural Differences

- **Filial piety**, i.e., respect and a feeling of responsibility for one's parents, is embedded in eastern cultures; such a general guiding principle is not found in the west

- Rapid population aging occurred in modernized western societies in the twentieth century; it will occur in developing eastern societies in the twenty-first century (it has already happened in Japan).

- In eastern cultures, the eldest son and his wife are usually responsible for caring for his parents; in western cultures a daughter or a daughter-in-law is more likely to be responsible.

- In eastern cultures, older family members often live in the household of a child, usually the eldest son; in western cultures, this seldom occurs.

- In western cultures, state-supported economic assistance, housing, and health care for older adults are common; these programs are just beginning to appear in eastern cultures.

Cultural Similarities

- The family is the primary support system for the social and daily lives of older adults.

- With population aging, an increasing number of older adults are economically dependent on the state and/or their families for survival in later life.

- Fertility rates are declining, and smaller families, including some with no children, are more typical than in the past. (China, for example, has a one-child policy.)

- Debates are common about what the relative responsibility of the state and the family should be in providing support to older adults.

Aging in a Multicultural Society

Canada's open-door immigration policy has created a diverse, multicultural society in which the mosaic of later life is changing rapidly. If we are to become a more tolerant society and design effective programs and policies for all older Canadians, the past, present, and future cultural diversity of our aging population must be understood. Our population mix is different in the early years of the twenty-first century than it was in the middle of the twentieth century. From the 1940s to the 1960s, most immigrants were white, they came from Europe, and they lived in both rural and urban communities. Many had little education, and they usually, at least among the first generation, found employment as labourers.

Over the past 30 years, our immigrant population has become more diverse (over 250,000 arrive each year) as members of many different cultural and linguistic groups arrived. There has been greater diversity in level of education and economic status on arrival (from Hong Kong millionaires to political refugees from impoverished, developing nations), and most settle in the three largest urban centres—Montreal, Toronto, and Vancouver. There are significant variations in the rate at which members of different groups are assimilated into mainstream society. Moreover, a general label, such as Asian, and one general policy that 'fits all' is no longer adequate when one is describing or serving a specific group because of the considerable diversity within the group. Furthermore, unlike the situation in earlier times, some immigrants are arriving late in life (under the family re-unification program) and are supported by children who emigrated to Canada in early adulthood. This diverse group of older immigrants, as well as others who emigrated earlier and are aging in Canada, are often not served fully in later life by policies and social institutions designed for the majority who make up mainstream society.

The language, cultural, and religious differences of immigrants create unique challenges for service workers and policy-makers who provide health care, community and home care, institutional care, and economic assistance. Some older members of ethnic minorities do not speak English; adhere to their traditional diet; are not knowledgeable about social or health-care services; and have specific cultural beliefs about health care, death and dying customs, and the responsibility of the family versus the state in supporting older people. These factors are especially challenging when one is trying to reduce or eliminate gender inequality in later life among diverse cultural groups. Many immigrant women are illiterate or don't speak English, they are economically disadvantaged, they experience transportation problems, and they adhere to traditional cultural beliefs about health care and social support in later life.

Not only is our older population culturally diverse, but the cultural differences both among and within the various groups are growing; this will make service delivery even more difficult throughout this century, especially in large metropolitan areas. An understanding of, and a sensitivity to, cultural diversity will reduce the barriers in the support systems designed to enhance the quality of life of *all* older Canadians. This is especially important if older immigrants are admitted to long-term care facilities where diet, language, and medical and palliative care are designed for life-long residents of Canada.

The Meaning of Culture

Culture and society are intimately linked. They reflect 'different sides of the same coin of social reality' (McPherson et al., 1989: 7). Whereas a society involves 'sets of social relationships', culture consists of 'the meanings' that develop when individuals or groups interact in these relationships. Because cultural elements are shared by a group of people, social relationships and a society change over time. Culture, which provides a symbolic order and a set of shared meanings to social life, includes values, beliefs, attitudes, norms, customs, and knowledge. These elements are represented in our language, art, dress, technology, literature, music, ceremonies, and games. The most highly valued elements of a culture become institutionalized and are transmitted from one generation to the next, and some are adopted by immigrants through a process of **assimilation** and **acculturation**.

Of particular importance in understanding the social organization of a society are its values, beliefs, and norms. **Values** are the internalized criteria by which members select and judge goals and behaviour in society. Values are trans-situational (that is, they can be held and used in many situations) and are found in most institutions in a society. They include principles such as democracy, freedom, achievement, competition, and respect for older people. **Beliefs** represent an individual's conception of the world. They are a statement about what is thought to be true as opposed to what is desirable (as in the case of values). Beliefs are unique to a given culture or subculture and are learned by observation, by adopting traditions, or by accepting ideas expressed by parents, teachers, and the mass media. **Norms** define acceptable or expected behaviour in specific social situations. Many norms concerning how we dress, how we spend our leisure time, or when we work are related to our chronological age or our social positions. Our values, beliefs (whether or not they are correct), norms, and attitudes generate stereotypes about people and can lead to discrimination toward members of a specific group, including older adults.

Some cultural elements are similar from one society to another, although they may be expressed differently. For example, all societies have some form of political, social, and economic organization, a set of values, a common language, and a way of socializing their members. On the other hand, some societies are democracies, others dictatorships; some value older people, others do not. In most societies there is a high degree of agreement about what people value and how they behave. This is reflected in the phenomenon known as **ethnocentrism**, in which members regard their mainstream culture as superior to all others. Ethnocentric beliefs influence how we behave toward people from other cultures, including members of subcultures in our own society, who themselves hold and express a unique, but different, set of values, beliefs, norms, and customs. Ethnocentrism fosters insensitivity to those in other cultural groups and leads to policies, such as pension and health-care systems, and practices, such as the kind of food served in long-term care settings, that serve primarily those in mainstream society.

Historical and Comparative Approaches to Understanding Aging Processes

Just as biologists identify and explain similarities and differences among different species in order to arrive at generalizations, scholars in the social sciences and humanities seek to understand the process of aging and the status of older people in different cultural and historical contexts. The study of aging from a comparative perspective began with the publication in 1945 of Simmons's classic study of elderly people in a variety of primitive societies. For many years after, scholars focused on a description of aging and the status of the elderly in a variety of societies. These studies found that chronological or perceived age is an important factor in the stratification of many societies and that the status of older people varies between societies and within a society at different historical periods.

Much of this early work was descriptive and did not explain *why* there were differences in the status of the oldest persons in different societies. Since the late 1970s, however, scholars have sought to explain cultural variations in the aging process. First, historians and sociologists identified patterns of thought and behaviour by older people that are repeated in many cultures, as well as those that are found only in a specific culture, subculture, or historical period. Historical studies of aging, for example, have verified that the status of older adults has not always been as low as it is today in some societies nor as high as it was once assumed to be in some societies.

A second development was the study of aging from an anthropological perspective. Focusing on cultural elements, anthropologists explain variations along a continuum of possible patterns of aging. The anthropology of aging investigates the social and economic status of older people in a society; the social roles of adults at different stages in life; the rituals associated with aging and dying; whether age grading and discrimination are factors in the social organization of a society; and how social behaviour throughout the life course is shaped by cultural elements. Anthropologists have identified over 3,000 societies in the world, with considerable variations found in both the process of aging and the status of older people (Fry, 1985). These societies are categorized according to their level of industrialization and modernization into one of three types: (1) primitive hunting-and-gathering societies; (2) pre-industrial societies; and (3) post-industrial and postmodern societies. Today, many international organizations (the United Nations, the World Health Organization) use a dichotomous category: *developed* and *developing* nations. Most studies describe variations within a specific society over time, and only a few have directly compared aging processes in two or more cultures.[2]

As the social structures of modern societies have become more complex, scholars have studied the diversity that is found *within* a society, especially that based on race, ethnic background, and religion. These structural factors influence the experiences and opportunities of aging adults, especially across social class and gender lines. In addition, aging and the status of older people vary between and within unique **subcultures**. Topics studied within unique cultural backgrounds include attitudes toward aging; the lifestyles of older people; aging problems unique to the group, such as diet, housing, health care, and income; and variations in access to informal support networks and to health and social services. These studies have shown that unique policies and services are often needed to enhance the quality of life of an older person in a specific cultural group and to reduce later-life inequities between members of the dominant group and minority groups.

The Modernization Hypothesis and the Changing Status of Older People

Before the Industrial Revolution, i.e., before about 1750, only two types of societies existed: primitive hunting-and-gathering tribes and agrarian-peasant communities. In primitive hunting-and-gathering societies the oldest members were considered to be a valuable source of knowledge about rituals and survival skills. Knowledge was a source of power, and when knowledge was no longer needed (when mechanization arrived with the Industrial Revolution) or when knowledge was acquired and held by the young, elderly people lost power and status. Social differentiation was based largely on age, and elders held influential positions in the social, political, and religious spheres of life (Goody, 1976). The oldest members of the community were expected to contribute as much as possible by assisting with economic and household chores; by teaching games, songs, traditions, and survival skills to the young; and, if a man, by serving as an 'elder' or 'chief' (Simmons, 1945, 1952). To illustrate the current importance of older people in developing countries, United Nations Secretary-General, Kofi Annan, at the opening of the World Assembly on Aging in April 2002, stated that 'in Africa, when an old man dies, a library disappears . . . without the knowledge and wisdom of the old, the young would never know where they come from, or where they belong.'

In agrarian-peasant societies the oldest citizens controlled the land and were considered the heads of extended families, which often included at least three generations. In these societies, the oldest people had the most knowledge about, and experience with, survival skills, animal care, growing crops, rituals, and laws. When no longer able to contribute as labourers, they 'retired' and transferred control of the family resources, usually to the oldest son. Then they were cared for by the family and the community because of their past contributions and because they were still a major source of knowledge.

With the onset of the Industrial Revolution, because of the need for labour in towns and cities, migration from rural to urban areas increased rapidly, especially among young adults. New social structures, cultural values, political and social systems, and social processes evolved, and these had a profound impact on the lives of all age groups, including older people. For individuals, industrialization generally resulted in more education; improvements in public health and living conditions, which increased longevity; independence from parents after late adolescence; greater personal wealth; and increased leisure time because of shorter working hours. For the social and economic system of a society, the Industrial Revolution led to six major changes (Burgess, 1960; Cowgill, 1974a).

1. A shift from home to factory production; that is, the family was no longer the centre of economic production (as it had been on farms). This meant a separation of work and home and a dramatic increase in the number of people, including older people, who became dependent on non-family employers for economic security.

2. Increased migration to cities, especially by young people, resulted in greater social differentiation, the development of multiple social groups (family, work, and neighbourhood), exposure to new values and norms, and the establishment of public schools.

3. A breakup of the extended family and the emergence of the nuclear family, often living in a different community from the parents.

4. The rise of large organizations (that is, factories and unions) and the creation of new occupations requiring skills that young people could acquire through apprenticeship or formal schooling. Many of the skills possessed by older people became obsolete, and

mandatory retirement was introduced. A minimum level of formal education became a prerequisite for employment in certain occupations.

5. A rapid spread of new knowledge, with the result that the knowledge and power held by older adults through experience was no longer relevant or valued.

6. An improvement in the quality of medical care, with a reduction in the rates of infant and childhood mortality, an increase in life expectancy, and a larger population.

The process by which a society moved from the pre-industrial to the industrial world was known as **modernization**. Cowgill and Holmes (1972) were among the first to argue that modernization and the accompanying social, political, and economic changes led to a decline in the status of older people. Older adults lost power and status because they no longer held essential roles and were no longer the major source of knowledge. Also, because adult children no longer lived in the family home, some believed they were no longer obliged to support their aging parents. To test their hypothesis that the status of older people declined with modernization, Cowgill and Holmes (1972) examined the status of older people in 15 different cultures and subcultures. They concluded that modernization does account for the declining status of older persons, except in societies where they continued to perform valued functions.

For many years this somewhat simplistic 'before and after modernization' explanation of the changing status of elderly people went unchallenged. However, in the 1900s, modernization theory was challenged and re-examined by historians and anthropologists interested in the societal aspects of aging.[3] First, they expressed serious doubts about the assumption that the status of *all* older people declined dramatically after the modernization of western societies. Quadagno (1982), presenting evidence from nineteenth-century England, concluded that the onset and degree of industrialization, or modernization, differed considerably by region and industry. She found that in some industries, and in some regions, the position of older people improved with increased mechanization. To illustrate, Quadagno (1982) noted that the invention of the sewing machine increased the output of older seamstresses who worked at home. Because economic conditions did not favour the construction of new factories, the contributions of these older women actually increased in the postindustrial era. This is a unique example of how the income and status of some older women increased while that of their male age peers decreased. That is, where physical labour is essential in a society, older men lose status before older women because they can no longer perform heavy physical work.

Similarly, Hendricks (1982) noted that modernization occurs first in core areas of a country or in core countries. Beyond this regional or international core is a peripheral region that fails to modernize at the same rate, and perhaps not at all. A current example is the rapid modernization of urban Beijing and Shanghai compared to the rural regions in China. As an alternative explanation for the all-or-none view of modernization, Hendricks (1982) proposed an 'internal colonialism' or 'dualistic development' model. According to this model, control over resources resides in the metropolitan regions of a nation. Older people living closer to a metropolitan area are the first to lose status, especially if they are members of an already devalued group. Those in peripheral (rural) regions may not lose status, although they may lack social assistance in later life if their children migrate to large urban centres or emigrate to other countries.

A second criticism of modernization theory noted that the social status of older people in pre-industrial societies was not always as high as assumed. For example, Stearns (1982) argued that in pre-industrial France elderly persons were never valued highly. A pessimistic image of old age

prevailed and was held by all age groups in France at that time (including by elderly people). This view resulted from the cultural belief that old age is an unpleasant time and that older people are a nuisance. Because these beliefs persisted before *and* after modernization in France, modernization cannot be held responsible for a change in the status of older people in that country.

Another perspective is that the status in modern societies is no lower and may be higher than it was before industrialization. In some post-industrial societies, such as Japan and Korea, older people are supported by their children, their economic status has improved because of income security plans, programs of social support have enhanced rather than diminished their position, and mandatory retirement has relieved them of the burden of work and rewarded them with freedom and leisure time. In short, the assumption of a difference in their treatment before and after modernization is misleading. Laslett (1985) concluded that any loss of status by elderly people occurred as much as a century or more *after* the beginning of industrialization. Any losses were due to changes in the age structure and in social values. Such changes coincided with the demographic transition to lower fertility and mortality rates that characterize postmodern societies.

More recently, Ng et al. (2002), in a study of Hong Kong, concluded that as societies modernize, changes in family structures and in traditional values weaken the informal social support network previously supplied by the family. The breakdown of the traditional multi-generational household (where an older parent often lived with an adult child) is due to smaller families, smaller living spaces, increased employment by daughters and daughters-in-law, and the emigration of children to other countries such as Canada. And there is less support across society for values associated with the Confucian teaching of filial piety, by which a son and daughter had a duty to serve and pay respect to parents in later life, and the parents expected this obligation to be fulfilled, especially by the eldest son. The reality in modern Hong Kong and in other Asian societies (Sung, 2001), is that older people now lead more independent lives without the immediate, available support of family members. This has occurred because of changes in family structures and traditional cultural values, and the fact that many children have emigrated. Highlight 2.1 examines the ideals and expression of elder respect in the modern East Asian societies of China, Japan, and Korea.

Finally, with respect to the impact of modernization, there are varying degrees of influence within a society because of different value systems. For example, because they adhere to a strict religious doctrine that rejects modern influences, elderly Old Order Mennonites in North America have retained leadership roles in the church, community, and family, even where some members of the religious group have adopted such elements of modernization as electricity in the home and the use of cars instead of horse and buggy.

In summary, there is conflicting evidence concerning the status of older people in pre-industrial societies. Just as some earlier societies held elderly people in high esteem while others abandoned them, similar patterns can be found in contemporary societies. Just as elderly persons were abandoned by some nomadic tribes, today some older persons are abandoned or 'warehoused' in long-term-care institutions.

The next two sections present brief descriptions of aging in selected pre-industrial and industrial societies. The descriptions are based on accounts from each society at a given point in history. Thus, we see only a snapshot of a specific period in a society's development. The descriptions also tend to ignore variations within cultural or regional groups. Most important, there may be a gap between the stated values, beliefs, or attitudes of respondents and their actual behaviour. Even when people tell an interviewer that they respect their elders and look after them, careful observations may or may not support this ideal view (Fry, 1985). Hence, as you read about, or interact with, members of different cultural groups, search for both hidden and alternative meanings about aging and about being an elderly person in that group. And do not base conclusions or provide assistance or services solely on the basis of your own cultural experiences or beliefs.

Aging in Pre-industrial Societies

Preliterate Societies

In preliterate societies (those in which there was no formal education system), knowledge, beliefs, and survival skills were located in the memories of those with the greatest experience: the elders. The economic system, whether the people were hunters and gatherers or farmers, was based on production and consumption within domestic kinship groups, and the dependence of children on their parents was linked to a degree of obligation toward the oldest people in the family or tribal unit (Goody, 1976).

The status of elderly people was highest in societies that had a surplus of food, and where the oldest members controlled property or had knowledge of survival skills, rituals, and customs. In societies where food was scarce, where property was nonexistent, or where leadership was based on ability rather than on longevity or family ties, older people were sometimes abandoned or put to death. In both types of preliterate societies, older men commanded greater respect than older women. Highlight 2.2 illustrates the status of elderly people in a variety of preliterate societies.

Literate Pre-industrial Societies

The status of older people in literate pre-industrial societies varied according to living conditions, religious beliefs, and cultural values. For example, elderly people appeared to have high status in early Hebrew, Roman, and North American societies. They lost that status as wars, migration, and changing values created higher status for youth and for those who acquired wealth and made

Highlight 2.1 The Ideals and Expression of Elder Respect in Three Modern East Asian Societies

Throughout history, respect for elderly people has been a common value in many societies. It is prevalent in societies where Confucian teachings prevail, such as China, Japan, and Korea. Filial piety requires children to acknowledge and appreciate the care and assistance they received from parents as children. In return, there is an obligation to respect one's parents, and all elderly people, and to provide support for one's parents in later life. But as Sung (2001) notes, 'respect' is an abstract concept. Hence, there is confusion as to how respect should be demonstrated, in general, and specifically in Asian societies. Sung (2001: 17–21) reviewed the literature and identified 14 types of respect for elders:

- Care respect: Providing care and services for elders.
- Victual respect: Serving food and drinks of elders' choice.
- Gift respect: Bestowing gifts on elders.
- Linguistic respect: Using respectful language in speaking to and addressing elders.
- Presentational respect: Holding courteous appearances.
- Spatial respect: Furnishing elders with honourable seats or places.
- Celebrative respect: Celebrating birthdays in honour of elders.
- Public respect: Respecting all elders of society.
- Acquiescent respect: Being obedient to elders.
- Salutatory respect: Greeting elders.
- Precedential respect: Giving precedential treatment to elders.
- Funeral respect: Holding funeral rites for deceased parents.
- Consulting respect: Consulting elders on personal and family matters, customs, and rituals.
- Ancestor respect: Worshipping ancestors.

Employing these categories, Sung (2001) analyzed how younger Asians in three societies express respect. While there is general adherence to the belief of elder respect at the level of society, i.e., towards elders in general, the amount of respect shown to elders in a specific family depends on personal beliefs, experiences, resources, and energy. The extent to which elders are actively or passively respected and the forms used to express respect vary by culture and age cohort. As Mehta (1997) and Sung (2001) found, there is a shift in the meaning of respect from obedience and subservience to courtesy and kindness; from listening to parents and obeying them, to listening but not always obeying or behaving as expected; from bending forward (bowing) to greet elders to shaking hands with them; and from treating *all* elders, *equally*, with respect, to treating those with more resources and greater achievements with higher respect. As acculturation occurs in Canada across generations of Asian immigrants, mandatory expressions of respect are likely to be modified, weakened, or abandoned.

Source: Adapted from Sung (2001: 17–21).

Highlight 2.2 The Status of Older People in Preliterate Societies

In nomadic societies, elderly people were devalued if they became a burden and had no specialized knowledge or skills, if cultural values dictated that they were no longer worthy of life (because of declining physical strength), or if children sought revenge on parents. Thus, abandoning ill and frail elderly people was relatively common. Holmberg (1969: 224–5) reported that the Sirino tribe in Bolivia abandoned elderly people when they became ill or unable to walk. The Yakuts of Siberia forced elderly people to become beggars and slaves. The Chukchee of Siberia killed frail elderly people in a public ceremony before the tribe (de Beauvoir, 1972).

In other societies, elderly people served as 'information banks' for the society and were held in high esteem if they passed on useful skills and information to younger people. Maxwell and Silverman (1970) identified six major functions that elderly people performed in preliterate societies: (1) hosts of feasts, games, or visiting groups; (2) consultants about survival skills or rituals; (3) decision-makers for groups; (4) entertainers; (5) arbitrators of disputes; and (6) teachers of the young. The authors found a strong relationship between the amount of useful information held by older adults and the respect accorded to them by other members of society.

Elderly people in preliterate societies might contribute to their tribes, even in old age, in the following ways: older chiefs conducted political or religious meetings; elderly Incas served as scarecrows in the fields; and elders educated and entertained children in the evenings (Simmons, 1960; Rosow, 1965; de Beauvoir, 1972; Goody, 1976). Moreover, in addition to performing functional roles, older people held higher status if the social organization or social structure of the society included a stable place of residence; a viable system of food production; low-skill functional roles (like those listed above); a nuclear family structure; and a system of religion in which older people were revered because they were thought to be able to communicate with the gods.

functional contributions to the society, regardless of age. Highlight 2.3 describes the status of elderly people in some literate pre-industrial societies.

Aging in Industrialized Societies

The onset of industrialization and modernization after about 1750 led to a phenomenon known as the 'epidemiological transition', characterized by lower morbidity and mortality rates from disease and an increasing life expectancy. This transition increased the demand for health and social services, especially by older people, who were more likely to live their last few years in poor health, with disabilities and with some loss of independence (Wister and Gutman, 1997). Some snapshots of modernization and its impact on different societies are described below.

Samoa

Traditional Samoan culture involved a subsistence economy comprised of extended families who lived in seaside villages and were headed by an elected chief. In each village sharing was common within and between families, and elders were respected by the extended family (Watson and Maxwell, 1977: 46–58; Rhoads, 1984).

In the early 1800s Christianity was introduced to the islands. Contact with westerners increased when the United States took control of Eastern Samoa after 1900. During and after the Second World War the literacy rate in Samoa increased, and older adults were no longer needed as repositories of information. Industries were established to provide employment and income. Western material goods were imported, and food

Highlight 2.3 The Status of Older People in Literate Pre-industrial Societies

The Ancient Hebrews

The ancient Hebrews are one of the earliest societies for which there are written records and well-preserved artifacts. This was one of the first societies to view long life as a blessing rather than a burden. In the years between 1300 BC and AD 100, the Hebrews were a nomadic desert tribe comprising large extended families. The family included a patriarch, wives, concubines, children, slaves, servants, and any others who attached themselves to the domestic group for protection. The patriarch served as ruler, religious leader, judge, and teacher. He controlled all aspects of political, religious, economic, and social life and was identified by a long, grey beard—a sign of wisdom and authority. In this relatively stable yet nomadic culture, aging, at least for men, represented increasing wisdom and power.

The City-States of Ancient Greece and Rome

According to ancient Greek literature, the Greeks feared old age. Greek gods were depicted as eternally youthful, and much of the literature commented on the declining physical and mental strength of older people. In ancient Greece, power was more likely to be associated with wealth than with age, and if an older man attained power, it accrued to him because of his wealth.

Elderly Romans, unless they were wealthy, lost power and influence as they grew older. This is not surprising, since evidence from burial remains indicates that average life expectancy may have been only 20 to 30 years. Death, even by suicide, was considered preferable to suffering the indignities of physical, mental, and social deterioration. In the later years of the Roman Empire, the threat from the barbarians placed a premium on youth and strength, and survival of the fittest prevailed as a necessity. Those who did not contribute to society were abandoned or put to death.

England

The Roman church, after the decline of the Roman Empire, became the ruling authority throughout feudal England and Western Europe. Although the status of older people should have improved with the rise of Christianity, this was not the case. The Church was more interested in recruiting new members than in performing social work. However, by the sixteenth and early seventeenth centuries, when longevity increased somewhat, values such as charity, hospitality, and care for others became basic tenets of parish life, regardless of denomination. This led to an increased concern for older people, especially if they were poor. Consequently, almshouses were created to provide institutionalized care for poor people. However, since caregiving resources were scarce, even the oldest people were expected to work as long as possible. The state became involved, formally, in supporting older people with the passage of the Elizabethan Poor Laws in 1603. Henceforth, elderly persons without families to care for them were looked after by a parish, with some limited financial assistance from the state.

Colonial America (1620–1770)

The rigours of colonial life placed a premium on strong, healthy adults. Consequently, the colonies were initially a young, male-dominated society, with a median age of about 20 years. Less than 2

continued

Hightlight 2.3 continued

per cent of the residents were over 65. Being highly religious, the Puritans adhered strictly to Biblical teachings. Elders were honoured by occupying leadership positions, and they sat in the most prestigious seats at town meetings. However, this status was not based solely on religious beliefs; it was also related to wealth—the oldest members owned the land and resources and thereby commanded respect from their families. Even in this religious society, sometimes the poor were driven from town so they would no longer be an economic burden. As in many societies, older women did not receive the same respect as older men.

According to Fischer (1977), the declining status of elderly people in North America began not with industrialization, urbanization, and higher levels of literacy, but with a change in cultural values after the American Revolution in 1776. This led to an emphasis on equality based on performance and income and to a westward migration away from the influence of parents. Many pioneers were sons of eastern colonials who moved away from the nuclear family to build a fortune and new life in their 'little house on the prairie'. One outcome of this trend was that many older people were left in the eastern colonies to fend for themselves. Some ended their lives alone, often in poverty.

sharing decreased. The promotion of tourism led to even more contact with Westerners. As a result of these influences, the power and authority of the elders in the community declined. However, they were still treated with respect within the family, and children continued to contribute to the economic support of the elders in their extended family.

The Anishinabe of Georgian Bay

The Anishinabe, a term meaning 'original people', inhabited the islands and mainland of Georgian Bay in Ontario (Vanderburgh, 1987). The elders played a traditional role by transmitting knowledge and culture to the children of the tribe. Specifically, they taught mythic and local history, the language, healing methods and beliefs, and traditional rituals.

With the arrival of Christian missionaries and the creation of schools on the reserves, missionaries and teachers began to control the knowledge and culture that was transmitted to the younger generations of Anishinabe. Skills needed for survival in the 'modern' world were taught: English, mathematics, and science. By the 1960s, the role of elder had disappeared, and the

older members of the tribe lost prestige and a sense of being useful and needed. As modern ways infiltrated the tribe, elderly Anishinabe gradually began to be neglected by their families and the tribe, and many were forced to enter non-Native long-term-care institutions.

In the 1970s, the Native elderly regained some importance when the federal government created Native Cultural/Educational Centres across Canada. Vanderburgh (1987) describes how, in 1974, the Native elders of the Anishinabe were recruited by the staff of a centre on Manitoulin Island to record and transmit elements of their traditional culture. The oldest-surviving Anishinabe became 'volunteer elders' in the traditional sense: passing on their knowledge to young children concerning rituals, crafts, language, and related anecdotal narratives about the early life and history of the Anishinabe.

Japan

Understanding the status of elderly people in Asian cultures requires an understanding of Asian philosophical and religious principles. While the cultures vary in many respects, they have some common elements. First, many Asians believe that age represents an accumulation of wisdom. In addition, the Confucian concept of filial piety, or respect for parents, is linked to the principle of ancestor worship, maintaining a link with the past and ensuring respect for parents, who will be the next ancestors to be worshipped. In these Asian societies, the unity of the family and the role of elderly people in society are valued.

Modernization began in Japan in the Meiji era (1868–1912) and was intensified during Japan's reconstruction after the Second World War. Today, Japan has a rapidly decreasing birth rate (about 1.7 children per couple) and the highest life expectancy in the world. Hence, it is the most rapidly aging society in the world. Life expectancy in Japan is 77 years for men and 84 years for women, and people 65 and over make up about 17 per cent of the population. But it is projected that by 2020 about 27 per cent of the population will be over 65.

The tradition of filial piety and the remnants of a hierarchical social structure continue to integrate elderly people into society and enable them to receive respect and support from younger age cohorts. But changes are happening. First, young adults are moving to large cities, far from their rural roots. Second, traditions such as respect for older people and caring for one's parents are weakening (Ogawa and Retherford, 1993). Third, because of a shortage of special housing for older people, retirement communities, a new concept in the 1990s, are being built. Finally, the role of Japanese women is changing as more young women earn university degrees and work full-time and consequently have less time to care for an aging parent or parent-in-law and less interest in doing so. Grassroots organizations are being created, as well, to improve the status of women, including older women. While the leadership and control of most senior citizen clubs in Japan (Silver Centres) still rests with men, these traditional rights are being challenged by women.

At the same time, elderly Japanese men and women seem to be expecting less from their children in terms of care, and because of increased longevity, many 'young' elderly people in their 60s may become responsible for the care of a very elderly parent. In Japan, friends and neighbours seldom provide support to elderly people, and the tradition of retirees at age 60 finding a second job is becoming less prevalent because of a depressed economy. Thus, many elderly people, especially men, are facing years of non-employment in which they must find meaningful ways to spend a vast amount of leisure time.

At the institutional level, the status of older people in Japan has not declined much since the onset of industrialization, as evidenced by September 15 being an official national holiday, 'Respect for the Elders Day'; the special celebration for a person's sixtieth birthday (*Kanrecki*); and the practice of giving up one's seat to an older person on public transit. In 1963 the Japanese government passed the National Law for the Welfare of the Elders, which requires that elderly people be given respect, the opportunity to work, and the right to participate in social activities. Since then, many other laws or national policies have been enacted to institutionalize the care of and respect for older people in Japan.

Researchers have suggested that the status of older adults in Japan is declining. Sparks (1975) found that although Japanese adults may care for their aging parents, an increasing number do so reluctantly. Indeed, some abandon their parents or pass them from one sibling to another, thereby meeting the minimal requirements of filial duty. Plath (1972) noted that even when elderly parents live with their children, they may not be included in family conversations and activities, in effect being reduced to the level of domestic labourers or servants. Consequently, the burden of care for elderly parents is increasingly being shifted from adult children, for whom it is a personal trouble, to the state or place of former employment, where it becomes a public responsibility. This shift in values and practice, whether real or desired, has created a need for more public social policies and programs for elderly people. Finally, as in other modern nations, rural-urban differences in the status of older people can be found in Japan. In the rural areas, long-standing values and practices tend to persist, and most elderly people live with their children if the latter have not migrated to a large city.

Israel: Aging in a Kibbutz

The first kibbutz in Israel was established in 1909 by Jewish immigrants. A kibbutz includes 50 to 1,000 people who live in a self-sustaining economic and household community. For the most part, kibbutzim are agricultural co-operatives (although some have established industries) characterized by common ownership of property and equality in production and consumption.

All members of the kibbutz must work to produce sufficient food and goods for themselves. The oldest men and women in the kibbutz are called *vatikim*. In addition to receiving the same benefits as regular members, the *vatikim* usually have better housing. They also benefit from close family bonds since two or three generations usually live within the kibbutz. These family bonds have been a source of support in the past. Other practices also contribute to successful aging: all members have equal standing with respect to their rights and obligations and hence, there is no mandatory retirement; informal and formal care is provided to all; there is a high quality of medical care; and there is stability in their lifestyle—in the worker role, in social and family ties, in the standard of living, in public involvement, and in the greater likelihood that their children will live in the same community.

Although elderly people are opposed to retirement because it represents a life without purpose or meaning, they nevertheless engage in a process of gradual retirement that involves lighter tasks and reduced hours of work. In this way they become more dependent on communal institutions, and as their numbers increase because of longevity, they become a greater economic burden. As a result, some kibbutzim have established industries in which older people are assigned easy but tedious tasks, thereby enabling them to continue contributing to the community in some functional capacity. However, for older women in particular, this has created a problem since some cannot adapt to the repetitive factory chores to which they are assigned.

The Israeli kibbutz represents a model in which many of the basic problems of aging—economic security, family and community relations, health care, and retirement—have been addressed and partially solved because of a religious and social commitment to equality and care, regardless of age. However, there are increasing reports of intergenerational conflict between younger members, who want farming to become more mechanized, and the *vatikim*, who adhere to a tradition that manual labour is needed to produce goods. This conflict is rooted in the changes that have been made to many kibbutzim: outsourcing of services (about 60 per cent by 1998), a greater emphasis on profits, the use of hired workers, less influence in decision making by all members on an equal basis, and differential rewards according to one's contribution or social position. Most older members are opposed to these changes and feel alienated and less satisfied with life in the kibbutz (Leviatan, 1999). Thus, structural changes in the kibbutz are leading to changes in social arrangements that have a negative effect on the older members. Like other segments of other societies, social changes induce stress and coping difficulties for older members.

Aging in Subcultures

The Concept of Subcultures

In multicultural societies such as Canada, differences among social groups are often due to unique cultural backgrounds and specific group identities and histories. These may be natural groups based on gender, age, religion, race, or ethnicity, or they may be created when members of a subgroup do not accept all or most elements of the dominant culture. Or they may be formed when some members of a society are formally or subtly excluded from mainstream society. These groups demonstrate the characteristics of a subculture rather than those of a social category.

Members of a subculture adopt a set of values, norms, customs, behaviours, and attitudes that differ from those of mainstream society. In some instances the subgroup may use a different language and may separate itself physically or socially from mainstream society in homogeneous communities, such as Chinatown. Although all people who are 65–75 years of age in a city or town represent a 'social category', they do not necessarily form a subculture, because they do not share a common identity or unique and specific values, norms, and daily experiences. However, if a group of 65–75 year-olds live in a commune, a trailer park, or a retirement village, they form a subculture if they adopt a common identity, i.e., as retirees, and hold unique values, norms, and experiences that make them different from those of the same age who live elsewhere.

Convergent subcultures are subcultures that are eventually assimilated into the larger culture. An example would be the descendants of Italian immigrants who arrived in Canada after the Second World War and who were assimilated over two or three generations. Other subcultures, such as the Old Order Mennonites or Hutterites, are *persistent subcultures* because they maintain a totally separate and unique identity, lifestyle, and place of residence, often in rural areas. In the following sections, issues of aging and the status of elderly people are examined for indigenous, racial, ethnic, and religious subcultures.

Indigenous Subcultures: The Aboriginal People of Canada

Cultures and Lifestyles

Aboriginal people are those whose ancestors were the original inhabitants of a region or country. Statistics Canada defines Aboriginal people as 'those who report themselves as identifying with at least one Aboriginal group (North American Indian, Métis or Inuit), and/or those who report as being a Treaty Indian or a Registered Indian as defined by the Indian Act, and/or those who were members of an Indian Band or First Nation' (Statistics Canada, 2001). Overall, there are more than 55 sovereign Aboriginal peoples in Canada.

According to the 2001 census, 1.3 million Canadians reported their ancestry as Aboriginal, and of these, 976,300 identified themselves as 'aboriginals', an increase of 22 per cent since 1996. Most live in Ontario and British Columbia in terms of absolute numbers, but Manitoba, Saskatchewan, and the three territories have the largest percentage of Aboriginal people. In total, Aboriginal people comprise 3.3 per cent of the population, but only 4 per cent of this population is 65 and over, compared to 13 per cent in the non-Aboriginal population. But while the population is growing, fewer people (25 per cent) are able to carry on a conversation in a native language. In 2001, 33 per cent of the Aboriginal population was under 15 years of age, largely because of a fertility rate 1.5 times higher than that for other Canadian women. First Nations people comprise about 68 per cent of the total Aboriginal population, the Métis about 26 per cent, and the Inuit about 5 per cent. Collectively, Aboriginal people appears to be the preferred label, although government reports and the popular press use Native and more specific terms such as First Nations, Indian, Treaty or Status Indians, Registered Indians, Métis, or Inuit.[4] While about 50 per cent lived in cities in 2001 (Newhouse and Peters, 2003; Statistics Canada, 2003), it is those who live in coherent communities in rural areas, in isolated northern settlements, or on reserves who constitute a subculture.

The Canadian Constitution recognizes three groups of Aboriginal people—Indians, Inuit, and Métis. These groups are three separate cultures with unique heritages, languages, cultural practices, spiritual beliefs, and degree of assimilation into mainstream society. They have experienced different life chances and lifestyles than non-Aboriginal Canadians. Thus, just as we should not label all people from Asia, India, and the Far East as 'Asians', not all members of all sovereign groups should be labelled as 'Aboriginal'.

In comparison to mainstream Canadian society, relatively little is known about the diverse subcultures in the Aboriginal population, or about elderly people in these small, often isolated communities.[5] There is considerable cultural diversity in beliefs, values, and customs, both among the various tribes, bands, and nations and between generations in each community. These differences are due to geographical isolation, economic conditions, out-migration of younger people, and the degree of government support or intervention in a community.

Nevertheless, there are some some common structural and cultural conditions that are common to many communities, and which have an effect on elderly Aboriginal people (Indian and Northern Affairs Canada, 1995). Traditional Aboriginal cultures share the following elements:

- a large kin network, with strong family ties and orientation
- a close-knit community, sometimes suspicious and resentful of mainstream society
- a respect for elders, who are a source of tradition and wisdom
- a preference for informal support from relatives over formal care from public services
- a wide variety of spiritual beliefs which guide everyday life
- a preference to remain in the community in later life, rather than to live in an institution in another community
- adherence to traditional healing practices and beliefs.

Demographically, Aboriginal communities are characterized by:

- high fertility rates, with infant mortality rates twice as high as the Canadian average
- families headed by a single parent (almost 20 per cent), of whom almost 90 per cent are women
- an earlier age at death because of an average life expectancy that is 6–7 years less than the national average, although the gap is narrowing (Health Canada, 2002)
- more disabilities in adult life than the general population
- a projected tripling in the number of Aboriginal 'seniors' by 2016 (Health Canada, 2002)
- less formal education than other Canadians (fewer than 5 per cent have a university degree)

From a structural perspective, Aboriginal people are faced with inequalities and a difficult lifestyle, characterized, in general, by:

- high levels of unemployment or irregular employment
- low average incomes, economic deprivation, and a dependence on government subsidies
- substandard housing, and few housing options, especially in later life
- few retirement, nursing homes, and geriatric-care facilities in remote communities
- poor health, including a high incidence of chronic diseases which are related to lifelong malnutrition, alcoholism, and misuse of drugs; and to inadequate health-care services and facilities, including a lack of hospitals and health- care workers in the community
- a higher incidence of being victims of crime, especially violent crime, and of spousal or child abuse

- the lack of formal community-based social and welfare services, such as home care, and an under-use of formal services even when they exist, owing to a preference for support from relatives.

Despite increased interventions through federal health and financial assistance programs (Health Canada, 2002: 33), Aboriginal people still suffer higher unemployment, much worse living conditions, and greater poverty than any other group in Canada. While other ethnic groups have been assimilated into the dominant culture, at least to some degree, most Aboriginal groups remain both culturally and physically isolated from mainstream society.

Because Aboriginal people have a shorter life expectancy than other Canadians, it has been argued that the eligible age for federal assistance should be lowered from 65 to 55 years of age (Ontario Advisory Council on Senior Citizens, 1993). In this way, fairness and need would be addressed, and a larger number of Aboriginal people would be eligible for social assistance earlier in life, at the time when it is needed.

The situation of older people in Aboriginal communities is generally much worse than that of the typical elderly person in Canadian society. Many Aboriginal elders attended residential schools which were designed to assimilate children into mainstream culture, thereby denying access to, and identity with, their language and culture. Some of these schools exposed some children to physical and sexual abuse, and to unhealthy living conditions and malnutrition. They also contributed to unstable family structures when they were admitted to these schools (Reading, 1999). Many have experienced stress through the loss of traditional 'ways of living' as the fish and game are depleted when mining or forestry companies enter their space. Other communities have been moved, and some individuals have been forced to migrate to cities or towns.

Total annual income is often below the poverty line, however it is measured, which is the minimum amount needed for bare subsistence. Very few have completed high school, and many have not completed elementary school. Many women are widowed early in life or have been a single parent for many years. Because the extended family is a central institution, many elders live with their 'family', which includes unemployed children and grandchildren. In this situation, the extended family often lives on a very small income. This living arrangement provides access to an informal support network in later life. Others, however, live alone, and often do so in substandard housing conditions. 'Elders' are still respected to some degree, because of their experience, their past contributions to the community, and their knowledge of traditions. However, the term 'elder' is increasingly being replaced by the term 'elderly'. Status, respect, and a meaningful social role are being eroded or lost as communities modernize and young people move away.

Inequality of Health Status

The health of Aboriginal people who live in cities and towns (the off-reserve Aboriginal population), is significantly poorer than that of the non-Aboriginal population with respect to self-perceived health, chronic conditions, long-term restrictions on activity, depression, and reported unmet health needs (Statistics Canada, 2002: 73–88; 2003a; 2003b).

In general, Aboriginal people living on reserves and in remote northern settlements have high levels of poverty, morbidity, and mortality. Life expectancy is lower than that of the non-Aboriginal population because of a number of demographic and lifestyle factors: high rates of infant mortality, alcohol and substance abuse, and family and community violence, especially involving young males; high suicide rates; and a high incidence of diabetes, HIV infection, obesity, and disability. The communities lack adequate health-care facilities, and it is difficult to recruit and keep health-care workers in remote regions. It is for these reasons that the Commission on the Future of Health Care in Canada (Romanow, 2002: 159–61), recommended that $1.5 billion be allocated to improving access to health care in rural and remote communities, including the use of Telehealth for access to specialists and health information via technology.

Elderly Aboriginal people are disadvantaged by high disability rates (twice the national average) and a lifetime of poor health, which is compounded by lack of access to health-care facilities (Health and Welfare Canada, 1992; Wister and Moore, 1998). They need high levels of care (Buchignani and Armstrong-Esther, 1999), thereby placing a burden on the middle generation, which, because of high fertility rates, still has many childcare responsibilities. Among Aboriginal elders, the prevalence of self-reported chronic conditions such as heart disease, hypertension, diabetes, and arthritis is often double or triple the rate reported by other Canadians in the same age group (Health Canada, 2002). These conditions are compounded by the fact that many elderly Aboriginal people prefer to receive 'traditional' health care from medicine people in the community. Moreover, many are not eligible for extended health plans that cover vision and dental care, prescription drugs, and new health technologies. Most reserves and many communities do not have nursing homes. Thus, elderly people who need continuing care must enter a nursing home away from the familiar life of their home community. There, they seldom receive the kind of food they prefer, and their family and friends are unable to visit frequently.

Racial and Ethnic Subcultures

In multicultural societies some ethnic or racial groups are labelled as **minority groups**. Because of prejudices and stereotypes, members of these groups often experience discrimination. However, not all members of a minority group experience discrimination. Rather, the relative status of a minority group in a society at any particular time determines whether a particular group is viewed as a 'minority' group and is therefore subject to some degree of discrimination and inequality. Moreover, individuals in the same ethnic or racial group are ranked differently depending on their gender, education, or occupation.

There are variations between and within groups in terms of the length of time a group has lived in the host country, the amount and type of discrimination directed toward members of a group, and the extent to which a group is assimilated into the host society. The location of a group in the ethnic and racial stratification system can change and thus can lead to changes across generations in the process of aging and in the status of elderly people in the racial or ethnic group. These differences arise because subsequent generations are likely to be assimilated into mainstream Canadian society. Later generations are better educated, have higher incomes, and may discard the traditional values, language, and customs of their parents and grandparents. If structural and cultural assimilation does not occur, cultural background remains an important ascribed factor that persists across the life course, especially where racial or ethnic identity is preserved. To illustrate, there are four distinct generational groups among Japanese North Americans: the *Issei* (first or immigrant generation); the *Nisei* (second generation, born in Canada); the *Sansei* (third generation); and the *Yonsi* (fourth generation). Each generation was socialized at a different period in history, and each experienced, if at all, different forms of discrimination and different social opportunities.

Some ethnic groups live primarily in an ethnic neighbourhood throughout their lives. While this housing location provides security and support in the early years in a new society, it can lead to isolation for older members in the later years as children move away from the ethnic neighbourhood. And as new groups move in, the ethnic and racial composition of the neighbourhood changes.

Most health and social welfare policies and services are designed for members of the majority group. In fact some racial or ethnic groups under-utilize the social services available in a community because they don't know what services are available, or because their language, customs, or beliefs make it difficult for immigrants to accept the service, especially in long-term-care institutions.

Racial subcultures are characterized by physical features, such as colour of skin or the shape of the eyes, that distinguish them from the dominant culture. However, it is not the physical characteristics that set members of racial subgroups apart socially, politically, or economically. Rather, it is the *social meanings* that the dominant group assigns to these features, combined with the extent to which members of the subgroup adhere to their unique values, identities, and attitudes.

Ethnic subcultures are groups that share cultural characteristics such as language, beliefs, religion, or national origin. Some ethnic groups that immigrated to Canada during specific historical periods have been assimilated into mainstream society and no longer constitute a major subculture. Some examples are the descendants of Irish immigrants who settled in Montreal, or Ukrainian immigrants in the Prairie provinces. Some large language and cultural groups, such as the French Canadians in Quebec, or the Chinese in a 'Chinatown', have formed a distinct, visible and persistent dominant culture, often with their own social, economic, and religious organizations.

Ethnic groups provide members with a framework of common values, identity, and history, as well as a social network for assistance and friendship. As with racial groups, membership in ethnic subcultures influences how specific individuals adapt to the aging process (Driedger and Chappell, 1987). For example, although Chinese and Japanese Canadians form two distinct subcultural groups, they have relatively similar cultural backgrounds. The first generation, born in China or Japan, adhere to traditional values—the importance of the family for social support, and the necessity of obedience to, and respect for, the eldest members of the family and community. Many of these first-generation Canadians have experienced difficulties as older adults in a foreign culture. Highlight 2.4 describes some of the unique features of aging in Chinese and Japanese subcultures. These groups are selected as examples because considerable research about them has been published in Canada. However, in a multicultural society like Canada, there is an urgent need for new studies on the many ethnic and religious groups that are 'invisible in aging research' (Salari, 2002). For example, in Arab, Middle Eastern, and Muslim immigrant groups there are many unique aging issues pertaining to family support, housing and health-care needs, use of services, discrimination (including racial profiling and stereotyping), and daily quality of life that require specific programs and policies. Some of these issues are related to religious beliefs about medicine or diet, others to economic status that prevents the purchase of drugs or private home care.

Currently, about 25 per cent of all Canadians over 65 years of age were born outside of Canada. But most of them immigrated as children or young adults and have lived in Canada for most of their lives. Others have come in recent years to be cared for by adult children who have lived in Canada for many years or who are arriving themselves with their parents. Recent elderly immigrants are often widowed and are more likely to be women than men. Many leave their village birth place and encounter a foreign culture, a different value system, and frequently, a family lifestyle that is foreign to their way of thinking. About 5 per cent of the women and 3.5 per cent of the men do not speak either English or French (Health Canada, 2002: 6). If they are unable or unwilling to learn English, and if the youngest generation cannot speak the language of their grandparents, communication with those inside and outside the home becomes difficult, if not

Highlight 2.4 Aging in Chinese and Japanese Subcultures

Chinese Canadians

The Chinese emigrated to Canada in three main waves. The first to come, the Cantonese, were young, illiterate, unskilled labourers who began to arrive in the 1850s to build the railways and work in western gold mines. Most intended to make a fortune and return to China in their old age. However, many settled here permanently. Experiencing discrimination and hostility in mainstream society, many withdrew into the relative security of urban Chinatowns or lived in small towns, where they opened laundries or restaurants.

The second wave of Chinese immigrants, the Mandarins, arrived after 1948 when the Communists occupied mainland China. Most of these immigrants were older, and because of their age, few learned English. As a result, they often lacked knowledge about services available to them in mainstream society and lived most of their life in the Chinatowns of larger cities. The third wave, many of them affluent, well-educated entrepreneurs from Hong Kong, have been arriving since the 1980s, settling mainly in Vancouver, Toronto, and Montreal. About 12 per cent of all immigrants who arrived in Canada between 1991 and 2001 came from Hong Kong or mainland China.

The situation of elderly Chinese people is often related to whether they spent their childhood in China or Canada. Those socialized in China are more likely to adhere to traditional Chinese values, which are often quite different from those of their children raised in Canada. They are ineligible for many forms of government financial and social assistance, and if single in later life, have limited incomes, often living with others in a single room in Chinatown. Others live in public housing, where security may be low and their neighbours may not speak Mandarin or Cantonese. They often lack information about social and medical services and may be unable to pay for medical care. Their later life becomes more difficult if they are moved to a nursing home, where they are often unable to communicate with staff or fellow residents, and where they are not served traditional foods. Here, they become even more isolated than they were in the larger society. To assist elderly Chinese in the later years, special housing and services are being established by and for members of the Chinese community. Increasingly, Friendship Clubs and Benevolent Aid Societies in Chinatowns provide leisure activities, social services, and housing for elderly Chinese.

More recent elderly Chinese immigrants, however, are more likely than non- Asians to live with their children or other Chinese families. Those between 55 and 59 years of age are nearly twice as likely to live with one of their children than non- Asians in the same age group, and by age 80 to 85 they are almost four times more likely to live with a child, especially if their income or wealth is near the poverty line. These living arrangements are most common in the case of elderly persons who are ineligible for pension benefits, who cannot speak English or French, and who are recent arrivals to repatriate the family (Pacey, 2002).

Japanese Canadians

Japanese immigrants first arrived in North America in the nineteenth century. The first wave (the *Issei*) were primarily unskilled labourers, many of whom migrated because their older brothers had inherited the family land and wealth in Japan. Unlike early Chinese immigrants, the *Issei* required their children to learn English and attain an education so they would obtain better jobs. Despite being interned as possible traitors and being forced to sell their property during the Second World

continued

War, Japanese Canadians have attained a higher socio-economic status than many other immigrant groups. Today, only about 15 per cent of elderly Japanese Canadians are foreign-born, compared to over 90 per cent of elderly Chinese Canadian (Kobayashi, 2000).

Most elderly Japanese people are widows who enjoy good health and live as independently as possible since housing is not generally a problem. Elderly Japanese of the *Issei* generation knew little English; the third (*Sansei*) and fourth (*Yonsei*) generations know little, if any, Japanese. This language gap creates communication problems for some elderly Japanese, but it does reveal that the Japanese are more acculturated and less tied to their cultural roots than the Chinese.

Despite the social mobility and cultural assimilation of second- and third-generation Japanese, the quality of relationships with elderly parents has not declined. Elderly parents receive assistance from their children and seem to adjust to a state of dependency and reduced authority without losing self-esteem. This occurs because both generations adhere to the tradition of group goal orientation, rather than to an individualistic ethic. Kobayashi (2000), who interviewed 100 second-generation (*Nisei*) and 100 third-generation (*Sansei*) Japanese Canadians, found that over 60 per cent have a high commitment to filial duty as a cultural value, even though only about 50 per cent report high identity as a Japanese Canadian. She found that this commitment influences the amount and quality of emotional support provided to parents, but has little or no influence on the financial or service support they provide.

impossible. In such a situation, they often become housebound and totally dependent on their offspring for survival and mobility in the community. Many cannot understand their children's busy 'western' way of life, and feel isolated and abandoned in their child's home. Older men, especially, miss the traditional power and status they enjoyed in their homeland, and older women, who are often lonely and depressed, feel that they live in an alien environment. Highlight 2.5 describes an elderly widow's unhappiness in later life after coming to Canada to live with one of her children.

There is a cumulative effect of the advantages or disadvantages acquired across the life course that influences coping and adapting in later life (Olson, 2001). Being a member of, and having a strong sense of identity with, a racial or ethnic group can be a liability or an asset in later life, depending on one's personal situation. For those with strong ethnic or racial identities and ties to the heritage group, there may be a conflict between adhering to traditional as opposed to mainstream practices with respect to the use of health-care services, or the use of family as opposed to formal support mechanisms.

As some ethnic elders are discovering, the formal support system in Canada can be insensitive to cultural needs. Many long-term-care institutions fail to serve the linguistic, dietary, or health-care needs of their ethnic residents. For example, Yeo (1993) found that bilingual nursing-home residents with advanced dementia often stop speaking English and revert to speaking their first language with staff and visitors. With over 200 different language and ethnic groups in Canada, culturally relevant services for an aging multicultural society must be developed. In particular, members of various ethnic groups must be hired as employees and volunteers in social and health-care settings for older people.

Religious Subcultures

In Canada and the United States, the Amish, Mennonites (Bond et al., 1987; Quadagno and

Highlight 2.5 A Mother's Plea for Independence

My Dear Family:

How happy I felt coming to Canada to live with you! I thought all my dreams would come true: Enjoying the company of my children, watching my grandchildren grow up, learning English, having a job, making new friends. . . . Look at me now. . . .

Oh! If you knew how many times I have tried to write this letter, my dear daughter, my beloved grandchildren. But I preferred to hide my feelings in order not to make you suffer, too. Did you ever think of the consequences when you sponsored me to come to this country? Why didn't you tell me how things really were? Then I could have thought twice before deciding to make this enormous change in my life. Now it's too late. I don't have my house, my friends, my independence. I don't have money I can spend freely, and I think I'm also losing my family!

Please do not think I don't value your efforts. I know you have to work hard and don't have much time for housekeeping or taking care of your children. But I did not know you wanted such help from me. It's my pleasure to babysit my grandchildren from time to time, but I didn't think this would be a daily obligation. When I told you that I wanted to learn English so I could go out by myself and feel more secure, your answer was, 'Mama, you are very old, you cannot learn English. Besides that, I need you here.' For years, I didn't venture to ask again. I thought the least I could do was help you, since I was already a burden on the family. But, to tell you the truth, I cannot stand it any more! I couldn't even go to church on Sundays, if your husband was tired or not in a mood to drive me there, because you were afraid that I would get lost if I went by bus.

You came to this country very young. You have already adapted to the culture and customs here. For me, as a senior, the process is very difficult. I cannot even communicate with my grandchildren because they haven't learned to respect the old ones. When I ask the eldest to go with me to a store, he refuses, because he doesn't want anyone to know that we speak Spanish. He's ashamed to go out with his grandma. I feel so lonely and frustrated. . . . When I lived in my homeland I used to go everywhere, saying hello to everybody, solving problems, helping people, receiving friends in my home. Now, when your friends come over, I prefer to go to the basement and cry silently in my room, because your friends aren't mine and I do not feel welcome to join you. You don't seem to care about talking in English, although you know I don't understand. And I don't have the confidence to invite over some people I have met at church. This is not my house. I just have a dark little room in the basement. . .

However, things are going to change now. A friend opened my eyes. She asked me, 'Why don't you go to school? Why don't you have coffee with us when we invite you? Why do you seem so sad?'

I know you were very surprised when I told you about my registration in a seniors' English class. I know you were mad at me because I wouldn't have lunch ready for the family, or be home to babysit your daughter until you returned from work. But dear one, I need to have a life, too. I can help you. As your mother, I am willing to do that. But you know, I need my own activities and friends, too. I know that I'm capable of learning English, although you laugh at me and try to convince me not to go back to classes because 'I'm wasting my time.' Now I ride the bus, I have joined a seniors' club and I don't need anyone to take me to church. Certainly I am old, but I have rediscovered the valuable person inside me. I hope you'll understand.

I want to lead my own life, a life worth living, as long as I am alive. Let me live,

Your loving mother.

Source: Herrera (1994). Reprinted by permission of the author.

Janzen, 1987), and Hutterites are examples of religious subcultures that live in rural areas, while Mormons, Jews, and Muslims tend to live in cities. In other societies, individuals and groups are formally or informally stratified by religion, and sometimes they are separated geographically (Sikh and Hindu in India, Catholic and Protestant in Ireland). These religious communities have a profound impact on the process of aging and on the rights, privileges, and status of older people, especially men. Highlight 2.6 illustrates the impact of a religious subculture on the status and lives of elderly Druze men and of Mennonites living in rural regions of Canada and the United States.

Highlight 2.6 Aging in Religious Subcultures

The Druze in Syria and Israel

The Druze, a minority religious sect (Gutmann, 1976), live in the highland villages of Syria and Israel. They follow a traditional way of life with an agricultural economy. To coexist with the dominant Muslim world from which they are geographically separated, their sons are raised to be policemen and soldiers for the government of Syria or Israel. Religion is central to their identity and way of life, particularly for men. The basic tenets of the religion are kept secret from the outside world, from all Druze women, and from young Druze males, who are labelled *hajil*, or 'the unknowing ones'.

When a Druze man enters late middle age, he is invited to become an *agil* and receives a copy of the sect's secret religious text. If the invitation is accepted, he gives up alcohol and tobacco and devotes a great deal of time to prayer, and his life becomes almost completely ruled by religious duties. Admittance to the religious sect gives men increasing power as they age, because they are thought to serve as a passive interface between their god Allah and the community. As Gutmann (1976: 107) notes, the older Druze 'switches his allegiance from the norms that govern the productive and secular life to those that govern the traditional and moral life.' Religion enables men to continue being active in the community, but on a different level and for a different purpose than when they were younger.

Old Order Mennonites in Rural Canada and the United States

Many Mennonites who immigrated to North America from Europe settled in rural areas of Canada and the United States. Isolated from mainstream society, the 'Old Order' Mennonites maintain traditional ways of life: clothing is simple but somewhat formal, electricity and farm mechanization is not used, and transportation is by horse and buggy.

Following the traditional teachings and practices of Mennonite law, Old Order Mennonites adhere to the codified practices of inheritance and caring for elderly parents that were established in Europe. Children respect their parents, to the extent that one child will remain single and live in the family home to care for aging parents. Parent-child relations are strong, and most children live close to their parents. Families are large, and religious teachings require that children inherit the farm property or an equivalent cash gift. Basic to this process of inheritance is a desire to preserve family stability, to support all members throughout their lives, and to provide security and care for parents in later life. If children are not present, others in the church provide assistance and care, either informally or through church-sponsored nursing homes.

Source: *Adapted from Bond et al. (1987) and Quadagno and Janzen (1987).

Summary

Understanding the historical and cultural differences experienced by older adults across the life course is important if we are to meet their needs. The meaning of aging, the situation of being older, and the processes of aging vary at different periods in history, as well as in different places, even in the same society. Although there are some universal commonalities in the aging process, the cultural and subcultural differences must be taken into account in the policies and programs for an older population. A sensitivity to cultural differences is essential for ensuring that all the members of an increasingly diverse mosaic of older Canadians will receive equal services. In Canada there are many ways to age and experience later life beyond that of mainstream society. The unique cultural beliefs, identities, values, traditions, and life-course experiences of Aboriginal people and immigrant groups present a challenge. Our goal, while creating a civil society, is to understand and respect diverse cultures and traditions and to incorporate them into our public policies and personal practices. In this way, all Canadians will experience a meaningful and satisfying later life.

For Reflection, Debate, or Action

1. If you are a member of an ethnic, racial, or religious group, or if you know someone who is, identify any unique cultural values, beliefs, norms, practices, or experiences pertaining to daily living, family values and interaction, health care, or religion that might influence the status and quality of life of elderly members.

2. Discuss with an elderly person outside your extended family whether there are any historical events or social changes during their lives that have had a major effect on how they have grown older or on how they are adapting to later life.

3. Interview a social or health-care worker to determine how cultural differences among their elderly clients or patients pose unique challenges in the delivery of services or programs.

4. Examine census data for your home community or province to identify the location and size of major cultural groups, and indicate the percentage in each group by age group (45–64, 65–79, 80+).

5. Visit an ethnic neighbourhood to observe and record the relative number and visibility of older people, the types of daily activities in which they engage, and who they interact with as they move about the neighbourhood.

6. Examine new policies or programs as they are announced by local, provincial, and federal agencies or organizations. Identify the extent to which they are likely either to serve or to neglect Aboriginal people and immigrant groups.

7. To what extent is Canada, as a diverse, multicultural society, becoming a model for a new mosaic of later life?

8. Identify some ideas from other cultures or earlier historical periods that might better serve and support older people in the future.

9. Identify some of the needs of aging people in Canada's racial, ethnic, and religious subcultures for housing, transportation, health care, and home care. Propose new or revised government policies that would meet these needs, especially policies that might improve quality of life and reduce language barriers.

Notes

1. Sources about the anthropology of aging include Fry (1980a, 1996, 1999); Keith (1985, 1990); Achenbaum (1996); Sokolovsky (1997); Elliott (1999); Ikels and Beall (2001); and Andersson (2002). Articles about aging processes and older people in a variety of countries are published in the *Journal of Cross-Cultural Gerontology.*

2. Some exceptions are Simmons (1945); Shanas et al. (1968); Havighurst et al. (1969); Cowgill and Holmes (1972); Fry (1980b); Keith (1982); Shin and Lee (1989); Keith et al. (1994); Sokolovsky (1997); and Bengtson et al. (2000).

3. For discussions of modernization, see Cowgill (1974b); Fischer (1977); Amoss and Harrell (1981); Quadagno (1982); Stearns (1982); Foner (1984); Achenbaum (1985); Fry (1985, 1988); Cowgill (1986); Albert and Cattell (1994); Fry (1996); and Ng et al. (2002).

4. In March 2002, Indian and Northern Affairs Canada published an extensive list of definitions (www.ainc-inac.gc.ca/pr/info/info101_e.pdf).

5. Sources of reports about Aboriginal people include the First Nations and Inuit Health Branch of Health Canada (www.hc-sc.gc.ca/fnihb-dgspni); Indian and Northern Affairs Canada (www.ainc-inac.gc.ca); the Aboriginal Canada Portal (www.aboriginalcanada.gc.ca); Newhouse and Peters (2003); White et al. (2003); and publications by Statistics Canada (2001, 2003), particularly, *2001 Census Aboriginal Population Profile*. This publication provides information on the Aboriginal-identity population for communities where their population is 250 or more people. Information is presented under the following categories: population, education, earnings, income, work, and families and dwellings.

References

Achenbaum, A. 1985. 'Societal Perceptions of the Aging and the Aged'. Pp. 129–48 in R. Binstock and E. Shanas (eds), *Handbook of Aging and the Social Sciences*. New York: Van Nostrand Reinhold.

———. 1996. 'Historical Perspectives on Aging'. Pp. 137–52 in R. Binstock and L. George (eds), *Handbook of Aging and the Social Sciences*. San Diego, Calif.: Academic Press.

Albert, S., and M. Cattell. 1994. *Old Age in Global Perspective*. New York: G.K. Hall.

Amoss, P., and S. Harrell (eds). 1981. *Other Ways of Growing Old: Anthropological Perspectives*. Stanford, Calif.: Stanford University Press.

Andersson, L. (ed.). 2002. *Cultural Gerontology*. Westport, Conn.: Greenwood.

Bengtson, V., et al. (eds). 2000. *Aging in East and West: Families, States and the Elderly*. New York: Springer.

Bond, J., et al. 1987. 'Familial Support of the Elderly in a Rural Mennonite Community', *Canadian Journal on Aging*, 6(1), 7–17.

Buchignani, N., and C. Armstrong-Esther. 1999. 'Informal Care and Older Native Canadians', *Aging and Society*, 19(1), 3–32.

Burgess, E. (ed.). 1960. *Aging in Western Societies*. Chicago: University of Chicago Press.

Cowgill, D. 1974a. 'The Aging of Populations and Societies', *The Annals*, 415 (September), 1–18.

———. 1974b. 'Aging and Modernization: A Revision of the Theory'. Pp. 123–46 in J. Gubrium (ed.), *Late Life: Communities and Environmental Policy*. Springfield, Ill.: Charles C. Thomas.

———. 1986. *Aging around the World*. Belmont, Calif.: Wadsworth.

———, and L. Homes. 1972. *Aging and Modernization*. New York: Appleton-Century-Crofts.

de Beauvoir, S. 1972. *The Coming of Age*. New York: Putnam.

Driedger, L., and N. Chappell. 1987. *Aging and Ethnicity: Toward an Interface*. Toronto: Butterworths.

Elliott, G. (ed.). 1999. *Cross-Cultural Awareness in an Aging Society*. Hamilton, Ont.: Office of Gerontological Studies, McMaster University.

Fischer, D. 1977. *Growing Old in America*. London: Oxford University Press.

Foner, N. 1984. *Ages in Conflict: A Cross-Cultural Perspective on Inequality between Old and Young*. New York: Columbia University Press.

Fry, C. 1980a. 'Towards an Anthropology of Aging'. Pp. 1–20 in C. Fry (ed.), *Aging in Culture and Society: Comparative Viewpoints and Strategies*. New York: Praeger.

————— (ed.). 1980b. *Aging in Culture and Society: Comparative Viewpoints and Strategies*. New York: Praeger.

—————. 1985. 'Culture, Behavior and Aging in Comparative Perspective'. Pp. 216–44 in J. Birren and W. Schaie (eds). *Handbook of the Psychology of Aging*. New York: Van Nostrand Reinhold.

—————. 1988. 'Theories of Age and Culture'. Pp. 447–81 in J. Birren and V. Bengtson (eds), *Emergent Theories of Aging*. New York: Springer.

—————. 1996. 'Age, Aging and Culture'. Pp. 117–36 in R. Binstock and L. George (eds), *Handbook of Aging and the Social Sciences*. San Diego, Calif.: Academic Press.

—————. 1999. 'Anthropological Theories of Age and Aging'. Pp. 271–86 in V. Bengtson and W. Schaie (eds), *Handbook of Theories of Aging*. New York: Springer.

Gee, E. 1999. 'Ethnic Identity among Foreign-Born Chinese Canadian Elders', *Canadian Journal on Aging*, 18(4), 415–29.

Goody, J. 1976. 'Aging in Nonindustrial Societies'. Pp. 117–29 in R. Binstock and E. Shanas (eds), *Handbook of Aging and the Social Sciences*. New York: Van Nostrand Reinhold.

Gutmann, D. 1976. 'Alternatives to Disengagement: The Old Men of the Highland Druze'. Pp. 88–108 in J. Gubrium (ed.), *Time, Roles and Self in Old Age*. New York: Human Sciences Press.

Havighurst, R., et al. (eds). 1969. *Adjustment to Retirement: A Cross-National Study*. Assen, The Netherlands: Van Gorcum.

Health Canada. 2002. *Canada's Aging Population*. Ottawa: Minister of Public Works and Government Services Canada.

Health and Welfare Canada. 1992. *Aboriginal Health in Canada*. Ottawa: Minister of Supply and Services.

Hendricks, J. 1982. 'The Elderly in Society: Beyond Modernization', *Social Science History*, 6(3), 321–45.

Herrera, E.1994. 'A Mother's Plea for Independence', *The Moment*, 21, 11. Toronto: Centre for Spanish-Speaking People.

Holmberg, A. 1969. *Nomads of the Long Bow*. Garden City, NY: Natural History Press.

Ikels, C., and C. Beall. 2001. 'Age, Aging and Anthropology'. Pp. 125–40 in R. Binstock and L. George (eds), *Handbook of Aging and the Social Sciences*. New York: Academic Press.

Indian and Northern Affairs Canada. 1995. *Highlights of Aboriginal Conditions, 1991, 1986*. Cat. no. R32-15411-1986E. Ottawa: Minister of Public Works and Government Services Canada.

Keith, J. 1982. *Old People as People: Social and Cultural Influences on Aging and Old Age*. Cambridge, Mass.: Winthrop.

—————. 1985. 'Age in Anthropological Research'. Pp. 231–63 in R. Binstock and E. Shanas (eds), *Handbook of Aging and the Social Sciences*. New York: Van Nostrand Reinhold.

—————. 1990. 'Age in Social and Cultural Contexts: Anthropological Perspectives'. Pp. 91–111 in R. Binstock and L. George (eds), *Handbook of Aging and the Social Sciences*. San Diego, Calif.: Academic Press.

—————, et al. (eds). 1994. *The Aging Experience: Diversity and Commonality across Cultures*. Thousand Oaks, Calif.: Sage.

Kobayashi, K. 2000. 'The Nature of Support from Adult Sansei (Third Generation) Children to Older Nisei (Second Generation) Parents in Japanese Canadian Families', *Journal of Cross-Cultural Gerontology*, 15(3), 185–205.

Laslett, P. 1985. 'Societal Development and Aging'. Pp. 199–230 in R. Binstock and E. Shanas (eds), *Handbook of Aging and the Social Sciences*. New York: Van Nostrand Reinhold.

Leviatan, U. 1999. 'Contribution of Social Arrangements to the Attainment of Successful Aging—The Experience of the Israeli Kibbutz', *Journal of Gerontology: Psychological Sciences*, 54B(4), 205–13.

McPherson, B. et al. 1989. *The Social Significance of Sport*. Champaign, Ill.: Human Kinetics Books.

Maxwell, R., and P. Silverman. 1970. 'Information and Esteem: Cultural Consideration in the Treatment of the Aged', *Aging and Human Development*, 1(4), 361–92.

Mehta, K. 1997. 'Respect Redefined: Focus Group Insights from Singapore', *International Journal of Aging and Human Development*, 44, 205–19.

Newhouse, D., and E. Peters (eds). 2003. *Not Strangers in These Parts: Urban Aboriginal Peoples*. Ottawa: Policy Research Initiative.

Ng, A., et al. 2002. 'Persistence and Challenges of Filial Piety and Informal Support of Older Persons in a Modern Chinese Society: A Case Study in Tuen Mun, Hong Kong', *Journal of Aging Studies*, 16(2), 135–53.

Ogawa, N., and R. Retherford. 1993. 'Care of the Elderly in Japan: Changing Norms and Expectations', *Journal of Marriage and the Family*, 55(3), 585–97.

Olson, L. (ed.). 2001. *Age through Ethnic Lenses: Caring for the Elderly in a Multicultural Society*. Lanhan, Md.: Rowman and Littlefield.

Ontario Advisory Council on Senior Citizens. 1993. *Denied Too Long: The Needs and Concerns of Seniors Living on First Nations Communities in Ontario*. Toronto: The Council.

Pacey, M. 2002. Living Alone and Living with Children: The Living Arrangements of Canadian and Chinese-Canadian Seniors. SEDAP Research Paper No. 74. Hamilton, Ont.: McMaster University (http://socserv2. mcmaster.ca/sedap).

Plath, D. 1972. 'Japan: The After Years'. Pp. 133–50 in D. Cowgill and L. Holmes (eds), *Aging and Modernization*. New York: Appleton-Century-Crofts.

Quadagno, J. 1982. *Aging in Early Industrial Society: Work, Family and Social Policy in Nineteenth Century England*. New York: Academic Press.

———, and J. Janzen. 1987. 'Old Age Security and the Family Life Course: A Case Study of Nineteenth-Century Mennonite Immigrants to Kansas', *Journal of Aging Studies*, 1(1), 33–49.

Reading, J. 1999. 'An Examination of Residential Schools and Elder Health'. Pp. 29–54 in *First Nations and Inuit Regional Health Survey*. Ottawa: Health Canada, Medical Services Branch.

Rhoads, E. 1984. 'Reevaluation of the Aging and Modernization Theory: The Samoan Evidence', *The Gerontologist*, 24(3), 243–50.

Romanow, R. 2002. *Building on Values: The Future of Health Care in Canada*. Ottawa: Commission on the Future of Health Care in Canada.

Rosow, I. 1965. 'And Then We Were Old', *Trans-Action*, 22(2), 20–6.

Salari, S. 2002. 'Invisible in Aging Research: Arab Americans, Middle Eastern Immigrants and Muslims in the United States', *The Gerontologist*, 42(5), 580–8.

Shanas, E., et al. 1968. *Old People in Three Industrial Societies*. New York: Atherton Press.

Shin, E., and J. Lee 1989. 'Convergence and Divergence in the Status of the Aged: An Analysis of Cross-National and Longitudinal Variations in 32 Selected Countries', *Journal of Aging Studies*, 3(3), 263–78.

Simmons, L. 1945. *The Role of the Aged in Primitive Society*. New Haven, Conn.: Yale University Press.

———. 1952. 'Social Participation of the Aged in Different Cultures', *The Annals of the American Academy of Political and Social Science*, 279 (Jan.), 43–51.

———. 1960. 'Aging in Preindustrial Societies', in C. Tibbits (ed.), *Handbook of Social Gerontology*. Chicago: University of Chicago Press.

Sokolovsky, J. (ed.). 1997. *The Cultural Context of Aging: Worldwide Perspectives*. Westport, Conn.: Bergin and Garvey.

Sparks, D. 1975. 'The Still Rebirth: Retirement and Role Discontinuity'. In D. Plath and E. Brill (eds), *Adult Episodes in Japan*. Leiden, The Netherlands: Brill.

Statistics Canada. 2001. *Aboriginal Peoples in Canada*. Profile Series cat. no. 85F0033MIE. Ottawa: Statistics Canada.

———. 2002. *How Healthy Are Canadians? A Summary 2002 Annual Report*. Cat. no. 82-003-SIE. Ottawa: Statistics Canada.

———. 2003a. *Aboriginal Peoples Survey 2001: Initial Findings: Well-being of the Non-Reserve Aboriginal Population*. Cat. no. 89-589-XIE. Ottawa: Statistics Canada.

———. 2003b. *Aboriginal Peoples of Canada, 2001 Census*. Cat. no. 94F00041XCB. Ottawa: Statistics Canada.

Stearns, P. (ed.). 1982. *Old Age in Preindustrial Society*. New York: Holmes and Meier.

Sung, K-T. 2001. 'Elder Respect: Exploration of Ideals and Forms in East Asia', *Journal of Aging Studies*, 15(1), 13–26.

Vanderburgh, R. 1987. 'Modernization and Aging in the Anicinabe Context'. Pp. 100–10 in V. Marshall (ed.). *Aging in Canada: Social Perspectives*. Markham, Ont.: Fitzhenry and Whiteside.

Watson, W., and R. Maxwell. 1977. *Human Aging and Dying: A Study of Sociocultural Gerontology*. New York: St Martin's Press.

White, J., et al. (eds). 2003. *Aboriginal Conditions: Research as a Foundation for Public Policy*. Vancouver: University of British Columbia Press.

Wister, A., and G. Gutman (eds). 1997. *Health Systems and Aging in Selected Pacific Rim Countries: Cultural Diversity and Change*. Vancouver: Simon Fraser University, Gerontology Research Centre.

———, and C. Moore. 1998. 'First Nations Elders in Canada: Issues, Problems and Successes in Health Care Policy'. Pp. 103–24 in A. Wister and G. Gutman (eds), *Health Systems and Aging in Selected Pacific Rim Countries: Cultural Diversity and Change*. Vancouver: Simon Fraser University, Gerontology Research Centre.

Yeo, G. 1993. 'Ethnicity and Nursing Homes: Factors Affecting Use and Successful Components for Culturally Sensitive Care'. Pp. 161–77 in C. Barresi and D. Stull (eds), *Ethnic Elderly and Long-Term Care*. New York: Springer.

CHAPTER 3

Individual Aging: Continuity and Change across the Life Course

Focal Points

- Are some diseases more prevalent in later life (see Chapter 12)? Is aging a disease?
- Do changes in the physical and psychological systems of aging individuals involve losses *and* gains?
- In what way do physical and cognitive changes across the life course have positive *and* negative influences on the social behaviour and social networks of aging individuals?
- Is the decline in the motor and sensory systems greater than that in the cognitive system?
- Does personality remain stable or change throughout a person's life?

Introduction

Why do some people 'age well', while others 'age poorly'? To understand fully how people interact with others and function within their environment in later life, we need to understand the normal changes that occur *within* individuals across the life course. Aging involves a process of change, from birth to death, in our interacting biological, physiological, and psychological systems. These normal changes take place at different rates and to varying degrees. The changes influence functional capacity, interaction with others, everyday life, and the quality of life in later life. These changes also influence a person's health, especially in the middle and later years.

Aging is not a disease, but some diseases, such as Alzheimer's disease, Parkinson's disease, and strokes are more prevalent in later life. The cumulative effect of having certain diseases, such as arthritis or diabetes, earlier in life can become devastating in later life. Adopting safe, healthy

habits in regard to diet, drugs, alcohol, smoking, sex, and physical exercise can slow the processes of aging, increase longevity, maintain independence, and help a person adapt to age-related changes in later life, such as loss of muscle and strength. In contrast, both genetic factors (McClearn and Vogler, 2001) and environmental factors (low socio-economic status, inadequate housing) can speed up the normal changes in aging or health for those who are predisposed to disease states and malnutrition. Issues related to individual and population health in later life are discussed in Chapter 12. In the present chapter the focus is on continuity and changes in the biological, sensory, perceptual, cognitive, and personality systems across the life course. These changes, involving both decline in vision, hearing, and mobility and growth in wisdom, experience, and knowledge, result in either cumulative advantages and disadvantages in later life.

It is beyond the scope of this chapter to present cellular-level explanations as to why changes occur in the human organism.[1] However, because these changes influence behaviour and cognition in aging adults and how we interact with a changing social and physical environment, the emphasis is on describing normal aging processes in order to separate myth from fact. The most prevailing myth is that aging involves degenerative changes in our physical and psychological systems that lead, *inevitably*, to frailty and ultimately to total dependence on others. While that may be true for some people (usually not until the the last few months or years before death), disabilities and frailties are observed at any age because of genetics, injuries, diseases, environmental factors, and living habits.

A **disability** is a 'reported' difficulty in performing the activities of daily life (ADLs) such as dressing, getting out of bed, grooming oneself, or using the toilet; or in performing instrumental activities of daily life (IADLs) such as shopping, banking, cleaning and maintaining a home, and driving a car. Or it is a physical or mental condition or a health problem that reduces the kind or amount of activity that can be completed (Statistics Canada, 2002). A reported disability can range from a backache to an inability to walk, even with an assistive device such as a cane or a walker. Older people report more disabilities than younger people, and more older women than older men report one or more disabilities. The 2001 Participation and Activity Limitation Survey (PALS) conducted by Statistics Canada (2002) found that 41 per cent (about 1.5 million) of all older Canadians 65 and over reported having at least one disability. The number of disabilities and their severity increases with age, and by age 75 and over, 53 per cent of older Canadians report having a disability. Among people over 65 years of age, the disabilities reported most often were mobility problems (80 per cent of those with a disability), pain, agility (difficulty getting dressed), and confusion (about 4 per cent of all problems). Although these disabilities restrict

functioning in later life, whether they increase dependence or lower one's perceived quality of life depends on such factors as tolerance of pain, personality and self-esteem, available support, type of environment, whether one lives alone, and energy.

Frailty, often associated with aging, is not well defined. It is *not* an inevitable consequence of aging, but rather is a disease state that is susceptible to intervention and reversal in some cases (Bortz, 2002; Morley et al., 2002). Frailty is characterized by muscle weakness, especially in the legs; fatigue and diminished energy reserves; decreased physical and social activity; loss of weight; and a slow or unsteady gait. Clinicians often label someone as frail if they have three or more of these characteristics. Frailty is strongly related to increased risks of falling, social isolation, dependence and institutionalization, and nearness to death. The causes of frailty include genetic traits related to the metabolic, cardiovascular, and immunologic systems; the onset of disease or injuries that limit physical activity; poor nutrition; sedentary living, where lack of regular physical activity in later life leads to loss of muscle strength and endurance in the legs; and the onset of normal aging processes such as dementia and sarcopenia (loss of muscle).

Having briefly discussed two possible outcomes of individual aging, disabilities and frailty, the remainder of this chapter presents an overview of normal aging processes that influence social and intellectual behaviour and performance in later life. As noted in Chapter 1, individual differences in traits, characteristics, and abilities increase with age. Some of this variation and diversity is attributable to variations in the rate and degree of change due to the normal aging processes. It is these differences that explain, partially, why some people age 'well' or better than others, and why individuals experience age-related changes at different rates and to different degrees.

All individuals, as they age, experience some decline in health and gradual losses of physical, motor, and cognitive efficiency and ability. Most people, at least until very late in life, do not experience functional losses that seriously change or affect their social or cognitive behaviour.[2] Most people do not spend their later years in a state of dependence. Rather, the varying degrees of physical, perceptual, or cognitive losses require some adaptation. This process of adaptation is influenced by a variety of past and present social and environmental factors, such as previous lifestyle, personality structure and coping style, support from significant others, socio-economic status, race, gender, and living arrangements (with a partner or alone). Adaptation to changes in the physical and psychological systems are influenced as well by historical events and social changes, such as wars and depressions, and by unique personal events or transitions, such as divorce, involuntary retirement, or widowhood.

Aging, Physical Structure, and the Physiological Systems

The structure and function of the human organism attains full maturity and its greatest strength and energy in early adulthood. From early adulthood on, there is a gradual and progressive decline in the structure and function of the body's various components and a resulting decrease in the general activity level of the organism. The rapidity of the decline is influenced by genetic and external factors, such as lifestyle, nutrition, and the quality of the environment, and, in general, with each aging cohort we have observed a compression of morbidity such that health and vigour are maintained until there is a sudden decline before death very late in life.

Some of these system changes, such as those to the elasticity and texture of the skin, are external and highly visible, but most are internal and are not noticed until they begin to influence the activities of daily living, social interactions with others, or work performance. Moreover, there are differences in the rate of decline for each organ or

system. For example, a person who is 65 years old may have the strength and energy of a 50-year-old and the external physical appearance of a 50-year-old but may have hearing or vision problems more commonly experienced by an 80-year-old.

This interaction of physical and physiological aging has a unique impact on the behaviour, attitudes, and performance of an individual. This is reflected in the dynamic interplay between the personality or personal coping style of an individual; the attitudes, perceptions, and interaction of others; and an individual's subsequent 'presentation of self' and type and frequency of social participation. The effect of these changes is related to the severity of change, the degree to which changes occur at the same time or rate, and the extent to which the changes are considered by an individual to be threatening or limiting. The reactions of significant others (social support, discouragement, lack of interest, and decreased interaction) influence, as well, the perceptions and behaviour of an older person.

Throughout this chapter, remember that modal patterns are presented, and that there are considerable differences within and between individuals. These differences are due to genetic, social and environmental factors, including socio-economic status, gender, diet, race, ethnicity, occupation, geographic location, body type, and age cohort.

Changes in the Structure and Composition of the Organism

External Changes

As we age, visible changes occur in the skin, the hair, and in the shape and height of the body. During middle age the skin becomes dry and wrinkled as it becomes thinner and losses elasticity and subcutaneous fat. Similarly, hair becomes thinner and loses its original colour. Because of negative social meanings frequently attached to the presence of wrinkles and grey hair, some people actively fight a 'cosmetic battle' so as to appear younger than their chronological age. Not surprisingly, a profitable cosmetics industry has evolved to meet this social need. As well, entrepreneurs actively market anti-aging gimmicks, programs, and products.

For many adults, body weight increases up to about 50 years of age, although there is often a decline thereafter because of a change in body metabolism. This increase in weight is due to an accumulation of fat and a reduction in muscle tissue which appears most frequently in the abdominal area for men, and in the limbs and abdominal area for women. Some of these changes are more pronounced with poor diets and lack of physical activity. As a result, body shape may change from a lean and youthful appearance to a more portly, rotund, or mature appearance. Obesity in later life has both physical and psychological effects on older adults (Himes, 2004).

Aging adults are faced with a cultural ideal of a youthful body and an active life. To cope with the changes observed in one's appearance and with the inner changes that are felt, such as less efficiency, decreased energy, and aches and pains, older adults adopt various cognitive strategies. Hennessy (1989), in a study of body culture and aging, identified two types of adapters. The 'active copers' continued or had begun a program of physical activity, and were conscious of how they dressed and appeared. The 'reactive copers' reported that they knew they 'should' or 'ought' to be active and to pay more attention to appearance, but for various reasons did not invest time in physical activity.

A visible change in body shape may cause a person to be considered by others to be older than his or her actual age. Attempts to mask these physical changes may involve dressing in loose clothes to hide the shape of the body. A healthier adaptation to changes in body composition or shape is to exercise regularly and eat properly. However, many people are unwilling or unable to invest the time and energy to do so.

Another visible sign of aging is a shortening of stature that begins in late middle age. This is caused by changes in the structure and composition of the spine: vertebrae collapse or intervertebral discs become compressed. These changes are seen in an increased 'bowing' of the spine, the loss of a few inches in height, rounded or stooped shoulders, and back pain.

External visible changes with age influence how a person perceives him- or herself and how others perceive and interact with that person. For those who are secure and live in a supportive social environment, physical changes are seldom traumatic. However, for those whose identity and social interaction are closely related to their physical appearance, attempts to alter the presentation of the physical self may become a time-consuming battle, particularly in the case of people who are separated, divorced, or widowed and anxious to date or attract a new partner.

Internal Changes

Internal physical changes have more effect on the performance of physical tasks than on social perceptions, attitudes, or behaviour. These changes include the following:

- a decrease in muscle mass and elasticity

- a decrease in water content and an increase in fat cells in relation to muscle cells

- a decrease in bone mass and minerals so that bones are more brittle; this increases the likelihood of fractures, especially among menopausal women

- a deterioration in the range, flexibility, and composition of the articulating surfaces and joints, which enhance the likelihood of fractures or arthritis, particularly after 80 years of age

Many of these changes lead to decreased mobility, changing leisure activities, and an inability to perform household tasks in the later years. They also can increase the incidence of accidents or falls, particularly if there are steep stairs, insufficient lighting, slippery floors, or a bathroom without grab bars. Even a fear of falling may restrict mobility and decrease one's independence (see Chapter 7).

Changes in Physiological Systems

Over time, most physiological systems become less efficient and less capable of functioning at maximum capacity. Decreased functional performance is usually noticed during strenuous work or leisure activities. However, a fitness or training program can delay or reduce the effects of physiological age-related changes. If physiological systems function efficiently, especially under physical or mental stress, self-image can be enhanced.

The Central Nervous System
This system begins to slow down with age, as evidenced by a longer response or reaction time, by earlier onset of fatigue, hand tremors, and a general slowing of the autonomic nervous system (Vinters, 2001). Changes in the autonomic nervous system may lead to changes in metabolism, in the structure and function of a number of organs, and in nervous receptors, processors, and reactors. Some of these changes are seen in the slower execution of a task, although, contrary to a popular myth, the quality of performance seldom decreases. Changes in the autonomic nervous system influence emotions and behavioural reactions and are related to the onset of senile dementia.

The Muscular System
Age-related changes in the muscular system result in a decrease in strength and endurance, although the rate and degree of loss depend on the frequency and intensity of physical activity. Sarcopenia (a major loss of muscle mass and loss of muscle function), which is an age-related process, is a major cause of falls, disability, and morbidity among older people. In addition, the time for a muscle to relax or contract, and the time required before it can be restimulated, increases in later life. This occurs partly because of changes in the contractile tissue in the muscle

and partly because of neurological changes. These changes reduce the ability to engage in endurance tasks or in tasks requiring repeated actions of the same muscle group, such as digging in the garden or washing windows. A decline in muscular endurance also reduces the efficiency of other body functions such as the respiratory system. Furthermore, a decrement in the muscular-skeletal system increases the likelihood of falls: there may be reduced leg lift when walking, which increases the chance of tripping, or there may be greater difficulty in regaining balance after stumbling. The efficiency of the muscular system can be enhanced in the later years by regular exercise and physical activity. Thus, it is possible to delay the onset of muscular changes with age and improve the ability to perform daily tasks in later life.

The Cardiovascular System
Among the many physiological changes that occur with age, the most visible (and the most significant for behaviour) are those in the cardiovascular system: there is a decrease in maximum heart rate attainable, a decrease in maximum cardiac output and stroke volume, and an increase in blood pressure. These factors combine to lower the efficiency of the system and to hasten the onset of fatigue during physical activity. These outcomes, in turn, limit the duration and type of work and leisure activities that can be pursued. These cardiovascular changes are not inevitable. It is possible, with a regular and sufficiently intense exercise program, to lower the resting heart rate, to increase the maximum heart rate during work, and to increase the cardiac output.

It is more difficult, however, to retard the onset of arteriosclerosis and atherosclerosis. *Arteriosclerosis*, a loss of elasticity in the arterial walls, restricts the flow of blood to the muscles and organs, thereby lowering endurance during work or play. *Atherosclerosis*, characterized by a hardening and narrowing of the arterial walls, results from the accumulation of fatty deposits that partially or completely block the flow of blood. These cardiovascular diseases, which are especially prevalent among men, are difficult to prevent or treat because their pathology is still not fully understood. However, low-cholesterol diets and regular exercise throughout one's life are related to a lower incidence of these diseases.

The Respiratory System

The efficiency of the respiratory system decreases with age for a number of reasons. These include decreases in elasticity of the lungs; in vital capacity (the amount of air that can be forcibly exhaled after a full inspiration); in diffusion and absorption capacities; and in maximum voluntary ventilation and oxygen intake. These changes reduce the efficiency of intake and inhibit the transportation of oxygen to organs and muscles.

The co-ordination and efficiency of both the respiratory and the cardiovascular systems are highly interrelated in determining a person's physical fitness capacity. Unless people engage in regular endurance exercise throughout the adult years, by 60 to 75 years of age there may be as much as a 50 per cent decrease in physical work capacity from the maximum value attained in early adulthood. In the absence of training, a less fit person has few reserves for emergencies, and during stressful situations fatigue begins earlier and the recovery period is longer. Obviously, these physiological deficiencies limit the type, intensity, and frequency of some forms of social activity, such as sports, playing with grandchildren, walking or hiking, gardening, sexual relations, or shovelling snow.

Involvement in Physical Activity by Age

Physical activity has a number of benefits for the aging person (Highlight 3.1). Many studies have found a positive relationship between the amount of participation in physical activity at work or play and the level of physical and mental health. And recent studies have found that more physically fit older people score higher on tests of cognitive functioning; thereby suggesting a relationship between physical activity and mental performance (a version of the 'sound body, sound mind' theme). Similarly, there is an inverse relationship between the amount of physical activity at work or play and mortality rates. Yet, as many studies have indicated, involvement in physical activity declines with age, especially among women and among those with lower levels of formal education. This pattern appears to be virtually universal, although it varies somewhat from nation to nation and from cohort to cohort.

Patterns of Physical Activity through the Life Cycle

Children in modernized nations are involved to some degree in regular sport or exercise programs at school or in the community. However, some never fully adopt the habit of this type of leisure activity, either because their parents do not place a high value on physical activity, or because they do not have an opportunity to become involved at an early age. Consequently, childhood obesity is a serious health problem.

The pattern of declining involvement in physical activity begins relatively early in life. Many children withdraw from involvement in physical activity because of unpleasant experiences in sport programs, because there is no alternative to elite sport for those who are less skilled, because they have experienced failure, because there is an overemphasis on elite performance rather than participation, or because facilities or programs are not available. For those who remain involved past childhood, physical activity has a lower priority as adolescents search for personal identity, assimilate into the youth culture, and reject some societal values, including those that advocate physical activity or sport as part of a healthy life.

Explanations for Varying Degrees of Involvement by Older Age Cohorts

Cohort differences in the type and frequency of participation in physical activity are accounted

Highlight 3.1 Physiological Benefits of Exercise

- increased blood flow through the capillaries
- increased muscle mass, endurance, and strength
- decreased percentage of body fat and a lower body weight
- increased flexibility and coordination
- increased cardiovascular endurance
- decreased systemic blood pressure
- increased and more efficient blood flow from the extremities to the heart
- increased maximal oxygen intake and physical work capacity
- lowered resting and exercising heart rate
- more rapid heart-rate recovery after strenuous exercise
- more rapid oxygen-debt repayment after strenuous exercise
- increased use of anaerobic energy reserves
- increased neural regulatory control, including faster reaction time

for both by declining physical capacity and by a number of sociological and psychological factors. This pattern of less involvement by successively older cohorts is more pronounced among the less educated, among those with lower incomes, among those in rural areas, among those in manual occupations, and among women (especially if married with pre-school-age children).

Negative attitudes toward physical activity, sometimes because of unpleasant experiences early in life, are also a factor in low participation rates. These attitudes can be reinforced by myths, namely: that the need for exercise decreases with age; that middle-aged and elderly people do not have, or have lost, the skill to perform most physical activities; that physical activity is dangerous to one's health; or that older people should 'take it easy' as they age. Even among adults who do exercise, many think they are getting enough exercise when, in fact, it is often insufficient to develop or maintain adequate fitness levels.

A person's commitment to leisure as well as to work influences the degree of involvement in exercise or sports. If not much spare time is available, physical activity may have a low priority, compared to, for example, time with the family.

From a societal perspective, the myth that an older adult is beyond help often discourages physical activity programs being established for older people. Because of **age grading** and the creation of age norms, there are few facilities and programs that enable adults to be physically active on a regular basis. 'Acting your age' at one time implied that participation in sports or physical activity is not socially acceptable in later life. If these age norms interact with gender-related norms, there are greater social barriers to prevent women from participating in sports or physical activity.

Age grading, or ageism, is entrenched further in a society when physically active role models are not available. However, the presence in recent years of physically active adults of all ages has weakened the restrictive age norms concerning involvement in physical activity in the middle and later years, for both men and women. Moreover, there is increasing scientific evidence that physical fitness can be improved at all ages and, more important, that it is beneficial to the enhancement of physical and mental health and of competence in later life (Stones and Kozma, 1996). Thus, physical activity is becoming more socially acceptable and desirable for adults of all ages. Highlight 3.2 illustrates the range of possible involvement in sport and physical activity by older people.

Aging and the Motor and Sensory Systems

In the previous section it was noted that changes in the central nervous system occur with increasing chronological age. The most noticeable of these changes is a general slowing of motor, cognitive, and sensory processes. A number of explanations for this phenomenon have been proposed, including a loss of neurons, which are not replaced; a decrease in the size and weight of the brain; diseases such as manic-depressive psychosis, coronary heart disease, strokes, or depression; hormonal changes; or loss of motivation or concentration.

Regardless of the cause, a general decline is observed in the speed of psychomotor performance, cognitive functioning, and sensory and perceptual processes. This is more pronounced as the required action becomes more complex. This occurs in abstract reasoning or when rapid decisions have to be made while performing a motor task such as in sports that require a reaction to a

---

Highlight 3.2 Physically Active Older Adults at Play

The mass media, given the increased interest in physical activity and sport by the general population, periodically report the accomplishments or unusual athletic feats of aging adults. These individuals, although still exceptions to the norm, show what can be accomplished in later life and set an example for other people their age.

- A 61-year-old potato farmer won the 875-kilometre Sydney-to-Melbourne marathon (in Australia).

- A 66-year-old, who holds 28 age-group track records, runs 20 miles every other day.

- A 71-year-old cycled 919 miles in 10 consecutive days, including the 12,095-foot Independence Pass to Aspen, Colorado.

- A 72-year-old sophomore on a college tennis team hits 130 practice serves daily and competes in slalom and giant slalom skiing events in the winter.

- A 77-year-old minister plays 'old-timers' hockey once a week from 11 p.m. to 2 a.m.

- A 70-year-old ran from Vancouver to Halifax in 134 days, 16 days faster than when he ran the same course at the age of 62.

- Sixteen men (62 to 77 years of age) and six women (49 to 70 years of age) bicycled 7,700 kilometres from Victoria, British Columbia, to St John's, Newfoundland, in 100 days at an average of approximately 90 kilometres per seven-hour day.

- Never physically active before age 65, a 75-year-old woman jogs nine miles four or five nights a week. Three mornings a week, she conducts aerobics classes for women aged 25 to 45.

- Wearing a T-shirt that read 'The Flying Nun', a 75-year-old nun finished sixth in a 1,500-metre race walk, thereby achieving her goal of winning a ribbon for placing in the top six.

ball, in assembly-line jobs, or when driving a car at high speed in heavy traffic. This observable slowing down has a direct effect on social behaviour and leads to stereotypes of older people such as the slow, overly cautious driver. In fact, with advancing age there may be a slowing of speed to ensure accuracy. This **cautiousness**, a generalized tendency to respond slowly or not at all because of the possible consequences of a mistake, occurs in many situations where a decision must be made. Regardless of the underlying mechanism, this slowing down reduces the chances of survival when fast reaction time is required, as in heavy traffic. It may also limit complex thinking because the mediating processes slow down to the point where some of the elements, or even the goal of the task, may be forgotten.

Motor Performance

Motor performance in a multitude of daily tasks on the job, at home, while driving, or at leisure depends on perceiving and evaluating information received from the sensory organs, storing and processing this information, and responding through the voluntary muscles. The most significant changes in motor performance with age are a loss of speed in making decisions and a concomitant increase in reaction time. These changes are most evident when a complex decision is required and when the individual must respond rapidly. This loss is compounded if the situation is stressful, such as driving under dangerous conditions or writing a test with implications for present or future employment.

Reaction time, the period from perception of a stimulus to reaction, is a complex phenomenon and is not well understood. A slower reaction time has been explained as a physical problem resulting from a number of possible physiological processes. These include a decline in signal strength as neurons and nerve cells die; an increase in reflex time for skeletal muscles; a loss of efficiency in central processing mechanisms so that more time is needed to monitor incoming

signals; and a general deterioration in the sensorimotor mechanisms. A loss of reaction time can be offset by practice and a strong desire to succeed at the task, and by spending more time monitoring the input stimuli before a response is made. However, not all situations permit unlimited reaction time, and errors result if sufficient time is not available. With unlimited time to perform a task, older people perform about as well as they did when they were younger. In fact, with unlimited time to monitor stimuli, an older person is often more accurate than a younger person.

If a job demands speed in decision making and performance, an older worker may be disadvantaged, more so than if an occupation requires merely physical strength. Although speed and accuracy at work decline slightly with age, experience can compensate for the onset of slowness. For those who cannot continue to perform, many voluntarily or involuntarily leave their job. This creates problems of unemployability and a lower income because of a loss of seniority or a shift to a lower occupational level.

In the social domain, a slowing of reaction time and decision making, especially if accompanied by some of the sensory changes noted in the next section, reduces the frequency, quality, and type of interaction with others and with the environment. That is, perception of the social world changes, and individuals are perceived by others as slow, old, or incompetent. These perceptions can lead to less social interaction and further sensory deprivation, resulting in emotional and behavioural problems such as loneliness, isolation, depression, and decreased mobility. In short, in situations where a fast reaction time is essential, most older people do not perform as well as they did when younger. This slowing down may, in turn, directly or indirectly influence job performance or the frequency and quality of social interaction.

Changes in motor control are related to mobility in later life. With normal losses in balance and a change in gait and in posture, which becomes less stable and upright, older people are more liable to fall. Balance is controlled in the cerebellum, which loses about 25 per cent of its cells with aging. Falls are a major cause of hospitalization and institutionalization, dependency, and premature death in later life. With advancing age, people walk more slowly, take shorter strides, and take more frequent strides (this gait is often referred to as shuffling). These changes in gait increase the likelihood of falls (Simoneau and Leibowitz, 1996; Ketcham and Stelmach, 2001). Once an older person has had a fall, he or she begins to be afraid of falling and may avoid physical activities and sports, as well as other social activities. However, a physical training program which increases muscle strength, flexibility, balance, and posture can help to prevent falls.

Sensory Processes

Communication with others, either face to face or indirectly, such as by television, telephone, or the Internet, is essential throughout one's life. To interact with the physical environment and with other people, an individual sends and receives information. This ability depends largely on sensory receptors that permit information to be received by and transmitted to the brain. As we age, greater stimulation is needed in order to send information to the brain.

Changes with age in the major sensory receptors and processors reduces the quality and quantity of information available to the organism. The efficiency of the receptors also influences the interest in communicating and the capacity to understand information. Changes in these systems are seldom abrupt, and may not even be noticed at first. If an impairment is not severe, the organism compensates for the loss by a variety of means: a person may use a different sense to a greater extent, such as lip reading to compensate for loss of hearing; or intensify the stimulus (e.g., with a hearing aid) or correct it (e.g., with eyeglasses); or use experience to predict or identify the stimulus (e.g., recognizing a stop sign by its shape).If two senses decline simultaneously, as

vision and hearing often do late in life, a person may have difficulty with their job, with walking, or with social interaction.

Vision

After middle age, structural and functional changes in the visual system have an effect on social behaviour (Kline and Scialfa, 1996; Fozard and Gordon-Salant, 2001). These changes include:

- a thickening of the lens and a decrease in the diameter of the pupil, both of which limit the amount of light reaching the retina;
- less flexibility in the lens (**presbyopia**), which decreases the ability to focus on objects at varying distances;
- a decrease in threshold adaptation to darkness, glare, and rapidly changing light levels; and
- a yellowing of the lens that filters out green, blue, and violet at the shorter wave-length end of the spectrum.

In addition, loss or impairment of vision is experienced by people suffering from glaucoma (less than 5 per cent of the population) or from some degree of cataract development (as much as 60 per cent of the older population).

As a result of these changes, a brighter light is needed for reading and working. A person may have difficulty in adapting to changes in illumination when walking or driving at dusk, or when moving from well-lit to dark areas. As many as 25 per cent of falls among older people are attributed to vision problems. Some people may be unable to perceive blue, green, and violet tones in the spectrum and may therefore have difficulty coordinating the colours of their clothing or appreciating works of art. While none of these changes are totally disabling, they detract from the pleasures of daily living. For example, if declining eyesight prevents people from driving at night, or at all, their mobility is limited and they are increasingly dependent on others. Living environments may need to be redesigned—with brighter lights, less glare, and larger lettering on signs and in books—to make the environment safer and more enjoyable for older people.

Hearing

Unlike visual problems, which can be observed and more easily corrected, hearing impairment is less noticeable to oneself and to others. The older person, unaware that his or her hearing is declining, may have communication problems. A major type of hearing loss is the progressive inability to hear higher-frequency sounds in music and speech (**presbycusis**). This impairment, caused by the loss of fine hair cells in the inner ear, appears after about the age of 50 and is more common among men, especially those who have been exposed to industrial noise. As many as 40 per cent of older people have impaired hearing. One must wonder about the hearing loss that will be exhibited by those who have used ear phones for loud music throughout adolescence and early adulthood.

A hearing impairment affects performance on the job, and the ability to function safely and efficiently in one's environment (if one is unable to hear doorbells, telephones, or car horns). Presbycusis creates stress in social situations, inhibits communication (especially if there is background noise), decreases the quality of social interaction (if one misses the punch line in jokes), causes fear and embarrassment, and leads to depression. Some older people with hearing difficulties begin to avoid social events, and what began as a natural hearing loss leads to social isolation. Hearing aids provide partial compensation for losses, but other adaptive means are also necessary, such as facing a speaker, lip reading, interpreting hand gestures and facial expressions, and overcoming the embarrassment of asking people to repeat what they have said.

Taste, Smell, Touch, and Pain

By about the age of 60, there is a higher taste threshold for all four taste sensations: salt, sweet, bitter, and sour. In addition, there is less saliva and a loss in the number of taste buds. These changes are compounded by smoking, wearing dentures, and by taking some prescription drugs. Furthermore, the ability to detect or identify odours declines with age.

When the sense of taste and smell decline at the same time, a person may enjoy their food less and may start eating less, with a consequent decline in nutrition. In short, mealtime is no longer an enjoyable social or culinary experience. In addition, a person who is widowed and living alone is less inclined to prepare food, especially if food and mealtime no longer provides pleasure. These changes in eating habits can result in medical problems. Moreover, a severe loss of taste and smell deprives people of an early warning system that alerts them to spoiled foods or dangerous odours, such as natural gas, propane, and smoke. And some older people not only have both a poor sense of smell and taste, but also have weaker cognitive tools to identify odours.

There is a loss of sensitivity in touch and to vibration in some, but not all, parts of the body with advancing age. Indeed, some older people who singe their fingers on a hot stove do not notice the pain or damage. However, the prevalence of pain increases with age; the main sources of chronic pain in later life are arthritis, rheumatism, angina, and vascular disease. Chronic pain has a serious effect on physical and emotional well-being, and when it becomes severe it affects all aspects of our everyday lives.

Although complaints about pain often increase with age, it is unclear about whether pain thresholds remain constant or decrease with age. Part of this uncertainty stems from a failure to separate the physiological variable of the pain threshold from the social and psychological elements of pain. It is not known whether observed age differences in pain perception are related to the processing capacity of the central nervous system, to changes in the peripheral receptors, to the source of the pain, to the personality and motivation of the individual, to changes in the cognitive processes interpreting the source and nature of the pain, or to some combination of those factors.

While pain thresholds may or may not decline with age, tolerance of pain is at least partly related to motivational and cognitive factors; hence, no valid conclusions can be drawn concerning changes in the pain threshold or pain tolerance with age. Some older people experience pain and refer to it often; others experience pain but live stoically with it and do not refer to it; others do not have any more pain than younger people. The social situation, the source of pain, and motivational and cognitive processes influence whether pain is perceived or reported. Some older people complain even about minimal levels of pain in order to receive attention from others, particularly from adult children or other caregivers. Others never complain for fear they will be viewed as unable to care for themselves.

Aging and Cognitive Processes

Just as aging individuals must adapt to physical and social changes, so too must they respond to normal changes in the cognitive systems, that is, memory, intelligence, wisdom, learning, and creativity (Birren and Schaie, 1996, 2001; Park and Schwarz, 2001). These changes occur at different rates and to different degrees within individuals (aging effects) and among different cohorts or generations (cohort effects). As in the physical domain, there is a generalized slowing down of the cognitive processes in later life, but some age-related slowing is specific to particular kinds of tasks (Albert and Killiany, 2001; Madden, 2001).

Conventional wisdom suggests that as people age there is an inevitable and severe decline in cognitive functioning and capacity. Such stereotypical views often lead younger people to think that older people are incapable of learning or thinking, are forgetful, and are unable to be creative or to solve problems. Yet, a large body of research shows that declines in cognitive processes are less rapid and less severe than declines in

the motor, physiological, and sensory systems. There is considerable diversity in cognitive functioning among older adults; in fact, there is more variability within any given age group than between younger and older people. Any declines in cognitive functioning are due to either normal aging or to dementia disease states. These states represent a general and major decline in cognitive functioning that is reflected in memory impairment and losses in the ability to use judgement or language and to engage in abstract thinking. Only about 8 per cent of Canadians between 65 and 74 years of age experience any form of diagnosed dementia at a mild, moderate, or severe level. However, this percentage increases to about 30 per cent for those 75 to 84, and to almost 66 per cent for those 85 and older. Moreover, changes in cognitive processes are influenced by illness or disease, motivation to perform, substance abuse, and educational attainment. For example, cohort differences are almost always observed since each successive cohort, especially among women, is better educated.

Intelligence

Intelligence is a multi-dimensional construct consisting of primary abilities such as verbal comprehension, reasoning, abstract thinking, perceptual speed, numerical facility, problem solving, and word fluency (Schaie, 1996). However, psychologists disagree on the number, meaning, and measurement of the primary abilities. Moreover, it is important to distinguish between **competence** and intelligence: intelligence refers to underlying abilities that can be applied to many situations, while competence refers to adaptive behaviour unique to a specific situation or class of situations.

Adults demonstrate two types of intelligence. **Fluid intelligence**, influenced by neurological capacity, represents incidental learning that is not based on culture. Fluid intelligence is the ability to adjust one's thinking to the demands of a specific situation and to organize information to solve problems. It is measured by performance tests that are scored according to accuracy and speed. **Crystallized intelligence**, a product of education, experience, and acculturation, is based on learning and experience. Consequently, there are individual differences that vary by level of education, socio-economic status, and gender. Crystallized intelligence is measured by verbal comprehension tests that stress vocabulary and the continual addition or restructuring of information within the cognitive system.

Both cross-sectional and longitudinal studies confirm that fluid intelligence peaks during adolescence. In contrast, crystallized intelligence increases with age, at least to the mid-70s, after which it may decline. Women experience an earlier decline in fluid abilities, whereas men experience an earlier decline in crystallized abilities. Most studies indicate that there is little significant decline in intelligence until at least after age 60. Studies indicate that more recent generations have experienced gains in both fluid and crystallized intelligence, but there are greater gains in fluid intelligence. Highlight 3.3 identifies factors that influence the intelligence test performance of older people.

Older people demonstrate a range of intellectual abilities. There are individual differences in intelligence from birth onward, and a decline in cognitive functioning is not inevitable for everyone. Whereas some individuals experience little or no decline throughout adulthood, others experience severe intellectual loss. Moreover, although some elderly people perform more slowly on intellectual tasks or have difficulty with novel tasks or situations, such as computer games or automated banking, normal aging processes do not significantly diminish the ability to solve problems (Willis, 1996). In fact, older people can use their accumulated knowledge and experience to offset any loss of speed in intellectual tasks.

Assuming normal health, differences in intelligence among older people are more closely related to heredity, education, and cohort differences than to chronological age. The greater intel-

Highlight 3.3 Factors Influencing Intelligence Test Performance in Later Life

In the absence of illness and disease states, the differences observed in intellectual performance can be accounted for by a variety of past and current social and environmental factors. Some factors that may either increase (+) or decrease (–) test performance include the following:

1. The amount of experience, motivation, and training concerning the material in the tests (+).
2. Higher levels of education completed, and fewer years since leaving school (+).
3. The absence of stress and fatigue in test situations (+).
4. The use of appropriate and meaningful test items (+).
5. The use of feedback, instruction, and practice in taking tests (+).
6. The presence of stereotypes that define the elderly as incompetent, thereby lowering expectations and the level of test motivation (–).
7. Living in an environment that is conducive to intellectual stimulation (+).
8. A decreased emphasis on speed of performance (+).
9. The onset of personal crises, including major changes in job, marital, financial, or health status (–).

These environmental explanations for performance on intelligence tests have led to remedial programs and attempts to change some elements of the environment in order to modify both crystallized and fluid intelligence (Schaie, 1997; Willis, 1997; Sternberg and Lubart, 2001).

ligence demonstrated by younger cohorts is due to more and better education, more experience in test situations, better health care during infancy and childhood, and a greater likelihood of having learned the skills demanded by intelligence tests. Given a stimulating and supportive environment, gains rather than losses in intelligence are the more typical pattern, at least until the last few years of life, when nearness to death (terminal decline and terminal drop) is often predicted by a decline in cognitive functioning (Berg, 1996).

Learning and Memory

Learning and memory illustrate the classic 'chicken-and-egg' dilemma. Learning involves the acquisition of information or behaviour, while memory involves the storage and retention of the learned behaviour. For material to be acquired and stored in memory it must be learned. Similarly, to demonstrate that material has been learned, the person must recall it from his or her memory before the material can be used to answer a test question. This illustrates the importance of distinguishing between learning and performance. When a person cannot perform what was learned earlier, it is difficult to determine whether the material was not learned; whether it was learned but not remembered; or whether it was learned and stored in the memory, but cannot be retrieved for performance. Performance, rather than learning or retrieving per se, is influenced by age-biased or unsuitable learning tasks in tests, anxiety in a test situation, temporary physiological or psychological states (such as fatigue, lack of motivation, or depression) and the need to perform or demonstrate learning in a short period of time.

Learning
The belief that 'you can't teach an old dog new tricks' is still widely held. However, research evidence suggests that while there are individual differences within and between age cohorts in learning ability, older adults can learn new skills, ideas,

and concepts if adequate personal and situational conditions are present. Older adults have the capacity to learn but it often takes them longer to search for, code, recall, and respond. Where individuals set their own rates of speed, learning is more likely to occur[3]. Learning potential is restricted, as well, because of a decreased ability to distinguish relevant from irrelevant information. This problem is more acute for women since they are more likely than men to attend to irrelevant stimuli. It is important to eliminate distractions in the environment for older learners, and to enhance the learning environment with supportive instructions and guidance.

Noncognitive factors also influence the ability to learn at all ages. First, there must be a willingness to use one's physical and mental capacities. The level of motivation is most likely to be high for meaningful and relevant tasks. However, overinvolvement or overarousal, resulting from an excessive drive state is more likely to detract from performance among older than younger learners. Second, learners must not only have a sufficient level of intelligence to acquire information, but must also have experience in learning situations. Learning capacity involves acquiring and using the habits and skills of learning. Thus, older adults who remain involved in learning, education, or retraining across the life course are more likely not only to want to learn but to do so more efficiently. Another important factor in learning in later life is health. Generally, healthier individuals learn with greater ease.

Memory
Memory is involved in almost all stages of information processing (Backman et al., 2001). A simple three-stage model of how memory works was developed by Murdock (1967). During the first stage, information is received and temporarily placed in 'sensory stores'. For example, auditory information (the sound of a siren) is stored in the 'echoic memory', while visual information (such as the face of someone you have just met) is stored in 'iconic memory'. In the second stage,

this information, if it is considered important and is not interrupted by competing stimuli, is transferred by the 'attention' process to 'short-term memory'. From here, by additional rehearsal of the stimuli, the information is transferred at the third stage to more permanent 'long-term memory'. Information can be lost in the first stage (sensory storage) by decay or replacement, at the second stage (short-term memory) by forgetting if the information is not repeatedly rehearsed, and in the third stage (long-term memory) through a failure of the retrieval system to find what has been stored. For example, there is often a decline with age in both recall and recognition tasks, thereby suggesting that both acquisition and storage processes may change with age.

Some theories suggest that there are specific types of memory. For example, 'episodic' memory represents the acquisition and retrieval of information acquired in a particular place at a particular time for a given individual (such as a trip, a meaningful event, or a first love). 'Semantic memory' represents common knowledge, vocabulary, or concepts that are shared by most people, such as the colour of stop signs or the meaning of 'caution' signs or the fact that a round object rolls.

Research suggests that a progressive decline in memory performance is not inevitable, nor irreversible when it does occur (Backman et al., 2001). Older people are more likely to have the ability to remember distant events (episodic memory) than recent materials. This type of memory is related to reminiscence, in which significant personal events from the past are frequently recalled and therefore rehearsed for later recall. There is considerable variability among the older population in the degree of impairment to episodic memory. Episodic memory is better among women, among those in good health, among those with more education, and for those who are more engaged in social, cognitive, and physical activities. However, as in learning experiments, older people need more time to retrieve information from both their short- and long-term memory, especially if there are many competing stimuli in the environment, or if stored material must be manipulated or reorganized before the question can be answered.

The apparent reasons for 'memory loss' or slower and less efficient recall are not clearly understood. However, it appears that such factors as lower intelligence, not using stored information, interference in the recall process while learning new information (retroactive interference), interference from the large amount of information already stored (proactive interference), or a lack of motivation (such as a belief that older people are forgetful) contribute to a decline in memory performance.

Slower and less efficient memory processes are not totally due to biological changes. Therefore, it is possible to diagnose a problem and improve the efficiency of the memory process in later years through practice and intervention. Memory can be enhanced by:

- adopting methods to facilitate memorization;

- providing more time for the acquisition, rehearsal, and retrieval of information;

- using meaningful material to be learned and remembered in experimental situations;

- relying more on recognition than on recall;

- reducing interference during the learning process; and

- informing older adults that 'forgetting' and 'memory loss' are not inevitable and that they do have the capacity to remember, although it might take longer to do so.

What people believe and feel about their memory may be as important as their actual memory. That is, a person who thinks that their memory is bound to deteriorate may feel anxiety and a loss of control and may make less effort in memory-demanding situations; all of that may, in turn, contribute to declines in memory performance in later life.

Cognitive Style: Thinking and Solving Problems

'Cognitive style' refers to the characteristic way that individuals conceptually organize their environment, manipulate the knowledge they possess, and make decisions or approach problems that have to be solved. Two contrasting cognitive styles have been labelled 'field-dependent' and 'field-independent'. 'Field-dependent' individuals are more aware of their social environment, more people-oriented, and generally more conventional in their behaviour. In contrast, 'field-independent' people are more analytical, more internally directed, and less constrained in their behaviour by tradition and convention.

An individual may be reflective (a longer response time and fewer errors is the norm) or impulsive (a fast response time with less accuracy is the norm). Cognitive style is revealed, as well, when a decision involves some risk. Older people are generally more cautious and cognitively rigid and are sometimes reluctant to make difficult decisions, especially when a situation is ambiguous, when speed is required, or when they are afraid of failing. Thus, in some situations older people react with caution by substituting accuracy for speed; in others they may be rigid in their thinking and resort to prior learning or experience, even if it is no longer suitable. Furthermore, it appears that if given the option of not making a decision, many select this alternative. It is not clear whether this rigidity and cautiousness among elderly people is an aging phenomenon or whether it is a cohort and historical factor; that is, these traits have been part of a lifelong cognitive style. An alternative interpretation of cautiousness is that it reveals an unwillingness to take risks, especially in situations where older people are less willing to be evaluated or they are afraid of making a mistake.

Complex thinking is limited by a general slowing down of behaviour because of changes in the central nervous system; a loss of speed in all stages of information processing; and a change in health, particularly with the onset of coronary heart disease or cerebrovascular disease. The slowing may also be due to 'divided-attention' deficits (such as difficulty in trying to listen to two conversations) or 'selective-attention' deficits (difficulty in ignoring irrelevant information, such as a conversation on the radio while talking to another person).

People may compensate for loss of speed in information processing by relying on past experience and knowledge, by employing memory aids, or by eliminating irrelevant stimuli. Charness (1981) argued that individual differences in cognitive aging are due to changes either in 'hardware' (processing mechanisms) or in 'software' (strategies and learning controlled by the performer). Since hardware changes generally result in a loss of speed or a decline in memory, difficulty in solving problems occurs unless software changes are learned and used. These compensating mechanisms are particularly important in problem-solving or decision-making tasks. Thus, with increasing age, adults become not only less accurate in problem solving but also slower.

The ability to solve problems declines with age because of a general slowing down of behaviour and because of an unwillingness or inability to use newer, more efficient strategies that might lead to a solution or decision (Willis, 1996). However, declines are related as well to education and to the type of task. There is less decline in ability among better-educated older people and for tasks similar to those used in one's occupation. Charness (1981) suggested that older people are inferior to younger people in solving problems, not because their ability has declined, but because they have always been less effective. A cohort effect is present because they have not acquired a skill when younger and have had less experience with the skill during their lifetimes.

Creativity and Wisdom

Creativity and wisdom are related to, but different from, intelligence, and they reflect a person's cognitive style. Often these two cognitive elements are thought to function at opposite ends of the life course—creativity is expressed when younger; wisdom when one is older. Both concepts are difficult to define and measure (Sternberg and Lubart, 2001). **Creativity** involves the ability 'to produce work that is novel, high in quality, and task-appropriate' (Sternberg and Lubart, 2001: 510). It involves knowledge, personality, cognitive thinking, motivation, and a consideration of environmental influences. Creativity can lead to a solution to an old problem; the identification of a new problem; the creation of a unique cultural product that is valued by others (such as a work of art, music, or literature or a scientific invention); or the development of a new concept, product, theory, or practice.

Creativity is usually measured by either the total productivity (or quantity) throughout a person's career, such as the number of articles published by a scientist or the number of books, poems, or paintings created, or by the highest-quality piece of work (such as a Nobel Prize–winning work). The study of creativity has been based primarily on retrospective studies of the career profiles of various occupational groups or on case studies of older people, such as Grandma Moses or George Burns, who have been defined as highly creative.

Creative 'potential' often peaks at about age 40, with a decline appearing after about age 50. However, there are individual differences by occupation. For example, the peak of creativity in mathematics and chemistry occurs in the 30s and 40s, while in literature and history, where experience and a larger investment of reflective time in a single project are necessary, the peak occurs in the 50s or 60s. Furthermore, the highest-quality work often appears when the largest quantity of work is being produced.

The pattern of creativity throughout a person's life is influenced by such factors as health, motivation, energy, personal lifestyle, competing interests, expectations of significant others, and the social environment. For example, older people may have a capacity for creativity but lack a social environment that provides the stimulation

to question and to create, or the opportunity to pursue ideas to completion. Nevertheless, with maturity and advancing age, many people become more reflective, integrative, and interpretive in their thinking and behaviour, thereby enhancing their creative potential.

With significant accomplishments by people in their 60s, 70s, or 80s, it is clear that, with the right environment, older people are capable of highly creative work well into their later years. Individuals who are producers of high-quality work in the later years have been referred to as 'Ulysseans' (McLeish, 1976). They view later life as a challenge and the production of further creative works as an adventure. Highlight 3.4 includes a few lines from Tennyson's poem 'Ulysses', which expresses the desire to continue creating, contributing, and performing at a high level in the later years.

Wisdom is defined as the 'power of judging rightly, and following the soundest course of action based on knowledge, experience and understanding' (Webster's New World Dictionary). Studies have suggested that wisdom involves some balance of intelligence and creativity, and that both can increase or decrease with age. Wisdom increases to a maximum at some point because of experience and creative energy. However, as cognitive functions of memory and reasoning begin to decline late in life, wisdom may be expressed or demonstrated less often.

Personality Processes and Aging

To explain changes in behaviour with age, social scientists have tried to determine the relative influence of personality factors. Perhaps nowhere else is the interaction of the personal system with the social system more evident than when personality is considered as a factor in the aging process. **Personality** involves individual differences in diverse human characteristics such as traits, emotions, moods, coping strategies, cognitive styles, goals, and motives that are unique to

Highlight 3.4 Ulyssean Adults: Motivation to Achieve in Later Life

How dull it is to pause, to make an end,
To rust unburnish'd, not to shine in use!

And this grey spirit yearning in desire
To follow knowledge like a sinking star. . .

Death closes all; but something ere the end,
Some work of noble note, may yet be done . . .

. . . but strong in will
To strive, to seek, to find, and not to yield.

(From 'Ulysses' by Alfred Tennyson)

an individual who interacts with others in a variety of social settings.

Most personality research focuses on the early developmental years of childhood and adolescence. It tries to describe and explain characteristic ways in which individuals think, that is, their cognitive style, and behave, that is, their lifestyle. Two questions dominate personality research: (1) Is behaviour determined internally by personality traits or externally by the social situation? (2) Is personality stable, once established, or does it change as people grow older? To understand the influence of personality on behaviour throughout later life we need to answer those questions.

Social Behaviour: A Function of Personality Traits or the Social Situation?

Is behaviour determined by personality traits or by the social environment? According to the 'trait' approach, individuals, through a combination of heredity, early socialization, and interaction with significant others, develop personal traits and characteristics, a cognitive style, and a temperament. These behavioural dispositions are thought

to be stable over time; and they enable individuals to respond consistently and predictably to their social and physical environments.[4]

In contrast, the 'situational', 'behavioural', or 'state' perspective argues that behaviour is determined by the social situation and that individuals learn to behave in a way that is appropriate to a given situation. According to this perspective, a 'personality' per se does not exist. Or, if it does, it has little stability, since the behaviour of an individual is determined by external social norms and sanctions unique to specific situations, such as the workplace, the home, or a leisure situation.

As with many bipolar views of the world, neither position has received overwhelming support in the research literature. Rather, an interactionist perspective evolved as a more realistic view in which behaviour results from continuous two-way interaction between a person with unique cognitive and emotional traits and a particular social situation. Thus, an individual's personality influences his or her behaviour and adaptation to specific situations, while the situation itself influences which traits from the available repertoire are expressed and in what way. Through an interactive process involving personal and social systems, individual lifestyles evolve.

Personality: Stability or Change across the Life Course?

This question is still being debated, although the available evidence, especially from longitudinal studies, suggests that after early adulthood, people demonstrate reasonable consistency in such personal characteristics as presentation of self, attitudes, values, temperament, and traits. Many individuals make a conscious effort to maintain consistency in the behavioural and cognitive presentation of self. When behaviour and personality are assessed and averaged over a large sample of situations, stability is the normal pattern in the absence of confounding health problems.

However, evidence from surveys and individual case studies indicates that some personality changes occur at or beyond middle age in some people. First, most members of a cohort exhibit changes over time in some trait, but a person's relative position in the group does not change. The most dependable person at age 20 is the most dependable person at age 50, even though the average score for the cohort may increase, perhaps because dependability has become a more valued and important cultural value. Second, all members of a cohort change, but some people change more than others. The person who was most aggressive at age 20 may be among the more passive at age 50.

How are these changes explained? A developmental perspective argues that people change and adapt as their individual lives evolve. A relatively new concept in personality research is **generativity**, a process that begins in mid-life and in which individuals become less concerned with self-identity, the self, and a focus on themselves and more concerned with mentoring and helping others—such as co-workers, older adults, children, or young colleagues. This is achieved by becoming a leader, mentor, and contributor in the broader community (Ryff et al., 2001).

Self-concept is a subset of personality that is the outcome of our motivations, attitudes, and behaviour relevant to our self-definition (how we define and present ourselves to others) and our personal meaning of life. The 'self' has three basic components (Giarrusso et al., 2001: 296): (1) cognitive (who we think we are); (2) affective (feelings about who we are); and (3) conative (our action on the basis of self-perceptions). There is both stability and change in the self-concept as we age. We use our physical, cognitive, and social resources to maintain or change our self-concept as social or cultural situations change. Historical and cultural trends influence the self-concept and self-motivated actions (Giarusso et al., 2001). George (1996) argued that there is a *reciprocal* relationship between life-course experiences and the content of the self as we age. Life-course events shape the self, and the content of the self influences life-course experiences. Moreover, the self is influenced not only by current social circumstances, but also by culture and our place in the social structure earlier in life.

Research about the self attempts to understand how adults cope with stressful situations that emerge in later life—retirement, widowhood, death of friends, failing health, dependency, and institutionalization.[5] Ruth and Coleman (1996: 309) defined coping as the 'constantly changing cognitive and behavioural efforts to manage specific external or internal demands that are appraised as taxing or exceeding the resources of the person'. But through self-evaluation processes we cope and adapt by making social comparisons and noting discrepancies in how we react, behave, or think compared to others in similar situations. This process involves *social* cognition; that is, we focus on the content and structure of social knowledge (our understanding of social reality) and on the cognitive processes involved in accessing such knowledge (Blanchard-Fields and Abeles, 1996).

Demonstrated changes in personality reflect underlying latent needs and characteristics that could not be or were not expressed earlier in life. As social situations change with age, people are less inclined to present the self in a traditional outmoded or inappropriate way. For example, as a person who was striving and ambitious in early adulthood moves into middle or later life, he or she may devote less time to work, becomes more relaxed in interpersonal situations, and demonstrate a different presentation of the self in all social situations. This change is more likely to occur if career goals have been attained, especially if at an earlier age than expected.

Another factor leading to an apparent change in personality is the lack of opportunity to demonstrate certain traits. For example, a need to be aggressive or achievement-oriented continues, but opportunities to do so are no longer as readily available at work or at play (such as sports). In addition, the physical and psychic energy needed to continue a pattern of aggressive and achievement-oriented behaviour may no longer be available.

Finally, emotions are at the 'heart' of social relations, and they influence how and why we care about outcomes. Joy, fear, anger, shame, guilt, and disgust are expressed to varying degrees across the life course, depending on the social context. In later life, emotions may be felt but not expressed, or only expressed with or against certain people. Age does not affect emotional intensity per se, nor does it bring with it a generalized negative mood (as in the stereotype of grumpy old men) or a decrease in positive mood (Magai, 2001).

So, does personality change as people age, or is it stable? The answer to the question is 'yes' and 'yes'. The evidence increasingly supports the 'co-occurrence of persistent traits and unfolding development linked to changing life tasks' (Ryff et al., 2001: 492). While most people do not experience major personality changes with age, some change their patterns of social interaction as situations or demands evolve. Similarly, others, aware of changing norms among younger cohorts, change their behaviour or cognitive pattern to 'fit' with contemporary lifestyles. Some personality changes may be related to physiological, medical, or cognitive changes; others reflect latent character traits, fewer opportunities, or a changing social environment.

Personality Traits

Many cross-sectional studies have measured single or multiple **personality traits**[6] to determine whether differences exist by age, or if age is a more significant factor in personality differences than other social variables, in particular, gender, socio-economic status, race, ethnic background, or birth order. Some common personality traits[7] are aggressiveness, anxiety, authoritarianism, cautiousness, conformity, conservatism, creativity, decision-making style, egocentrism, ego strength, emotionality, extraversion, happiness, introversion, irritability, need for achievement, passivity, perceived locus of control, reminiscence, rigidity, risk taking, self-concept or self-image, self-esteem, and sociability.

For most traits, the evidence in favour of either age differences or age changes is equivocal. Some studies find differences between age groups or changes with age, while others are unable to demonstrate any differences or changes. Despite the inconsistency of the findings, the current cohort of older people are generally more conservative, cautious, egocentric, introverted, and passive and less emotional than younger age groups. It is unclear whether these differences are due to lifelong characteristics related to cohort effects, learned changes with age, or forced changes with age because of decreasing opportunities, stereotypes, or changing interaction patterns with younger cohorts.

In addition to the above factors, which are primarily internally determined, other personality traits are more dependent on social learning and social interaction. These externally induced factors are more likely to change with age. For example, consider the concept of self-esteem, that is, how people think and feel about themselves and how they think others view them. Self-esteem is a learned characteristic, a product of lifelong social interaction and social experiences. Most older people report a positive sense of self-esteem. However, the degree of self-esteem is related to such factors as socio-economic status, educational attainment, and health. Thus, it is not surprising that a loss in self-esteem may accompany the loss of a job, being discriminated against as an older worker, a decline in health, a divorce, the onset of a disability, or declining independence. Moreover, withdrawal from, or less frequent interaction with, significant others also reduces self-esteem. Some personality traits are highly dependent on social learning and interaction, and when losses or changes occur in these areas, older people, like younger people, begin to question their worth and competence. This, in turn, lowers their self-esteem or changes their self-concept, thereby leading to further changes in behaviour and to changes in other personality dimensions.

While there appear to be some age differences and age changes in personality traits, these are not universal or inevitable. Individual differences in personality traits (within and between age cohorts) are influenced by the social environment. Recently, psychologists have been finding evidence that for some personality traits there are intra-individual differences in the *rate* of change. Some people are stable; others change; and those who change on one personality dimension may not change on another (Mroczek and Spiro, 2003). Similarly, Small et al. (2003) found substantial personality change in old age that could be attributed to changes in health or to such major events as retirement or widowhood.

Personality Types

The early years of social gerontology were characterized by attempts to identify **personality types** that would explain life satisfaction or 'successful' aging.[8] This body of descriptive research generated many labels for older people who appeared to think and behave in similar ways—stable, rocking-chair, passive-dependent, integrated or unintegrated, disengaged, active-competent, and husband-centred (for women!). The labels were thought to describe lifestyles that had been built over the life course and that persisted in later life

and explained 'adjustment' to the demands of aging. Most of these 'types' were derived from a single research study, usually with men, and using samples of fewer than 100 older people. Unfortunately, these labels were sometimes adopted by the media, practitioners, and older people, thereby contributing to ageism in society and to self-fulfilling prophecies about behaviour in later life. This perspective on personality is not well accepted today since 'labelling' is considered ageist and inaccurate, and unable to account for diverse personalities in later life. Moreover, life-long stability in personality is considered less likely as generativity and changes in the self occur across the life course in response to cognitive, physical, or health changes or to events that influence a person's ability to cope with a changing social world. Finally, *if* successful aging could be defined or explained, it would involve many other factors, not just personality.

Summary

Aging is not a disease. As people go through life, they experience inevitable, but normal, changes in physical structure, such as height, posture, and shape, and in their motor, sensory, cognitive, and personality systems. There are variations, both within and between individuals, in the rate and amount of loss or gain in these domains because of personal factors—heredity, health, education, gender, and lifestyle—and environmental factors—work, housing, and neighbourhood—that require coping strategies and adaption. These normal changes that take place with age influence personal behaviour and lifestyles, as well as the way in which others react to the aging person. Personality is both somewhat stable and subject to change across the life course in different social situations, and as health changes or major transitions occur. In short, the rate, degree, and nature of individual aging has an influence on social interactions and lifestyles throughout life, as well as in later life.

For Reflection, Debate, or Action

1. Go to www.aging.unc.edu/ioalearning, and complete the modules in the 'Aging Body Quiz'.

2. Using information in this chapter, develop an argument to support or refute the claim that the human lifespan can be extended beyond its current limit of about 120 years.

3. Can any of the many cognitive processes be altered in early or later life to slow the amount of cognitive loss or impairment? If so, which processes, and how might interventions slow down such losses or impairments?

4. If you think of two or three older people in your family, to what extent does personality, lifestyle, and health distinguish those who are adapting well to growing older from those who are having some difficulty?

5. Develop a plan to enable more older adults to share their wisdom for the betterment of society.

6. Looking ahead 40 years, to what extent do you expect that you, as an individual, will have changed, and in what ways? Consider appearances and characteristics you observe in your parents, and reflect on whether this will be you in the future—why or why not?

NOTES

1. For detailed discussions of psychological and biological changes, see the *Handbook of the Psychology of Aging* (Birren and Schaie, 1996; 2001), the *Handbook of the Biology of Aging* (Masoro and Austad, 2001), and current and past issues of the *Journal of Gerontology: Biological Sciences* and the *Journal of Gerontology: Psychological Sciences*.

2. This does not imply that gross changes in behaviour do not occur because of organic deterioration or the reaction to physically or mentally stressful events. Rather, it suggests that, contrary to the prevailing myth, most older people do not encounter such problems. Indeed, less than 10 per cent of elderly people are ever institutionalized, and when they are, it is most often in the last few years or months before death.

3. For example, university-level correspondence courses in which lectures are provided on tape and with printed learning aids may be a more effective learning situation, not only for older people, but for all adults who have been away from formal schooling for many years. This method allows people to learn at their own pace, without having to take notes in a classroom from a professor who speaks rapidly, and they can replay the tapes as many times as necessary.

4. Although most studies have focused on measures of one or more personality *traits* (for example, introversion, sociability, aggressiveness, egocentrism, achievement orientation, dependency, etc.), a few studies have used multi-dimensional scales to arrive at personality *types* (Type A versus Type B; or, integrated, passive-dependent, work-centred, person-oriented, and rocking-chair). Moreover, a variety of instruments have been used to measure personality traits or types. These include clinical case studies obtained through interviews; personality inventories like the Cattell 16PF; projective techniques like the Thematic Aperception Test or the Rorschach inkblot test; laboratory behavioural tests; and content analyses of life histories, diaries, memoirs, or autobiographies.

5. For a discussion of the self in later life, see Ruth and Coleman (1996), Ryff and Marshall (1999), and Giarrusso et al. (2001).

6. The instruments used most often are the Guilford-Zimmerman Temperament Survey; Cattell's 16 Personality Factor (16PF) Inventory; Eysenck's Personality Inventory; and the Minnesota Multiphasic Personality Inventory.

7. Sometimes traits are measured as isolated characteristics; at other times they are measured in such

a way that clusters are formed. For example, on the 16PF instrument, sociability, impulsiveness, and dominance combine to represent the personality factor of extraversion. Many question whether it can be assumed that personality traits are independent of one another, or whether the traits are interrelated to create a personality structure.

8. For a discussion of the influence of personality types on successful aging, see Reichard et al. (1962), Neugarten et al. (1964), Havighurst (1969), Maas and Kuypers (1974), and Friedman (1980).

References

Albert, M., and R. Killiany. 2001. 'Age-Related Cognitive Change and Brain-Behaviour Relationships'. Pp. 161–85 in J. Birren and W. Schaie (eds), *Handbook of the Psychology of Aging*. San Diego, Calif.: Academic Press.

Backman, L., et al. 2001. 'Aging and Memory: Cognitive and Biological Perspectives'. Pp. 349–77 in J. Birren and W. Schaie (eds), *Handbook of the Psychology of Aging*. San Diego, Calif.: Academic Press.

Berg, S. 1996. 'Aging, Behaviour and Terminal Decline'. Pp. 323–37 in J. Birren and Schaie (1996).

Birren, J., and W. Schaie (eds). 1996. *Handbook of the Psychology of Aging*. San Diego, Calif.: Academic Press.

———— (eds). 2001. *Handbook of the Psychology of Aging*. San Diego, Calif.: Academic Press.

Blanchard-Fields, F., and R. Abeles. 1996. 'Social Cognition and Aging'. Pp. 150–61 in J. Birren and W. Schaie (eds), *Handbook of the Psychology of Aging*. San Diego, Calif.: Academic Press.

Bortz, W. 2002. 'A Conceptual Framework of Frailty: A Review', *Journal of Gerontology: Medical Sciences* 57A(5), M283–8.

Charness, N. 1981. 'Aging and Skilled Problem Solving', *Journal of Experimental Psychology: General* 110(1), 21–38.

Fozard, J., and S. Gordon-Salant. 2001. 'Changes in Vision and Hearing with Aging'. Pp. 241–66 in J. Birren and W. Schaie (eds), *Handbook of the Psychology of Aging*. San Diego, Calif.: Academic Press.

Friedman, M. 1980. 'Type A Behavior: A Progress Report', *The Sciences* 20(2), 10, 11, 28.

George, L. 1996. 'Missing Links: The Case for a Social Psychology of the Life Course', *The Gerontologist* 36(2), 248–55.

Giarrusso, R., et al. 2001. 'The Aging Self in Social Contexts'. Pp. 295–312 in R. Binstock and L. George (eds), *Handbook of Aging and the Social Sciences*. San Diego, Calif.: Academic Press.

Havighurst, R. 1969. 'Research and Development in Social Gerontology', *The Gerontologist*, 9(4), 1–90.

Hennessy, C. 1989. 'Culture in the Use, Care and Control of the Aging Body', *Journal of Aging Studies* 3(1), 39–54.

Himes, C. (ed.). 2004. 'Obesity in Later Life', *Research on Aging* (special issue), 26(1), 3–176.

Ketcham, C., and G. Stelmach. 2001. 'Age-Related Declines in Motor Control'. Pp. 313–48 in J. Birren and W. Schaie (eds), *Handbook of the Psychology of Aging*. San Diego, Calif.: Academic Press.

Kline, D., and C. Scialfa. 1996. 'Visual and Auditory Aging'. Pp. 181–203 in J. Birren and W. Schaie (eds), *Handbook of the Psychology of Aging*. San Diego, Calif.: Academic Press.

Maas, H., and J. Kuypers. 1974. *From Thirty to Seventy*. San Francisco, Calif.: Jossey-Bass.

McClearn, G., and G. Vogler. 2001. 'The Genetics of Behavioral Aging'. Pp. 109–31 in J. Birren and W. Schaie (eds), *Handbook of the Psychology of Aging*. San Diego, Calif.: Academic Press.

McLeish, J. 1976. *The Ulyssean Adult: Creativity in the Middle and Later Years*. New York: McGraw-Hill.

Madden, D. 2001. 'Speed and Timing of Behavioral Processes'. Pp. 288–312 in J. Birren and W. Schaie (eds), *Handbook of the Psychology of Aging*. San Diego, Calif.: Academic Press.

Magai, C. 2001. 'Emotions over the Life Span'. Pp. 399–426 in J. Birren and W. Schaie (eds), *Handbook of the Psychology of Aging*. San Diego, Calif.: Academic Press.

Masoro, E., and S. Austad (eds). 2001. *Handbook of the Biology of Aging*. San Diego, Calif.: Academic Press.

Morley, J., et al. 2002. 'Something about Frailty', *Journal of Gerontology: Medical Sciences*, 57A(11), M698–704.

Mroczek, D., and A. Spiro. 2003. 'Modeling Intraindividual Change in Personality Traits: Findings from the Normative Aging Study'. *Journal of Gerontology: Psychological Sciences* 58B(3), P153–65.

Murdock, B. 1967. 'Recent Developments in Short Term Memory', *Quarterly Journal of Experimental Psychology* 18(3), 206–11.

Neugarten, B., et al. 1964. *Personality in Middle and Later Life*. New York: Atherton Press.

Reichard, S., et al. 1962. *Aging and Personality*. New York: John Wiley.

Park, D., and N. Schwarz (eds). 2001. *Cognitive Aging: A Primer*. Philadelphia: Taylor and Francis.

Ruth, J-E., and P. Coleman. 1996. 'Personality and Aging: Coping and Management of the Self in Later Life'. Pp. 308–22 in J. Birren and W. Schaie (eds), *Handbook of the Psychology of Aging*. San Diego, Calif.: Academic Press.

Ryff, C., and V. Marshall (eds). 1999. *The Self and Society in Aging Processes*. New York: Springer.

Ryff, C., et al. 2001. 'Personality and Aging: Flourishing Agendas and Future Challenges'. Pp. 477–99 in J. Birren and W. Schaie (eds), *Handbook of the Psychology of Aging*, San Diego, Calif.: Academic Press.

Schaie, W. 1996. 'Intellectual Development in Adulthood'. Pp. 266–86 in J. Birren and W. Schaie (eds), *Handbook of the Psychology of Aging*. San Diego, Calif.: Academic Press.

Simoneau, G., and H. Leibowitz. 1996. 'Posture, Gait and Falls'. Pp. 204–17 in J. Birren and W. Schaie (eds), *Handbook of the Psychology of Aging*, San Diego, Calif.: Academic Press.

Small, B., et al. 2003. 'Stability and Change in Adult Personality over 6 Years: Findings From the Victoria Longitudinal Study', *Journal of Gerontology: Psychological Sciences* 58B(3), P166–76.

Statistics Canada. 2002. *Participation and Activity Limitation Survey (PALS): A Profile of Disability in Canada, 2001*. Ottawa: Statistics Canada. Cat. no. 89-577-XIE.

Sternberg, R., and T. Lubart. 2001. 'Wisdom and Creativity'. Pp. 500–22 in J. Birren and W. Schaie (eds), *Handbook of the Psychology of Aging*. San Diego, Calif.: Academic Press.

Stones, M., and A. Kozma. 1996. 'Activity, Exercise and Behavior'. Pp. 338–52 in Birren and Schaie (1996).

Vinters, H. 2001. 'Aging and the Human Nervous System'. Pp. 135–60 in J. Birren and W. Schaie (eds), *Handbook of the Psychology of Aging*. San Diego, Calif.: Academic Press.

Webster's New World Dictionary. 1997. S.v. 'Wisdom'.

Willis, S. 1996. 'Everyday Problem Solving'. Pp. 287–307 in J. Birren and W. Schaie (eds), *Handbook of the Psychology of Aging*. San Diego, Calif.: Academic Press.

CHAPTER 4

Population Aging:
A Demographic and Geographic Perspective

Focal Points

- Why do populations age, at what rate do they age, and how do we measure population aging?

- Why is population aging a global concern?

- How can demographic statistics be misused and misinterpreted?

- Where do the elderly live in Canada—rural or urban areas, central city or suburbs, eastern or western provinces, metropolitan areas or small towns and cities?

- To what extent do older people emigrate to Canada?

- How can demographic statistics and indices be used to develop or revise policies, programs, and practices?

Introduction

Population aging statistics illustrate past trends, the present situation, and what the future might be like. This information is extremely useful for planning policies and programs, both current and future. However, these same statistics can be misleading or be misinterpreted, or they can cause irrational fears about the future (fears that have been attributed to 'apocalyptic' or 'voodoo' demography). In recent years, demographic facts have been used to raise concerns about the possibility of rapidly increasing costs of pension plans and health care; intergenerational conflict over scarce resources; and public policies that will advantage or disadvantage one age cohort more than another. This chapter introduces demographic indices, trends, and projections pertaining to the size, composition, and distribution of the population in Canada and throughout the world.

To understand the social processes associated with aging, we must understand, as well, the present and possible future age structure of our country and of other parts of the aging world. We live in an interdependent global society where global aging is, and will be, increasingly tied to the global economy, geopolitics, and global humanitarian issues. Worldwide, the elderly population is increasing by about 800,000 a month. Nationally, regionally, and locally, changes in age structures and in the geographical location of older people due to immigration or migration require that public policies and service programs for an aging population be designed or redesigned. Some of these policy domains include pensions, education, health care, housing, home care, long-term care, public transportation, mandatory retirement, immigration, and leisure services. For example, a community might have to decide whether to build a new elementary school, a senior citizen centre, or a chronic-care hospital. Whatever is built must meet the needs of a specific segment of the population in that community for the next 30 to 50 years. Demographic trends and projections can provide objective facts to help politicians reach the best decision for the future.

To avoid or solve economic and social problems arising from population aging, federal governments debate questions such as these:

- Should the retirement age be raised or eliminated?

- Should public pension benefits be reduced?

- Should pension contributions be increased?

- Should the number of immigrants be increased?

- Should incentives be created to encourage couples to have more children?

These questions illustrate how, on a societal level, population aging is posing significant challenges for the labour force, the economy, the health care system, and the family, all of which must adapt to an age structure that is becoming older. With advance planning because of demographic projections, society will meet these challenges. History has shown that the school and university systems adapted when the baby boom entered school; and later, the labour force absorbed this large birth cohort. Now, society must adapt as the baby boom cohort leaves the labour force and enters the later years of life.

In developing countries, however, demographic indices illustrate that a major social problem is rapid population growth due to high fertility, not rapid population aging due to low fertility rates and enhanced life expectancy as in developed countries. In developing countries different policies are required to slow population growth through lowered fertility rates. Thus, India promotes sterilization, while China has a 'one child per family' policy.

An awareness of demographic trends can influence personal decisions—to move to a region or country where there are greater employment opportunities or to move to another community for a safer, healthier, more active retirement. Moreover, entrepreneurs monitor demographic trends to decide what type of new products to develop; where to sell new products in the health care, travel, leisure, housing, or clothing sectors (Foot and Stoffman, 1998); and where, geographically, to locate new businesses so as to serve specific age groups.

To preview your future life course, take the year you were born and add 25. In that year, you will probably be a full-time member of the labour force. Add 40 to your year of birth; at this point you will probably be a parent and a homeowner. Add 60 or 65 to your birth year, and this will give you the period during which you will likely retire. You now have an approximate profile of when you and your birth cohort will experience some major life transitions.

This chapter presents a brief, non-technical introduction to the field of **demography**. Demographers conduct cohort analyses to understand the unique social and historical events affecting the life course of specific age cohorts (such as the baby-boomers, who were born between 1947 and 1966), the effect of such a unique cohort on the age structure over time, and their interaction with earlier or later birth cohorts (Foot and Stoffman, 1998). They also study why and how populations change over time, becoming smaller, larger, or older. For example, with declining fertility rates and very little immigration, later in this century Japan and many countries in Europe will experience a slow but significant *decrease* in population size as the baby boom cohort dies. In contrast, with decreasing fertility rates, medical advances in child care and the treatment of AIDS, better public sanitation and disease control, and more educational and economic opportunities, many of the developing countries will age rapidly in the next 50 years.

To analyze these issues, demographers study fertility rates, mortality and morbidity rates, causes of death, and immigration and internal migration patterns. Then, they present a 'current' demographic snapshot or profile of a nation, region, or community; explain the changes and trends of many past decades; and, using varying assumptions, make projections, but not predictions, about the future size, composition, and location of the population. Often these projections include economic, social, and policy issues to be addressed, or the possible consequences, positive or negative, of demographic changes for a society or community (Foot and Stoffman, 1998; Serow, 2001; Rosenberg, 2000; Connidis, 2003).

Tables and figures are used by demographers to illustrate demographic trends and patterns, for Canada and the world, about the past, and also about the future.[1] The demographic facts illustrate important ideas or patterns, particularly if reliable comparative information is available for different periods and different regions or countries. It is not essential to memorize the numbers. Rather, examine and interpret the trends and consider possible social, political, or economic implications for older people and for cohorts at all ages. Recent statistics and trends for your region, town, and neighborhood can be found in the government publications section of most libraries[2] and on the Statistics Canada web site (www.statcan.ca).

Demographic facts, whether at the international, national, regional, or local level, should be interpreted to identify possible implications for you, your parents, the oldest citizens in your community or region, and younger age cohorts who will follow. In such an analysis, you should be interested not just in those who are over 65 at present, but rather in the current and future characteristics of age cohorts who will be 65 and older

in the next 20 to 30 years. And the statistics should be interpreted with knowledge of the values, beliefs, situations, lifestyles, and past experiences of different cohorts. To illustrate, Easterlin (1996) stressed that lifestyle and value differences between the baby boomers and their parents are quite significant—boomers spend more of their income; fewer of them marry; there are more divorces and re-remarriages; they have fewer children; there are more childless couples and people who have never married; there are more dual careers; and some will inherit vast amounts of money or property from their frugal parents or grandparents. Consequently, as the baby-boom cohort enters later life, their financial, family, and leisure circumstances will be quite different from those of their parents and grandparents—some will have only limited savings whereas others will have large inheritances; they will have fewer children or, in some cases, none at all, to look after them; and a larger percentage will live alone because they are divorced or never married or had a permanent relationship. They are also very consumer- and leisure-oriented.

Some textbooks on aging include many pages of demographic statistics, but even as you read this book, 'current' published statistics are becoming dated. For example, there is often a two-year delay from the time data are collected through a census[3] or survey until the information is published. And statistical summaries can be as confusing as they are illuminating since there are often differences in the source of the data and the year in which data were collected, in how the data are categorized in tables or figures, in how many age categories are used, or in how indices are computed.[4] For example, data in tables may be presented for one-, five-, or ten-year cohorts. Some reports place all those over 65 in one category; others use over 60; others use five-year intervals, such as 61–5 and 66–70 or ten-year intervals, such as 60–9, 70–9, and so on.

Whereas some reports publish the percentage of older people, others present the absolute number of older people. These inconsistencies create problems in understanding and applying demographic knowledge since a report about a small percentage increase in the total older population may mask a rapid increase in their absolute numbers. To illustrate, in Africa, projections for the period 2000 to 2015 indicate only a 0.3 per cent increase in those 65 and older. But, in absolute numbers, the increase may range from 19 million to 29 million; many of whom will need social, medical, or financial assistance in the near future. These variations in the way data are reported make it difficult to understand trends or changes, or to compare information from a variety of studies. Consequently, we must be careful in how we interpret and use such information.

Global Demographic and Epidemiological Transitions

In many developed countries until the beginning of the twentieth century, fertility rates were high and large families were common, although many children died in infancy or they succumbed to epidemics, acute infectious diseases, or food shortages in early childhood. Even those who survived beyond early or middle childhood often died in early or middle adulthood because of epidemics, wars, or food shortages before reaching 'old' age. It is for these reasons that average life expectancy at birth was only about 30 years in 1800, and barely reached 50 years until after 1900 (Riley, 2001). By the late 1850s and thereafter, mortality and morbidity rates declined and populations started to grow larger and older. Then, as land became scarce in the United Kingdom and Europe, many young adults emigrated to North America, thereby enlarging the population of Canada and the United States.

In the late 1800s and beyond, changes in the size and age structure of many developed nations occurred because of four interrelated demographic elements (Hauser, 1976), all of which contributed to a '**demographic transition**'. The first element of the transition was a **population explo-sion**, in which the world's population increased from about 1 billion in 1800 to about 6 billion at the beginning of the twenty-first century. It is projected that if fertility rates remain constant in most developed countries and decline in developing countries, the world population will total about 9 billion by 2050. Of this total, 17 per cent will live in the more developed countries and 83 per cent in the developing countries. Where fertility rates remain high, population growth will be greater, and population aging will occur at a slower rate.

A second element was **population implo-sion.** That is, the population of most countries became concentrated in a relatively small area, primarily when young adults migrated to cities in search of work and an urban lifestyle. **Population displosion**, the third element, began when the population of a specific geographic area became increasingly heterogeneous owing to in- or out-migration and immigration. Population implosion and displosion are seen in the geographic distribution and migration of people in a nation, region, or community. Finally, as a country modernized, a **technoplosion** (the rapid spread of new technological developments) created major changes and improvements in public health (such as disease control, public sanitation, and health promotion), individual health and longevity, work and leisure lifestyles, and quality of life.

In conjunction with a demographic transition, there are often improvements in the health of a nation—a health transition. As a population ages, the leading causes of death usually change from infectious, parasitic, and acute illnesses to chronic and degenerative diseases. This phenomenon, known as an **epidemiologic transition**, begins once there are improvements in nutrition, personal health care, public sanitation, education and economic development. In the developing countries, epidemics of infectious diseases, famines, and lack of sanitation are common, but once those conditions improve, death rates begin to decline, especially among infants, children, and women during childbirth. As a result, life expectancy at birth rises and the leading causes of death become the chronic and degenerative diseases of later life. In Canada, during the twentieth century, the leading causes of death changed from pneumonia, tuberculosis, and infectious diseases in early life to cardiovascular diseases, respiratory diseases, and cancer in later life.

It is important to note that these demographic and epidemiologic changes, especially the increase in life expectancy, happen at different rates in different societies, and are primarily the result of human agency, plus public health policy. As Riley (2001: 24) notes, the quality of life improves and life expectancy increases as a result of both personal and public-policy actions. The end result is an improved standard of living (better nutrition, housing, and clothing); more community resources devoted to sanitation, public health, and disease control; and enhanced research to develop drugs and medical technology to resist and control disease. Today, we have yet to eradicate cardiovascular diseases, cancer, dementia, and AIDS. But, if and when we do, longevity in the later years should increase and survival rates in the early years will increase dramatically in developing countries where AIDS is an epidemic.

Demographic Variations among Age Cohorts

Demographic analyses enable us to understand some of the variations in the life styles and life chances of different birth cohorts. Often the analyses involve a comparison of the size and composition of one birth cohort with those of earlier and later cohorts. For example, Foot and Stoffman (1998: 19–31), who describe the life circumstances of nine birth cohorts born between 1914 and 1995, devote special attention to three sequential and unique cohorts. Since the size of these cohorts varied considerably, the members of the 'boom', 'bust', and 'echo' cohorts might have different life trajectories and life chances:

- The 'baby-boom' cohort, born between 1947 and 1966, had about 9.9 million members in

1998 (about 32 per cent of the Canadian population), and at its peak was 36 per cent larger than the baby-bust cohort (1967–79). Members of the baby boom cohort range from their late 30s to late 50s at present, and some are already retired.

- The 'baby-bust' cohort, born between 1967 and 1979, comprised about 5.6 million in 1998. Members are currently in their mid-twenties to late thirties.

- The 'baby-boom-echo' cohort (children of the baby boomers), born between 1980 and 1995, included about 6.5 million in 1998. Members are currently 9 to 24 years of age.

At the height of the baby boom, Canadian women were averaging about four children each, the highest fertility rate in the industrialized world at that time. The baby-bust cohort was characterized by significantly lower fertility rates, which were due to the introduction of the birth control pill, combined with changing values about large families, as well as increased education and employment opportunities for women. The baby-boom-echo cohort repeated some of the fertility patterns of their grandparents, which resulted in a small population bulge between 1980 and 1995.

There is considerable diversity within the large baby-boom birth cohort. Thus, when decisions or projections are being made about economic investment, social services, or public policies, one policy may not fit all those born in the 'boom' period. For example, those born in the late 1940s, the 'front-end' boomers, have always had an economic and social advantage (Owram, 1996). Currently, the first members of this subgroup are in their mid-fifties and are perhaps contemplating retirement. The 'back-end' boomers, the approximately 3.2 million people born between 1961 and 1966, are now in their late thirties and early forties; they have been labelled 'Generation X' (Foot and Stoffman, 1998: 26–8). When members of Generation X were ready to enter the labour force in the late 1970s and early 1980s, Canada was in a major economic recession, and they experienced high rates of underemployment and unemployment. Out of economic necessity many of these adult 'back-end' boomers returned to live with their parents at some point. Sometimes this living arrangement fostered conflict between Generation Xers and their parents, who are at the peak of their careers and earning power and do not understand or appreciate why their children are unable or unwilling to work.

As in the case of the baby boomers, there is diversity within the older age cohort. Thus, research analyses and projections should divide the older cohort into a number of sub-cohorts to obtain more precise information about this segment of the population. To illustrate, over a theoretical 40-year age range that might constitute the older age cohort (55 to 95), the age groups for analysis might be 55–64, 65–74, 75–84, and 85–100. Each group has had different life experiences and opportunities, and they are at different stages in later life with respect to interests, needs, capacities, and potential. Yet, they all could be combined and defined as 'elderly', 'older', 'retired', or 'seniors'. But, this gross aggregation for statistical purposes might not capture nuances that are essential for developing effective policies and programs for older adults.

Policy-makers and entrepreneurs should study not only the current generation of older Canadians but also the following age cohorts— namely, the 'pre-retirees' or 'early retirees', who are 45 to 64 years of age. In Canada, this group numbered about 7.3 million in 2001. For most people in this age group, child rearing is complete; many have high incomes and large amounts of disposable income; and they are among the most active consumers in Canadian history. On the negative side, over the next decade, death and disability rates will begin to increase for this age group; their incomes will begin to decline, especially for those who retire early; and more women in this age group will become widows. An analy-

sis of this cohort affords a preview of the characteristics and lifestyles of the elderly population in the next 20 to 30 years, and of how and why they may have different needs and lifestyles in their retirement years.

But the study of aging does not involve only two distinct groups—those under 65 and those over 65. Rather, the relationships among age cohorts within the age structure must be understood. For example, in periods of high unemployment, if a large proportion of the population between 18 and 25 is unemployed and if a large proportion over 50 is also unemployed owing to downsizing, conflict between these two cohorts could emerge as they compete for a scarce resource, namely, a job. An increase in the number or proportion of one cohort, such as those over 65, can result in a number of possible social changes that must be addressed. These include:

- in the economic domain, a need for more pension funds, or if high rates of inflation emerge, more older adults may seek work after they retire;

- in the political domain, the development of advocacy groups for older people, and the election of older candidates to political office;

- in the educational domain, the need for adult education, the closing of elementary schools, and an increase in the use of distance learning through television and the Internet;

- in the legal domain, an increase in the number of crimes committed by old people (stealing to obtain necessities); an increase in crimes against the elderly in urban areas; a need for legal assistance, including divorce and remarriage contractual agreements, by older people; and

- more generally, the need to provide more health, social, and recreational services to an older client group.

Demography Is Not Destiny: The Misuse of Demographic Statistics

The possible implications of demographic aging for public policy and for the lifestyles and life chances of different age cohorts has led to some misuse or misinterpretation of demographic facts about aging and older people. Sometimes facts are manipulated by the press, which uses alarmist headlines to increase newspaper sales; by politicians to justify increasing taxes, reducing pension or health care costs, or transferring more elder care responsibilities from the state to the family; or by the health care system to justify requests for larger budgets and more facilities. The use of demographic statistics for these purposes has been called 'alarmist' (Friedland and Summer, 1999) or 'apocalyptic' or 'voodoo' demography (Gee and Gutman, 2000).

Alarmist or apocalyptic interpretations argue that older people, as the fastest-growing segment of the population, are becoming a burden and a problem to society. Political economists and critical gerontologists who study aging phenomena argue that a negative and unrealistic view of aging is being created by these catastrophic projections. The elderly are being blamed for the current social and economic problems facing society. As a result, they argue, older people may be marginalized to an even greater extent than at present. Such projections, and the resulting media headlines, fuel the argument that generations are being treated unequally, or that there is 'generational inequity'. Some of these crisis-oriented and alarmist projections can be seen in the following headlines that have appeared in the North American press, especially in the 1990s:

- 'Retiring Boomers Set to Detonate a Demographic Time Bomb'
- 'Population Aging Creates Intergenerational Inequities'
- 'Age Limits Needed for Expensive Health Treatments'

- 'Baby-Boom Pensioners Will Bankrupt the Pension System'
- 'Intergenerational Age War Erupts'
- 'Grey Power Creates a Voting Bloc'
- 'Health-Care Costs Escalate Due to Aging Population'
- 'Elderly Create Housing Crisis'
- 'Aging Workers Deprive Youth of Job Opportunities'
- 'Elderly Caregiving Costs (Time and Money) Escalate'
- 'Aging Immigrants and Refugees Deprive Older Canadians of Social Services'
- 'Do Women Live Too Long?'

Some demographic changes that elicited fears about population aging in Canada during the 1990s were identified by Cheal (2000, 2003):

- The public pension system will have to support an increased number of recipients. Therefore, if the system is to remain viable, an unfair burden will be placed on people of working age to contribute to Canada's 'pay-as-you-go' pension system (those currently employed must make sufficient contributions to pay benefits to those currently retired).

- Older people will create a large unsustainable demand for costly medical services.

- The increase in the number of elderly people who will need public assistance cannot be met by current budgets.

- The economic output of Canada will be greatly reduced because so many older workers are leaving the labour force.

- The social and economic burden of responsibility for the care and support of older adults will fall on fewer people.

Most of these alarmist scenarios have been triggered by fears about the impact of the baby boom cohort moving into later life over the next 30 years. There is particular concern that the health care and pension systems may become bankrupt as this unique cohort ages. But as Northcott (1992: 60) succinctly stated, 'There are really three "villains" in this alleged bankruptcy scenario: population aging, federal and provincial budget deficits, and high interest rates.' More recently, stock market losses have contributed to a fear of pension bankruptcy. For example, in the first six months of the 2002 fiscal year, the Canada Pension Plan lost $4 billion in value because of a decline in the stock market. Similarly, most company and individual pension plans or retirement savings lost a proportionate amount. Yet, nobody blames the stock market for possible future problems in meeting the commitment to support retirees through public or private pensions. Another economic concern is the national, provincial, regional, or community debt that must be repaid in the future, primarily by younger cohorts. Thus, demographic changes per se must be separated from other historical or period effects which increase the debt or deficit of a nation, and thereby contribute to real economic concerns in the future, for *all* age cohorts.

To separate reality from rhetoric and myth, the alarmist projections require a more balanced, comprehensive analysis, not only of demographic facts, but also of how individuals behave and make decisions and of how political, economic, and social welfare institutions react to changing population dynamics (Friedland and Summer, 1999; Gee and Gutman, 2000; Hayward and Zhang, 2001; Cheal, 2003). Yes, population aging creates economic pressures for a society because of increased pension payments, increased expenditures for social and health services, and loss of tax revenue when large numbers of people retire or when revenue is forgone as a result of subsidies for older people (such as 'senior' rates for public transportation). But as Cheal (2000) noted, 'there is more to the future than just demographic trends.' These trends must be placed in a social context. For example, Northcott (1992: 61–3)

suggested that there are at least five alternative scenarios for delaying, avoiding, or solving a future economic crisis:

1. Gradually eliminate the deficit and debt to improve the economy.

2. Increase revenues (through taxes, clawbacks, and higher thresholds for eligibility) and reduce services.

3. Increase community and home care services to delay or avoid the assumed high cost of elder care in institutions.

4. Increase the amount of volunteer services provided by family and others—but this might take more women out of the paid labour force, and thereby reduce the tax revenues and expenditures that can stimulate the economy.

5. Redefine the age or criteria upon which benefits or services are provided—for example, delay retirement or pension payments to age 70; pay benefits only to those who are classified as 'frail' or 'dependent'.

Similar fears have been generated about how an increased life expectancy and increased numbers of elderly people will be a 'drain' on the health care system. But, as Fries (1980) and others have argued, with increased life expectancy there is 'compression of morbidity' into the final few years of life. That is, with a healthier environment, healthier lifestyles, and increased education and health promotion, morbidity is delayed so that individuals remain healthy for an increasing proportion of their lives. For most, it is argued, there is a relatively short period of acute illness before death, which can be costly in terms of drugs, surgery, hospitalization, and long-term care.

Health economists in Canada argue that our health-care system will not become bankrupt if managed properly, including using the wealth and savings of the boomers to help pay the increased costs their increased numbers will generate. In what is perhaps the most definitive study of this question, which was based on data from

British Columbia, Evans et al. (2001) concluded that in the past, changes in the age structure have not been major contributors to increased per capita use of health care services. Rather, increased health care costs are attributed to inflation in the cost of drugs and to more prescribing of these drugs, along with high capital and operating costs for new medical technologies (such as MRI machines and staff), which all age groups use. Evans and his colleagues argue that the largest problem facing the health care system will be a shortage of physicians, especially those trained in geriatric medicine. There are many ethical issues concerning whether to extend life or postpone death for untreatable physical diseases and dementia through the use of costly life-support systems. The legal and ethical issues surrounding end-of-life decisions are discussed in Chapter 12.

As you read demographic projections, and the media's coverage of these projections, question and verify the assumptions that are used and the interpretations that are drawn from the demographic facts. Are there hidden political, economic, or policy agendas in the publicized interpretations? While the facts may be accurate, the interpretations may be incorrect or self-serving (for example, to support the introduction or elimination of a specific policy, program, or product). Many countries in Europe, which are much 'older' today than Canada will become, have adapted successfully to population aging and are providing high-quality support to their older citizens. Highlight 4.1 summarizes the main messages and policy principles from a report entitled *Demography Is Not Destiny* (Friedland and Summer, 1999). Although based on an analysis of US data, the messages apply to any modernized country, including Canada.

The Demography of Aging

Introduction: An Aging World

The United Nations (2002b) reported at the Second World Assembly on Ageing that popula-

tion aging (1) is *unprecedented* in the history of humanity, and the number of older people in the world will exceed the number of young people for the first time by 2050; (2) is *pervasive*, globally, and will have an impact on every citizen, regardless of age; (3) is *profound* and will have an impact on all aspects of human life—economic, social, political, health, housing, migration; and (4) is *enduring* and likely irreversible, with the proportion of older people projected to increase from 10 per cent in 2000 to about 21 per cent in 2050. This global aging, which is caused by lower fertility rates and increased longevity, produces changes in the age structure of all societies and presents nations and communities with both enormous challenges and opportunities as we move toward the middle of the twenty-first century.

Population aging affects the economic and social development of a nation. How each nation and community adapts to changes in the age structure requires careful planning and rational decisions by political leaders and international agencies, such as the United Nations, the World Health Organization, and the World Bank, and other financial institutions that invest in different regions of the world. To understand the evolving socio-cultural, economic, health, and population conditions of the twenty-first century, a demographic foundation is needed.

In the twentieth century, from a global perspective, most interest in population aging was focused on the 'developed' or 'more developed' countries or regions; in this century most interest will be focused on the 'developing' or 'less developed' countries and regions.[5] These two categories of country are used for comparative purposes, but they are crude measures that may not accurately reflect differences at a given time because of different rates of economic and social development (Hong Kong versus mainland China; western rural China versus the Shanghai region or the new 'economic development' regions).

Employing census[6] data and vital-statistics registrations,[7] demographers examine rates of fer-

Highlight 4.1 Demography Is Not Destiny

Drawing on the discussions and conclusions of a 13-person Expert Working Group, Friedland and Summer (1999) identified five messages and five policy principles that policy-makers should include when considering the future needs of a rapidly aging population.

Messages

- Population projections are fraught with uncertainty, especially those for the distant future. Projections vary widely in their accuracy, depending on the assumptions employed.

- Projections are not statements of absolute facts. They are based on assumptions, which are conditional statements about what will happen, if and only if certain other things happen. As more information becomes available, the accuracy of those assumptions will become clearer and the uncertainty of the projections decreases; therefore demographic facts must be monitored constantly.

- In the past few decades, in many countries, the older population has grown dramatically in absolute size and as a proportion of the population without dire consequences.

- It is easier to make statements about the future that are based only on demographic facts than on all the interactions among people, communities, and institutions. Factors such as economic growth; changes in people's values, expectations, and behaviour; and changes in public policies can also alter the future situation for older and younger citizens.

- Today is different than the past. The elderly of today and those in the future are and will be, in general, healthier, wealthier, and better educated than previous generations. However, this does not mean that all older persons are coping well or having their needs met. Hence, future policies must strive to eradicate inequities in service, support, and assistance for older adults.

Policy Principles

- Policies that promote economic growth, redistribute incomes, influence individual behaviour, or alter the demographic age-sex structure will change our future.

- An aging and longer-living population may lead to higher public and private expenses.

- Sufficient economic growth should mean that projected government spending will be no larger as a percentage of national income than it is today.

- There are financial risks associated with health care, long-term care, and pension income regardless of financing decisions.

- Prudent public policy for an aging population requires action today but should be flexible enough to be adjusted as circumstances change.

Source: Adapted and reprinted with permission from Friedland and Summer (1999:1, 55).

tility, mortality, migration, and immigration to describe the size, shape, and geographic distribution of past, present, and future age structures. They also collect and analyze statistics such as labour-force participation rates, birth and death rates by sex, and internal migration rates. They are also interested in the distribution of the population by geographic region, age, sex, income, language, occupation, race, and ethnic background. But the goal of demographers is not merely to record the status quo and describe changes in the age structure; rather, they search for possible explanatory factors, such as social, political, economic, or historical events, that lead to changes in fertility, mortality, and immigration and migration rates, and they examine the consequences of these changing rates. These consequences include significant political, social, or economic changes for society and individuals.

To arrive at plausible and realistic projections,[8] demographers use a variety of demographic, social, economic, political, and environmental factors as 'assumptions'. They usually incorporate a range of assumptions to arrive at low, medium, or high projections of fertility, mortality, and immigration rates; population size; the sex ratio; and so forth. For example, the current fertility rate in Canada (the average total number of children born to each woman during her childbearing years—15 years to the early forties) is

about 1.5. However, low, medium, and high projections about population size might be based, respectively, on fertility rates of 1.3 (low), 1.5 (medium), or 1.8 (high). Each scenario would result in a different population size in the year 2050. Highlight 4.2 illustrates the assumptions underlying the population projections made by Statistics Canada for the year 2026.

Aging in the Developing Nations

The proportion of the total population 60 years of age and older in 2002 in developing regions was 8 per cent, with a projected increase to 19 per cent by 2050; in developed regions it was 20 per cent, with a projected increase to 33 per cent by 2050 (United Nations, 2002). The changes in age structure in developing countries began in the early 1950s as fertility rates began to decline from an average of about 6.2 births per woman. This rate is projected to decline to 2.1 births per woman by 2050. At the same time, average life expectancy is projected to increase from 40 to 74 years for men, and from 40 to 78 years for women

---

Highlight 4.2 Population Projections: Three Scenarios for 2000–2026

Population projections are important in the strategic decisions of business owners, city planners, politicians, or anyone concerned about the size and characteristics of the population. Statistics Canada routinely provides three possible growth scenarios for population projections:

- *High-growth scenario*—Assumes an increase in fertility to 1.8 children per woman by 2026; life expectancies at birth of 81.5 and 85.0 years in 2026 for men and women, respectively; and an annual immigration of 270,000 by 2005 (most of the immigrants will be young adults when they immigrate).

- *Medium-growth scenario*—Generally assumes that current trends will continue: a constant fertility rate of 1.48 births per woman; life expectancies of 80 and 84 years for men and women, respectively, by 2026; and annual immigration of 225,000.

- *Low-growth scenario*—Fertility is assumed to decline to 1.3 births per woman; life expectancies are 78.5 and 83.0 years for men and women, respectively, and annual immigration is assumed to decline to 180,000 by 2005.

Source: George et al. (2001).Reprinted by permission of Statistics Canada.

(Hayward and Zhang, 2001). It is estimated that by 2050 nearly 80 per cent of the world's older population will live in the less developed nations, compared to about 60 per cent today (AARP, 2002). In China, which has about 20 per cent of the world's total population, 7 per cent of the current total population is 65 and older. But, this proportion is projected to rise to 13 per cent by 2025 and to 23 per cent by 2050 (AARP, 2002: 13), largely because of the 'one-child per couple' policy.

To put this speed of aging in perspective, Table 4.1 illustrates, for a number of countries, the number of years that were required, or will be required, for the population 65 years of age and older to increase from 7 per cent to 14 per cent of the total population. Compared to the speed of aging in France and Sweden, developing countries will experience population aging over a very short period (20 to 41 years). Thus, the less

developed regions of Africa, Latin America and the Caribbean, Asia (excluding Japan and Hong Kong), Melanesia, Micronesia, and Polynesia are aging more rapidly than the more developed regions of the world. This does not give these countries much time to create policies and an infrastructure to meet the needs of older citizens.

In the year 2000, an estimated 800,000 people in the world turned 65 each month, 77 per cent of this gain occurring in the developing countries (Kinsella and Velkoff, 2001). Such rapidly aging societies must prepare to meet the economic and social challenges that will arise concerning health care, social security, and housing. Finally, as noted earlier, percentages can mask reality, and therefore absolute numbers, real and projected, for a country or region need to be known (Kinsella and Velkoff, 2001; United Nations, 2002). To illustrate, while the projected number of elderly people in Uganda will increase

Table 4.1 Speed of Population Aging

Country	Years for Population 65+ to Double from 7% to 14%
Developed Countries	
France (1865–1980)	115
Sweden (1890–1975)	85
United States (1944–2013)	69
Canada (1944–2009)	65
United Kingdom (1930–75)	45
Japan (1970–96)	26
Developing Countries	
Azerbaijan (2000–41)	41
China (2000–27)	27
Jamaica (2009–33)	24
Thailand (2003–25)	22
Columbia (2017–37)	20

Source: Adapted from Kinsella and Velkoff, (2001: Figure 2.6).

slightly from 2 per cent in 2002 to 5 per cent in 2050, the absolute increase may be 3.3 million people—a sevenfold increase (United Nations, 1999).

The future growth of population aging in a developing country such as China, where the population of older people is likely to increase from an estimated 134 million in 2002 to about 232 million in 2030 and to 330 million by 2050, could be described as a tidal wave. Many developing countries like China are currently still young and have the task of providing education and jobs for young people. In a few decades, however, they will be faced with an aging society. Yet, China may be ill prepared to address these changes for a number of reasons:

- China's economic development was delayed.
- There is no formal pension system.

- There is no comprehensive health care system.
- The population is less well-educated than in the developed countries.
- Young adults are emigrating to developed countries or migrating to urban regions of the home country, thereby becoming unavailable to care for their aging parents.
- Jobs previously held by older people, often until nearly the end of their lives, will be eliminated and as a result there will be economic hardship for older people without pensions.

These changes will have even more pronounced effects in rural regions, where fewer older people have pensions, where there is limited access to health care, and where poor nutrition prevails. Highlight 4.3 depicts a bleak scenario for the old-

---

Highlight 4.3 Aging in Ukraine

The situation for older people in Ukraine, like many others in the population, is bleak. The gross domestic product fell more than 52 per cent from 1990 to 1995; output of industrial goods dropped, as did agricultural production. In 1995, 63 per cent of the population had a per capita income below the official subsistence level. Birth rates declined, and death rates are climbing. Life expectancy dropped by more than three years from 1989 to 1997, and the proportion of those aged 65 and over in the total population has virtually levelled off.

The income gap between workers and pensioners has widened. In 1985, the average pension was 40 per cent of the average wage; by 1995, it was only 15 per cent. Yet, the size of the total workforce has fallen, and the number of older employees in 2000 was little more than half of what it was in 1989. Older people with jobs usually work for outdated collective industries. The new private ventures, which offer better jobs and wages, discriminate on the basis of age.

The effects of this deepening poverty are felt throughout society. More working-age adults provide financial support to older family members. In 1980, 5 per cent of working older people and 10 per cent of non-working older people received assistance from their adult children; today 30 per cent of all older people receive assistance.

Financial transfers from the oldest to the youngest generation have fallen. In 1980, 65 per cent of working pensioners and 26 per cent of non-working pensioners contributed to the financial well-being of their adult children. Today, only 15 per cent do so. Family structures are under siege. Marriage rates have fallen; the incidence of divorce and widowhood has risen. One study estimated that the average age of beggars in Kiev, Ukraine's capital, was between 64 and 65 years of age, while another study estimated that two-thirds of the nation's homeless are 60 years of age or over.

Source: AARP (2000: 5). Reproduced with permission.

est citizens of another impoverished developing country, Ukraine.

An Expanding Older Population

A Global Perspective

In 2002, of the 6 billion people in the world, the number of people over 60 was estimated at 600 million (10 per cent of the total population), with about 8 per cent in developing countries and 20 per cent in developed countries (United Nations, 2002b). It is projected that the world's older population will reach 1 billion by 2025 and nearly 2 billion by 2050[9] (22 per cent of the total population), with about 75 per cent living in developing regions. Table 4.2 illustrates the current and projected growth of the global older population. The 'oldest old', those 80 and over, are increasing at the fastest rate, with an annual growth rate of 3–4 per cent (compared to 2 per cent for the 60+

group in total) being projected from 2000–20. In 2002, the oldest old made up about 12 per cent of the world's older population; 22 per cent of them lived in developed countries and 13 per cent in developing countries. At the beginning of the twenty-first century, about 53 per cent of those 80+ in the world live in just six countries: China, the United States, India, Japan, Germany, and Russia.

Unlike an individual, who can only grow older, a nation can grow either 'younger' or 'older'. Like an individual, the population of a nation as a whole may be categorized as 'young' (up to 4 per cent of the population 65 and over), 'youthful' (4–6 per cent), 'mature' (7–9 per cent), or 'old' (10+ per cent). The onset of lower fertility rates and decreased immigration rates increases the proportion of older people in the total population, whereas an increase in fertility and immigration rates decreases their proportion of the total population. Currently, there are at least 25 countries where at least 14 per cent of the popu-

Table 4.2 Size of the Older Population (60 and over) by World Region, 2002–2050

Region	Number (1,000s) of Population 60+		% of Total Population 60+		% of 60+ Population 80+	
	2002	2050	2002	2050	2002	2050
World	628,874	1,963,76	10	21	12	19
More developed regions	235,523	395,106	20	33	17	29
Less developed regions	393,351	1,568,66	8	19	9	17
Least developed regions	34,419	175,713	5	9	7	10
Africa	42,221	204,776	5	10	8	11
Asia	338,084	1,226,714	9	23	10	18
Europe	148,319	221,079	20	37	15	27
Latin America and aribbean	43,678	181,191	8	22	11	18
North America	53,321	119,015	16	27	20	28
Oceania	4,250	10,992	14	23	17	24

Source: Adapted from United Nations (2002). Reprinted with permission of United Nations Population Division.

lation is 65 years or over. The countries with the oldest populations are Italy (with 18.1 per cent of the population aged 65 years and over), Greece (with 17.3 per cent), Sweden (with 17.3 per cent), Japan (with 17 per cent), and Spain (with 16.9 per cent) (Kinsella and Velkoff, 2001). Canada is not likely to reach these levels, if at all, until the entire baby boom cohort reaches 65 years of age. Most of these countries, unlike Canada, do not encourage or permit immigration. Hence, their younger age groups are not replenished as fertility rates decline.

In most countries, especially the developing countries, the older population is growing faster than the total population. Between 2000 and 2030, large percentage increases are projected in the older population in such developing countries as Singapore (372 per cent), Malaysia (277 per cent), Colombia (258 per cent), Mexico (277 per cent), Bangladesh (207 per cent), and China (170 per cent). But even some developed nations will have moderate increases in the next 30 years, such as Canada (with 126 per cent) and Australia (with 108 per cent). In the already 'old' European countries there will be smaller increases (Sweden, 45 per cent; Greece and Italy, 43 per cent; Ukraine, 21 per cent; and Bulgaria, 14 per cent).

A Canadian Perspective

In 2001, of Canada's 31 million residents, 3.9 million (or 13 per cent) were 65 years of age or older. Only 4 per cent of this older population were Aboriginal people. It is projected that the percentage of older Canadians will increase to 15 per cent by 2011, when the first wave of baby boomers retire; to 21 per cent by 2026; and to 25 per cent by 2031, when the last wave of boomers retire. In absolute numbers, it is projected that there will be 8 million people 65 and over by 2026, and 9 to 10 million by 2051 (Health Canada, 2002; Statistics Canada, 2002a). The number in the 80-and-over age group will grow from about 900,000 in 2001 to 1.6 million by

2041, when many of the survivors of the baby-boom cohort are between 75 and 95 years of age. Highlight 4.4 describes some of the demographic and social characteristics of the oldest age cohort.

In 2001, for the first time in Canada, the working-age population includes more people in the older-worker category (45–64 years) than in the youngest category (25–34 years). From 1991 to 2001, the population 45 to 64 years of age increased 35.8 per cent, mainly because the oldest baby boomers were entering this age category. It is projected that the population of the 45–64 year age group will increase another 30 per cent, to about 9.5 million, by 2011. At the same time, there are fewer younger people entering the working-age population to replace those nearing retirement. From 1991 to 2001 there was an 18 per cent decrease in the number entering the 25-to-34-year category.

Demographic Indices

In this section a number of the common indices used by demographers are introduced. These indices show past trends, the current situation, and projections of the future; or they are used to make comparisons between different countries or parts of countries.

Median Age

Median age is the chronological age at which the population is divided into equal numbers of younger and older people. If the median age is rising, that is further evidence that a population is aging. Today, the median age for the world is about 26.5 years, and is expected to rise to 36 years by 2050. The youngest country is Yemen at 15 years and the oldest is Japan at 41 years, although Italy is expected to reach a median age of 52 years by 2030 (Statistics Canada, 2002a; Kinsella and Velkoff, 2001). The median age in Canada was 37.6 years in 2001, and it is projected to rise to 39.5 years by 2006 and to 41.1 years

Highlight 4.4 The Oldest Cohort (80+0

The number of people around the world over 80 years of age is increasing rapidly. They constitute about 17 per cent of the world's elderly population, 22 per cent in developed countries, and 13 per cent in developing countries. In some countries, over 25 per cent of those over 65 years of age are in this oldest age group; most of them are women. It is projected that by 2050 the 80-and-over cohort will make up 29 per cent of the older population in Canada, 32 per cent in Sweden, and 36 per cent in Japan. As we enter the second decade of this century, the *proportion* of 'oldest old' in many countries will stop increasing, although the *absolute numbers* will continue to grow.

In Canada, over 430,000 people were 85 years of age and over in 2001, and 70 per cent were women. This represents a 58 per cent increase in this age group since the 1981 census. In 2001, there were 3,795 centenarians in Canada (740 men and 3,055 women), a 21 per cent increase from 1991 (Statistics Canada, 2002a). It is projected that Canada will have about 7,400 centenarians by 2011 (NACA, 1993). Globally, the number of centenarians is projected to increase from 210,000 in 2002 to about 3.2 million by 2050.

Much of the increase in the number of older people 85 and over is attributable to heredity. But, long life is also associated with having a higher-than- average education and occupational status, having an intact marriage until death, having a smaller-than-average number of children, being the first-born, and living in a healthy manner (that is, exercising regularly, eating a healthy diet, abstaining from smoking and alcohol, and living in the same geographical area throughout life) (Perls, 1995; Perls and Silver, 1999).

Despite such rapid current and expected future growth, this segment of the population has received relatively little research attention, often because the 80- and-over group is hidden in statistical analyses that report data for those 60 or 65 and over. Many in this cohort are often the healthiest of the entire cohort of older people because they are survivors—many of their birth peers did not survive into their 70s or 80s because of illness, disease, or accidents. Some of these survivors may be living on nothing but small old-age pensions.

While some in this oldest age cohort live in their own homes, others cannot live independently. If they lack strong family support (because, for example, their children are deceased or are frail themselves or live far away), they are likely to be moved to a residential institution. This cohort often needs both informal and formal support services, especially since more than 70 per cent are women and over 80 per cent of the women are widowed. Many live alone and have one or more physical disabilities that prevent them from driving or using public transit. Not surprisingly, members of this oldest age group eventually become the heaviest users of the health-care system, particularly with respect to acute hospital stays and treatment of chronic illness and disabilities.

The size of the oldest cohort will continue to grow until well into this century, and their unique needs require specific policies and programs. In the future, more members of this older age cohort will be better educated, more economically secure, and healthier. As a result, they will increasingly remain independent as long as they can and will demand adequate home-support services and alternative housing options.

by 2011. The youngest region in Canada is Nunavut, with a median age of 22.1 years. Here, there are high fertility rates and only 2 per cent (about 600 people) of the population is 65 years of age or older. The highest median age is 38.8 years in Quebec and Nova Scotia.

Life Expectancy

Life expectancy is the average number of years of life remaining for an individual at a given age. It is determined by recording the death rates for each age at a particular time and then constructing 'life tables', which make it possible to project the 'average' number of years of life remaining for a male or female.[10] Remember that life expectancies are 'averages' based on chronological age—some of us do not live as long as the average; others live longer owing to gender, education, wealth, and genetics; healthier ways of living; or to disease control or the eradication of a disease.

The two most frequently cited statistics are life expectancy at birth and life expectancy at age 60 or 65. Obviously, a low death rate for a certain age group means a correspondingly higher life expectancy. Therefore, as infant mortality has fallen, the average life expectancy at birth has increased. In modernized nations, life expectancy has increased because of the improved prevention and treatment of chronic diseases in the later years, and because of healthier ways of living throughout the life course.

It has been argued that as more people live closer to the theoretical maximum life span (about 115–20 years for humans), there has been a 'rectangularization of the survival curve' (Fries and Crapo, 1981; Nusselder and Mackenbach, 1996). According to this view, which has generated much controversy, illness leading to death occurs closer to the end of life, and we experience a shorter period of disability, illness, or infirmity before death than did people in the past. But increased life expectancy can be due to both a later onset of illness leading to death and to an increased ability and willingness to treat the illness and prolong life. Through technology, drugs, and medical advances, a higher percentage of older people survive illnesses, and some are kept alive for long periods, even though they may live in a state of extreme frailty or disability. The debate continues about whether the survival curve is accurately depicted by a rectangular or by an angular decreasing slope in the later years. Much of the debate centres on the quality of life that is considered to be ideal or possible in later life, and at what cost such a quality of life is achieved. Most of the improvement in life expectancy has occurred over the past few decades, primarily because of declines in infant mortality (especially in developing nations), reduced mortality at all ages, and to reduced morbidity in the later years. There is little likelihood that the curve will flatten much further, if at all.

In early Roman times, the world's average life expectancy at birth was about 20 years; by 1800 it was about 30 years, by the 1900s it had increased to 45 to 50 years; in 2000 it was 67 years, and it is projected to rise to 76 years by 2050 (Riley, 2001). Among the 'developed' countries of the world, current life expectancy at birth varies for males and females, respectively, as illustrated by Japan (77 and 85), Australia (77 and 83), and Hungary (67 and 76). In 'developing' countries, life expectancy, in general, is lower, as illustrated by India (62 and 63); Uganda (42 and 44); Brazil (59 and 68); and South Africa (50 and 52). Where the HIV/AIDS epidemic is prevalent, as in Botswana, Namibia, and Zimbabwe, life expectancy at birth may be reduced by more than 30 years (Kinsella and Velkoff, 2001: 27). In Sierra Leone, because of poverty and disease, average life expectancy is 40 years, and the disability-free life expectancy is only 26 years.

Variations in life expectancy throughout the world at any time are influenced by social, health, and living conditions, and by whether new technologies like water sanitation, birth control, medical diagnostic tools, and drugs are available. Events such as famines, wars, epidemics of infectious diseases like AIDS, and economic depressions can have a profound impact on the life expectancy of a specific age cohort in a specific country. At the same time, the event may have little or no influence on the life expectancy of another age cohort in the same society. For example, a long war could change the life expectancy and size of birth cohorts that are 18 to 25 years of age but would have considerably less effect, if any, on those over 40 years of age.

In North America, in general, life expectancy at birth is higher for women, for urban residents, and for those with more education and a higher income. Life expectancy also varies within a country by region or municipality. These differences are due to variations in wealth, education, standards of living, climate, or the migration patterns of particular age groups. To illustrate, the Canadian average life expectancy is about 79.7 years, with life expectancy at birth for women being 82.2 years, and for men, 77.7 years.

Average life expectancy varies by community, and even within different sectors of a metropolitan area. Life expectancy is an indirect indicator of a population's health, and people living in the largest cities and urban centres are among the healthiest in Canada. However, the poorer the neighbourhood, the shorter the life expectancy of its residents at birth; although the gap between rich and poor neighbourhoods is narrowing. Currently, life expectancy varies from 83.1 for women and 78.1 for men in British Columbia to 71.0 for women and 66.4 for men in Nunavut (Statistics Canada, 2003b. Life expectancy can vary by as much as four years above or below the national average, often because of differences in income, living conditions, and nutrition among different social groups. As a cohort ages, life expectancy at later stages in life (beyond age 65) is influenced by current and past lifestyle factors such as nutrition, exercise, marital status, health status, education, occupation, and income.

Given the gains in life expectancy in the twentieth century, can we expect the same in this century? Olshansky (2001) concludes that future gains will be measured in days or months, not years, and that average life expectancy is unlikely to rise above 85 years. He concluded that any significant gain will occur only if there are large reductions in mortality among older people, and that any more significant gains cannot be achieved by lifestyle modifications. In contrast, Oeppen and Vaupel (2002) assert that given past

gains, it is reasonable to assume life expectancy will continue to increase by about 2.5 years per decade, as in the past. If this projection held, average life expectancy would reach about 100 years around the year 2060.

An improvement in life expectancy does not necessarily mean, however, that the health or quality of life of the population has improved (Crimmins et al., 1996; Hogan and Lise, 2003). Rather, it may be that ill or disabled people experience a prolonged illness and a delayed death. Thus, life expectancy should be measured, as well, by qualitative indices. To illustrate, measures of disability-free, healthy, or active life expectancy are used to assess *quality* of life more than *quantity* of life.

Healthy, active, or disability-free life expectancy is a measure of the average number of years a person can expect to live without chronic disability (Verbrugge, 1997; Kinsella and Velkoff, 2001). This measure reveals how longevity and morbidity interact to influence differences in the quality of life. The most commonly used measures assess the ability to perform the activities of daily living (ADLs) such as eating, using the toilet, and walking; and such instrumental activities of daily living (IADLs) as shopping, cooking, and using private or public transportation. Globally, healthy life expectancy varies from less than 26 years in Sierra Leone to a high of 74.5 years in Japan.

In Canada, compared to an average life expectancy of 79.7 years, the disability-free life expectancy is about 68.6 years. This means that many Canadians can expect to live almost 11 years with some mental or physical disability before they die (Statistics Canada, 2002b). Those with higher education and those who live in urban areas have a higher disability-free life expectancy, as do people who live in certain geographical regions. To illustrate, the disability-free life expectancy index ranges from a high of 72.8 years in Richmond, British Columbia (where life expectancy is 81.2) to a low of 61 years in the Nunavik region of Quebec (where life expectancy is 65.4).

In a 2001 Participation and Activity Limitation Survey conducted by Statistics Canada (Statistics Canada, 2002b), at least one disability was reported by 40 per cent (about 1.5 million) of the population 65 and over, 31 per cent of those 65 to 74, and 53 per cent of those 75 and over. Within this older population reporting disabilities, 1.1 million (about 8 in 10 seniors) reported problems with walking, over 1 million reported difficulty getting dressed or cutting up food, and more than 887,000 reported they were disabled because of pain. An estimated 573,000 seniors, or 40 per cent of all those with disabilities, reported having 'severe' or 'very severe' limitations. The majority of these were women, reflecting women's longer life expectancy. This means that women experience more disability as part of of living longer.

Birth and Death Rates

A population grows or declines (without immigration as a factor) as changes occur in the number of births and deaths in a society. For much of human history there were more births than deaths in any one year, but this ratio is changing. When fertility rates were high, especially above the natural replacement ratio of 2.1,[11] populations grew. But, the worldwide average number of children per woman has decreased from about 5 in the 1950s to about 2.7 in the first few years of this century. Of course there are still wide variations, ranging from 7.6 in Yemen to 1.1 in Armenia, Bulgaria, Latvia, Spain, and Ukraine (United Nations, 2002a).

In Canada, the national fertility rate is about 1.5, with a high of almost 3 in Nunavut. In 2001, there were about 333,000 births in Canada, compared with about 219,000 deaths. But if projections hold for 2025, the number of deaths (338,000) will exceed the number of births (336,000) for the first time in that year, thereby leading to a zero or negative natural growth rate. Thus, before 2025, if continuing growth of the population is desired, higher immigration or greater incentives to have more children will be on the agenda of public policy discussions. Table 4.3 illustrates different child-bearing patterns in different age cohorts in Canada.

Crude birth and crude death rates record the number of births and deaths per 1,000 people during a one-year period. They provide relative measures by which frequencies of births and deaths can be compared over time. Generally, in developed and developing societies, both rates have fallen since the early 1900s, with the exception of the increase in birth rates during the baby-boom years (see Highlight 4.5). If birth and death rates stabilize at low levels, over a number of years population aging will cease. In Canada, crude birth and death rates for 2001 were 10.8 and 7.4 per 1,000 people, respectively (Statistics Canada, 2002c).

Crude birth rates fluctuate, depending on religious beliefs, the use and availability of birth control, and social norms concerning marriage and size of family. Crude death rates vary because of such factors as the quality of sanitary services, the quality and availability of health care, and the incidence of degenerative and infectious diseases, wars, and natural disasters. If, for example, cardiovascular diseases, cancer, and other lifestyle-related diseases were eliminated in industrialized countries, crude death rates would decrease and life expectancies would increase substantially. These decreases would be similar to the changes that occurred after tuberculosis and influenza were virtually eliminated as causes of death. The effect of a reduction in mortality on the age structure depends on the ages where the changes occur. If death rates decline for infants, as they did in the nineteenth and twentieth century, there is an increase in the number of young people. If death rates decline in later life, as suggested above, through the elimination of cardiovascular diseases, cancers, and other diseases related to lifestyle, population aging will be accelerated (Serow, 2001).

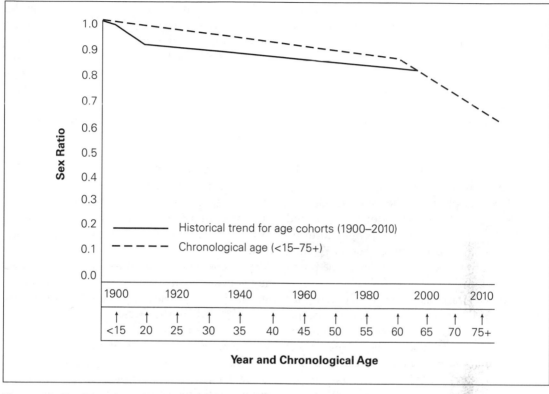

Figure 4.1 The Decreasing Sex Ratio by Year and by Chronological Age in North America

Source: Adapted from reports by Statistics Canada and the United States Bureau of the Census.

jected to increase in developed countries as the gender gap in life expectancy *narrows*, and to decrease in developing countries as the gender gap in life expectancy *widens*.

The sex ratio for the entire Canadian population in 2001 was 96 males per 100 females, with the ratio ranging from 94:100 in Nova Scotia to 100:100 in Alberta, to 107:100 in Nunavut (Statistics Canada, 2002a). For the population 65 years of age and older, the sex ratio at the time of the 2001 census was 75 males for every 100 females; which continues the decline in the ratio of 104 men per 100 women in 1941, to 94 in 1961 and 75 in 1981. At age 100 and above, there are only 25 men per 100 women.

The Dependency Ratio

Two periods in which one is *not* employed in the labour force are childhood/adolescence and the post-retirement years. Allegedly, during these stages individuals are 'dependent' on their family and/or the state for economic support. Dependency ratios are a crude approximation of the ability of a population to support itself financially. Consequently, these measures have been used to support the apocalyptic-demography argument that an aging and dependent population will become a financial burden to society. Both the overall (total) dependency ratio and the older-population dependency ratios indicate the number of non-workers who are supported, directly or indirectly, by those in the labour force, that is, by health and economic assistance programs in the private and public sectors. This measure assumes that there is mandatory retirement at age 65 in all jurisdictions, but that is no longer true.

The total dependency ratio is constructed by dividing the number of people under 19 and over 65 years of age (the young and old dependents) by the number of people who are 'eligible' to be in the labour force, namely, all those between 20 and 64 years of age. The *older-population* dependency ratio is the number of people 65 and over divided by the number of people 20 to 64 years of age. It is usually expressed as the number of dependents for every 100 people in the population of working age.

In 2001, the total dependency ratio for Canada was 62, which means that 62 people under age 19 and over age 65 were supported by 100 people 19 to 64 years of age. This ratio is projected to increase to about 65 in 2021 and to 71 by 2026 (Rosenberg, 2003). The older-population dependency ratio was 21 in 2001 and is projected to increase to 31 in 2021 and to 37 by 2026 (Rosenberg, 2003). These ratios may become even higher than projected if more workers retire early (before 60 or 65), or if others are forced out of the labour force in their mid- to late 50s. If, on the other hand, mandatory retirement was delayed or eliminated, older people might remain in the labour force, and the ratio would decrease.

The 'potential support' ratio (PSR) is the number of people 65 and over per 100 people divided by the number of people 20 to 64, all of whom are theoretically employed in the labour force. This measure of dependency is used quite often when comparing the number of support people available in different countries. Globally, the PSR fell from 12 to 9 people from 1950 to 2002, and is projected to fall to 4 working-age people for each person 65 and over by 2050. This ratio varies dramatically by type of region. In the more developed regions, the PSR was 5 in 2002 and is projected to decrease to 2 by 2050; but in the less developed regions, where fertility rates are still high and just starting to decline, the PSR was 12 in 2002 and is projected to decrease to 5 by 2050.

These ratios are used to imply that there may be an increasing, and perhaps unfair, financial burden on those of working age—*if* the elderly are really 'dependent' as the index implies. But many are not. Although a dependency ratio provides an approximate index of the economic burden placed on a society by its dependent members, it is, at best, a crude estimate. The index ignores financial contributions of the so-called 'dependent' population through taxes, savings, investments, capital accumulated, and voluntary unpaid labour provided by young people, retired people, and housewives. Paid employment should not be the sole measure of productivity or of whether cititzens are contributing to their society. The ratio does not account for changes in age of retirement. For example, those who retire before age 65 and do so voluntarily, should not be included in dependency ratio statistics; yet they are, at present.

The calculation of dependency ratios includes arbitrary ages in the denominator, which can vary depending on when transitions from schooling to work, and from work to retirement, occur. There are considerable numbers of people who are unemployed at different times between 20 and 65 years of age, and these people do not get factored out even though they become 'dependent' during this period of unemployment. In contrast, some older people are employed after 65 years of age, and therefore not 'dependent'. Dependency ratios provide a historical picture or make projections within a society if the measures at each point in time employ the same factors and assumptions. Increasingly, this is less likely to be the case, and therefore, they are often inaccurate.

Geographic Distribution of the Aging Population

Geographic data are collected to provide a snapshots of the current composition and distribution of the population in specific communities or regions; to analyze changes since previous snapshots; and to project future scenarios that may require new policies or programs. Most geographic information is presented at the national level. However, any change in population composition or size is felt most directly at the provincial, regional, or local level. Hence, policy decisions are essential at the local level (even though the funds may come from the federal or provincial government) if changes in the composition of, or number of residents in, the local population are to be accommodated in the areas of health care, social services, housing, transportation, and leisure. In this section the geographic location of the older population, globally, and by region

within Canada, is noted, as are changes over time in the proportion of older people in specific cities, regions, or countries. In addition, immigration patterns of older adults are described. Information on the migration decisions and patterns of older Canadians is introduced in Chapter 7 when later life changes in housing location are discussed.

A Global Perspective

As previously noted, global statistics record the number and proportion of older people by whether they reside in a 'more' or 'less' developed region, or in a 'least developed' country. The level of economic development is a key factor in categorizing the size, location, and health of the older population. Table 4.4 shows the distribution of the world's population by geographical region and by rural versus urban location.

Internationally, migration is at an all-time high, whether it results from labour migration, family reunification, refugee asylum, or illegal

Table 4.4 Geographic Distribution of the World's Population 60 and over, 2000 and 2050 (Percentages)

Region	2000	2050
Oceania	1	1
Africa	6	1
Latin America and Caribbean	7	9
North America	8	6
Europe	24	11
Asia	53	63

	2000	2025	More Developed (2000)	Less Developed (2000)
Urban	51	62	74	37
Rural	49	38	26	63

Source: Adapted and reprinted with permission from United Nations (2000).

immigration. The Population Reference Bureau (1999) reported that about 145 million people lived outside their native country in the mid-1990s and that the number is increasing by 2 to 4 million people a year. Whereas the largest immigration flows used to be from Europe to North America, the largest flows are now from Latin America and Asia into North America; and from eastern Europe, the former Soviet Union, and North Africa into northern and western Europe. Most of these immigrants go to large urban centres. Among the small proportion of older migrants, most are seeking asylum as refugees or are joining their children who emigrated earlier.

A Canadian Perspective[12]

From 1996 to 2001, the total population of Canada increased by 4 per cent. But there were significant differences among the provinces and territories over this period—in Alberta the population grew by 10.3 per cent, in Nunavut by 8.1 per cent, in Ontario by 6.1 per cent, and in British Columbia by 4.9 per cent. At the same time, the population of Newfoundland and Labrador fell by 7 per cent, that of the Yukon by 6.8 per cent, and that of the Northwest Territories by 5.8 per cent. At present, five out of six people 65 and over live in the four most populated provinces (Ontario, Quebec, British Columbia, and Alberta). Table 4.5 reports the provincial and territorial variations in the geographic distribution of those 65 and older in Canada in 2000, and as projected for 2021.

The majority (75 per cent) of people 65 and over live in a metropolitan or urban area, especially in suburban areas built in the 1950s and 1960s. Some notable examples of 'older' communities are Qualicum Beach on Vancouver Island, with 38 per cent of its population 65 and over, and a median age of 58.1 years; Victoria, British

Table 4.5 Geographic Distribution of Canadians 65+, 2000 and 2021

Province/Territory	2000 (%)	Projected for 2021 (%)
Newfoundland and Labrador	11.6	22.5
Nova Scotia	13.2	21.3
Prince Edward Island	13.1	19.9
New Brunswick	12.9	22.2
Quebec	12.8	21.0
Ontario	12.6	17.7
Manitoba	13.5	18.8
Saskatchewan	14.4	19.5
Alberta	10.1	17.1
British Columbia	13.0	18.8
Nunavut	2.6	7.2
Northwest Territories	4.1	11.0
Yukon	5.4	14.5

Source: Adapted from the Statistics Canada publications Population Projections for Canada, Provinces and Territories, 2000–2026, Catalogue 91–520, March 2001, and from A Portrait of Seniors in Canada, Third Edition, Catalogue 89–519, October 1999.

Columbia, with 17.8 per cent of its population 65 and over and a median age of 41.0 years; and Niagara-on-the-Lake, Ontario, 25 per cent and 46.3 years. At the other extreme, Mackenzie, Alberta, is the 'youngest' community with a median age of 22 years; while Brampton, Ontario, has a median age of 32.9 years because of an active regional recruitment policy by that city to create jobs and cheaper housing for young adults outside metropolitan Toronto.

In 2001, for the three largest metropolitan areas, the median age of the population was 37.9 in Montreal, 37.4 in Vancouver, and 36.2 in Toronto. There have also been subtle but important population shifts within large metropolitan areas that have long-term implications for the planning of leisure facilities, transportation, subsidized housing, home care, and health care. In the Toronto suburbs of Etobicoke, North York, and Scarborough, for example, the population 75 to 79 years of age grew from 25 to 32 per cent between 1996 and 2001, and the population aged 85 and older grew by at least 20 per cent. This growth illustrates the tendency of most older people to 'age in place'—that is, in the home and neighbourhood where they have lived most of their adult years. Many of these residents are widows who live alone in the family home.

From one census to the next, the size and composition of the population changes in regions, provinces, and municipalities. These changes are monitored, and explanations are sought for any large growth or decline in the relative proportion of older and young adults. Are the changes due to increased or decreased economic opportunities in the labour force for young adults, who may, for example, leave Nova Scotia and move to Alberta; to lifestyle choices of the young, who may move from small towns to large cities; or to migration by retirees, who may move either temporarily or permanently to a more temperate climate or less expensive region; or a return migration to a community where they lived earlier in life? Less than 5 per cent of adults 65 and over moved from one province to another between 1996 and 2001

(Statistics Canada, 2003a). These migration issues are addressed further in Chapter 7.

Rural-Urban Distribution

In Canada, 80 per cent of the population lives in an urban area; while about 75 per cent of those 65 and over live in urban areas. But among Canadians who live in rural areas, a large percentage are people 65 and over who 'age in place'. In 2001 the median age of the population of rural areas and small towns was 39 years, compared to 41 years in metropolitan areas. Moreover, the median age of rural areas and small towns rose by 3.5 years from 1996 to 2001, compared to a rise of 1.8 years in metropolitan areas (Statistics Canada, 2002a).

The suburban areas around large Canadian cities grew rapidly in the 1950s and 1960s. In the early years of suburban development, the residents were generally under 40 years of age. Over time, the suburban population ages, leading to a 'greying of the suburbs', with different shopping, transportation, and social service needs. When the original owners are no longer able to look after a house or a spouse dies, the property is sold, often to a younger couple, thereby beginning a new cycle in the age structure of a neighbourhood. Because neighbourhoods are developed at different times, variations between neighbourhoods in the average age of the residents is common. If the proportion of elderly residents increases in a neighbourhood or community, resources need to be shifted to meet the needs of retirees. For example, community recreation departments may increase spending on facilities and programs for middle-aged and older adults. Similarly, owners of businesses will change the type of merchandise or services they offer to cater to a 'grey' market.

Immigration in Later Life

Although less important than fertility and mortality rates in determining the size and composition of the age structure, immigration has contributed to the diversity of both the total and the older population. Immigration has also contributed to population growth in Canada, but the effect on total population aging is minimal (Moore and Rosenberg, 2001). Throughout history, because of different waves of immigration from different home countries, Canada has become a multicultural nation.

Until the 1970s, most immigrants came from European countries. In the past decade, immigrants were more likely to come from Asia, especially India and China. Consequently, an increasing proportion of new immigrants are identified as allophones by Statistics Canada—that is, their 'mother tongue', or native language, is neither English nor French. In the 2001 census, Canadians reported more than 100 languages under the category mother tongue; about 5.3 million (1 out of 6 Canadians) were identified as allophones, an increase of 12.5 per cent since 1996. After English and French, the top five languages spoken in Canada are

- Chinese (872,000),

- Italian (494,000),

- German (455,000),

- Punjabi (285,000), and

- Spanish (261,000).

According to the 2001 census, Toronto is home to 41 per cent of the people in Canada whose mother tongue is Chinese (34 per cent live in Vancouver), 42 per cent whose first language is Italian, and 35 per cent who first spoke Punjabi (32 per cent live in Vancouver). According to the 2001 census, immigrants settling in Toronto, Montreal, and Vancouver are increasingly living in 'ethnic' neighbourhoods. Statistics Canada defines 'ethnic neighbourhoods' as those where more than 30 per cent of the population is from one ethnic group. The 2001 census found that the number of ethnic neighbourhoods in the three cities increased from 6 in 1981 to 254 in 2001, with 157 being Chinese (most are not located in the traditional inner-city Chinatowns), 84 South Asian, and 13 black. To what extent this housing pattern contributes to isolation, less integration, and service-delivery issues in later life remains to be seen. This linguistic concentration and diversity presents a challenge to those serving the needs of Canada's future older population.

Approximately 4 per cent of those 65 and over in 2001 spoke neither English nor French, and many of these were women. Many older immigrants use only their first language and adhere more closely to their ethnic culture than do younger generations in the family. Older immigrants are likely to be economically disadvantaged in later life. This is especially true of refugees, some of whom arrive after 50 years of age with little or no formal education. Some ethnic groups, as measured by the proportion of older people, are much 'older' than others. This may result from their earlier time of arrival, or it may be due to low fertility rates after they arrived, which would raise the proportion of older people in the ethnic group.

Since 1901 Canada has admitted more than 13 million immigrants, of whom almost 2 million arrived between 1991 and 2001. Over 70 per cent of these immigrants settled in Canada's three largest cities: Montreal received 12 per cent; Toronto, 43 per cent; and Vancouver 18 per cent. Today, there are more than 200 different ethnic origins represented in the total population. In 2001, Canada's foreign-born population was 5.4 million, or 18.4 per cent of the total population, an increase of 17.4 per cent since 1996. It is projected that by 2020, visible minorities will account for 20 per cent of Canada's population. In Toronto, 44 per cent of the current population was born in another country, and about 60 per cent of the residents of Richmond, British Columbia, are members of a visible minority (primarily Chinese and south Asian).

About 25 per cent of Canadians who are 65 and older were born outside Canada; most of them immigrated as young adults. At first they increased the proportion of people under 65, but as they have grown older, they have contributed to the growth in size of the oldest age cohorts. In 2001, about 19 per cent of all adult immigrants were 65 years of age or older, but this is somewhat higher than the normal percentage. Many older immigrants come to Canada to join their children, and most come from developing countries. At the same time, some older people who immigrated to Canada earlier in life, leave, perhaps returning to their homeland.

Summary

The number and proportion of people 65 and over in every developed country grew significantly in the twentieth century. This aging trend is primarily the result of lower fertility rates; but longer life expectancy due to better health care and higher standards of living and changing immigration policies and rates also contributed to the growth. During the next 20 to 30 years, this pattern of increasing longevity and a proportional growth in the number of people over 65 will occur quite rapidly in developing countries as fertility rates fall in these countries and the standard of living rises.

Although older people are a numerical minority, they make up an increasingly large proportion of the population in all countries. In this century, an increasing number will be 80 years of age and older, and more will reach 100 years of age. Women live longer than men, and the ratio of women to men increases over the life course. Most older people live in urban centres where they have lived for most of their adult years. In small towns, villages, and farm communities, older people make up a higher than average proportion of the population (20–25 per cent).

To understand aging phenomena, and to plan policies and programs for the future, policymakers need demographic and geographic facts. Successful planning of policies and programs requires accurate interpretations of the assumptions used to make demographic projections, and a constant updating of the information at the local and regional level. Policies for an aging population must be constantly revised in the light of new demographic data if Canada is to meet the needs of our aging population.

For Reflection, Debate, or Action

1. Search for current demographic and geographic facts and indices about your home community or the community where one of your grandparents lives. Develop a demographic profile and analyze these facts to suggest what public policies and programs for older residents might be needed in that community in the next 10 to 15 years.

2. Visit www.beeson.org/Livingto100/default.htm and complete the 'Living to 100 Life Expectancy Calculator'. Then complete the Northwestern Mutual Life Insurance Company 'Longevity Game'

(www.nmfn.com/tn/learnctr-lifeevents-longevity). What do the results of these assignments tell you about life-course planning?

3. Examine census data for your community or province to determine if there are census tracts (neighbourhoods or towns) that have a large proportion of people over 65 years of age. Then, tour this area to determine whether there are sufficient services and facilities for an older population.

4. Employing demographic projections from Statistics Canada, government reports, and research articles,

construct a demographic profile of what the demographic situation might look like for Canada, or for your home community, on your sixty-fifth birthday. How might this information help you plan for a secure and satisfying later life?

5. Think about the future needs of your grandparents and parents, and identify three products or services that could generate a profitable financial investment for you or a business or industry.

6. Identify demographic, social, economic, and technological developments that might dramatically

increase the life expectancy of men over the next 30 to 50 years.

7. Statistical reports, tables, or figures, especially demographic projections, are sometimes interpreted in more than one way, or they are misinterpreted. Examine one or more of the tables or figures in this book and suggest how the data could be interpreted in at least two different ways. Discuss the implications for policies, programs, or beliefs and attitudes if one or the other of those interpretations is widely accepted.

Notes

1. Appendix A contains a simple but useful overview of how to read and interpret statistical tables or graphs.

2. Recent statistical sources available in the periodical or government publication sections of most libraries, include publications from the United Nations Social Development Division (www.un.org/esa/socdev/aging), such as the *Annual Demographic Yearbook*; Statistics Canada (www.statcan.ca), including the *Canada Yearbook*, *Annual Report on the Demographic Situation in Canada*, *Social Trends*, and the *Daily Bulletin* (available on the Internet); the World Bank (www.worldbank.org/publications); the US Census Bureau (www.census.gov); city or provincial social and government agencies; *Info-Age*, published periodically by the National Advisory Council on Aging (www.hc-sc.gc.ca/seniors-aines/seniors/english/naca/naca.htm); journals such as *American Demographics*(www.demographics.com), *Demography*, the free on-line *Demographic Research* (www.demographic-research.org), and *Canadian Public Policy*; and numerous gerontology journals and demography sourcebooks that publish recent research on individual and population aging (McDaniel, 1986; Myers, 1990; Northcott, 1992; World Bank, 1994; Martin and Preston, 1994; Elliot et al., 1996; Foot and Stoffman, 1998; Moore and Rosenberg, 1997; Kinsella and Velkoff, 2001; Health Canada, 2002; United Nations, 2002a, 2002b).

3. The most recent Canadian census was conducted in the summer of 2001; the data were released late in 2002 and throughout 2003.

4. The old-age dependency ratio mentioned later in this chapter has been compiled at different times using the following age ranges in the denominator: 15 to 64, 18 to 64, and 20 to 64. Thus, the specific ratio for a year may vary because different numbers are used in the denominator. Greater standardization is needed around the world, and in each country, in how demographic measures are compiled.

5. The United Nations classifies countries as 'more developed' (all nations in North America and Europe, including some nations that were part of the former Soviet Union; and Japan, Australia, and New Zealand) or 'less developed' (all the remaining nations of the world). Other agencies use the terms 'developed' and 'developing' countries, but the countries in each category are the same as in the UN classification.

6. Most countries conduct a census every 10 years and attempt to count every citizen. In Canada, a complete census is conducted in years ending in 1. In addition, there is often a partial census halfway between the complete censuses (in 1986 and 1996 for example). Unfortunately, every census slightly undercounts the population because of inaccuracies in reporting and the unavailability of some people, including illegal aliens, those who

cannot speak English or French, or those who are out of the country.

7. Vital statistics are collected when a birth, death, or marriage is registered; or when a person immigrates, obtains a driver's licence, buys a house, files an income tax return, or pays property tax. Population estimates vary in accuracy, especially in the developing countries, because of incomplete or inaccurate vital-statistics registration, and severe under-counting in censuses.

8. Population projections are made by taking the existing population and then making assumptions about future fertility, mortality, and immigration rates. These assumptions make it possible to project the size and proportion of the population at some point in the future. See Foot and Stoffman (1998: 282–6) for a brief summary of how demographers make projections. Globally, projections are made regularly by the United Nations, the United States Census Bureau, the World Bank, and the International Institute for Applied Systems Analysis. The assumptions used and the number of outcome scenarios vary greatly among these four agencies (O'Neill et al., 2001).

9. According to United Nations projections, the world population by 2050 would be 10.7 billion in a high-fertility scenario (2.5 children per woman); 8.9 billion in a medium-fertility scenario (2.0); or 7.3 billion in a low-fertility scenario (1.6) (Population Reference Bureau, 1999: 16).

10. In the reference section of a library, consult life tables for Canada. To determine your own life expectancy, find the row in a specific life table for your sex, race, and year of birth. Move across to the column that matches your current chronological age. This figure indicates the average number of years you can expect to live. Generally, if you were born in North America between 1980 and 1990, you can expect to live, on average, about 73 years if you are male and about 80 years if you are female.

11. The 'replacement level' fertility rate in developed societies is 2.1. This represents the rate necessary to maintain the current population size if there is no immigration or emigration (McKie, 1993).

12. There are some excellent, but, until the 2001 census results are fully released, somewhat dated sources of geographical and regional demographic statistics in Canada. These include: Northcott (1992), Elliott (1996), Centre on Aging (1996), Moore and Rosenberg (1997, 2001), Northcott and Milliken (1998), Gutman et al. (2000), and Moore et al. (2000).

References

AARP (American Association of Retired Persons). 2000. *Global Aging Report*, 5 (May/June), 5. Washington, DC: AARP.

———. 2002. *Global Aging: Achieving Its Potential*. Washington, DC: American Association of Retired Persons.

Centre on Aging. 1996. *Manitoba Fact Book on Aging*. Winnipeg: Centre on Aging, University of Manitoba.

Cheal, D. 2000. 'Aging and Demographic Change', *Canadian Public Policy*, 26 (Supplement 2), S109–22.

——— (ed.). 2003. *Aging and Demographic Change in the Canadian Context*. Toronto: University of Toronto Press.

Chui, T. 1996. 'Canada's Population: Charting into the 21st Century', *Canadian Social Trends*, 42 (Autumn), 3–7.

Connidis, I. 2003. 'The Impact of Demographic and Social Trends on Informal Support for Older Persons'. Pp. 105–32 in D. Cheal (ed.), *Aging and Demographic Change in the Canadian Context*. Toronto: University of Toronto Press.

Crimmins, E., et al. 1996. 'Differentials in Active Life Expectancy in the Older Population of the United States', *Journal of Gerontology: Social Sciences*, 51B(3), S111–20.

Denton, F., et al. 1987. 'The Canadian Population and Labour Force: Retrospect and Prospect'. Pp. 11–38 in V. Marshall (ed.), *Aging in Canada: Social Perspectives*. Markham, Ont.: Fitzhenry and Whiteside.

———, et al. 1998. 'The Future Population of Canada: Its Age Distribution and Dependency Relations',

Canadian Journal on Aging, 17(1), 83–109.

———, and B. Spencer. 2000. 'Population Aging and Its Economic Costs: A Survey of the Issues and Evidence', *Canadian Journal on Aging*, 19 (Supplement 1), 1–31.

Easterlin, R. 1996. *Growth Triumphant: The Twenty-First Century in Historical Perspective*. Ann Arbor, Mich.: University of Michigan Press.

Elliot, G., et al. 1996. *Facts on Aging in Canada*. Hamilton, Ont.: Office of Gerontological Studies, McMaster University.

Evans, R., et al. 2001. 'Apocalypse No: Population Aging and the Future of Health Care Systems', Research Paper no. 59. Hamilton, Ont.: McMaster University, Program for Research on Social and Economic Dimensions of an Aging Population (http://soc-serv2.mcmaster.ca/sedap).

Foot, D., and D. Stoffman 1998. *Boom, Bust and Echo 2000: Profiting from the Demographic Shift in the New Millenium*. Toronto: Macfarlane Walter and Ross.

Friedland, R., and L. Summer 1999. *Demography Is Not Destiny*. Washington, DC: National Academy on An Aging Society.

Fries, J. 1980. 'Aging, Natural Death and the Compression of Morbidity', *New England Journal of Medicine*, 303(3), 130–5.

———, and L. Crapo. 1981. *Vitality and Aging: Implications of the Rectangular Curve*. San Francisco: Freeman.

Gee, E., and G. Gutman (eds). 2000. *The Overselling of Population Aging: Apocalyptic Demography, Intergenerational Challenges, and Social Policy*. Don Mills, Ont.: Oxford University Press.

George, M., et al. 2001. *Population Projections for Canada, Provinces and Territories, 2000–2026*. Cat. no. 91-520-XPB. Ottawa: Statistics Canada, Demography Division.

Gutman, G., et al. 2000. *Fact Book on Aging in British Columbia*. Burnaby, BC: Simon Fraser University, Gerontology Research Centre.

Hauser, P. 1976. 'Aging and World-Wide Population Change'. Pp. 59–86 in R. Binstock and E. Shanas (eds), *Handbook of Aging and the Social Sciences*. New York: Van Nostrand Reinhold.

Hayward, M., and Z. Zhang 2001. 'Demography of Aging: A Century of Global Change, 1950–2050'. Pp. 69–85 in R. Binstock and L. George (eds), *Handbook of Aging and the Social Sciences*. New York: Academic Press.

Health Canada. 2002. *Canada's Aging Population*. Ottawa: Minister of Public Works and Government Services.

Hogan, S., and J. Lise. 2003. 'Life Expectancy, Health Expectancy, and the Life Cycle', *Horizons*, 6(2), 17–20.

Kinsella, K., and V. Velkoff. 2001. *An Aging World: 2001* (US Census Bureau, Series P95/01-1. Washington, DC: US Government Printing Office.

McDaniel, S. 1986. *Canada's Aging Population*. Toronto: Butterworths.

McKie, C. 1993. 'Population Aging: Baby Boomers into the 21st Century', *Canadian Social Trends*, 29 (Summer), 2–6.

Martin, L., and S. Preston (eds). 1994. *Demography of Aging*. Washington, DC: National Academic Press.

Moore, E., and M. Rosenberg. 1997. *Growing Old in Canada: Demographic and Geographic Perspectives*. Ottawa: Statistics Canada.

———, and M. Rosenberg. 2001. 'Canada's Elderly Population: The Challenges of Diversity', *The Canadian Geographer*, 45(1), 145–50.

———, et al. 2000. *Geographic Dimensions of Aging: The Canadian Experience 1991–1996*. SEDAP Research Paper no. 23. Hamilton, Ont.: McMaster University (http://socserv2.mcmaster.ca/sedap).

Myers, G. 1990. 'Demography of Aging'. Pp. 19–44 in R. Binstock and L. George (eds). *Handbook of Aging and the Social Sciences*. San Diego, Calif.: Academic Press.

NACA (National Advisory Council on Aging). 1993. *Position on Canada's Oldest Seniors: Maintaining the Quality of Their Lives*. Ottawa: NACA.

Northcott, H. 1992. *Aging in Alberta: Rhetoric and Reality*. Calgary.: Detselig.

———, and P. Milliken. 1998. *Aging in British Columbia: Burden or Benefit*. Calgary: Detselig.

Nusselder, W., and J. Mackenbach. 1996. 'Rectangularization of the Survival Curve in the Netherlands, 1950–1992', *The Gerontologist*, 36(6), 773–82.

Oeppen, J., and J. Vaupel. 2002. 'Enhanced and Broken Limits to Life Expectancy', *Science*, 296 (May 10), 1029–31.

Olshansky, J., et al. 2001. 'Prospects for Human Longevity', *Science*, 291 (February 23), 1491–2.

O'Neill, B. et al. 2001. 'A Guide to Global Population Projections', *Demographic Research*, 4 (no. 8, 13 June). (www.demographic-research.org)

Owram, D. 1996. *Born at the Right Time: A History of the Baby Boom Generation*. Toronto: University of Toronto Press.

Perls, T. 1995. 'The Oldest Old', *Scientific American*, January, 70–5.

————, and M. Silver 1999. *Living To Be 100: Lessons in Living Your Maximum Potential at Any Age*. New York: Basic Books.

Population Reference Bureau. 1999. *World Population: More Than Just Numbers*. Washington, DC: Population Reference Bureau.

Riley, J. 2001. *Rising Life Expectancy: A Global History*. New York: Cambridge University Press.

Rosenberg, M. 2000. 'The Effects of Population Ageing on the Canadian Health Care System'. Hamilton, Ont.: McMaster University, SEDAP Research Paper no. 14 (http://socserv2.mcmaster.ca/sedap/).

————. 2003. Personal communication indicating overall (total) and older population dependency ratios for census 2001 data, and projections for 2021 and 2026.

Serow, W. 2001. 'Economical and Social Implications of Demographic Patterns'. Pp. 86–102 in R. Binstock and L. George (eds). *Handbook of Aging and the Social Sciences*. New York: Academic Press.

Statistics Canada. 2002a. *Profile of the Canadian Population by Age and Sex: Canada Ages*. Cat. no. 96F0030 XIE2001002. Ottawa: Statistics Canada (www.statcan.ca).

————. 2002b. *A Profile of Disability in Canada, 2001*. Cat. no. 89-57-XIE. Ottawa: Statistics Canada (www.statcan.ca).

————. 2002c. *Report on the Demographic Situation in Canada, 2001*. Cat. no. 91- 209-XPE. Ottawa: Statistics Canada.

————. 2003a. *Canada: A Nation on the Move*. Ottawa: Statistics Canada.

————. 2003b. *The Daily*, 25 September.

United Nations. 1999. *World Population Prospects: The 1998 Revision*, Vol.1. New York: United Nations, Department of Economic and Social Affairs, Population Division.

————. 2000. *The Sex and Age Distribution of the World Populations: The 1998 Revision*, Vol. II: *Sex and Age*. New York: United Nations, Department of Economic and Social Affairs, Population Division.

————. 2002a. *Population Aging, 2002*. New York: United Nations Population Division (www.unpopulation.org).

————. 2002b. *World Population Ageing, 1950–2002*. New York: United Nations, Department of Economic and Social Affairs Population Division.

Verbrugge, L. 1997. 'A Global Disability Indicator', *Journal of Aging Studies*, 11(4), 337–62.

World Bank. 1994. *Averting the Old Age Crisis*. New York: Oxford University Press.

PART 2

The Social and Environmental Context of Aging

Part 2 examines the social and environmental context in which individuals age, as well as the context in which we learn about, and attempt to understand, older adults and aging phenomena. Chapter 5 introduces the main perspectives and theories that describe, explain, and interpret aging phenomena from a social science perspective. Two levels of analysis are required for a full understanding of aging processes: the micro- (or personal) level, which pertains to individual aging, and the macro- (or societal) level, which pertains to the aging of a cohort or population. These are not separate processes—throughout life and history there is constant interaction between individual and population aging and among individuals, their culture, and the social structures in which they age. To enable you to interpret research findings and conduct research yourself, the chapter introduces the goals and methods of scholarly inquiry and specific methodological issues that arise in the study of older persons and aging processes. Ethical procedures and practices that must be employed to protect older participants in research studies are also discussed.

Our social world involves a number of interacting social structures that influence a person's life chances, lifestyle, health, and actions throughout his or her life. Society is stratified by social class, gender, race and ethnicity, and age interacts with these dimensions of social differentiation to create opportunities and barriers across the life course. Chapter 6 discusses the influence of social structures on the process of aging, both for age cohorts (at the societal level of analysis) and for generations (within extended families). This discussion examines such outcomes as social differentiation due to age and aging; age-segregated and age-integrated structures; and ageism, age grading, and age norms across time. Social processes and issues such as cohort flow, structural lag, the changing status of older persons, intergenerational equity and transfers, and the myth or reality of a generation gap are introduced.

The lived environment influences the quality of our life throughout the life course, but even more in later life. As we grow older, an ideal person-environment fit requires adaptation if we are to 'age in place' in the family home rather than move to an institution, such as a retirement or nursing home. Some older people suffer falls, lose their means of transportation, and develop a fear of crime, all of which limit their mobility and the way they live. Thus, it is essential that as one ages, the home and neighbourhood environment be as safe as possible. Chapter 7 examines relationships between the aging individual and elements of his or her housing environment. Issues addressed include urban versus rural living; age-integrated versus age-segregated housing and neighbourhoods; transportation options; fear of crime; the risk, avoidance, and outcome of falls; technology and independence; and homeless older people. The chapter also discusses a range of housing options in later life (from independent living to assisted living to dependent living) and the mobility and migration of older people.

CHAPTER 5

Understanding Older People and Aging Processes: Theory and Research

Focal Points

- What is a theory? Why are theories constructed, and how are they used to explain and interpret aging phenomena?

- Which theories explain and interpret individual *and* population aging, and the link between individual aging and the social structure?

- Why and how do we conduct research?

- Are unique research methods required for studying older adults?

- How can an older person's rights be protected through ethical research practices?

Introduction

As you consume and assimilate information from research journals, scholarly books, government reports, and the mass media, many facts, patterns, and observations about discrete elements of individual and population aging are *described*. Describing elements of the social world is important, but description represents only the first level of understanding. We also need to know *why* a fact or observation exists (for example, why women are the primary caregivers for the elderly); *why* a process, problem, or event occurs repeatedly, usually in similar situations (such as why young adults leave rural communities); and *why* there are variations in the facts, patterns, and observations—whether by gender, age, class or ethnic background; by rural versus urban place of residence; or by country or region of the world (why, for example, do older people have higher status in some ethnic groups and in developing countries). The search for explanation is the ulti-

mate goal of research and scholarly inquiry. If we can understand, explain, and interpret the meaning of a phenomenon, then we are more likely to change the status quo and improve the everyday life of older people by developing effective and efficient policies and programs that equitably meet the needs of all older persons.

To enlarge the knowledge base and enhance our understanding about individual and population aging, theoretical perspectives and well-established research methods are employed. Theoretical perspectives stimulate and guide our thinking as we move from a description to one or more explanations for some recurring fact or pattern. Theories also provide a set of concepts by which scholars working in different places all have common tools and meanings with which to study and interpret a phenomenon. In a similar way, common research methods enable us to answer a specific question, interpret social reality, or solve a specific problem within our social world. The theories and methods presented in this chapter represent the current thinking in our field.

The Goals of Scholarly Research

The ultimate goal of scholarly inquiry is to offer plausible and complete interpretations of, and explanations for, observations or empirical findings in our social world. Scholars theorize and engage in research for the following reasons:

- To satisfy an innate curiosity and a need to know about some question, pattern, problem, or observation. Why and how, for example, does a social pattern or problem occur? Why do people, individually or collectively, behave in a specific way?

- To refute myths or verify assumptions, such as, for example, that the elderly are impoverished or that elder abuse is an outcome of caregiving.

- To identify inequities in the social world— such as the poverty of elderly widows or the lack of adequate health care and housing for older people—and suggest how they might be reduced or eliminated.

- To produce reliable and valid information for the evaluation, development, and implementation of policies and programs.

The most crucial goal of research is to explain observed relationships or patterns and interpret the meaning of a **social phenomenon** observed in everyday life. Examples of social phenomena studied in this book include ethnic, gender, and social-class differences in aging; cross-cultural variations in the status of older people in a society; population aging; fear of crime among older adults; aging in place in the family home; and adaptation to retirement and widowhood in later life. Arriving at one or more explanations or inter-

pretations for a phenomenon enables us to understand *why* the relationship or event occurs, and the meaning of the situation for those involved. Since different scholars study a given phenomenon or problem by using different theories, assumptions, or methods, alternative interpretations or explanations of the same phenomenon evolve over time. These different and often competing interpretations or explanations confuse students or laypeople. However, they are necessary, at least in the early stages of discovering knowledge about a phenomenon. The presence of alternative theoretical perspectives and the emergence of alternative explanations for the same issue or question stimulate researchers to find more complete explanations or interpretations of aging phenomena. Unfortunately, unlike researchers in the natural and physical sciences, social scientists seldom reach one ultimate explanation of some facet of the social world that could be expressed as a law.

Laypeople and journalists also pursue the goals of description and explanation as they study or observe aspects of aging behaviour in everyday life. However, the major difference between a scholarly and a non-scholarly approach to understanding is the use by scholars of well-defined concepts and theoretical perspectives to guide their thinking and rigorous and standardized methods to help them reach their conclusions. Moreover, researchers are seldom satisfied with one explanation—they constantly search for alternative, more complete, and more succinct explanations. Scholars are competitive, intellectual craftspeople who employ theories and rigorous research methods to gain insight about social or physical phenomena, and to discover a more comprehensive explanation or interpretation of a specific phenomenon, situation, or problem.

Although there is no universally accepted definition, a theory is a set of interrelated ideas that present a logical, systematic, and reasonably complete understanding of a process, situation, or observed fact. A theory represents 'a broad view of the fundamental processes underlying social structure and social life' (George, 1995: 51), and is both a research tool and an outcome of scholarly inquiry. As a research tool, a theory

- provides assumptions and definitions;
- summarizes, connects, and synthesizes existing facts, meanings or observations to help build a coherent, systematic, and cumulative body of knowledge;
- provides a focus on large, highly relevant questions or issues facing society (such as age and inequality);
- summarizes what is essential and relevant in order to understand a given phenomenon;
- guides and stimulates thinking by introducing new research questions and identifying gaps or flaws in the existing state of knowledge; and
- stimulates the search for more complete or alternative explanations, and for generalizations that apply in many places or historical periods.

As a product of scholarly activity, a theory

- provides a model of how the complex social or physical world operates;
- represents a conceptual system to be accepted or rejected, and therefore further stimulates the development and accumulation of knowledge;
- interprets and explains findings, observations, and meanings;
- facilitates social interventions through the development and implementation of policies and programs grounded in theoretically based knowledge.

General Theoretical Perspectives

Dawe (1970) identified two contrasting perspectives that have guided general sociological

research for many years and, to some extent, much of the research on aging: the *normative* perspective and the *interpretive* perspective. The normative perspective assumes that **norms** (established rules) and **status** levels exist in society to provide social control or social order. This order is deemed necessary for the survival of a society. According to this perspective, individuals learn social roles by internalizing shared norms (such as to listen before speaking) and values (such as respect for older people) through a process of **socialization**. Most individuals in a society adhere to these roles without question (that is, conformity prevails). When rules are broken (that is, there is a deviation from the norms), varying types of sanctions are imposed by the formal agents of social control (such as parents, teachers, or the police). This perspective is associated with the positivist approach to understanding, which assumes that the social world is similar to the physical world of chemistry, biology, or physics in that there is cause and effect.

In contrast, the interpretive perspective views individuals as social actors who, through a process of negotiation, define, construct, interpret, and control their place or situation in society. In this way, individuals, through agency, create and change the social order. Institutions and structures are changed when human agency is used and when people engage in interaction. Here, the focus is on interpreting and understanding the meaning of everyday life as expressed and interpreted by actors in the situation. Here, the emphasis is on definitions of a situation (the meanings) and how they emerge and are managed through social interaction (Berger and Luckmann, 1966). According to this perspective, sometimes labelled the social constructionist or social phenomenological perspective, the world is composed of 'meanings', not 'things' (Gubrium and Holstein, 1999). The facts themselves are not essential for understanding social life. Rather, what matters is how the facts are interpreted by those in the situation. Interpretations shift over time, and different interpretations of the same fact or situation can occur because of social differentiation (for example, men and women view caregiving differently), and different cultural experiences, beliefs, and values.

A third general theoretical perspective, the critical perspective, argues that there are inherent inequities in the social structure that have important consequences for the life chances and lifestyles of some members of a society. Advocates of this perspective critically study and interpret (by gender, class, race, age, and ethnicity) the experiences, meanings, and actions of the disadvantaged and less powerful members of a society.

Just as different research methods are needed to answer different questions, different theoretical perspectives are necessary to advance our understanding. Each perspective or theory is based on different assumptions and employs different concepts, and one perspective may be more effective than another in helping us understand a specific phenomenon. Competing theoretical perspectives are necessary to increase our knowledge.

Theories about aging represent either a micro-level (individual) *or* a macro-level (societal) view of the world. In reality, if aging processes and the situation of older people are to be completely understood, both micro and macro levels of analysis are required. That is, we need to link the lives of individuals (human agency) with social structures across the life course (Marshall, 1999). To date, much of the research has focused on aging individuals and on how they adjust to or cope with their micro-worlds. Hagestad and Dannefer (2001) argue that we need to move away from this 'microfication' in aging research and pay more attention to the wider social context, namely, the processes influencing stability and change in the culture and social structure of communities, nations, and the global village in different historical periods. This approach reinforces Mills's (1959) plea to connect the 'personal troubles' of individuals with the 'public issues' inherent in the structures and institutions of society. The everyday aging experiences of individuals, which are the subject of the micro-level of analysis, are connected with the historical, cultural, demographic, political, economic, and social situation in which aging occurs, which is the subject of the macro-level of analysis. Or, from another perspective, individual biographies and social history are interconnected (Marshall and Mueller, 2003).

Throughout most of the history of gerontology, theories were developed at *either* the micro- or macro-level, although some have served a 'bridging' or 'linking' function between the two levels (Marshall, 1996; Bengtson et al., 1997, 1999). Figure 5.1 illustrates, by level of analysis, the historical development of the major theories used to study aging phenomena.

Developing Knowledge: The Use of Perspectives and Theories

This section introduces a number of conceptual tools for understanding aging phenomena from both the individual and societal perspective. Although terms such as 'theory', 'model', 'perspective', and 'framework' are often used interchangeably, in this book a 'theory' or 'model' refers to a formal, specific explanation of some facet of the social world. A 'perspective' or 'framework' is a more general or global view, which includes one or more theories or models that, in general, take a similar approach to the study of social phenomena. Perspectives, sometimes labelled as schools of thought, such as functionalism, symbolic interactionism, and the critical perspective, provide a general orientation to developing research questions, explaining research findings, and interpreting observations or meanings about aging phenomena. No attempt has been made to categorize the perspectives and theories into a dichotomous micro-macro classification system with its artificial and potentially misleading boundaries.[1] Moreover, each of the following subsections summarizes the main ideas about a particular perspective. Consequently, they constitute an overview rather than a comprehensive

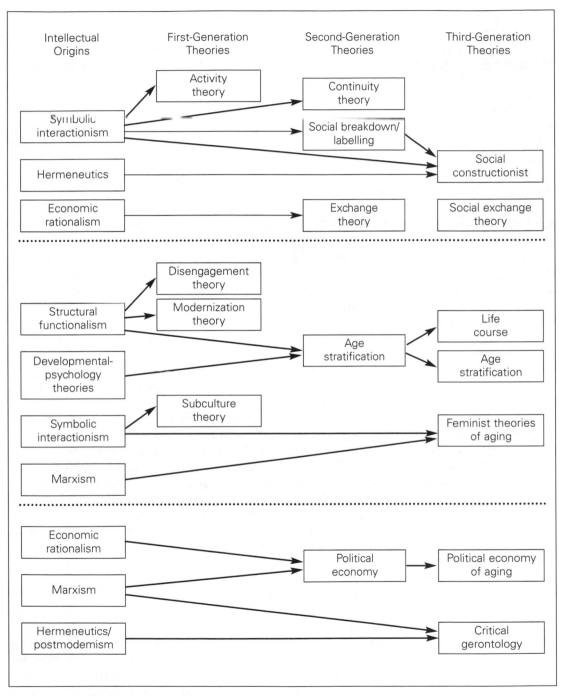

Figure 5.1 The Historical Development of Theories in Social Gerontology

Source: Reproduced with permission from Bengtson et al. (1997). *Journal of Gerontology*, 52B (March 1997), S72–88.

analysis or critique of the various approaches sometimes found within a given perspective.

Theoretical Perspectives[2]

The Life-Course Perspective[3]

This perspective provides an analytical framework for understanding the interplay between individual lives and changing social structures, between personal troubles and public issues, and between personal biography and societal history (Holstein and Gubrium, 2000; Elder and Johnson, 2003; Heinz and Marshall, 2003; Marshall and Mueller, 2003; Settersten, 2003). The approach requires a consideration of the interaction among historical events and social changes, individual decisions (human agency), and the opportunities we have and the constraints we face in decision making. These opportunities and constraints are influenced by social-structural factors, that is, age, gender, and class; cultural factors, such as ethnicity or race; and the impact of early life experiences and decisions on later life. As George (1996a) noted, 'we are architects of our own lives', but our choices are linked inevitably to social structure and culture. Or as Settersten (1999) succinctly stated, 'there can not be agency without structure.'

It was once assumed that the life course involved timely, orderly, and sequential transitions along a relatively clearly defined and common trajectory or path. These transitions, significant life events, or turning points usually happened at a certain age or time in life and were often accompanied by rites of passage, such as a wedding. Or the transitions occurred with the onset of critical events or experiences such as retirement, divorce, or widowhood. According to this perspective, life follows a series of branching points until death (Schroots, 1995). Some examples of major branching points are the decision to attend a particular university and enrol in a specific program; location and type of first job; age at marriage; a divorce or widowhood; or a move to another region or country.

Today, there are many possible pathways through the life course. A given route depends on which events occur at the branching points and when; on individual or group decisions made at each point; and on reactions or adjustments to the critical event or experience. Our life course is composed of multiple, interdependent trajectories relating to education, work, family, and leisure. What happens along one trajectory, such as education, often has an effect on other trajectories, such as work and leisure. The branching points, when connected, represent an inverted tree, and many trees of different shapes and sizes are possible for individuals, groups, or cohorts. The life-course trajectory changes direction or shape when a new event leads to a branching point. The decision to move in a new direction may be voluntary or involuntary, due to external historical, geographical, social, or political circumstances.

Compared to the past, fewer transition points today are related to age. And the trajectories are less orderly, especially in education, family, and careers, and more diverse: older people date and remarry or live common-law after being divorced or widowed; men father children at age 60; people become unemployed at 40 or retire at 45; adults graduate from university after age 60; women are widowed or become grandmothers at 40 years of age. These asynchronous transitions, which may create strains in relationships or personal stress, can be the result of individual decisions, such as a teenage pregnancy or dropping out of school at 16; actions taken by others, such as an employer that downsizes a company or a husband or wife who asks for a divorce; or because of a war or a baby boom, which may lead to either more or fewer jobs for the members of a specific birth cohort.

The influence of early life events on one's life path and on later life is not well understood because there have been few longitudinal studies.[4] Using an extensive longitudinal analysis of the meaning of the Depression for those who were children during this difficult economic period, Elder and Johnson (2003: 57–71) derived five principles that can guide our study of aging and later life:

1. Human development and aging are life-long processes—many early experiences, meanings, events, and transitions are linked to later life opportunities and experiences.

2. Human agency prevails—individuals construct their own life course through the choices they make and the actions they take within the opportunities and constraints of history and their personal circumstances, such as their advantages or disadvantages due to their location in the social structure (based on age, gender, race, ethnicity and social class).

3. The life course of individuals is embedded in, and shaped by, the historical times and places they experience over their lifetime. Individuals and birth cohorts at the micro-level are affected by large-scale macro-historical events like wars, economic depressions, or natural disasters.

4. The antecedents and consequences of life transitions, events, and behaviour patterns vary according to when they happen in a person's life. Thus different but adjacent birth cohorts can be affected differently by the same historical event.

5. Lives are lived interdependently, and social-historical influences are expressed through these shared relationships—lives are not lived in isolation. Our actions are determined by, and in turn influence, the actions of those to whom we are closely linked. Losing a job in middle age can create stress in a marriage or make it difficult for children to attend university.

One approach to studying aging from a life-course perspective is to reconstruct the life of individuals or cohorts within the context of a specific social structure and history. In this approach, people are interviewed about their life histories, and lifelines are drawn to identify crucial events and turning points at each chronological age and stage of life, thereby providing a biography, or journey, for an individual. Respondents are asked what important events happened at a specific time or age, and why, and what the event meant to them at that time and later in life (Schroots, 1996: 123; Giele and Elder, 1999); and they are asked about possible future pathways. For example, important historical events (a war, an epidemic, a depression) often interact with significant personal events (first job, birth of a child, divorce). Thus, a personal event such as getting married at the time of a major historical event (war) may alter the expected life course for an individual or age cohort. To better understand this approach, interview a grandparent or an elderly neighbour in order to find out how a few significant decisions or social or historical events at one stage in life influenced his or her life history and life opportunities. What were the 'roads taken, or not taken', and why?

The Symbolic-Interactionist (Social-Constructionist) Perspective

Symbolic interactionists seek to understand social life by interpreting the meaning of cognitive, symbolic, or behavioural acts. They are more concerned with challenging common assumptions and asking new questions than in perpetuating the social order as prescribed by the positivists in their normative approach to understanding. Understanding is reached when an individual defines the social situation in terms of what it means to him or her (Thomas, 1931). Through verbal or symbolic interaction with others, such as type of dress, gestures, language, and mannerisms, a specific situation is defined in personal terms. Individuals also observe and interact with others in order to arrive at a definition of the 'self' (Cooley, 1902). Through this process meanings emerge as we interpret and evaluate how we are viewed by others. As a result of this evaluation and interpretation, we arrive at what Goffman (1959) refers to as 'the presentation of self'.

Individuals define the situation and then decide how they will present themselves to others in terms of dress, manner, content of verbal interaction, and general and specific behaviour. For example, as university students you may present yourself differently to others during a job interview, when at home with your parents, or when at a party with people your own age.

The symbolic-interactionist perspective, also known as the social-constructionist perspective (Bengtson et al., 1997: S77), is used to study individual processes of aging in a natural setting. The social definition and meaning of the setting and of aging are derived through observations and through an interpretation of the personal narratives of older people. This perspective does not normally consider the larger social system in which the specific individual is found. Rather, it is interested in how individuals in a setting interpret and assign meaning to specific events, behaviours, or situations; and in how these meanings influence the person's life. A classic study that used this perspective was Gubrium's (1993) analysis of life stories to understand the quality of life experienced by residents of a nursing home.

The Social-Exchange Perspective

At both the individual and society level, social interaction is viewed as a process in which we seek to maximize the rewards we receive and to reduce the costs, whether they be material (money, goods, or services) or non-material (friendship or social support). Social interaction involves reciprocity (give and take), whereby each actor in a relationship brings resources (often unequally) and strives to balance his or her costs and rewards. While the quantity element is important, increasingly, the emphasis is on the quality of exchange relations. Today, research analyzes how exchange relationships are influenced by emotional, social, financial, and altruistic resources.

A basic assumption of the social-exchange perspective is that individuals search for social situations in which valued outcomes are possible, and in which their social, emotional, and psycho-logical needs can be met. Since this goal may involve acquiescence and compliance by an individual or group, a fair exchange may not be readily apparent, or possible, in every social relationship. Thus, social scientists seek knowledge about past experiences and present personal needs, values, and options before they determine the equality of a specific social exchange relationship. This is especially the case when one attempts to explain exchange behaviour among individuals of different ages, particularly where roles, decision-making, and resources shift with advancing age. (Emotional, physical, and financial support is often reversed between aging parents and adult children.)

According to this view of the world, after an interaction has begun, it continues as long as it is rewarding to both parties, even though the rewards may not be equal. When one actor gives more than the other and the interaction continues, that person gains power in the exchange relationship.

In reality, most social relationships are not reduced to participants seeking a 'balanced' budget. Rather, most relationships include some imbalance where one side cannot or will not reciprocate equally. In most exchange relationships participants strive to maximize their power while maintaining a fair outcome. Not surprisingly, some status characteristics—for example, being white, male, highly educated, wealthy, or young—strengthen one's position in the negotiation process. If one is black, female, illiterate, poor, or elderly, he or she is often at a disadvantage in social interactions. Having two or more of these less highly valued status characteristics leads to even greater disadvantages in social-exchange relationships.

Although one theory cannot explain all phenomena on all levels, the social-exchange perspective is applied to both the individual and cohort levels of analysis. Consequently, this theory is increasingly being used to explain many facets of the aging process, including informal social support or family caregiving in the later years. One outcome of exchange relationships is that older people may become increasingly dependent on others, and their social power may diminish. For example, at the macro-level, if the occupational skills of older workers become outmoded or obsolete, they are forced to accept early retirement in return for a modest pension benefit, social assistance, and leisure time. Similarly, when individuals are considered to be no longer able to care for themselves, they are forced into residential institutions and cared for as a repayment for past contributions. In reality, however, most older people have resources to exchange, including love, experience, wisdom, time, skills, money, and real estate, and they do continue to participate in an exchange process, although the resources exchanged change over time.

The Structural-Functionalist Perspective

Created by North American sociologists in the 1950s and 1960s, this perspective focuses on the relationships between social structures and social institutions and the resulting influence on the individual. For example, advocates of this perspective might ask what purpose the family, as a social institution, serves in society, and what influence the family has on individual behaviour as we age in a particular society. Not only the function but the structure of the family varies among different societies, particularly when developing and highly modernized societies are compared. This perspective argues that there is a commonly accepted social order (or structure) in a society; that it is essential to maintain the existing forms and functions of social institutions, such as the family, the political system, or the economic system; and that each element of the structure can be viewed analytically as having a manifest (that is, intended) or latent (unintended) function. Social action by an individual is determined and regulated by a formal yet abstract set of rules derived from the structure of the society. From this perspective, human agency is considered to have little or no significance in determining social behaviour.

The essential concepts of functionalism are norms, roles, and socialization. This perspective assumes that all components of the social structure are necessary, are interrelated, and exist to maintain consensus and conformity within the social system. Social norms determine the roles available to different age groups. For example, mandatory retirement, which removes older individuals from a major social role is 'functional' because it enables younger people to enter the labour force. Since the older worker is required to accept and adapt to this role loss, society creates and legitimizes the non-work of the 'retiree', and in many societies provides an economic reward in the form of a pension. The individual is expected to accept this process without question or opposition because the transition is necessary for a society to function and maintain order.

For structural-functionalists, aging is a process in which an individual adjusts to inevitable new roles, such as a retiree or widow. This perspective argues that an individual's failure to adapt to role changes (such as from worker to retiree) represents an inability to fit into the existing social structure, not that the structure is ineffective or unsuitable for that individual or period in history. However, it must also be recognized that not all social relationships are functional. Some are dysfunctional and detract from the stable functioning of society. For example, elder abuse occurs in dysfunctional families or relationships. Mandatory retirement could be viewed, as well, as a dysfunctional process in that it eliminates from the labour force those who have the most experience and knowledge.

Structural functionalism employs quantitative research methods and adheres to the principles of scientific discovery used by the physical sciences. Increasingly, this perspective is criticized as being too reductionist, too static, too deterministic, and too objective. Consequently, scholars have proposed alternative perspectives that focus on the possibility of conflict, change, inequality, and diversity in a society. Most of these perspectives use methods of analysis that are observational, qualitative (rather than quantitative), and historical.

The Conflict Perspective

Whereas functionalism sees the social world as normative and static, the conflict perspective views society as dynamic and changing. According to this perspective, conflict is inevitable since society is composed of competing groups. One group controls authority, power, and money; others believe that they are deprived, exploited, or manipulated, and therefore try to wrest some or all of the resources from those in control. Conflict theorists believe that changes must be made so that all groups have an equal share of the resources. In the conflict perspective, social interaction involves negotiation and compromise to resolve conflict, and only in extreme cases does conflict lead to a civil war or a revolution.

Adherents of the conflict perspective search for power groups and attempt to explain how they manipulate or control other social groups. For example, it has been argued that modern industrialized societies are controlled by white, middle-aged, wealthy males. This has led to conflict between young people, who have yet to gain power, and middle-aged people, who have the most power; and more recently, between older people, who have lost their power and authority, and middle-aged people. In fact, it has been suggested that a voting coalition of younger and older people could form in the years ahead if the economic status of these two disadvantaged groups does not improve. That is, conflict between age groups evolves because of perceived inequities in power and inadequate access to valued resources. Another example of conflict is that between women and men for power and money. It is this power struggle over gender inequity that fostered the feminist movement and feminist theories.

The Postmodern Perspective

Originating in philosophy, but now used widely in the social sciences and humanities, postmodern thought challenges the assumptions of the positivist science perspective. The postmodern perspective questions the notion that reason and empirical science provide an objective, reliable, and universal way of understanding human behaviour. Postmodernists employ two basic intellectual approaches to understanding: social construction and deconstruction (Hazan, 1994). Both of these processes are interpretive, analytical, interactive, critical, and change-oriented. The social-constructionist approach argues that truth and reality are dynamic and cannot be observed directly or discovered objectively. Rather, reality is socially constructed and evolves as we actively interact with others or record our thoughts and meanings. As Hare-Mustin and Marecek (1994: 52) note, 'our understanding of reality is a representation, not an exact replica. . . . Representations of reality are shared meanings that derive from shared language, history and culture.' For example, Ray (1996) argued that the conclusions of some scholars and practitioners about the experience of later life may reflect their own perceptions or interpretations rather than those of older people themselves.

The deconstructionist (or post-structuralist) approach contends that language is a social concept that must be deconstructed in order to understand and explain the 'real' meaning of thoughts and behaviour. In this approach, literature, laws, policies, contracts, speeches, value systems, and so on are analyzed. An understanding of the real meaning of social life is acquired by emphasizing what is included and not included and by highlighting inconsistencies and consistencies in what has been written and said by others. To illustrate, Ray (1996: 677) suggests that a postmodern feminist who deconstructs the term 'caregiving' might find that the activity involves intimacy and connection (care), and that the care is offered freely (is given rather than demanded) to meet the physical needs of another person. She could find, as well, contrary to public opinion, that the term excludes the notion of care as hard work performed for remuneration (by a home nurse), or that care begins because of a sense of duty or responsibility (by a daughter). Similarly, postmodernists critique the language and discourse of the research and policy literature that ignores or constricts our knowledge about older women.

The Feminist Perspective[5]

This perspective argues that, across the life course, unequal opportunities, unequal access to resources, and differential social status accrue to individuals according to gender. Through gender stratification in work, leisure, the family, politics, and other social domains, women are oppressed and disadvantaged compared to men. In gender relations, men hold power that is derived from participation in the public sphere of social life; women lack power and have been restricted, at least in the past, to the private world of the home.

Feminist scholars emphasize that the male view of the world should not be the norm and that the situation of women can be understood only through an examination of women's social experiences, by women or by men, using a feminist perspective. They argue that understanding and equality can be attained only through analysis, theory development, and political and social action based on a unique understanding of the female world. Hence, the goals of feminist research are to understand social reality through the eyes and experiences of women, to eliminate gender-based oppression, and to improve the lives of women. The process involves a consciousness-raising experience for the researcher and the participants (Neysmith, 1995). Feminist scholars and practitioners seek explanations for how gender hierarchies are created and sustained and why women are subordinated. They also develop strategies and actions to confront and eliminate the inequalities created by a gendered social world, and seek to construct new images and possibilities for women by changing attitudes and eliminating stereotypes.

Although feminists have emphasized the diversity among women based on race and ethnicity, class, health, and sexual orientation, few have considered age, aging, or the situation of older women. Nor have they devoted much attention to gender-based age relations in later life, including the gendered component of aging for men (Thompson, 1994; Arber and Ginn, 1995; Bengtson et al., 1996, Kimmel, 2000). Rather, as McMullin (1995: 31) observes, gender has been an 'add-on' to other theories in mainstream sociology and in gerontology. Consequently, she argues for the development of a theory that explains the link between gender and age-based systems of inequality. Feminist scholars interested in aging have criticized general gerontological theories as being incomplete since they are based on the experience and interpretations of white, middle-class males. Similarly, scholars and practitioners are criticized for failing to study gender relations, or the experiences of women in the context of aging.[6]

Studies of older women that employ a feminist approach focus on their everyday experiences, or on the economic and power relations between women and men. This approach leads to new ways of studying and understanding problems heretofore examined solely from a male perspective. To illustrate, Blieszner (1993), employing a socialist-feminist perspective, examined the economic and other consequences of widowhood. *Both* widows and widowers from different classes, racial or ethnic backgrounds, and age-cohorts were studied to understand the 'meaning' of widowhood. Blieszner examined, as well, how capitalism and patriarchy, which encourage class exploitation and the gendered division of labour, influence the experience of widowhood.

Feminists argue that the factors influencing the onset of poverty in later life are different for women than for men (McDaniel, 1989, 2004). First, elderly women, because of their irregular work histories, have few if any pension benefits. Second, some older women are not eligible for survivor's benefits when their spouse dies. Third, women live longer than men and are more likely to exhaust their savings. Fourth, when older women become ill they seldom have a partner to care for them. Poverty, as seen from this perspective, is less an aging problem and more an issue for women who live a long life. Feminists conclude that older women are devalued and powerless in a male-dominated society that oppresses all women and that this situation is even worse for women who live a long life. In reality, the impoverishment of older women is socially constructed and imposed. Hence, feminist perspectives allow us to view the experiences of aging through the eyes of women, rather than by considering the experiences of men to be normative and ideal. The life course and later life are experienced differently by men and women.

Socialist feminists argue that women occupy an inferior status in later life because they live in a capitalist and patriarchal society in which they have been disadvantaged throughout their lives. Power relations between the genders influence the *current* situation of older women (MacQuarrie and Keddy, 1992) for a variety of reasons, including the following:

- Most women in older age cohorts have accepted, without question, the patriarchal structure and the domination by men of their social and work lives.

- Gendering processes in organizations throughout the life course determine what types of jobs are available to women (mainly part-time and clerical) and the size of the pension they receive because of the type of job they held, and their irregular work history due to pregnancy, childrearing, or responsibility to care for elderly parents.

- A conflict exists between production (work) and reproduction (family) because of the gendered division of labour and gender ideology.

- In a gendered welfare system most benefits accrue to men or to women through a husband or father.

These factors suggest that social reform is needed to change the social and economic structure, as well as gender relations, so that there will be social, economic, and political equality for both genders (Lynott and Lynott, 1996). Gender inequities are socially constructed, institutionalized, and perpetuated by dynamic social, economic, and political forces, rather than by individual choices (agency). Both genders experience ageism and patriarchy, but they experience it differently because of different life experiences, meanings, and expectations in relation to work, family, and leisure. And gender-based public policies usually favour males in terms of eligibility and benefits. To illustrate, feminists argue that the burden of caring for elderly parents falls on women, not because of natural (biological) nurturing needs, but because of a gendered socialization process. This process, reinforced through public social policies, creates an expectation that this type of labour is the responsibility of women, perhaps because they have been socialized to perform, or are willing to engage in, unpaid domestic work (Stoller, 1993; Ray, 1996).

Theories to Explain Aging Phenomena

Since the 1960s, a number of theories have been developed to explain aging phenomena. Most of the early theories (activity, disengagement, and continuity theories) focused on individual adaptation in later life, whereas more recent theories (age stratification, political economy, and critical gerontology) focus on the macro-aspects of aging—age and social structures, the state, and social inequality.

Activity (Substitution) Theory

This was the first theory that sought to explain 'successful' or ideal aging in the later years of life. The idea of slowing down but remaining active and thereby adjusting successfully to aging was first suggested by Havighurst and Albrecht (1953). This theory argued that individual adaptation in later life involved continuing an active life. Continued social interaction would maintain the self-concept and, hence, a sense of well-being or life satisfaction. Later, Burgess (1960) suggested that old age should not be viewed as a 'roleless role', but that individuals should replace lost roles or social activities with new ones. Maintaining an active life involved replacing lost roles by either re engaging in roles played earlier in life or learning new ones. Engaging in activities provides opportunities for role-related interaction, and one's identity is confirmed by receiving positive feedback from others (Reitzes et al., 1995). The basic assumptions of this theory are that: (1) high activity and maintenance of roles is positively related to a favourable self-concept; and (2) a favourable self-concept is positively related to life satisfaction, that is, experiencing adjustment, successful aging, well-being, and high morale.

For a number of years, this theory was accepted without question and, in fact, was the basis for many of the social programs and services provided to older people—on the assumption that if they were kept busy with a range of activities and social roles, they would age 'successfully'. Although some studies have supported activity theory and others have failed to support it, few have refuted the theory by finding support for the idea that high activity is related to low levels of satisfaction.

Because the evidence to support activity theory has not been overwhelming, a number of criticisms and reservations about the theory have been expressed. Opponents of activity theory argue that activity levels can decrease without a loss of morale; that some people have never been socially active in their lives, yet exhibit satisfaction; and that not everyone has the economic or interpersonal resources to replace lost roles. Moreover, there has been little consideration of the quality or meaning of the activity that serves as the substitute activity. To keep busy at mundane, repetitive, socially sanctioned tasks may not result in a high sense of morale or life satisfaction if these activities have little intrinsic meaning to the individual. Another criticism is that the theory is not a theory at all. Rather, it represents a set of assumptions that may apply only to some people as they age. It has also been noted that activity theory illustrates the chicken-and-egg dilemma: Are older people satisfied because they are active; or are people who are satisfied more likely to be involved in social roles and activities? Most evidence suggests that aging involves selective replacement of, *and* selective disengagement from, some roles and activities, as well as the acquisition of new roles.

Disengagement Theory

Disengagement theory (Cumming et al., 1960; Cumming and Henry, 1961), constructed as an alternative to activity theory, was presented as an alternative explanation for 'successful' aging. This theory represented a shift from an emphasis on the individual to an emphasis on the interaction between the individual and society. Disengagement theory was derived from both a developmental and a functionalist perspective and was based on the assumption that change and adaptation in the later years of life are necessary, both for the individual and for society. The inevitability of death, the probable decrease in physical and/or mental ability as one ages, and the high value placed on youth led to the belief that both the individual and society benefit from disengagement.

This theory argued that only through a process of disengagement by older people can young people enter the labour force, and if this withdrawal is mandatory and occurs at a specific age, namely, 65, the loss of older individuals at death is less disruptive to society. Thus, for the mutual benefit of individuals and society, aging should involve a functional and voluntary process by which older people disengage from society, and society disengages from the individual. In reality, however, many forms of disengagement, including mandatory retirement, are not voluntary.

Theoretically, the process of disengagement results in less interaction between an individual and others in society and is assumed to be a universal process. Disengagement is believed to be satisfying to the individual because he or she is released from pressures to behave as expected (on the job), and there is more freedom to deviate from societal norms without criticism. Through disengagement, it is argued, individuals experience a high level of satisfaction and well-being in the later years of life.

To support or refute this explanation of successful aging, many research studies were conducted in the 1960s and 1970s, resulting in some revisions and clarifications of the theory by the original authors (Cumming, 1963; Henry, 1964). The major criticisms of the theory were that the process was not universal, voluntary, and satisfying and that not everyone disengages from his or her previously established role set. Clearly, a comparison of pre-industrial societies, where there is no retirement and older people have a high status, with modern industrialized societies suggests that the process is not universal across time.

A number of studies found that withdrawal is not a typical pattern. Moreover, there are different types of disengagement, and people in different social situations disengage to varying degrees. For example, a person may be physically engaged in a job but psychologically disengaged if work no longer has interest, meaning, or value for the individual. Similarly, a person may be disengaged organizationally from religion if he or she no longer attends religious services but may be engaged non-organizationally if he or she prays in private or participates in religious services via radio or television. Some older people are forced to disengage when their health or financial means decline, or when friends die or move away. Disengagement may also occur at early stages in the life cycle, as in the case of a person who drops out of mainstream society to live as a homeless person, or those who move to a rural area to live alone. Moreover, some individuals are socially or psychologically 'disengaged' all through their lives, while others are fully engaged in work, volunteer activities, and social interaction until they die, although the nature of the activities may change as they adjust to the aging process.

Another criticism of the theory is directed at the assumed cause-and-effect relationship. Is the process initiated by an individual or by society? An individual may be socialized to disengage, to learn that this is an expected pattern of behaviour in the later years, and to conform, voluntarily, by behaving as expected. In contrast, it may be that society withdraws from the individual by preventing or discouraging access to social roles (such as through mandatory retirement), to power, or to interaction with other age groups.

Other criticisms of disengagement theory have commented on the logical weakness of the theory and on the methodology used to test the theory (Passuth and Bengtson, 1988: 336–7; Achenbaum and Bengtson, 1994; Hendricks, 1994; Marshall, 1994). Most of the studies have been cross-sectional, and there has been no attempt to distinguish between age effects and cohort effects. And the theory has been tested mainly from the perspective of the individual, rather than from that of the society. In addition, chronological age has been used as the major independent variable, when, in fact, failing health, perceived imminence of death, or economic hardship may lead to disengagement. Other criticisms are that disengagement has been variously interpreted to imply isolation, loneliness, or passivity and that disengagement has been interpreted as the opposite of activity, when, in fact, an individual can be disengaged but still be active in a number of smaller roles or activities. Finally, disengagement theory, as originally proposed, did not examine the importance of psychological commitment to, or the meaning of involvement in, social interaction. The conscious thoughts and feelings of individuals about aging have seldom been considered as factors in whether disengagement occurs or not.

In summary, there is little research evidence to support the idea that decreased role involvement and social interaction are universal and inevitable processes. Nor is there evidence that this decreased interaction or disengagement is related to higher levels of life satisfaction or morale. Nevertheless, the 'concept' of disengagement, more than the 'theory' of disengagement, may be useful in explaining individual behaviour rather than universal, inevitable behaviour. For example, older people in poor health have less opportunity to be engaged in social roles and may consciously narrow their social world by withdrawing from social roles (Johnson and Baier, 1992). While some older individuals disengage, others remain highly active. Whether, why, and to what extent these two patterns lead to more or less life satisfaction is not understood. In all likelihood, the way in which an individual adapts in the later years may be related to maintaining role flexibility. That is, some roles and activities are continued, some are discontinued, some are intensified, some are reduced, and some are begun for the first time. In order for aging individuals to achieve this role flexibility, a combination of structural disengagement from work or organizations and the adoption of new forms of social interaction may be more typical of modern life in the later years, especially for the more advantaged members of society.

Continuity Theory

This theory argues that as people age, they strive to maintain continuity in their lifestyle. Indeed, there are pressures within society to seek and maintain continuity in lifestyles, role relationships, and activities throughout one's life. This theory argues that people adapt more easily to aging if they maintain a lifestyle similar to that developed in the early and middle years (Atchley, 1971, 1989). Thus, it may be unreasonable to expect that a person who has always preferred solitary activities will adjust to retirement by becoming more socially active, joining voluntary associations, or taking a trip with a tour group. Similarly, a person who has led an active life will not likely disengage unless there is a strong reason for doing so, such as failing health.

At first, continuity theorists ignored the possible effect on behaviour of such societal factors as social change in cultural values and modern-ization, and the possibility of acculturation by immigrants. In reality, aging involves both continuity and change. Continuity does not imply an absence of change. Rather, maintaining continuity involves adapting to both internal changes (i.e., in attitudes, values, beliefs, temperament, and identity) and external changes (i.e., in role relationships, activities, and the environment) and coping with discontinuity because of illness, disability, role loss, or loss of skills.

Age Stratification—The Aging and Society Paradigm.[7]

This model of aging has evolved over a 30-year period from a static to a dynamic view of aging, with new concepts being added as further knowledge about aging processes emerged.[8] This approach was developed to link people's lives with social structures[9] as aging processes evolve across the life course (Riley, 1971, 1985, 1994; Riley et al., 1972, 1999). More specifically, Riley et al. (1999: 327) argued that 'the paradigm is a conceptual framework, or approach, for designing and interpreting studies of age and illuminating the place of age in both lives (as people age) and the surrounding social structures. . . . Changes in people's lives influence and are influenced by changes in social structures and institutions. These reciprocal relationships are linked to the meanings of age, which vary over time.'

According to this theory of aging, society is segregated by age, and the common example given by Riley and her colleagues was that there were three main age strata, each with a specific purpose: childhood and adolescence for education; young and middle adulthood for work; and the later years for retirement and leisure (see Figure 6.1, p. 183). Through a process of role allocation or age grading, individuals gain access to social roles on the basis of chronological, legal, or social age. Age is a criterion for entry into, and exit from, many social roles. However, such an age-related status system can lead to inequality since the right to work is severely limited before the age of 16 or 18 and after age 65. In this model, structures and institutions provide opportunities and barriers at particular ages in people's lives, and tend to force people to interact primarily with those in the same age stratum. In the early static stages of developing the theory, human agency was ignored, and it was assumed that individuals passively accept and adhere to social norms based on age. Hence, conflict between the age strata was not likely.

In the second phase of development, Riley and others recognized that cohort differences arise when cohorts born at different times experience a different life course as societal changes occur in values, economic and educational opportunities, and in the use of technology. That is, the lives of those who are older today (your grandparents) are not the same as the lives of those who were older 30 years ago (your great-grandparents) or those who will be older in 20 years (your parents) or in 40 years (your own cohort). The process of **cohort flow** and succession (Riley, 1973) was introduced to account for the aging of cohorts in a dynamic world characterized by social, economic, political, and structural changes. These changes may or may not have an influence on specific age cohorts.

These interdependent changes in people's lives, and in structures and institutions pertaining to age norms for social behaviour and the allocation of social roles, changed our thinking from a society that is age-segregated to one that is age-integrated. Highlight 5.1 illustrates one example of a change in age-based norms concerning both the pursuit of formal education and interaction among diverse age cohorts.

A third stage of development moved the age-stratification model beyond a consideration of only age stratification to a consideration of other structural elements in a society. One of the early criticisms of age-stratification theory was not only that it ignored the possibility of conflict between age strata, but that it failed to account for the interaction of age with other social categories—such as race, ethnicity, gender and social class—that could also produce conflict within or across

age cohorts. Age conflicts occur when members of subsequent birth cohorts have different opportunities, such as more formal education; different attitudes, for example about equality in society; and different beliefs, such as whether women should pursue careers. These beliefs arise when unique social and historical experiences suggest that resources, rewards, and social roles should be allocated in different ways. If an age-stratum consciousness develops, a cohort interprets events through its own unique experiences, thereby generating a cohort-centric view of the world. Cohort-centrism makes it difficult to understand or accept the views of other cohorts, and the possibility of resolving differences becomes more difficult. Thus, age-cohort conflict may emerge over differing values, beliefs, experiences, or interests.

Similarly, within age cohorts and across age cohorts, social differentiation by class, gender, race, or ethnic background may lead to cohort conflict or social change. To illustrate, the counterculture movement of the 1960s involved primarily middle- or upper-middle-class university students in their late teens or early 20s. This generational unit rebelled against the middle-aged and older cohorts of society, which they believed held too much economic and political power.

But age strata interact with other elements of social stratification to initiate change across society. For example, cohort norms and age meanings change across the life course, and within many age cohorts, as a result of new social movements such as the women's movement, which has changed gender roles in an attempt to eliminate inequalities based on gender. This continuous process of cohort norm formation involves 'behaviours and attitudes that develop within a cohort in response to social change, and they become crystallized as new norms or ideologies—new meanings—that then pervade and influence all age strata and social structures' (Riley et al., 1999: 339).

Another development in the third stage of the evolution of this theory was the recognition that age-based changes in individual lives and in

Highlight 5.1 It Is Never Too Late

The first day of classes our professor challenged us to get to know someone we didn't already know. As I stood up to look around, a gentle hand touched my shoulder. I turned around to find a wrinkled little old lady beaming up at me with a smile that lit up her entire being. She said, 'Hi handsome. My name is Rose. I'm eighty-seven years old. Can I give you a hug?' I laughed and enthusiastically responded, 'Of course you may!' and she gave me a giant squeeze. 'Why are you in college at such a young, innocent age?' I asked. She jokingly replied, 'I'm here to meet a rich husband, get married, have a couple of children, and then retire and travel.' 'No, seriously', I asked. I was curious as to what may have motivated her to be taking on this challenge at her age. 'I always dreamed of having a college education and now I'm getting one!' she told me.

After class we walked to the student union building and shared a chocolate milkshake. We became instant friends. Every day for the next three months we would leave class together and talk nonstop. I was always mesmerized listening to this 'time machine' as she shared her wisdom and experience with me. Over the course of the year, Rose became a campus icon and easily made friends wherever she went. She loved to dress up and she reveled in the attention bestowed upon her from the other students. She was living it up.

At the end of the semester we invited Rose to speak at our football banquet, and I'll never forget what she taught us. As she began to deliver her prepared speech, she dropped her three by five cards on the floor. Frustrated and a little embarrassed, she leaned into the microphone and simply said 'I'm sorry I'm so jittery. I gave up beer for Lent and this whiskey is killing me! I'll never get my speech back in order so let me just tell you what I know.' As we laughed, she cleared her throat and began: 'We do not stop playing because we are old; we grow old because we stop playing. There are only four secrets to staying young, being happy, and achieving success. You have to laugh and find humor every day. You have to have a dream. When you lose your dreams, you die. We have so many people walking around who are dead and don't even know it! There is a huge difference between growing older and growing up. If you are nineteen years old and lie in bed for one full year and don't do one productive thing, you will turn twenty years old. If I am eighty-seven years old and stay in bed for a year and never do anything I will turn eighty-eight. Anybody can grow older. That doesn't take any talent or ability. The idea is to grow up by always finding the opportunity in change. Have no regrets. The elderly usually don't have regrets for what we did, but rather for things we did not do. The only people who fear death are those with regrets.' She concluded her speech by singing 'The Rose.' She challenged each of us to study the lyrics and live them out in our daily lives.

At the term's end, Rose finished the college degree she had begun all those years ago. One week after graduation Rose died peacefully in her sleep. Over two thousand college students attended her funeral in tribute to the wonderful woman who taught by example that it's never too late to be all you can possibly be.

Source: www.geocities.com/koalagrey_au/never.html. Accessed 30 March 2000.

social structures do not occur simultaneously. There are differences in timing. This asychrony creates 'imbalances between what people of given ages need and expect in their lives and what the social structures have to offer. These imbalances exert strains on both the people and the social institutions involved, creating pressures for further change' (Riley et al., 1999: 336). Most of this imbalance is at the social structural level and is known as 'structural lag' (Riley et al., 1994). For example, women seeking careers and career advancement may find that economic institutions block their opportunities or cannot create enough opportunities to meet individual needs. Or with rapid population aging, sufficient community services and institutional facilities cannot be provided to meet the needs of the increasing number of older people who are no longer able to live independently in their homes. Imbalances created by structural lag, once recognized, become a stimulus for further and faster change to improve the connection or restore the balance between individual lives and social structures.

The Political Economy of Aging

To understand the status of older people in a modern welfare state, researchers study the social institutions, structures, and processes that influence the meaning and experiences of aging and that contribute to inequality in later life.[10] According to this view, politics and economics, not demography (demography is not destiny), determine how old age is constructed and valued in a society. This theory argues that the onset of dependency and a diminished social status and self-esteem in the later years are an outcome, not of biological deterioration, but of public policies, economic trends, and changing social structures, which result in the unequal distribution of society's resources. A core assumption is that the social construction of old age is a product of public policy and that public policies concerning retirement income (that is, pensions), health care, and social services are an outcome of power relations and social struggles within political institutions.

According to Estes (1991: 31), a political-economy approach to aging is based on the following premises:

- The social structure shapes how older individuals are viewed and how they view themselves, thereby affecting their sense of worth and power.
- Labels such as 'the elderly' or 'seniors' shape not only the experience of old age, but also society's decisions concerning public policy.

- Social policy and the politics of aging mirror both the inequalities in a social structure and the outcomes of power struggles that emerge because of structural factors, such as gender, class, and racial stratification. Thus, social policy is an outcome of the perceived advantages and disadvantages, experienced variously by those representing capital and labour, by whites and non-whites, and by men and women.
- Social policy embodies the dominant ideologies and beliefs that enforce, support, and extend the advantages or disadvantages in the larger economic, political, and social order.

This approach links the structural and personal aspects of aging, and it has been effective in studying such aging issues as the following:

- the amount and type of public expenditure required by retired people for health care, pensions, housing, and home care
- the social, political, economic, and legal rights of older people
- how population aging changes the distribution of public funds, sometimes creating a heavy public debt for later generations
- the issue of voluntary versus mandatory retirement
- the differentiation of the industrial sector of a nation into a core and a peripheral sector in which different conditions for employers and workers influence the experience of older workers and their patterns of retirement (see Highlight 5.2)
- equal pension accessibility
- age-restrictive policies that marginalize older workers in the labour force or exclude them from the labour force.

Another assumption of the political-economy perspective is that older people, as an age group,

Highlight 5.2 Retirement in Canada: A Political Economy Perspective

The political economy perspective, with its emphasis on structural, socioeconomic, and political processes, adds a further dimension to the more traditional micro explanations of retirement patterns and adjustments (see Chapter 9). The traditional view of retirement, in which people are individually responsible for maintaining their lifestyle and economic status in later life, is being challenged by proponents of the political economy perspective. According to this perspective, when people are forced to retire and accept a pension as a reward, they begin to occupy a marginal and dependent position in society. The political economy perspective argues that individuals are not responsible for retirement policies that force them to leave the labour force, or for the inflation that erodes their pension savings. Rather, public policies are responsible for changing their status from worker to retiree.

The labour force is often divided, conceptually, into two main sectors (core and peripheral), which creates disparity in wages, varying patterns of employment, and unequal fringe and pension benefits. McDonald and Wanner (1987, 1990) found that men employed in the core sector (manufacturing and construction) had better career opportunities, higher wages, and were more likely to retire early and receive a private pension than men employed in the peripheral sector (agriculture, retail sales, and self-employed). Core sector employees were less likely to need Guaranteed Income Supplement (GIS) payments. These results also applied to women employed in the core sector, although more women who had been employed in this sector received GIS payments. In addition, more women than men in the core sector continued working past 65 years of age. McDonald and Wanner argue that the dual structure of Canada's economy influences when, and with what resources, an individual will retire.

Source: Adapted from McDonald and Wanner (1987, 1990).

are impoverished and lack power. Yet this view conflicts with the experiences and feelings reported by many older people. Like other perspectives, this macro-level approach to the study of aging must be integrated with micro-level approaches to account for the variety of individual and cohort aging experiences in modern industrialized societies (Passuth and Bengtson, 1988: 344). In effect, the political economy perspective illustrates how private troubles become public issues, and how public issues create private troubles. To understand whether public policy reduces, removes, or increases social inequalities in later life, we must consider the interaction of age, gender, and race, all of which intersect across social classes. Some social welfare policies and programs have the potential to reinforce gender, age, and racial stratification, thereby reproducing inequality across the life course, or introducing unequal experiences and opportunities in later life. Thus, this perspective on aging phenomena must be used in conjunction with a life-course and historical perspective for individuals and cohorts who live their lives within a specific but changing, political, social and economic context.

Critical Gerontology

This theory emerged when scholars[11] began to question the assumptions of much of the social gerontology research of the 1970s and 1980s, especially the ideas based on essentialism—a position that seeks a universal, single, or multiple cause for some social phenomenon (Laws, 1995). Critical theorists critique the prevailing ideology and social order. They challenge the status quo, including prevailing myths and assumptions about pervasive and unacceptable social conditions, and the hidden interests and goals of power groups. This approach involves praxis— active involvement in understanding and changing the social construction or meaning of everyday life. To critical theorists, the search for causes of a social phenomenon ignores the complexity of our daily lives, which are lived in unique historical, social, cultural, and geographical circumstances. This approach, which views aging as a socially constructed dialectical process involving the individual and society, seeks to empower older people and to emancipate them from all forms of economic and social domination and discrimination.

Baars (1991) defined critical gerontology as 'a collection of questions, problems and analyses that have been excluded by established (mainstream) gerontologists'. Some examples of questions that critical gerontologists have addressed are the role of the state in the management of later life; the purpose and meaning of old age and growing old; the meaning and outcome of the lack of power in later life among disadvantaged members of society, and the inequities in later life around the world in access to health care, technology, and wealth. By questioning and analyzing the historical and cultural forces that underlie social phenomena, critical gerontology focuses on either the humanistic dimensions, that is, the meanings in the everyday life of older people, or the structural components of aging, that is, the emancipation and empowerment of older people.

Much of the early thinking and research in gerontology emphasized the views of white, urban-dwelling, middle- and upper-class older people, primarily men. Critical gerontology, like many of the more recent perspectives, tries to be inclusive and emphasizes the experiences of older people who are underrepresented or disadvantaged within a number of social institutions, including the labour force and leisure activities; who need supportive housing, health care, and social services; and who live in developing rather than developed countries. This critical approach has generated knowledge of what it means to grow old within specific class, gender, racial, and ethnic boundaries, as well as how to empower older people to improve their lives. For example, Calasanti (1996) stressed that the 'voices' of retirees whose power in social relations is reduced because of race, ethnicity, gender, or class must be included in our research and policy agendas. She argued that a more inclusive approach to the study of aging phenomena enables us to understand that aging experiences are fluid, contextual, dialectical, and changeable through human agency and political action. Moreover, to allow the views of advantaged groups to be seen as the ideal norm and as the basis of policies and programs presents a distorted image of the lives of *all* older people in a community or society.

Research Methods: The Search for Answers

The Link between Theory and Research

To advance our understanding of aging phenomena, previous sections introduced a number of concepts, theories, and perspectives. But theories alone cannot guarantee that we will understand social reality. Rather, research is needed so that we can discover, describe, explain, and interpret facts, patterns, and relationships that we observe our social world.

Philosophers of science have often debated which comes first: theory or research. While there is no agreement on this question, there is agreement that *both* theory and research are essential components of scholarly inquiry and that they are linked in a creative dialectical process. The nature and importance of this link was summarized by the social theorist, Derek Layder (1994: vi), who wrote:

> My guiding assumption is that theory is never completely isolated from problems of empirical research, any more than empirical

research is free from theoretical assumptions. The really interesting questions concern the nature of the relations between theory and empirical research and not whether either domain has some divinely given priority.

Theory suggests ideas, provides concepts, and helps to explain and interpret observations. Research discovers and identifies facts, patterns, and meanings, and it attempts to provide explanations and interpretations for situations or events in our social world. Research refutes or supports theories and perspectives; initiates the revision of existing theories or perspectives; or leads to the construction of new theories and perspectives that will help us more fully understand and interpret social phenomena. In practice, most scholars employ a composite approach: observations, surveys, interviews, and textual analyses begin after some preliminary theoretical work; and theory construction and revision do not proceed too far without testing the linked ideas or concepts through some type of research.

Many critics argue that much research in the social sciences and in social gerontology is 'theoretically sterile' (George, 1995), 'atheoretical', and mainly descriptive. As Featherstone and Wernick (1995: 1) warned, we must avoid an approach to generating knowledge that is 'data rich and theory poor.' Therefore, as you read articles, books, or reports about aging phenomena, question the content and completeness of the theories and theoretical perspectives; critique the research methods upon which conclusions are based; and search for explanations and interpretations rather than mere description about the problem or issue. Above all, strive in your own thinking and actions to incorporate a theoretical approach and to expect or demand explanations and interpretations for the phenomena you observe.

The Research Process

Research 'matters' because it is an essential part of the development and advancement of knowledge-based societies. Research is a way of knowing and understanding our social world and of verifying the reality of what we observe in everyday life. Research can be 'curiosity-driven' by scholars who, as specialists on a topic, have an innate need to know more about the topic without any immediate practical applications. Or it can be more 'applied' or practical when it is undertaken to evaluate service programs or to evaluate and change current policy (Martin Matthews and Gee, 1997). 'Action' research is undertaken to change and improve the situation of people living in particular circumstances, such as elderly people who are homeless, poor, or living in inadequate housing. Such action research often leads to changes in programs or policies (McWilliam, 1997) that can improve the lives of older people.

Research agendas, whether created by scholars, practitioners, or policy-makers, influence the research questions that are asked, or not asked, and influence how findings and observations are interpreted (Connidis et al., 2000). In order to advance knowledge, an integrated research agenda, involving many theoretical perspectives, disciplines and research methods is employed. Figure 5.2 illustrates an intellectual framework developed by the Canadian Institutes of Health Research to guide health research on topics related to four primary research sectors. To illustrate, when the intellectual framework is applied to aging research, the horizontal axis represents a continuum of research from the cellular and molecular level, namely, biology and genetics, to the community or population level, that is, history, demography, epidemiology, sociology, and economics. The vertical axis represents a range of different types of research from basic, that is, research in chemistry or biology, to applied, such as program evaluation, clinical procedures and practices, and public-policy analysis.

The Selection of Research Methods

Selecting which research method or methods to use in a study is guided by the research question

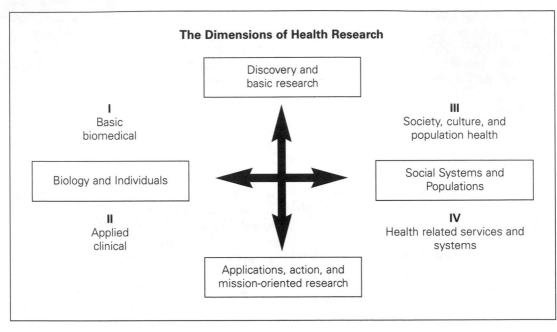

Figure 5.2 A Model to Guide Research

Source: Halliwell and Lomas (1999). Reprinted with permission.

to be answered. A decision to ask a specific question or to study a particular setting is influenced by observations of everyday life, reviews of the literature, or critical analyses of a program and policy. Once a question is asked or a gap in knowledge is identified, the creative insight of a scholar frames the question within some theoretical perspective and selects a method or methods. For example, a sociologist interested in understanding how women adapt to widowhood is unlikely to study such factors as colour of eyes, maiden name, or whether her sign of the zodiac is Pisces or Scorpio. Rather, drawing on accumulated knowledge in the literature about widowhood, plus everyday observations of, or reports by, widows, the researcher designs a study that may include such factors as a widow's income, education, ethnicity, perceived health, number and location of friends and children, and history of participation in the labour force.

Many different research methods can be employed to study aging processes and older people. Often, they are classified as 'qualitative' (based on observations, open-ended interviews, or analyses of textual material to interpret the meanings of what people say, do, or think) or 'quantitative' (based on surveys or analyses of existing data to generate numerical data from which conclusions are derived). In the early years of research on aging topics, quantitative methods dominated. More recently, qualitative methods or a combination of both approaches is more common because more complete knowledge about the same individuals or groups can be provided over time (Martin Matthews, 1995; Cutler and Schaie, 2001; Singer and Ryff, 2001; Krause, 2002). Singer and Ryff (2001) argue that the blending of 'numbers' from quantitative research and 'narratives' from qualitative research enables us to more fully understand life histories, aging processes, and older people. A specific method may be more suitable at one stage or level of research—for example, qualitative methods for understanding at the individual level, and quantitative methods for understanding at the societal level. The advantages of a multi-method approach are illustrated in an early, creative, ground-breaking study of social isolation among residents of a nursing home (Marshall, 1981). Whether and why a resident was isolated, or not, within the home was determined through *observations* about how frequently he or she visited public places in the home; *interviews* to determine the person's social interaction with the residents and staff; and *analyses* of daily staff reports about the frequency and type of social interaction for each resident.

Qualitative and Quantitative Research: Toward a Synergy

As interpretive theoretical approaches emerged, new methods of inquiry were needed to answer questions posed by scholars employing these perspectives. To answer their questions, qualitative researchers enter a natural, real setting, such as a retirement home, or study a unique social group, such as older gays or lesbians. They observe, listen, ask questions, or examine documents. The preferred methods of qualitative research are the following:

- ethnography, which describes a culture and the meaning of behaviour in a cultural context, such as a nursing home or a Chinatown

- grounded theory, where the goal is to develop a theory inductively and 'ground' it in evidence collected through direct observations, interviews, or textual material

- phenomenology, where in-depth interviews identify the essence and meaning of lived

experiences (Cobb and Forbes, 2002: M198–9).

The goal of qualitative, interpretive researchers is to understand, as fully as possible, how people in a specific situation or group view and experience their social world. This approach is particularly useful for examining the 'quality' and meaning of social interactions or of later life in general. Through an analysis of letters, diaries, interviews, reports, or what is said or done in the setting, the process of research systematically searches for, and interprets, the meanings of the situation from the perspective of the participants. Then, the process involves searching for and interpreting commonalities, diversity, and variations in the experiences and meanings of aging, of being old in a particular environment, or of having certain characteristics, including class, race, ethnicity, sexual orientation, or state of health, that influence meanings and opportunities in later life.

The quantitative researcher, who is often quite remote from his or her 'respondents' (they may never meet face-to-face), employs statistical analyses; the qualitative researcher, on the other hand, interacts directly with the 'informants', and analyzes and interprets their words, symbols, experiences, beliefs, and actions in the context of their social setting. Thus, whereas research reports based on quantitative studies contain graphs, tables, and figures, reports by qualitative researchers contain many quotations that reflect the voices of older adults. Finally, there are also differences in how the two types of research are evaluated and assessed as contributions to knowledge. For quantitative research, the criteria for evaluation are internal and external validity, reliability, generalizability, and objectivity. For qualitative research, the evaluation criteria are credibility, transferability, dependability, and confirmability (Lincoln and Guba, 1985; Cobb and Forbes, 2002). But for both types, the main criterion is whether we understand the phenomenon more completely and accurately as a result of the research.

Types of Research Methods

Secondary Analysis of Data Sets

In secondary analysis, the researcher, to answer emerging research questions, re-analyzes data sets, such as surveys or a census, that were collected at an earlier time and often for some other purpose. The goal may be to answer new research questions, to analyze data that were not used when the original study was completed, or to study changes by comparing earlier data with current data. A serious weakness of secondary data analyses is that the data set may lack essential independent or control variables that could provide a more complete and valid explanation for any age differences or age changes that are discovered.

Secondary Analysis of Textual Materials

In this method, the researcher analyzes textual material such as diaries, letters, photographs, films, biographies, or newspapers for qualitative themes to understand a social phenomenon. Highlight 5.3 illustrates how an analysis of letters to and from family members were used to understand family ties at an earlier period in history.

Historical and Literary Methods

These methods are used to describe and analyze an individual, setting, or issue over a period of years, to understand a process or event of everyday life in an earlier period or in another society, or to develop case studies or biographies of aging individuals or institutions across their life course. This time-consuming method involves detailed

---

Highlight 5.3 A Content Analysis of Letters Exchanged within a Mennonite Family, 1877–1912

Using a life-course perspective on aging and family relationships, Quadagno and Janzen (1987) analyzed the role of religious and ethnic traditions in preserving family stability, in providing support and security in old age, and in shaping the life course of descendants. Based on an analysis of a series of letters written between an eldest son and his parents, from 1877 until 1912 when the father died, the authors reconstructed the life course for two generations of a Mennonite family who migrated from Russia to the Kansas plains in 1874. The letters, stored in a Mennonite library in North Newton, Kansas, recorded family events and crises, community events, and Mennonite beliefs. Any gaps in the correspondence were filled in by examining land transaction records, birth and death records, and census records.

The authors found that, because of a strong belief in family support and the traditional Mennonite pattern of inheritance, accumulated property or wealth was transferred fairly to offspring. In return, children provided considerable social support to the parents. Through a content analysis of letters stored in a library, we learn how traditional values and practices brought from Russia were handed down from one generation to the next. At the same time, we learn that as social, political, and economic conditions changed over a 34-year period in the U.S. midwest, some of the traditional patterns of inheritance and family support were altered because of the mobility and changing needs of the offspring. Had only quantitative data been available (place of residence of each son and daughter, marital and occupational status of the children), the actual amount of family support and the feelings expressed toward parents and offspring would not have been known. However, a qualitative analysis—an examination of the content of the family letters in detail—captured the strength and meaning of family support as it evolved over three decades.

Source: Summarized from Quadagno and Janzen (1987).

interviews with older respondents about their life course; an examination and interpretation of relevant personal documents such as photos, letters, and diaries; and interviews with relatives and other significant others in their life. Similarly, literary and discourse scholars in cultural studies and in aging studies[12] analyze books, poems, plays, and letters to discover meanings about aging and being old, about attitudes toward older people, and about social relationships in later life, for example, between older parents and their adult children.

Narrative Gerontology

Both a method and a way of thinking about and studying aging processes, narrative gerontology assumes we are biographical beings with stories to tell and that in the process we become the stories.[13] The stories told by individuals function as a lens through which continuities and discontinuities, transition points, crises, and the meaning of those events in our lives are revealed 'from the inside' (Kenyon and Randall, 1999). Advocates of this method often justify such an approach to understanding phenomena with the phrase 'we are biographical as well as biological entities'. Narrative gerontology considers human agency to be important in our lives but stresses that 'when we are told a tale, we do not necessarily have to believe it' (Biggs, 2001: 315). That is, narrative gerontologists must tease out the truth in the stories they are told. One weakness of this method is that it may not work with people who are very reserved or who are not very articulate, not highly educated, or not very fluent in English. Highlight 5.4 illustrates how the biographical method interprets the broader context of a person's life by understanding the meaning of physical activity in an older woman's life.

Survey Research

This method, which uses random or restricted samples, employs face-to-face or telephone interviews or questionnaires that are mailed or deliv-

---

Highlight 5.4 A Narrative Approach to Understanding Physical Activity Involvement in Later Life

To understand the meaning of physical activity as a leisure or social activity in later life, Grant (1999) used a life history approach, based on the interpretive perspective, to get 'inside' the concept of active aging, as expressed by those living this type of lifestyle. Through interviews he reconstructed their sport and physical activity experiences and the role of physical activity in the lives of older adults across the life course. Then, these biographical narratives were placed within the broader social context of an older person's social world (see paragraph one below). Based on interviews with Beryl, a 78 year old, we learn that her experiences with active aging in later life were not due to any single set of determinants. As you read the thoughts expressed below by Beryl, Grant suggests that you try to 'identify some experiences that have been influential in shaping how she makes meaning about the role of physical activity in her world.'

- Monday morning was washing day. I used to chop wood to heat the water to do the washing. The clothes were boiled, put in a tub of rinsing water, then put through the wringer. Then they were hung on the line . . . Then the ironing would start and that took time. So that was Monday gone. Tuesday was similar but another routine and so the week went. Different chores but very busy. Of course it was also my job to organize the kids and be responsible for all the meals. I had many years of that lifestyle. It was all I knew and compared to others I thought I had a great life. But when I look back . . . well it's hard to imagine how I coped.

continued

Hightlight 5.4 continued

- For years Roy and I used to play bowls at the same club and I loved it, we had lots of fun. However, a few years ago, after he died, I had my left hip done [replaced] and couldn't play like I used to. I got so frustrated that I eventually stopped playing. . . . As you can imagine I was a bit low for a few years, quite lonely . . . didn't really do anything at all. Had to get some help from the hospital but I'm fine now. I still get a bit down.

- It was during one of those lonely moments when self pity takes over that I decided life needed to change. I used to just sit around, it wasn't me. . . . I needed a thrill in my life, take a risk; I wanted to do something different. So I arranged to go sky diving, you know, strapped to the instructor. My friends thought I had lost my marbles, but the doctor gave me a clearance, probably wanted to get rid of me . . . What an amazing experience, such a beautiful feeling, just floating along like a bird.

- After sky diving I got a new lease on life, that was about 4 or 5 years ago, and realized I could do things if I was determined. I joined a dancing group, although I hadn't danced since probably my daughters' wedding back in the mid 60's. I also signed up for a plant propagation course and played around with that for a while, but it was too complex. Recently I went to a daytime class on interior designing because I wanted to paint the bathroom. But you know what surprised me the most? On my walk one damp morning, I popped into the local gym. I'm still not sure why, maybe it was to get dry or the weird music aroused my curiosity. I had sometimes seen others about my age going in there and wondered what they did. After a tour of the place and a chat I signed up. It didn't cost much for an oldie!

- On my next visit they took my blood pressure and I was asked to fill out a card about do I smoke, have stress, and that sort of stuff. They also gave me a few pamphlets to read about blood pressure, osteoporosis, and some stretching exercises to do at home . . . never do them. I told them not to worry about my health, as the doctor said I was fine. . . . It was strange at first. I mean there was the clothing, difficult for an old girl to change her habits. When I'm there I just love playing around on the rowing machine. They [instructors] know me now and just leave me to myself. It's funny though because even after a couple of years my friends still don't understand why I bother going and I don't understand why they don't want to go.

- I was 75 when I started doing most of those things. I think I found a new freedom. You know, sometimes I can hardly believe myself. Up until a few years ago I would have shied away from all this. But now I feel like a flower that's about to bloom. Roy would be so proud of me.

Source: Adapted from Grant (1999) and Grant and O'Brien-Cousins (2001).

ered to a respondent. Survey research is conducted for the following reasons:

- To describe or discover social facts, such as the number of widows over 70 years of age who live below the poverty line.

- To discover whether a relationship exists between variables, such as between chrono-logical age and voting behaviour in a local election

- To determine attitudes, beliefs, or behaviour before and after specific events. For example a questionnaire or interview with people shortly after they retire might be repeated one year or five years later to discover whether their attitudes or behaviour has changed.

A major advantage of survey research is that information is collected from small samples that represent much larger populations. However, this method can be very expensive and time-consuming, especially if every respondent has to be interviewed. If a survey involves a mailed questionnaire, it is less expensive than personal interviews, but researchers are unable to probe and obtain a more detailed interpretation of what is meant by a particular answer to a question. Nor can it be determined whether a respondent understood every question in the survey.

There are also a number of disadvantages or limitations when surveys are used with older respondents. For example, older people are more likely to agree than disagree with some statements; to use a small proportion of the response categories on a five- or seven-point scale; to use extreme response categories (high or low); or to give the same answer to all the questions in a set of questions that have similar response categories. The reason may be fatigue in the case of long questionnaires or interviews, declining health, lack of experience with multiple-choice questions, or a desire to be viewed as co-operative. Older respondents are also less likely to answer questions about income or savings, death, personal health problems, or sexual matters, all of which they view as private and confidential matters (Martin Matthews et al., 1991). However, this may be a cohort effect that will dissipate as succeeding age cohorts move into the later years.

Participant Observation

In this method, scholars observe, or interact with, individuals as they carry out everyday living in one or more natural social settings over a period of time. This method is most commonly employed to understand the meanings and context of aging in a special setting, such as a retirement home or community, or a senior citizen centre. In some studies, the researcher's role is not disclosed to the people being studied until after the project is completed. This unobtrusive

approach may prevent the subjects from behaving unnaturally or misrepresenting information. In other studies, a researcher's identity is disclosed, and he or she participates, often as a regular member of the staff, such as by leading an exercise class or serving as a volunteer or as a passive but visible observer. Participant observation enables a researcher to

- obtain information about specific cultural or subcultural environments;
- understand the nature, quality, and meaning of social interactions, not just their frequency;
- study topics where direct questions or measurements are not possible;
- study phenomena about which informants or respondents may be unwilling or unable to report accurately; and
- adapt and change the design or emphasis of the study as the research progresses.

The main limitations of this method are that (1) often it does not use standardized instruments, such as a questionnaire or interview schedule, consequently, other scholars will find it difficult to repeat the study; (2) it is very time-consuming; (3) the sample is small and may not be representative of the situation in another similar setting (Luborsky and Rubinstein, 1995); and (4) the participant observer must be highly skilled in observation, conversation, listening, analysis, and interpretion. Moreover, these studies are seldom replicated in similar settings to verify that the interpretations of thoughts and behaviours are typical and representative of the phenomenon in question.

Evaluation and Intervention Research

This method is a form of applied research that evaluates or provides feedback about the effectiveness of a specific program, policy, or service. This type of research is increasing because policymakers are under growing pressure to use public funds efficiently and fairly. And with the aging of the population, it is essential to know which policies and programs are effective, why they work, with whom they work, and where they work best (Pillemar et al., 2003: 5). This type of research is used to make informed decisions about whether or not specific programs or policies should be changed, continued, or eliminated when budget cuts are required. However, sometimes such evaluations are funded by an agency that has an interest in either terminating or continuing a policy or program. Thus, we must be alert to possible hidden agendas when program or policy evaluations are commissioned.

Evaluation research is conducted for the following purposes:

- to assess needs before a policy or program is started

- to determine whether any progress has been made toward a specific goal, such as greater independence or well-being among older residents or participants

- to measure if and how a program's objectives have been attained, if a policy is effective, or if an intervention has been successful

- to measure the cost-effectiveness at any stage of a program or policy after it has begun

- to identify gaps or inequities in existing policies or programs.

Evaluation research can alert us to social change and to the diverse needs of different age cohorts. For example, an intervention program designed to address the transportation needs of urban residents over 60 years of age living in the central core of the city in 2004 may be totally inadequate to meet the needs of the same age group who live in the suburbs of the same city.

Cross-National Research

A comparison of cultures, social structures, policies, statistical data, or individual characteristics in different countries is a useful way to discover and understand differences and similarities among older people throughout the world. Cross-national research provides a comparison of where we stand in comparison to other social systems, and it enables us to acquire new ideas from countries where some aging issues we will encounter in the future have already been addressed. To provide valid, reliable, and useful comparative knowledge, this type of research, using any of the methods described above, must employ common concepts, definitions, measurements, and language in the collection of data or in the observations made in each country. In aging research, cross-national comparative research has studied similarities and differences in cultural characteristics; work and retirement patterns; private savings and wealth; family, work, and leisure structures; inter-generational transfers of wealth; health and disability statistics; and general well-being in later life (National Research Council, 2001).

Methodological Issues in Aging Research

The Interpretation of Data and Observations

The production of new knowledge involves not only asking 'relevant' and 'interesting' questions, but also answering the research questions with the proper procedures. The interpretation or explanation of observations must be valid and not extend beyond the information provided by the data or the observations. Most aging research examines differences among age groups on one or more characteristics; changes in meaning, behaviour, status, or lifestyle within age groups or individuals as they pass through various stages of life; or the past or present situation of those in a specific age cohort or setting. Social scientists, and you as readers of their work, must conclude whether the research findings are due to aging effects, cohort differences, or period effects, that is, the influence of historical or societal events. As noted earlier, aging does not occur in a vacuum. Therefore, as we seek to explain and interpret the results of a specific research study, we must consider the possible influence of historical events, cultural factors, and social, structural, and environmental circumstances.

Aging varies within and among individuals, cohorts, and cultures. To understand *why*, universal processes of aging must be separated from culture-specific processes. For example, there are different conceptual and methodological issues to consider when research is conducted in a rural environment rather than a large urban community. (What is the definition of rural? How long have the respondents lived in the rural setting?) Moreover, the heterogeneity within an ethnic or racial group by class, gender, income, or education must be recognized. Similarly, it is a major conceptual error to classify all older people in Canada who come from mainland China, Hong Kong, Vietnam, southeast Asia, or Korea as 'Asian'. Similarly, not all older Aboriginal people have common backgrounds, values, or experiences. Such labels mistakenly imply that those with the same label have had the same kind of common cultural and lifelong experiences.

Issues in Quantitative Research Designs

Cross-Sectional Designs: Identifying Age Differences

A cross-sectional design involves recording observations or responses of individuals at different ages at one point in time and reporting the results for each age group. For example, the results of a descriptive study of the relationship between age and attendance at movies in 2004 might be reported as in Table 5.1.[14] While a quick reading of this table might lead to the conclusion that movie attendance declines with age, the method of collecting data means that we can not conclude that the differences between age groups are due to growing old, that is, to an aging effect. Rather, we can only conclude that at one point in history (in 2004) there were *age differences* in the frequency of movie attendance. The table shows that younger age cohorts are more likely to attend movies three or more times a year. Depending on the questions asked, it is often possible to identi-

Table 5.1 A Cross-Sectional Design: Age and Movie Attendance, 2004

Age	% of Those Who Attended Movies Three Times or More per Year in 2004		
	Males and Females	Males	Females
14–19	58	65	52
20–24	54	62	50
25–34	45	52	39
35–44	33	41	25
45–54	20	31	14
55–64	15	20	10
65–74	11	19	9
75 and over	8	12	6

Note: The data reported here are hypothetical.

fy variations *within* age groups that are significantly different than those *between* age groups. For example, Table 5.1 shows that males of all ages attend movies more often than females. Thus, the low frequency of attendance by those over the age of 55 could be explained by the fact that there are more women than men in the older age groups.

A cross-sectional design identifies differences between age groups but does not enable us to explain *the reason* for the differences. Nor can it provide explanations about the process of aging experienced by a given cohort. For example, those over 65 years of age may never have attended movies to any great extent at any time in their lives. This pattern may have evolved either because going to the movies was not popular in their early years, or because they could not afford to go to movies when they were young. In either situation, this cohort, unlike later generations, may never have acquired the habit of going to movies. Consequently, in later life, they do not spend any of their fixed income on movies.

A cross-sectional design alerts us to patterns of behaviour that vary by age group. The differences among age groups could also indicate generational or cultural differences (for example, immigrants may be less inclined to attend movies), changes with age, or the influence of specific historical events (such as a depression or an energy crisis) on a particular age group at some point in their life. Therefore, alternative research designs are needed to determine whether attendance at movies declines with age, and is, therefore, an aging effect.

Longitudinal Designs: Identifying Changes with Age

Longitudinal, or panel, designs provide more accurate and complete explanations of the aging process because they study the same individuals or groups over a number of years (a panel study). However, few longitudinal studies have been conducted because they are expensive and time-consuming.[15] Moreover, subjects in these studies

often die, move away, or refuse to continue participating in the research project.[16] Longitudinal research allows direct observation of changes in individuals and groups as they age, either in prospective studies, in which the subjects are studied at regular intervals over a period of years, or, although these are less desirable, in retrospective studies, in which individuals reply to similar questions pertaining to earlier stages in their lives. This method is used, as well, to examine the rate at which events occur or to illustrate that changes occur across time. This latter technique, known as event history analysis (Campbell and O'Rand, 1988), enables us to study how much time passes before a consequent event occurs—such as the length of time between marriage and the birth of a child, between a serious illness or disability and retirement, between divorce or widowhood and remarriage. Using a longitudinal design, researchers can study variations by gender, social class, education, place of residence, or ethnicity for aging-related events.

Table 5.2 presents hypothetical data for a longitudinal study of two birth cohorts. These data, collected from 1925 to 2005, indicate the frequency of movie attendance across the life course for two birth cohorts, one born in 1910 and one in 1940. Note that few in the 1910 cohort attended movies before 1945. Yet, after the Second World War, a larger percentage of this age cohort attended movies. This effect on a particular age cohort at a particular point in the life course is known as a 'period' effect. It represents a change in behaviour resulting from environmental, historical, or social events, rather than from reaching a specific chronological age (35 in this case). But unless a research project has a large sample, studied over a long time frame, period effects at a particular stage may be missed.

Table 5.2 also illustrates how to avoid 'cohort-centrism'—interpretations in which generalizations about the aging process and the status or behaviour of older people are derived on the basis of studying only one age cohort. Since each birth cohort experiences a different life course,

Table 5.2 Longitudinal Design: Age and Movie Attendance by Birth Cohort

Year	Age	1910 Birth Cohort Attending 3 Times or More per Year (%)	Year	Age	1940 Birth Cohort Attending 3 Times or More per Year (%)
1925	(15)	10	1955	(15)	58
1935	(25)	15	1965	(25)	62
1945	(35)	42	1975	(35)	60
1955	(45)	40	1985	(45)	57
1965	(55)	30	1995	(55)	52
1975	(65)	22	2005	(65)	40

Note: The data reported here are hypothetical.

longitudinal studies should include at least two age cohorts to control for possible cohort differences in life experiences, that is, period effects and socialization differences. Unless more than one age cohort is included, possible between-cohort differences may be missed, and conclusions based on the study of one cohort can be misleading or inaccurate. For example, Table 5.2 shows that the 1940 birth cohort attended movies more frequently at all ages than the 1910 cohort. Furthermore, the 1940 cohort demonstrates a relatively stable pattern of movie attendance across the life course, with only a slight decline in attendance occurring in the later years. Are they an atypical or typical cohort with respect to patterns of movie attendance?

As in cross-sectional designs, any intra-cohort variations by gender, social class, marital status, ethnicity, educational attainment, or other relevant variables should be studied and reported. However, these controls are often neglected in longitudinal studies since more emphasis is placed on changes or differences at subsequent time periods. That is, variation within a cohort may increase or decrease because of either maturation or specific period effects. For example, movie attendance at age 35 may be significantly lower than at age 25 for those in each cohort who become parents, and therefore have less time or money for leisure outside the home (this is a maturation or life course effect). Or attendance may decrease at a certain point in history for all adults, regardless of chronological age, perhaps because the movie industry at a certain period produces movies that appeal primarily to children or adolescents (a period effect). Or the extensive use of home videos and satellite dishes may reduce actual movie attendance by specific age cohorts more so than for other cohorts.

Cohort Analysis: Isolating Age Changes and Age Differences

Cohort analysis was developed in response to the limitations of cross-sectional and longitudinal designs for studying aging processes across time (Schaie, 1965, 1988). This sequential design accounts for age changes, cohort differences, and period effects, thereby reducing or eliminating any confusion as to whether results are due to age changes or age differences. To control for possible explanatory factors, this design collects similar information from different individuals who were born at different times and who are studied at different times.

While this approach should involve a longitudinal, prospective study over three or more generations, many cohort analyses involve a retrospective, cross-sectional analysis of information stored in archives. For example, national surveys, such as opinion polls and the census, often ask the same questions at regular intervals. However, at each interval different people represent the specific birth cohort. This eliminates the need for a longitudinal study in which the same individuals must be followed for many years. To illustrate this design, imagine we are in the year 2015 and have constructed a table based on one item (movie attendance) that has been included in a national survey every 10 years since 1945. Table 5.3 illustrates hypothetical patterns of movie attendance across the life course for three birth cohorts that might represent three generations within a family: grandparents, parents, and grandchildren.

In this type of analysis,[17] it is possible to do all of the following:

- to observe cross-sectional age differences (read down column 5 for the year 1985)
- to study age changes within a cohort over time (read across rows a, b, or c)

- to compare patterns of movie attendance by cohorts of the same chronological age (at 35 years) at different points in history (compare cells 3a, 5b, and 7c)
- to note whether patterns of attendance over time vary among different cohorts (compare rows a, b, and c)

For example, the hypothetical data in Table 5.3 suggest that, except for the 1930 cohort, which began to attend movies relatively late in life (compare cells 1a and 2a versus cell 3a), there seems to be increasing frequency of movie attendance by the younger birth cohorts, both initially (compare cells 1a, 3b, 5c) and later in life (compare cells 4a, 6b, and 8c). Moreover, despite increasing attendance by the younger cohorts, attendance is lower among all cohorts after age 35 (see cells 3a to 7a, cells 5b to 8b, and cells 7c to 8c). For the two most recent cohorts this trend begins sooner in that the peak for attendance is reached at about age 25 and age 15 respectively (compare cells 4b and 5b, and cells 5c and 6c).

A cohort analysis compares the influence of period effects on each cohort. For example, to determine whether high ticket prices during a

Table 5.3 Cohort Analysis: Age and Movie Attendance by Birth Cohort

Birth Cohort	% Attending Movies Three Times or More per Year (age in years)							
	1945 (1)	1955 (2)	1965 (3)	1975 (4)	1985 (5)	2005 (6)	1995 (7)	2015 (8)
a) 1930 (grandparents)	10 (15)	12 (25)	33 (35)	30 (45)	21 (55)	11 (65)	4 (75)	–
b) 1950 (parents)	–	–	58 (15)	62 (25)	60 (35)	41 (45)	52 (55)	40 (65)
c) 1970 (children)	–	–	–	–	72 (15)	60 (25)	69 (35)	61 (45)

Note: The data reported here are hypothetical.

period of high unemployment might have been a factor in decreased movie attendance around 1995, an investigator might note that there was a sharp decrease in attendance by the 1930 cohort. But this might be expected because of retirement and having less discretionary income, and the decrease might be found in all cohorts when they reach 65 years of age. However, an examination of cells 5b, 6b, and 7b and cells 5c, 6c, and 7c suggests that for both the 1950 and 1970 birth cohorts, as well, attendance fell in 1995, before rising slightly and then continuing the overall pattern of declining by age. Therefore, we might be able to argue that there were unique period and historical events around 1995 that explain why all three cohorts went to movies less often.

Issues in Qualitative Research Designs

Emergent Research Designs

Rather than the more formal and formulaic research designs used in quantitative research, qualitative research employs an 'emergent' research design (Marshall and Rossman, 1999). This type of design is more flexible and can be modified as new ideas and understandings emerge during the research study. The process of qualitative research moves from broad questions at the start to more specific questions as the study evolves.[18] Unlike quantitative designs, where data are analyzed after being collected, in qualitative research, interpretation and analysis are continual and are subject to re-interpretation as new evidence or observations emerge. Rather than the large random samples that are necessary in quantitative research, qualitative research employs smaller, snowball samples in which key informants, identified by others in a setting, are added at any time. Thus, the sample size is seldom predetermined, as it is in quantitative research, where formal statistical methods dictate the minimum sample size that is required in order for the findings to be generalizable to the larger population.

Researcher as Participant

Unlike the quantitative researcher, who strives for objectivity and distance from the research participants, the qualitative researcher is part of the study. He or she must be a sensitive, adaptable, patient, and astute observer and listener and must be tenacious in probing for more information. Yet, at the same time, the researcher must be aware of, and avoid, his or her personal prejudices and preconceptions in gathering and interpreting the evidence (Cobb and Forbes, 2000). In quantitative research the researcher could be fooled by responses to poorly worded or misinterpreted questions. In qualitative research, the researcher uses interviews with respondents and significant others, observations of the respondents in the setting, and a review of any available or relevant personal data to help verify an observation or a verbal response given by a respondent, and to revise an earlier interpretation of the phenomenon being studied.

The Setting

Because the setting or context is so essential to the interpretation of evidence, it must be fully and accurately described and analyzed, including both the physical and social structure. Within the setting, activities and interactions are observed and any events, including those which might negatively influence the success of the study, are noted. In short, this method is a complex, dynamic process that requires a complete understanding of the assumptions, language, and procedures of qualitative research. This approach does not merely involve adding a few open-ended questions to a survey, or 'hanging out' and watching older people in some social setting.[19]

Sampling Issues: The Selection of Respondents and Participants

When studying older people, one must consider the heterogeneity of the elderly population before reaching any conclusions. If a representative sample is needed in quantitative studies where the intent is to apply the findings back to the general population, lists of those in the population who are 65 years of age and older may not be available. Hence, researchers often depend on readily available and visible older people, such as volunteers or people who are active in churches or senior citizen centres. Consequently, those who are less visible, less active, or less healthy, or who live in nursing homes are less likely to be included. Moreover, people of any age who volunteer are often better educated, healthier, more mobile and social, and perhaps more liberal in their values, beliefs, and lifestyles. These sampling matters can introduce bias and non-representativeness into a research study, and thereby limit the generalizability of the findings.

In qualitative studies, while the intent is to understand the actors and the social interaction in a particular setting, sometimes settings are selected for reasons of convenience; for example, the researcher may know a resident of a particular retirement home or may have met the director at a professional meeting. The selection of one setting rather than another may not be an issue for some aging topics, but it may be for some types of research questions. For example, the findings of a study involving older Aboriginal people in a northern settlement will not be applicable to older Aboriginal people, in general, since many now live in large cities. Or to study older gays and lesbians in a small university community, because that is where the researcher is located, may not yield findings that are representative of the lives of most gays and lesbians, who live in large metropolitan centres, or of those who live in conservative, rural communities. Similarly, to study the residents of a single retirement home may be to ignore the unique circumstances of retirement-home residents elsewhere who are members of a particular ethnic, religious, or racial group; or who are gay or lesbian; or who live in a rural setting.

Regardless of whether a study is qualitative or quantitative, potentially relevant characteristics of all older people and real situations in their everyday lives are often under-represented or neglected in aging research. For example, studies often neglect frail and institutionalized older people; members of less well-known immigrant groups, such as East Indian, Vietnamese, or Brazilian; or members of minority religious groups, such as Muslims and Hindus (Salari, 2002); those in the lower socio-economic stratum, including homeless older persons; those living in a household with family members; gay and lesbian older people; divorced or never-married older men and women; those whose first language is neither English nor French; widows or widowers living alone in their home; and those living on farms in small towns or in remote areas of the country. These characteristics and situations need to be incorporated into research studies because they are important elements of the diverse mosaic of older Canadians. Moreover, even when a study seeks to understand only one segment of the older population, possible diversity within this segment must be incorporated into the selection of a sample. To illustrate, in a study of the leisure lifestyles of older women, differences in occupational, marital, and family histories must be considered because these factors do influence leisure behaviour. Contrary to common assumptions, all women over 65 are not retired, married or widowed, and grandmothers. Rather, the following differences might be found within a group of 65- to 70-year-old women who live in the same neighbourhood. Some may be:

- never-married and still employed
- married and employed part-time
- widowed and retired
- widowed, remarried, and employed
- married, with a single daughter and grand-child living at home while the daughter attends university or works
- remarried to an older man in ill health who requires a high level of care

Issues in Collecting Information from Older Adults

Special skills, techniques, and instruments are needed for research involving older people. First, trust and a good rapport with older respondents must be established since research personnel may be viewed suspiciously as strangers, especially if they telephone or arrive at the older person's home without warning or permission.

Surveys conducted by mail may not be completed for a variety of reasons: the respondent has literacy problems, the print is too small, the sentences are too complicated or contain jargon, the respondent is unable to choose a single answer to a multiple-choice questions, or he or she refuses or forgets to return the survey. Even if the survey is completed, the answers may not be accurate since older respondents may give what they think are socially acceptable responses. In addition, they may be more likely to respond with 'no opinion' or 'don't know'; and they may be unwilling to answer very personal questions about death, finances, health, sexual relations, or family relationships.

Interviews are a much more effective way to gather information from older people because a face-to-face situation builds rapport and enables an interviewer to clarify the questions or ask them in different ways, and to probe for clarification or additional information. But even with interviews there can be difficulties. First, once rapport is established, the respondent must be kept focused on the topic. He or she may want to share all kinds of information or to turn the interview into a social visit. This lengthens the interview and may increase the cost of doing research. Or when interviews are conducted in the respondent's home, a spouse or other person in the household may interject his or her opinions or answers, or influence the responses of the interviewee. Second, the gender of the interviewer matters. For some topics, older people may feel more comfortable responding to interviewers of the same sex, or they may mention or emphasize different issues or give quite different answers, depending on whether the interviewer is of the same or opposite sex (Stephenson et al., 1999). Similarly, the age, race, and ethnicity of the interviewer may matter. An interviewer of the same age, race, or ethnic background can increase the depth and quality of information collected.

Regardless of whether a questionnaire or an interview is used, language is an essential component of the research process. Ageist language and labels should be avoided. Similarly, questions that ask, 'When you were 'younger . . .' do not elicit as detailed and useful responses as more specific questions that ask, for example, 'When you were 25–30 years of age, . . .'. The language used when studying older people from a specific subcultural or cultural group must be appropriate for the respondents. Interviews and questionnaires should be conducted in the first language of the respondents. Those whose English is not entirely fluent may not fully comprehend the questions in an oral interview or a questionnaire. Similarly, when religious or ethnic groups are studied, members of the specific group should be involved in the design and pre-test of a questionnaire or interview guide, as interviewers, and in the interpretation of the information collected.

The very old (85 and over), including those who are frail, regardless of their age, are difficult to find and are often excluded from research studies. Yet they constitute an important and growing segment of the older population. These segments of the older population are important for the study of such issues as loss of independence, elder abuse, adequacy of social support and caregiving, and the quality of life in residential institutions. If a frail older person is to be interviewed, an interpreter, caregiver, or family member can be used when deafness, lack of comprehension, or confusion on the part of the older interviewee might otherwise interfere with the collection of information (Russell, 1999b). One recent approach to studying this sub-population is to use the Minimum Data Set for comparing health outcomes among frail older people. This procedure involves implementing a standardized assessment for all patients in chronic-care hospitals or nursing homes (Hirdes and Carpenter, 1997; Hirdes et al., 1999). Finally, the frail, institutionalized elderly person is often viewed as powerless and dependent by staff and administrators, and not worthy of being studied, or it is assumed they are unable to provide information. Moreover, administrators, who fear what residents might say about the quality of care, may refuse a researcher's request to interview or observe residents in their institution.

Ethics in Research: Procedures to Protect Older Participants

Regardless of the setting or the competence of potential research participants, participation in research must be voluntary. Older adults who participate in research projects must understand what is expected of them, and why, and must give their consent freely and without coercion to be interviewed or observed or to have their personal records examined. For some older people, the ability to understand and give consent to an interview or observation may fluctuate from day to day due to health reasons. The process of acquiring informed consent must allow participants time to consider whether they wish to be involved or not. And if the potential participant has dementia, the concept of informed consent may not be understood, in which case a family member or a guardian who has the legal power to make such a decision may give consent.

All research involving older respondents must ensure privacy and guarantee protection from harm. The research process must protect participants from any physical or mental harm, such as worry, anxiety, or mental anguish. Those who live in a retirement or nursing home or who are cared for by others in their own home, must be protected from any possible retaliation by caregivers, who during an interview, may be criticized by an older person. Protection from harm also involves refraining from asking questions, especially questions about death, if they appear to disturb the respondent; and ending an interview or observation immediately if the older person becomes severely disturbed or appears uncomfortable.

A particularly difficult ethical issue involves how to respond if the observer or interviewer suspects, or is told by the older person, that physical, psychological, or financial abuse or neglect is occurring. Who should be informed, how, and when are difficult decisions, especially if concrete evidence is lacking. These are issues that researchers and their staff must resolve before entering the field to conduct interviews or observations of older people.

Summary

This chapter introduced theories and perspectives to help you think about, interpret, and understand data and observations about aging processes and the situation of older people in a variety of settings. At present, no single theoretical perspective or methodological approach dominates. Rather, as in many fields of study, a variety of methods and theories are needed to stimulate creative thinking, to increase our knowledge, and to provide alternative explanations or interpretations of a process or situation. Some theories and methods are used primarily to study micro-level (i.e., individual) aging questions; others are used for macro-level questions (i.e. issues at the level of society or the population). Increasingly, the micro- and macro-levels are interdependent, and theories and methods must address and answer questions at both levels. And we must take a longer and broader view of aging phenomena, at both the individual and societal level, across historical periods, in different cultural settings, and across the life course of a specific individual or age cohort.

You may never become a theorist or a career researcher. However, an understanding of current theoretical perspectives and research methods is essential for your development as a creative and critical thinker, as an informed citizen, as a student, and later in a career that may or may not relate to aging issues. Use theoretical perspectives and theories and their concepts to critique what you read and observe in the mass media, government reports, and research articles. Theories and perspectives can also guide your thinking about policies, programs, and decisions concerning the older population. Similarly, an understanding of research methods and their inherent strengths and weaknesses will enable you to assess more accurately the quality, reliability, and credibility of the information you read about in research articles and the print media, or that is reported in the electronic media, including the web. Finally, do not always accept what you read as the truth or the only explanation for an outcome or event. Interpret and critique the ideas and conclusions of others, and search for new or more complete explanations or interpretations for phenomena you observe about aging and older people.

For Reflection, Debate, or Action

1. Select a fact, pattern, or observation about aging or older people that is of interest to you, and employing concepts from one or more of the theories about later life and aging, attempt to explain or interpret why the phenomenon occurs regularly.

2. Select a public policy and use one of the theoretical perspectives on aging to explain why the policy is, or may not be, successful in meeting the intended objectives.

3. Select an article from a recent issue of the *Canadian Journal on Aging*, and critique the research design and methods used. Are they suitable for the research questions being asked? Do they facilitate or inhibit a more complete understanding of the topic? What other design or method might have been used to address the same topic, and why?

4. Develop an argument as to which specific theory or theoretical perspective would help you to understand more about some specific aging phenomenon.

5. Select one theoretical perspective, and with a classmate, debate why and how the perspective can or cannot contribute to better policy-making for Canada's aging population.

6. Select a newspaper or magazine article about an aging topic and state whether and how the article reflects a particular theoretical perspective. If the article is atheoretical, suggest a theoretical perspective that might have been employed to provide a more in-depth, consistent, and accurate interpretation or explanation of the issue being discussed.

7. Which micro- and macro-theories of aging would a policy-maker in Health Canada find most useful, and why, in the development and delivery of a new health-related policy?

8. On the basis of your current knowledge about adults 65 and over in Canada, which theoretical perspective or theory fits best with your current views on aging and the status of older people in our society?

9. Among the many theories and theoretical perspectives, which ones, and why, would be most useful in addressing the perennial question as to whether support in later life is a public issue or a private trouble?

Notes

1. For a detailed and historical discussion of theoretical issues in the social gerontology and sociology of aging literature, see George, 1995; Bengtson et al., 1997, 1999; Calasanti, 1996; Lynott and Lynott, 1996; Marshall 1996, 1999; Schroots, 1995; Bengtson and Schaie, 1999; Minkler and Estes, 1999; Garner, 1999; McMullin, 2000; Hagestad and Dannefer, 2001; Marshall and Mueller, 2003).

2. Additional perspectives and theories are introduced throughout the text to explain specific phenomena such as modernization (Chapter 2), environmental press (Chapter 7), intergenerational family dynamics (Chapter 8), and caregiving (Chapter 11).

3. 'Life course', 'life span', and 'life cycle' sometimes are used interchangeably in the literature (Hagestad, 1990). However, from a sociological and gerontological perspective, life course is the preferred term, whereas psychologists employ life span and life cycle to refer to universal, somewhat inevitable 'stages' of development across the life span from infancy to old age.

4. One notable exception is the classic study by Elder (1999) about the effects in later life on those who experienced the Depression as children.

5. The feminist perspective includes many theoretical approaches—micro, macro, normative, interpretive, and critical-socialist (Gee and Kimball, 1987; Calasanti, 1993; Hamilton, 1993; Osmond and Thorne, 1993; Lopata, 1995; Marshall, 1996; Ray, 1996; Bengtson et al., 1997; Garner, 1999; McDaniel, 2004)—and many research methods (Reinharz, 1992; Neysmith, 1995; Calasanti, 1996). Articles representing the different approaches can be found in the *Journal of Women and Aging*, the *Journal of Aging Studies*, and *Canadian Woman Studies*.

6. For feminist critiques, see Gee and Kimball, 1987; McDaniel, 1989, 2004; MacRae, 1990; Calasanti, 1992, 1993; MacQuarrie and Keddy, 1992; Calasanti and Zajicek, 1993; Arber and Ginn, 1995; McMullin, 1995; Ray, 1996; Garner, 1999.

7. Originally called 'age stratification theory' when first proposed in 1972 (Riley et al., 1972); more recently it has been re-labelled as the 'aging and society paradigm' in recognition of its evolving, broader view of aging (Riley et al., 1999).

8. The work of Riley et al. (1999) provide an illustration of how theoretical developments occur over a period of time.

9. In the work of Riley and her colleagues, social structures refer to 'societal institutions, such as the family, the economy, and educational, political and religious organizations; their component roles; their rules and resources; their built-in culture and values; and, the social environments' (Riley et al., 1999: 341, n.5).

10. Adherents of the political economy of aging perspective include Myles, 1989; Minkler and Estes, 1991; Estes, 1991; Estes et al., 1996; Quadagno and Reid, 1999; and Walker, 1999.

11. For examples of the critical perspective, see Moody, 1988, 1993; Baars, 1991; Minkler and Estes, 1991, 1999; Cole et al., 1993, 2000; Calasanti, 1996; Minkler, 1996; Phillipson, 1998; Ray, 1998; Estes, 1999; and, Holstein and Minkler, 2003.

12. Examples of this type of research are found in the *Journal of Aging Studies*.

13. Narrative gerontology is represented by the work of Cole et al., 1993, 2000; Birren et al., 1996; Kenyon and Randall, 1999; and Biggs, 2001.

14. Please note that the data reported in Tables 5.1, 5.2, and 5.3 are fictitious. These hypothetical results are presented to illustrate research designs and possible interpretations of the data.

15. To explain whether social, cognitive, or physical differences among individuals or cohorts at a particular age have always been present, or whether these change with age, we need longitudinal data. In 2006, the Canadian Longitudinal Study on Aging will be launched under the auspices of the CIHR Institute on Aging.

16. Because respondents are lost over the course of the study, it can always be asked whether the final sample is similar to the original sample. For example, in a longitudinal study of movie attendance, those who no longer wish to be in the study may be those who no longer attend movies because of such factors as low income, declining vision, or loss of mobility.

17. Ideally, this type of analysis is done for both males and females and with controls for relevant factors, such as race, income, education, or religion. However, to simplify the explanation of cohort analysis, I have included only patterns for the total population in Table 5.3.

18. Some excellent sources for learning how to design and interpret qualitative studies include Lincoln and Guba, 1985; Hendricks, 1996; Gubrium and Holstein, 1997; Crabtree and Miller, 1999; Marshall and Rossman, 1999; Russell, 1999a; Denzin and Lincoln, 2000; Munhull and Boyd, 2000; Cobb and Forbes, 2002; and Rowles and Schoenberg, 2002.

19. An excellent recent example of qualitative research is Sarah Matthew's in-depth study of how siblings (sisters *and* brothers) support their aging parents (Matthews, 2002). Highlight 12.5 (page 425; reprinted from Matthews, 2002) offers an excellent example of insights about a situation, namely the concerns about and care for a parent with Alzheimer's disease, that can be acquired through the use of qualitative research.

References

Achenbaum, A., and V. Bengtson.1994. 'Re-engaging the Disengagement Theory of Aging: On the History and Assessment of Theory Development in Gerontology', *The Gerontologist*, 34(6), 756–63.

Alwin, D., and R. Campbell.2001. 'Quantitative Approaches: Longitudinal Methods in the Study of Human Development and Aging. Pp. 22–43 in R. Binstock and L. George (eds), *Handbook of Aging and the Social Sciences*. New York: Academic Press.

Arber, S., and J. Ginn (eds). 1995. *Connecting Gender and Ageing: A Sociological Approach*. Philadelphia: Open University Press.

Atchley, R. 1971. *The Social Forces in Later Life*. Belmont, Calif.: Wadsworth.

———. 1989. 'A Continuity Theory of Normal Aging', *The Gerontologist*, 29(2), 183–90.

Baars, J. 1991. 'The Challenge of Critical Gerontology: The Problem of Social Constitution', *Journal of Aging Studies*, 5(3), 219–43.

Bengtson, V., et al. 1996. 'Paradoxes of Families and Aging'. Pp. 253–82 in R. Binstock and L. George (eds), *Handbook of Aging and the Social Sciences*. San Diego, Calif.: Academic Press.

———. 1997. 'Theory, Explanation and a Third Generation of Theoretical Development in Social Gerontology', *Journal of Gerontology: Social Sciences*, 52B(2), S72–88.

———, and W. Schaie (eds). 1999. *Handbook of Theories of Aging*. New York: Springer Publishing Co.

———., et al. 1999. 'Are Theories of Aging Important? Models and Explanations in Gerontology at the Turn of the Century'. Pp. 3–20 in V. Bengtson and W. Schaie (eds). *Handbook of Theories of Aging*. New York: Springer.

Berger, P., and T. Luckmann.1966. *The Social Construction of Reality*. Garden City, NY: Doubleday.

Biggs, S. 2001. 'Toward Critical Narrativity: Stories of Aging in Contemporary Social Policy', *Journal of Aging Studies*, 15(4), 303–16.

Birren, J., et al. (eds). 1996. *Aging and Biography: Explorations in Adult Development*. New York: Springer.

Blieszner, R. 1993. 'A Socialist-Feminist Perspective on Widowhood', *Journal of Aging Studies*, 7(2), 171–82.

Burgess, W. 1960. *Aging in Western Societies*. Chicago: University of Chicago Press.

Calasanti, T. 1992. 'Theorizing about Gender and Aging: Beginning with Women's Voices', *The Gerontologist*, 32(2), 280–2.

———. 1993. 'Introduction: A Socialist-Feminist Approach to Aging', *Journal of Aging Studies*, 7(2), 107–9.

——— (ed.). 2004. 'New Directions in Feminist Gerontology', *Journal of Aging Studies*, 18(1), 1–121.

————. 1996. 'Incorporating Diversity: Meaning, Levels of Research, and Implications for Theory', *The Gerontologist*, 36(1), 147–56.

————, and A. Zajicek. 1993. 'A Socialist-Feminist Approach to Aging: Embracing Diversity', *Journal of Aging Studies*, 7(2), 117–31.

Campbell, R., and A. O'Rand. 1988. 'Settings and Sequences: The Heuristics of Aging Research'. Pp. 58–79 in J. Birren and V. Bengtson (eds), *Emergent Theories of Aging*. New York: Springer .

Cobb, A., and S. Forbes.2002. 'Qualitative Research: What Does It Have to Offer to the Gerontologist?', *Journal of Gerontology: Medical Sciences*, 57A(4), M197–202.

Cole, T., et al. (eds). 1993. *Voices and Visions of Aging: Toward a Critical Gerontology*. New York: Springer.

————. (eds). 2000. *Handbook of the Humanities and Aging*. New York: Springer.

Connidis, I., et al. 2000. 'Editorial: Beyond 1999: A Research Agenda', *Canadian Journal on Aging*, 19(3), i–xi.

Cooley, C. 1902. *Human Nature and the Social Order*. New York: Scribner's.

Crabtree, B. and W. Miller (eds). 1999. *Doing Qualitative Research*. Newbury Park, Calif.: Sage.

Cumming, E. 1963. 'Further Thoughts on the Theory of Disengagement', *International Social Science Journal*, 15(3), 377–93.

————, and W. Henry. 1961. *Growing Old: The Process of Disengagement*. New York: Basic Books.

————, et al. 1960. 'Disengagement: A Tentative Theory of Aging', *Sociometry*, 23(1), 23–35.

Cutler, S., and W. Schaie. 2001. *Research Methods in Aging: A Selective Annotated Bibliography*. Washington, DC: Association for Gerontology in Higher Education.

D'Arcy. C. 1980. 'The Manufacture and Obsolescence of Madness: Age, Social Policy and Psychiatric Morbidity in a Prairie Province'. Pp. 159–76 in V. Marshall (ed.), *Aging in Canada: Social Perspectives*. Don Mills, Ont.: Fitzhenry and Whiteside.

Dawe, A. 1970. 'The Two Sociologies', *British Journal of Sociology*, 21(2), 207–18.

Denzin, N., and Y. Lincoln (eds). 2000. *The Handbook of Qualitative Research*. Thousand Oaks, Calif.: Sage.

Doherty, W., et al. 1993. 'Family Theories and Methods: A Contextual Approach'. pp. 3–30 in P. Boss et al. (eds), *Sourcebook of Family Theories and Methods: A Contextual Approach*. New York: Plenum Press.

Elder, G. 1999. *Children of the Great Depression: Social Change in Life Experience*. 25th anniversary edition.

Chicago: University of Chicago Press.

————, and M. Johnson.2003. 'The Life Course and Aging: Challenges, Lessons and New Directions'. Pp. 49–81 in R. Settersten (ed.), *Invitation to the Life Course: Toward New Understandings of Later Life*. Amityville, New York: Baywood.

Estes, C. 1991. 'The New Political Economy of Aging: Introduction and Critique'. Pp. 19–36 in M. Minkler and C. Estes (eds), *Critical Perspectives on Aging: The Political and Moral Economy of Growing Old*. Amityville, NY: Baywood.

————, et al. 1996. 'The Political Economy of Aging'. Pp. 346–61 in R. Binstock and L. George (eds), *Handbook of Aging and the Social Sciences*. San Diego, Calif.: Academic Press.

————. 1999. 'Critical Gerontology and the New Political Economy of Aging'. Pp. 17–35 in M. Minkler and C. Estes (eds), *Critical Gerontology: Perspectives from Political and Moral Economy*. Amityville, New York: Baywood.

————. 2001. 'Political Economy of Aging: A Theoretical Framework'. Pp. 1–22 in C. Estes et al. (eds), *Social Policy and Aging: A Critical Perspective*. Thousand Oaks, Calif.: Sage Publications.

Featherstone, M., and C. Wernick. 1995. *Images of Aging*. New York: Routledge.

Ferraro, K. 2001. 'Aging and Role Transitions'. Pp. 313–30 in R. Binstock and L. George (eds) *Handbook of Aging and the Social Sciences*. New York: Academic Press.

Garner, J. 1999. *Fundamentals of Feminist Gerontology*. New York: Haworth Press.

Gee, E., and M. Kimball. 1987. *Women and Aging*. Toronto: Butterworths.

George, L. 1995. 'The Last Half Century of Aging Research and Thoughts for the Future', *Journal of Gerontology: Social Sciences*, 50B(1), S1–3.

————. 1996a. 'Missing Links: The Case for a Social Psychology of the Life Course', *The Gerontologist*, 36(3), 248–55.

————. 1996b. 'Social Factors and Illness'. Pp. 229–53 in R. Binstock and L. George (eds), *Handbook of Aging and the Social Sciences*. San Diego,Calif.: Academic Press.

Giele, J., and G. Elder (eds). 1999. *Methods of Life-Course Research: Qualitative and Quantitative Approaches*. Newbury Park, Calif.: Sage.

Goffman, E. 1959. *The Presentation of Self in Everyday Life*. New York: Doubleday.

Grant, B. 1999. 'Physical Activity and the Meaning to Self', Presented at the 5th World Congress on Physical

Activity, Aging and Sports, Orlando, Florida, August 10–14, 1999.

———, and S. O'Brien-Cousins 2001. 'Aging and Physical Activity: The Promise of Qualitative Research', *Journal of Aging and Physical Activity*, 9(3), 237–44.

Gubrium, J. 1993. *Speaking of Life: Horizons of Meaning for Nursing Home Residents*. New York: Aldine de Gruyter.

———, and J. Holstein. 1997. *The New Language of Qualitative Methods*. Oxford: Oxford University Press.

———. 1999. 'Constructionist Perspectives on Aging'. Pp. 287–305 in V. Bengtson and W. Schaie (eds), *Handbook of Theories of Aging*. New York: Springer.

Hagestad, G. 1990. 'Social Perspectives on the Life Course'. Pp. 151–68 in R. Binstock and L. George (eds), *Handbook of Aging and the Social Sciences*. San Diego, Calif.: Academic Press.

———, and D. Dannefer 2001. 'Concepts and Theories of Aging: Beyond Microfication in Social Science Approaches'. Pp. 3–21 in R. Binstock and L. George (eds), *Handbook of Aging and the Social Sciences*. New York: Academic Press.

Halliwell, J., and J. Lomas. 1999. 'Dimensions of Health Research: The Four CIHR Sectors—Perspectives and Strategies—A Discussion Paper', Ottawa: Social Sciences and Humanities Research Council of Canada and Canadian Health Services.

Hamilton, R. 1993. 'Feminist Theories', *Left History*, 1(1), 9–33.

Hare-Mustin, R., and J. Marecek. (1994. 'Gender and the Meaning of Difference: Postmodernism and Psychology'. Pp. 49–76 in A. Herrmann and A. Stewart (eds), *Theorizing Feminism: Parallel Trends in the Humanities and Social Sciences*. Boulder, Colo.: Westview Press.

Havighurst, R., and R. Albrecht. 1953. *Older People*. New York: Longmans, Green.

Hazan, H. 1994. *Old Age: Constructions and Deconstructions*. Cambridge: Cambridge University Press.

Heinz, W., and V. Marshall (eds). 2003. *Social Dynamics of the Life Course: Transitions, Institutions, and Interrelations*. New York: Aldine De Gruyter.

Hendricks, J. 1994. 'Revisiting the Kansas City Study of Adult Life: Roots of the Disengagement Model in Social Gerontology', *The Gerontologist*, 34(6), 753–5.

———. 1996. 'Qualitative Research: Contributions and Advances'. Pp. 52–72 in R. Binstock and L. George (eds), *Handbook of Aging and the Social Sciences*. San Diego, Calif.: Academic Press.

Henry, W. 1964. 'The Theory of Intrinsic Disengagement'. Pp. 415–18 in P. Hansen (ed.), *Age with a Future*. Philadelphia: F.A. Davis.

Hirdes, J., and I. Carpenter. 1997. 'Health Outcomes among the Frail Elderly in Communities and Institutions: Use of the Minimum Data Set (MDS) to Create Effective Linkages between Research and Policy', *Canadian Journal on Aging/Canadian Public Policy*, Supplement, 53–69.

———, et al. 1999. 'Integrated Health Information Systems Based on the RAI/MDS Series of Assessment Instruments', *Healthcare Management Forum*, 12(4), 30–40.

Holstein, J., and J. Gubrium. 2000. *Constructing the Life Course*. Dix Hills, NY: General Hall.

Holstein, M., and M. Minkler. 2003. 'Self, Society and the New Gerontology', *The Gerontologist*, 43(6), 787–96.

Johnson, C., and B. Baier. 1992. 'Patterns of Engagement and Disengagement among the Oldest Old', *Journal of Aging Studies*, 6(4), 351–64.

Kenyon, G., and W. Randall 1999. 'Introduction: Narrative Gerontology', *Journal of Aging Studies*, 13(1), 1–5.

Kimmel, M. 2000. *The Gendered Society*. New York: Oxford University Press.

Krause, N. 2002. 'A Comprehensive Strategy for Developing Closed-Ended Survey Items for Use in Studies of Older Adults', *Journal of Gerontology: Social Sciences*, 57B(5), S263–74.

Layder, D. 1994. *Understanding Social Theory*. Thousand Oaks, Calif.: Sage.

Laws, G. 1995. 'Understanding Ageism: Lessons from Feminism and Postmodernism', *The Gerontologist*, 35(1), 112–18.

Lincoln, Y., and E. Guba 1985. *Naturalistic Inquiry*. Beverly Hills, Calif.: Sage.

Lopata, H. 1995. 'Feminist Perspectives in Social Gerontology'. Pp. 114–31 in R. Bleiszner and V. Hilkevitch Bedford (eds), *Handbook of Aging and the Family*. Westport, Conn.: Greenwood Press.

Luborsky, M., and R. Rubinstein. 1995. 'Sampling in Qualitative Research', *Research on Aging*, 17(1), 89–113.

Lynott, R., and P. Lynott. 1996. 'Tracing the Course of Theoretical Development in the Sociology of Aging', *The Gerontologist*, 36(6), 749–60.

McDaniel, S. 1989. 'Women and Aging: A Sociological Perspective', *Journal of Women and Aging*, 1(1–3), 47–67.

———. 2004. 'Generationing Gender: Justice and the Division of Welfare', in 'New Directions in Feminist

Gerontology', special issue, *Journal of Aging Studies*, 18(1), 27–44.

McDonald, L., and R. Wanner. 1987. 'Retirement in a Dual Economy: The Canadian Case'. Pp. 245–61 in V. Marshall (ed.), *Aging in Canada: Social Perspectives*. Markham, Ont.: Fitzhenry and Whiteside.

———. 1990. *Retirement in Canada*. Markham, Ont.: Butterworths.

McMullin, J. 1995. 'Theorizing Age and Gender Relations'. Pp. 30–41 in S. Arber and J. Ginn (eds), *Connecting Gender and Ageing: A Sociological Approach*. Philadelphia: Open University Press.

———. 2000. 'Diversity and the State of Sociological Aging Theory', *The Gerontologist*, 40(5), 517–30.

MacQuarrie, M., and B. Keddy. 1992. 'Women and Aging: Directions for Research', *Journal of Women and Aging*, 4(2), 21–32.

MacRae, H. 1990. 'Older Women and Identity Maintenance in Later Life', *Canadian Journal on Aging*, 9(3), 248–67.

McWilliam, C. 1997. 'Using a Participatory Research Process to Make a Difference in Policy on Aging', *Canadian Journal on Aging*, 16 (Supplement), 70–89.

Marshall, C., and G. Rossman 1999. *Designing Qualitative Research*. Thousand Oaks, Calif.: Sage.

Marshall, V. 1981. 'Participant Observation in a Multiple-Methods Study of a Retirement Community: A Research Narrative', *Mid-American Review of Sociology*, 6(2), 29–44.

———. 1994. 'Sociology, Psychology, and the Theoretical Legacy of the Kansas City Studies', *The Gerontologist*, 34(6), 768–74.

———. 1996. 'The State of Theory in Aging and the Social Sciences'. Pp. 12–30 in R. Binstock and L. George (eds), *Handbook of Aging and the Social Sciences*. San Diego, Calif.: Academic Press.

———. 1999. 'Analyzing Social Theories of Aging'. Pp. 434–55 in V. Bengtson and W. Schaie (eds), *Handbook of Theories of Aging*. New York: Springer.

———, and M. Mueller 2003. 'Theoretical Roots of the Life Course Perspective'. Pp. 3–32 in W. Heinz and V. Marshall (eds), *Dynamics of the Life Course: Sequences, Institutions and Interrelations*. New York: Aldine de Gruyter.

Martin Matthews, A. (ed.). 1995. 'Methodological Diversity', *Canadian Journal on Aging*, 14 (Supp. 1), 1–212.

———, and E. Gee (eds), 1997. 'Policy and Research on Aging: Connections and Conundrums', *Canadian Journal on Aging*, 16 (Supplement), 1–186.

Matthews, S. 2002. *Sisters and Brothers / Daughters and Sons: Meeting the Needs of Old Parents*. Bloomington, Indiana: Unlimited.

———, et al. 1991. 'Obtaining Income Information from Elderly Respondents: An Assessment of Non-Response and Reliability', *Canadian Journal on Aging*, 10(2), 177–98.

Mills, C.W. 1959. *The Sociological Imagination*. New York: Oxford University Press.

Minkler, M. 1996. 'Critical Perspectives on Aging: New Challenges for Gerontology', *Ageing and Society*, 16(2), 467–87.

———, and C. Estes (eds). 1991. *Critical Perspectives on Aging: The Political and Moral Economy of Growing Old*. Amityville, NY: Baywood.

———, and C. Estes (eds). 1999. *Critical Gerontology: Perspectives from Political and Moral Economy*. Amityville, NY: Baywood Press.

Moody, H. 1988. 'Toward a Critical Gerontology: The Contributions of the Humanities to Theories of Aging'. Pp. 19–40 in J. Birren and V. Bengtson (eds), *Emergent Theories of Aging*. New York: Springer.

———. 1993. 'Overview: What Is Critical Gerontology and Why Is It Important?' Pp. xv–xii in T. Cole et al. (eds), *Voices and Visions: Toward a Critical Gerontology*. New York: Springer.

Munhall, P., and C. Boyd 2000. *Nursing Research. A Qualitative Perspective*. New York: Jones and Bartlett.

Myles, J. 1989. *Old Age in the Welfare State: The Political Economy of Public Pensions*. 2d edn. Lawrence: University of Kansas Press.

National Research Council. 2001. *Preparing for an Aging World: The Case for Cross-National Research*. Washington, DC: National Academy Press.

Neysmith, S. 1995. 'Feminist Methodologies: A Consideration of Principles and Practice for Research in Gerontology', *Canadian Journal on Aging*, 14 (Supp. 1), 100–18.

Osmond, M., and B. Thorne. 1993. 'Feminist Theories: The Social Construction of Gender in Families and Society'. Pp. 591–623 in P. Boss et al. (eds), *Sourcebook of Family Theories and Methods: A Contextual Approach*. New York: Plenum.

Passuth, P., and V. Bengtson. 1988. 'Sociological Theories of Aging: Current Perspectives and Future Directions'. Pp. 333–55 in J. Birren and V. Bengtson (eds), *Emergent Theories of Aging*. New York: Springer.

Phillipson, C. 1998. *Reconstructing Old Age*. Thousand Oaks, Calif.: Sage.

Pillemar, K. et al. 2003. 'Finding the Best Ways to Help: Opportunities and Challenges of Intervention Research on Aging', *The Gerontologist*, 43 (Special Issue I), 5–8.

Quadagno, J., and J. Janzen. 1987. 'Old Age Security and the Family Life Course: A Case-Study of Nineteenth-Century Mennonite Immigrants to Kansas', *Journal of Aging Studies*, 1 (1), 33–50.

———, and J. Reid 1999. 'The Political Economy Perspective in Aging'. Pp. 344–58 in V. Bengtson and W. Schaie (eds), *Handbook of Theories of Aging*. New York: Springer.

Ray, R. 1996. 'A Postmodern Perspective on Feminist Gerontology', *The Gerontologist*, 36(5), 674–80.

———. 1998. 'Introduction: Critical Perspectives on the Life Story', *Journal of Aging Studies*, 12(2), 101–6.

Reinharz, S. 1992. *Feminist Methods in Social Research*. New York: Oxford University Press.

Reitzes, D., et al. 1995. 'Activities and Self-Esteem: Continuing the Development of Activity Theory', *Research on Aging*, 17(3), 260–77.

Riley, M. 1971. 'Social Gerontology and the Age Stratification of Society', *The Gerontologist*, 11(1), 79–87.

———. 1973. 'Aging and Cohort Succession: Interpretations and Misinterpretations', *Public Opinion Quarterly*, 37(1), 35–49.

———. 1985. 'Age Strata in Social Systems'. Pp. 369–411 in R. Binstock and E. Shanas (eds), *Handbook of Aging and the Social Sciences*. New York: Van Nostrand Reinhold.

———. 1994. 'Aging and Society: Past, Present, and Future', *The Gerontologist*, 34(4), 436–46.

———, et al. 1972. 'Elements in a Model of Age Stratification'. Pp. 3–26 in M. Riley, M. Johnson, and A. Foner (eds), *Aging and Society. Vol. 3: A Sociology of Age Stratification*. New York: Russell Sage Foundation.

———. 1994. *Age and Structural Lag: Society's Failure to Provide Meaningful Opportunities in Work, Family and Leisure*. New York: Wiley.

———. 1999. 'The Aging and Society Paradigm'. Pp. 327–43 in V. Bengtson and W. Schaie (eds), *Handbook of Theories of Aging*. New York: Springer.

Rowles, G., and N. Schoenberg (eds). 2002. *Qualitative Gerontology*. New York: Springer.

Russell, C. 1999a. 'Introduction: Perspectives on Using Qualitative Research in Aging Studies', *Journal of Aging Studies*, 13(4), 365–8.

———. 1999b. 'Interviewing Vulnerable Old People: Ethical and Methodological Implications of Imagining Our Subjects', *Journal of Aging Studies*, 13(4), 403–18.

Salari, S. 2002. 'Invisible in Aging Research: Arab Americans, Middle Eastern Immigrants, and Muslims in the United States', *The Gerontologist*, 42(5), 580–8.

Schaie, W. 1965. 'A General Model for the Study of Developmental Problems', *Psychological Bulletin*, 64(2), 92–107.

———. 1988. 'The Impact of Research Methodology on Theory Building in the Developmental Sciences'. Pp. 41–57 in J. Birren and V. Bengtson (eds), *Emergent Theories of Aging*. New York: Springer.

Schroots, J. 1995. 'Psychological Models of Aging', *Canadian Journal on Aging*, 14(1), 44–66.

———. 1996. 'The Fractal Structure of Lives: Continuity and Discontinuity in Autobiography'. Pp. 117–30 in J. Birren et al. (eds), *Aging and Biography: Explorations in Adult Development*. New York: Springer.

Settersten, R. 1999. *Lives in Time and Place: The Problems and Promises of Developmental Science*. Amityville, NY: Baywood.

——— (ed.). 2003. *Invitation to the Life Course: Toward New Understandings of Later Life*. Amityville, NY: Baywood.

Singer, B., and C. Ryff 2001. 'Person-Centered Methods for Understanding Aging: The Integration of Numbers and Narratives'. Pp. 44–65 in R. Binstock and L. George (eds), *Handbook of Aging and the Social Sciences*. New York: Academic Press.

Stephenson, P., et al. 1999. 'A Methodological Discourse on Gender, Independence, and Frailty: Applied Dimensions of Identity Construction in Old Age', *Journal of Aging Studies*, 13(4), 391–401.

Stoller, E. 1993. 'Gender and the Organization of Lay Health Care: A Socialist-Feminist Perspective', *Journal of Aging Studies*, 7(1), 151–70.

Thomas, W. 1931. 'The Definition of the Situation'. Pp. 41–50 in W. Thomas (ed.), *The Unadjusted Girl*. Boston: Little, Brown.

Thompson, E. (ed.). 1994. *Older Men's Lives*. Thousand Oaks, Calif.: Sage.

Walker, A. 1999. 'Public Policy and Theories of Aging: Constructing and Reconstructing Old Age'. Pp. 361–78 in V. Bengtson and W. Schaie (eds), *Handbook of Theories of Aging*. New York: Springer.

CHAPTER 6

Social Structures and the Life Course:
Social Inequality and Social Change

Focal Points

- In what way do social structures and human agency interact to influence social relationships and to shape life-course trajectories?

- Does chronological age matter? How does age define and structure much of our lives and influence social relations and opportunities across the life course?

- Why and how are life chances and social relations across the life course, and in later life, influenced by social inequalities based on social class, gender, race, or ethnicity?

- For some members of disadvantaged groups in society, why is there a cumulative disadvantage in later life?

- How much of our daily social life is age-segregated as opposed to age-integrated, and why?

- To what extent are there generation gaps in society?

- How do public and private intergenerational transfers maintain social order, family stability, and generational equity?

Introduction

Chronological age and apparent age influence relationships in many social situations. Through interactions with others in a variety of social institutions, our identities are created and modified within social structures that guide and limit the nature and type of social relationships. As people engage in social relationships they acquire or are assigned unequal amounts of power and status because of the rights or duties attached to their social positions, such as professor versus student, or parent versus child. A social structure is created when a pattern of interrelated statuses and roles coalesce to constitute a relatively stable set of socially constructed relations.

Personal histories are constructed within evolving and intersecting social structures based on social class, race, ethnicity, gender, and age. These dimensions organize social life in a hierarchical structure in which, at the societal level, rewards can be allocated and distributed unequally. These elements of social structure are viewed as having 'master' status and are crucial determinants of social identity and social opportunities. They influence how, and to what extent, we gain access to power and other valued resources in a society or organization. Or, as McMullin (2000) succinctly argued, class, age, gender, ethnicity, and race are interlocking sets of power relations that structure social life and therefore contribute to, and perpetuate, social inequality. Social class, gender, race, age and ethnicity are not just individual properties or characteristics that create differences among people. They are basic structures inherent in the foundation of a society, and they often foster conflict among social groups.

This chapter is concerned with age structures, socially structured relations among individuals and age cohorts, and structural-level processes such as cohort flow, intergenerational transfers, age grading, and structural lag. Age is the structural dimension of interest in this chapter. However, age interacts, conceptually and theoretically, with class, race, gender, and ethnicity to create power relations and life chances across the life course. These links are especially important for an understanding of the later years, where lifelong disadvantages are often cumulative and thereby create more difficult situations for some members of older age cohorts.

Before we examine age structures and their effect on an individual, three caveats must be noted. First, while the focus here is on the structures or power relations based on age, class, race, gender, and ethnicity, we must not ignore human agency. Structures do not fully determine or control an individual's life course or outcome. The structural elements establish boundaries within which human agency is invoked by individuals or groups. Social movements, such as the feminist, black power, or grey power movements; changing roles and norms; and changing status systems over time present different opportunities and barriers to individuals or cohorts as they invoke agency across the life course. Do not, then, fall into the trap of believing that the life course is completely predetermined by our situation at birth or that one of these dimensions of inequality ensures that one is forever doomed to a disadvantaged status in society. Human agency can change life trajectories and facilitate social mobility. Agency is invoked when we acquire and develop social, human, and cultural capital

through the pursuit of higher education and by joining social networks. At one time, members of the dominant social class (those with more education and/or wealth) and the dominant gender (male) reproduced their position in society by the direct transmission of economic capital to their children through gifts and an inheritance. Although that still happens, agency enables individuals to change society or to improve their social status by acquiring social, human, and cultural capital.

A second caveat is that, at present, no one single theory or perspective can guide our thinking about social structures and aging. The age-stratification perspective focuses on inequality but minimizes the interaction of age with other systems of inequality. Similarly, the political economy and feminist perspectives focus on power relations in society, but devote less attention to age per se and to the interaction of age with other dimensions of power. And, while exchange theory may help us to understand intergenerational transfers in the family, it is not very effective in accounting for transfers at the societal level. As McMullin (2000: 526) notes, one set of these power relations, whether based on age, class, gender, ethnicity, or race, does not have more weight than the others, at least theoretically. Hence, she and others argue that a theoretical framework that fully integrates class, age, gender, and ethnicity and race is needed. Until a new macro-theory emerges, we, as students of aging phenomena, must conceptually consider all five dimensions as interacting sectors when designing research projects, social policies, or programs for older people (McMullin, 2004).

A third caveat is that social structures and processes unique to aging at the societal level must be differentiated, at times, from those unique to aging in an extended family. For example, a generational difference, or a generation gap, may be found on some attitude, belief, or value when the responses of unrelated individuals who are 65, 45, and 25 years of age are compared. However, these differences may not be observed if we compare the responses of those who are 65, 45, and 25 years of age in the same extended family. That is, differences between cohorts may be more pronounced, or real, at the societal level than at the personal level of the extended family. Thus, when employing cohort and generational analyses, we need to consider both similarities and differences at two levels: at the macro-level of society and at the micro-level in extended kinship systems.

Social Structures and Aging

Social Differentiation: Variation in Life Chances and Lifestyles

Without the influence of social structures on regular and enduring patterns of social interaction, our society might be unstable. To survive and attain its goals by ensuring social order and stability, every social system—whether a married couple, a business organization, a university, or a society—requires a division of labour and responsibility among its members. Hence, different social positions are created within social institutions. Different degrees of status are assigned to each position on the basis of the importance, power, or responsibility given to them in the social system. Positions are ranked, formally or informally, according to whether they have more or less status, power, or prestige than other positions, and whether there is variation in the rewards (that is, salary and prestige attached to a position). Associated with each position are rights and obligations, together with types of behaviour that are expected of an individual who occupies the position. Social norms evolve that represent common agreement on how individuals should behave, and these norms, in turn, provide clues as to how others will interpret and react to the individual.

Being assigned to, or achieving certain positions and not others reflects inequality in a social structure. This differentiation influences our life chances and lifestyles and facilitates or inhibits social interaction within and between the various strata of the social structure (O'Rand, 1996, 2001). This structural differentiation fosters either the integration or isolation of individuals or groups in a variety of social systems. For example, a 55-year-old man whose occupation is defined as labourer may have a moderately high status in the age structure because of his chronological age; a very high status in the family structure because he is the patriarch and primary wage earner; but a low status, responsibility, or power at his place of employment or in the community at large because of his low level of education and type of job.

Social Stratification: Unequal Access to Opportunities and Rewards

In pre-industrial societies, a simple three-tiered social structure based on age and gender often prevailed: a group of elderly men who ruled as a gerontocracy; all other adults; and children and adolescents who had not been declared 'adults' by some rite of passage. Today, the social structures of modern societies represent a complex mosaic of intersecting dimensions on a variety of social attributes and across a number of social institutions—family, education, work, leisure, the state, and religion.

Individuals in a society, organization, or group are ranked higher or lower than others on the basis of social class, race, gender, ethnicity, or age. When this ranking occurs, a system of unequal access to opportunities and rewards is created, and is usually perpetuated across time. Social positions, with variations in status and power, are assigned on the basis of either *ascribed* attributes, that is, race, gender, ethnicity, or *achieved* attributes, that is, class, age, and education, all of which represent social constructs. On the basis of these attributes, individuals are evaluated as inferior or superior to others when different values, beliefs, and experiences are 'constructed' around these attributes in a specific culture, organization, or institution. Once these evaluations of social worth become institutionalized, or a part of the culture and everyday life, individuals are ranked and systems of stratification are created. In North American and most modern societies, individuals are generally considered to be 'better', 'superior', or 'more worthy' (Tumin, 1967: 27) if they are

- white rather than black,
- male rather than female,
- educated rather than uneducated,
- wealthy rather than poor,
- white-collar workers rather than blue-collar workers,
- young adults rather than older adults,
- urban or suburban rather than rural dwelling,
- of Anglo-Saxon origin rather than members of other racial or ethnic groups,
- native-born rather than foreign-born,
- employed rather than unemployed, and
- married rather than divorced.

These stratification systems mean that some people have higher (or lower) status and more (or fewer) opportunities to acquire valued rewards, and they experience different lifestyles, challenges, and opportunities as they move through life. This leads to competition, and sometimes conflict, for scarce resources among occupants of the various social strata (O'Rand, 1996, 2001). These status differences are reinforced, if not created, by government policies that allocate resources and define the eligibility for rewards on the basis of the status (and therefore need) of certain lower-status groups—minority racial groups, poverty groups, children, elderly people, or women. But changes can and do take place in status rankings and in the composition of a social structure as a result of population aging, changes in the number and type of immigrants, and changes in gender, class, and racial relations.

Inequality involves an uneven distribution of wealth and poverty; unequal opportunities for education, health care, and leisure; differential access to power and rewards; and differential use of human agency. It would be much easier to understand the emergence and perpetuation of inequality if it were due to only one stratification system. However, in our complex social world, stratification systems interact and intersect to create and perpetuate structured social inequality (McMullin, 2004). Thus, we must understand how the age stratification system and chronological age interact with other stratification dimensions across the life course. As each age cohort passes through the life course, it represents a heterogeneous mixture of individuals who vary along interconnecting gender, class, racial, ethnic, religious, educational, and marital dimensions. These dimensions produce, maintain, and transfer elements of social inequality from one generation to the next, and they interact to influence opportunities, challenges, and lifestyles in later life. For example, economic security and health in later life are related to lifelong constraints imposed by gender, race, ethnicity, and class (especially the level of education); and to one's marital and employment history across the life course. The following sub-sections discuss relationships between age and the 'master status' stratification systems (class, gender, race, ethnicity), and discuss the possible cumulative effect of these status systems in later life.

Social Class and Age

Most societies are structured into a number of interlocking social classes, or strata. The number of strata range from two (aristocrats and peasants) or three (professionals, white-collar workers, and blue-collar workers) to a more complex structure with many divisions (upper-class, upper-middle class, middle-class, lower-middle-class, upper-lower-class, and lower-class). All the divisions are arbitrary and are socially constructed. In modern societies, the social-class structure is strongly influenced by the level of formal education, the prestige allocated to each occupation, and the wealth of an individual, family, or social group. Education, as an investment, leads to skills, employability, a healthier and longer life, and higher standards of economic and social well-being. Educational status influences attitudes, values, behaviour, friendships, job opportunities, health, and income throughout life. Different age cohorts and specific members of each cohort have had differential access to education throughout history, often because education has been valued differently by different families and age cohorts. In general, few people, especially women, used to have a university education. But that changed in the late twentieth century, and many members of the baby-boom cohort, especially women, have at least an undergraduate degree.

In each class, common values, beliefs, types of behaviour, and lifestyles emerge, many of which are passed from generation to generation by the family of origin. Thus, unequal or disadvantaged status early in life can contribute to unequal situations and hardships later in life (O'Rand, 2001). However, social mobility in middle or later life is possible through human agency; for example, a person who invests in an education, works hard, and achieves upward mobility in a career, or marries into a wealthy family can rise above his or her family of origin in the class-stratification system. Class and age interact to influence structured social relations, finances, health, and work and leisure opportunities across the life course, including the later years. Highlight 6.1 illustrates the influence of social class on the lives of two elderly widows—one from a lower-class background; the other having the advantage of an upper-middle-class background throughout her life.

Gender and Age

Sex refers to the genetic and biological difference between males and females. **Gender**, however, is a socially constructed concept that defines what it *means* to be male or female in a given society, and what types of behaviour and roles are expected of females and males at different stages in their lives.[1] Pyke (1996: 530) defined gender as:

> an emergent property of situated interaction rather than a role or attribute. Deeply held and typically nonconscious beliefs about men's and women's essential natures shape how gender is accomplished in everyday interactions. Because those beliefs are molded by existing macrostructural power relations, the culturally appropriate ways of producing gender favor men's interests over those of women. In this manner, gendered power relations are reproduced.

Gender shapes social life through agency and gender stratification; it is a central organizing principle of our social world, like class and race. Throughout the life course, and in all societies, males and females play different roles, receive different rewards, and experience different realities. For women, these gendered realities include

- less access to education, income, property, power, and pensions;
- more responsibility for unpaid family caregiving and less involvement in the paid labour force;
- more poverty, in general, and in later life;
- more victimization through violence, abuse, or neglect; and
- a more difficult later life—being widowed, being poor, living alone, being institutionalized or homeless—owing to cumulative disadvantages, many of which originate earlier in life as a result of being divorced or being absent from the labour force.

Highlight 6.1 Social Class Matters: Diversity in Widowhood

The transition to widowhood, itself a traumatic experience, can lead to unforeseen changes in the way one lives because of variations in social class. Alma and Betty are 70 years of age, live in the same city, and have both been widowed for five years. Here the similarities end, partly because of class differences and their related life experiences and opportunities.

Alma is among the invisible poor in society, since, when her husband died, his meagre pension benefits were lost. A housewife most of her life, Alma lacks her own pension, has few savings left, and is totally dependent for her survival on the old-age pension and the guaranteed income supplement. Since she was unable to find work, she has recently moved from her rented house into a sparsely furnished rooming house. In her small room she cooks, eats, and sleeps, sharing a bathroom with other lodgers. Faced with declining strength and mobility, the climb to the third floor is becoming more difficult, as is shopping for food and other necessities. She lives in a deteriorating neighbourhood with a high crime rate, and so she never ventures out at night. She has become a 'prisoner in her own room' because her children and friends live too far away to provide help and transportation. For Alma, the 'golden years' have not materialized. The next transition will probably be a move to publicly funded housing, where, in fact, her quality of life may improve.

Betty, in contrast, having raised her family, entered university at age 50, and upon graduation began a career as a journalist. Now, at 70, she is constantly seeking new challenges and adventures. She has written a successful novel and contributes a weekly column to a number of newspapers. Betty lives in a downtown condominium, consults her stockbroker weekly, takes tennis lessons three times a week, has a wide circle of female friends, and dates regularly. Volunteer work at a local elementary school one day a week keeps her in touch with the younger generation. She has considered 'wintering' in the south, but she prefers to take three or four trips a year to more exotic destinations in Europe or the Far East. For Betty, widowhood does not represent a loss of economic or social resources. In reality, the transition to being single has provided freedom and an incentive to reap the benefits of later life.

Definitions of gender vary by culture; in a society over time; across the life course (different issues matter to teenage girls versus elderly widows with respect to some elements of femininity); and within a society by race, class, ethnicity, sexual orientation, education, and region of the country. Our gendered selves (males and females) interact in gendered institutions of education, work, family, leisure, politics, the military, and religion to create a gendered world.

It must be stressed that gender, as a concept, includes men as well as women (Thompson, 1994). Men are not genderless, but their gendered experiences and social lives are different from those of women in the same age cohort. Men tend to be advantaged in terms of education,

income, career opportunities, health, having a partner throughout life to care for them, and having power in many social institutions—business, sports, politics, religion, and education (Thompson, 1994).

When age and gender intersect to create gendered social processes and outcomes across the life course, including the later years, women, in general, are more disadvantaged; and gender inequalities are most cumulative and visible among older women. Because of gendered pathways through life and the situation of women in later life, aging has been described as 'a woman's issue'. Calasanti (1999: 45) argued that 'gender relations are socially-constructed power relations between men and women which become institutionalized in various social arenas.' These power relations emerge in the family, education, work, leisure, and politics. They spill over into society at large, becoming embedded, as well, in the larger context of differences by race, class, ethnicity, and age at different stages in life, including the later years.

Kimmel (2000) defined gender as the study of masculinities and femininities. Stressing diversity in the gender stratification system, he argued that there is greater diversity *among* men and women than *between* men and women. That is, there are different levels and meanings of masculinity and femininity, and it is through differential socialization experiences that men and women exhibit different masculinities and femininities. The gender differences we observe or that individuals experience are the outcome of gender identities interacting in gendered institutions to create gender inequality. As gender inequality is reduced, gender differences between women and men will shrink, although they are unlikely ever to fully disappear, at least in the immediate future. Men and women are not from different planets as one popular culture book would have us believe—*Men are from Mars, Women are from Venus* (Gray, 1992)! We are more alike than different, and in some social groups and in some institutions the gender gap is narrowing (Kimmel, 2000).

Thus, despite social change and progress, there remain 'enduring inequalities by gender across the life course, producing for women an accumulated disadvantage, and a lifetime of cumulative advantage for men' (Moen, 2001: 184). Gender matters because men and women, as gendered individuals, are differentially located in gendered social structures that foster different roles, relationships, and the accompanying opportunities and barriers. Gender reflects power differences in which inequities are created so that some men have power over women; some women have power over other women *and* men; and some men have power over other men. Consequently, Kimmel (2000) concludes that not all masculinities and femininities are created equal. To illustrate, because of life-long gender differences and experiences, women

- are valued less in society,
- are victims of discrimination and sexist attitudes and practices,
- are victims of violence,
- are under-employed or unemployed,
- engage in unpaid labour in the home, which deprives them of pension benefits,
- assume major responsibility for family caregiving,
- have fewer educational opportunities, and
- have truncated or random work careers.

In later life these gender differences are further magnified because women followed different life trajectories at work, leisure, and in the family, and experienced different lifestyles than men. To illustrate, older women generally:

- live part of their later life alone—widowed, divorced, never-married
- lack full public or private pension benefits, and many experience poverty
- are burdened with the responsibility of caring for a parent, a spouse, or a grandchild when a son or daughter dies or is divorced
- retire when their spouse retires, despite having spent less time in the labour force
- have a higher incidence of chronic health problems
- are more likely to suffer in silence as they are less aware of societal inequities in social, health, or financial status

These differences reflect the 'feminization of later life'. Clearly, more, but not all, older women are vulnerable in later life because of life-long gender differences. The financial and health implications of having less education, moving in and out of the labour force, and having the responsibility for home, child care and parent care are magnified in later life. Inequalities are more likely to occur if an older woman survives her spouse, receives a reduced pension when she is widowed, and depletes her savings if she lives into her eighth or ninth decade. The economic situation of older women is compounded by gender-based pension policies, which heretofore have been based on the assumption that all women are married and dependent on their husband. Those who are divorced or widowed and those who never married or are childless are especially disadvantaged because age and gender interact in later life to produce inadequate pension income and a reduced quality of life (see Chapter 9).

As with most aspects of aging, descriptions of ideal, generalized patterns of aging by one social category, gender, are not sufficient. Women are not a homogeneous group, but rather vary by age, education, wealth, marital status, ethnicity, race and social class, just as men vary on the same attributes. Gender relations do foster gender differences, but gender relations in terms of roles, power, and prestige are changing, at least in domains like the family and leisure, and in some sectors of the labour force. In later life, if older people, in general, are valued less and assigned a low ranking by society, their life situation becomes even more difficult if they hold, as well, another lower-status attribute, such as being a woman with little education, a gay woman, an Aboriginal woman, or an immigrant widow. Consequently, the intersection of these various stratification systems must be understood when one is developing research, policies, or programs that pertain to older women.

At one time, scholars and practitioners in the field of gerontology labelled this multi-dimensional impact as double jeopardy (age and gender), triple jeopardy (age, gender, and race), or multiple jeopardy (age, gender, race, class). Serious difficulties in later life were attributed to the interaction of racism, sexism, and ageism. They argued that these discriminatory processes

merged in later life to lower the quality of life for many older people. But two of these inequalities—racism and sexism—are experienced across the life course, and ageism may or may not become a factor in later life. You may still encounter the 'jeopardy' label when you read the literature. However, a more useful way of understanding later life is to realize that stratification systems interact to create structural inequalities for some individuals as they move through the life course, including the later years.

Today, research and policy analysis focus on the extent to which the outcomes of the stratification systems are cumulative and additive throughout the life course (O'Rand, 1996; Ferraro, 2001). Inequality in power, prestige, and privileges exists throughout the life course within and between all cohorts. The effects of these risk factors accumulate through a person's life to increase the heterogeneity of older cohorts, and thereby increase the inequality experienced by some older people. Inequalities in later life are not random. Economic or health disadvantages later in life are partially attributable to the cumulative effect of early structural disadvantages, such as poverty, less education, and child-care responsibilities; institutionalized discrimination; and individual agency (that is, decisions or actions taken or not taken at transition points).

As with many topics in gerontology, it is difficult to separate aging effects from cohort effects. An elderly woman with lower-class roots in a racial or ethnic group may be among the most impoverished people in later life with respect to income, housing, and health. But she is also likely to be among the least educated, and she has probably had a low income and poorer than average health all her life. Being female, poorly educated, and a member of a minority ethnic or racial group has created lifelong disadvantages, and the later years may not significantly increase her already disadvantaged situation. Some of these heightened disadvantages in later life can be offset by policies that provide income or services based on need. Such policies, if delivered fairly and effectively, have the potential to reduce disparities, at all stages of life, but especially in later life (O'Rand, 1996).

Race, Ethnicity and Age

Canada's 'open door' immigration policy contributes to considerable variation in the number of language and cultural groups in most age cohorts. Some immigrants never become fully assimilated into Canadian society; others, often those in the second generation, become structurally assimilated. For many first-generation members of racial or ethnic groups in Canada, and for some individuals in subsequent generations, poverty, in other words, lower-class status, is synonymous with race and ethnicity, thereby fostering and perpetuating social inequality across the life course. Labelled as minority groups, they are really poverty groups. Because of prevailing prejudices and stereotypes in mainstream society, members of these groups may experience discrimination in access to services and opportunities. With less education, lower incomes, and a lower quality of housing all their lives, they are more likely to experience poor health and poverty in their later years (Williams and Wilson, 2001). This situation is compounded further at all ages, including later life, if a household is headed by a woman who is a single parent, the sole wage earner, and a member of a minority group. An inability to read or speak English or French can create difficulties in later life—either in seeking services or health care or if a person is forced to live in an institution where the staff do not speak the primary or sole language of some residents.

Nevertheless, not all members of a racial or ethnic group are disadvantaged. It depends on educational attainment and opportunities for social mobility, especially for those in second and third generations. But for those who are born into a family with low income, little education, and little power, there is a lifelong negative impact on employment opportunities and income, health, quality and location of housing, and access to health care and other services. The lifelong disadvantages accumulate to create additional hardships in the later years as health and income decline further.

The location of a specific group in the ethnic and racial stratification system changes over time, and leads to variations among generations in the process of aging and in the status of older people. Moreover, the status of one group improves when other even more disadvantaged groups arrive in Canada, when the amount or type of institutionalized discrimination directed toward a group decreases, or when the group becomes assimilated into mainstream society, often over a period of two to three generations after arriving in Canada.

Finally, some members of minority ethnic and racial groups experience inequality in the receipt of public benefits and social services since most social policies are developed for those in mainstream society. This form of systemic inequality is subtle and often unintended. But if policies and formal services are insensitive to varying cultural or language needs, members may be unaware of, or not know how to obtain, some service or benefit. For older people who need institutional care in nursing homes, such facilities may not meet their needs with respect to diet, health care practices and beliefs, or language. Yeo (1993) found, for example, that bilingual nursing home residents with advanced stages of dementia often revert to speaking their first language with the staff and visitors.

Age Structures and the Life Course

Introduction: Concepts and Social Processes

Concepts

To understand the influence of age structures across the life course in a society or a social institution such as the extended family, three major concepts are employed: 'cohort', 'generation', and 'generational unit'. A **cohort** is composed of everyone who was born in a specified year or in a specific period of years (2000-5). We are often interested in the size and socio-demographic characteristics of an age cohort and whether these elements influence the life chances and lifestyles of cohort members at different stages of their lives.

A **generation** is more than a group of people (an age cohort) born during the same period (Mannheim, 1952). It represents a unique grouping of adjacent birth cohorts, many of whom have experienced a significant socio-historical event, such as a depression or war, in a similar manner or whose members tend to think and behave in a similar way because they interact frequently or adopt similar values. Members of a generation often develop a historical or social consciousness or bond that gives unique meaning to their lives and sets them apart from other birth cohorts. Some generations create significant conflict and change in a society or institution. The social construction of a generation does not occur among all adjacent age cohorts that emerge. There have been four significant generations[2] in North America in the twentieth century:

1. Adults who had just entered or were about to enter the labour force during the Depression of the 1930s (the 'Depression' generation).

2. People who were children of this Depression generation and who were influenced throughout their lives by the fact they were children during this calamitous economic period in history. Many became parents of the baby boomers (Elder, 1999).

3. The large baby-boom generation born in the years following the Second World War (Foot and Stoffman, 1998).

4. Children of the baby-boomers, who were born after 1970 (Adams, 1997) and variously labelled in the 1990s as 'Generation X', 'Twentysomethings' (Coupland, 1992; Thau and Heflin, 1997), 'Generation Next'

(Kotash, 2000), or the 'Nexus Generation' (Barnard et al., 1998), primarily because of their unique values and lifestyles, which were depicted in comedy television series in the late 1990s.

When scholars, the media, and laypeople use the term generation, they may be discussing three quite different groups (Alwin, 2002: 43).

- All people born in the same year (1985)

- A unique position in a family's line of descent (the second or third generation to attend a specific university or enter a specific occupation, or be employed by a specific company)

- A group of people self-consciously defined, by themselves and by others, as part of a historically based social movement, such as the 'hippie' generation of the sixties, the baby boomers, or Generation X.

It is important to note that in the media, and sometimes in scholarly research, 'generation' and 'cohort' often are used interchangeably.

To this point, we have implied that a generation defines a group at the societal level of analysis. However, as a concept, generation applies, as well, to different age groups in an extended-family system (Marshall, 1983; Price et al., 2000; Connidis, 2001). The structure of a family lineage system influences the interaction patterns within and between generations. Most kinship systems include two generations (parents and young children or adolescents) or three generations (grandparents, parents, and children). But with increasing longevity in modern societies, a four-generation family (great-grandparents, grandparents, parents, and children) is also possible, at least for a brief time. However, with childless marriages or never-married children among the second generation, a new type of two-generation family is emerging, consisting of parents and adult children. In time, this latter group will become a one-generation family consisting of older adults with no children, ultimately leading to the extinction of a particular kinship system.

At the societal level, each generation may include subgroups with different world-views or with a unique group consciousness, such as university students compared to people of the same age working in blue-collar occupations. These unique subgroups are known as **generational units** (Mannheim, 1952). In some generations there may be no generational units, or a number may form depending on the social, political, or economic circumstances of a particular historical period. For example, in North America, among the youth generation of the 1960s, variously labelled the 'hippie', 'beat', or 'counter-culture' generation, it was college students, rather than working-class youth, who were the more radical generational unit in seeking social change. In contrast, in England, working-class youth were the more radical and rebellious generational unit in the youth culture of that period. In short, generational units coalesce and form around existing social characteristics such as class, race, or ethnicity; and they are related to political or social perspectives such as liberalism, conservatism, or socialism, which, in turn, are often class-based.

Social Processes

Three interrelated social processes are influenced by age structures: cohort analysis, generational analysis, and lineage effects. **Cohort analysis** refers to the use of quantitative or qualitative methods to study the characteristics of, or meanings associated with, a specific birth cohort, whether for a single year or for a five- to ten-year period, as it moves across the life course. Cohort analysis is used, as well, to study social change and stability over time. The relative size of a cohort compared to others born earlier or later shapes the experiences of its members. To illustrate, the baby-boom cohort, compared to the baby-bust cohort, experienced crowded classrooms and much more competition for a finite number of jobs when they entered the labour force.

Generational analysis involves combining subgroups of specific cohorts or groups of adjacent cohorts on the basis of common socio-historical experiences; two examples of such subgroups are the baby-boom and the baby-bust generations. This approach, at the macro-level of society, seeks to understand how cohorts maintain continuity in the existing social order, or how and why they initiate change in the social order. These outcomes are known as **cohort effects**. This type of generational analysis examines the influence of emerging age cohorts on the stability of social structures and considers interaction patterns within and between members of age strata. Generational analysis examines the impact on society of social consensus, conflict, change, or inequality among cohorts. It also examines the extent to which age stratification interacts with other dimensions of social differentiation and how this interaction affects individuals or cohorts.

Generational analysis has also been used to study similarities, differences, or conflicts among generations in an extended family. Here the outcomes are known as **lineage effects**. For some family members, particularly adolescents and young adults, the influence of the family as opposed to that of the peer group, which may adhere to different values and practices, creates strain for some individuals, and perhaps leads to social conflict and change for society if a generational consciousness emerges. Interaction (more at some stages in the life course than at others) between the family-lineage structure and societal age structures becomes even more complex when age structures interact with class, racial, ethnic, or gender stratification systems. Thus, when generational 'conflicts' or generation 'gaps' are observed, the explanation for differing values or behaviour concerning work, politics, sexual practices, or religion may reflect either a cohort gap across society or a lineage gap in an extended family (Henretta, 1988). For example, parental and grandparent views about premarital sex generally conflict with those of teenagers and young adults. Are these differences due to aging effects, different cohort values, or a more deep-rooted difference based on changing cultural or religious values in specific extended families?

Age Grading and Age Norms

Age grading is the process by which chronological age influences elements of social life such as social positions, roles, norms, and structured social relationships. This process results from a system of age stratification that is present not only in the society at large, but also in social groups, organizations, and institutions (O'Rand, 1990, 1996, 2001). Age grades provide a cultural definition of the expected rights, behaviour, and responsibilities of an individual at a particular stage or age in the life course. These age-based cultural definitions become the basis for self-identification and for allocating positions in a society or institution. For example, though nothing in the law prevents any professor at a university from being appointed president of the university, those under 50 years of age likely would be considered 'too young' for such a position, however well qualified they might be.

Two types of age norms are internalized and adopted to varying degrees across the life course. *Ascriptive age norms* are based on rules and constraints determined for a specific chronological age, such as retiring at 65, voting at 18, or driving at 16. *Consensual age norms* provide an approximate age range in which specific roles or types of behaviour are appropriate or should be given up. They define the approximate age for transitional events such as leaving home, entering the labour force, getting married, having children, or retiring. Age norms also influence lifestyle factors such as what kind of dress, language, or type of social or leisure activities are considered suitable for different ages.

Age norms provide some degree of social control and stability by constraining our behaviour in social situations (act your age!'). However, there appear to be relatively few age-related norms that define acceptable and unacceptable behaviour for older people. Where clearly defined norms for older people are present, and accepted, they often refer to behaviour that should be avoided at a particular age, such as dating or wearing certain styles of clothing. Obviously, age norms change over time with changes in socialization practices, societal values, or economic conditions; or with increased knowledge about the physical or cognitive capacity of older people. Moreover, all members of a particular age cohort may not adhere to age norms, and age norms vary in a cohort by class, race, gender, ethnicity, and place of residence. Highlight 6.2 illustrates a remarkable later-life change in attitude and behaviour following surgery.

Highlight 6.2 A Certain Age

My mother loves to describe her favourite cartoon. Two old women stand at a bus stop, one dowdy and stooped, the other flashy and brazen in a get-up designed for someone half her age. The flashy one says to the little old lady, 'I was old, too, once, but it didn't suit me'. My mother laughs, clearly seeing herself in the company of the flashy and brazen.

In the way oft-told tales seem to shape the lives of their tellers, my mother became a character in her own cartoon. But she became the stooped old woman, and changing her mind didn't appear to be an option. Ambushed out of nowhere, pursued by demons beyond her control, she

continued

Hightlight 6.2 continued

increasingly retreated into a world that was blurred around the edges. We could read in her eyes a reflection of our own terror, our own pain at so suddenly losing our family's mother and grandma.

It had started with little telltale signs that, taken singly, might have slipped by unnoticed, camouflaged by the normal process of growing old. The vacant look we passed off as distraction: 'Mom's not hearing a word we are saying.' The occasional non sequitur that brought first laughter, and then an exchange of worried looks. The bathroom emergencies that we thought we just had to accept as one of the inconveniences—no, humiliations—of aging. The unbalanced, shuffling gait that eliminated long striding walks around Stanley Park. Her once razor-sharp mind slipping.

My mother has always been a bit of a Pollyanna and, like so many of her generation, she denies anything is wrong. Getting her to admit to a cold is like getting her to admit she has syphilis. She has always equated feeling unwell—never mind being really sick—with full-blown moral failure, and certainly something never to be willingly acknowledged. So the idea of asking her how or what she was feeling, with the expectation of getting a useful answer, was out of the question. My mother's particular idiosyncrasies aside, it is almost impossible to ask anyone, let alone your mother, if she thinks she is losing her mind. At the point where the question really needs to be asked, it is immaterial whether you're trying to avoid her fears or your own.

I spoke with my brothers and sisters, trying to decide if we were overreacting, simply having trouble with our mother's aging, or whether what we could all see was happening was really cause for alarm. I spoke to our family doctor. Feelings of disloyalty came up against my need to fix things; a belief that I knew best what was going on clashed with a socially prescribed deference to the specialized knowledge of doctors. We discussed normal aging, depression, nutrition, build-up of uric acid from kidney problems, strokes, brain tumours, Alzheimer's disease.

After much delay, CAT scans and MRIs diagnosed blockage of her cranial-spinal fluid, enlarged ventricles and excess fluid on the brain, damage to brain cells. I tortured myself with 'if only's'. If only I had listened to my heart, if only I had confronted her denial, if only I had deferred less, we would have had this knowledge sooner and less damage would have been done. But the truth is that of all the terrifying things that can grab hold of an old person's—or any person's—mind and not let go, enlarged ventricles in the brain are probably the best thing that could have happened to her.

The neurosurgeon, Dr Honey ('And he truly is a honey,' mom assured us), told her that surgery to install a shunt in her head to drain the fluid into her abdomen couldn't guarantee reversal of the damage already done, but would stop it from progressing. The danger of stroke as a result of the operation was slight, but present. Mom consulted with all her kids. Finally, she asked Dr Honey, 'What would you do if I was your mother?' His response: 'I'd tell her to do it.' So mom did.

The results were better than anything any of us had dared to hope for. Dr Honey called her his star patient. She glowed and crowed and assured us that she had never really been worried in the first place. But she did admit that was probably because she really wasn't too clear about what was going on. We were the ones acutely aware of her terrifying tailspin. Her awareness and her memory of that time are blessedly fuzzed by the demons that were destroying her brain cells.

She was lucky. We were lucky. She got old—really old—once, but she changed her mind. And she was right. It didn't suit her. Fate decided to give her another chance. She came back, to sparkle a little longer—a little older, for sure, a little less brazen, wearing her 83 years a little more vividly, perhaps—but she came back.

Source: Reprinted with permission of the author, Linda Light. First published in the Facts and Arguments page of *The Globe and Mail* 15 July 1999: A22.

Age Structures: Segregated or Integrated?

Age structures include people who are of different chronological ages and who are at different stages in the life course. The strata are interconnected, and there are varying degrees of interaction between the strata.[3] An individual's location in the age structure influences his or her behaviour, attitudes, and values in a number of domains. Similarly, age creates behavioural expectations in structured relations with others, both in and outside the age stratum to which an individual belongs by virtue of year of birth. Some age-related expectations become institutionalized and lead to self-fulfilling prophecies and stereotypes that magnify the differences between age strata. For example, at one time it was believed that retirees should 'relax' and cease being productive. However, today, more older people have the potential and desire to be creative and to remain productive, including as volunteers. This need would not be fulfilled if they accepted a socially constructed age norm that expected them to 'take it easy' or 'disengage' after they retire.

A long-standing debate in the aging literature has been the question of whether a society and its institutions should be age-segregated, as university residences and nursing homes are, or age-integrated like families and workplaces.[4] This debate was stimulated by age-stratification theory, which conceptualized society as age-segregated, and by the related question of whether an age-segregated structure stimulated or prevented age or generational conflict. Riley and Riley (1994) conceptualized two 'ideal' types of social structures across the life course; one was more typical of the past (age-segregated), and one reflects the present and future structure (age-integrated). Figure 6.1 illustrates that in an age-segregated structure, different periods or stages in life were associated, in general, with specific activities or responsibilities—youth with education, middle-age with work) and old age leisure. In contrast, the contemporary view is that age structures are integrated and should permit, as well as encourage, opportunities for education, work, and leisure at all ages.

Over time, age-graded roles and expectations have become blurred as people of different ages interact more frequently and develop more com-

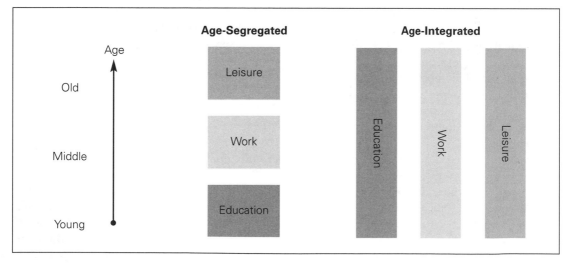

Figure 6.1 Ideal Types of Age Structures

Source: M.W. Riley and J.W. Riley, Jr (1994). Copyright © 1994. This material is used by permission of John Wiley & Sons, Inc.

mon interests. Public policies also change the meaning and significance of age for structured relations, and thereby either reduce or enhance barriers for age-based interaction (Walker, 2000). Age integration has been fostered through formal intergenerational programs in which people of different ages interact frequently and thereby come to understand and respect people of other ages (Newman et al., 1997). Some examples include:

- Adopt-a-grandparent programs where young children are paired with older non-relatives in their community.

- Retired people serving as teacher assistants in elementary schools or as volunteers in youth after-school programs.

- Older people attending university classes (see Highlight 5.1, page 143).

As Hamil-Luker and Uhlenberg (2002) note, later-life educational pursuits promote age integration and increase the likelihood that older people will make a productive contribution to society either as employees or as volunteers. However, they caution that there are still many age-related role expectations that create barriers or lead older people to believe they should not enter formal education programs. As we will learn in Chapter 10, Silver Colleges, Universities of the Third Age, and Elderhostel programs have provided educational opportunities for older people, but they reinforce an age-segregated society. In contrast, at the institutional level, many universities encourage those over 60 or 65 years of age to attend age-integrated classes where they share life experiences with young adults. Are there any older people in your classes? If so, introduce yourself and spend some time learning from these life-long or later-life learners.

The family and extended kinship system is the only fully age-integrated institution that facilitates and encourages interaction across age and cohort boundaries. However, other sectors of society are becoming more age-integrated. This process is facilitated and advanced if chronological age is not used, directly or indirectly, as a criterion for participation in an organization or institution (Uhlenberg, 2000: 261). Perceived or real age barriers result in a perpetuation of the age-segregated form of age structure (Figure 6.1). In contrast, a reduction or elimination of age barriers fosters a more linked, age-integrated age structure across the life course. When age is used as a criterion for participation, a structural barrier to interaction with others is created, and this barrier often becomes institutionalized. In reality, there is much less segregation by age than there is by race or gender in most sectors of society, but it still exists, especially in some workplaces. As more age-integrated structures evolve, it is more difficult to make the argument that there is age-based conflict at the societal level (see 'Age Structures and Social Change' below for a discussion of intergenerational transfers and the generational equity issue).

Age Structures and Social Change

Structural Lag

Over time there have been changes in the number of age strata, in the shape of the age structure, and in the relative prestige of positions, both in the same or different age strata. For example, in pre-modern societies the oldest men generally held the most prestige and power. In modern societies, with more age strata, power has shifted to middle-aged men. That is, social meanings based on age vary from one culture and historical period to another. To illustrate, in earlier centuries those over 40 years of age were considered old, whereas in the twentieth century people were not defined as old until about 65 years of age. At present, the definition of old age is moving toward 70 or 80 years as life expectancy increases and the health of older people improves. But many policies and programs lag behind changing definitions and the needs of older adults. For example, because of healthier lifestyles acquired throughout the middle years, new programs and facilities for a healthier, active, and more heterogeneous older population are required. But they may not be available because of outdated policies or programs. The process by which individual or cohort needs change faster than social values and norms or institutional structures is known as **structural lag** (Riley et al., 1994; O'Rand, 1996; Cutler and Hendricks, 2001). In developed countries, 'there is a disjuncture between opportunity structures and the capabilities of older persons, and between roles open to them and their potential contributions' (Cutler and Hendricks, 2001: 465). In the developing countries, public pensions and health-care facilities lag far behind the needs of a rapidly increasing number of older people.

Social structures and values often lag behind changes in family values, such as the filial obligation to care for one's elderly parents. In Taiwan, Hsu et al. (2002) found that this practice was declining as children emigrate or establish their own household after marriage rather than living with a parent. Adult children are much less likely to live with their aging parents than previously, and hence, they are more likely to contribute financial support, paid household services, and emotional support. Hsu et al. (2002) quote an old Chinese proverb that expresses the new reality and a need for new policies: 'nearby neighbours are better than faraway relatives.' They argue that volunteer support networks and community care systems should be established quickly to eliminate the structural lag in caregiving. In Taiwan, the needs of elderly people are not being met by the family nor by government policies and programs. Consequently, there is structural lag in meeting the needs of an aging population.

Some examples of structural lag where policies and programs for older people have not kept up with emerging needs are the following:

- opportunities for formal education throughout the life course, rather than only during childhood and adolescence

- leisure facilities or programs for people of all ages

- flexible pension and retirement systems for a work history that involves many jobs, with many employers, rather than one career in the same organization

- flexible work schedules and pension rights for women that recognize the time they spend on child rearing and caregiving

- employment options to permit both early retirement and working beyond 65 years of age

- social support for dual-career couples who have to care for or help their aging parents

- age-neutral policies to recognize a shift from an age-segregated society to an age-integrated society, in which age structures and age norms become less important

Changing historical and personal circumstances create pressure for social change. But individual life-course changes usually occur before institutional changes, leading to structural lag. How individuals *and* institutions adapt to structural lag and how structural lag can be reduced or eliminated is a challenge for policymakers.

Cohort Flow

Cohort flow is the process by which birth cohorts succeed one another over time. As cohorts pass through life, they become smaller and comprise a larger percentage of women. Each cohort experiences the life course in different ways (Uhlenberg and Miner, 1996). While each cohort contains individuals with different social characteristics and experiences, all members of a cohort experience some similar events, thereby making them different from members of other cohorts—especially older or younger cohorts far removed from the trajectory of the cohort being studied.

Cohort and Generational Effects

Social structures are relatively static at specific periods in history but over time they are changed by social conflict or change. As a result of social changes, cohorts and generations age in different ways and have the potential to introduce further social change into an organization, a community, a social institution, or a society. As noted in earlier sections, a society and the social institutions in that society are characterized by social differentiation and social stratification. At the societal level, whether there is change, and if so how much, is influenced by whether successive cohorts accept, redefine, or reject the values and status quo that preceding cohorts have institutionalized. Newer cohorts initiate change when elements of the social stratification systems are no longer considered acceptable or just. Social change when it occurs can be controversial or harmonious. For example, when older people perceive ageism, discrimination, segregation, or isolation, they seek to change the status quo by educating others, by political processes (see Highlight 6.3), or by rebellion and no longer conforming to social expectations.

Sometimes change involves generational conflict. This conflict may be unavoidable because members of two or more competing generations are at different stages of socialization, because they live during unique historical periods where competing values or conditions prevail, or because one generation experiences social inequalities which they seek to reduce or eradicate. Generational conflict may also arise because of cohort-centrism, in which members of a cohort interpret all social or historical events from their own point of view (Henretta, 1988). Cohort-centrism may develop an age-group consciousness and solidarity, thereby leading to possible discontinuities or conflict between age groups. Ultimately, this may lead to social or political change. Highlight 6.3 illustrates the increasing political involvement and empowerment of older

Highlight 6.3 Grey Power: A Process of Social Change by Older Adults

Political participation across the life course generally involves low involvement beginning in late adolescence, an increase through late middle-age, followed by a decrease in the post-retirement years. In recent decades, however, older adults have expanded their political consciousness and activism. Inspired by the charismatic leadership of Maggie Kuhn, who founded the Gray Panthers in 1970 (www.graypanthers.org), people over 65 began to lobby and speak out on their own behalf. Most of this activism, labelled as 'grey power', focusses on inadequate government policies and programs on such issues as taxes, old-age security systems, housing, home care, drug plans, and health care.

Active and persuasive older people participate in public dialogue on radio and television, in mail campaigns to MPs, and in protest marches and sit-ins to bring their concerns to the attention of politicians, private-sector entrepreneurs, the media, and younger age groups. They have also formed advocacy groups to promote the needs, interests, and rights of older people (Canadian Pensioners Concerned, Canada's Association for the Fifty Plus—CARP). Governments, to seek advice, have created local, provincial, and national advisory groups (such as the National Advisory Council on Aging—NACA). These groups are composed of older adults who are invited to participate in the decision-making process and to comment on existing and future government policies. These government-created bodies seek to empower 'senior' voters.

Older people do have ideas, needs, and dreams, and they need to be heard, now and in the future. Visible and vocal advocacy groups sensitize governments to the important issues that affect the quality of life of middle-aged and older Canadians.

age cohorts, which has resulted in social and political change.

Generations, like gender, class, race or religion, become a common explanatory factor to account for differences among groups in a society or for why a society changed. Too often change or differences are attributed to generational succession; that is, the characteristics common to one or more older age cohorts are replaced by those of younger age cohorts. Alwin (2002), however, notes that changes in attitudes, beliefs, and behaviour result also from historical events, such as September 11, and from normal oucomes of aging. People, through agency, change as they grow older and respond to specific social movements or historical events. Alwin argues that social change results as much from shifts in thinking and behaving in individual lives, due to either aging or historical event, as it results from generational succession. Clearly, the onset of the civil rights movement and the women's movement were unique and distinctive experiences for those who were young adults at that time. These events influenced the development of unique world views among many, and these views remain an influential force as these cohorts age. But these world views also changed the lives of older cohorts, not just the lives of those in much younger cohorts. This helps to support the generational-succession explanation for social change.

Most studies of generational succession and social change are based on cross-sectional rather than longitudinal studies. Hence, most conclusions about the influence of generations are based on a snapshot at one time. Moreover, the specific issue or question addressed in a survey at one point in time can influence interpretations. Thus, Alwin concludes that whether generational succession explains social change depends more on the issue or question being used to represent change:

> Generational replacement seems to explain
> why fewer Americans now than 30 years ago

say they trust other people, but historical events seem to explain why fewer say they trust government. Similarly, historical events, in interaction with aging effects (or life cycle change), may explain lifetime changes in church attendance or politicial partisanship better than generational shifts (Alwin, 2002: 42).

Lineage Effects

In the family and extended-kinship system, there are likely more similarities in values, ideals, behaviour, and stratification elements (such as class and race) than are observed at the societal level. These similarities, despite age and gender differences, provide some continuity and stability across generations in the extended family.

Structured social relations in the extended family involve negotiation, and the provision of opportunities for agency, especially by younger members. Thus, conflict in the family due to age differences is a possibility, either periodically or permanently, with a concomitant disruption in the frequency or intimacy of structured relations. In some families there are people who have nothing to do with those in the older or younger generations, perhaps because of conflict based on differences in values, ideals, beliefs, or experiences.

Lineage conflict can be initiated or increased when intergenerational debates and conflicts at the societal level spill over into the family domain. This happens when the media highlight different values, beliefs and norms, and different cultural 'tastes' and practices among younger people—in music, clothes, body piercing, hair styles, sexual activity, racial or gender equality, and political ideologies. There is usually some difference in values and lifestyles between most generations, at both the society and family level, because each cohort was socialized at a different period in history. It is the inability or unwillingness to accept changes or new ways of thinking and behaving that lead to further changes or conflict, at the societal or family level, in structured social relations between generations. Often these changes are triggered by agency, usually on the part of younger members who seek to express their individuality. For the most part, changes are brought about and institutionalized through peaceful debate and calm discussion over a period of time, or by persistent behaviour, rather than through violent conflict. Believe it or not, at one time in this author's lifetime, jeans were considered work clothing. They were never worn by women, by middle-aged or older people; nor were they worn to school, in an office, in restaurants, or on airplanes. The public acceptance of jeans as a form of leisure or work apparel took place quietly over a period of years, first at the family level, and then at the societal level. Even today, however, as silly as it seems, there are some private clubs, religious institutions, or places of employment where the wearing of jeans is discouraged or forbidden.

Generation Gaps: Myth or Reality?

Is there a 'generation gap' in the extended family, or at the societal level, among the young, middle-aged, and older segments of the population? When intergenerational strain arises, it could lead to generation 'gaps' or 'inequities'. To understand why this might happen, it is necessary to examine social, economic, political, and historical events, or changes in values and beliefs, which create social dissension among generations at the lineage or cohort levels. Each new generation experiences existing social institutions with a new perspective—this is the phenomenon of 'fresh contact' (Mannheim, 1952)—and they may or may not attempt to change social, political, or economic conditions to meet evolving needs and interests.

Lineage Gaps
Discussions between members of two or three generations in a family concerning differences in opportunities, values, rights, and behaviour can lead to action and change, or they may remain at the level of interesting and at times frustrating

debates. Where a gap is perceived ('I don't understand my kids'; 'My parents are out-of-date'), the size and seriousness of the gap are evaluated differently by each generation. The older generation tends to minimize the gap, arguing that it is merely due to differences in maturity and experience on the part of the younger generation. They also believe that any differences in values, behaviour, or dress are temporary and will eventually disappear. In contrast, members of younger generations exaggerate perceived differences that they wish to change. They claim that members of the older generation do not understand and that middle-aged and older people interfere with their need and right to establish values, identities, and lifestyles that are more suitable in the current period in history.

Conflict often occurs in immigrant families when the cultural values and experiences of different generations begin to clash. Second- or third-generation Canadian-born youth, socialized by parents or grandparents who were born and raised in another country, face the dilemma of having to choose between traditional values held by older members of their family, and the customs of their peers, mainstream society, and the media. In such a situation, intergenerational strain and conflict does arise in the family. However, these generational differences tend to narrow and disappear as subsequent generations become assimilated and adopt the cultural norms of mainstream Canadian society.

A generation gap may be reported if different generations live together. That is, frequent daily interaction can create intergenerational disagreements, which may be seen as a generation gap. Of course, such a housing relationship can create, as well, a greater understanding and appreciation of generational differences. That is, such disagreements may be due to living arrangements and to differences in behaviour because of one's stage in the life course, rather than to a real generation gap.

There appear to be three possible explanations for apparent lineage gaps in an extended family. First, differences in values and attitudes arise because generations are at different stages of development or maturation. In this situation, members of the older generation expect (or hope) that young people will grow out of their adolescent values and attitudes as they move into early adulthood.

A second explanation is that differences arise because of a generational or cohort effect. Members of a particular generation, socialized at a different time in history, acquire habits, attitudes, and beliefs that are needed and valued in that era. Each generation acquires a unique view of the world, and variations of these acquired differences are demonstrated during subsequent stages of the life course.

A third possible explanation for generational differences is based on historical or period effects. That is, social, economic, or political events, such as a war, a major new public policy, or the election or defeat of a corrupt government, change the behaviour and beliefs of a specific generation. In this situation, even though the event has an influence on other generations, one generation may be more involved or influenced than others. For example, many of those who were young adults during the Depression of the 1930s have tended, throughout life, to be thrifty and cautious in personal financial management. They saved much of what they earned, and they cannot understand the consumer spending habits of their children or grandchildren.

One reason why there appear to be fewer differences in the family is that conflicts tend to be resolved through daily negotiation and compromise between parents and their children. At the family level, individuals usually coexist peacefully with respect to value or behavioural differences. Tensions are more likely to develop over visible interpersonal and lifestyle matters such as etiquette, dress, study habits, or music preferences rather than over political or religious issues. Differences in political and religious beliefs and affiliations generate healthy debates and are often viewed as a normal and desirable part of matur-

ing. Often, these differences between parents and children persist only during adolescence or young adulthood, although they can last a lifetime.

Societal Gaps

Any attempt to determine whether a generation gap exists at the societal level must control for social class, ethnicity, educational attainment, religion, gender, and place of residence. These factors, rather than age differences, could account for major observed generational differences in society, since people who have similar life experiences are more likely to share the same world view, regardless of age.

Another limitation in understanding whether generational differences exist at the societal level is the diversity in attitudes, values, beliefs, norms, and lifestyle behaviours throughout modern societies. We cannot conclude that a generation gap exists on the basis of studying only one or two of these factors, such as a specific political, religious, or sexual belief, or only one or two groups in a society. There may be a generational difference on one value dimension but not on others. Similarly, there may be differences among elements of a specific domain, such as politics. For example, there may be a disagreement about which political party to support, but agreement about the performance, positive or negative, of a current political leader or a particular government policy. In addition, there may be a gap between particular segments of society but not among others (lower class versus upper class; women versus men; rural versus urban).

The debate continues as to whether real and persistent generation gaps exist, whether there are societal or only lineage gaps, and to what extent a gap, if it exists, leads to generational conflict, social disharmony, or social change. Most of the evidence from studies that have examined both societal and lineage differences among three-generation families suggests that a significant gap does *not* exist at either the societal or lineage level (Bengtson et al., 1990, 1996). The generation gap is more imaginary than real, and there is more consensus than conflict among and between generations. If studies find that a generation gap exists, it usually centres on specific values, beliefs, and behaviour. Moreover, reported generation gaps are more evident when they do not involve family members. A common reply of respondents in this type of study has been 'Yes, there is a generation gap, but not in my family.' (Bengtson and Cutler, 1976: 145).

Role Transitions

Our journey through the life course involves learning and playing a sequence of social roles, many of which interact in the family and work structure. This process of acquiring and discarding roles is often influenced by either chronological or social age norms. Some major role transitions include those from school to work, from being single to being married, from having children at home to having an empty nest, from being married to being divorced or widowed, and from working to being retired. For some of these transition points, rites of passage such as a wedding or a retirement party celebrate the transition. Throughout the life course, in each society or subculture, there are relatively well-accepted beliefs concerning the right age and order for such events as completing an education, leaving the parental home, entering an occupation, marrying, or retiring.

The ideal timing and sequence of events and role transitions across the life course is socially constructed (Gee, 1990; Settersten and Hagestad, 1996a, 1996b; Ferraro, 2001; Hareven, 2001; Moen, 2001; Marshall and Mueller, 2003). Informal and formal age norms evolve to create an approximate timetable for events in key areas of social life across the life course (Foner, 1996). Today, age norms are viewed as flexible guidelines for the timing and order of how life trajectories might evolve, and are less likely than in the past to be viewed as rigid and compulsory. There is

more room for human agency. There are also fewer and less severe consequences if one ignores an age norm, such as by remaining single until age 40 or 50; skips an expected life event, as in the case of a married woman who has no children; or experiences a life event in a different sequence, such as having children before or without being married, or completing a university education in mid- or late life.

Ideal age-related deadlines are mentioned more often, by both men and women, concerning family matters than those related to work, education, or leisure (Settersten and Hagestad, 1996a, 1996b). However, men refer to social deadlines more often than women, and the reported variation in meeting deadlines or timetables was greater for men than women. Settersten and Hagestad (1996b) concluded that there is not a strong set of age-based norms for transitions in work and education, that timetables are not enforced through mechanisms of social control (that is, rewards and sanctions), and that the existence of multiple-age timetables for work and education reflects the increasing diversity of modern societies.

Generally, the order of family-related events is more clearly defined and expected—for example, completing school, leaving the parents' home and demonstrating independence through a job, marriage, and having children (Gee, 1990). However, changes have occurred due to the women's movement, an unstable economy, and increased opportunities for pursuing an education. For example, Gee (1990) found that women with higher levels of education, and women in younger birth cohorts preferred a later age for such life events as completing one's education, getting married, and having children.

Intergenerational Transfers

We all function in a complex web of intergenerational relationships, first in the family, and later at work and in society at large (McDaniel, 2002).

Social order and the stability and continuation of a society, institution, or organization are dependent on intergenerational transfers, which are 'the essence of societal reproduction, continuity, interaction and exchange' (McDaniel, 1997: 2). Transfer of money, property, formal services, or 'in-kind' donations (child or parent care, housework, or a material gift of some value that can be converted to money or services) is a long-standing tradition in family units. Intergenerational transfers represent, as well, an inherent principle of a welfare state where public transfers are made to pay for education, health care, home care, and income assistance.

Some transfers are directed to the oldest generation, others to the youngest; some are compulsory, others voluntary; some involve everyone in an age cohort, whereas some apply only to those who can demonstrate need; and some are taxed, while others are tax-free. McDaniel (1997: 14–15) proposed four criteria for evaluating intergenerational transfers:

1. The direction of the transfer—old to young, young to old, middle-aged to old or young. Most are downward, but some are upward.

2. The sector—public or private, or both in some proportion (e.g., pensions and an inheritance from their parents to support older people in their later years).

3. The content of the transfer—money, services, in-kind gifts, or time.

4. The nature of the transfer—direct or indirect; voluntary or coerced; from the individual or family rather than from the public or the workplace; planned or unplanned; and large or small.

Table 6.1 illustrates the types of transfers along two dimensions: (1) upward or downward across three generations; and (2) transfers from the public (government or employer) or private (family) sectors.

Intergenerational transfers are related to the concept of 'linked lives', the idea that different cohorts at the societal level and different individuals in the family are linked together over time. Over time, a social compact, if not a legal contract, emerges by which 'we repay the generosity of the preceding generations by giving to our successors' (McDaniel, 1997: 6).[5]

Public Transfers

Public transfers from the state to eligible citizens are made to families that cannot provide financial or social support for all its members at every stage in the life course. And because of the inherent inequality and diversity in intergenerational relationships (Tindale et al., 2002), changes in values and beliefs led to arguments that society's resources must be redistributed to those who are disadvantaged. Some examples of such public transfers are public education for children, adolescents, and young adults from kindergarten to the level of either an undergraduate education or a specific job skills training program; public pensions, and, for retired people in the lower-income group, the guaranteed income supplement; and subsidies to retirees for health care, home care, institutionalized housing, and transportation. Most public transfers are funded by those currently in the labour force and are made to those who are not working, i.e., children and young people, unemployed adults, and older people.

Maintaining public transfer systems, especially in periods of population aging when the public debt or unemployment rates are high, is expensive. Transfer payments lead to debates about 'generational inequity', 'generational conflict', or the 'apocalyptic', 'catastrophic', or 'voodoo-demography' warnings that the public pension and health care systems are in danger of going bankrupt. Individuals who pay much of the cost of supporting older people begin to question the society's guiding principles and policies. They forget, however, that they, too, will some day be eligible to receive such transfers and will perhaps

Table 6.1 A Typology of Intergenerational Transfers

	Receiving Generations		
	Children	Parents	Grandparents
Giving Generations			
Children			
Private		Social joys/continuity Community links	Social Joys, continuity
Public		Public debt* Support, transfer potential	Support, transfer potential
Parents			
Private	Child support Attention, care Socialization	Security Attention, care	Attention, care Support
Public	Education Health care Transfers, i.e., social assistance, public health, etc.	Transfers, i.e., employee insurance, regional equities, social assistance, etc.	Pensions, health care Public debt[a]
Grandparents			
Private	Attention, care Bequests, gifts Values, heritage	Attention Bequests, gifts, support Values, heritage	Attention, care Pooling resources
Public	Public infrastructure Societal wealth	Public infrastructure Societal wealth	Transfers from well-off to less well-off

[a]Cremer, Kessler, and Pestieau treat public debt as a transfer from children to parents, or from parents to grandparents, since they see the latter benefiting from taxes and the former paying taxes without benefiting as much from public expenditure

Source: Adapted from Cremer et al. (1994:218) and McDaniel (1997).

have a greater need than the current cohort for similar transfers. Often these arguments are made by the more advantaged members of the society, who forget or ignore the inequalities in society due to race, ethnicity, age, or gender. It is these inequities, especially those based on gender and class, that are not captured fully in the intent of many public policies. Members of younger generations argue that their generation is being penalized by having to bear the cost during difficult

economic times. But, as McDaniel (2000) and others stress, population aging is not the cause of inequities. Rather, it reveals underlying weaknesses in the funding and coverage of safety net policies in a welfare state.

Concomitantly, at various periods in history, a state may question whether it can still afford its various transfer systems. At these times, the mantra of C.W. Mills (1959) is raised again: what is the right balance of public (a public issue) versus private (a private trouble) responsibilities and transfers? In recent years, the boundary between public and private transfers is becoming blurred as adjustments in financial support are made. When this debate emerges, the state looks for ways to offload costs or services to the family, for example, through home care for the elderly rather than hospitalization or institutionalized housing. These public debates are examined further in the section below on generational equity.

Private Transfers

In many traditional, pre-industrial societies, private transfers in the family took place when land was passed to the eldest son and when the eldest son (or daughter) took care of aging parents in return for housing or some other component of wealth. Today, intergenerational family transfers involve caregiving and care receiving, as well as financial transfers. Caregiving transfers primarily involve time and work, rather than money, and are usually one-way, from parents to young children or from adult children to aging parents (Martin-Matthews, 2000).

Transfers begin in childhood when parents or grandparents give the children gifts, money, or opportunities like music lessons, trips, or participation in competitive sports. The practice continues with encouragement and financial support to attend university, financial assistance for the purchase of a car or home, and the inheritance of accumulated wealth when the grandparents and parents die.

In a recent study of why and how older people make financial transfers in the family, Ploeg et al. (2003) found that the oldest generation provides funds to grandchildren primarily for education (in the form of cash or RESPs), discretionary spending, or for trips; and to adult children for the purchase of a home or car, a wedding, living expenses, trips, or cash for spending or investing. Many transfers are made either at a time of need, such as a divorce, illness, or unemployment; or in relation to a major life course transition, such as marriage, purchase of a first home, birth of a child, or a return to school). Transfers are more likely to be made by an older married couple than by a widow, and to be made when there are enduring, stable, and high-quality relationships in the extended family.

A common reason for family transfers is a desire by older parents to help their adult children and grandchildren to build or rebuild secure lives and futures. In some cases they believe that societal opportunities are fewer today, compared to the advantages they enjoyed throughout their lives. Therefore, financial transfers are necessary so that their offspring can maintain a similar relative position in society. Other reasons for making a financial transfer include a desire to help, especially if they had been helped by their parents; a sense of family responsibility and love; the passing of an inevitable inheritance when it is needed most and can be enjoyed, rather than later in the adult child's life; and a desire to ensure that the grandchildren can pursue higher education.

In the family unit, transfers have the potential to maintain the relative economic advantage from one generation to the next or to facilitate higher standards of living than those experienced by earlier generations. But there is also the potential for conflict if some or all members of a younger generation do not receive transfers, or equal transfers and if they harbour feelings of resentment. This situation occurred in earlier times when the eldest son or the first-born child inherited the land, while his or her siblings were left to fend for themselves. The inability of parents to leave enough wealth to all their children, or their failure to do so, was one reason for the creation of almshouses, homes for the elderly, a public pension system, and immigration by children to other countries.

Generational Equity at the Societal Level

Most discussions of generational equity are linked to fears generated by apocalyptic demography (see Chapters 1 and 4). Issues in this debate were publicized in a *Globe and Mail* article entitled 'A

Generation Bequeaths a Terrible Mess to the Next' (Simpson, 1997: A14). This article described how people under the age of 65 have to pay significantly more into the Canada Pension Plan than did the oldest generation, which is now receiving pensions from the Plan. The alleged inequity occurs because those in the middle-aged and oldest cohorts created the large government deficits and debt that now must be reduced or eliminated by subsequent generations. But, as McDaniel (2000) noted in the previous section, population aging is only a triggering event for this discussion. The generational equity debate—about how to achieve equity, whether equity can be achieved, and whether there should be equity between generations—is really about how to fund transfers such as income assistance, health care, subsidies to needy individuals, and the social safety net in general (Williamson et al., 1999).

Over time in a society, an informal or formal intergenerational 'social contract' emerges, which assumes that generations with relatively common expectations and obligations work together to ensure solidarity, support, and an orderly generational succession across the life course. In this way, regardless of stage in life, generations are treated equally in terms of their economic, social, and political needs, especially in later life, when some members have greater needs.

With the onset of population aging, increasing concern has been expressed about the loss of equity, for a number of reasons:

- the rising cost of elder care, which will have to be borne by younger generations

- a decline in the economic status of many young people owing to high unemployment and underemployment

- the unequal distribution of wealth, which favours a small segment of the middle and oldest generations

- public policies that favour members of one generation more than another—such as tax deductions for retirees and lower fares for older people on public transit

- an increase in poverty rates among the youngest and oldest generations (especially among widows)

- a shift in government policy in which responsibility for social welfare and health care has changed from being a 'public issue' to being a 'private trouble'

In recent years each of these issues has been magnified by escalating government deficits and debts. Some argue that these debts can be eliminated

- if those now in the labour force pay higher taxes than previous workers (that is, retirees);

- if higher tax rates are imposed on those over 65 for the accumulated wealth, pensions, and income supplements they 'earned' earlier in life; or

- if a combination of the two approaches is used.

In either scenario, there is potential for complaints of unfairness by those most affected by such policy changes. Specifically, there has been a growing feeling among younger generations that older people receive benefits from publicly funded programs that are disproportionate to their current or past contributions or to their real need. The opinions expressed include the following:

- Eligibility for social benefits should be based, not on age, but rather on need.

- The eligibility rules for benefits are changing as public support systems are being dismantled.

- Tax-sharing responsibilities are shifting too fast from older to younger groups.

- Other groups in society, such as single mothers and the homeless, need public benefits or services more than older people.

- Too many older Canadians are wealthy, greedy, and uncaring.

Generational equity is the subject of a continuing debate in Canada as part of the discussion of changes in intergenerational relations and of population aging, both of which are complex issues. Often, apocalyptic demography is invoked to justify shifting responsibility for transfers from the public to the private domain (Gee, 2000). At the same time, less recognition is given to past intergenerational contributions by older people at the family and societal level, and not enough effort is being made to ensure that society's resources are more equitably distributed to account for differences in class, gender, age, race and ethnicity in the total population. Consequently, scholars and those in the public sector continue to monitor intergenerational relations and the possible effect of public policies on these relations; to identify structural inequities and the generation that is affected; and to change policies to ensure that the needs of all generations are met equitably.

Summary

This chapter has used cohort and generational analysis to examine the influence of the social structure and a number of social processes on aging and the status of older people. Lifelong social or economic differentiation is important in understanding the situation and status of older people, especially women and members of disadvantaged groups.

Chronological age, which influences an individual's location and status in society and in specific social institutions, is one criterion for entering and leaving social positions. Laws based on chronological age impose responsibilities, prescribe eligibility for benefits or programs, and influence our life chances and lifestyles (Law Commission of Canada, 2004). In an age-stratification system, age-based norms provide a cultural definition of expected rights, kinds of behaviour, and responsibilities of individuals at particular times in their lives. To some extent, these norms regulate social interaction and help define when life events should occur and in what order. But there are few age-related norms to guide the behaviour of older people. The few norms that do exist usually specify what behaviour should be avoided after a particular chronological age.

A generation gap, especially in extended families, appears to be more imaginary than real. There is little empirical evidence to support the existence of a generation gap at either the societal (cohort) or family (lineage) level of analysis. When a cohort or generation gap is noted, however, it tends to be at the societal level and to involve specific values, beliefs, or behaviour. When lineage differences are observed, they are often related to lifestyle and developmental issues, many of which disappear with the transition to early adulthood.

For Reflection, Debate, or Action

1. Find two or three situations in your social world where age interacts with class, gender, ethnicity, or race to disadvantage some members of society. How would you eliminate these disadvantages to render aging a more equitable process?

2. Identify possible sources of structural lag in your social world, and suggest how the lag might be reduced or eliminated.

3. Debate whether, why, and in what way there is a generation gap in your family and/or in society, in general.

4. Identify ascribed and achieved attributes that create unequal access to opportunities in your world. Would a person in his or her 60s share the same view about the existence of these inequities as someone in his or her 20s? In what instances

might an older person have more opportunities than the younger person, and when might an older person have fewer opportunities?

5. Think about the generations in your extended family and describe any differences in behaviour, attitudes, or beliefs that you could attribute to aging or cohort effects.

6. Interview someone from another generation in your family and ask their opinion about the younger generation's beliefs, values, and lifestyle; and about their taste in movies, music, and dress. Do their responses differ from your views, and if

so, how? Why do you think there are differences, if any?

7. With an age peer, or with an older person in your family, discuss whether public transfers to older people should be replaced by private transfers, partially or totally, and in what areas of support.

8. Debate whether it is reasonable to use age as a criterion in legislation, laws, public policies, or public programs. Do age-based laws create unfairness and become outdated or ineffective for a changing society (because of structural lag)?

Notes

1. For a discussion of gender, see Matthews, 1979; Gee and Kimball, 1987; Hendricks, 1993; Thompson 1994; Nichols and Leonard, 1994; McMullin, 1995, 2004; Moen, 1995, 2001; Arber and Ginn, 1995; Calasanti, 1999; Hatch, 2000; Kimmel, 2000; Worell et al., 2000; Calasanti and Slevin, 2001; Sinnott and Shifren, 2001; and Arber et al., 2004.

2. Only one generation throughout history may acquire a specific label, and the label does not apply in all societies to those who belong to that generation. That is, particular social or historical conditions may not occur in all societies at the same time, or ever, and the historical conditions (that is, the Depression, the sexual revolution, and

the feminist revolution) that spawned the generation may never occur again.

3. For a discussion of age strata see Foner, 2000; Riley and Riley, 2000; Uhlenberg, 2000; and Walker, 2000.

4. Interaction among people of different ages can be measured or classified according to frequency, duration (how long it lasts), equality (whether it is one-way or two-way), intimacy (the nature of the topic discussed), complexity, and outcome (cooperation, conflict, or consensus).

5. This discussion is based on the political economy perspective and exchange theory as described in Chapter 5.

References

Adams, M. 1997. *Sex in the Snow: Canadian Social Values at the End of the Millennium*. Toronto: Viking.

Alwin, D. 2002. 'Generations X, Y and Z: Are They Changing America?', *Contexts* (Fall/Winter), 42–50.

Arber, S., and J. Ginn (eds). 1995. *Connecting Gender and Aging: A Sociological Approach*. Philadelphia: Open University Press.

———, et al. (eds). 2004. *Gender and Aging: Changing Roles and Relationships*. Maidenhead, UK: Open University Press.

Barnard, R., et al. 1998. *Chips and Pop: Decoding the Nexus Generation*. Toronto: Malcolm Lester.

Bengtson, V., and N. Cutler. 1976. 'Generations and Intergenerational Relations: Perspectives on Age Groups and Social Change'. Pp. 130–59 in R. Binstock and E. Shanas (eds), *Handbook of Aging and the Social Sciences*. New York: Van Nostrand Reinhold.

———, et al. 1990. 'Families and Aging: Diversity and Heterogeneity'. Pp. 263–87 in R. Binstock and L. George (eds), *Handbook of Aging and the Social Sciences*. San Diego, Calif.: Academic Press.

———. 1996. 'Paradoxes of Families and Aging'. Pp. 253–82 in R. Binstock and L. George (eds), *Handbook of Aging and the Social Sciences*. San Diego, Calif.: Academic Press.

Calasanti, T. 1999. 'Feminism and Gerontology: Not Just for Women', *Hallym International Journal of Aging*, 1(1), 44–55.

——, and K. Slevin (2001. *Gender, Social Inequalities and Aging*. Walnut Creek, Calif.: AltaMira Press.

Connidis, I. 2001. *Family Ties and Aging*. Thousand Oaks, Calif.: Sage.

Coupland, D. 1992. *Generation X: Tales for an Accelerated Culture*. New York: St Martins Press.

Cremer, H., et al. 1994. 'Public and Private Intergenerational Transfers: Evidence and a Simple Model'. Pp. 216–31 in J. Ermisch and N. Ogawa (eds), *The Family, the Market and the State in Ageing Societies*. Oxford: Clarendon Press.

Cutler, S., and J. Hendricks. 2001. 'Emerging Social Trends'. Pp. 462–80 in R. Binstock and L. George (eds), *Handbook of Aging and the Social Sciences*. New York: Academic Press.

Dowd, J. 1980. *Stratification among the Aged*. Monterey, Calif.: Brooks/Cole.

Elder, G. 1999. *Children of the Great Depression: Social Change in Life Experience*. 25th anniversary edn. Chicago: University of Chicago Press.

Ermisch, J., and N. Ogawa (eds). 1994. *The Family, the Market and the State in Aging Societies*. Oxford: Clarendon Press.

Ferraro, K. 2001. 'Aging and Role Transitions'. Pp. 313–30 in R. Binstock and L. George (eds), *Handbook of Aging and the Social Sciences*. New York: Academic Press.

Foner, A. 1984. 'Age and Social Change'. Pp. 195– 216 in D. Kertzer and J. Keith (eds), *Age and Anthropological Theory*. Ithaca, NY: Cornell University Press.

——. 1996. 'Age Norms and the Structure of Consciousness: Some Final Comments', *The Gerontologist*, 36(2), 221–3.

——. 2000. 'Age Integration or Age Conflict as Society Ages?', *The Gerontologist*, 40(3), 272–6.

Foot, D., and D. Stoffman. 1998. *Boom, Bust and Echo 2000: Profiting from the Demographic Shift in the New Millennium*. Toronto: Macfarlane Walter and Ross.

Gee, E. 1990. 'Preferred Timing of Women's Life Events: A Canadian Study', *International Journal of Aging and Human Development*, 31(4), 279–94.

——. 2000. 'Population and Politics: Voodoo Demography, Population Aging, and Canadian Social Policy'. Pp. 5–25 in E. Gee and G. Gutman (eds), *The*

Overselling of Population Aging: Apocalyptic Demography, Intergenerational Challenges and Social Policy. Don Mills, Ont.: Oxford University Press.

——, and M. Kimball. 1987. *Women and Aging*. Toronto: Butterworths.

Gray, J. 1992. *Men Are from Mars, Women Are from Venus: A Practical Guide for Improving Communication and Getting What You Want in Your Relationships*. New York: Harper Collins.

Hamil-Luker, J., and P. Uhlenberg. 2002. 'Later Life Education in the 1990s: Increasing Involvement and Continuing Disparity', *Journal of Gerontology: Social Sciences*, 57B(6), S324–31.

Hatch, L. 2000. *Beyond Gender Differences: Adaptation to Aging in Life Course Perspective*. Amityville, NY: Baywood.

Hareven, T. 2001. 'Historical Perspectives on Aging and Family Relations'. Pp. 141–59 in R. Binstock and L. George (eds), *Handbook of Aging and the Social Sciences*. New York: Academic Press.

Hendricks, J. 1993. 'Recognizing the Relativity of Gender in Aging Research', *Journal of Aging Studies*, 7(2), 111–16.

Henretta, J. 1988. 'Conflict and Cooperation among Age Strata'. Pp. 385–404 in J. Birren and V. Bengtson (eds), *Emergent Theories of Aging*. New York: Springer.

Hsu, H-C, et al. 2002. 'Age, Period, and Cohort Effects on the Attitude toward Supporting Parents in Taiwan', *The Gerontologist*, 41(6), 742–50.

Kimmel, M. 2000. *The Gendered Society*. New York: Oxford University Press.

Kotash, M. 2000. *The Next Canada: In Search of Our Future Nation*. Toronto: McClelland and Stewart.

——. (2004). *Does Age Matter? Law and Relationships between Generations*. Ottawa: Law Commission of Canada.

Mannheim, K. 1952. *Essays in the Sociology of Knowledge*. London: Routledge and Kegan Paul.

McDaniel, S. 1997. 'Intergenerational Transfers, Social Solidarity, and Social Policy: Unanswered Questions and Policy Challenges', *Canadian Journal on Aging*, Supplement, 1–21.

——. 2000. 'What Did You Ever Do for Me: Intergenerational Linkages in a Reconstructing Canada'. Pp. 129–52 in E. Gee and G. Gutman (eds), *The Overselling of Population Aging*. Don Mills, Ont.: Oxford University Press.

——. 2002. 'Intergenerational Interlinkages: Public, Family and Work'. Pp. 22–71 in D. Cheal (ed.), *Aging and Demographic Change in Canadian Context.* Toronto: University of Toronto Press.

McMullin, J. 1995. 'Theorizing Age and Gender Relations'. Pp. 30–41 in S. Arber and J. Ginn (eds), *Connecting Gender and Ageing: A Sociological Approach.* Philadelphia: Open University Press.

——. 2000. 'Diversity and the State of Sociological Aging Theory', *The Gerontologist,* 40(5), 517–30.

——. 2004. *Understanding Inequality: Intersections of Class, Age, Gender, Ethnicity and Race in Canada.* Toronto: Oxford University Press.

Marshall, V. 1983. 'Generations, Age Groups and Cohorts: Conceptual Distinctions', *Canadian Journal on Aging,* 2(3), 51–62.

——, and M. Mueller. 2003. 'Theoretical Roots of the Life Course Perspective'. In W. Heinz and V. Marshall (eds), *Dynamics of the Life Course: Sequences, Institutions and Interrelations.* New York: Aldine de Gruyter.

Martin-Matthews, A. 2000. 'Intergenerational Caregiving: How Apocalyptic and Dominant Demographies Frame the Questions and Shape the Answers'. Pp. 64–79 in E. Gee and G. Gutman (eds), *The Overselling of Population Aging.* Don Mills, Ont.: Oxford.

Matthews, S. 1979. *The Social World of Old Women: Management of Self-Identity.* Beverly Hills, Calif.: Sage.

Mills, C.W. 1959. *The Sociological Imagination.* Oxford: Oxford University Press.

Moen, P. 1995. 'Gender, Age and the Life Course'. Pp. 171–87 in R. Binstock and L. George (eds), *Handbook of Aging and the Social Sciences.* San Diego, Calif.: Academic Press.

Moen, P. 1996. 'Gender, Age and the Life Course'. Pp. 171–87 in R. Binstock and L. George (eds), *Handbook of Aging and the Social Sciences.* San Diego, Calif.: Academic Press.

——. 2001. 'The Gendered Life Course'. Pp. 179–96 in R. Binstock and L. George (eds), *Handbook of Aging and the Social Sciences.* New York: Academic Press.

Newman, S., et al. 1997. *Intergenerational Programs: Past, Present and Future.* London: Taylor and Francis.

Nichols, B., and P. Leonard (eds). 1994. *Gender, Aging and the State.* Montreal: Black Rose.

O'Rand, A. 1990. 'Stratification and the Life Course'. Pp. 130–48 in R. Binstock and L. George (eds), *Handbook of Aging and the Social Sciences.* San Diego, Calif.: Academic Press.

——. 1996. 'The Cumulative Stratification of the Life Course'. Pp. 188–207 in R. Binstock and L. George (eds), *Handbook of Aging and the Social Sciences.* San Diego, Calif.: Academic Press.

——. 2001. 'Stratification and the Life Course: The Forms of Life-Course Capital and Their Interrelationships'. Pp. 197–213 in R. Binstock and L. George (eds), *Handbook of Aging and the Social Sciences.* New York: Academic Press.

Ploeg, J., et al. (2003. 'Helping to Build and Rebuild Secure Lives and Futures: Intergenerational Financial Transfers from Parents to Adult Children and Grandchildren'. SEDAP Research Paper No. 96. Hamilton, Ont.: McMaster University. http://socserv2.mcmaster.ca/sedap.

Price, S. et al. (eds). 2000. *Families across Time: A Life Course Perspective.* Los Angeles, Calif.: Roxbury.

Pyke, K. 1996. 'Class-Based Masculinities: The Interdependence of Gender, Class and Interpersonal Power'. *Gender and Society,* 10(5), 527–49.

Riley, M. 1985. 'Age Strata in Social Systems', pp. 369–411 in R. Binstock and E. Shanas (eds), *Handbook of Aging and the Social Sciences.* New York: Van Nostrand Reinhold.

——. 1987. 'On the Significance of Age in Sociology', *American Sociological Review,* 52(1), 1–14.

——, and J. Riley. 1994. 'Structural Lag: Past and Future'. Pp. 15–36 in M. Riley et al., (eds), *Age and Structural Lag.* New York: John Wiley and Sons.

——, and J. Riley. 2000. 'Age Integration: Conceptual and Historical Background', *The Gerontologist,* 40(3), 266–70.

——, et al. 1994. *Age and Structural Lag.* New York: John Wiley and Sons.

Settersten, R., and G. Hagestad. 1996a. 'What's the Latest? Cultural Age Deadlines for Family Transitions'. *The Gerontologist,* 36(2), 178–88.

——. 1996b. 'What's the Latest? II: Cultural Age Deadlines for Educational and Work Transitions', *The Gerontologist,* 36(5), 602–13.

Simpson, Jeffrey. 1997. 'A Generation Bequeaths a Terrible Mess to the Next', *The Globe and Mail,* February 18, A14.

Sinnott, J., and K. Shifren. 2001. 'Gender and Aging: Gender Differences and Gender Roles'. Pp. 454–76 in J. Birren and W. Schaie (eds), *Handbook of the*

Psychology of Aging. New York: Academic Press.

Thau, R., and J. Heflin (eds). 1997. *Generations Apart: Xers vs. Boomers vs. the Elderly*. Amherst, NY: Prometheus.

Thompson, E. (ed.). 1994. *Older Men's Lives*. Thousand Oaks, Calif.: Sage.

Tindale, J., et al. 2002. 'Catching Up with Diversity in Intergenerational Relationships'. Pp. 223–44 in D. Cheal (ed.), *Aging and Demographic Change in Canadian Context*. Toronto: University of Toronto Press.

Tumin, M. 1967. *Social Stratification*. Englewood Cliffs, NJ: Prentice-Hall.

Uhlenberg, P. 2000. 'Introduction: Why Study Age Integration?' *The Gerontologist*, 40(3), 261–6.

———, and S. Miner. 1996. 'Life Course and Aging: A Cohort Perspective'. Pp. 208–28 in R. Binstock and L. George (eds), *Handbook of Aging and the Social Sciences*.

San Diego, Calif.: Academic Press.

Walker, A. 2000. 'Public Policy and the Construction of Old Age in Europe', *The Gerontologist*, 40(3), 304–8.

Williams, D., and C. Wilson. 2001. 'Race, Ethnicity and Aging'. Pp. 160–78 in R. Binstock and L. George (eds), *Handbook of Aging and the Social Sciences*. New York: Academic Press.

Williamson, J., et al. (eds). 1999. *The Generational Equity Debate*. New York: Columbia University Press.

Worell, J., et al. (eds). 2000. *Encyclopedia of Women and Gender*. Vols 1 and 2. New York: Academic Press.

Yeo, G. 1993. 'Ethnicity and Nursing Homes: Factors Affecting Use and Successful Components for Culturally Sensitive Care'. Pp. 161–77 in C. Barresi and D. Stull (eds), *Ethnic Elderly and Long-Term Care*. New York: Springer.

CHAPTER 7

The Lived Environment: Community and Housing Alternatives in Later Life

Focal Points

- With whom, and where, do older people live?
- What are the environmental challenges older people must conquer to remain independent and mobile in their community?
- Why is aging in place the preferred housing choice in later life?
- How do different housing and living arrangements influence quality of life in the later years?
- To what extent, and why, do older people move—to a different kind of housing or to new neighbourhoods or communities?

Introduction

Throughout life, well-being and quality of life are influenced by the community and neighbourhood in which one lives, the type of living arrangement (with whom one lives), the quality and type of housing, and the availability of transportation and community services. These elements in our physical and social environment become even more important in later life as changes in physical and cognitive capacities, and in the physical environment itself, require us to make adaptations in order to remain as independent, mobile, and safe as possible. The study of the two-way interaction between the aging individual and his or her environment[1] is an *ecological* approach to understanding later life. If the living environment of older adults is understood and enhanced, their independence and the quality of their lives can be maintained for longer, and the 'warehousing' of older people in long-term care institutions can be delayed or avoided.

Not all older people age in place, although this is the most common pattern. Some older people move to new communities in later life, often in sufficient numbers to change the demographic profile of the community they leave or enter. Whereas the migration patterns for younger adults are influenced by the availability of jobs and affordable housing, the migration patterns for older people are influenced by the climate, the availability of health and social services and recreational facilities, and, to some extent, by economic status or a desire to live near their children.

To study or evaluate the environment in which older people live, we must consider all of the following:

- the physical characteristics, social characteristics, and location of the community, neighbourhood, and place of residence—type; quality; size; composition of residents (age, ethnicity, socioeconomic status); urban, suburban, rural, or remote

- the contents of the housing unit, that is, furnishings, art, and collectibles that define our identity and family history

- the 'meaning' of community to older people

- the availability and accessibility of transportation, and social, leisure, and health care services

- the physical layout (number of levels, size of rooms) and safety features of a living unit which inhibit or facilitate the instrumental activities of daily living, such as cooking and walking

- dangers in the home and community, such as crime and the risk of falls or other accidents

- adaptive interventions for the home—technology, renovations, home-care services

- the living arrangements of older people—independent housing for a couple, a single person, or a family; or assisted or dependent housing

- 'aging in place' or local moves or migration to another community

- the availability and cost of suitable housing alternatives in the community

These elements influence whether the environment is 'senior-friendly'. One's environment can maintain, support, and stimulate older people; or it can introduce unsafe and unsatisfying constraints and barriers to independent living, thereby lowering the quality of life and forcing the person to move to a new housing environment in later life. There is no 'ideal' environment that meets the needs or wishes of most older people. When people move, they have to adapt not only to a different physical milieu, but also, in most cases, to a new social network. To meet the needs of a heterogeneous older population as personal capacities and housing conditions change, a variety of housing and living arrangements should be available in a community.

The Meaning of Community

'Community', as a concept, has a number of meanings that must be understood if we are to have successful policies and programs for older people. On the simplest level, a community is a geographical space defined by political, municipal, or natural geographical boundaries. A community may range in size from a few adjacent streets in a neighbourhood, to a small city, or to large metropolitan areas like Vancouver. Some even refer to the world as a global community or a global village. A community can vary, as well, in location—rural, remote (as in Canada's northern areas), urban, or suburban—and each kind of location poses different challenges for individuals and for those responsible for public policies and social services.

A community is also a concentrated settlement of people, within a defined area, who believe that most of their needs are satisfied through a system of interdependent relationships. For some, but not all residents, a community represents a group identification with the geographic area and with each other. This sense of 'community' arises through meaningful and persistent social relationships in which members engage in mutual cooperation and have shared interests, goals, values, and traditions. Thus, one can live physically in a community but not feel part of it if there is little or no meaningful social interaction with other people.

Across the life course, community matters to individuals because it represents an anchor point and is a source of cumulative advantages, as in the case of a safe, upper-middle class area, or disadvantages, as in the case of an unsafe, deteriorating lower-class area. Thus, there are differences in the kinds of communities in which aging occurs, and these differences have implications for the social and economic health and well-being of older residents (Robert, 2002). Although most older people prefer to age in place for as long as possible, the quality of the community either makes them move to a different place or remain in the same place and community. Life-long inequalities for people who live in disadvantaged communities or neighbourhoods have implications for the types of services that may be needed in later life.

Communities may be 'age-integrated', that is, consisting of people of varying ages who work and live together. Or they may be 'age-segregated', that is, consisting mainly of people of similar ages, as in a retirement home or a village where most of the residents are older people. In general, age-integrated communities are favoured by most older people, unless they are forced to move to age-segregated housing for health or financial reasons.

One goal of public policy should be to create 'healthy senior-friendly' communities where all citizens can age well and live independently for as long as possible. Societies should ensure that older people have an equal opportunity to participate in as much of community life as possible if they choose to do so, regardless of age, gender, health, or wealth. If healthy, active-living communities are created, health care costs are reduced, and fewer older people are housed, for fewer years, in long-term care institutions.

Living in Rural or Remote Communities

Rural communities vary in size, location, availability of public services, occupations of residents, types of housing, and economic base (Keating et al., 2001a). Different challenges and opportunities face those who age in such diverse rural settings as an isolated Newfoundland fishing outport, a farm in northern Saskatchewan, or a rural village in southern Ontario. In Canada, some rural communities, such as those in the northern territories, are also 'remote', that is, far from cities. This diversity in size, location, and economic base means that one policy for rural Canada will not meet the needs of all rural or remote residents. Moreover, among older rural residents, some have lived in the area all their lives, whereas others may be affluent recent migrants to a rural retirement area (Bowles et al., 1994).

This diversity in location and in the composition of residents makes it difficult to agree on a definition of 'rural'. Keating (1991: 11–19) argues that any definition of rural life has three components. First, occupations in rural communities have expanded and become more diverse, and we need to distinguish between 'farm' and 'nonfarm' occupations. In the Canadian census 'farm', as an occupational category, is defined as 'all persons living in rural areas who are members of the households of farm operators living on their farms for any length of time during the twelve month period prior to the census' (Statistics Canada, 2003a).

Second, population density and distance from a metropolitan centre must be considered. In rural areas, population densities and living conditions are quite diverse. Statistics Canada (2003c) considers rural areas to include:

- small towns, villages, and other populated places with less than 1,000 population according to the current census;

- rural fringes of census metropolitan areas and census agglomerations that may contain estate lots, as well as agricultural, undeveloped and non-developable lands;

- agricultural lands; and

- remote and wilderness areas.

A third component of rural life is the presence of a rural ideology and culture—the values and beliefs rural residents hold about their land, the community, the interaction between people and nature and among other people in the community, and the links between the economic unit and the extended family (Keating, 1991: 15–18). Keating (1991: 100) also argued that the social, cultural, and economic history of a community must be taken into account, while Joseph and Martin Matthews (1994) stressed the importance of a community's migration history—does a rural community become 'elderly' because young people have left, because older people have moved in, or for both those reasons?

To analyze the influence of rural living on the aging process and on later life, avoid the dichotomous Statistics Canada distinction between rural and urban areas. With variations in the size, density, location, and history of communities, definitions of 'rural' and 'urban' sometimes merge or overlap when we speak about the people (rather than the geographic area) who live in small towns within 100 kilometres of a large urban centre. Moreover, there is considerable diversity in the backgrounds and lives of older residents in both urban and rural communities.

Most research about older people has focused on residents of large urban communities. Consequently, we know much less about older people who live on farms, in villages, in the remote northern regions, or in the outlying communities of large cities. Fewer than 20 per cent of older Canadians live in rural communities. Of these, fewer than 3 per cent actually live on a farm. However, in some villages and towns, as many as 25 to 30 per cent of the residents may be over 65 years of age. These communities often include a large proportion of older widows. Some rural communities have aged because many of the young people have left to seek work and a different lifestyle in cities. Other communities have aged because of the in-migration from urban areas of older retirees who seek an alternative lifestyle and a more economical cost of living.

Older residents of rural communities are disadvantaged in some ways compared with their urban counterparts. Some of these disadvantages include lower incomes; little, if any, public transportation; inadequate housing options; and fewer

social and health services because of a lower tax base and the closure of small hospitals. An inability to drive isolates older people in rural areas and increases their dependence on others.

Those who have lived their entire lives in rural settings are part of a unique subculture. This subculture is characterized by a strong sense of independence; a willingness to help neighbours and relatives and to accept help from them; and a greater acceptance of the status quo, such as inadequacies in housing, income, health care, or transportation. When informal caregivers can no longer provide enough assistance, and when formal services are not available, older people often move from the rural community to a larger town or city. Such a move can be traumatic for lifelong rural residents. Thus, expanded policies and programs for older rural residents are needed so they can live longer in their familiar rural environment.

Living in Urban Communities

Since 1991, more adults 65 and over have lived in the suburbs than in the central core of Canadian cities. Among those 75 and over, the number of suburban residents has increased twice as fast as in the core areas (Hodge, 1991). Many of these older residents are 'overhoused' in 'empty nests', and an increasing number are widows who live alone in houses that are now 30 to 50 years old. As in rural areas, those who live in the suburbs are likely to need a car for shopping, leisure, and medical appointments.

Older people continue to live, as well, in the central core of cities because they cannot afford to rent or buy in newer areas. However, some of these older residents are forced to move because of urban renewal projects or increases in taxes or in the cost of heating and repairs. In the latter situation, the proportion of older people living in the central core decreases through the process of 'gentrification' (Henig, 1981)—inner-city houses are purchased, renovated, or demolished and a new, more expensive house is built on the lot. The composition of these neighbourhoods changes because new residents tend to be younger, well-educated professionals, many of whom are dual-income, childless couples. At the same time, rents in the area increase, and older residents living on fixed incomes have to move elsewhere.

In stable neighbourhoods, especially in low-income areas, there is a high degree of homogeneity with respect to age, race or ethnicity, and class. This homogeneity fosters the development of a network of neighbours who provide mutual support and assistance in later life. But when a neighbourhood experiences a rapid turnover in homeowners, or where homes are purchased by members of a different ethnic or racial group, heterogeneity increases and a sense of community may be lost. In this situation, older people who age in place lose the social support system they had assumed would be available from their neighbours. Consequently, in the later years, an older person who ages in place may live in a non-supportive environment.

Aging in Place

In general, older people have three general choices of where to live—remain in the house or apartment where they have lived for many years; move to another living unit in the same neighbourhood or community; or migrate to another community in a different part of the province or country.

For a variety of reasons, most older people, especially in urban areas, strive to live in the family home unless forced to move late in life (Moore et al., 2000). Over time, our home comes to represent a defined, personal place that provides independence, security, and a sense of belonging (Kontos, 1998). People establish ties to the place and to the people and the physical setting of the neighbourhood or community. Aging in place allows older people to form and maintain a sense of identity and autonomy that institutionalized living does not permit or often encourage. When older people are faced with declining personal abilities or a deteriorating neighbourhood or home, they engage in psychological adaptation to

convince themselves and others that they can remain in their current environment. According to Wister (1989), this psychological adaptation involves accepting or denying health-related disabilities or difficulties; developing strategies to cope with an environment that is becoming more challenging; changing their expectations about what constitutes an ideal or adequate environment; denying the loss of competence to fully cope with the environment; or believing that, with a short time left to live, a change in housing is not necessary, possible, or worth the effort.

Living in a familiar environment can become more difficult if a person becomes unable to walk or drive; becomes unable to perform the activities of daily living or to maintain the interior or exterior of the home; is afraid of crime in the area; or if there is a lack of services needed to ensure a safe and healthy life. In these situations, decisions must be made about a change in housing or in living arrangements. Despite the likelihood of human agency acting in most domains of life, most older people resist making a decision to move to more suitable housing. As a result, family members or community agencies are sometimes required to make the decision to move an older person or couple from the family home to alternative housing. But, before such a drastic move is made, assistance may be available from family, neighbours, friends, or community agencies. Such help may include doing house cleaning and repairs; shopping and providing some or all meals; driving an older person to medical appointments or to social activities; bathing and dressing; and a neighbourhood watch program where neighbours phone or drop in daily to make sure those who live alone are coping and safe.

An Ecological Model of Aging: Person-Environment Interaction

To explain the links between aging individuals and their environment, a number of theories and models have been proposed.[2] These theoretical perspectives focus either on the 'meaning' that an environment evokes in an older person (that is, whether it is satisfying and contributes to a desire to age in place), or on how individual competencies and environmental factors interact to foster adaptation in later life. These latter theories argue that individuals either change their personal environment, or they adjust to it through adaptive behaviour that maximizes the 'fit', or congruence, between their personal needs and the demands of a specific environment.

People who live in an environment that meets their needs usually report a high level of well-being. Incongruence and discontent result from major personal changes—a housing move, a sudden decline in health, a personal loss such as a divorce or widowhood, or an inability to drive or to manage tasks around the home. When there is deviation from some ideal balance between personal needs or abilities and the environment, a change in either personal needs or the environment is necessary to restore congruence.

Environmental Press and Individual Competence

Lawton and his associates developed an 'ecological model of adaptation and aging', which included the *macro-environment* , that is, the community where older people live, and the *micro-environment*, that is, the housing where they spend most of their time (Lawton 1980, 1985; Lawton et al. 1982).

This model is based on the premise that adaptation involves the interaction of *individual competence* and *environmental press*. Individual competence includes health, sensori-motor functioning, perception, and cognitive skills; it is measured by observable behaviour that reflects the presence of these states and abilities.

Environmental 'press' includes an assessment of five components in later life (Lawton, 1980: 17–18):

- the personal environment, including significant others such as a spouse, children, and friends

- the group environment, which provides social norms and reference groups

- the supra-personal environment, or the average characteristics of individuals in the immediate neighbourhood; that is, similarities or differences in age, income, race, and ethnicity

- the social environment, which includes cultural values, political events, and economic cycles

- the objective physical environment, whether it be small (one room) or large (a metropolitan or regional area)

Each environment creates different demands, or 'press', for older people.

In addition to the objective environment, the subjective or perceived environment is also important for successful adaptation in later life. Whether a neighbourhood is perceived as safe or dangerous depends on an individual's subjective judgement, which is based on knowledge and experience, together with an assessment of one's ability to cope with any changes in personal abilities or the environment. These subjective experiences influence behaviour in addition to, and independently of, the 'objective' environment. For example, an older person who feels that the stairs are becoming 'too long or steep' and therefore avoids using them may reduce his or her daily interaction with others in the neighbourhood. Another older person, however, may be unwilling or unable to perceive that the stairs are dangerous given his or her personal ability. In this situation, the stairs may cause a fall, which may lead to hospitalization, death, or the need to move to another type of housing unit.

The ecological model of aging (Figure 7.1) illustrates that the level of individual competence can vary from low to high, while the degree of environmental press can range from weak to strong. The outcome of the interaction between competence and environment influences adaptive behaviour and affect (emotional or mental state); the slope represents ideal behavioural adaptation and positive affect. The slightly fan-shaped curve indicates that as the level of competence increases, the ability to tolerate higher levels of environmental press increases. The less competent an individual, the more the environment influences adaptation and quality of life. Point A, which represents maladaptive behaviour and negative affect, is illustrated by the situation in which

highly competent people experience sensory deprivation (such as solitary confinement). Point B represents a low level of competence and strong environmental press. This situation leads, as well, to maladaptive behaviour and negative affect; it is illustrated, in the extreme, by an elderly, homeless person in a northern region who spends the winter trying to survive by living on the street.

Individual competence and environmental press are influenced by individual differences in needs and by the extent to which environments vary in their ability to satisfy these needs. Where competence and press are balanced, there is con-

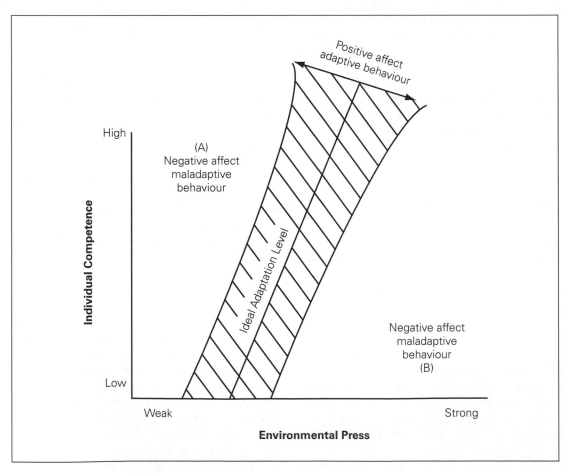

Figure 7.1 An Ecological Model of Aging

Source: Adapted from Lawton and Nahemow (1973).

gruence and a positive mental state. A lack of balance suggests person-environment incongruence and a negative mental state.

In later life, individual competence declines because of losses in cognitive or sensory-motor abilities or in general health. Consequently, an aging person may experience a reduced capacity to cope with environmental press, especially if the press involves a deterioration in the physical condition of the home.

A major criticism of the ecological model of aging is that it assumes that people are passive and do not try to meet their needs or preferences through the use of environmental resources, or human agency. It is assumed that individual needs, attitudes, knowledge, preferences, and perceptions are not considered until the environment creates a high degree of press. The original conception of the model was based on a 'docility' hypothesis whch implied that older people only react to a changing environment or to decreasing competence. The model has been criticized, as well, for not taking into account a person's high degree of familiarity with their current environment or a person's willingness to take behavioural risks in their environments (Wister, 1989).

In response to criticism, Lawton (1987, 1990) introduced the concept of *environmental proactivity*. In this process, older people actively adapt or change their physical or social environment before the environment creates pressure for change. He argued that how they do that depends on their personal, social, and economic resources to reduce 'press'.

While an environment often becomes more restrictive and difficult as one ages, new forms of housing are available, and more formal and informal support mechanisms are provided by the family or the state. Thus, individuals have freedom of choice, but they may need assistance in making decisions about where and how to live in later life. Ideally, such decisions about housing are made in advance of changing competencies or environmental press (Haldemann and Wister, 1994). Often, however, decisions are made after a

crisis, such as illness, economic hardship, or the loss of a spouse. Moreover, past experience with an environment influences present perceptions and coping skills, and human agency ensures that voluntary or forced decisions are made concerning where to live, and with whom, as personal and environmental resources change (Svensson, 1996). In reality, however, the wish to 'age in place' often overrides any rational decisions concerning housing in later life.

Most recently, Cvitkovich and Wister (2002) argued that a life-course perspective must be incorporated within the person-environment (P-E) model of aging since both individual competence and environment resources can change. Consequently, the timing, duration, and sequencing of person-environment transactions and thresholds vary across the life course, particularly in later life. Their multi-level P-E model of aging involves an individual's subjective perception of the relative importance of three environmental domains: structural resources (housing, the neighbourhood and the community); social support (from family, friends, and neighbours); and service support (from home care, community agencies, and health services). When their model of aging was tested against three other P-E models, they found that the multi-level model, which placed more emphasis on the subjective interpretations of aging individuals, increased the prediction of well-being among a group of frail participants attending an adult day centre (Cvitkovich and Wister, 2001).

Coping with the Environment: Challenges and Adaptations

Elements of environmental press and changes in personal competencies interact to create difficulties for aging people in remaining independent and moving about the environment, whether it be their home or the larger community. On a personal level, as people age, in order to carry out the essential activities of daily living (ADLs) such as bathing, eating, using the toilet, and walking about the home, they may need assistance from others or they may need to use mechanical aids— a cane, a walker, a wheelchair, a riding chair for stairs, a chair and grab bars in a bathtub or shower, or a raised toilet seat with grab bars. Similarly, older people lose their ability to perform instrumental activities of daily living (IADLs) such as house maintenance, preparing meals, shopping, or banking because of difficulty in walking or standing, cognitive impairment, or an inability or unwillingness to drive. In such cases, older people need help if they are to continue living in their home.[3] Some of these losses can be offset by using the Internet for banking and shopping; by lowering the cupboards in the kitchen and installing seating for food preparation; by moving the laundry room to the main floor; and by cooking with a microwave rather than a traditional stove.

This section discusses five environmental challenges facing older people: (1) injuries and falls, (2) the loss of private transportation; (3) crime against older adults and the fear of crime among older people; (4) the adoption of technology by older people to help them live in a safe and familiar environment; and (5) homelessness among older citizens.

Injuries and Falls: Risk Factors and Prevention

Injuries and falls among older adults are a costly public health problem, and a major reason why older people lose their independence and move into institutions (Fletcher and Hirdes, 2000; Morley, 2002). Older people suffer burns from cooking, knife cuts from preparing foods, muscle and joint injuries as a result of overexertion, poisoning from improper medication; and injuries resulting from loose wires and unsafe tools or appliances.

Among those 65 years of age and over who live in the community (rather than in institutions), falls are the leading cause of injury and death. For those 71 years of age and older, over 87 per cent of injuries resulting in hospitalization are caused by falls, and 75 per cent of these injuries lead to death (Health Canada, 2002c). About 33 per cent of older people have a fall each year, and the percentage is much higher in long-term care institutions (Fletcher and Hirdes, 2002). Women are more likely to fall than men. Gallagher et al. (1999), in a random survey of 1,285 'seniors' in British Columbia, found that, among women, the rate was 18.6 falls per hundred people compared to 13.3 per hundred for men. The estimated annual direct and indirect costs to the health care system for fall-related injuries by older adults is nearly $3 million (Health Canada, 2002c).

At home, people fall on stairs, when getting in and out of bed or chairs, in bathtubs and showers, on slippery floors, when dressing, and when suddenly changing direction while walking. Outside the home, they fall on uneven ground, at curbs when crossing streets, in malls when they are jostled, or on escalators. A single fall may not cause a broken wrist, arm, leg, or hip, but repeated falls increase the risk of serious injury. Once a person is injured, he or she may become frightened and confused, become less independent, and begin to be unwilling to move about the home or community or unable to do so safely. Fear of falling leads, as well, to further inactivity and social isolation.

There are three types of risk factors related to injuries and falls among older people: personal, home, and community. The main *personal* risk factors are loss of strength, flexibility and balance; being female; being poor; having limited vision, cognitive impairment, or physical illness (such as strokes or Parkinson's Disease); lack of concentration; unsuitable medication; impaired mobility due to problems with the feet, knees, or hips; living alone; drinking alcohol; and haste (such as when crossing a street or performing some task). Risk factors in the *home* environment include poor lighting; steep and slippery stairs; slippery floors; the absence of grab bars in bathtubs and showers; loose rugs; and the use of high cupboards that require the person to reach. *Community* risk factors include high curbs; sidewalks with cracks and raised sections; traffic lights with a short time duration for pedestrians; snow or ice on walkways; inadequate lighting; and slippery or high stairs in public transit vehicles and buildings.

Preventive measures can reduce the incidence and seriousness of falls.[4] On the personal level, adaptations include the use of assistive devices such as a cane or walker; moving slowly when changing position from lying or sitting to standing; exercising to improve strength and flexibility; reducing alcohol consumption; using safe, well-fitting footwear; and avoiding medication that has such side effects as loss of balance or judgement.

In the home, interventions and adaptations include grab bars and railings; ramps instead of stairs; brighter lights and movement-sensor lights for nighttime; alarm and monitoring systems; using portable hand-held telephones to avoid rushing to the phone; and keeping traffic areas clear of obstructions.

Falls will never be eliminated among older people, but through the use of assistive devices, education on how to move and live safely, and interventions to change the environment, the incidence and severity can be reduced.

Private and Public Transportation

Being able to move about the community is essential in maintaining independence and freedom in later life; and in not seeing oneself as a burden to others. As an elderly woman stated, 'independence is power . . . to move around when you want to' (Finlayson and Kaufert, 2002: 82). Becoming dependent on others for transportation results in a loss of spontaneity in social involvement with others outside the home.

Transportation must be available and accessible across the life course so that older people can remain independent; obtain the goods and services they need; do volunteer work; engage in social activity (such as visiting their children and friends, going to shops, to church, and to clubs); and fulfil the obligations of later life (such as visiting a spouse or friend in a hospital or nursing home, attending funerals, or visiting a grave). Yet, access to, and personal availability of, transportation declines with age. Those who are most likely to have reduced access to private or public transportation in later life are widows, those in poor health, those over 80 years of age, rural residents, and those with low incomes. Among older people there is a strong and consistent relationship between access to transportation and reported quality of life (Flaherty, 2003) (see Highlight 7.1).

If private or public transportation is not available, older citizens become isolated and housebound, and social interaction and access to necessary services or goods is limited. Older people who continue to drive often provide transportation to friends their age who cannot drive.

Older people who no longer drive or who never drove (many women in current older cohorts) have three transportation alternatives: be driven by volunteers, friends, or children; take taxis or public transportation, or use specialized transit services that provide door-to-door service. Public transportation is generally available only in cities, and even suburbs have less public transit than the urban core. Rural residents who are unable to drive are even more likely to be housebound and dependent than urban residents. Moreover, isolation in a rural area increases when train and bus services between rural communities and urban centres are reduced or eliminated, and during the winter.

Where public transportation exists in urban or suburban areas, routes needed by older people may not be available or convenient, or the fare may be too expensive, even if reduced fares are available for 'senior citizens'. In addition, a fear of crime on the subway and physical barriers (large crowds, high steps onto a bus) may discourage older adults from using public transit. Partly for

---

Highlight 7.1 The Meaning of Loss of Transportation

'I can drive to see my old friends because I still have my licence. But I am afraid I may not be allowed to keep it. There is no local bus and there are no shops or amenities nearby. For six months a year the snow and cold make the winter hard, and sidewalks are slippery.' (An 82-year-old widow living in a large housing complex for seniors.)

'When my driver's licence was revoked, it was a terrible loss of independence. I just don't have the money to spend on taxis and am too frail to use public transportation. My friends get tired of taking me where I need to go.' (An 89-year-old widow living alone in her home.)

'I had to give up driving my car eight years ago. I'm very frail now and things have gotten worse since I fractured my hip last year. I can get into a car fairly well, but riding on city streets is very rough on my back. Any sudden stops and starts are very painful. Buses are impossible because of my back pain and the height of the steps.' (A 92-year-old living alone in her apartment.)

Source: Adapted from the Statistics Canada publication *Growing Old in Canada* (1991 Census monograph series), Catalogue 96–321, December 1996.

---

those reasons, 'dial-a-ride' programs with door-to-door service have been set up in many communities.

The Older Driver

In recent years, increasing attention has been directed to the habits of, and risks associated with, older drivers (Bess, 1999b; Munro, 2000; Bedard et al., 2002; Klavora and Heslegrave, 2002; NACA, 2003). When and where older people drive is influenced by what they consider to be risks in the local environment. Risks that are predictable—such as volume of traffic on certain roads or at specific times of day, the weather, reduced vision while driving at night, crime in certain districts, construction work on particular streets—influence when older people drive (not during rush hours or at night), what routes they take, and where not to travel in a large city. Other risks, however, are unpredictable and cannot be avoided—such as a sudden change in the weather, an accident that increases the traffic volume, an irritable driver, or a breakdown.

Much of the interest in older drivers has been stimulated by the following headlines: 'The Driver Is Miss Daisy' (*National Post*, 19 April 2000); 'Licensed to Kill' (*The Globe and Mail*, 18 April 2000) and, 'Too Old to Drive? (*Time Magazine*, 21

July 2003); and by newspaper reports of serious accidents involving older drivers:

- A 75-year-old veered on to a sidewalk, injuring several pedestrians.

- An 80-year-old pressed the gas pedal instead of the brake and drove off a pier, killing his wife, who was in the passenger seat.

- An 86-year-old lost control at a farmers' market, injuring 40 people and killing 10.

- An 80-year-old was stopped while driving the wrong way on a four-lane highway.

- An 87-year-old drove into a group of children on a field trip, killing one child, and injuring 77 others.

Interest in this topic has increased as well, because there are, and will be, more older drivers, especially those 80 and older. According to the latest statistics (1996–7), about 60 per cent of people over 65 have a driver's licence (71 per cent of those 65–9 compared to 23 per cent of those 85 and over). Just 40 per cent of those 65 and over drive three or more times a week, and distances driven tend to be, on average, 11 to 17 km a day (NACA, 2003). For the average number of kilometres driven, older drivers have more accidents than any other age group (Bess, 1999b; Munro, 2000). The reasons cited include reduced vision, especially at night; poor hearing; dementia; side effects of medication (such as drowsiness); slower response time; shorter attention span, and an inability to make quick decisions.

How to ensure that older drivers are competent is a difficult task for families and public policy. Family members should ride with older relatives or follow them while they are driving (to see whether they drift from lane to lane, go through stop lights, bump curbs, or fail to signal a turn); and check for recent dents in their car. Or they should consult with their doctor or local police and ask them to take action.

From the point of view of public policy, this issue is a classic case of whether policies should be based on age or competence. General approaches are to identify problem drivers and de-license them; use a graduated license system like that for beginning drivers that would not allow them to drive at night or on highways with a speed limit over 80 km; require older drivers to take retraining; require annual testing; and increase the use of such aids as wider mirrors, pedal extensions, booster seats, and visual enhancement systems. However, there are many unresolved issues concerning any attempt to monitor or control older drivers: (1) how do we define an 'older' driver; (2) how do we balance the rights of individuals to remain independent and drive against the need to ensure public safety; (3) who is responsible for de-licensing—the family, the police, or the physician; (4) what tests and criteria should we use when testing older drivers (medical and visual exam, written test, on-road tests); and (5) how can tests be conducted without making the driver so nervous that he or she may under-perform given the importance of the outcome? In some jurisdictions, these issues have become highly political, with 'seniors' groups lobbying against restrictions on elderly drivers (Cobb and Coughlin, 1998). As a sign that older drivers are becoming a serious public issue,

a senior driver website has been created in the United States to provide information to families, older drivers, and policy-makers, and to post the latest research and resources about older drivers (www.seniordrivers.org).

Victimization and Fear of Crime among Older Adults

Interest in the incidence of crime against older citizens has been stimulated by news reports of assaults or fraud involving older people and by the number who report that they have fears about being victimized, either in their home or in the community. In some cases this fear may be so great that they become a prisoner in their home, afraid to walk in their neighbourhood during the day or night. This real or imagined unsafe environment reduces social interaction, thereby lowering the quality of life of older people.

Victimization of Older Adults

Many crime statistics do not record the age of victims. Hence, we do not have an accurate picture of how many crimes are perpetrated against older people. They are sometimes referred to as 'hidden victims' because they are less likely than younger people to report crimes—for fear of retaliation, for fear that their children or friends will think they are no longer able to take care of themselves, or from reluctance to admit they were exploited by a fraudulent investment scheme.

Many studies find that the absolute number of crimes against older people is increasing. However, when compared with all other age groups, the prevalence rates are lower, especially for violent crimes such as homicide, rape, or assault with robbery. In 2001, there were 157 reported violent crimes per 100,000 people 65 and older; which was 14 times lower than the 2,226 per 100,000 for 18- to 24-year-olds. The rate for 55- to 64-year-olds was 395 per 100,000 (Johnson and Au Coin, 2003). Among those 65 years and older in 2001, there were 35 homicides, 19 of which were committed by family members. More than half of older female homicide victims are killed by their spouse or ex-spouse; whereas most older men are killed by an adult son (Au Coin, 2003; Dauvergne, 2003). About one-third of homicides involving elderly people are related to a prior history of domestic violence.

According to the 1999 General Social Survey, 8 per cent of those 65 and older reported having been the victim of at least one crime (personal and household victimization, including spousal violence) in the preceding 12 months. This 8 per cent compares with 40 per cent for those 15–24 years of age, 31 per cent for those 25–44, and 20 per cent for those 45-64. Those 65 years of age and over were 21 times *less* likely to be victims of violent crimes and 9 times *less* likely to be victims of personal property theft than those in the 15–24 age group (Statistics Canada, 2001a). Only 1 per cent of older Canadians living in private dwellings reported that they had been physically or sexually assaulted by a spouse, adult child, or caregiver in the five years prior to the study, and only 7 per cent reported any form of emotional or financial abuse by the same group.[5]

How can these patterns of victimization be explained? The likelihood of personal victimization is related to environment and lifestyle. First, older people may be victimized less than younger people because they are not as likely to spend large amounts of time moving about the community, especially at night; because they avoid high-crime environments such as parks or poorly lit areas; and because the lifestyles of younger people expose them more frequently to environments or situations conducive to crime. Older people who experience a higher risk of victimization are often those who are more socially disadvantaged. Their chance of being assaulted increases if they live in or near neighbourhoods with high crime rates, if they live alone, and if they are dependent on walking or on public transportation rather than driving.

Older citizens are often victims of fraud (CARP, 1998; Donahue, 2001), which may be conducted by mail, the Internet, telemarketing, or door-to-door salespeople. Fraud against older people involves credit cards, bank accounts, donations to fake charities, assuming a new mortgage on a mortgage-free home, completing unneeded home repairs, and even love affairs where young women gain the affections of vulnerable octogenarians and acquire money or property that might otherwise be left to adult children. Donahue (2001) reported that older people in some ethnocultural communities are especially vulnerable because they have less education or cannot speak English; because they fear retaliation or intimidation if they say no; and because they may not know to whom a fraudulent act should be reported. Being a victim of larceny, property loss, or a fraudulent crime is very traumatic for older persons, partly because the loss often represents a larger percentage of their financial resources than it does for a younger person. Such crimes also generate fear and anxiety about the security of their environment.

To reduce incidents of crime against older people, educational, social support, and safety programs are being developed. These include: special police units in neighbourhoods where there is a high percentage of middle- and low-income older residents; voluntary escort services to and from the home; dial-a-bus services; neighbourhood home-watching services; the education and training of professionals and older people about avoiding crime; support services for victims; and public education about crime in later life. Electronic security systems make the home and neighbourhood a safer environment; there are also call-for-help devices to be used when a person is walking at night or is alone in their home. In Calgary, the Kerby Rotary House provides shelter for older victims of family violence and maintains a crisis line for older people who need to seek help. In the first two years that the shelter was open (1999–2001), 112 women and 19 men sought shelter from abusive family members, and the crisis line handled 40 to 50 calls a month; the average age of the callers was 67 years (Au Coin, 2003).

Fear of Victimization

One indirect result of greater publicity about crime against older people and the creation of special support systems to prevent or discourage crime, is an increase in the number of older citizens who report a fear of being victimized. Although older people are victimized less than other age groups, some studies have shown that a large number (as many as 50 per cent in some studies) express fear that they may be victimized and say that fear of crime is one of their most serious personal problems.

Fear is generally reported more frequently by older women who are poor, who live alone, who live in high-crime neighbourhoods, or who live in subsidized age-integrated or racially integrated housing complexes.[6] Fear is higher among those who have been, or know someone who has been victimized, who are physically disabled, or who use public transportation. Fear of crime is linked, as well, to other fears and insecurities associated with later life such as illness, falls, and living or walking alone. The characteristics of the neighbourhood environment also influence the incidence and level of fear—where the street lights are not very bright, where there are few pedestrians, where there is little or no police surveillance, or where young people congregate. Fear of crime is another example of how declining personal competence and an environment that is or appears to be dangerous can interact to influence the quality of life in the later years.

Technology in Later Life[7]

Assistive Devices

Various devices maintain or increase functional capabilities among people with impaired vision or hearing or who have difficulty walking. Other devices provide assistance with personal care, homemaking, and leisure activities. Some devices, such as canes or walkers, are more likely to be used in the home than in the community since an older person often does not want to appear to be losing the ability to walk or to demonstrate independence (Sutton et al., 2003). Yet, the primary purpose of these devices is to enhance independence and facilitate the activities of daily life in the community (Health Canada, 2002b).

Mechanical and technological aids for the home include non-slip floors, walkers, canes, chairs for bathtubs or showers, raised seats for furniture and toilets, L-shaped door handles, grab bars, personal emergency-response systems, telephones and books with large print, kitchen utensils with larger handles, talking books, hearing aids, wheelchair-accessible vans, movement-activated lights, and security systems. These aids contribute to a safer and more functional environment, especially for those living alone (Chappell, 1994; Zimmer and Chappell, 1999; CAG, 2000; NACA, 2001; Charness and Schaie, 2004), and enable older people to remain living in their home.

'Smart-home systems' assist and monitor older people with cognitive decline, difficulty in walking, and declining health. Hidden sensors in clothing, jewellery, furniture, kitchen utensils, rugs, or walls collect and report data; they can be programmed to prevent the person from entering a kitchen or bathroom alone, going outside, or stepping onto stairs. Aids reduce, as well, the stress of caregiving and provide some relief to a spouse who may not be able to constantly monitor the safety or health of a partner, or lift a partner who falls or has difficulty standing up from a sitting position. Such devices enable older people to extend the period of independence at home, to improve their sense of self-worth and autonomy if they can perform the activities of everyday life, and to facilitate mobility in the home and community.

While some technologies are not introduced until health and coping problems emerge, others are part of normal daily living; they include banking machines; cell and portable phones with voice mail and caller ID; and the Internet for e-mail, shopping, banking, stock trading, and information retrieval. However, not all older people are able or willing to use the new technology. Those less likely to adopt or use technology are usually less educated, poor, women, rural residents, those with little prior experience with technological devices, and renters rather than home owners (Zimmer and Chappell, 1999). In this sense, there is a 'digital divide' within the older population between those who have access to, and use, technology to help them adapt to their environment; and those who do not know about the technology, or who know about it but do not have access to it, cannot use it if accessible, or refuse to use it. The introduction of more technology into rural Canada could reduce some of the isolation of rural living for older people (NACA, 2001).

A good example of the adoption of new technology by older people is the World Wide Web. Each year more older adults are using the web to communicate with friends and relatives; for travel, health, and leisure information; for entertainment; for dating; and for everyday activities such as banking and grocery shopping (Health Canada and the Canadian Association on Gerontology jointly sponsor a website to provide health information for older people—www.canadian-health-network.ca/1seniors.html). No longer are newspaper headlines such as 'Cyber Granny', 'Surfing Seniors', or 'Wired and Retired' surprising. Among adults 55 and over, 19 per cent reported using the Internet in 2000 (23 per cent were men; 15 per cent were women). The percentage ranged from a high of 28 per cent in British Columbia to a low of 8 per cent in Newfoundland (Statistics Canada, 2001b). Many grandparents regularly talk to their children and grandchildren by e-mail. While older men are more likely than older women to use the Internet, the gap is narrowing as more 'seniors' groups offer instruction and provide 'Internet cafes' at senior citizen centres (Silver, 2001). Moreover, most public libraries now provide Internet service.

Although the availability of technological aids is increasing, cost, lack of knowledge about their availability, an unwillingness to adopt a technology, and the perceived stigma of using assistive devices such as a hearing aid limits their widespread use. If motivated, older people can learn to use a new technology, including computers for communication, information, or monitoring their safety. However, a debate has emerged as to whether *impersonal* technology or *personal* help should be used to provide assistance to older people. For some, the answer is easy—to enhance mobility and help a person remain in the family home, an electric seat for going up or down stairs, a wheelchair, a walker, or a monitoring system is essential. But if assistance with cooking, eating, dressing, or bathing is required, technology will be less useful, if at all.

The Homeless Elderly

Although they are invisible to most members of a community, a growing number of older people live and sleep in public shelters or in streets, parks, subways, or abandoned buildings, especially in large cities. Homelessness among older people is usually a continuation of a life begun in youth or early adulthood. This lifestyle adds new meaning to 'aging in place'—growing old without a home. For a smaller number, homelessness is a new living arrangement triggered by relatively recent financial, health, or personal trauma that caused the person to leave his or her permanent residence.

Most older homeless people are men, but an increasing number are women, especially those who have been physically or sexually abused, are mentally ill, or have been abandoned by partners or family. Other factors that contribute to homelessness in middle or later life are drug and alcohol abuse, discharge from a penitentiary or mental institution, lack of close family ties, and lifelong poverty. Many homeless 'older' people are under 65 years of age since life expectancy is much lower than for most of their peer group because of chronic illnesses and lack of access to health care. Many former homeless people over 65 years of age have become wards of the state and are no longer living on the streets.

There are only a few studies of homeless older people in Canada (CMHC, 2000a), and therefore we depend on American and British studies and reports (Cohen, 1999; Crane, 1999) for much of our information. We do not know how many homeless elderly people there are in Canada, but estimates in the United States range from 3 to 27 per cent of the older population (Cohen, 1999). It is likely that the absolute numbers will increase as the older population grows, especially if social support programs for older homeless people are not developed. For example, CMHC (2000a) reported that the use of Toronto's emergency shelter system by homeless older women increased by 13 per cent from 1988 to 1996, and that older homeless women seldom have access to subsidized housing. The number of homeless women with a history of severe mental illness and substance abuse is increasing, according to the same report. Of the 10 older homeless Toronto women who used shelters for over a year, almost all reported some form of physical or sexual abuse in childhood that prompted them to leave their home and family at an early age. Others reported being on the streets because of family or marital breakdowns. More than half reported being the victim of recent assaults 'on the street', or in a co-ed shelter or drop-in centre. Thus gender-segregated shelters are essential because many women avoid shelters or low-cost hotels because they fear being raped or assaulted. These women seek shelter in more visible public spaces like store fronts, which they consider to be safer.

Homeless elderly people are difficult to reach with social services. Many are transients who live from day to day or week to week in single-room-occupancy hotels (SROs) in poor, high-crime sections of a city. Here, they may develop an informal social support system consisting of the staff and fellow residents of the hotel. Many live in the same hotel for years. Such living arrangements are not easily replaced if a hotel is demolished for urban renewal or is destroyed by fire. And if SRO tenants are unable to pay daily or weekly rents, they are forced to return to the streets and lose the hotel staff as their support system.

Members of this vulnerable aging and poor subculture pose an interesting challenge for the social-welfare system, which is faced with large annual increases in the number of homeless youth who must be served and protected. Youth often receive priority in terms of facilities, programs, and policies. The lifelong experience of rootlessness, mental illness, or poverty makes it difficult for older homeless people to adjust to traditional long-term-care institutions when they are no longer able to live on the street. Many, especially in the northern parts of Canada meet an early death and are often buried as 'unknown' paupers.

To serve this unique subculture of older people, structural risk factors need to be eliminated through income subsidies, low-cost housing, outreach social support programs, health assessments with follow-up medical and dental care, and counselling or rehabilitation services. For some, learned helplessness has become a way of life. But job training and help finding a low-skill job can alter the behaviour of some older homeless people.

Living Arrangements in Later Life

Throughout the life course, living arrangements vary as human agency and life events, such as marriage, divorce, widowhood, poor health, poverty, or never having been married, interact to influence with whom we live, if anyone. In later life, options include living in a kinship unit—with a spouse only, with adult children, with a grandchild, with siblings or other relatives, or in multi-generational households; living alone; living with non-family, often in some type of group setting; or living in an institution.

The majority of older Canadians who are not in an institution either live with a family member, usually a spouse; or they live alone if they are widowed or divorced or have never been married

(Connidis, 2001; Pacey, 2002). Table 7.1 illustrates the living arrangements of older Canadians as reported in the 2001 census.

These data are in contrast with living arrangements in earlier times, and with those in the developing countries at present, where older people tend to live in multi-generational households (Bongaarts and Zimmer, 2002). In Asia and Latin America, fewer than 10 per cent of older adults live alone; although the percentage living alone in Japan and Taiwan is increasing as filial piety declines and fewer children are available or willing to house an aging parent, and as more housing options become available for older citizens.

In earlier times, multi-generational family households were common because elderly parents controlled the property, and inheritance was awarded to the child who lived with their aging parent(s). It was also expected that, after the death of one parent, the surviving parent would live with an adult child. Over the past century, multi-generational households have decreased for a number of reasons: more opportunities for children to migrate to other regions or countries; declining parental control over adult children; lower fertility rates and therefore fewer children; longer life expectancy for parents; an unwillingness of parents to be a burden on a child; and more urban living with more housing options for older, single adults.

In 1996, only 3 per cent of all family households in Canada included three generations—grandparents, adult child, and grandchildren. Of those that did, 31 per cent included a widowed parent, an adult child and partner, and grandchildren; 48 per cent included a single parent and children with one or two grandparents; and 21 per cent included two grandparents, an adult child and partner, and grandchildren. Over 80 per cent of these households were in cities (Che-Alford and Hamm, 1999). And contrary to common assumptions, these households were not formed exclusively because of the activity limitation of an aging parent. Rather, it was found that of the 40 per cent of three-generation households that included someone with an activity limitation, in 25 per cent of households the limitation was among the children, in 38 per cent it was in the middle generation, and in 37 per cent, in the oldest generation (Che-Alford and Hamm, 1999). Thus, the three-generation household is formed as a family support system for those in all age groups.

Over half of the three-generation households are headed by immigrants, most of whom are Asian where both a cultural tradition of extended family living and economic necessity prevail. Chinese-Canadians between 55 and 59 years of age are nearly twice as likely to live with adult children, and those 80 to 85 are nearly four times more likely to live with children than non-Asian people of the same age (Pacey, 2002: 21–3). Recent immigrants are more likely to live with children or in multiple families when there are lower levels of acculturation and when they do not speak English.

Table 7.1 The Living Arrangements of Older Canadians (percentages)

	With Spouse or Partner	With Children	Alone		In Institution	
	65+	65+	65+	85+	65+	85+
Women	35	13	35	38	9	23
Men	61	12	16	23	5	35

Source: Statistics Canada (2002b). Adapted from the Statistics Canada Web site <http://www12.statcan.ca/english/census01/Products/Analytic/companion/fam/canada.cfm>.

Living with at least one other person provides social interaction and stimulation, maintains autonomy and independence, delays the need for formal support and institutionalization, and is more economical than living alone. Yet, an increasing number of older people, especially women, are living alone, either because of social structural changes or because of personal abilities and preferences. At the structural level, decreasing fertility rates, more childless marriages, increased divorce rates, and more never-married women leave older women with fewer relatives in later life. On the personal level, more older adults have sufficient wealth to live alone and to buy assistance and services as needed; more value privacy and autonomy; and most widowed people prefer to remain in their family home and familiar neighbourhood (Bess, 1999a; Connidis, 2001; Pacey, 2002).

In 2001, 78 per cent of the population 65 and over (more than one million), most of whom were widows, lived on their own. The increase from about 39 per cent living alone in 1971 is due to an increased ability to pay for independent living and less stigma to living alone at all ages (Clark, 2002). By gender, 38 per cent of older women compared to 17 per cent of older men live alone. Men are more likely to remarry, live with a woman, or live with a family member (Connidis, 2001: 40–2; Clark, 2002: 4). Older women without much income are much more likely to live with an adult child (Pacey, 2002). For older women who never married or who were divorced or widowed in mid-life, living alone or living with an unrelated person represents a lifestyle adopted long before the onset of later life. Hence, later life living arrangements are not very different than earlier in life unless economic or health factors necessitate a change. Highlight 7.2 describes the lives of two centenarian women who live alone.

Today, there are many viable and socially acceptable living arrangements in later life, including living alone, living in a temporary or permanent common-law relationship, living with relatives, or living with non-relatives in a non-institutionalized setting. While the majority of older people live in a family, alternatives are appearing as fewer family options are available and as more older people seek to maintain their independence. Living arrangements are a personal matter, and agency is invoked across the adult stages of the life course. Later in life, however, declining health or financial insecurity often necessitates a change in living arrangements. Often the decision is made, not by the elderly person, but by a relative or physician, although the older person is often consulted and involved in the decision if he or she is mentally competent. The next section examines the many types of housing available to older Canadians—from private homes to long-term-care geriatric settings.

Housing Alternatives in Later Life

Historically, 'aging in place', moving in with a child, or 'institutionalization' were the possibilities for housing in later life. Today, many older people are demanding the right to decide where and how to live and are looking for more housing options. In response, the public and private sectors are developing new forms of housing and community-based services to help elderly people live safely, independently, and in the style they prefer within the constraints of their individual health and finances (Haldemann and Wister, 1994). These initiatives have been stimulated by the impending needs of the large baby-boom generation that will have retired by 2030 (CMHC, 2002a).

Housing possibilities in later life range from 'fully independent' housing to 'supportive' housing to 'fully dependent' housing. Since the needs of older people in regard to health, mobility, safety, and social life are likely to change from time to time, there is no single housing policy or type of housing that can meet the needs and preferences of older people, especially women who live into their 90s, often alone.

Highlight 7.2 Living Alone As a Centenarian

A.B. 105-year-old Still Lives By Herself[1]

A cake topped with a small flame lit up a restaurant as A.B. celebrated her 105th birthday with family and friends. She still lives by herself in the house she bought in 1932, is in excellent health, and takes no medication. She never got her driver's licence but continues to do her own shopping and attributes her longevity to will power, perseverance, determination, and faith. 'She wasn't able to walk or talk til, she was eight but certainly makes up for that now,' a friend said Saturday, adding no one knows why she couldn't speak. 'She does everything by herself and needs less help than people 40 years younger.' When asked why she never married, the Liverpool-born woman described a boyfriend she once had. 'He was an older man but all he wanted was a servant and I had done enough of that so I got rid of him.'

M.T. *Still Going Strong at 102*[2]

Her birthday just passed and she can't touch her toes. She's disappointed. 'That's what getting older does to a person,' she says, sighing. 'Last year, I could touch my toes. This year, I can't.' It's not all that surprising, considering that M.T. is 102 years old and still lives independently in her own home. Her two-bedroom bungalow is surrounded by daffodils and tulips ready to bloom. This woman is a treasure. She doesn't need a cane to walk. She hears perfectly without a hearing aid. She does not need glasses. To demonstrate this, she gleefully picks up a needle and threads it with hands that are steady and quick.

Born in Ukraine on 31 March 1900, she has vivid memories of her life as a young girl. 'It was the best time of my life!' she says, eyes shining. 'My parents had two houses and my life was carefree. I attended lots of parties and danced and danced and danced.' She married and had nine children. She loves to tell the story of how she delivered every child but one herself. She tied the umbilical cords with string from the grocery store. Her husband worked at sea for great lengths of time. This left her alone to work the farm and tend the children. 'I taught my children to eat their pasta one noodle at a time. This would give me time to whip out and milk the cows!'

Her husband died more than 50 years ago, and she has been on her own ever since. After his death, she moved to town. Until last year, she was able to tend her own garden, and plant and harvest her own potatoes. There are some things that, at 102, she can't do any more. But she runs her home basically by herself. She still gets all her own meals and loves to cook perogies and chicken stew. A community care nurse comes in about once a week, but M.T. says the woman can't find anything to do once she gets there, so she measures her pulse and has a cup of tea. M.T. exercises with two-pound weights, one weight in each hand, swings her arms back and forth, and marches around the house.

She misses the days of her youth. She loved the parties and says she's looking forward to the greatest party of them all: her funeral. She's got it all arranged and paid for—the hall, the food, the music. There will be two priests at the service. And she shows off what she'll be wearing: a pink chiffon dress. She has embroidered a coffin-size pillow and a shawl that matches her dress. Also in her funeral folio are two delicate white lace slippers. She shows them off with a smile, explaining she will not, under any circumstances, go barefoot into the hereafter. This last party, she says, is coming soon.

[1]Adapted and reprinted with permission from *The Record*, 31 July 1997. Reprinted by permission The Canadian Press.
[2]Adapted and reprinted with permission from *The Toronto Star*, 27 April 2002, L3.

A Typology of Housing Options

The location and type of housing environment influences the social life and the well-being of older people, and determines what services are available in later life. Housing for older adults can be categorized and assessed along three intersecting dimensions: from independent to dependent, from age-integrated to age-segregated, and from low- to high-quality. The first two dimensions are illustrated in Figure 7.2.

Various housing options are shown in each quadrant. In quadrant A, the dwelling unit is age-integrated and consists of either privately owned or rented dwellings, as well as subsidized low-rent, age-heterogeneous housing. This latter type of housing provides inexpensive shelter, but social services and assistance programs are seldom provided. For those living in 'granny flats' (see below), family support is available as needed.

Most residents of the dwellings in quadrant A 'age in place', and generally they report high levels of social interaction and satisfaction with their lives. If the quality of the neighbourhood has deteriorated, or if there has been a change in the composition of the population, there may be less

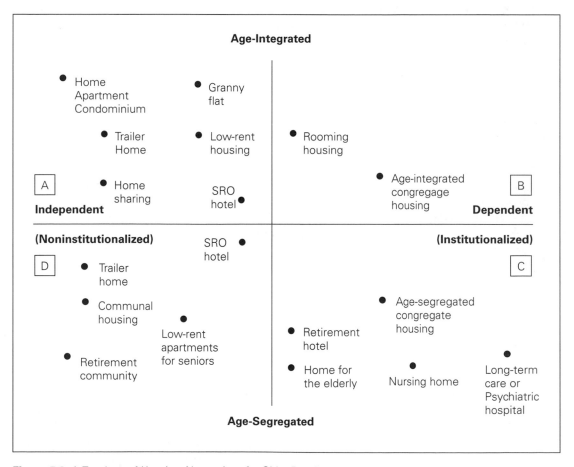

Figure 7.2 A Typology of Housing Alternatives for Older People

Source: Adapted from Lawton and Nahemow (1973).

interaction and less satisfaction expressed—the environment is considered to be less safe, friendly, or supportive. In this situation, residents maintain their independence, but they feel that the quality of their lives is deteriorating. For those who live in age-integrated single-room occupancy (SRO) hotels, social interaction with others is low, but life satisfaction is reported as acceptable because hotel staff provide support and a sense of security.

Quadrant B represents two types of housing that combine age integration with supportive housing. This type of housing varies according to the services offered and the rules imposed on residents. The congregate or sheltered housing option is exemplified by the Abbeyfield concept (see Highlight 7.4 below).

The types of housing listed in Quadrants C and D are age-segregated, with varying degrees of dependency and institutionalized living. They consist of housing that is planned to enchance person-environment fit for older residents. Many of the units provide assistive devices, supervision, and programs for older residents who previously lived in age-integrated, independent settings such as a house, or an apartment. Planned housing of this nature expands the lifestyle opportunities for older people and generally has a positive influence on their well-being.

Quadrant C represents non-institutionalized, age-segregated housing and independent lifestyles. These range from inexpensive trailer parks to affluent retirement communities in warm regions, to subsidized housing for older people, to SRO hotels that serve older men and women. The options in quadrant D range from retirement hotels and condos that offer minimal services such as maid service and security; to retirement homes and congregate housing that provide all meals and necessary personal services; to nursing homes and long-term care facilities for geriatric patients. In short, there are a variety of possible types of housing for older people, but not all forms are equally available in each community. Nor will each type provide personal satisfaction or meet the daily needs of all older people.

Independent Housing

Over 90 per cent of older people in Canada live in private households for most of their later years. Of these, over 60 per cent live in detached houses, 28 per cent in apartments, 10 per cent in semi-detached houses or townhouses; and 1 per cent in mobile homes (Health Canada, 2002a: 17). Over 66 per cent own their home, and most of these homes are mortgage-free. Of the approximately 33 per cent of those over 65 who rent, about half live alone. For retirees who rent, the proportion of total income allocated to rent is higher than it is for renters in other age groups (Health Canada, 2002a: 17). Thus, most older Canadians are homeowners and age in place in the family home.

A small minority of older Canadians opt to live in age-segregated retirement communities, usually in temperate climates in southern Ontario or British Columbia. An even smaller percentage move seasonally or permanently to retirement communities in the southern United States (Streib, 2002). These seasonal migrants are discussed later in the section on migration. But, as Van den Hoonard (2002) found, these communities may offer a satisfying life only to those who are couples and permanent residents of the community. She observed that 'newcomers' (those who have been in the community for less than five years), 'snowbirds' (seasonal residents), and those who are widowed are not fully accepted by the year-round residents. That is partly because groups have already formed for bridge or golf, most activities are 'couple-oriented', and because seasonal residents are viewed as less involved and committed to community issues and problems.

The home is a major asset, which helps retired or widowed owners to live on a reduced income. However, it can also be a liability because of increased operating costs, because a high percentage of the owner's income is required for maintenance, or because, with declining health, a person is unable to maintain the house and garden. Over 75 per cent of houses owned by older Canadians appear to meet or exceed Canada's housing standards. This means 'that their housing was in adequate condition, requiring no major repairs; suitable in size to meet their needs; and affordable, consuming less than 30 per cent of their total before-tax household income' (CHMC, 2002B; Health Canada, 2002a: 17). For older women with a small or declining pension, it may become financially difficult to stay in the family home. That is why the controversial concept of 'reverse mortgages' has emerged. There are various plans, but basically, equity in the home is used to provide monthly cash payments to the owner or owners while they are alive. Upon their death, the estate pays off the mortgage, including interest; or, under other types of agreements, the house becomes the property of the company that provided the reverse mortgage. In either case, the homeowners acquire needed income while alive, but the value of their estate for their surviving relatives is significantly reduced.

Most people prefer to remain in the family home in their later years. This dwelling is a symbol of independence; a repository of family history, artifacts, and memories; a familiar and supportive social and physical environment; and a link to a 'community' that is valued (Maddox, 2001; Wahl, 2001). Even though objective measures may suggest that a home is no longer safe or accessible, many older people subjectively assess their situation differently and report being 'satisfied' or 'well-accommodated' in their place of residence—even in the face of objective evidence which rates the housing as 'unsatisfactory', 'unsuitable', or 'unsafe'. That is, they are too attached to their home and to aging in place to make a rational decision. Or they may not want to become a burden to their children by living with one of them; or they are not aware of viable and economical housing alternatives that may be available in their community. The next section introduces the concept of 'supportive housing', which provides varying degrees of assisted living.

Supportive Housing

For older adults who experience difficulty living in the family home because of their health or their finances, home-care programs and alternative housing are provided in some communities. Such housing arrangements are sometimes referred to as 'supportive housing'. The term is a broad one that can refer to housing in which assistive programs or home renovations are available; to new living arrangements in the current place of residence; or to institutionalized forms of housing for community-dwelling older people (CHMC, 2000b; Maddox, 2001; Carder, 2002; NACA, 2002).

A move from the family home is one of the most difficult and important decisions in later life since relocation can be stressful and unsatisfying. Before a move from the family home is initiated, whether voluntary or not, the home can be renovated to make it safer and more accessible.[8] In addition, home-care workers can help with household chores, bathing and other personal care, and therapy; and a 'meals on wheels' program can ensure that the older person is getting proper food and some companionship every day. Alternatively, a relative or roomer may move into the home of an older single person. Highlight 7.3 illustrates two examples of home-sharing arrangements.

A second level of supportive housing is the 'accessory' apartment, either in the home of a child or attached to it. This type of housing enables the older person to retain some privacy but to benefit from a large measure of security and unobtrusive supervision. Another version is a garden suite[10] or a 'granny flat', which is a self-contained cottage-like unit consisting of one bedroom, a kitchen, bathroom, and living room, that is built on the property of an adult child or other relative. In the United States these units are known as ECHO housing (Elder Cottage Housing Opportunity). Originally conceived in Australia, they are more common in rural and suburban areas since smaller lots in many cities make them unfeasible. Indeed, even where the lot is large enough and the flat is intended as a short-term

Highlight 7.3 Home Sharing in Later Life

An Age-Integrated Arrangement

Sharing his or her home with a university student or a young adult in the labour force, an older person acquires income, companionship, and security and receives assistance with household tasks. This living arrangement is a way to use housing stock more effectively, especially in university communities where housing is in short supply. The younger person spends less money on housing, contributes to the community, and, hopefully, learns about life from the wisdom and experience of an older person. And, one or both may become 'confidants' for the other in matters of personal and private concerns.

An Age-Segregated Arrangement

Faced with living alone in a large house or being forced to move out of the family home, single older people, especially women, acquire a 'housemate' of about the same age. This form of shared housing is a way to reduce costs, to be sociable and active, and to remain in safe and familiar surroundings. In some cases, tenants provide companionship or services in exchange for lodging rather than paying rent. The housemate may be a sibling or an old friend, but, more often, he or she is a stranger. With careful screening and selection, a friendship may evolve from the tenant-landlady arrangement.

Some communities have agencies to facilitate house sharing.[9] They function like a matchmaking or dating service for younger adults, and are operated as a private business, by a religious institution or social agency, or through a large organization. Some offer mediating and monitoring services to help a housemate relationship grow and survive.

arrangement while a parent can live alone, neighbours may oppose the building of such suites.

This type of housing enables an older person to live near, but not 'with' a child, and therefore not interfere with the adult child's life. In addition, such an arrangement enhances grandparent-grandchild relationships, reduces travel time for family visiting, reduces guilt on the part of an adult child for 'abandoning' a parent, and provides a temporary facility that is wheelchair-accessible and meets other specific needs created by physical disabilities.

The third level of supportive living is 'congregate' housing.[11] This takes the form of retirement homes, which usually consist of a self-contained one- or two-room unit in a building with support services. These facilities emphasize a phi-

losophy of caring rather than the 'warehousing' of older people in expensive long-term care facilities. There is an emphasis on 'service', stimulation, and activation for the residents. Meals, housekeeping, and social and recreational programs are provided by qualified staff. The resident furnishes the suite with his or her possessions, the door can be locked, and there are common areas, such as a dining hall, library, chapel, fitness rooms, and social-activity rooms. Residents are not viewed as 'patients', as they are in nursing homes, and they are involved, to some degree, in decisions about their 'home' through a resident council and periodic consultations. This type of housing preserves the older person's autonomy, freedom of choice, dignity, privacy, individuality, and independence in a home-like environment (Carder, 2002). Most rooms are equipped with emergency call buttons, and assistive devices, if needed, are provided. Additional services—laundry, administration of medication, therapy, help with dressing, help with bathing, and hair and skin care—are available for a fee, as needs change. These facilities often include an 'assisted-living' floor for those with a cognitive or physical impairment who require 24-hour supervision but are not bedridden. Many of these facilities are operated by the private sector and can be quite expensive, costing, for example, more than $4,000 a month per person. Others are subsidized by the government, but waiting lists and careful screening for admission often delay a needed or desired move into these subsidized units.

With the aging of the baby boomers, CMHC (2000b) estimates that by 2031 there will be about 4 million people over 75 and about 1 million over 85 needing a variety of housing options. Many of these oldest Canadians will have activity limitations—CMHC estimates that 50 per cent of the 74–84 year age group and 75 per cent of those 85 and over will have difficulty performing one or more of the activities of daily living. An unpublished report (KPMG Consulting, 2000) projected that if home care and supportive housing are not expanded, the need for long-term beds in 2041 will increase by 170 per cent over the number available in 1999. But, if enough home care is provided, and *affordable* supportive housing units are constructed, the need will be only 61 per cent higher than in 1999. This report also estimated that the cost of constructing a supportive housing unit is 20 to 30 per cent *less* than the cost of building and servicing *one* bed in a long-term care facility.

Not only is congregate housing more economical than long-term care, but it offers relief to family caregivers; reduces the demands on the formal health care system; enables an older person to live independently in a community; and improves the health, sociability, mobility, and safety of many who are struggling to live alone or as a couple in the family home (NACA, 2002). As indicated above, the demand for these facilities

will increase. To meet the demand, facilities must be available for low- as well as high-income citizens; they should be located in neighbourhoods close to where the person lived most of his or her adult life; and consumer-protection mechanisms regarding contracts, billing for add-on services, staff-resident relations, and residents' rights and obligations must be developed and enforced (NACA, 2002). Highlight 7.4 describes some other forms of supportive housing.

Dependent Living: Institutionalized Living in Later Life

In the late nineteenth and early twentieth centuries, most assistance or care for frail elderly people was provided by religious or charitable organizations in the local community. Or the government established 'poorhouses' or 'houses of refuge' for those who were poor, homeless, or in ill health (Haber, 1993; Snell, 1996: 36–72). In Canada, these shelters offered little more than custodial care for the infirm and destitute, and many poorhouses were located in farming areas so that residents could grow much of their own food.

In 1931, for the first time, the Canadian census included a survey of institutionalized elderly persons (Snell, 1996: 67–8). At that time there were 118 'homes for adults' in Canada, most of which specialized in serving elderly persons, and another 79 institutions that served both adults and children, such as unwed mothers and orphans. For older adults who needed chronic care, few hospitals or nursing homes were available until the 1940s and 1950s (Forbes et al., 1987; Rudy, 1987). However, with the passage in 1957 of the federal Hospital Insurance and Diagnostic Services Act, provinces were required to provide coverage for chronic and convalescent care. As a result, nursing homes for frail older people were established by the provinces and by charitable organizations.

Highlight 7.4 Supportive Housing Options in Later Life

Abbeyfield Homes

Originating in England, this type of housing consists of a large renovated house in a residential neighbourhood, where 7 to 10 older, independent adults, each with a separate lockable room, can live together. A housekeeper is hired to prepare meals and do housekeeping and shopping. As in a family home, the residents eat together and provide mutual support. This type of home, which is most common in British Columbia and Ontario, is a less expensive kind of congregate housing than retirement homes.

A Campus Model of Integrated Living and Graduated Assistance

This model, primarily developed by the private sector, provides a range of housing and assistance options on one site. This integrated facility provides a continuum of supervision, care, and assistance. At the most independent end of the housing continuum are self-contained apartments or condos where residents live independently of others in the complex, unless they decide to participate in some of the communal meals and social activities provided to the retirement-home residents. Connected to the apartment or condo building is a building composed of congregate suites where all meals are provided, as are a range of services and programs. This retirement home usually includes an assisted-living floor for those requiring more assistance and supervision, including a locked floor for those with Alzheimer's disease who are prone to wandering. The third element of the interconnected complex is a nursing home to which residents can be moved, when necessary, to receive long-term nursing care. In this type of facility, it is possible for an older couple to live in connected facilities where one person, who requires nursing care and supervision lives on an assisted-living floor or in the long-term care facility, while the totally independent partner continues to live in their apartment or condo unit or in the retirement-home section.

An Apartment for Life

This concept, developed in the Netherlands where the building of facilities for older people is heavily subsidized, is a more compact version of the campus model of housing. Older people move into a one-bedroom apartment in a highrise building that is usually located in the centre of a city. Different services and levels of care are delivered to the person in his or her apartment as needed, no matter how ill or disabled he or she becomes. This practice eliminates the need to move older people to another building or floor as their needs change. Only residents with severe dementia who wander or become aggressive are moved. Those with mild forms of dementia are not 'locked in' or 'overly supervised' as they might be on an assisted-living floor in a retirement home in Canada. Three groups of older people live in each building: independent seniors 55 and older; those who need some assistance with ADLs; and those who, because of frailty or severe physical or cognitive impairment, would be candidates for a nursing home in most countries. All three groups are integrated and are likely to be found on the same floor. The apartment-for-life building is integrated into the neighbourhood and includes a grocery store, restaurant, clinic, and social centre, which all residents in the neighbourhood, as well as those living in the building, can use. In this system, older people in the apartment building are integrated with the wider community.

Some of the major issues concerning the institutionalization of older people include the following:

- how to delay or prevent institutionalization by providing home care in the community

- determining the best level of care for an individual

- enhancing the quality of life in nursing homes and long-term care institutions

- improving survival rates following admission

- meeting the needs of an ethnically and linguistically diverse older population

- designing institutions to facilitate autonomy, privacy, social interaction, and dignity in the later years of life

- defining 'levels of care' with respect to the placement of individuals, and the funding of institutions for the type of services they offer

- retaining employees and improving staff morale in retirement and nursing homes, where low wages (about $13 to $18 an hour) are common in a very profitable industry. Highlight 7.5 describes the reflections of an employee about life in a nursing home.

A major problem in understanding the issues associated with institutionalized living is that long-term care is defined in a variety of ways. For example, the same level of care may be provided in facilities with different names, both in different provinces and in the same province; or a facility may provide more than one level of care (Forbes

Highlight 7.5 Life in a Nursing Home

I have just finished my shift at the nursing home. I see Mrs M. offering to feed her roommate, who is no longer able to feed herself. I see a kiss on the cheek offered to H., who wants to go home. 'This *is* your home' we say, and often the crying stops. And D. with her infectious chuckle is stripping for me as I wash her and put her to bed. She plays peek-a-boo with the covers as I say goodnight. I know that if I try to relate these images to my family and friends, I will be met with uncomfortable silences, even groans. The fact is that nursing homes bring to mind images of suffering and death.

This is about the *life* in a nursing home, not the dying. As long as we exist, we live, and our final years are as precious as any other time. When we meet old people, we tend to see only that they are old. It is familiarity which reveals the residents' individuality. Mrs L. does not look to us like Mrs Y. simply because they are both small, old, and have grey hair. Mrs L. is 95 and quite alert. Her table is filled with pictures of her youth, provided by her daughter, who visits almost every evening. At bedtime, Mrs L. explains to me that she is getting married in the morning and must be up early. She is very verbal and occasionally bursts into tears and can't explain why.

Routines become rituals with the old; small details are meaningful. Y., whose lower legs have been amputated, has six brightly coloured crocheted blankets which must be neatly arranged over her knees when she is put to bed. Her 'documents' (an assortment of folded toilet paper and paper towels) must be arranged 'just so' on her table. Without these nightly comforts, Y. becomes mildly asthmatic and will not sleep.

There is a fine line between those who require supervision and those who can live more or less independently. Establishing the appropriate relationship with the residents is part of our task. When I go to assist W. to bed, she is generally jovial and warm. I change her diaper and then offer to put on her pajamas. 'I do myself,' says W. firmly. She is supporting herself with her arms on her

continued

Hightlight 7.5 continued

wheelchair. I am so afraid she will fall. I open her drawer to get her pajamas. 'No, no, I do myself!' she says, louder. I watch quietly for a few moments, as she examines her clothes, then decide to leave. I check back in a few minutes, and find her in the bathroom, brushing her teeth. 'She manages,' I think to myself, with wonder.

But there are behavioural problems as well. How do you manage D., who hates to be washed, kicks, spits, and scratches? Some nights we can skip washing him, but eventually he will begin to smell. In order to wash him, we often need three caregivers—two to hold his arms and prevent injury to the third. None of us are comfortable with this work, which is against his will.

Most of the women who work here are gentle and polite, intelligent and hard-working. They muster discretion and kindness with family members, creativity and patience with irrational behaviour. In these regards, my co-workers are a constant source of inspiration to me. Of all our activities, meals are the most highly defined, and potentially chaotic. One hundred and fifty residents must be transported by elevator to the dining room, where a variety of diets are accommodated. Salt-free, diabetic, lactose-intolerant, regular, minced, purée. S. eats only hot dogs; W. and her fruit plates; Mrs N. gets rice instead of potatoes. I observe that almost all residents show a preference for some kind of food.

On my break, my mind returns to the nursing home where I trained. My first impression was that it was dark, with a pervasive smell of 'oldness'. Fragile bodies, pale faces. Unanswered calls for help. Now I wonder at how those impressions have evaporated. Warmth and familiarity have replaced the darkness. I have not tried to paint a cheery picture of the nursing home. There are many problems: stress-related tempers, suspicious family members, unrealistic regulations—the nursing home is not a playground. But becoming familiar with it, and the many paths of aging, has enriched my life.

Adapted and reprinted with thanks to the author, Ms Gail Landau, and with permission from the *Globe and Mail*, 22 September 1998: A24.

et al., 1987: 20; Charles and Schalm, 1992a, b; MacLean and Klein, 2002). The level of financial support, the size and qualifications of staff, the type of services provided, the size of the facility, and the needs of the residents are all factors in defining the level of care provided by a facility. In reality, an older person may, over a period of time, require low, medium, and high levels of care in an institution. Although some facilities are designed to provide all three levels, many elderly people are admitted to a retirement home, which provides a low level of care but, eventually, they must be moved to a facility that provides a higher level of care, that is, a nursing home or long-term care geriatric facility.

In general, the lowest level of institutional care is provided in privately operated retirement homes, where an assisted living floor is often available for those who need regular supervision but only low-level nursing and personal care. This level of care is also available in homes operated by non-profit organizations. These homes provide beds for residents who do not require more than about one-and-a-half hours a day of nursing care. If more care is needed, extra services can be purchased, or the person must be transferred to a nursing home.

Housing at the medium- or extended-care level is provided mainly by privately owned, profit-oriented nursing homes subsidized by a provincial government. A few homes are operated on a non-profit basis by ethnic or religious groups in order to meet the need for particular languages, diets, or customs. The highest level, extended or chronic care, is provided to those who are chronically ill or who have one or more major functional disabilities that necessitate 24-hour nursing and personal care. In many communities, especially in aging rural areas and small towns, there is often a shortage of long-term-care beds. This results in long waiting lists, delays in placement, unsuitable placements, or the need to move to another community. Highlight 7.6 describes a new concept in housing for dependent older people, specially designed long-term-care bungalows, which are much less expensive than such care in a geriatric ward of an acute- or general-care hospital.

The Incidence of Institutionalization

In the 2001 Canadian census, 4.4 per cent of men and 8.4 per cent of women over 65 lived in an institution. However, up to 75 per cent of frail elderly people may live in some type of institution for part of their later years, especially if they have been living alone. The percentage of the older population that is institutionalized varies by gender, country, province, and region, and is determined, to some extent, by government policies with respect to the subsidization of such facilities (Forbes et al., 1987: 43–4).

Accommodation in a retirement or nursing home which provides custodial care is more likely with increased severity of chronic disease, a high level of cognitive impairment, and increasing dependence on others for help with the basic activities of daily living (ADLs). In Canada, the main chronic conditions that increase the inci-

---

Highlight 7.6 Long-Term Care Bungalows

Long-term care is defined as 24-hour nursing and personal care, with recreation, leisure, and therapy programs. The Peter D. Clark Centre in Ottawa is a municipal long-term-care facility for people who require ongoing care. The average age of the residents is 89, they are very frail, and 85 per cent suffer from Alzheimer's disease or related dementia. The entire Centre has 216 residents, of whom 48 live in four bungalows, 12 in each.

The bungalow concept emerged from a partnership between the municipality and the Alzheimer Association of Ottawa-Carleton. They recognized that an institution can be more confusing for people with dementia. Five principles guided the design of the Centre and the four bungalows:

- support normal activities
- maximize functioning
- involve family and volunteers
- promote social interactions
- create a sense of comfort and security

The design features of the bungalows include private rooms, rummaging closets, locked closets for important articles of clothing, short hallways, small dining rooms, home-like kitchens, camouflaged exits, family dining rooms, and common spaces. The bungalows, which adjoin the Centre's core building, can be closed off from the main Centre or open to it. At the end of the first year, the Centre conducted a survey with families, which indicated 85 per cent satisfaction with the bungalow concept.

dence of institutionalization are arthritis and rheumatism, Alzheimer's disease, heart disease, high blood pressure, strokes and osteoporosis (Lindsay, 1999).

Decisions about who should be, or must be, admitted to publicly funded long-term-care institutions are made difficult by increases in daily housing and caring costs and a shortage of long-term-care beds. (In Chapter 11, alternative ways of providing care in the community are proposed.) To provide objective assessments of relative need before admission to a facility, and to monitor the changes in personal needs, Resident Assessment Instruments (RAIs) have been developed (Hirdes et al., 1999b, 2001; Warren, 2000; Fries et al., 2002). These instruments are used, as well, to assess the quality of care in an institution (Hirdes et al., 1998) and to plan for the future health care needs of an aging population.

Each assessment provides a comprehensive profile of a person's needs by means of an instrument such as the Minimum Data Set (MDS). Then, on the basis of the needs identified in the assessment, a comprehensive care plan is proposed. The RAI must be administered to all residents in all nursing homes in the United States at admission, after any significant change in health status, and at least annually. In Canada, however, RAI's are not required, as yet, in many jurisdictions.

There are four different RAIs used in Canada: MDS 2.0 for use in long-term care facilities; MDS-HC for assessing home-care needs; MDS-MH for assessing mental health; and MDS-PC for assessing palliative-care needs. As of 2004, the first three will be required in Ontario. In other provinces and territories, some RAI's are 'recommended' and others are 'mandated' by provincial legislation. In all provinces and territories, it also possible that they are being used voluntarily in some communities or facilities.

Quality of Care

Nursing homes are subsidized and regulated by the provincial and territorial governments (retirement homes operated by the private sector are not regulated), but inspection standards vary greatly. Consequently, the quality of living and care can range from 'excellent' to 'atrocious' in terms of sanitation, use of medication, quality of nutrition, and the qualifications of, and treatment by, the staff (Kane and Kane, 2001; Quadagno et al., 2003). Occasionally, the media carry stories about physical or psychological abuse, epidemic infections, unsanitary conditions, neglect of residents, over-medication, or theft by the staff. For this reason, there are government regulations to ensure that residents have the right to privacy and some control over their own lives. For example, in many jurisdictions nursing homes and homes for the elderly are required by law to establish residents' councils to provide feedback to the operators and to consider complaints. In reality, however, many of these councils are controlled by the staff and hence, some jurisdictions have ombudspersons and 'Bills of Rights' to protect residents of long-term care facilities.

The definition and measurement of quality in long-term-care institutions is a contentious issue,[12] and many factors and perspectives must be taken into account.[13] The various interests of residents (the clients), the staff, the resident's family, the owner (in the case of a private institution), and government policy-makers are all factors in the definition and measurement of quality. For example, staff and residents may have quite different opinions about the need for autonomy and privacy, about personal space, and about the quality and variety of food. Other factors include the scheduling of meals and bathing; who lives with whom, and where, in the facility; who can visit a resident and when; whether mobility and activity are permitted and encouraged to enhance self-esteem and self-care; and whether constraints are used to 'control' residents (Hirdes et al., 1999a; Quadagno et al., 2003).

Some of these quality issues are environmental—the arrangement of furniture and the provision of public space to encourage interaction with other residents, and the use of assistive devices to encourage and help residents to leave their bedrooms. Other issues of quality can be addressed by staff training to improve attitudes and services; by orientation programs for clients and their families before admission; by providing recreational and therapeutic programs as well as 'care'; and by regular consultation with residents and their families.

Ethical Issues in Long-Term Care Facilities

Most residents of a long-term care facility have significant levels of physical or mental impairment. They are dependent and vulnerable, and many are confused. Once admitted, they lose some or all independence because of institutional rules and practices. They have little, if any, choice about when they can eat or bathe, where they can travel within or outside the residence, who they live with (if they are sharing a room), or who provides their personal care. To ensure the dignity, freedom, autonomy, safety, and legal rights of residents (Clements, 2002), bills of rights have been enacted. These rights establish standards about the quality of care and the treatment of dependent human beings, and they ensure that institutions 'are homes for the people who live there' (Chernin, 1996). A bill of rights should be posted in every institution as a reminder that the rights and dignity of residents must be respected.

A contentious issue in long-term care facilities is whether restraints should be used to protect residents from self-harm. Often, it is argued, these devices are employed to make life easier for staff. However, it is the dignity of the person and the competing values of autonomy versus safety that must be at the core of any debate or decision as to whether chemical (sedatives) or physical restraints should be used to prevent wandering, falls, or aggressive behaviour. Physical restraints such as bed rails, straps, or confining chairs are used to restrict movement. These restraints may cause physical pain, may violate the moral right of an individual to freedom of movement, and may cause humiliation and anger. If the person is mentally competent, informed consent is required for the use of restraints. Chemical restraints may add to the existing confusion, fears, and anxiety of a resident.

A person may be declared 'mentally incompetent' if he or she is unable to manage personal financial affairs; understand information regarding personal or medical care; judge the suitability of a recommended medical treatment; or make a decision about personal or financial matters. An individual can be declared mentally incompetent only by a court after application by a spouse, child, or caregiver. If a person is declared mentally incompetent, a guardian is appointed by the court. This person, or a committee, assumes legal responsibility for decisions concerning place of residence, finances, medical treatment, social relations, and/or choice of activities. A decision can be appealed, or it can be reviewed and reversed in the future. If a judge subsequently finds that a guardian is not performing his or her responsibilities adequately, a new guardian or a public trustee may be appointed to assume responsibility for an older person's welfare.

Adjustment to Institutionalized Living

Moving in the later years from independent, private living to any type of institutional housing represents a major change in a person's life. Most people have difficulty adjusting to the lack of privacy, the reduction in personal and physical space, the regimented, monotonous daily routine, the 'institutional' food, and the impersonal custodial care. Entering an institution is quite stressful, especially if the move is involuntary. The loss of one's home or apartment entails a loss of personal possessions, and it symbolizes vulnerability and frailty, loss of independence, and perhaps the imminence of death. For some, continuing to live is felt to be a burden—to oneself and to others. For example, consider the thoughts of a 94-year-old widow who moved into a nursing home because she lost her balance and fell frequently:

> I'm a bump on a log. I'm absolutely useless. I'm just sitting here, a menace, just, you

might say, worthless. Just sitting here and I have to be cared for. I'm not able to contribute to anything. I hope I don't live the rest of the year out because there's no point in it. There would just be more worry and more trouble for my son and his wife. They never miss visiting. They're just as faithful . . . they come every week no matter how busy they are. . . . But things like that are a burden to other people. They have to look after me. Life don't mean anything now. There's nothing to look forward to. All you've got is your memories to look back on. (Gubrium, 1993: 57).

The stress of being moved to an institution can be reduced by preparing an older person for the move with a tour of the facility, by temporary trial visits of a week or more, and by ensuring that the family maintains contact. Ongoing decision making and monitoring by the family are essential to the well-being of institutionalized residents. Family members can provide on-site services and transportation to off-site medical appointments, and they can monitor the quality of care received and the specific needs of the resident (Keating et al., 2001b). Better adjustment is achieved by those who receive social support from friends and relatives; by those who move voluntarily; by those who were socially isolated and lonely in the community; and by those who are given some control over their daily lives in the institution. Many new residents become more active after moving into an institution and experience an improvement in their psychological, social, and physical well-being.

Adjustment is facilitated by the presence of a personally designed interior environment that is familiar and non-threatening rather than an impersonal, sterile institutionalized setting. Rooms should be personalized by permitting residents to bring objects from their homes to decorate and furnish the living area, and by providing more environmental stimulation throughout the institution, such as soothing colours; music; and

colour codes, signs, and symbols to identify floors and corridors. Some institutions provide an illuminated 'memory box' outside each room for the display of personal objects belonging to the resident. This provides an identity for the resident, helps them find their room, and serves as a starting point for conversations with the staff and fellow residents. Many institutions now permit pets to visit or even have their own pets, thereby enhancing the emotional health of some nursing-home residents, especially those who previously owned a pet (Banks and Banks, 2000).

Changing Places: Local Moves and Migration in Later Life

Aging in place is the most common living pattern in later life. Only about 10 per cent of older Canadians move or migrate more than 200 kilometres from where they lived before they retired. Of those who have moved in the previous five years, 76 per cent move no more than 50 kilometres from their previous home. (Che-Alford and Stevenson, 1998). But future older cohorts may be more mobile. Many baby boomers have moved often, they will be more affluent and healthier than previous older cohorts, and more later life housing options will be available, especially housing developments which promote 'amenity living' and the 'good life'—by providing exercise facilities, security, and social programs. Some of these developments will be located in the home community or nearby; others will require a move of more than 100 kilometres or permanent or winter migration to another province or country.

After a major transition such as retiring or being widowed, an objective and subjective appraisal by the individual or couple of housing needs, living arrangements, and preferred lifestyle should be made. This can lead to a voluntary and rational (at least at the time) decision to age in place or to move, locally or long distance. Some older people who would like to move, however, become 'involuntary stayers' (Moore and Rosenberg, 1997). These individuals do not have the financial resources, the health, or the freedom to move because their adult children or very elderly parents live in the community, or they need some personal care and support. Many of those who are unable to move are older single women. In general, moving in later life is influenced and shaped by earlier experiences of moving (frequency, distance, and adjustment), by current emotional ties to the neighbourhood or community, by the location of key family members, by personal and spousal health, by wealth, and by the kind of life the person wants.

Litwak and Longino (1987) identified three general types of moves in later life. An 'amenity-oriented' move is voluntary and enables older people to live in a better climate or community, to live near relatives or friends, to live in smaller, more accessible, safer or cheaper housing, or to pursue a more active life, especially during the winter. The most popular amenity destinations for Canadians are Vancouver Island or the Okanagan Valley in British Columbia; the Niagara region in Ontario; Florida; or the southern and western regions of the United States.

A second type of move occurs when an older person or couple begin to have difficulty in performing instrumental activities of daily living (IADLs), such as preparing meals, maintaining the house, or shopping. The home environment becomes too difficult and perhaps unsafe for their personal abilities (that is, there is environmental press). The third type of move occurs with the onset of a severe physical or mental disability that forces the older adult to move—to a child's home, to supportive housing, or to a long-term-care institution. In the past, many of these moves took place prematurely because a suitable support network or adequate polices and programs were not available in the community. Because communities and families are increasingly developing a greater variety of support systems as needed, moving to an institution can be prevented or delayed.

Local Moves

The majority of moves in later life are local, often within the same county or metropolitan region. For urban-dwelling retirees, an increasing number of moves are to non-metropolitan 'rural' or small towns to begin a 'new' life that is safer, more economical, and healthier. However, later in the retirement years, local moves are made most often because of declining health or because more economical or accessible housing is required. Many of these late-in-life moves are by elderly widows, partly because of financial difficulties, and most involve a move to an institution or community where social and health-care services are available. Few older people move as long as they have enough money and the physical abilities to live in their current home.

These local moves represent increasing dependence and the need for a new type of housing arrangement: from a house to an apartment or condominium; from a house, apartment, or condominium to supportive housing; and from the family home or supportive housing to an institution that provides a needed level of care. Those most likely to make a local move late in life, in addition to women who are single, separated, widowed, or divorced, are renters rather than homeowners; those with low incomes and little education; those with a history of moving often; and those who are becoming more dependent on others because of declining physical or mental capacity. A person who is deciding whether to move is influenced by environmental considerations, which can operate as 'push' factors (such as declining safety and security, urban renewal, or gentrification) or as 'pull' factors (such as availability of financial or health assistance or higher-quality shelter).

Migration

Migration is defined as a move across political boundaries to another county, province, or country, either seasonally or permanently. Seasonal migration usually takes place in the winter and often consists of moving to a milder climate.[14] Some affluent Canadians, however, not only go south in the winter, but also migrate in the summer to a cottage or summer home outside an urban area, after a short spring or fall stay in a 'permanent' residence. Because older people today are more mobile, especially on a seasonal basis, geographers, community planners, economists, and gerontologists monitor migration patterns and the redistribution of where older people live, the motivations and characteristics of migrants, and the economic and social impact of migration on the 'sending' and 'receiving' communities.[15] A high concentration of older residents in a community is the result of three processes (Longino, 2001): 'accumulation', or aging in place, when older people remain in the community while young people leave in large numbers; 'recomposition', which happens when older people settle permanently in areas that younger people are leaving; and 'congregation', when migrants of all ages arrive in the community, but older people arrive in significantly greater numbers.

In Canada, most permanent interprovincial migration among the older population is westward, although there is a small amount of return migration from Ontario to the Atlantic provinces. As a result of migration patterns, there is a concentration of the elderly population in British Columbia (especially Victoria and the Okanagan Valley), Alberta, and Ontario (especially in smaller cities and in the St Catharines–Niagara Falls region). For example, in British Columbia only 20 per cent of all residents over 65 were born in that province, and of those 85 and older, only 12 per cent were born there. Statistics Canada (2003b) reports that from 1996 to 2001, for those 65 and over, the largest number (individuals) of net losses were in Quebec (5,350), Manitoba (1,495), and Saskatchewan (1,860). The largest net gains were in Alberta (3,685), British Columbia (2,915), and Ontario (1,285). At the level of Census Metropolitan areas (adjacent municipalities in a major urban core with a population of at least 100,000), for those 65 and over, the communities with the largest net losses from 1996 to 2001 were Toronto (12,470), Montreal (4,095), and Vancouver (2430). Those with the largest net gains were Hamilton (1,735) and Ottawa-Hull (1,620) in Ontario, Edmonton (1,230) in Alberta, and Victoria (1,005) in British Columbia.

The major migration pattern for older Canadian 'snowbirds' tends to be a seasonal path to the southern United States or Mexico for the winter months (November to March). An estimated 225,000 or more older Canadians visit Florida each year, mostly as seasonal residents who stay from one to five months (Martin et al., 1992; Tucker et al., 1988, 1992). However, these numbers vary annually, often in relation to the exchange rate on the Canadian dollar.

While both personal and environmental 'push' and 'pull' factors stimulate migration in the later years, the pull factors tend to be more influential in a decision to seek an alternative or higher-quality lifestyle. Moreover, it appears that non-economic factors are most influential in determining who migrates and to what regions. Most later-life migration occurs within the first 10 years of retirement, and for most older people, the decision is reached after visits to the area, or after consulting with friends who migrated earlier to the area. Those who migrate primarily for lifestyle reasons are more likely to be wealthier; to be married; to have previously migrated or travelled extensively during adulthood; to have more education; and to be in good health. Older adults seeking an active, leisure-oriented retirement lifestyle in another community tend to be highly independent individuals.

For a community, the arrival or departure of large numbers of older people significantly changes the economic resources of, and the infrastructure demands on, the community. Some communities, for purposes of economic development, actively encourage older people to migrate to the community (Longino, 2001). In these receiving communities, older people are less likely to be perceived as outsiders or a financial burden on local housing, health, leisure, transportation, library, or social welfare budgets, whether they are permanent or seasonal residents. Many older migrants are healthy, affluent married couples who contribute significant economic benefits to the receiving community by purchasing goods and services and by paying rent or property taxes. As well, they indirectly stimulate the local tourism industry when their family and friends visit them.

The 'home' or 'sending' community, however, loses a significant amount of revenue for up to six months a year. Studies have shown that seasonal migration usually ends or is shortened as health or financial resources decline (Longino and Serow, 1992). In this scenario, the original home community or region is a two-time loser—it loses the spending income of lifelong residents during their healthy, affluent retirement years; and it must absorb the high costs of health care, social services, and institutionalization when the migrants return as partially or totally dependent residents. At the same time, the seasonal retirement-destination region has benefited from the retirees' spending during their healthy, affluent years of retirement, yet does not have to absorb the costs for those who have returned home to seek assistance during the frail, dependent years of later life.

Summary

The lived environment, including living arrangements, quality of housing, and the geographical location influence well-being and the quality of life in the later years. Where one lives, and with whom, are valued highly by older people. Most prefer to age 'in place', that is, in the family home in a familiar neighbourhood and community. But increasingly, after retirement, older people are more mobile. Hence, either permanent or seasonal migrations are increasing. For those who age in place, there are more housing alternatives and community-care services, which help to delay or prevent institutionalization in costly extended- or long-term care facilities.

As health declines and disabilities increase, independence and autonomy are weakened. An older person is more likely to move to more suitable housing in later life if he or she becomes unable to drive, develops a tendency to fall, is unwilling or unable to adopt technological or mechanical assistive devices, is afraid of crime, or has difficulty walking because of unsafe or inaccessible parts of their environment, such as the sidewalks or buildings. The availability of a range of types of housing, rather than only two choices (living in the family home or with a child, versus institutionalization), enables older people to live in suitable, accessible, affordable, safe, and satisfying surroundings. A range of options reduces the burden on the family, and from the perspective of the state, reduces the high costs of hospital stays and long-term care facilities. In short, a prime goal of enlightened community leaders should be to ensure that older people live in suitable and affordable housing in their community, and not in an institution.

For Reflection, Debate, or Action

1. Employing the ecological model of aging (Figure 7.1), identify some elements of environmental press that could present adaptation difficulties for older people in your community.

2. Assess the housing alternatives available for older adults in your home community, and identify the type and amount of housing stock that will be needed in order to meet the needs of two or three

different generations of older people in 2030 when the entire baby boom generation has retired.

3. Debate the pros and cons of multi-generational housing for older people in your family and community.

4. Make a list of emerging technological developments and social changes, and indicate if, and why, they will have an impact on the aging process or on older people, today and in the future.

5. How can older people use new technologies to enhance their quality of life, and what are some of the disadvantages of technology for older age cohorts?

6. Debate the pros and cons of whether there should be mandatory driving tests and de-licensing for older adults. If you advocate de-licensing, what criteria should be employed to ensure that assessments and decisions are fair and objective?

7. Visit a retirement home and a nursing home in your community, and identify the different level of care and services provided. Determine to what extent residents are involved in decisions, and to what extent RAI instruments are used for admission and for on-going care decisions.

8. If you were a community planner responsible for housing development, why would you advocate either age-segregated or age-integrated housing for older adults?

9. Visit a local nursing or retirement home and volunteer half a day of your time for 10–12 weeks. At the end of the period make at least 10 recommendations as to how the social and work environment might be altered to:

   • improve the quality of life of the residents; and

   • increase the efficiency and improve the quality of service provided by the staff.

Notes

1. This chapter focuses on the spatial and physical characteristics of the 'designed' or 'built' environment and on the social environment as influenced by the physical environment. This does not mean that a the natural environment is not important to older people (Wright and Lund, 2000). Indeed, respect for nature has long been a concern of many older people, including Aboriginal people who make decisions with seven future generations in mind.

2. Theories about aging and the environment can be found in Gubrium (1973), Windley and Scheidt (1980), Kahana (1982), Lawton et al. (1982), Golant (1984), Haldeman and Wister (1994), Scheidt and Windley (1985, 1998), Cvitkovich and Wister (2001, 2002), and Wahl and Weisman (2003).

3. In Chapter 11, sources and types of social support to assist with ADLs and IADLs are discussed. Here the emphasis is on adaptations to the environment through the use of mechanical or technological devices or through alterations to the physical environment.

4. See Robson et al. (2003) and Health Canada publications *An Inventory of Canadian Programs for the Prevention of Falls among Seniors Living in the Community* and *A Best Practices Guide for the Prevention of Falls among Seniors Living in the Community* (www.hc-sc.gc.ca/seniors-aines/pubs/inventory/intro_e.htm).

5. Elder abuse is discussed in Chapter 11.

6. This statistic may partially reflect the fact that men are less likely to admit to being afraid. There are also more women than men in the older population.

7. *The International Journal of Technology and Aging*, published since 1988, provides information about the use of technology by older adults in a variety of residential, work, and leisure settings.

8. CMHC, the federal housing agency, provides financial assistance up to $2,500 to help low-income homeowners and landlords pay for home adaptations to extend the time they can live independently in their own home or a rented house or apartment. This program, Home Adaptations for Seniors' Independence, provides funds to install handrails, grab bars, walk-in showers, bath and stair lifts, wheelchair ramps, and widened doorways for wheelchair access.

9. In the United States, the American Association for Retired Persons (AARP) operates the National Shared Housing Resources Center, which runs home-sharing programs in over 200 communities (www.aarp.org/getans/consumer/homeshare.html).

10. See www.cmhc-schl.gc.ca and click on 'Garden Suites' for a description and floor plan of garden suites and information about relevant legislation and the financing of garden suites in Canada. This site also provides access to CMHC publications (Reports and Research Highlights), housing programs for older people, and the Housing in Canada Electronic Data Series. The National Association of Home Builders Research Centre (www.nahbrc.org) gives examples of unique housing design features for older people, such as those shown in the Life Wise Home demonstration project. Click on 'Seniors Housing'.

11. Congregate housing provides a semi-independent living arrangement where each individual or couple has an apartment or room with a bathroom, and sometimes cooking or laundry facilities. Congregate housing provides services that includes one to three meals a day, laundry and maid service, private transportation, security service, minor health care, and recreational programs. The congregate concept usually means that the residents eat at the same time in a common dining room. Recent developments in this area are described in journals such as *Assisted Living Today*, *Provider*, *Contemporary Long Term Care*, and *Journal of Housing for the Elderly*.

12. Many facilities are operated as private enterprises, and the owners seldom permit outsiders or researchers to study the facility or its residents. As a result, many studies on this topic involve non-profit institutions or, less frequently, those where the residents are affluent, are in better health, and pay high fees. These latter settings are atypical in that the environment and the quality of care are generally superior to those of most for-profit institutions, which have a mission to generate profits rather than enhance the quality of care for residents. Institutions operated by voluntary organizations or religious groups on a not-for-profit basis are often more person-oriented and less bureaucratic, and therefore have higher levels of quality of care.

13. The outcome of an evaluation of the quality of care provided by an institution depends on whether the evaluation includes the views of a resident, a resident's relative, a staff member, and/or a government inspector. The most thorough type of evaluation considers all of those views. Evaluations may consider the amount of personal space; degree of privacy; safety of the physical structure; type, availability, and quality of health and medical care; degree of emotional interest in and concern for residents on the part of staff; the availability and variety of social, recreational, and therapeutic programs; the variety and nutritional quality of food; and the policies of the institution concerning visitors, sex, alcohol, and tobacco.

14. Canadians who winter in the United States stay less than six months in order to meet the requirements of Canadian tax laws and to remain eligible for health insurance.

15. For a discussion of migration by older people see Moore and Rosenberg, 1997; Longino, 2001; Longino et al., 2002; Walters, 2002; Statistics Canada, 2003a, 2003b.

References

Au Coin, K. 2003. 'Family Violence against Older people'. Pp. 21–32 in H. Johnson and K. Au Coin (eds), *Family Violence in Canada: A Statistical Profile, 2003*. Cat. 85-224-XIE. Ottawa: Statistics Canada, Canadian Centre for Social Justice.

Banks, M., and W. Banks. 2002. 'The Effects of Animal-Assisted Therapy on Loneliness in an Elderly Population in Long-Term Care Facilities', *Journal of Gerontology: Medical Sciences*, 57A(7), M428–32.

Bedard, M., et al. 2002. 'Traffic-Related Fatalities among Older Drivers and Passengers: Past and Future Trends', *The Gerontologist*, 41(6), 751–6.

Bess, I. 1999a. 'Widows Living Alone', *Canadian Social Trends*, Summer, 2–5.

———. 1999b. 'Seniors Behind the Wheel', *Canadian Social Trends*, Autumn, 2–7.

Bongaarts, J., and Z. Zimmer. 2002. 'Living Arrangements of Older Adults in the Developing World: An Analysis of Demographic and Health Survey Household Surveys', *Journal of Gerontology: Social Sciences*, 57B(3), S145–57.

Bowles, R., et al. 1994. *Retiree Migrants to a Small Ontario Community*. Ottawa: Canada Mortgage and Housing Corporation.

British Columbia Ministry of Health and Ministry Responsible for Seniors. 1999. *Supportive Housing in Supportive Communities: The Report on the Supportive Housing Review*. Victoria, BC: The Ministry.

CAG. 2000. *Policy Statement on Assistive Devices for Seniors*. Ottawa: Canadian Association on Gerontology (CAG).

Carder, P. 2002. 'The Social World of Assisted Living', *Journal of Aging Studies*, 16(1), 1–18.

CARP. 1998. *CARP's National Forum on Scams and Fraud: Report and Recommendations*. Toronto: Canadian Association of Retired Persons (CARP).

Carrière, Y., and L. Pelletier. 1995. 'Factors Underlying the Institutionalization of Elderly Persons in Canada', *Journal of Gerontology: Social Sciences*, 50B(3), S164–72.

Chappell, N. 1994. 'Technology and Aging'. Pp. 83–96 in V. Marshall and B. McPherson (eds), *Aging: Canadian Perspectives*. Peterborough, Ont.: Broadview.

Charles, C., and C. Schalm. 1992a. 'Alberta's Resident Classification System for Long-Term Care Facilities. Part I: Conceptual and Methodological Development', *Canadian Journal on Aging*, 11(3), 219–32.

———. 1992b. 'Alberta's Resident Classification System for Long-Term Care Facilities. Part II: First-Year Results and Policy Implications', *Canadian Journal on Aging*, 11(3), 233–48.

Charness, N., and W. Schaie (eds). 2004. *Impact of Technology on Successful Aging*. New York: Springer.

Che-Alford, J., and K. Stevenson. 1998. 'Older Canadians on the Move', *Canadian Social Trends*, (Spring), 15–18.

———, and B. Hamm. 1999. 'Under One Roof: Three Generations Living Together', *Canadian Social Trends*, (Summer), 6–9.

Chernin, S. 1996. *Every Resident: Bill of Rights for People Who Live in Ontario Long-Term-Care Facilities*. Toronto: Advocacy Centre for the Elderly, and Community Legal Education Ontario.

Cvitkovich, Y., and A. Wister. 2001. 'Comparison of Four Person-Environment Fit Models Applied to Older Adults', *Journal of Housing for the Elderly*, 14 (1 and 2), 1–25.

———, and A. Wister. 2002. 'Bringing in the Life Course: A Modification to Lawton's Ecological Model of Aging', *Hallym International Journal of Aging*, 4(1), 15–29.

Clark, W. 2002. 'Time Alone', *Canadian Social Trends*, 66 (Autumn), 2–6.

Clements, G. 2002. 'Ethical and Legal Issues: A Legal Perspective'. Pp. 333–60 in M. Stephenson and E. Sawyer (eds), *Continuing the Care: The Issues and Challenges for Long-Term Care*. Ottawa: CHA Press (www.cha.ca).

Cobb, R., and J. Coughlin. 1998. 'Are Elderly Drivers a Road Hazard? Problem Definition and Political Impact', *Journal of Aging Studies*, 12(4), 411–27.

CMHC. 2000a. *Women on the Rough Edge: A Decade of Change for Long-Term Homeless Women*. Research Highlights No. 54. Ottawa: Canada Mortgage and Housing Corporation.

———. 2000b. *Supportive Housing For Seniors*. Research Highlights No. 56. Ottawa: Canada Mortgage and Housing Corporation.

———. 2002a. *Housing the Boom, Bust and Echo Generations*. Research Highlights No. 77. Ottawa: Canada Mortgage and Housing Corporation.

———. 2002b. *Seniors' Housing Conditions*. Research Highlights No. 78. Ottawa: Canada Mortgage and Housing Corporation.

Cohen, C. 1999. 'Aging and Homelessness', *The Gerontologist*, 39(1), 5–14.

Connidis, I. 2001. *Family Ties and Aging*. Thousand Oaks, Calif.: Sage.

Crane, M. 1999. *Understanding Older Homeless People*. Philadelphia: Open University Press.

Dauvergne, M. 2003. 'Family Violence against Seniors', *Canadian Social Trends*, 68 (Spring), 10–14.

Donahue, P. 2001. *Fraud in Ethnocultural Seniors' Communities*. SEDAP Research Paper No. 37. Hamilton, Ont.: McMaster University (http://socserv2.mcmaster.ca/sedap).

Finlayson, M., and J. Kaufert. 2002. 'Older Women's Community Mobility: A Qualitative Exploration', *Canadian Journal on Aging*, 21(1), 75–84.

Flaherty, J., et al. 2003. 'A Consensus Statement on Nonemergent Medical Transportation Services for Older Persons', *Journal of Gerontology: Medical Sciences*, 58(9), 826–31.

Fletcher, P., and J. Hirdes. 2000. 'Risk Factors for Falling among Community- Based Seniors Using Home Care Services', *Journal of Gerontology: Medical Sciences*, 57A(8), M504–10.

———., and J. Hirdes. 2002. 'Risk Factors for Serious

Falls among Community- Based Seniors: Results from the National Population Health Survey', *Canadian Journal on Aging*, 21(1), 103–16.

Forbes, W., et al. 1987. *Institutionalization of the Elderly in Canada*. Toronto: Butterworths.

Fries, B., et al. 2002. 'A Screening System for Michigan's Home- and Community- Based Long-Term Care Programs', *The Gerontologist* 42(4), 462–74.

Gallagher, E., et al. 1999. 'The Nature of Falling among Community Dwelling Seniors', *Canadian Journal on Aging*, 18(3), 348–62.

Golant, S. 1984. *A Place to Grow Old: The Meaning of Environment in Old Age*. New York: Columbia University Press.

Gubrium, J. 1973. *The Myth of the Golden Years: A Socio-Environmental Theory of Aging*. Springfield, Ill.: Charles C. Thomas.

———. 1993. *Speaking of Life: Horizons of Meaning for Nursing Home Residents*. Hawthorne, NY: Aldine de Gruyter.

Haber, C. 1993. 'Over the Hill to the Poorhouse: Rhetoric and Reality in the Institutional History of the Aged'. Pp. 90–122 in W. Schaie and A. Achenbaum (eds), *Societal Impact on Aging: Historical Perspectives*. New York: Springer.

Haldemann, V., and A. Wister. 1994. 'Environment and Aging'. Pp. 36–50 in V. Marshall and B. McPherson (eds), *Aging: Canadian Perspectives*. Peterborough, Ont.: Broadview.

Health Canada. 2002a. *Canada's Aging Population*. Ottawa: Minister of Public Works and Government Services Canada.

———. 2002b. *Go for It! A Guide to Choosing and Using Assistive Devices*. Ottawa: Minister of Public Works and Government Services Canada.

———. 2002c. *Healthy Aging: Prevention of Unintentional Injuries among Seniors*. Ottawa: Health Canada.

Henig, J. 1981. 'Gentrification and Displacement of the Elderly: An Empirical Analysis', *The Gerontologist*, 21(1), 67–75.

Hodge, G. 1991. 'The Economic Impact of Retirees on Smaller Communities', *Research on Aging*, 13(1), 39–54.

Hirdes, J., et al. 1998. 'Use of the MDS Quality Indicators to Assess Quality of Care in Institutional Settings', *Canadian Journal on Quality in Health Care*, 14(2), 5–11.

———. 1999a. 'International and Regional Variations in Restraint Use: Implications for Selecting Benchmarks', *Canadian Journal on Quality in Health Care*, 15(2), 19–23.

———. 1999b. 'Integrated Health Information Systems Based on the RAI/MDS Series of Assessment Instruments', *Healthcare Management Forum*, 12(4), 30–40.

———. 2001. 'Development of the Resident Assessment Instrument—Mental Health (RAI-MH), *Hospital Quarterly*, 4(2), 44–51.

Johnson, H., and K. Au Coin (eds). 2003. *Family Violence in Canada: A Statistical Profile, 2003*. Ottawa: Statistics Canada, Canadian Centre for Justice Statistics (Cat. #85-224-XIE).

Joseph, A., and A. Martin Matthews. 1994. 'Growing Old in Aging Communities'. Pp. 20–35 in V. Marshall and B. McPherson (eds), *Aging: Canadian Perspectives*. Peterborough, Ont.: Broadview.

Kahana, E. 1982. 'A Congruence Model of Person-Environment Interaction'. Pp. 97–121 in P. Lawton et al. (eds), *Aging and the Environment: Theoretical Approaches*. New York: Springer.

Kane, R., and R. Kane. 2001. 'Emerging Issues in Chronic Care'. Pp. 406–25 in R. Binstock and L. George (eds), *Handbook of Aging and the Social Sciences*. San Diego, Calif.: Academic Press.

Keating, N. 1991. *Aging in Rural Canada*. Toronto: Butterworths.

———. 2001a. 'A Good Place to Grow Old? Rural Communities and Support to Seniors'. Pp. 263–77 in R. Epp and D. Whitson (eds), *Writing Off the Rural West: Globalization, Governments and the Transformation of Rural Communities*. Edmonton: University of Alberta Press.

———. 2001b. 'Services Provided by Informal and formal Caregivers to Seniors in Residential Continuing Care', *Canadian Journal on Aging*, 20(1), 23–45.

Klavora, P., and R. Heslegrave. 2002. 'Senior Drivers: An Overview of Problems and Intervention Strategies', *Journal of Aging and Physical Activity*, 10(3), 322–35.

Kontos, P. 1998. 'Resisting Institutionalization: Constructing Old Age and Negotiating Home', *Journal of Aging Studies*, 12(2), 167–84.

KPMG Consulting. 2000. 'Canadian Continuing Care Scenarios, 1999–2041'. Edmonton: KPMG. Unpublished report.

Lawton, P. 1980. *Environment and Aging*. Monterey, Calif.: Brooks/Cole.

———. 1985. 'Housing and Living Environments of Older People'. Pp. 450–78 in R. Binstock and E.

Shanas (eds), *Handbook of Aging and the Social Sciences*. New York: Van Nostrand Reinhold.

———. 1987. 'Aging and Proactivity in the Residential Environment'. Paper presented at the American Psychological Association Annual Meeting, New York.

———. 1990. 'Residential Environment and Self-Directness among Older People', *American Psychologist*, 45(5), 638–40.

———, et al. (eds), 1982. *Aging and the Environment: Theoretical Approaches*. New York: Springer.

———, and L. Nahemow. 1973. 'Ecology and the Aging Process'. Pp. 619–74 in C. Eisdorfer and P. Lawton (eds), *The Psychology of Adult Development and Aging*. Washington, DC: American Psychological Association.

Lindsay, C. 1999. 'Seniors: A Diverse Group Aging Well', *Canadian Social Trends*, (Spring), 24–6.

Litwak, E., and C. Longino. 1987. 'Migration Patterns among the Elderly: A Developmental Perspective', *The Gerontologist*, 27(2), 266–72.

Longino, C. 2001. 'Geographical Distribution and Migration'. Pp. 103–24 in R. Binstock and L. George (eds), *Handbook of Aging and the Social Sciences*. New York: Academic Press.

———., and W. Serow. 1992. 'Regional Differences in the Characteristics of Elderly Return Migrants', *Journal of Gerontology: Social Sciences*, 47(1), S38–43.

———, et al. 2002. 'Pandora's Briefcase: Unpacking the Retirement Migration Decision', *Research on Aging*, 24(1), 29–49.

MacLean, M., and J. Klein. 2002. 'Accessibility to Long-Term Care: The Myth versus Reality'. Pp. 71–86 in M. Stephenson and E. Sawyer (eds), *Continuing the Care: The Issues and Challenges for Long-Term Care*. Ottawa: CHA Press.

Maddox, G. 2001. 'Housing and Living Arrangements: A Transactional Perspective'. Pp. 426–43 in R. Binstock and L. George (eds), *Handbook of Aging and the Social Sciences*. New York: Academic Press.

Martin, H., et al. 1992. 'Sociodemographic and Health Characteristics of Anglophone Canadian and US Snowbirds', *Journal of Aging and Health*, 4(4), 500–13.

Moore, E., and M. Rosenberg. 1997. *Growing Old in Canada: Demographic and Geographic Perspectives*. Ottawa: Statistics Canada.

———., et al. 2000. *Geographic Dimensions of Aging: The Canadian Experience, 1991–1996*, SEDAP Research Paper No. 23. Hamilton, Ont.: McMaster University (http://socserv2.mcmaster.ca/sedap).

Morley, J. 2002. 'A Fall Is A Major Event in the Life of an Older Person', *Journal of Gerontology: Medical Sciences*, 57A(8), M492–5.

Munro, M. 2000. 'The Driver Is Miss Daisy', *National Post*, 19 April, A17.

NACA (National Advisory Council on Aging). 1993. *The NACA Position on Canada's Oldest Seniors: Maintaining the Quality of Their Lives*. Ottawa: Minister of Supply and Services.

———. 2001. *Seniors and Technology*. Ottawa: NACA.

———. 2002. *The NACA Position on Supportive Housing for Seniors*. Position Paper No. 22. Ottawa: National Advisory Council on Aging.

———. 2003. 'Let's Get Moving', *Expression*, 16(1), 4–8.

Pacey, M. 2002. *Living Alone and Living with Children: The Living Arrangements of Canadian and Chinese-Canadian Seniors*. SEDAP Research Paper No. 74. Hamilton, Ont.: McMaster University (http://socserv2.mcmaster.ca/sedap).

Quadagno, J., et al. (eds). 2003. 'Challenges in Nursing Home Care', *The Gerontologist*, 43 (Special Issue II), 4–131.

Robert, S. 2002. 'Community Context and Aging: Future Research Issues', *Research on Aging*, 24(6), 579–99.

Robson, E., et al. 2003. 'Steady As You Go (SAYGO): A Falls-Prevention Program for Seniors Living in the Community', *Canadian Journal on Aging*, 22(2), 207–16.

Rudy, N. 1987. *For Such a Time as This*. Toronto: Ontario Association of Homes for the Aged.

Scheidt, R., and P. Windley. 1985. 'The Ecology of Aging'. Pp. 245–58 in J. Birren and W. Schaie (eds), *Handbook of the Psychology of Aging*. New York: Van Nostrand Reinhold.

——— (eds). 1998. *Environment and Aging Theory: A Focus on Housing*. Westport, Conn.: Greenwood Press.

Silver, C. 2001. 'Older Surfers', *Canadian Social Trends* (Winter), 9–12.

Snell, J. 1996. *The Citizen's Wage: The State and the Elderly in Canada, 1900–1951*. Toronto: University of Toronto Press.

Statistics Canada. 2001a. *Seniors in Canada: Canadian Centre for Justice Statistics Profile Series*. Ottawa: Minister of Industry.

———. 2001b. *Overview: Access to and Use of Information Communication Technology*. Catalogue no. 56-505-XIE. Ottawa: Statistics Canada.

————. 2002a. *Victims and Persons Accused of Homicide By Age and Sex*. CANISM II, Table 253-0003. Extracted from Stats Can website on 11 Dec. 2002. (http://www.statcan.ca/English/pgdb/legal10a.htm).

————. 2002b. *Profile of Canadian Families and Households: Diversification Continues*. Catalogue no. 96F0030XIE2001003—22 Oct. Ottawa: Statistics Canada.

————. 2003a. *Net Migrants and Net Migration Rates by Age Group, Provinces and Territories, 1996–2001*. Extracted from Statistics Canada website (http://www12.statcan.ca/english/census01/products/analytic/companion)

————. 2003b. *International Migration for Census Metropolitan Areas by Age Groups, 1996–2001*. Extracted from Statistics Canada website (http://www12.statcan.ca/english/census01/products/analytic/companion/mob /tables/ migage).

————. 2003c. *2001 Census Dictionary*. Catalogue no. 92-378-XIE. Ottawa: Statistics Canada.

Streib, G. 2002. 'An Introduction to Retirement Communities', *Research on Aging*, 24(1), 3–9.

Sutton, D., et al. 2003. 'Medical and Everyday Assistive Device Use among Older Adults with Arthritis', *Canadian Journal on Aging*, 21(4), 535–48.

Svensson, T. 1996. 'Competence and Quality of Life: Theoretical Views of Biography'. Pp. 100–16 in J. Birren et al. (eds), *Aging and Biography*. New York: Springer.

Tucker, R., et al. 1988. 'Older Anglophone Canadian Snowbirds in Florida: A Descriptive Profile', *Canadian Journal on Aging*, 7(3), 218–32.

————. 1992. 'Older Canadians in Florida: A Comparison of Anglophone and Francophone Seasonal Migrants', *Canadian Journal on Aging*, 11(3), 281–97.

Van den Hoonard, D. 2002. 'Life on the Margins of a Florida Retirement Community: The Experience of Snowbirds, Newcomers, and Widowed Persons', *Research on Aging*, 24(1), 50–66.

Wahl, H. 2001. 'Environmental Influences on Aging and Behavior'. Pp. 215–40 in J. Birren and W. Schaie (eds), *Handbook of the Psychology of Aging*. New York: Academic Press.

————, and G. Weisman. 2003. 'Environmental Gerontology at the Beginning of the New Millennium: Reflections on Its Historical, Empirical, and Theoretical Development', *The Gerontologist*, 43(5), 616–27.

Walters, W. 2002. 'Place Characteristics and Later-Life Migration', *Research on Aging*, 24(2), 243–77.

Warren, S. 2000. Editorial. 'Resident Assessment Instruments: Their Use for Health Care Planning and Research', *Canadian Journal on Aging*, 19 (Supplement 2), i–xv.

Wilmoth, J. 2000. 'Unbalanced Social Exchanges and Living Arrangement Transitions among Older Adults', *The Gerontologist*, 40(1), 64–74.

Windley, P., and R. Scheidt. 1980. 'Person Environment Dialectics: Implications for Component Functioning in Old Age'. Pp. 407–23 in L. Poon (ed.), *Aging in the 1980s*. Washington, DC: American Psychological Association.

Wister, A. 1989). 'Environmental Adaptation among Persons in Their Later Life', *Research on Aging*, 11(3), 267–91.

Wright, S., and D. Lund. 2000. 'Gray and Green?: Stewardship and Sustainability in an Aging Society', *Journal of Aging Studies*, 14(3): 229–49.

Zimmer, Z., and N. Chappell 1999. 'Receptivity to New Technology among Older Adults', *Disability and Rehabilitation*, 21(5/6), 222–30.

PART 3

Aging and Social Institutions

Social institutions, as cultural products that persist from generation to generation, provide value orientations, norms, and a structure for interaction in our daily lives. In pre-industrial societies, the family and the tribe (and perhaps religion) were the principal institutions; today, our lives are influenced by a number of socializing, regulative, and cultural institutions.

Socializing institutions, such as the family, the peer group, and the educational system, normally have the greatest influence from childhood to early adulthood. During adulthood, the family continues to be an important institution, in which relationships change as we become or cease to be a partner, parent, or grandparent. *Regulative* institutions include the economic, legal, and political systems. During adulthood, the economic system influences when we work, our work history (i.e., our employability), and our earnings. Changes in labour force policies and practices influence the nature of work, and along with public policies, the time at when we must or could retire. Sometimes labour force and public policies disadvantage some members of the labour force, such as women, the working class, and particular ethnic groups. *Cultural* institutions, including the mass media, religion, voluntary associations, the arts, and sport provide a milieu for social participation during a person's leisure time across the life course.

Part 3 examines social relationships across the life course, and the effect of transitions on individuals in the family, at work, in retirement, and during their leisure time. Involvement in family, the labour force, and leisure settings creates opportunities for, or barriers to, social interaction, and influences our quality of life in the middle and later years. Transitions such as parenting, the empty nest, divorce, unemployment, retirement, or widowhood have the potential to create personal crises or opportunities for growth that change lifestyles and life chances. How an individual adjusts to these transitions is influenced by socio-demographic characteristics, past history, and the amount of social support available, especially from within the family.

Chapter 8 examines aging in the context of family interaction and intimate ties, such as relations between generations and within the same generation; marital satisfaction; and the effect of divorce, the empty nest, retirement, and widowhood on the individual and the family. What were once considered unique family ties and relationships (never-married, gay or lesbian couples, or childless couples) are no longer seen as unusual. Chapter 9 reviews the effect of employment history on social interaction and lifestyles in later life and examines the process of retirement and the economic status of retired people and their dependents. Workers are becoming older, and some of these older employees experience discrimination in the workforce. Similarly, women have experienced discrimination in work opportunities and wages, Thus, special attention is directed to gender issues in the workforce and in retirement, including the feminization of poverty. In Chapter 10, the structure and size of social networks and diverse patterns of social participation in later life are described. Older adults are involved in such diverse 'leisure' activities as crime, religion, politics, education, the media, voluntary associations, tourism, and gambling. But, with increased life expectancy, how to fill one's time in a meaningful way is a personal trouble for some, especially those who were work-oriented for most of their adult life.

CHAPTER 8

Family Ties, Relationships, and Transitions

Focal Points

- If kinship structures change, what influence does this have on intergenerational relationships in later life?
- Is marital satisfaction across the life course represented by a straight or curved line?
- Why are more grandparents raising young grandchildren?
- If one is single, childless, gay, or lesbian, to what extent, and why, do these situations influence family relations and support across the life course?
- Which family transitions in the middle and later years influence interpersonal relationships, and why?
- Why are widowhood and divorce so influential in the lifestyle and quality of life of older women?
- To what extent, and in what circumstances, do older adults date, cohabit, or remarry?

Introduction

The family, as a fundamental social institution, influences daily life and life chances through the life course. Families provide stability, emotional support, and financial assistance; age-integrated social interaction; socialization concerning values, morals, and life skills; and legal rights and obligations. But families can also be a source of tension and conflict. Families provide a structure in which we experience many life transitions, including marriage, raising children, the empty nest, divorce, widowhood, and remarriage. We have already learned about intergenerational family conflict and transfers (see Chapter 6) and about household composition and living arrangements in a family context (see Chapter 7). Later

we will see how the family interacts with work and retirement (Chapter 9), with social participation (Chapter 10), with caregiving and social support for frail and dependent parents, including elder abuse (Chapter 11), and with issues such as guardianship and end-of-life decisions (Chapter 12).

Many books on aging discuss 'family' in the context of intergenerational conflict, the problems and burdens of caring for frail parents, or the unique stressful situation of those in the 'sandwich' generation. Yes, family stress and conflict can result in domestic abuse and violence against children, spouses, and elderly parents. Yes, children and a spouse may be abandoned.

Yes, divorce occurs in many families. And yes, caring for an aging parent can be stressful and burdensome. But as Rosenthal (2000: 45) notes, 'there is more to family life than caregiving'; a contention reinforced by Matthews' (2002) study of adult siblings, who, for the most part, reported that caring for and assisting their parents was not a burden. There is a big difference between providing assistance to, versus custodial care of, elderly parents. Rather, help to parents is seen as an extension of normal family interaction. Most older people are not abandoned by their children; and support and assistance characterize most family relationships across the life course. Moreover, the 'sandwich' generation is more myth than fact—that is, there are relatively few middle-aged woman who are employed full-time, have a child at home, *and* have an aging parent needing daily help, supervision, and care (Rosenthal, 2000: 57–9).

This chapter discusses continuity, changes, and diversity in family structures and networks; the type, frequency, meaning, and quality of both intra- and inter-generational relations; and the timing, sequencing, and duration of family-related transitions throughout life, especially those which have implications for later life. Intimate ties and relationships that are family-like but are seldom recognized in legal terms as such, are discussed. Throughout, families are viewed as social networks that vary in structure, size, and gender composition. Consequently, more emphasis is placed on understanding the quality and meaning of family ties and interaction, than on the frequency or quantity of interaction across the life course (Matthews, 2002). This emphasis on relationships enables us to understand more fully who does what, with whom, and for whom; and whether the amount of assistance and interaction is considered to be fair by people who are caring for grandchildren, frail parents, or grandparents. Perceptions of relationships also help family members decide how and when to provide support to meet children's or parent's needs. Family life involves caring *about*, and caring *for*, blood relatives, and others, across the life course.

Definitions of Family

At one time **family** meant a social group in which membership is determined by blood or marriage ties. Often, only a married couple with children, together with any of the couple's surviving parents, were included. Family-life trajectories were relatively constant and common: an adult child moved from the family of orientation to a family of procreation after marrying; raised children; experienced the 'empty nest' when children left home as young adults; and later became a grandparent and likely a widow or widower in later life. However, over the course of the twentieth century, considerable change and diversity emerged in the structure and generational relations within kinship groups.[1]

Discontinuities and irregularities in the traditional family life course have resulted in a social reconstruction of the family. Family structures and relationships are changed by divorce, single parenting, permanent family conflict, remarriage, childlessness, never-marrying, engaging in serial or long-standing common-law partnerships (whether same-sex or opposite-sex), and by the return of adult children to live in the family home.

Rather than live in the same home as their adult children, most older people prefer intimacy at a distance, that is, living independently yet being close enough to visit. Even when health or financial losses force older people to leave the family home, they still prefer some form of independent living. To illustrate, 78 per cent of Hamilton-area adults interviewed by Rosenthal (as cited in NACA, 1986) said that if the time came when they could not live on their own, they would rather live elsewhere than with their children. Similarly, in a study of older adults in London, Connidis (1989: 5–7) found that living alone was the preferred arrangement. Moreover, 80 per cent of the older people in this study reported that if they were no longer able to live in their own homes, they would prefer to live in a seniors' facility rather than with a child. In contrast, older members in some ethnic groups prefer to live with their children; or they do so because they have no choice for financial reasons. Highlight 8.1 illustrates 'intimacy at a distance', and why five older persons in Ottawa selected an independent life in a seniors' residence rather than live with one of their children.

In addition to family relationships, informal family-like relationships emerge with neighbours or friends over time. Some of these relationships evolve to a level where a friend or neighbour is almost like a relative. These people, known as **fictive kin** (MacRae, 1992), become a core part of the social network of older adults, especially if relatives are not available to provide companionship or assistance; or to serve as a confidant. Women tend to form and value such relationships more than men, especially if they are divorced or widowed. Fictive kin are an important source of assistance and support in later life for men and women who never married, are widowed, who

are childless, who are gay or lesbian, or who are estranged from their children. Indeed, an emerging type of household involves older women living with friends. Often these are long-standing friendships that lead to co-habiting arrangements in later life.

As a legal term, family defines certain rights and obligations for those who are biologically related. Some of these rights and obligations include health and pension benefits, survivor benefits, and access to a share of accumulated family wealth after being divorced or widowed. In contrast, those who are not in a 'legal' family relationship (those in a same- or opposite-sex cohabiting partnership for a short period of time, or in a series of relationships) seldom have legal rights to wealth or benefits. For example, cohabiting partners, whether same-sex or opposite-sex, may not be allowed to visit a partner in the intensive-care ward of a hospital or to make decisions about treatment, even though they may be closer to the patient than a more distant blood relative (Fox and Luxton, 2001).

Highlight 8.1 Intimacy at a Distance: The Choice of Independent Seniors

A.T.: When my doctor advised me that I shouldn't be living alone, my daughter was willing to have me move in with her, but I prefer the independence we have here.

V.S.: My son lives in Toronto, and he used to worry about me, but now he knows that someone looks in on me every day. I looked after my mother-in-law for 14 years, and I decided that no one was going to go through that with me.

H.T.: My son-in-law and grandsons are very supportive, but they respect my independence. They're only a phone call away if I need them, but I wouldn't want to be waiting around for them to call, nor would I ever want them to feel that they have to call me. I have my own life to live.

W.C.: My family felt I shouldn't be living alone. My daughter has been very supportive, and I wouldn't want to have to get along without her—we speak on the telephone every day. She no longer worries because she knows we're well taken care of here.

V.W.: I lived with my granddaughter and her husband and that would have worked out except that I began to feel isolated because they were away at work all day. We didn't live close to public transportation, and I began to feel I couldn't get out, especially in winter. I decided to move here because I'm the kind of person who likes to have other people around.

Source: NACA (1986).

Social definitions of a family have evolved over the years. Since many studies of family units are based on Statistics Canada data, their two definitions are important (Statistics Canada, 2002a). Statistics Canada defines a 'census' family as 'a husband and wife (including common-law couples), with or without children who are unmarried, or, a lone parent with or without children who have never married (regardless of age); and who are living in the same dwelling.' An 'economic' family is 'a group of two or more persons who are related to each other by blood, marriage, common law or adoption, and who live in the same dwelling' (Fox and Luxton, 2001).

At one time common-law partners, both opposite- and same-sex, were excluded from census questions, even if in a permanent and long-standing relationship. Today, the above definitions recognize common-law partnerships (about 30 per cent of all couples in Quebec are common-law), and, as of the 2001 census, data are collected about same-sex common-law couples. Inclusion in the census, however, does not necessarily give these persons the full legal rights of marriage. Today, 'couples' living in separate households, for whatever reason, are not recognized as a family unit; nor, are never-married adults who are childless. Clearly, family and kinship units are social constructions, not products of biology. Therefore, more inclusive definitions are being developed for collecting census data, for establishing legal rights, and for conceptualizing research and policies about family units across the life course (Connidis, 1994). As the next sections illustrate, in the twenty-first century there is considerably more diversity in family structures and relationships than in the early or middle years of the twentieth century.

Kinship Structures

To understand and describe changing or emerging family structures across the life course, Hagestad (2003: 142) stated that we need the following information:

- the number of generations, and the fertility rates and timing of births in each generation
- the relative age difference between and within each generation (age-condensed or age-gapped)
- the gender composition of each generation
- the number of single, never-married individuals in each generation
- marital patterns due to divorce, widowhood, remarriage, and cohabitation.

The life-course perspective enables us to examine change and stability in the structure, transitions, and relations within family units across time. Continuity and change in family structures and relationships across the life course influences who provides companionship and care in the later years.

During the first half of the previous century, kinship structures usually involved two or three generations, and each couple usually remained married and raised two to four children. With life expectancy in the low 70s, grandparents seldom survived to see their grandchildren marry or have children. However, as health improved and longevity increased, family structures became longer, and at least one member (usually a woman) in the oldest generation often lived into their 80s. Then, after the baby boom, fertility rates declined and each generation became narrower. As well, more women entered the labour force, more men and women delayed marriage, and more divorces occurred. Consequently, average age at marriage and age when a first child was born was delayed to the later 20s or beyond. And more women did not marry and more couples did not have children. Other couples married, had children and then divorced, and often one or both partners remarried, thereby creating another branch to an existing kinship system. All of these changes have had an impact on the size and shape of the kinship structure.

Four major changes in kinship structures have occurred in recent decades (Uhlenberg,

1993; Hagestad, 2003). First, the kinship system has become longer (at least three and perhaps four generations), with more vertical ties and intergenerational relationships. This trend toward verticalization means that family structures and family relationships have become more complex. For example, at different stages in life, a married woman might be a daughter, sister, granddaughter, wife, daughter-in-law, aunt, mother, mother-in-law, grandmother, great-grandmother, or widow. Today, with single-parent households, childless couples, divorce, and remarriage in all generations, the same woman, once separated or divorced, may be an ex-wife, single parent, step-mother, or step-grandmother.

A second change in kinship structures is a shift from an 'age-condensed' structure to an 'age-gapped' structure in some extended families. In an 'age-condensed' structure successive generations in a family have children at an early age (21 and under), leading to a narrow age difference (often about 20 years) between children, their parents, and their grandparents. More common is delayed childbearing over several generations (childbirth when the mother is 30 or over) wherein 'age-gapped' structures emerge, with a gap between each generation of about 30 years. This structure is most likely in families where the women are highly educated and have full-time careers. The 'normative', or most typical, structure is one where childbearing occurs between 22 and 29 years of age, with the average age at first child being about 27 years, at present (Caputo, 1999; Martin Matthews et al., 2001). In Canada, about 55 per cent of family structures are normative, 32 per cent are age-condensed, and 13 per cent are age-gapped (Martin Matthews et al., 2001).

A third structural change is the emergence of truncated families, where a specific family lineage eventually disappears when the youngest generation is childless by choice or chance. The fourth emerging change is the increased number of reconstituted or blended families as a result of remarriage following divorce or widowhood. This family structure creates a complex set of family relationships. For example, a child may have four, six, or eight sets of grandparents (for children, a dream in terms of birthday gifts; for parents, a nightmare in terms of visiting!). Thus, while there may be fewer grandchildren, there are more grandparents (Kemp, 2001). However, some grandparents (and aunts or uncles) are abandoned or isolated when the biological parents remarry or when a custodial parent moves to another community.

Today, few people reach the later stages of life with no surviving kin.[2] The oldest surviving members of kinship systems are located in many types of family structures, including the following:

- a married male with a wife, one or more married children, one or more siblings, and many grandchildren

- a never-married woman with or without surviving siblings and perhaps with a few distant relatives

- a very elderly widow with no surviving children or siblings, but with some grandchildren and perhaps great-grandchildren

- an elderly man cohabiting with an older or younger woman

- two widowed siblings living together.

Factors Influencing Family Relationships

The family life of older people is influenced by structural and personal factors that affect the quantity, quality, and type of interaction among family members across the life course. Connidis (2001: 16) identified four dimensions of family relationships central to intimate ties and to relationships between and within generations in later life:

- First, how many relatives are available, and what their relationship is to the older person (spouse, child, sibling, grandchild).

- Second, what the past and present patterns of contact and interaction are (how many and how frequent) between older persons and available kin.

- Third, what types of communication, assistance, and support are given and received among members of different generations, and in what direction the exchange flows.

- Fourth, what the quality of family relationships is across the life course. This quality could range from a supportive and emotional caring relationship (parent to infant, or adult child to parent) to an abusive or neglectful relationship involving adult children and their parents (see Chapter 11).

Gender, class, race, and ethnicity influence family relationships across the life course. These elements create diversity in family-based norms, beliefs, and values, and they have the potential to create either barriers or opportunities for kin relationships. For example, class, race, and ethnicity influence whether aging parents and adult children live in the same household or nearby; the amount and type of emotional and instrumental support, as opposed to financial support, that is exchanged; and whether daughters and daughters-in-law work or care for elderly parents. The frequency and quality of interaction with parents, in-laws, and other relatives is stronger among women. Mother-daughter ties are stronger and more intimate than son-parent ties. Widows generally have more contact with their children than do older married or divorced women.

Kinship interaction is often facilitated and promoted by one or two members of the extended family, usually women, who take on the role of **kin keeper** (Rosenthal, 1985; Spitze and Logan, 1989). This person makes sure that members of the family keep in touch with one another, reminds people about birthdays, co-ordinates the care for a sick or aging family member, and keeps in touch with various relatives by telephone, letter, e-mail, or visits. Much of this responsibility

within the extended family of orientation is assumed by a grandmother or an older daughter, while kin keeping with in-laws is usually done by a daughter-in-law. The kin keeper often serves as a confidant or caregiver for aging parents or other family members, thereby providing care, emotional support, and advice within the extended family. One outcome of a divorce in the middle or oldest generation is that a kin keeper may disappear for some members of the kinship unit, thereby leading to decreased interaction between family members within and across generations.

The importance of gender in later-life family relationships is partially related to the fact that women are more involved in expressive than instrumental relationships at all stages of life. Although sons act as caregivers in the absence of daughters, they tend to provide less direct support. Aging parents without a daughter may be at a disadvantage in the later years when they need assistance, especially in terms of the quality or type of assistance. For example, parents may receive financial aid from a son to hire a homemaker or nurse, but they are less likely to receive personal care (such as help with dressing, bathing, shopping, or feeding) that a daughter might have provided. The contributions of men in aging families is seldom studied. Matthews (2002), whose work is a notable exception, argues strongly that men must be included in research on family ties and family relationships. Similarly, Campbell and Martin-Matthews (2003: S357) stress 'the importance of examining the gendered nature of care tasks to better understand how motivating and obligating factors influence men's involvement in different types of filial care.' With some men becoming more involved in family responsibilities throughout the life course, they likely will assume increased responsibilities for the monitoring and care of aging parents. But will the gendered nature of individual caregiving tasks change, and if so, when?

But as women enter the labour force and remain in it, the level and type of social support and interaction between parents and adult children decreases. With changing social norms and values, and increased levels of education, there are more opportunities for more women to begin careers early in life, or to renew their careers in mid-life once their children are in school. Hence, fewer middle-aged daughters or daughters-in-law are available for daily phone calls or visits or to provide daily or weekly personal care for parents or in-laws.

Social class also affects the frequency and nature of intergenerational relationships. Regular face-to-face visits are more common among those in the lower classes because of greater geographic proximity, and less career mobility. And where lower class is linked to ethnic groups, there may be a greater sense of obligation to provide personal care. Members of the higher social classes keep in contact more by phone and e-mail, and offer financial rather than instrumental assistance to their aging parents.

Racial and ethnic background are structural dimensions that influence family relationships across the life course. There is great diversity between and within (by generation or cohort) ethnic and racial groups in values and cultural expectations about family obligations and interactions. To create effective policies, both the cultural heritage and the degree of assimilation of various ethnic groups into the host society must be understood.

Most studies of ethnic- or racial-minority families have found that there is a high value placed on kinship ties and a greater dependence than in mainstream society on family members for social relationships, housing, and financial support throughout life, especially in the later years. Perhaps because of minority-group status and unique cultural values, a closely knit extended family serves as the primary resource for assistance and support, rather than friends or social organizations. But this dependence on family creates a stressful paradox for older members, especially those who are widowed. Elderly parents in immigrant families are well integrated into the kin network, often living in a child's household. But often they report being lonely, isolated, and bored in this type of living arrangement (Treas and Mazumdar, 2002). Many are dependent on kin for emotional, social, and financial support, and some report they are only servants for their children and grandchildren. If they don't speak English and if they live in non-ethnic, suburban communities, where they have no contact with age peers from their cultural group, their only social contact may be the family (review Hightlight 2.5, page 62). However, as cultural values are weakened across generations through acculturation and assimilation, the primary resource for older people changes from the family to friends or social agencies in the ethnic or racial community.

Family Ties and Relationships

Marriage generally constitutes the most intimate and enduring family tie across the life course. As a result of marriage, subsequent relationships emerge involving children and parents, grandparents and grandchildren, siblings, and other relatives, including in-laws. However, not all adults in middle and later life are involved in a marital relationship. Rather, they may engage in serial or long-term monogamous ties that involve cohabiting in a heterosexual or homosexual relationship. Others live alone, with or without an intimate relationship with another person. The diversity of intimate family or family-like relationships requires that we examine various types of partnerships across the life course.

Marital Status and Marital Relationships

Marital status influences much of adult social life and is related to living arrangements, health, and general well-being (Connidis, 2001: 45–8). Being married usually means having a companion who will share one's life and provide care, especially if that is necessary late in life. Table 8.1 indicates the marital status of older Canadians in 2001.

Table 8.1 Marital Status by Sex and Age Group[a]

Age	Women				Men			
	Single	Married[2]	Widowed	Divorced	Single	Married[2]	Widowed	Divorced
50–54	7.7	75.3	3.7	13.2	9.6	79.8	0.9	9.7
55–59	6.2	73.2	7.4	13.1	7.1	81.6	1.7	9.6
60–64	5.4	69.8	13.7	11.1	6.2	82.0	3.0	8.8
65–69	5.3	62.8	23.0	8.9	5.9	81.1	5.5	7.5
70–74	5.6	52.3	35.4	6.8	6.0	78.8	9.3	5.9
75–79	5.8	39.9	49.6	4.7	5.6	74.9	15.3	4.2
80–84	6.5	26.5	63.9	3.1	5.1	67.9	23.9	3.0
85–89	7.9	13.8	76.7	1.6	5.4	56.9	35.6	2.1
90+	8.9	4.2	86.1	0.7	6.1	36.3	55.9	1.7

[a]Includes common-law relationships.

Source: Adapted from the Statistics Canada publication *Legal Marital Status (5), Age Groups (12A) and Sex (3) for Population 15 Years and Over Living in Common-law Unions, for Canada, Provinces, Territories, Census Metropolitan Areas and Census Agglomerations, 1996 and 2001 Censuses – 100% Data (Marital Status of Canadians, 2001 Census)*, Catalogue 97F0004, October 2002.

The family network for married people is generally larger, even if there are no children, than for those who never married or who live common-law. Over 75 per cent of adults 75 years of age and over have at least one living child, and about 80 per cent are grandparents. Because of increased life expectancy, more grandparents, especially grandmothers, have adult grandchildren in their 30s or 40s, which increases the likelihood they are or will become great-grandparents.

Marital Satisfaction in Later Life

Marital satisfaction in the later years is related to how close one feels to the spouse as a confidant and as a source of emotional support, and to how much agreement there is in the partnership about marital closeness (Tower and Kasl, 1996). Among the current cohort of elderly people, high levels of marital satisfaction are generally reported more by men than by women. Connidis (2001: 54–5) reports that marital satisfaction increases with age and that those who are more satisfied with their marriage enjoy better mental health and well-being. Conversely, those in a conflicted marriage may experience depression and lower levels of physical and mental health.

While there are likely to be cycles of satisfaction and dissatisfaction in any marriage, there are two general, but different, patterns of satisfaction reported across the life course[3] (see Figure 8.1). First, there may be a gradual decline in marital satisfaction through all stages of the marriage (pattern A) that may or may not lead to separation or divorce. The alternative pattern, with variations in the slope that reflect the time at which changes begin (B1, B2, B3), suggests that the relationship is curvilinear. These possible patterns are supported by both anecdotal reports and research findings (Rosenthal and Gladstone, 1994). There is continuing debate as to whether satisfaction is actually higher in the later years than it is during the early years before children are born. This hypothetical pattern is represented by the extension upward (dotted lines) of the three curvilinear paths. Curve B1 suggests that the low point occurs when children are adolescents; B2 sug-

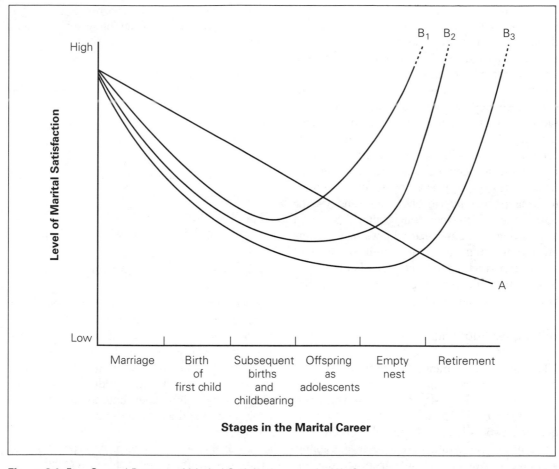

Figure 8.1 Four General Patterns of Marital Satisfaction over the Life Course

ªIncludes common-law relationships.

gests that it occurs after the last child leaves home (the empty nest); and B3 suggests that it occurs just before or after the husband retires, or when one partner becomes very ill.

In a detailed discussion of whether reported improvements in marital satisfaction across the life course are 'real', Connidis (2001: 56–60) notes that satisfaction may be reported to increase because people adapt and are less critical and more accepting of a partner's faults as they age. Or, the change may be due to cohort differences in the meaning of marital quality and in the importance of marital stability, rather than to differences over time in the course of all marriages (Glenn, 1998). Indeed, among younger cohorts, divorce rates have increased (see Table 8.1), and although older couples are more likely to remain married, there is no evidence of an *improvement* in marital quality in the later years of long marriages (Glenn, 1998). Moreover, the number of divorces after the age of 60 is increasing, often at the time that one or both partners retire.

When one of the partners becomes cognitively or physically impaired, rather than a divorce, a form of 'separation' occurs when one partner is moved to a long-term care institution. The partner who continues to live alone in the community is viewed as a married widow or widower. That person may experience guilt, anger, sadness, resentment, and self-pity, all of which are tempered by feelings of relief from burdensome caregiving responsibilities. The non-institutionalized partner recognizes that marriage and companionship are over, and yet he or she must continue to be a partner by caregiving and and visiting (Gladstone, 1995). Increasingly, after a period of years living alone, married widows or widowers are forming intimate or quasi-intimate relationships before their spouse dies. Or, after the death of a partner and a brief mourning period, they begin a new relationship.

Sibling Relationships

Like marriage or common-law relationships, sibling interaction is an intra-generational relationship, unless there are step-siblings, in which case there may be differences of 10 to 20 years between two different sibling cohorts. Over 80 per cent of older adults have at least one sibling, although for women over 80 years of age, the possibility of having a surviving sibling, especially a brother, is less likely. Siblings represent a long-lasting family bond, with a shared genetic and cultural heritage from early childhood to death. With lower fertility rates and more only children, there are fewer siblings in absolute numbers. But with increasing divorce rates and re-constituted families, there are more step-siblings and half-siblings than in the past. Thus, the study of sibling relationships in later life is important both for the companionship relationship, and for emotional and instrumental support to aging parents. Yet, with few exceptions (Matthews and Heidorn, 1998; Campbell et al., 1999; Connidis, 2001: 207–41; Matthews, 2002), we know very little about relationships involving sisters and brothers

across the life course or in later life.

Sibling relationships can follow four possible patterns:

1. frequent interaction in the family home during childhood and adolescence; then little or no interaction after leaving home;

2. frequent interaction in childhood is continued throughout the life course if they are 'best friends', especially along a sister-sister or brother-brother link, and if spouses get along well;

3. a slow drifting apart during mid-life after entering the labour force and getting married; and

4. a renewal of contact and closeness in later life.

The degree of drifting during mid-life depends on such factors as living far apart, relations with brothers- or sisters-in-law, differences in careers or lifestyles, and whether a sibling needs support after being divorced or widowed. Later-life renewal increases after the children leave home, when siblings jointly contribute to the care of an ailing parent, and after the death of one or both parents.

Until the death of one or both parents, siblings often maintain indirect contact with each other through the parents and by attending annual or periodic family celebrations. However, after the death of a parent, particularly their mother who may have been the kin keeper, sibling communication and interaction often increases, thereby renewing the relationship. However, contact is unlikely to be renewed for more than practical reasons if the relationship was characterized by rivalry and conflict in the past, if the respective spouses are considered to be unfriendly or incompatible, if care of a frail parent or settlement of a parent's estate creates strain, or if distance or health prohibits regular visiting. In general, siblings who are close throughout early life tend to remain close in later life if health and mobility permit communication and interaction; and rivalry tends to decline over the life course (Connidis and McMullin, 1992).

Sibling relationships in the later years are influenced by gender, marital status, and differences in age. Ties are stronger between sisters than between brothers or a sister and a brother. However, just as most studies of widowhood and retirement involve women and men, respectively, very few studies of sibling ties in middle or later life examine ties between brothers. Most of what we know about brothers in sibling relationships is derived from studies of their involvement in the monitoring and care of elderly parents. Matthews and Heidorn (1998) found that in brother-only families, sons promoted self-sufficiency by the parents, were less involved in the monitoring of parents, and helped only if asked by their parents. If care was needed, sons provided traditional 'masculine' services (home repairs, driving, or financial assistance), while their wives, if there was a history of good relations with the parents-in-law, performed the more 'gender- appropriate' services of bathing, dressing, feeding, and shopping.

Cultural values and historical practices influence the quantity and quality of sibling relationships among members of some racial or ethnic groups. Within cultural groups that place a high value on family solidarity and mutual assistance, sibling links are more likely to be strong and continue throughout life and to increase in later life if one of the siblings becomes widowed or experiences a decline in health or financial status.

Siblings, especially if widowed, never married, or childless, may be the only source of support for each other in the later years. Older widowed or never-married sisters sometimes create a common household in the later years to provide each other with social, emotional, and economic support. Older siblings may provide financial and social security for a sibling who is unmarried or widowed. Although only a minority of siblings report having received support from a brother or sister, many say that their siblings are an available source during a crisis, especially if they live nearby (Connidis, 2001). With families becoming smaller and greater geographical mobility in later life, siblings may be less readily available in the future. Highlight 8.2 illustrates some thoughts about sibling relationships.

Parent-Adult Child Relationships

Most older people (more than 80 per cent) have at least one living child of their own, and they may have acquired step-children through remarriage. The 2001 census found that

- there were almost half a million step-families in Canada, representing about 12 per cent of all couples with children;
- there were 1.3 million single-parent families; and
- 20 per cent of all children were living in a single-parent household (Statistics Canada, 2002a).

These demographic household facts, combined with increased geographical mobility by

Highlight 8.2 Sibling Relationships in Later Life

Sibling companionship and support are an untapped resource in later life, often because siblings have drifted apart over the adult years. With family ties essential for the care and support of elderly parents and perhaps, as well, for a never-married, childless, or divorced sibling in later life, sibling relationships are sometimes rediscovered and reconstructed (Connidis, 2001: 207-41; Matthews, 2002). Matthews (2002: 5) notes that just as adults continue to be 'children' to their parents, they continue, as well, to be brothers and sisters to their siblings. Connidis (2001: 207-8) makes the addi-

continued

tional point that marriage creates siblings-in-law, and that through divorce and reconstituted families, adults acquire half siblings or step-siblings. Thus, in some families there are many siblings or quasi-siblings with whom elderly people could connect. The following comments illustrate different themes at the heart of sibling relationships in later life.

Drifting Apart and Coming Together

When we were younger, we were all quite close. . . . And then, for some reason that none of us know about . . . we drifted apart. . . . And we had very little in common. . . . But starting again, oh, I don't know, 10, 12 years ago or something, we've really got back and got pretty much the relationship we had when we were kids (Connidis, 2001: 217).

If you develop relationships in the community where you live and you're very involved with your family, you don't have much time for siblings. But then, after your children grow up, you probably think of your siblings more just because you are fond of each other, and you just want to maintain that relationship (Connidis, 2001: 218).

The Sharing of Intimate Moments

Many widows and retired sisters end up living together again with the same kind of intimacy as they shared in childhood. At the end of her life, as at the beginning, a sister may be privy to the small, personal details about the other—her eating, sleeping and washing habits—to which possibly no other person, except a long-term sexual partner, ever has access (McConville, 1985: 56).

You don't mind having them (siblings) know what you've gone through. This is something (a divorce) that you need to talk about inside the family (Connidis, 2001: 228).

Sharing Parent Care

We probably drew closest together during the time we looked after our elderly mother. . . . We did it together. It was a joint decision (Connidis, 2001: 234).

Too much falls to me (a sister with four brothers). I don't think any of them are doing their fair share. Money doesn't take the place of giving of themselves. . . . All the work is left to me . . . but I have learned to accept it (Matthews, 2002: 178).

My brother and I are both available. . . . I organize it. I ask him to do things for Mom. He and I both do what we can to help her. He makes every effort to take on half the responsibility (Matthews, 2002: 184).

Mother relies on us which, lately, I've been resenting mainly because I'm not the favorite, and I'm the one who gives her the most help and attention. . . she doesn't appreciate what I do for her. My sister goes every day for a meal, but I have to get the food. . . . I think I would like to divide responsibilities with her, but I can't discuss that with her (Matthews, 2002: 193).

both children and parents, and increased labour-force participation by women, have helped to change the relations between parents and adult children in recent decades. In some cases, divorce, single-parenting, reconstituted marriages, and geographical mobility weaken or eliminate parent-child relations. In other cases a relationship is strengthened because a transition creates closer parent-child bonds; provides increased assistance and support, including co-residence; or creates larger family networks in reconstituted families when two sets of parents and additional sets of grandparents may be available.

Across the life course, a parent-child dyad represents a relationship bound by ties of proximity, affection, legal responsibilities and rights, and moral responsibilities. The relationship is built on emotional bonding, communication, reciprocity of exchange, and interdependence of the two generations. A parent-adult child relationship involves constancy and change across the life course. As children pass through adolescence and the early adulthood years, sources of conflict and tension revolve around the communication (or lack of) and interaction styles of parents (reported most by children), the habits and lifestyle choices of children (reported most by parents), child-rearing practices and values, work habits and orientations, household standards and maintenance, and differing perspectives on political, religious, or other ideological issues (Clarke et al., 1999). Most of these intergenerational tensions, as we saw in Chapter 6, are temporary and do not lead to lifelong conflict or estrangement between parents and children. Moreover, strong relations in childhood persist through adulthood, even if frequency of contact diminishes because of geographical distance or a child's marriage (Townsend-Batten, 2002).

Although the possibility of overt and long-standing conflict exists within a parent-child relationship, we seldom know the degree or type of such conflict because family matters are kept private and confidential, especially by older people. With increasing longevity and the likelihood of family crises in more generations, the incidence of family stress or conflict may increase. Nevertheless, the prevailing evidence suggests that the relationship is not usually characterized by conflict, and that most elderly people are not abandoned by, or alienated from, their children.

Crises such as an acute illness, the death of one parent, financial difficulties experienced by an elderly parent (often a widow), or a divorce or financial crisis involving an adult child increase parent-adult child interactions. Relations are continued and intensify when a parent is moved into a residential care facility, even if the parent is cognitively impaired and unable to recognize a son or daughter who visits. With higher divorce rates in middle-age, a divorced person's relationships with his or her parents and grandparents can become closer or more distant. A divorced child may become dependent on his or her parents for emotional and financial support, and for helping to look after their children. Divorce also has negative, long-lasting effects on parent-child relations, especially for a biological father who is divorced when his children are young. If the mother has custody, birth fathers, voluntarily or involuntary, may eventually lose contact with their children. Hence, a potential source of assistance and care in later life is lost.

Adult children represent the predominant monitoring system and source of physical, emotional, and financial support for elderly parents. The parent-child dyad is a two-way reciprocal support network, and a small mutual-aid system. Throughout life, these reciprocal relations involve giving and receiving love, social and instrumental support, and financial assistance in the form of cash or property. In family-owned businesses, reciprocity within the family involves childhood contributions to the business, which may, in early or mid-adulthood, result in a transfer of ownership or operational responsibility to a son or daughter (Highlight 8.3).

A past history of receiving or giving wealth, care, knowledge, or other resources across generations builds a reservoir of debt or tradition that is, or should be, continued into later life. In later life, however, an adult child becomes more of a giver than a receiver. Thus, over the life course, reciprocity and interdependence emerge among linked lives in a kinship structure (Hagestad, 2003). The direction, frequency, type, and amount of exchange varies across time, depending on personal needs and on opportunities to interact with and assist others in the family unit.

Most reciprocity involves unequal and variable transfers across the life course, and different points of view often emerge about the amount, direction, equity, or appropriateness of the transfers. Most of the flow is from parent to child, although in later life the balance shifts as children give more emotional and instrumental aid to parents, and parents report receiving more help (Stone et al., 1998). However, until their death, and at death through a will, parents who have wealth continue to pass it on to their children or grandchildren.

Four main issues concerning relationships between older parents and adult children have been emphasized in recent years:

1. the amount of contact and the quality of interaction while an aging parent is independent, healthy, and mobile (Connidis, 2001: 120–58);

2. the type and amount of exchanges provided by aging parents to adult children who experience a crisis or traumatic event, such as a divorce, the death of a child, unemployment,

---

Highlight 8.3 Family Reciprocity: Operation and Ownership Transfer of the Family Farm

There are many types of family business, but none is so intimate as a family farm, which is normally passed from generation to generation (Keating, 1996). This legacy and commitment begins when children are old enough to assume responsibilities on the farm and thereby contribute to family labour while attending school.

The transfer of the family farm fosters intergenerational harmony as members strive to keep the farm in the family, especially if they have owned it for two or more generations (Munro et al., 1995). Increasingly, this is more difficult as small farms are bought by large agricultural corporations, or as children show less interest in farming.

The process of transferring farm ownership to a son or daughter begins during his or her mid-life. The parents, to keep at least one child on the farm, reduce their management and work responsibilities while maintaining sufficient control and involvement to generate an adequate income for their retirement years. The long-standing economic goal of farmers who value family continuity of ownership has been to build sufficient equity and income to support two generations: the parents and the child and his family (usually a son or son-in-law). If the farm doesn't provide an adequate income, the children are likely to leave to pursue a more stable career elsewhere.

Many farmers put off the actual transfer of ownership as long as possible, sometimes until after their death through an inheritance. This delay can create dissension between the generations, especially in an era of gender equity, in which a daughter may claim a share of the farm yet not be viewed as an eligible successor (Keating, 1996). Where that happens, the mother often has to mediate between the father and the children to facilitate a more harmonious transfer of ownership and responsibility.

Source: Adapted from Keating (1986, 1996) and Munro et al. (1995).

or widowhood in early or middle adulthood (Ganong and Coleman, 1998; Connidis, 2001: 185–203);

3. the amount and quality of support provided to cognitively or physically frail parents who require increasing levels of physical, emotional, or financial assistance in the later years (see Chapter 11); and

4. the shocking finding that, while it is not common, family members, rather than care workers, are the most frequent perpetrators of elder abuse, fraud, or neglect (see Chapter 11).

Most older parents, especially after the age of 80, have one child living nearby, and most have contact at least once a week by telephone, letter, or a visit with at least one child. About 70 per cent of adult children engage in frequent contact with their mother, while 60 per cent report frequent contact with their father (Townsend-Batten, 2002) If a daughter is employed full-time, there is less face-to-face contact. Parents with a strong religious affiliation and working-class parents tend to have more frequent contact with adult children.

If an adult child has an elderly divorced parent, the amount of help provided, and the sense of obligation to help are influenced by the amount and quality of contact they have had over the years with the divorced, non-custodial parent. One study found that the needs of one's own family were a higher priority than any responsibility for a divorced parent or step-parent (Ganong and Coleman, 1998). Connidis (2001: 185–203) reports

- that divorced parents, especially fathers, have less contact than married parents with their adult children;
- that divorced mothers receive more assistance and support from their children than do divorced fathers; and
- that divorced parents generally provide less financial aid and support to their adult children.

If an adult child divorces, it is a distressing experience for most parents, especially if they were unaware of problems in the marital relationship. Most parents offer emotional and social support to a divorced child and to any grandchildren (see next section). But the divorce of an adult child requires renegotiating the parent-adult child relationship, especially if co-residency and/or grandchildren are involved (Connidis 2001: 190).

Grandparent-Grandchild Relationships

At birth, about 66 per cent of children have four living grandparents (including step-grandparents), and by 30 years of age, 75 per cent still have at least one grandparent (Connidis, 2001: 167). The 2001 census found that among the estimated 5.7 million grandparents in Canada, 80 per cent of women and 74 per cent of men over 65 years of age are grandparents. In total, 6.5 per cent of grandparents (almost half a million) live in the same household as their grandchildren. In 12 per cent of these grandparent-grandchild households, both biological parents are absent. In absolute numbers, almost 57,000 grandparents in Canada are living with one or more grandchildren with no parental involvement (see below), and in 50 per cent of these households a single grandparent is raising a grandchild alone. Between 1991 and 2001, the number of children under 18 living only with their grandparents increased 20 per cent. Family units where a middle generation (that is, parents) is missing are known as 'skip-generation households' (Milan and Hamm, 2003). These are increasing because of more drug abuse by one or both parents, more divorces, and more reporting of child abuse and neglect.

With declining birth rates (as reflected in smaller families and more childless marriages), older people in the future will have fewer grandchildren than they do now, or none at all. However, step-grandchildren are acquired when a divorced or widowed child remarries. In contrast, with more common-law relationships, never-married children, childless adult children, and children who are divorced, some older people never became grandparents. Moreover, face-to-face grandparent-grandchild interaction is less frequent than it was in the past because both the grandparents and their adult children live at greater distances, or the grandparents are less available because of more active lifestyles.

Grandparents provide kinship continuity and contribute to the preservation and perpetuation of family rituals and history. The age at which one becomes a grandparent varies by class, education, and the age at which children marry. With delayed marriage and childbearing in age-gapped families, some people may not become grandparents until after they retire, if at all. However, in age-condensed families, people often become grandparents in their late 30s or early 40s.

The lifestyle of grandparents has changed, as have social norms regarding what is expected from a grandparent (Kemp, 2003). Grandmothers in their 50s who work have less time to look after their grandchildren. Once retired, many grandparents prefer to spend more time travelling, doing volunteer work, and dating if they are widowed, rather than taking care of grandchildren. Mueller et al. (2002) argued that there is more to the grandparent and grandchild relationship than how often they see each other. The quality of the relationship is what matters and therefore measuring frequency of contact is less useful for understanding the relationship, especially because contact with young grandchildren is mediated through the parents. Mueller et al. (2002) found that intimacy, helping behaviour, instrumental acts, and being involved in discipline as an authority figure are important indicators of the meaning and quality of this relationship.

The degree to which grandparents interact with their grandchildren and consider the relationship to be important is influenced by how far apart they live; by their lifestyle and whether they are employed; by the number of sets of grandchildren they have; and by the age of the grandchildren. The relationship tends to be close from

birth to the teenage years, and then weakens as grandchildren become busy with their friends, education, career, and marriage. If a grandparent has been highly involved in child care during the pre-teen years, the relationship often continues to be quite close into the later years of life.

Maternal grandparents are generally more involved with their grandchildren, and these ties often are closer, more meaningful, and more satisfying than those with paternal grandparents (Chan and Elder, 2000; Rosenthal and Gladstone, 2000). This stronger maternal tie is related to the fact that the mother-daughter tie is usually stronger than the parent-son tie, and is often reflected in a stronger grandmother-granddaughter tie, especially on the matrilineal side of the family. Increasingly, however, being a grandparent is viewed as a gender-neutral experience, and there is little difference in how grandmothers and grandfathers interact with grandchildren. Both engage in child care, teaching, and friendship with one or more of their grandchildren, and most grandparents describe their relationship with grandchildren as 'warm and close'.

The divorce of an adult child can change relationships with grandchildren. Usually the daughter gains custody of children, and the maternal grandparents often become more involved through support and financial assistance. In contrast, paternal grandparents are more likely to have less contact, or perhaps none, with their grandchildren, especially if the custodial parent moves to another community, or remarries and a new set of step-grandparents assume the grandparenting role. For a child, the remarriage of one or both parents often results in the acquisition of step-grandparents. Indeed, teachers have heard elementary school children boast about how many grandparents or great-grandparents they have after both biological parents remarry!

Grandparents may have to acquire legal visitation rights through the courts if they are not allowed to see their grandchildren after a divorce. Some jurisdictions now guarantee grandparent access to grandchildren through civil laws pertaining to separation and divorce. Under Canada's Divorce Act, grandparents have the right to apply for access to, or custody of, grandchildren after the biological parents divorce. But if a parent is abusive, is incarcerated, or dies, legal access for grandparents varies greatly according to provincial laws. Consequently, volunteer organizations, such as GRAND (Grandparents Requesting Access and Dignity) in Ontario, have been formed to help grandparents who are denied access to their grandchildren.

Regardless of who has custody of the grandchildren, divorce is a challenging transition for all three generations. For grandparents, especially in the 1980s and 1990s, divorce was not compatible with their belief that marriages should last forever, in good times and bad. They also had difficulty accepting the failure of a child's marriage. The following comment by an elderly widow explains why she did not tell her dying husband about the dissolution of their son's marriage:

> My second son was separated and my husband never knew. . . . I was prepared for my husband's death; it's natural, but I found my son's divorce is not something you expect, and . . . it was a terrible blow at the time (Martin Matthews, 1991: 19).

Even if parents suspected or knew their child's marriage was unhappy, a divorce is a shock and they experience considerable ambivalence— they are pleased their child is no longer in an unhappy or abusive relationship, but they are worried about the future of their child and their grandchildren, who will not have a 'normal' home and family life. Often the transition requires considerable re-negotiation of a parent's relationship with both the adult child and the grandchildren.

If one or both grandparents are moved to a residential care facility, this often changes the relationship with their grandchildren. In many cases, active grandparenting ceases when the older person enters a nursing home. In order to compensate for this loss or for the unavailability of a grandparent at any time after birth, foster-grandparent programs have been established. For active elderly people living in the community or in retirement homes, having a foster grandchild enhances self-esteem and morale, decreases feelings of loneliness and isolation, and creates an emotional bond and an extended family that benefits both the youngest and oldest generation. Similarly, to provide companionship for both pre-school children and older people, some day-care centres are located within, or adjacent to, retirement or nursing homes. Here, elderly volunteers teach or play with preschoolers, acting as surrogate teachers, grandparents, or simply as older friends and confidants.

Relationships between grandparents and grandchildren have been examined primarily from the grandparents' perspective. However, studies that examine the experiences of grandchildren reveal that children who interact with grandparents view the relationship as 'warm and close'; they have fewer prejudices about elderly people and growing old; and over time, they view their grandparents less as babysitters and gift-givers and more as companions and confidants. However, in three-generation immigrant families where the first or second generation emigrated to Canada, third-generation grandchildren often say they are not close to their grandparents, especially as teenagers and sometimes even when they live in the same household. In this situation, both grandchildren and grandparents claim they live in two different social worlds because of differences in acculturation and assimilation, and because language differences make communication difficult, if not impossible.

Grandparents Raising Grandchildren

There is an important difference between grandparents looking after their grandchildren while a parent works, and grandparents being responsible for raising one or more grandchildren. In this latter situation they become surrogate parents and primary caregivers for grandchildren. As such, they view themselves more as a parent involved in education and discipline and as an authority figure than as a grandparent who can indulge and entertain the child. Many in this situation regret the loss of the typical grandparent's role, as well as the time they would like to have for the grandchildren of other sons or daughters (Connidis, 2001: 178–83).

In 'skipped-generation' households where there is no biological parent (Minkler, 1999),[4] the grandparents have no choice but to become parents to their grandchildren. This happens when an adult child is terminally ill or dies, is divorced and abandons his or her children, becomes addicted to alcohol or drugs, physically abuses the child, is incarcerated for a crime, or enters a long-term health-care facility because of a chronic mental or physical illness. These events lead to three general types of 'parenting' by grandparents (Jendrek, 1994): (1) living with a child and providing formal and informal care, as needed; (2) providing day and evening care for young children while a parent is temporarily absent; or (3) obtaining legal custody so that a grandchild can live with the grandparent or grandparents—in this situation the child may or may not have legal access to his or her biological parents.

This forced parental role is not a preferred or ideal situation, but it may be the only solution for young children if the extended family is to remain together as a unit. The fight for legal custody can be costly and may create conflict between the grandparents seeking custody and one or both of the biological parents; between the grandparents seeking custody, usually on the matrilineal side, and the patrilineal grandparents; and even between the grandparents and a grandchild if he or she is in the pre-teen or teenager years and does not want to live with grandparents, especially in another neighbourhood or community. But legal custody is essential since in some jurisdictions the absence of legal guardianship means access is denied to social services, and even the right to attend the neighbourhood school.

The entry of a grandchild into a grandparent's household can create stress and uncertainty for older people. It changes their retirement plans

and reduces their retirement savings;[5] it interferes with their customary leisure and social activities with the result that they may lose friends and become socially isolated; and it can harm the caregiver's health and the marital satisfaction of one or both partners in the older parenting couple. The relationship with the biological parent or parents can be stressful, especially if they periodically and randomly reappear and wish to start acting as parents once more. Many grandparents worry about the future of the infant or child if their health fails and they can no longer continue to be the primary caregiver.

Common-Law Relationships

In the 2001 census, about 14 per cent of couples in Canada and 30 per cent of all couples in Quebec reported that they were living common-law (Milan, 2003). Such relationships are more typical among males and in younger age cohorts, often as a precursor to marriage, but sometimes these relationships are never converted to a legal marriage, even if the relationship persists into the middle or later years. For others, a common-law relationship develops after separation, divorce, or widowhood. Among such relationships that begin earlier in life and persist into later life, the partnership and kin network is very similar to that of married couples. Many of these relationships produce children, and grandparents are as involved as in families where the parents are married. The number of common-law relationships in later life is quite low at present. But the number will increase as more adults enter the later years having lived in one or more common-law relationships in earlier stages of life. Indeed, Dumas and Bélanger (1997) projected that by 2022 there will be as many common-law relationships as marriages.

Common-law relationships tend to be less permanent than marriages, and therefore the partners often sign agreements concerning property rights, access to wealth accumulated during the relationship, guardianship rights for children born during the relationship, and inheritance rights if one partner dies. Such contracts are especially important for ensuring that a woman in this type of relationship has economic security in later life.

Gay and Lesbian Common-Law Partnerships

In 2001, for the first time, the Canadian census asked respondents to identify whether they were living in a same-sex common-law partnership. While there were likely a number of Canadians who did not disclose that they were in a same-sex union, approximately 34,000 said they were living in such a partnership. This represents about 3 per cent of all cohabiting common-law pairs, and about 0.5 per cent of all married and common-law pairs. This arrangement was reported most often in Quebec and Ontario. Of the 34,000 same-sex partners, 45 per cent were women, and 15 per cent of the women and 3 per cent of the men said there were children in the household (Statistics Canada, 2002a). At present, we do not know the number of such partnerships among older adults, but we do know that there is under-reporting by those over age 60 (O'Brien and Goldberg, 2000; Connidis, 2001: 60–5, 119, 223–4). This cohort effect could disappear in the future as gay and lesbian partners who declared their sexual orientation earlier in life continue such relationships into later life.

The traditional kin network available to older gays and lesbians is generally small, and the composition depends very much on their personal history. Some have children from a failed heterosexual marriage, as a single person, through adoption of a child as an individual or as a couple, or, for lesbian couples, through artificial insemination to produce a child. Hence, children may be available for companionship and support throughout the middle and later years of the life.

The family ties of gay and lesbian adults with their family of origin is an understudied topic (Kimmel and Lundy Martin, 2002; Cruz, 2003; Connidis, 2004). Anecdotal evidence and a few case studies suggest that gay and lesbian adults are often estranged from or rejected by family members. Connidis (2004) states that this marginalized status requires the negotiation of family ties across the life course by *all* family members—the gay or lesbian member, siblings, parents, grandparents, and in-laws. If older gays and lesbians were abandoned by their family earlier in life because of their sexual orientation, they may have no family support in later life. However, as Laird, who is a mother, a grandmother, and partner of a lesbian notes, many who are gay or lesbian have good, though sometimes complicated, relations with parents, siblings, and other relatives:

> Ours is not an unusual story. Lesbians and gays come from families and are connected to these original families. . . . Most of us are not cut off from our families—not forever rejected, isolated, disinherited. We are daughters and sons, siblings, aunts and uncles, parents and grandparents. Like everyone else, most of us have continuing, complicated relationships with our families. We participate in negotiating the changing meanings, rituals, values, and connections that define kinship. (Laird 1996: 90)

As well, many gays and lesbians create a 'surrogate' family comprising a network of gay, lesbian, and heterosexual friends. But whether this network provides personal assistance, financial help, and personal care in later life, as a family would, is not known.

Among all older gays and lesbians, but especially among gay men because of AIDS, access to medical care, home care, and community services can be fraught with discrimination. Partners also have limited legal rights and may be denied access to employer drug and health benefit plans, to medical and financial records, or to visitation rights in hospitals (Claes and Moore, 2001; Brotman et al., 2003). Indeed, most medical record forms assume all clients are heterosexual and include such questions as, 'Are you married, and who is your next-of-kin?' A lifelong partner may be denied an inheritance or the right to participate in a hospital discharge or end-of-life decision normally made by family. Similarly, they may experience verbal harassment from the staff, or the staff may be unwilling to touch, bathe, or treat gay men or lesbians in a hospital or nursing home. Administrators of rental housing or long-term care facilities may reject their applications, and there are very few, if any, retirement or nursing facilities that serve the gay and lesbian communities. Thus, supportive housing in later life, and less discriminatory treatment in housing and medical care are needed by gays and lesbians as they age.

Never-Married Older Persons

Currently, about 7 per cent of men and women over 65 have never been married. In absolute numbers, the population of ever-single older adults is likely to increase in the next 20 years. More women are never married, although earlier in life, some may have lived in a common-law relationship. Although it is commonly assumed that an older person who never married is childless and without a history of intimate relationships, this may not be the situation for all single people in later life. Increasingly, some are single mothers or fathers through childbearing or adoption. In later life, most adults who never married report that they are not lonely or socially isolated because they have developed friendships with non-relatives, fictive kin, or extended family. They are used to living alone and being independent, although many do live with another person in a household. Often they have siblings. Some do regret not having children (Connidis, 2001: 89), and if they need assistance in later life, there are few surviving family members to provide instrumental or social support (Wu and Pollard, 1998). Connidis (2001: 79–90) notes that older, never-married women are likely to be highly educated, and to have earned a pension and achieved economic independence. They do not perceive being single as a stigma because their identity as a single

person was defined and accepted much earlier in life. In contrast, more older single men have little education and are less financially secure than married men of their age. For many who are childless and never married, the transition to singlehood represents 'an unanticipated change in social identity that is associated with aging and must be negotiated with a marriage-oriented cultural context' (Davies, 2003: 351). Davies found that the transition to 'singlehood' is accompanied by a conform with, and an acceptance of, being single that often occurs after 30 years of age. For women, buying a home was often reported as a marker as to when they began to identify more with singlehood, and to accept the transition.

Childless Older Persons

Childlessness is not restricted to those who do not form long-term unions. Married and common-law couples may also be childless, whether by choice or not (Connidis, 2001: 159–65). In total, about 14 per cent of the elderly population is childless (Connidis and McMullin, 1996). Those who cohabit in serial relationships are more likely to be childless than those who married or formed permanent long-standing common-law relationships. Not only are these individuals childless, but they lack grandchildren as well. Most are socially engaged with a partner, with aging parents, with siblings and their children, with extended kin, and with friends who serve as fictive kin.

In general, childless older persons report high levels of well-being and do not exhibit signs of loneliness or dependency in later life (Connidis and McMullin, 1992, 1999; Wu and Pollard, 1998; Zhang and Hayward, 2001). However, childless, unmarried older men report more loneliness than do women who are childless (Zhang and Hayward, 2001). In later life, those without children often receive support from family or friends, but once over 85, they are less likely to have someone close who can provide personal care, especially if they are widowed. Consequently, the risk of being admitted to a long-term care facility is higher among childless elderly women.

Increasingly, as new cohorts emerge, there is less stigma attached to being childless, even for married couples. Moreover, some speak of themselves as being 'child-free' (www.childfree.net) rather than 'childless', which implies missing something they want. Those who call themselves 'child-free' report that they made a conscious decision not to have children. The 2001 General Social Survey found that among 20- to 34-year-olds, 7 per cent of the women and 8 per cent of the men said they did not intend to have children (Stobert and Kemeny, 2003). Among older people, three commonly reported advantages of being childless are having fewer worries and problems, financial wealth, and greater freedom; and three disadvantages are lack of companionship, lack of support and care, and missed experiences and feeling incomplete (most likely reported by women) (Connidis and McMullin, 1999). As Connidis concluded (2001: 165):

> Clearly, it is not necessary to have children to have a satisfying old age. But, for those who wanted to have children and could not, a sense of regret about being childless continues into later life and lowers subjective well-being. In short, neither having children nor remaining childless guarantees happiness in later life.

Life Transitions in a Family Context

Family life changes when individuals and couples experience transitions across the life course. Major family transitions include cohabiting with an intimate partner, marriage, birth of a child, an empty nest when adult children leave home, a refilled nest when adult children return to live in the family home, divorce, widowhood, retirement, and remarriage. These events have both positive and negative outcomes for those who are directly involved, for other family members, and for the quality of family relationships, especially those involving parents, children, siblings, and grandparents. These transitions illustrate how lives within the extended family are linked and interdependent. In the following sections, the effect of some major family transitions on individuals and family members are examined. The effect on the family of two other major transitions is discussed in later chapters—retirement in Chapter 9, and deteriorating health and the need for family support and care in Chapter 11.

The Empty and Refilled Nest

When the last child leaves home, formal childrearing is thought to be completed and parents are described as living in an empty 'nest'. For parents, the transition is often gradual because most have more than one child, and all children rarely leave home at the same time. Often, the departure of the last child takes place when he or she marries, begins to live in a common-law relationship, or acquires a permanent job for the first time. Generally, sons leave the family home later than daughters. With smaller families and increased longevity, parents can expect to live in this empty-nest stage for a much longer time than their parents.

The empty nest is less common outside North America. Because of a housing shortage in many countries, single children remain at home until they marry, and living on one's own or with roommates is much less common. In many developing countries, in Europe, and especially in Asia, where filial piety remains a revered family value, it is common for one child, even if married, to form a household with his or her parents. For parents in some ethnic groups in Canada, especially for the first two generations following immigration, the empty nest is seldom experienced. Rather, one member of the second generation lives with his or her parents, or elderly parents move to the home of an adult child when they are no longer able to live independently.

The empty-nest stage brings relief from domestic chores associated with child rearing, a reduction in financial and parenting responsibilities, and the potential to begin living in a different way. Some have suggested that the transition represents a loss of the 'mothering' role and that women become depressed and bored because their main responsibility and source of life satisfaction is gone. Others argue that the transition brings enhanced freedom, especially for women, to pursue new opportunities outside the home through full- or part-time employment, volunteer work, a hobby, or attending university.

For most parents, the transition to the empty-nest stage is a positive experience. After the children leave home, a marriage may improve because a couple have more time for leisure interests and for each other. Conversely, an empty nest has the potential to magnify existing marital tensions or dissatisfactions. While this transition may not be the direct cause of a divorce, the empty-nest stage provides an opportunity to resolve long-standing differences. In an unhappy marriage, divorce is considered more feasible at this stage because it is no longer necessary to 'stay together for the sake of the children'. Some of these post–empty-nest separations or divorces, especially in the middle class, are initiated by women who seek a higher-quality relationship, or who wish to have more freedom to pursue their own occupational or educational goals.

In recent years there have been an increasing number of both 'crowded' nests (Boyd and Norris, 1999), in which children continue to live in the family home into their 30s, sometimes with a 'partner', and 'refilled' nests, in which 'boomerang' children return home after an assumed permanent departure (Mitchell and Gee, 1996, Mitchell, 2000). The 2001 census reported that owing to a 'delayed emptying' or 'refilling' of the parental nest, 41 per cent of 20- to 29-year-olds live in the parental home, an increase from 27 per cent in 1981 (Statistics Canada, 2002a). These situations occur most often in Ontario and Newfoundland, where 47 per cent and 51 per cent respectively of those in their 20s live in the parental home. This tendency is more common among sons, especially in urban centres.

Despite the oft-cited phrase, 'you can't go home again', many adult children do return to the family nest in early or middle adulthood, often after a personal crisis, or because they cannot adjust to living on their own. In the 1990s, about one-quarter of 19- to 35-year-olds who had left home returned for four months or more (Mitchell, 2000: 84). Some reasons for the return include: financial difficulties, unemployment, underemployment or the unexpected loss of a job, the ending of a common-law relationship, a divorce or early widowhood, or the ill health of an adult child or parent which necessitates daily caregiving.

Living longer with one's parents before leaving home or returning to live at home is more common among some ethnic groups; among parents and children who, for financial reasons, need to pool their resources; among those who are close to their mother; and among those who complete university with a large debt. Living with parents at age 20 or 30 occurs, as well, when the cost of housing escalates, especially in urban centres, and when apartments are in short supply. Most accounts of these living arrangements, both by parents and the adult child, suggest that the relationship is positive and harmonious. The parents receive instrumental help and companionship from the child, and they experience gratification in helping a child live comfortably, safely, and economically. Some parents, however, find that a refilling of the nest is stressful because their privacy and freedom disappear, especially if grandchildren also move into the house. They may also be forced to assume unexpected financial responsibilities at a time when they were allocating more of their income to leisure or retirement savings. Nevertheless, most parents do assist a divorced or unemployed child.

The media and some social scientists have suggested that 'boomerang kids' and those who delay leaving home represent a family crisis or a social problem, that they are immature, unable to assume independence, or lazy. In reality, most relationships fostered by these living arrangements are not conflictual or stressful, although mothers are generally happier with the situation than fathers (Mitchell, 2000). However, we do not know how many parents refuse to be part of such an arrangement or how many end such an arrangement because of conflict or stress. For example, about 20 years ago my next-door neighbour 'emptied' the family nest by selling the family house and moving into a condominium because his three adult children would not establish their own permanent households.

Divorce in Middle and Later Life

Marital transitions occur at any age, and they have long-standing implications for the individuals concerned and for their relatives, both close and more distant, including children, siblings, in-laws, parents, and grandparents (Connidis, 2001: 102–7, 185–95; Connidis, 2003). Divorce usually occurs earlier rather than later in life, although divorces among those 60 and over are increasing. With longer life expectancy, older adults may divorce to reduce stress and boredom, to improve their physical and mental health, because their interests and values have become too divergent, or because retirement triggers conflict and a desire for different lifestyles. With 20 or 30 years to live after retirement, one or both members may no longer wish to continue an unhappy or unsatisfying relationship. As of 2001, about 6 per cent of all older adults are divorced, with the percentage being relatively equal among men and women in the current cohort of adults 65 and over. However, the 2001 census indicated that among those between 50 to 64 years of age (the baby boomers), 9 per cent of men and 13 per cent of women were divorced. This suggests that in the future more members of each older cohort will be divorced, especially women (see Table 8.1).

Divorce in later life has both positive and negative consequences for the divorcing partners (Connidis, 2001: 24, 105; Chipperfield and Havens, 2001; Jenkins, 2003). For a man, a divorce is especially traumatic when it is initiated by his wife at or about the time he retires because he loses two sources of companionship and social support at the same time. Increasingly, because of the mandatory sharing of accumulated marital assets (including savings, property, and pensions) in divorce settlements, older women are less disadvantaged financially by a divorce than in the past. This is especially true if they have had a career and are entitled to their own pension, plus a share of their former husband's pension. Consequently, more women than previously are initiating a divorce in later life.

Widowhood in Later Life

Becoming and being widowed in later life is primarily a gendered experience. For many, if not most, older married women it is an 'expectable life transition' because of gender differences in life expectancy, and the tendency of women to marry older men (Martin Matthews, 1987). For many women, widowhood is often preceded by long periods of caregiving and the institutionalization of a partner. Most studies of widowhood have concentrated on how widows adjust to a change in their financial situation and in their social and psychological adaptation to living on their own.[6]

A widow's financial situation is most likely to change if she is ineligible for health-care or pension benefits earned by her husband. The losses are compounded if she did not generate her own personal savings and private or public pension benefits while employed in the labour force. McDonald (1997) refers to retired widows as the 'invisible poor' because they often lose financial benefits if they outlive their husband. Whereas the public retirement-income system is designed to provide an adequate income for married couples, it often fails to support widows to an adequate level, especially if they were poor before they were widowed. Some widows have to move because they cannot afford property taxes, utility costs, or essential home repairs. Others have difficulty in learning how to manage and make decisions about financial matters because their husband 'did all the financial work'.

In continuing or establishing new social relationships, however, widows generally fare better than widowers. Widows usually have a peer group of other women, including those already widowed, who provide social and emotional support and serve as confidants. But they often lose social connections associated with the husband's workplace or relationships involving 'couple' activities. As well, widows become closer to their children, especially their daughters, after losing their husband. In contrast, widowers seldom have close confidants nor a large group of friends; they have fewer emotional ties to their family; and they are generally less willing to share personal thoughts or needs with a confidant or family member. Men, in general, however are more likely to date, cohabit, or remarry after a period of bereavement.

These gender differences in financial status and social involvement will narrow in the future—more older women will have participated in the labour force and accumulated savings, property, and pensions; they will be more independent and be better able to make decisions; they will have greater financial knowledge and a higher level of education; and they will experience more liberal norms concerning dating, cohabiting, and remarriage in the later years.

Adapting to Single Life

Widowhood, like marriage and divorce, is more than a single event. It involves a *process* of learning and adapting to being single again. The process may begin with looking after a frail partner and the consequent realization, if not acceptance, that the partner is likely to die in the relatively near future. Then, following death, the process involves mourning and bereavement (see Chapter 12); negotiating a new identity as a 'single' person; and learning new tasks and responsibilities (financial and legal; home and car mainte-

nance in the case of widows; homemaking and keeping in touch with one's family in the case of widowers). The process, for both men and women, involves a renegotiation of relationships with children concerning both the child's and the widowed parent's need for support, privacy and independence; with other married couples; and with single and married persons of the opposite sex. If a woman's identity has been closely linked to the status and occupation of her husband, she may have difficulty changing from this identity to that of a single person. A woman must engage in identity work to determine 'who she is now, given who she was' while attempting to rebuild her sense of self, her life and her social world[7] (van den Hoonaard, 2001). In same- or opposite-sex common-law unions, surviving partners experience much the same grieving process, but rebuilding an identity, renegotiating relationships, and not having legal rights makes the process somewhat different.

For widows and widowers, the mourning and adjustment period can last for a year or more. This period is characterized by shock, depression, and anger. Loneliness and lack of companionship are frequently expressed feelings in the early stages of being on one's own, as noted in the following thoughts of widows (Martin Matthews, 1991: 18):

- It's the loneliness. No one else takes the place of your spouse. There is no one to share with. (Widowed for seven years)

- Even though I have a great family, I find loneliness hard to bear, especially on weekends and holidays. (Widowed for 18 years).

In addition to losing a partner, a widow or widower often loses married friends, who continue to socialize as 'couples' (van den Hoonard, 2001: Chapter 4). Sometimes a widow's friends 'drop' her because she is considered to be less interesting or pleasant than her husband, and it was the couple that was the basis of the relationship; or a widow continues to mourn and is not a pleasant social companion. In other cases, a widow herself fails to keep in touch with her friends and views the world as belonging to couples. Some widows believe that it is not possible or feasible to attend social events as a single person. Phrases such as 'a fifth wheel', 'the third person', 'an outsider', or 'the odd person out' express these feelings of discomfort that restrict social interaction. Moreover, some widows believe that their married female friends consider widows as a threat to their marriage. Some of these feelings are illustrated in the following comments recorded in an Ontario study (Martin Matthews, 1991: 27):

- Most of the people I associate with now are widows.

- Most couples stick together and leave us widowed ladies alone.

- You see someone else with a partner and you know yours is gone. You feel alone, on the outside. If you are with other widows, you don't feel so out of place.

Indeed, two common responses to the narrowing of a widow's social world are embitterment and a resignation that former friends, especially couples, have been lost. Even in a condominium retirement community, where widowhood occurs frequently, married couples have more interpersonal relations with other couples than do widowed people, and those who are widowed see themselves as marginalized, isolated, and having lower status (van den Hoonaard, 1994, 2001).

In rural areas, elderly widows experience loneliness and isolation if their children have moved away from the region. In addition, they may live far from health, leisure, and social services. The lack of public transportation and living at a great distance from social facilities creates barriers that inhibit the reconstruction of an active life. In small towns, a place of worship often becomes an important centre for a widow's

social involvement (van den Hoonaard, 2001: Chapter 8).

There are few formal rituals or community resources in modern societies to help widowed persons adapt to a new identity and to single life. Moreover, the expected mourning time has decreased as life in modern societies has become more hurried. For example, 'in 1922 Emily Post instructed that the proper mourning period for a mature widow was three years. Fifty years later, Amy Vanderbilt urged that the bereaved be about their normal business within a week or so' (Gibbs, 1989: 49). To help elderly widows adapt, 'widow-to-widow' programs provide emotional support and knowledge. These programs involve widowed volunteers who visit recently bereaved persons; telephone help lines for information and assistance; group sessions to discuss common problems; and public education to inform the widowed person about available services and resources, including written materials on living alone, employment, and financial and legal matters. For some widows, a sudden requirement to become self-sufficient and live independently is viewed as a challenge and an opportunity for growth. Women who expected or permitted their husbands to perform most tasks and to make all major decisions often experience freedom and acquire confidence when they perform financial and household tasks or make decisions about where or how to live as a single person.

Programs to assist widowers are less effective because there are fewer widowers available to provide support, and because men are more reluctant to discuss their feelings with a confidant. Although men usually need less assistance in coping with financial and legal matters after the death of their wife, they are more likely to need help with homemaking (cooking meals, doing the laundry, and cleaning the house) and with keeping in touch with their family.

Once widowed, people often are faced with decisions concerning where and how to live as a single person, and whether to seek employment. The decision to work is usually based on economic necessity, age, employment status at widowhood, and the psychological need for a new focus in life and a new social network. Most older widows, at least initially, decide to live alone in their homes and to maintain intimacy with their children at a distance. However, if a widow is poor, frail, poorly educated, and has strong ethnic and cultural ties, she is more likely to share a household with a relative. A recent trend is for elderly widowed siblings, especially sisters, to reunite and form a household, or if not living together, to spend more social time together (Connidis, 2001: 207–39).

Dating, Cohabitation, and Remarriage in Later Life

A majority of older men have partners, whereas the majority of older women do not. This gendered difference in later life partnerships is partly due to the fact that women live longer and fewer eligible men are available. But the difference is also due to the belief among many current older people that it isn't proper to have an intimate relationship, especially outside marriage, after being widowed. As well, an increasing number of older widows report that they enjoy the freedom and independence of being single. As one elderly widow stated, 'I wouldn't get married again for all the tea in China' (Connidis, 2001: 109). While some older widows are interested in an intimate relationship, most are either opposed to remarriage or consider it unlikely or impossible (Talbot, 1998). Common reasons cited for not becoming intimately involved following widowhood include: respect for the former partner; the previous marriage was 'perfect'; lack of support from children; possible loss of spousal pension benefits; not wanting to 'nurse' another frail partner; and a desire for freedom and independence to live a different lifestyle.

Given that the number of unattached older men and women is growing, and that an increasing number consider it socially acceptable to 'date', cohabit, or remarry, intimate partnerships are being created in later life. This is much more common among those who are divorced than those who are widowed, and it is five times more likely to occur for men than for women (Connidis, 2001: 107). As well, more men than women report being interested in a new marriage. Indeed, as many as 20 per cent of widowers over 65 cohabit or remarry within five years compared to about 6 per cent of widows. Reasons cited for creating new partnerships include a need for companionship and intimacy; love and sexual attraction; to share financial resources (on the assumption that two can live more cheaply and efficiently than one); and security, safety, and comfort (a man acquires a homemaker as well as a companion). Highlight 8.4 illustrates how a 72-year-old widower's life was suddenly enriched by falling in love.

A decision to date, cohabit, or remarry is not easy for older divorced or widowed people. Nevertheless, an increasing number of elderly people are actively seeking new relationships by attending singles clubs or senior citizen centres,

---

Highlight 8.4 Later-Life Romance

How strange it is to be 72 and in love again. What kind of craziness is this? Just a few months ago I was living alone and perfectly happy. Well, maybe not perfectly happy. My wife had died a couple of years before and I had settled in Victoria, expecting to spend the rest of my life appreciating the beauty of the place, feasting on the arts, reading the great books I had missed, and generally wandering in the land of the mind.

continued

Hightlight 8.4 continued

But that turned out to be not so easy. When one has been half of a long union that suddenly comes to an end, there is confusion about what was hers, what is mine and what were the compromises that made it work for so long. When the sharp pain of grief receded into kind remembrance, I was surprised and a little chagrined to find it replaced with an exhilaration I had not experienced since the day I left home to go to college. I could do as I pleased and go where I liked and make decisions unhampered by the restraints imposed by a relationship, however loving and caring it might have been.

At some point, the sense of exhilaration left me but I had the good sense to realize that losing a spouse after so many years is a life-changing episode, like adolescence, but deeper and more fundamental. I needed time and solitude to regain a sense of perspective, and the way I chose to heal was to drive alone across the country at a time when the crops were ripening into gold on the long prairies. The slanting sun was warm in the daytime, the first frosts cool at night. If I learned anything on that trip it was that I can be my own best friend—in fact, maybe I have to be before I can be a friend to anyone else. I also learned that things matter less.

Yet how one hates to think of oneself as being alone. All the arts in the world do not take the place of a warm human relationship, and though I felt healed and to some extent content, I still hoped that in some miraculous way I could again drink from that enchanted cup we call love.

Then, mysteriously, at exactly the right time, she appeared. Well, to tell you the truth, there was nothing mysterious about it. A woman I once worked with telephoned from Vancouver. 'I'm coming to Victoria and I was wondering if we could have dinner?' she asked. 'Do you mind if I bring along a friend?' she asked. 'I'd like to see her too and that will be my only chance to do that.' 'The more the merrier', I said. As it turns out, she fed the same line to Jill, who also responded positively, and the future became inevitable for both of us. I sat beside her that evening and though not many words passed directly between us, I recognized in her a quality of happiness and adjustment to everything about her—to the beauty of the day, to the dark and to the sunlight, to the ordeal of meeting strangers. But there was something more—a chemistry, something as mysterious as true love always is.

In everyone's life there will come a moment of decision, of opportunity, when a second will decide the fate of that person for all remaining time. My moment came the next morning. I called her and like a stammering teenager made plans for another date. And after that, another and another and another. I did not know that life could once again hold such happiness.

As we came to know each other, we spent time walking the beaches of Oregon and Vancouver Island's west coast. And a year after my lonely drive across Canada, we did it together, visiting friends and relatives along the way. Being together is like a party that has made us both forget that we were ever lonely. Jill has the capacity for joy—a zest for living that in turn made my life active, buoyant, and vigorous.

We will see some of the world together starting this fall and we will plan another trip next year. We know we cannot forever 'sing in the sunshine', We have discussed that—not for long—but each of us knows that we are more to each other than a mere absence of loneliness in a lonely world, more than compatibility, more than profound comfort to each other, more than sex. You can't spend 24 hours a day in bed.

When life has less length, it seems to have more depth and more beauty; the colours are brighter, the air purer, the view cleaner and the love sweeter.

Source: Adapted and reprinted with permission of the author, Maurice Walford, and the *Globe and Mail* (10 October 2002: A26).

by using introduction or dating agencies, or by placing personal ads in local newspapers, in magazines for retired people, or on the Internet (Highlight 8.5).

For some single older people, socializing with another person is initiated for practical reasons, and is not, at least initially, perceived as a 'date'. Rather, to help another person or to fill their own time, they engage in social interaction through shared driving to events; inviting someone to share a 'pair' of tickets to the theatre or a concert; helping a recently widowed friend or neighbour 'get out of the house'; or sharing a drink or a meal with a neighbour or friend. Sometimes, adult children encourage a widowed parent to bring a neighbour or a widowed friend to a family event; or former lovers reconnect after a failed marriage or being widowed. Other places where new relationships in later life begin are cruise ships, funerals of friends, supermarkets and laundromats, retirement communities, adult recreation centres, nursing homes (Highlight 8.6), or blind dates arranged by friends.

Cohabiting is becoming more prevalent among older adults, perhaps because of earlier life experiences and fewer social constraints that discourage cohabitation. Some of these arrangements are permanent, some are seasonal (while 'down south' as a snowbird); some are long-distance and periodic (one partner lives in Germany, the other in Canada); and some involve independent living by each partner, with overnight visits on weekends or certain nights of the week. This latter arrangement is common among

---

Highlight 8.5 Being 'Single' in Later Life: In Search of a Socially Active Lifestyle

An increasing number of unattached older adults seek an active social life. Rather than rely on friends or relatives to make introductions, some older people place an advertisement, like the following, in the personal column of a newspaper, in magazines for older adults, or on the Internet:

- 46-year-old lady would like to meet non-alcoholic and non-drug addict gentleman, aged 45–55, for companionship or lasting friendship.

- Gentleman, early 60s, loves horses, old songs, walking, wishes to speak to lady with same interests by telephone.

- Male, 68 years old, seeking female companionship, 55–70 years old. I enjoy bowling, cards, home-cooked meals, quiet walks and times.

- Widower, 63, good health, financially secure, owns modern home on country acreage. Would like to meet lady, 55–65, interested in country living, animals, some travel.

- Widower, 69, 5 ft. 10 in., 175 lbs., seeking companionship with lady 60–70, who enjoys dining, travelling, theatre, and quiet conversation.

- Widow, 60s, looking for companionship of gentleman 60–70, who enjoys cards, travelling, dancing.

- Would like to meet an honest, sincere widower, 65–70 years. Good sense of humour, social drinker, with car. PS: A way to a man's heart is through his stomach. My cooking includes garlic and onions.

- Attractive, vibrant, secure widow with class and grace, enjoys the outdoors, social activities, and travel. Seeks sincere, refined, stable gentleman, over 50, with the same interests, for a meaningful relationship.

Highlight 8.6 Extended-Care Love: Nursing Homes as a Social Context for New Relationships

The Oldest Generation

John, age 89, and Adrienne, age 93, met at a 'senior's' residence, and decided to marry since they were spending most of their time together in the residence. He had been widowed once, she had been married twice before. Friends and family blew bubbles at the 'newlyweds' as they walked to a reception with cans and a sign, 'Just Married', tied to each of their walkers. Commenting on the age difference, the new groom stated, 'It doesn't bother me falling in love with an older woman. I stayed with my first wife for more than 50 years. I think, at our age, it may be a little less than 50 years this time, but you never know. I'm pretty easy to get along with.'

The Middle-Aged Generation

This couple, in their 40s, did not meet at a singles bar, at work, or at a social event with age-peers. Rather, they met while taking their mothers for a wheelchair ride on a sunny day in May. Their mothers had lived on the same floor in a continuing-care facility for six years, but it was three years before their children met. Ironically, both children were divorced, worked in the same industry, and knew many of the same people in their field. Yet they had never met until they began bumping into each other while visiting and caring for their mothers. After about two years of dating, the couple were married in a synagogue next to the centre, and they invited staff, other residents, and their families to the ceremony and reception. As the bride noted, 'I can truly say it's a blessing that my mother is here, because if not, I would never have met the man for me.'

Centenarian Love

Many residents who move into a nursing home see the move as a symbol that their lives are ending or almost over. But for Fred, who entered the nursing home at 101 years of age in March, and Ida, who moved in at age 88 in May, the summer brought a whirlwind romance, a six-day engagement, and a September wedding. Both spend their days in wheelchairs, and Ida has been blind for 10 years. She had been a widow for 30 years, and never had a child, but does have many nephews and nieces. He was married to his first wife for 60 years. He re-married within six months of becoming a widower, but his second wife died two years before he moved into the nursing home. He has three sons, eight grandchildren, 14 great-grandchildren, and two great-great grandchildren. For both it was love at first meeting. Says Ida, 'I can't believe that I met someone so nice and fell in love at my age. He is so caring and loving.' Fred declares, 'She had an awfully nice voice and I found her pretty attractive and pretty nice.' The courtship involved eating dinner together and sitting in the sun holding hands, sharing stories about their past. As for their wedding night, Ida thinks they will 'just cuddle' in their new shared apartment.

Source: Adapted from news stories in the *The Record*, 20 and 25 September 2000. Reprinted with permission from The Record of Kitchener, Waterloo, and Cambridge, Ontario.

younger adults between the ages of 20 and 29, But the 2001 General Social Survey found that 42 per cent of the men and 11 per cent of the women living as 'non-residential partners' were 50 years of age or older (Milan and Peters, 2003). This arrangement enables each partner to maintain some independence and privacy while enjoying the benefits of an intimate relationship.

Most older adults who remarry consider the marriage to be successful (Connidis, 2001: 107–11). Success is often dependent on both partners having a high level of motivation to remarry, the support of adult children and friends, and having higher levels of education and health. Most older brides and some older grooms report that they never intended or expected to remarry. Some men remarry because they have difficulty adjusting to widowhood and prefer not to live alone. Older widowers often have little experience with domestic responsibilities, and they remarry to have someone take care of them. For older widows, the need for companionship, financial support, and intimacy, especially if their adult children are not close, are motivating factors. Cohabitation rather than marriage occurs if a widow will lose the pension benefits of her deceased husband when she remarries, or if her adult children discourage her from remarrying.

Adult children oppose a remarriage if they believe it represents a loss of respect and love for the deceased partner, or if they fear they will lose their inheritance when their surviving parent dies. Others fear that if their mother remarries she will become a nurse and a housemaid for another man, who will eventually become ill and disabled and die. On the other hand, some adult children recognize that a remarriage reduces some of their responsibilities for looking after or helping their parent since he or she no longer lives alone.

Although economic, social, legal, religious, or demographic factors discourage or prevent remarriage among older people, a number of factors increase the probability of, and the success of, a remarriage later in the life. Neither adult children nor an aging parent prefer a living arrangement whereby the widowed person lives in the home of an adult child. Yet, many older men and women need daily companionship in a family, and some may desire sexual intimacy.

Therefore, remarriage or cohabitation is viewed, increasingly, but not by everyone, as a socially acceptable and viable alternative to living alone. For residents of a retirement or nursing home, cohabitation or remarriage is usually more difficult, often because the staff and the policies of the institution do not encourage, support, or permit such arrangements.

Summary

The extended family is an essential element of social life and social support throughout the life course. Relationships within and across generations are influenced by common transitions such as marriage, common-law cohabitation, divorce, the emptying of the nest when children move out, widowhood, and declining health in later life. The structure, definition, and meaning of family as a social construct is evolving as family structures and relationships change across the life course and in late life. More research is needed about those who never married, gay and lesbian family members, those who are childless or child-free, sibling ties in adulthood, and the many combinations of step- and step-like relatives following divorce, widowhood, remarriage, or subsequent cohabitation relationships. With changing social norms, more older adults are dating, cohabiting, or remarrying, including those who live in retirement or nursing homes. An analysis of family relationships illustrates the gendered nature of family experiences. Mother-daughter-granddaughter ties are the strongest; women function as the kin keepers and confidants in most families; divorced or widowed women are more likely to experience economic hardship, and to have fewer chances or options or desire to remarry; and women in a divorce settlement usually gain custody of children and the accompanying life-long responsibility for their welfare as a single parent.

For Reflection, Debate, or Action

1. Identify those whom you consider your 'family', and indicate how frequently you have contact with each member. What are the purposes of this contact, and where does it take place? What meaning does this contact hold for you?

2. Much research about the family across the life course has been atheoretical. Do you agree or disagree with this statement, and why?

3. Identify the kin keeper in your family. Interview that person to learn about their experiences and how they define their responsibilities. Why do they, and you, think this person, rather than other members of the family, has become the kin keeper?

4. What are the social norms and barriers that impede dating, cohabitation, or remarriage in later life? How can the barriers be reduced or eliminated so that more older adults can participate if they choose to do so? Why might dating be a pleasant or unpleasant experience for older people? Are these reasons any different than those that apply to younger people?

5. There are few Canadian studies about common-law relationships in later life. Design a study to gain an understanding of the meaning and interaction patterns of common-law relationships for older adults (review the sections on methods and theory).

6. Interview a number of grandparents (both men and women) to develop an overview of their experiences and expectations about their relationships with grandchildren. Ask if their expectations fit with those of their children and grandchildren, and if not, determine why and where there are differences in expectations about the relationship.

7. Are there any fictive kin in your family network? If so, what support do they provide, and to whom?

Notes

1. The structure of kinship systems is discussed by Blieszner and Hilkevitch Bedford(1995); Bowen et al. (2000); Price et al. (2000); Connidis (2001); Fox (2001); Hareven (2001); Phillipson et al. (2001); and Matthews (2002).

2. Among older institutionalized residents, many do not have any relatives to look after them, and it is this situation that increases the likelihood that they must move into a residential care facility.

3. Most cross-sectional studies suggest that the relationship is between age and marital satisfaction. However, the degree of satisfaction may reflect, as well, the number of years a couple has been married and the stages in the marriage career that have been completed.

4. Discussions of grandparents raising grandchildren can be found in Kruk, 1995; Cox, 1999; Minkler, 1999; Hayslip et al., 2000; Connidis, 2001: 192–195; Fuller-Thomson and Minkler, 2001, 2003; Climo et al., 2002; Hill, 2002; and Milan and Hamm, 2003.

5. To assist poor older couples who are responsible for raising grandchildren, the city of Boston created GrandFamilies House—a supportive housing unit with 26 apartments and a social-work infrastructure to enable grandchildren to grow and mature in a safe and supportive environment.

6. For a discussion of widowhood (primarily widows), see Lopata, 1987a, 1987b; Martin Matthews, 1987, 1991; van den Hoonaard, 1999, 2001; Connidis, 2001: 93–102; Hungerford, 2001; Hurd and Macdonald, 2001; and Jenkins, 2003.

7. Martin Matthews (1991), Hurd and Macdonald (2001), and van den Hoonaard (1999, 2001) quote many insightful comments by widows. These qualitative studies present the 'voices' of widows at various stages in the process of losing their identity as a wife and accepting their identity as a single and widowed person.

References

Blieszner, R., and V. Hilkevitch Bedford (eds). 1995. *Handbook of Aging and the Family*. Westport, Conn: Greenwood Press.

Boss, P., et al. (eds). 1993. *Sourcebook of Family Theories and Methods: A Contextual Approach*. New York: Plenum Press.

Bowen, G., et al. 2000. 'Families in the Context of Communities Across Time'. Pp. 117–28 in S. Price et al. (eds), *Families across Time: A Life Course Perspective*. Los Angeles, Calif.: Roxbury.

Boyd, M., and D. Norris. 1999. 'The Crowded Nest: Young Adults at Home', *Canadian Social Trends*, 52 (Spring), 2–5.

Brotman, S., et al. 2003. 'The Health and Social Service Needs of Gay and Lesbian Elders and their Families in Canada', *The Gerontologist*, 43(2), 192–202.

Caputo, R. 1999. 'Age-Condensed and Age-Gapped Families: Coresidency with Elderly Parents and Relatives in a Mature Women's Cohort', *Marriage and Family Review*, 29(1), 77–96.

Campbell, L., et al. 1999. 'Sibling Ties in Later Life: A Social Network Analysis', *Journal of Family Issues*, 20(1), 114–48.

———, and A. Martin-Matthews. 2003. 'The Gendered Nature of Men's Filial Care', *Journal of Gerontology: Social Studies*, 58B(6), S350–8.

Chan, C., and G. Elder. 2000. 'Matrilineal Advantage in Grandchild-Grandparent Relations', *The Gerontologist*, 40(2), 179–90.

Chipperfield, J., and B. Havens. 2001. 'Gender Differences in the Relationship between Marital Status Transitions and Life Satisfaction in Later Life', *Journal of Gerontology: Psychological Sciences*, 56B(3), P176–86.

Claes, J., and W. Moore. 2001. 'Caring for Gay and Lesbian Elderly'. Pp. 217–29 in L. Olson (ed.), *Age through Ethnic Lenses: Caring for the Elderly in a Multicultural Society*. New York: Rowman and Littlefield.

Clarke, E., et al. 1999. 'Types of Conflicts and Tensions between Older Parents and Adult Children', *The Gerontologist*, 39(3), 261–70.

Climo, J., et al. 2002. 'Using the Double Bind to Interpret the Experience of Custodial Grandparents', *Journal of Aging Studies*, 16(1), 19–35.

Connidis, I. 1989. *Family Ties and Aging*. Toronto: Butterworths.

———. 1994. 'Growing Up and Old Together: Some Observations on Families in Later Life'. Pp. 195–205 in V. Marshall and B. McPherson (eds), *Aging: Canadian Perspectives*. Peterborough, Ont.: Broadview.

———. 2001. *Family Ties and Aging*. Thousand Oaks, Calif.: Sage.

———. 2004. 'Bringing Outsiders In: Gay and Lesbian Family Ties over the Life Course'. In S. Arber et al. (eds), *Gender and Aging: Changing Roles and Relationships*. Maidenhead, UK: Open University Press.

———. 2003. 'Divorce and Union Dissolution across the Life Course: Reverberations over Three Generations', *Canadian Journal on Aging*, 22(4), 353–68.

———, and J. McMullin. 1992. 'Getting Out of the House: The Effect of Childlessness on Social Participation and Companionship in Later Life', *Canadian Journal on Aging*, 11(4), 370–86.

———. 1996. 'Reasons for and Perceptions of Childlessness among Older Persons: Exploring the Impact of Marital Status and Gender', *Journal of Aging Studies*, 10(3), 205–22.

———. 1999. 'Permanent Childlessness: Perceived Advantages and Disadvantages among Older Persons', *Canadian Journal on Aging*, 18(4), 447–65.

Cox, C. (ed.). 1999. *To Grandmother's House We Go and Stay: Perspectives on Custodial Grandparents*. New York: Springer.

Cruz, J. 2003. *Sociological Analysis of Aging: The Gay Male Perspective*. Binghampton, NY: Haworth Press.

Davies, L. 2003. 'Singlehood: Transitions within a Gendered World', *Canadian Journal on Aging*, 22(4), 343–52.

Dumas, J., and A. Bélanger. 1997. *Report on the Demographic Situation in Canada, 1996*. Ottawa: Statistics Canada.

Fox, B. (ed.). 2001. *Family Patterns, Gender Relations*. Don Mills, Ont.: Oxford University Press.

———, and M. Luxton. 2001. 'Conceptualizing Family'. Pp. 22–33 in B. Fox (ed.), *Family Patterns, Gender Relations*. Don Mills, Ont.: Oxford University Press.

Fuller-Thomson, E., and M. Minkler. 2001. 'American Grandparents Providing Extensive Child Care to Their Grandchildren: Prevalence and Profile', *The Gerontologist*, 41(2), 201–9.

———. 2003. 'Housing Issues and Realities Facing Grandparent Caregivers Who Are Renters', *The Gerontologist*, 43(1), 92–8.

Ganong, L., and M. Coleman. 1998. 'Attitudes Regarding Filial Responsibilities to Help Elderly Divorced Parents and Stepparents', *Journal of Aging Studies*, 12(3), 271–90.

Gibbs, N. 1989. 'How America Has Run Out of Time', *Time* (April 24), 48–55.

Gladstone, J. 1995. 'The Marital Perceptions of Elderly Persons Living or Having a Spouse Living in a Long-Term Care Institution in Canada', *The Gerontologist*, 35(1), 52–60.

Glenn, N. 1998. 'The Course of Marital Success and Failure in Five American 10-year Marriage Cohorts', *Journal of Marriage and the Family*, 60(6), 569–76.

Hagestad, G. 2003. 'Interdependent Lives and Relationships in Changing Times: A Life-Course View of Families and Aging'. Pp. 135–59 in R. Settersten (ed.), *Invitation to the Life Course: Toward New Understandings of Later Life*. Amityville, NY: Baywood.

Hareven, T. 1994. 'Family Change and Historical Change: An Uneasy Relationship'. Pp. 130–50 in M. Riley et al. (eds), *Age and Structural Lag*. New York: John Wiley and Sons.

———. 2001. 'Historical Perspectives on Aging and Family Relations'. Pp. 141–59 in R. Binstock and L. George (eds), *Handbook of Aging and the Social Sciences*. New York: Academic Press.

Hayslip, B., et al. (eds). 2000. *Grandparents Raising Grandchildren*. New York: Springer.

Hill, T. 2002. 'Social Structure and Family Law: The Underlying Factors of Grandparent Legislation', *Journal of Aging Studies*, 16(3), 259–78.

Hungerford, T. 2001. 'The Economic Consequences of Widowhood on Elderly Women in the United States and Germany', *The Gerontologist*, 41(1), 103–10.

Hurd, M., and M. Macdonald. 2001. *Beyond Coping: Widows Reinventing Their Lives*. Halifax: Pear Press.

Huyck, M. 1974. *Growing Older*. Englewood Cliffs, NJ: Prentice-Hall.

Jendrek, M. 1994. 'Grandparents Who Parent Their Grandchildren: Circumstances and Decisions', *The Gerontologist*, 34(2), 206–16.

Jenkins, C. (ed.). 2003. *Widows and Divorcees in Later Life: On Their Own Again*. Binghampton, NY: Haworth Press.

Keating, N. 1986. 'Valuing Intergenerational Transfer of the Family Farm'. Paper presented at the annual meeting of the Canadian Association on Gerontology, Quebec City, November.

———. 1996. 'Legacy, Aging, and Succession in Farm Families', *Generations*, 20(3), 61–4.

Kemp, C. 2001. *The Social and Demographic Contours of Contemporary Grandparenthood: Mapping Patterns in Canada and the United States*. SEDAP Report #62. Hamilton, Ont.: McMaster University (http://socserv2.mcmaster.ca/sedap).

———. 2003. 'The Social and Demographic Contours of Contemporary Grandparenthood: Mapping Patterns in Canada and the United States', *Journal of Comparative Family Studies*, 34(2), 187–212.

Kimmel, D., and D. Lundy Martin (eds). 2002. *Midlife and Aging in Gay America*. Binghampton, NY: Haworth Press.

Kruk, E. 1995. 'Grandparent-Grandchild Contacts Loss: Findings from a Study of 'Grandparent Rights' Members', *Canadian Journal on Aging*, 14(4), 737–54.

Laird, J. 1996. 'Invisible Ties: Lesbians and Their Families of Origin'. Pp. 89–122 in J. Laird and R. Green (eds), *Lesbians and Gays in Couples and Families: A Handbook for Therapists*. San Francisco, Calif.: Jossey-Bass.

Lopata, H. (ed.). 1987a. *Widows*. Volume 1, *The Middle East, Asia and the Pacific*. Durham, NC: Duke University Press.

———. (ed.). 1987b. *Widows*. Vol. II, *North America*. Durham, NC: Duke University Press.

McConville, B. 1985. *Sisters: Love and Conflict within the Lifelong Bond*. London: Pan Books.

McDonald, L. 1997. 'The Invisible Poor: Canada's Retired Widows', *Canadian Journal on Aging*, 16(3), 553–83.

MacRae, H. 1992. 'Fictive Kin as a Component of the Social Networks of Older People', *Research on Aging*, 14(2), 226–47.

Martin Matthews, A. 1987. 'Widowhood as an Expectable Life Event'. Pp. 343–66 in V. Marshall (ed.), *Aging in Canada: Social Perspectives*. Markham, Ont.: Fitzhenry and Whiteside.

———. 1991. *Widowhood in Later Life*. Toronto: Butterworths.

———, et al. 2001. *Age-Gapped and Age-Condensed Lineages: Patterns of Intergenerational Age Structure among Canadian Families*. SEDAP Research Paper #56. Hamilton, Ont.: McMaster University (http://www.socserv2.mcmaster.ca/sedap).

Matthews, S. 2002. *Sisters and Brothers/Daughters and Sons: Meeting the Needs of Older Persons*. Bloomington, Ind.: Unlimited.

———, and J. Heidorn. 1998. 'Meeting Filial Responsibilities in Brothers-Only Sibling Groups',

Journal of Gerontology: Social Sciences, 53B(5), S278–86.

Milan, A. 2003. 'Would You Live Common-Law?' *Canadian Social Trends*, 70 (Autumn), 2–6.

———, and B. Hamm. 2003. 'Across the Generations: Grandparents and Grandchildren', *Canadian Social Trends*, 71 (Winter), 2–7.

———, and A. Peters. 2003. 'Couples Living Apart', *Canadian Social Trends*, 69 (Summer), 2–6.

Minkler, M. 1999. 'Intergenerational Households Headed by Grandparents: Contexts, Realities and Implications for Policy', *Journal of Aging Studies*, 13(2), 199–218.

Mitchell, B. 2000. 'The Refilled 'Nest': Debunking the Myth of Families in Crisis', Pp. 80–99 in E. Gee and G. Gutman (eds), *The Overselling of Population Aging*. Don Mills, Ont.: Oxford University Press.

———., and E. Gee. 1996. 'Boomerang Kids and Midlife Parental Marital Satisfaction', *Family Relations*, 45(6), 442–8.

Mueller, M., et al. 2002. 'Variations in Grandparenting', *Research on Aging*, 24(3), 360–88.

Munro, B., et al. 1995. 'Stake in Farm and Family: A Generation Perspective', *Canadian Journal on Aging*, 14(3), 564–79.

NACA. 1986. 'The Way It Is: All in the Family', *Expression*, 3(1), 3, Division of Aging and Seniors, Health Canada.

O'Brien, C-A., and A. Goldberg. 2000. 'Lesbian and Gay Men Inside and Outside Families', Pp. 115–45 in N. Mandell and A. Duffy (eds), *Canadian Families: Diversity, Conflict and Change*. Toronto: Harcourt Brace.

Phillipson, C., et al. 2001. *The Family and Community Life of Older People*. London: Routledge.

Price, S., et al. (eds). 2000. *Families across Time: A Life Course Perspective*. Los Angeles, Calif.: Roxbury.

Rosenthal, C. 1985. 'Kinkeeping in the Familial Division of Labor', *Journal of Marriage and the Family*, 47, 965–74.

———. 2000. 'Aging Families: Have Current Changes and Challenges Been 'Oversold'?', Pp. 45–63 in E. Gee and G. Gutman (eds), *The Overselling of Population Aging*. Don Mills, Ont.: Oxford University Press.

———, and J. Gladstone. 1994. 'Family Relationships and Support in Later Life', Pp. 158–74 in V. Marshall and B. McPherson (eds), *Aging: Canadian Perspectives*. Peterborough, Ont.: Broadview.

———, and J. Gladstone. 2000. *Grandparenthood in Canada*. Ottawa: Vanier Institute of the Family.

Snell, J. 1993. 'The Gendered Construction of Elderly Marriage, 1900–1950', *Canadian Journal on Aging*, 12(4), 509–23.

Spitze, G., and J. Logan. 1989. 'Gender Differences in Family Support: Is There a Payoff?', *The Gerontologist*, 29(1), 108–13.

Statistics Canada. 2002a. *Profile of Canadian Families and Households: Diversification Continues*. Cat. #96F0030XIE200/003—22 October 2002. Ottawa: Statistics Canada.

———. 2002b. *Annual Demographic Statistics*. Cat. no. 91-213. Ottawa: Statistics Canada.

Stobert, S., and A. Kemeny. 2003. 'Childfree by Choice', *Canadian Social Trends*, 69 (Summer), 7–10.

Stone, L., et al. 1998. *Parent-Child Exchanges of Supports and Intergenerational Equity*. Cat. no. 89-557-XPE. Ottawa: Statistics Canada.

Talbott, M. 1998. 'Older Widows' Attitudes towards Men and Remarriage', *Journal of Aging Studies*, 12(4), 429–49.

Tower, R., and S. Kasl. 1996. 'Gender, Marital Closeness, and Depressive Symptoms in Elderly Couples', *Journal of Gerontology: Psychological Sciences*, 51B(3), P115–29.

Townsend-Batten, B. 2002. 'Staying in Touch: Contact between Adults and their Parents', *Canadian Social Trends*, Spring, 9–12.

Treas, J., and S. Mazumdar. 2002. 'Older People in America's Immigrant Families: Dilemmas of Dependence, Integration, and Isolation', *Journal of Aging Studies*, 16(3), 243–58.

Uhlenberg, P. 1993. 'Demographic Change and Kin Relationships in Later Life'. Pp. 219–38 in G. Maddox and P. Lawton (eds), *Annual Review of Gerontology and Geriatrics*, Vol. 13. New York: Springer.

van den Hoonaard, D. 1994. 'Paradise Lost: Widowhood in a Florida Retirement Community', *Journal of Aging Studies*, 8(2), 121–32.

———. 1999. 'No Regrets: Widows Stories about the Last Days of Their Husbands' Lives', *Journal of Aging Studies*, 13(1), 59–72.

———. 2001. *The Widowed Self: The Older Woman's Journey through Widowhood*. Waterloo, Ont.: Wilfrid Laurier University Press.

Wu, Z., and M. Pollard. 1998. 'Social Support among Unmarried Childless Elderly Persons', *Journal of Gerontology: Social Sciences*, 53B(6), S324–35.

Zhang, Z., and M. Hayward. 2001. 'Childlessness and the Psychological Well-Being of Older Persons', *Journal of Gerontology: Social Sciences*, 56B(5), S311–20.

CHAPTER 9

Work, Retirement, and Economic Security

Focal Points

- Are older workers less efficient, productive, reliable, or creative than younger workers?

- To what extent is there discrimination in the hiring, promotion, or retraining of older workers and in their salary and benefits?

- Will there be enough workers to ensure a productive society once the baby boomers retire?

- Is there an ideal retirement age for individuals and for society?

- Are flexible, innovative retirement policies and practices needed to sustain the needs of the workforce and to maintain the viability of the Canada Pension Plan?

- What is an 'adequate' income in later life?

- To what extent is poverty a reality in later life, especially among women— is the 'feminization of poverty' fact or fiction?

- Does our pension system (private and government) require an overhaul, and, if so, should there be a shift in relative responsibility for income security in later life (this is the private trouble or public responsibility debate)?

Introduction

Until the 1980s, work life for men, from entry into the workforce until retirement, was usually continuous and relatively predictable. After completing his formal education, a man entered the workforce and remained employed, often with the same company, until he retired at age 65. For many women, especially those without a university education who married and raised children, participation in the workforce was random and discontinuous, and at age 65, a pension was not guaranteed.

The timing and pattern of transitions into and out of the workforce, the meaning of work,

the nature of careers, and economic security in later life resulting from a particular work history, have all changed in recent decades. These changes, at both the individual and the social-structural level, have an impact on older workers, the retirement process, the amount of individual economic security in later life, and the productive capacity of a society. These changes include the following:

- More retirees have increased economic security because of enhanced public and retirement benefits.

- There are more frequent and rapid shifts in the economy, leading to job losses, mergers, downsizing, and outsourcing of work to other countries where labour is cheap.

- There have been considerable stock-market fluctuations, which have a major effect on the value of public and private pension plans, personal retirement savings plans, and the timing of retirement.

- There are continuing but decreasing gender differences in work opportunities and histories, wages, and eligibility for retirement benefits—women are disadvantaged and more vulnerable, especially if they are divorced or widowed (Anisef and Axelrod, 2001).

- Combined with the influence of structural forces (gender, class, ethnicity, the economy), there is increased individualization of the work life—individuals, not just employers, help to make the decisions concerning entry to and exit from the workforce on the basis of personal interests, ambitions, and abilities (agency and personal choice are invoked) to seek a 'work-life balance'—see http://labour-travail.hrdc-drhc.gc.ca/worklife/work-life-balance-en.cfm.

- There is increased labour-force participation by women, especially women with higher levels of education, and among those who have never married or are divorced.

- Gender relations are changing at home and at work—men are more involved in family responsibilities because of two-career couples; women are more involved in management and leadership positions at work.

- Increasingly, lives are 'linked' across generations and institutions (Heinz, 2001)—entry to the workforce is delayed because of educational pursuits or a weak economy; family events or decisions are arranged around careers or work demands; women postpone entering the labour force or leave it early to care for children, grandchildren, or elderly parents.

- A knowledge-based economy with increased technology reduces the physical labour in jobs, necessitates retraining, stimulates organizational change, and requires fewer workers or more specialized skills (Chan et al., 2001).

- Retirement is more a family decision because of dual careers and family responsibilities versus a male-only individual decision, as in the past.

- Retirement is no longer, for many, a predictable event which occurs on or about the sixty-fifth birthday.

This chapter examines the links between the work history and meaning of work among older workers, the process of retiring from the workforce, and the influence of work history and the timing of retirement on economic security in later life. Particular attention is directed to gender differences in work opportunities and patterns, and the effect of these differences on the economic situation of older women. Throughout, the use of a life-course perspective reminds us that jobs and careers can change; that the meaning and importance of work in our daily lives can change because of family responsibilities, leisure interests, health, or the challenge of the job itself; that retirement from the workforce is increasingly a complex and prolonged process; and that human agency is an important element in decisions about work and careers at transition points. Transition points can arise when a person is offered a promotion that requires moving to a new city or extensive travel; when a company downsizes and offers incentives for early retirement; when a personal or family crisis, such as an illness, death, divorce, or accident, requires time away from work; or when rapid technological change necessitates retraining if one is to remain employed.

Older Workers in the Pre-retirement Years

Twenty to thirty years ago, research on the topic of older workers (those over 45 years of age) focused on individual issues—pre-retirement attitudes to retirement, planning for retirement, and characteristics of the minority who retired before 65 years of age. Today, the issues are both structural and individual:

- What is the effect on older workers of a changing work environment, where there is downsizing, contracting out, off-shore manufacturing, a contingent workforce, and employment in small companies without unions, pensions, or contracts to protect workers?

- Are older workers discriminated against in the workforce?

- Are older workers as productive and reliable as younger workers? Can they adapt to change and be retrained?

- Will there be a labour shortage once the baby-boom generation retires in the next 20 years, and will older workers need to be retained in the labour force?

- What is the impact of emerging corporate and public policies on the retention or retirement of older workers?

- How do older workers survive in a linked global economy?

- Has the prevalence of early retirement (Freedom 55) prematurely removed productive workers from the workforce?

- What is the influence of work history (such as periods of unemployment or part-time work and 'bridge' jobs) on retirement decisions and on economic security in later life?

A Changing Work History

The traditional age-segregated view of the life course (education, work, and retirement) was considered normative and ideal for much of the twentieth century. After completing his formal education (high school or university), a young man was expected to enter the labour force and to work continuously throughout his life. Women, on the other hand, after completing their education, were expected either to marry and raise children or to work; although part-time work was acceptable. Once employed, most of one's career was spent with the same company, for loyalty and to maximize one's salary and pension benefits. Then, at age 65, unless declining health or disability required an earlier exit, a man retired, if eligible, with full public and/or private pension benefits. Since the 1980s, however, working life in the developed countries has been, and continues to be, restructured (Marshall et al., 2001a). Young people are spending more years acquiring an education, and many earn a graduate degree or a specialized post-baccalaureate diploma. Thus, many enter the workforce at a later age than their parents. Moreover, because of economic conditions late in the twentieth and early in the twenty-first century, younger workers may be unemployed or underemployed for a few years after completing their education. Hence, the transition to a working life is delayed further.

Once a person is in the labour force, working life may include periods of unemployment, voluntary or involuntary job changes, and, perhaps, a voluntary or forced early retirement. Early retirement is sometimes encouraged by incentives offered by companies. Such incentives shorten a person's working life and, when combined with increased life expectancy, increase the time spent in retirement—if one remains unemployed in later life. In some occupations, because of a long period of education, late entry to the workforce, and early retirement, some workers spend only about 50 per cent of their life at work compared to their parents or grandparents, who spent 65 to 70 per cent of their life at work. Consequently, some older people engage in paid or volunteer work after early or 'on time' retirement.

Another emerging feature of work histories is that employees, voluntarily or involuntarily, 'individualize' their careers. Rather than progressing through various positions and levels in one company, they move across jobs and companies to fashion a career, or to survive as the labour force changes. In this situation, there is less loyalty and long-term commitment to one employer.

The Meaning and Form of Work

Despite the changing nature of work lives, work remains a central life focus, although its meaning and importance ebb and flow across the life course. Where and how we work influences income and savings, place and type of residence, social status, lifestyles, friendships, and economic security later in life.

Work also has the potential to influence life satisfaction or dissatisfaction, although this varies by the type of job. For example, employees in high-prestige, decision-making positions and those in the professions generally report high levels of job satisfaction. In contrast, workers engaged in repetitive manual labour are more likely to report lower levels of job satisfaction and less commitment to the job. Part of this dissatisfaction and lack of commitment result from a low income, the unchallenging nature of the job, impersonal employee-employer relations, and an early attainment of the highest position (the career peak) they can achieve in their working life. In addition, those at the lower occupational levels are more concerned throughout their work careers with job security, income, and friendships with colleagues than with the meaning and satisfaction they derive from the job. Regardless of work orientation, workers with a continuous and stable work history generally enjoy work more, and face retirement with a more positive attitude. Those most likely to express regret about retiring and try to delay it are those with little economic security and poor health and those for whom work has been the central interest in life.

Different attitudes toward work are held by those who have had an unstable or interrupted work history, that is, a work pattern characterized by cyclical periods of full-time employment, unemployment, part-time employment, or underemployment. In the 1990s, when downsizing was at its peak (employers reduced the size of their labour force to reduce costs), many older workers (45 and over) who became 'chronically' unemployed eventually gave up searching for work and said they were 'retired' (Marshall, 1995b).

Although most older workers are *not* alienated from their work, the meaning of work to them and their attitude to work can change with age. For example, there may be a decline in the amount of intrinsic work satisfaction during the later stages of labour-force participation. If they are not challenged at work, or if work is no longer their main interest, some workers decide to retire, either partially or completely. To counteract this loss of interest in work, employers may introduce new work options: flextime, sabbatical leaves, reduced loads, job sharing, job exchanges, graduated retirement, working at home, or contract work. Or, early-retirement incentive plans are offered so that employees can change jobs or careers with some financial security.

Flextime enables employees to begin and end the workday at their own selected hours (for example, they may begin work at any time between 7:00 and 9:00 a.m. and leave work at any time between 4:00 and 6:00 p.m.); or they can work the weekly maximum number of hours over a four-day week. Moreover, it is often possible within this system to accumulate extra credit hours to provide time off in addition to regular vacations. This option is appealing for women, and even more so for single parents, where it helps them to manage the combined responsibilities of work, child care, parent care, and housework.

A sabbatical leave provides fully or partially paid time away from work to engage in professional or personal development. Sometimes this leave is offered by a company to temporarily reduce its payroll costs during slow economic growth.

A reduced load represents a three-quarter or half-time appointment at a proportionately reduced salary. Job sharing involves two persons who each work part-time to meet the responsibilities of one position. These various plans permit employees to pursue alternative leisure or career interests or to meet the temporary demands of a family crisis, such as caring for an ill or dying parent or a grandchild whose parents have divorced. A major attraction of reduced loads is that the employees usually receive a full pension when they retire, despite not having worked full-time for a few years before retirement. From the perspective of the employer, a reduced-load policy lowers salary costs and permits the hiring of younger employees, who can be trained by experienced workers.

Mid-life Career Changes

Some occupations encourage or require a mid-life career change. For example, after a specified number of years of employment, combined with age, teachers, members of the armed forces, and some unionized blue-collar workers are eligible in their mid- to late 50s to retire with full pension benefits. This creates opportunities for the hiring and promotion of younger people. Other mid-life career changes result from being laid off through downsizing or restructuring, the onset of a disability that requires a change in occupation, age-related occupational requirements (such as those for airline pilots), or company policies (partners in many law and accounting firms must retire at 60 or 62).

Though it was once believed that a male 'mid-life crisis' triggered voluntary career changes, research has refuted the myth that men experience a crisis in mid-life. Rather, such voluntary moves occur mainly among middle- or upper-class workers who are financially independent and well educated.[1] Many of these career changes involve a voluntary shift from a professional position (for example, as a lawyer, engineer, or professor) or managerial position, where an individual is unsatisfied with his or her work life, to a more independent, challenging, or less structured occupa-tion, for example, as a writer, craftsperson, or self-employed businessperson. During this period they are supported financially by savings, investments, inheritances, or consulting fees as they search for a higher quality of life or new work challenges. Most are motivated by a change in lifestyle, not by a need for increased income. In fact, many move to careers that offer less prestige and income but greater personal freedom and satisfaction. Some of these people, in fact, choose to be unemployed and make no attempt to re-enter the labour force.

A Changing (Greying) Labour Force

Information about the Canadian labour force is acquired from the census, government labour force surveys, and case studies of specific firms or industries (McMullin and Marshall, 1999, 2001). In general, labour force participation rates for older men are decreasing, while for older women they are increasing. Women's involvement rose from 46 per cent to 59 per cent from 1976 to 2000. Unstable labour force involvement, that is, moving in and out of the labour force, is becoming more common among men, while continuous, stable involvement is more likely among women.

The choice of 65 as the age for mandatory retirement goes back many decades to a time when life expectancy was much lower than it is today, and when few women were in the labour force. Today, however, when the average life expectancy is about 80 years of age and the workforce is aging, it is being debated whether mandatory retirement at age 65 is still reasonable and whether it should even be legal. Mandatory retirement can be expensive for a society that is faced with the cost of supporting a growing number of retirees, and the loss of productivity for a nation when the labour force ages and shrinks in size.

The labour force is both aging and becoming more highly educated. In 2001, 2.5 million of the 15.5 million jobs in Canada required a university education. This represents a 33 per cent increase since 1991, and demonstrates the trend toward a knowledge-based economy. In 2001, the average

age of Canada's labour force was 39 years, an increase of two years since 1991. About 7.3 million Canadians were 45 to 64 years of age in 2001, a 4 per cent increase since 1996. Workers 55 years and older comprised 11.8 per cent of the labour force, with a range from 8 per cent in Nunavut to 13 per cent in British Columbia to 15 per cent in Saskatchewan (Statistics Canada, 2003a). In 2001, 15 per cent of Canada's workforce was within 10 years of retirement. By 2011, 50 per cent of the baby boom generation will be 55 and over, and 18 per cent will be over 60 years of age. It is projected that by 2021, 25 per cent of the labour force will be 45–54 years of age, and 1 in 7 workers will be 55 to 64 years of age.

Another trend is that the labour force is shrinking because there are fewer workers owing to lower fertility rates, a linked global economy where more work is performed 'off-shore', increased use of technology, and earlier retirement by older workers. The average or median age at retirement is declining. From the 1960s to the end of the 1990s, the labour force participation rate of 55- to 64-year-old men fell from 87 per cent to 61 per cent; and for those 65 and over, the decrease was from 30 per cent to 10 per cent (Baker et al., 2001). The median retirement age in 2001 was 61 years (Duschene, 2002), although there were variations by occupational group (public administration, 58.4 years; educational services, 57.4; and farming, 68.8).

Those most likely to work beyond 65 years of age are men; those with more education, especially advanced degrees; self-employed persons; those employed in farming, sales, and accounting sectors; and those in specific occupations, such as judges, family doctors, legislators, and religious leaders (Duchesne, 2002). Many of these older workers continue working until 70 or 75 years of age. A recent study (Statistics Canada, 2004) found that 8.4 per cent of seniors were working (an estimated 305,000 people aged 65 and over) in 2001, which reprensented a 20 per cent increase from 1996. About 18 per cent of these senior workers were 75 and older.

The most dramatic shrinkage in Canada's labour force has yet to happen. Over the next 20 to 30 years a retirement wave will evolve as 9.5 million baby boomers retire, with the crest occurring around 2011–12 (MacKenzie and Dryburgh, 2003). Even increased immigration and increased participation rates by women will not offset the projected shortage since fewer younger workers are entering the labour force. Some sectors, such as education, health care, public administration (government employees), and the forestry, mining, oil and gas sectors, will be more affected than others by an aging workforce and the large number of retirements in the next decade (Marshall, 2001a; Hicks, 2003; MacKenzie and Dryburgh, 2003). In 2003, for example, over 50 per cent of those employed in the education and health care sectors were in their late 40s and a large number were managers and professionals. These are leaders in their profession, and they will be difficult to replace all at once.

Both the private and public sectors need to address the changing age structure of the labour force, both in general and in specific occupations and industries. Current social policies encourage people to spend more time in school and retirement and less time in the workforce. Since the skills of older persons are underused, perhaps work opportunities should be more evenly allocated across the life course for those who wish to keep working (Hicks, 2003). Plans to recruit or retain workers in particular sectors and occupations, ranging from bricklayers to family doctors, need to be developed. The projected shortfalls in labour supply by 2011 could be offset by recruiting and attracting highly skilled immigrants for specific occupations; by recruiting, training, or retraining younger workers for specific jobs; or by creating incentives for older workers to delay their retirement or to return to work either full- or part-time.

Another emerging labour force trend is that work and careers are less institutionalized (Henretta, 2003). There is more self-employment; more small 'start-up' companies; and more 'individualized' careers, which are characterized by changing jobs, being in and out of the labour force, and early or partial retirement; and more portable pension plans, which facilitate job mobility. In addition, the location of work is changing. In the 2001 census, over 1.2 million Canadians, or 8 per cent of all workers, reported that they work at home. The likelihood of the home becoming the workplace increases with age, although some companies are encouraging sales and knowledge workers to work from home, thereby reducing office overhead costs for the employer, and the cost of travel, meals, and clothing for the employee.

In addition to concerns raised by the federal government as to whether a shrinking labour force can sustain a pension system for large numbers of retired boomers, additional questions are being asked by employers:

- Will higher wages attract youth or immigrants into occupations where there is a labour shortage or keep older workers in those occupations?

- Will incentives for early retirement need to be replaced by incentives for late retirement?

- Will there be a decline in national productivity and global competitiveness as the workforce gets older and smaller?

- What is the capacity and potential of older adults to continue working, to be retrained, or to be recruited back to work?

- Do older workers experience age discrimination in the workplace?

- Should government and employer policies concerning mandatory retirement be revised?

- Are retirees interested in returning to work and, if so, under what conditions?

Women and Work Histories

In developed countries like Canada, the labour-force participation rate of women has risen dramatically in the last few decades, with over 70 per cent of all Canadian women working part-time or full-time outside the home. Most working women are employed in what are often considered traditional 'female' occupations: clerical, sales or service, teaching, and nursing. However, with increased education, about 20 per cent of women entered 25 non-traditional (previously 'male) occupations between the 1970s and 1990s, with over 80 per cent entering occupations classified as management, professional, or sales. Others entered male-dominated occupations where men were leaving the occupation and where earnings or status were declining (Hughes, 2001). The percentage of employed women in non-standard jobs increased from 35 per cent in 1989 to 41 per cent in 1999. On average, women in these non-traditional occupations earn less than their male co-workers. In effect, many occupations are becoming either more gender-neutral or gender-integrated, and some that were previously dominated by men, such as optician and bartender, are now dominated by women. After 65 years of age, only 3 per cent of women are in the Canadian labour force; for men, the figure is 10 per cent (Statistics Canada, 2002). But, of the workforce aged 65 and over, women's share was 32 per cent in 2001, and will continue rising as younger women enter their senior years (Statistics Canada, 2004).

Although an increase in women's labour-force participation was one of the significant social changes that followed the Second World War, the study of workforce involvement among women was a neglected area of research until the women's movement in the 1970s. Until this time, male work and retirement experiences were considered more important, and male career patterns were used to explain women's experiences in the workforce. In recent years, more research[2] has been devoted to issues concerning labour-force participation rates and patterns of women, the meaning of work for women, gender-based inequities in opportunity, the discontinuous pattern of work for women and its impact on economic security, and the balancing of family and work responsibilities, especially in two-career families. This research has shown that the life course pathway for women at work is neither orderly nor neatly segmented into education, work, and retirement. Rather, career paths for women are closely embedded in, and linked to, family and work responsibilities (Moen and Horn, 2001).Highlight 9.1 summarizes a number of facts about women's participation in the workforce.

Cultural norms, structural inequities, historical events, and personal biographies (involving a partner, raising children, and caring for parents) influence the meaning of work and the career path for women more than for men. Thus, whereas studies of men's involvement in work or careers focus almost exclusively on the work domain, to understand women's involvement in work we must look as well at their family situation across the life course. Although more childless and never-married women pursue continuous and

Highlight 9.1 Women's Participation in the Canadian Workforce

Labour Force Facts and Trends

- More than 81 per cent of women in their prime childbearing years (aged 25–44) were in the paid labour force in 2002.
- Among women aged 45–54, 78 per cent were in the paid work force in 2002.
- Employment rates for women aged 25–44 (percentage of those in the age group who have paid jobs) have increased from 60 per cent in 1982 to 76 per cent in 2002.
- Employment rates for women aged 45-54 rose from 51 per cent in 1982 to 74 per cent in 2002.
- The percentage of women with paid jobs who are employed part-time has changed very little over the past 20 years (27.5 per cent in 1982; 27.7 per cent in 2002).
- Among employed women aged 25–44, the percentage working part-time actually declined from 28 per cent in 1982 to 21 per cent in 2002.
- Among women aged 25–44 who are working part-time, 33 per cent gave caring for children as the reason, but another 29 per cent said they were working part-time because of business conditions or inability to find full-time work.

Work and Family Responsibilities[1]

- Only 23 per cent of mothers of newborns in 2001 were not in the paid labour force.
- Among mothers in paid employment prior to the birth of their child, more than 80 per cent returned or planned to return to paid work within two years.
- Less than 20 per cent of women who gave birth did not plan to return to paid employment; were planning to return but did not know when; or were planning to take longer than two years off.
- Time off for maternity/parental leave is closely related to availability of benefits through Employment Insurance. Since the EI benefit period for maternity/parental benefits was extended from six months to one year in December 2000, the median time at home for women with benefits increased from six months in 2000 to 10 months in 2001.
- Median time off work for self-employed women (who don't qualify for EI benefits) was only one month in both years. Five per cent of mothers of newborns were self-employed in 2001.

[1] These facts, cited by Monica Townson in the workshop, were compiled from a report by Marshall (2003).

Source: Adapted with permission from Monica Townson, based on her presentation at a Gender and Retirement Workshop at Statistics Canada, 6 September 2003.

successful life-long careers, most women still acquire or assume family responsibilities or experience life transitions that significantly influence their work history—marriage, children, divorce, an empty nest, widowhood, parent or grandchild care. Many transitions into and out of the labour force are influenced by these family transition events. Consequently, some mid- and later-life work transitions for women represent a response to earlier unfulfilled life goals once a woman has fewer family responsibilities after her children leave home or if she is divorced or widowed.

The meaning of work and the opportunities for work vary for women in different birth cohorts. Mothers of the baby boomers were less likely to separate work and family experiences and responsibilities. Women in this cohort generally married and followed one of three work patterns: family-oriented and were never employed, even part-time; work-oriented, but took time off from work to look after their children or elderly parents; and continuous work, especially by those with higher levels of education or who were single or who were widowed early in life (Pienta et al., 1994).

In contrast, female baby boomers are 'a generation at work' (Galarneau, 1994). Table 9.1 illustrates the work history of these women into the early 1990s. The first wave (born between 1946 and 1955) entered the labour force in the 1960s, when favourable employment opportuni-ties were available. If married, they gave birth to a first child relatively late in life, but many were childless. The second wave (born 1956 to 1965) joined the labour force earlier and entered occupations with a higher status (the professions, managerial positions, science, and engineering), primarily because of their high educational attainment, combined with more opportunities owing to affirmative-action and pay-equity policies and to less gender discrimination in hiring and promotion.

Recent cohorts of women entering the labour force have encountered less discrimination in the workplace than previous cohorts. As Bernard et al. (1995: 59) noted, the rules, norms, and outcomes of work have traditionally been 'socially constructed and give males an advantage over females.' But as social gains are earned, gendered ageism and discrimination in the workplace are decreasing somewhat, at least, in some sectors of the economy. Consequently, younger cohorts of women experience a 'convergence' model of work in which their work experiences across the life course are more similar to men. At the same time, some younger male peers are assuming a 'convergence' model of family involvement in which there is more sharing of parenting and housework. This more equitable division of family labour has facilitated, to some extent, more gender-equitable opportunities in the labour force, although gender differences

Table 9.1 Employment Rates of Female Baby Boomers (%)

	Age and Year of Employment		
	1971	1981	1991
First Wave (1946–55)	(16–25) 54%	(26–35) 65%	(36–45) 80%
Second Wave (1956–65)		(16–25) 70%	(26–35) 80%

Source: Adapted from Galarneau (1994: Chart 2.1).

remain more pronounced among those in the lower social strata, who have fewer work options (Tremblay, 2001).

Work for some older women late in life may be more important than it is for older men, especially if participation in the labour force began late in life, or if they reach their 'career peak' later in life (Gee and Kimball, 1987: 70–3). However, because of structural constraints and subtle practices of age, gender, and wage discrimination, many middle-aged and older women were forced into marginal occupations, often in the secondary, low-paying service sector rather than in manufacturing or the professions (McDonald and Wanner, 1987, 1990). Recent research suggests that there are few, if any, significant gender differences in the importance of work to an individual and that work is a meaningful, expressive, and satisfying role for women.

To facilitate work opportunities, a variety of work schedules enable women to participate full- or part-time in the labour force in a more continuous pattern throughout the life course. At the *personal* level, a number of factors influence the frequency and pattern of labour-force participation by women in the middle and later years of life. Marital status has the most profound effect. Women who are single, separated, divorced, or widowed are more likely to work, to work full-time, and to work later in life. Married women are most likely to work if they have achieved high levels of education, and if they have a supportive partner. Health and age of children also play an important role in a woman's decision to participate or not in the labour force. At the *societal* level, women are more involved in the labour force because of legislation that prohibits or discourages income and occupational discrimination; the greater availability of day-care or elder-care centres; and the recognition that women can be successful in occupations previously assumed to be the exclusive domain of men, such as engineer, business executive, pilot, or law-enforcement officers.

Older Workers

'Older workers' are defined by most government agencies as those over 45 years of age. Consequently, this category now includes the *entire* baby-boom generation, most of whom are still in the workforce. Yet, with higher levels of education, improved health, and fewer strenuous jobs in most industries (because of automation and new technology), there is no longer a biological or social basis for those in their 40s and 50s to be considered 'older workers' or for age 65 to remain as the retirement age.

At one time, when much of the workforce was engaged in manual labour, people worked until beyond the age of 65 (in agriculture and self-employed situations) without any questions being asked about the competence or productivity of older workers. However, late in the twentieth century, for a number of reasons, it began to be alleged that older workers were, or could be, less productive, less adaptive to change in work requirements, less motivated, and less able or willing to be retrained. These concerns were raised as the economy weakened and downsizing and restructuring were necessary. Reasons were fabricated to justify the unemployment of older versus younger workers, and incentives were used to encourage older workers to retire. Indirectly, retirement incentive packages, along with investment advertisements promoting early retirement (the Freedom 55 theme), created a culture of early retirement wherein employers began to believe that employees wanted an early departure from the labour force. Such views reinforced the emerging devaluation of older workers. Very few employers expressed concern about the loss of experience, knowledge, and skills; the loss of mentors for younger workers; and the loss of an institutional 'memory' when older workers prematurely left the labour force. Moreover, older workers were less likely to be hired or to be offered promotions since younger workers were less expensive and were viewed as better trained and better able to learn new ways of working (McMullin and Marshall, 2001).

The competence and productivity of older workers is referred to whenever the elimination of mandatory retirement is discussed. Those who favour the continuation of mandatory retirement argue that employers should not be forced to keep incompetent, less productive, and unmotivated older employees, and that it would be difficult to assess competence if a case had to be made for firing a 70- or 80-year-old. Ironically, some of these statements are made by politicians or business executives who are older than employees who are forced to cease working at 65 years of age.

These interacting events generate ageism in the labour force through prejudices against older workers and age discrimination by individuals, corporations, the government, and the media. Indeed, mandatory retirement is viewed by many as the most blatant form of age discrimination. Age discrimination is manifested in stereotypical negative views of older workers held by employers and younger workers; in fewer opportunities for older workers to be trained or retrained; in fewer older workers being hired in open competitions; and in restructuring strategies that force older workers to accept an early retirement package. Once out of work, unemployed older workers take longer to find another job, receive a lower salary and fewer benefits than in previous positions, and find that the new job may be only a contract position or temporary or seasonal work. Some of these unemployed older workers eventually abandon the search for work and 'slide' into retirement without ever returning to the labour force (Marshall and Clarke, 1996; Underhill et al., 1997). Ageism in the workforce marginalizes older workers and increases their feelings of powerlessness. On the basis of a study of older garment workers in Montreal, McMullin and Marshall (2001: 114–21) concluded that ageism represents the 'intersection of structured age relations and individual actions. . . . Individuals act

within the structure of age relations to both reinforce and challenge it [ageism]'.

In the United States, the 1967 Age Discrimination in Employment Act (and subsequent revisions) banned discrimination against workers 40 to 70 years of age, and numerous cases of wrongful dismissal due to age have been won by older adults. In Canada, there is no formal labour legislation or law that requires a specific retirement age, except for those in some professions, such as pilots, firefighters, and judges. Rather, forcing an employee to retire because of their age is an issue covered by human rights acts. Canada's Human Rights Act does *not* view retirement at a specific age as discriminatory. And, as of 2004, four provinces (Ontario, Saskatchewan, Newfoundland and British Columbia) do *not* specifically protect workers 65 or older against age discrimination. Thus, in Alberta, Manitoba, New Brunswick, Nova Scotia, Prince Edward Island, Quebec, and the three territories, that mandatory retirement is viewed as a form of age discrimination. To challenge this provincial authority, cases have been taken to the Supreme Court of Canada. But, in a landmark ruling in 1990 that still prevails, the Supreme Court ruled that provincial mandatory retirement policies are a legitimate legal limit on worker's rights and do not violate the Charter of Rights and Freedoms. In support of this majority decision (5–2), it was argued that while the practice of mandatory retirement is inherently discriminatory, overthrowing the traditional retirement age would cause 'social upheaval' and a change such as this should be made by legislation. It was also stated by one member of the Court, who supported the majority decision, that 'work is inextricably tied to the individual's self-identity and self-worth.' This same judge, after he retired, argued that there should be no age discrimination! Obviously, social upheaval has not taken place in the United States, Australia, New Zealand, or in the provinces or territories that have eliminated mandatory retirement. This issue remains on the political agenda—Ontario was considering such legislation as of February 2004.

The Capacity and Performance of Older Workers

Discrimination in the workforce is based on the belief by employers that older workers are less productive, lack physical strength, are slow to learn, have slower reaction times, are forgetful, are afraid of new technology, fear change, are less motivated, and are resistant to re-education or retraining, and that older workers should step aside so that younger people can enter the workforce (Underhill et al., 1997: 32–4; Prager, 2002). What is the evidence concerning the abilities and productivity of older workers? First, most studies find that productivity does not decline with age, assuming average health and motivation. The amount and rate of any decline in physical or cognitive ability is highly variable (Marshall, 2002). Where there is some decline, it is often compensated for by experience or increased motivation in order to remain in the job. Most older workers can adapt to changing work requirements or conditions if they are so motivated. Adaptation varies within individuals at any age and is influenced by such factors as economic necessity, health, family demands, retraining opportunities and support, and the physical demands of the tasks. In reality, there are individual differences in work-related skills and motivation among both younger and older workers.

Work performance at any age is influenced by knowledge, experience, abilities, and personal factors unrelated to work, such as health, marital stress, and alcohol or drug use. Moreover, the stereotypes about older workers are not based on reliable objective measures of productivity, performance, or potential. Some of these views are based on the subjective ratings of performance by supervisors, who may have negative attitudes toward older workers. Stereotypes are often a function of the age of the evaluator: younger evaluators may assess older workers less favourably ('they are less productive or creative than my age peers'), while older evaluators may evaluate older workers more favourably ('older people like myself are loyal, efficient, and experienced workers'). Some older workers, who experience discrimination in hiring after being let go, may leave items off their resume or delete dates to conceal or disguise their chronological age. Highlight 9.2 summarizes research findings about older workers.[3]

Attitudes about, and toward, older workers on the part of managers and Human Resource personnel are changing, especially in small companies where there is more direct contact with older employees. But accurate knowledge is still lacking among some who are responsible for the hiring, supervision, and promotion of all employees. Not only does more research-based information help, but as Marshall (2001) noted, attitudes toward older workers will change and improve as the workforce continues to age; as successive cohorts enter the older-worker category (45 and over) with more education, technical and IT skills; and if the demand for labour creates the need to retain or recruit older workers. In summary, discrimination against older workers is probably due less to personal abilities and chronological age, and more to the economy and the cost of hiring, training, and employing more expensive older workers.

Interventions to Retain or Recruit Older Workers

To enhance the ability of older workers to perform effectively until retirement, or to recruit retirees if labour shortages emerge in specific occupations or sectors, various actions by employers have been proposed:

- moving employees to a new job that is better suited to their abilities
- redesigning jobs, workplaces, or equipment that may make the work unnecessarily difficult and unsatisfying and the workers less productive than they could be.

Highlight 9.2 The Performance and Ability of Older Workers

Prevailing myths concerning the inabilities of older workers, and isolated examples of older adults who perform poorly at work, are invoked to justify the continuation of mandatory retirement, or the dismissal of older employees. The following summary represents research-based facts about older workers.

- In most aspects of work functioning there are age-related declines, but the decline is usually gradual, and most jobs do not require constant performance at the maximum level or capacity.

- On specific measures related to age-performance differences, many older adults function at the same level as younger adults or even above that level.

- Most older people are receptive to using new technology and can acquire the skills if given an opportunity to train and practice. They may, however, need more time to learn and perform than younger people, who are more experienced with information technology.

- Chronological age is not an accurate predictor of job performance. Within all age groups, there are wide differences in productivity. Changes that occur with age may be due to health or personal problems (e.g., the burden of looking after children or parents) or to the type of work, which may involve physical labour or an increasing use of technology.

- Reaction time becomes slower with age, but experience at the task can offset the losses.

- Cognitive capacity at work can improve in later life, and there is little decline in intelligence that affects job performance.

- Older workers are generally more satisfied with their jobs and are less likely to leave an organization for another job.

- Declines in job-related aptitudes or skills do not occur at the same rate. For example, a hearing loss may not be accompanied by a slower reaction time or by a decline in eyesight, and losses that do occur may be compensated for by experience.

- Older workers are absent less often and have fewer accidents than younger workers.

- Older workers score as well as, or better than, younger workers in such areas as creativity, flexibility, and information processing.

- The productivity of older workers can be maintained or enhanced by retraining and by improvements in the workplace, such as better lighting, larger type sizes for printed materials, high-quality computer monitors, or the elimination of background noise.

- developing innovative training strategies adapted to the age of the worker

- allowing working from home, flextime, job sharing, longer vacations, seasonal work, or contract work

- accommodating workers with discontinuous work histories (in particular women and older workers) by offering more flexible pension and health benefits, with job counselling

- developing policies to encourage older workers to remain employed

- making work more meaningful and attractive than full-time leisure for those who enjoy retirement, but whose skills are needed in the workforce

• accommodating older employees who have parental responsibilities through flexible hours, and such benefits as payment for caregiving time away from work, for subsidized home-care workers, or for geriatric care consultants or case managers to perform in-home assessments of older parents.

One innovative mechanism for retaining older workers or facilitating re-entry into the labour force is the establishment of employment centres for retirees who seek volunteer or paid work In Japan, for example, Silver Human Resources Centres are established by the government (Highlight 9.3) to help older people looking for work (Bass and Oka, 1995). In Canada, some private employment agencies specialize in placing older workers in part-time or temporary posi-

tions. These part-time workers fill temporary or seasonal needs ranging from general office tasks to contract positions for experienced executives.

Such centres could be part of new public policies wherein a high value is placed on human capital and the work potential of all citizens, regardless of age. Such a policy could include both paid work and unpaid volunteer work. As part of such a policy, mandatory retirement could be abolished or the age raised; incentives might be introduced to encourage working beyond the normal retirement age; or the payment of retirement benefits could be delayed. In fact, in the United States, anyone born after 1966 will not be eligible to receive a government pension until age 67; and Sweden allows postponement, without penalty, of a pension until 70 years of age (Walker, 2000).

Highlight 9.3 Silver Human Resource Centres in Japan

In Japan, about 30 per cent of men and 15 per cent of women over 65 years of age work, despite mandatory retirement at age 60. Pensions are comparable to those in other industrialized nations, and a strict means (need) test reduces pension payments for 62- to 65-year-olds who work. There are two possible reasons for this high level of labour-force involvement. First, Japan values its older workers, and, second, the government has a policy of expanding the employment options of older people.

Since 1975, Silver Human Resource Centres (SHRCs) have promoted and facilitated the hiring of older part-time workers. In 1986 the Law for the Stability of Employment for the Elderly was passed, and the number of SHRCs increased significantly thereafter. Today, there are over 1,600 SHRCs in local communities throughout Japan, with over 700,000 registered members, who pay annual dues of about ¥5. Each Centre has between 200 and 3000 members. The average age of members is 69 for men and 67 for women. The centres are subsidized by Japan's Ministry of Labour, with a matching grant from the local government, and each SHRC is expected to become self-supporting. A centre creates contract jobs by working with local businesses and individuals. The job categories include technical, semi-skilled, clerical, caretaking services, canvassing, light manual, and home help. In 2001, 67 per cent of the jobs were in the private sector, and 33 per cent in the public sector. About 50 per cent of the jobs could be classified as blue-collar, 30 per cent as office or service work. There are twice as many male members, perhaps because of greater family obligations by women, fewer jobs for women, and the Japanese custom for older women to confine their work to the home. Nevertheless, changes are taking place: over 20 per cent of the women employed through SHRCs had previously never held a job outside the home. Thus, the SHRCs provide work opportunities for older women, even if their work experience is limited.

Source: Adapted from Bass and Oka (1995).

The Process of Retirement

Introduction

Retirement emerged as a social institution with the establishment of social security payments in welfare states,[4] the growth of industrialization and unions that obtained rights to a pension and retirement, and an increased importance attached to leisure and consumption in daily life.[5] Today, this ideal is promoted commercially as 'freedom 55' by the investment and travel industry—save and invest wisely (with us!) so you can retire and enjoy a life of leisure by age 55.

At the institutional level, retirement is shaped by social and economic factors across time, and at specific periods in history. Government legislation and employer pension plans provide incentives or requirements to retire at specific ages. Even where mandatory retirement has been abolished, employers use pension incentives to encourage the retirement of some or all employees (Klassen and Gillin, 1999; Henretta, 2003). As well, retirement and the economic 'benefits' attached to retirement are intimately linked to an individual's location, throughout the life course, in the gender, class, and ethnic structure of society (Phillipson, 1998). Retirement is yet another example of how the life course is a gendered experience and of how a social process is influenced by class and ethnic background. McDonald and Wanner (1990: 15) noted that 'retirement not only concerns older Canadians, it concerns all of us and is inextricably bound to the socioeconomic and political structures of Canadian society, which have been shaped by particular historical circumstances.'

Retirement will continue to be shaped by the political, economic, and social forces operating throughout your life. Indeed, your retirement and economic status in later life will not be determined solely by your working life, your biography, or your lifetime earnings and savings. Rather, your later life will be influenced by factors beyond your individual control, such as global and national inflation and unemployment rates; fertility rates, which influence the dependency ratio and the size of the labour force; the national debt; public- and private-sector policies concerning retirement and pensions; the degree of gender inequality in work and career opportunities, wages, and pension; and immigration policies that affect the size and composition of the labour force. In 2003, for example, after four years of significant stock market losses, some people approaching retirement began postponing their retirement. Many lost 25 per cent or more of their retirement nest egg and joked about a new slogan, 'Freedom 95, Feet First', as a replacement for the 'Freedom 55' theme.

Historically, government and employers have controlled the institution of retirement and individuals have had little choice as to when and how to retire. In recent years, however, there is more individual choice as to when and how one leaves the workforce. Some people have sufficient savings to retire early. Some retire fully; others become part of the 'contingent workforce' (Quadagno and Hardy, 1996) where they work casually or seasonally through short term contracts or consulting. Others may start their own business. Primarily, it is those with higher levels of education, greater savings, and some managerial experience who are successful in this type of contingent work. More often the decision is 'forced' when firms offer early retirement incentive packages, either through a collective agreement, or when the economy weakens and the labour force needs to be reduced.

For some, the economic benefits of accepting an early-retirement package are preferable to refusing the package and risking being laid off as a result of downsizing. A more common type of forced retirement in recent years results from being 'laid off' or 'fired' if one is 50 or older. Unable to obtain full-time employment thereafter, these people work at a series of full- or part-time 'bridge jobs' in later life for financial or psychological reasons. Usually, these 'bridge' positions pay a low wage and offer few or no benefits, but they span the period until the person is eligible for a government pension (Henretta, 2001).

The Concept of Retirement

In addition to being an important economic institution, retirement is an event, a process, and an increasingly lengthy stage in life. Retirement is one of the best examples of the constant interaction between the processes of individual and population aging. It is yet another example of how individual biographies intersect with institutional requirements and benefits. The meaning and experience of retirement, within and across

cohorts, varies depending on the personal situation of the retirees, and on societal policies, social norms, and cultural traditions pertaining to retirement at a given period in history. Just as the retirement experience of your parents may differ from that of your grandparents, so too may your work history and retirement experiences differ from those reported in the current literature. Highlight 9.4 itemizes the many individual and societal-level factors influencing retirement decisions and lifestyles.

Because work is often viewed as a central organizing principle of life, the departure from the labour force is considered a major transition in the life course (Henretta, 2003). Thus, much of

---

Highlight 9.4 Individual and Societal Factors Influencing Retirement Decisions and Lifestyles

Individual

- Work history (regular versus irregular, full-time versus part- time)
- Partner's work history, and age
- Economic status (earnings, savings, investments, entitlement to public and private pensions)
- Health status (perceived, objective)
- Leisure interests and experiences
- Informal support (family, friends)
- Attitudes toward retirement
- Personal factors
  - Age
  - Sex
  - Social class
  - Education
  - Race or ethnicity
  - Marital status

Societal

- Labour-force requirements (past, present, and future re: unemployment benefits)
- Economic history (periods of inflation, recessions, amount of government debt)
- Leisure opportunities (government programs and services)
- Formal support (subsidized housing, transportation, home care)
- Legislation and policies for retirement and social security (mandatory versus voluntary, availability of private and public pensions, vesting, portability)
- Demographic factors
  - Fertility rates
  - Mortality rates
  - Immigration rates and policies
  - Life expectancy
  - Disability-free life expectancy
  - Sex ratio
  - Dependency ratio

the early research on retirement concentrated on the (male) individual's preparation for, and adjustment to, mandatory retirement at age 65 or on the meaning of the 'event'. Today, retirement is thought of as a process, linked to one's work history and economic status, that occurs over a period of time, rather than being a one day event and a final stage in life.

The transition from work to retirement has become blurred, and there is considerable diversity in how and when working life ends, if it ever ends. Consequently, it is much more difficult to determine the percentage of people who are retired, and to arrive at a clear definition of 'retired'. Some older adults are refusing to retire if given a choice, while others retire but then return to work full- or part-time for a salary or as a volunteer. Statistics Canada (2002) reported that almost half of those who have retired are back in the workforce within two years. This is especially likely for men and for those who left involuntarily.

As a process, retirement is a moral or legal requirement that, sooner or later, most workers experience. In return for leaving the workforce, some financial security is provided by the government and perhaps, depending on work history, by a pension from the public or private sector. In addition, by attaining the age of 60 or 65, some people are eligible for varying levels of subsidized health care, social services (such as housing subsidies), or leisure activities through 'senior' discounts. The payment of a guaranteed wage through social-security benefits after retirement was introduced to shift the burden of support from the individual and the family to the state. These payments were intended to release older workers from the burden of work and to enable younger workers to enter the labour force (Snell, 1996). Today, as we will see later, governments are attempting to shift more of the responsibility for financial support in later life back to the individual.

As a dynamic process, retirement involves interaction between individual and societal factors. Much of the early research focused on individual factors—occupational differences, health, financial situation, and attitudes toward work and retirement. Today, retirement is thought of as an interactive process involving the individual, the employer (who sets policies and provides benefits), and society through cultural values, legislation regarding mandatory retirement, the state of the economy, and social security regulations. Consequently, we study the effect of retirement on individuals, the place of employment, and society.

Pre-Retirement Attitudes and Preparation

Most studies find that, before the transition, over 80 per cent of older respondents report favourable attitudes toward retirement. Generally, positive attitudes toward retirement are associated with good health, high income, a high level of education, and a high degree of support from significant others in the family and from peers at work concerning the approaching event. Those with unfulfilled leisure interests often report more favourable attitudes to retirement and look forward to 'pursuing their leisure dreams' while they are still healthy. They seldom think, 'What if I remain healthy until 85 or 90, yet retire at 55 to 60?' Generally, studies find that the younger the age at which a respondent is questioned about retirement, the more favourable the response. The reason may be that the event is further away, retirement and early retirement are becoming more socially acceptable, or pension plans may be more satisfactory than those available to earlier retiree cohorts. In short, retirement is being viewed less and less as a crisis by most people.

In contrast, negative attitudes are often related to a fear of financial difficulties in retirement, to a high degree of interest in, and satisfaction with work, or to work being the major or only life interest. For these individuals, retirement is an unwanted crisis that is to be postponed or avoided. Thus, a person's attitudes towards work or retirement influences the timing of retirement. Highlight 9.5 illustrates three types of pre-retirement images (positive, ambivalent/uncertain, and negative) expressed by 50- to 60-year-old professionals.

Theoretically, planning for retirement should help with decisions as to when and how to retire and should ensure a smooth transition, at a time compatible with an older worker's wishes. In reality, older workers do not devote much, if any, time to planning for retirement, nor do many take part in pre-retirement planning programs. Thus, as workers approach the normal retirement age, there is avoidance and a lack of strategic planning concerning timing and how they will spend their later years. Indeed, many do not know or enquire far in advance about their retirement benefits, especially income (Ekerdt and Hackney, 2002). The topic is avoided to some degree because of the many uncertainties about what might happen during retirement—the declining health of one or both partners; financial needs if retirement continues for 20–30 years before death; the state of the economy during the retirement years; and how to use time in an interesting and meaningful way without five days of work to fill much of the week.

To help people adjust to retirement, pre-retirement programs are offered by some employers or by private entrepreneurs. These programs range from a brief conversation about retirement benefits between the retiree and a human resources officer during the last week of work, to comprehensive educational programs that begin a number of months or years before the retirement date. The more comprehensive programs involve discussions about finances, health, post-retirement employment options, leisure opportunities, and community resources. Programs that provide facts and information are usually presented to a large group through lectures or printed material. Programs that offer assistance in personal adjustment are conducted in small discussion groups or personal counselling sessions. Most are voluntary and may or may not include a spouse or common-law partner.

Although it has been demonstrated that pre-retirement planning through informal or formal programs is an important factor in the initial adjustment to retirement, few employers offer this service. To fill this void, pre-retirement planning programs are provided by private consultants. Some of these programs involve the purchase of some type of investment plan; others offer seminars for a fee. Whether these programs are effective and lead to a successful retirement remains to be confirmed, especially since they tend to ignore individual differences in health, finances, and past lifestyle. The following guidelines can help older workers plan for and adjust to retirement:

- Plan early.
- Maintain flexibility in interests and social roles.
- Remain physically and socially active.
- Plan a gradual transition from work to retirement.
- Take a 'trial run' before a final commitment is made to a new community or lifestyle.
- Consult with spouse, friends, and children about short- and long-term retirement plans.

Retirement Decision Making and Timing

Decision Making

As early retirement becomes more common, whether voluntary or imposed, decisions about retirement are becoming more embedded in mid-life (Ekerdt et al., 2000). This results in a greater emphasis on saving money, trying different leisure skills or visiting vacation sites, developing skills for a subsequent job, and the development of an individual's and couple's timetables for leaving the workforce. Agency is a factor in the transition, and retirement timing is becoming more individualized. Highlight 9.6 lists structural and individual factors to consider when making a decision to retire before the mandatory age.

Highlight 9.5 Images of Retirement among 50- to 60-Year-Old Professionals

Positive Images

'I'm 59 and pretty much committed to the idea of retirement at 63. I think I want to try out new experiences. In retrospect it's what I've done all along, trying this and then that . . . not out of a feeling of frustration but more curiosity. I've always had the exploring urge. I'm interested in getting involved more in world government in an active way rather than just passive support.'

'I pick up the newspaper every day and see a couple of guys in their early fifties are dying. So, you say to yourself, wouldn't it be a lousy thing to work all this time and never get to travel or read the books [you want to]? And it would be wonderful to finally have the time to sit down [and do what you want]. When you're 30 life stretches out forever.'

Uncertainty or Ambivalence Images

'Barring unforeseen events, I'll continue what I'm doing, adding variety where I can and building in what you may call retirement activities. I've toyed with the idea—don't tell my wife—of an art gallery, where I could bring in money. I became interested in business when I started my practice and realized how much of a business it is.'

'Well, you know, I keep reading these things about how one should be ready [for retirement]. At the same time I don't dwell on it. But you can't help think about it. Many of my friends are retired or close to retiring. Many of them are extremely productive in their sixties and seventies. I mean, these things come to my mind.'

'When I think about it [retirement], I think that I'm not prepared for it. I'm a little bit concerned about it. If I can work until 70 I will work, assuming that one still has one's marbles. For me work is really very important. . . . I guess the time to think about retirement would be about five years before you do it. [But] I can't imagine ever giving up work.'

Negative Images

'I was surprised to see how many retired people . . . I knew who would come back and talk about it. They all appeared to be happy, but when you asked them, all they did was play golf down in Florida with the same people all the time. I couldn't think of anything more appalling than to have that at 60 years old. I made up my mind that I wasn't going to get myself into that trap. I wasn't frightened in any way of death, but of retirement. What the hell would I do?'

'I get shivers thinking about not working. I'd hate to sit in a park. I just can't think of getting to that point. Retirement is death. As I see retirement, I don't see it as a happy time at all.'

'The way I think about retirement is that it's not a period of my life. I don't plan to retire [laughs]. I don't need to. I'm having lots of fun now. The things I'm doing I should be able to do fairly long. I can play the piano until I'm 90. People keep operating as a therapist as long as they keep their head.'

Highlight 9.6 Factors That Encourage an Early Retirement

Institutional and Structural Factors

- A labour market characterized by high unemployment among all ages. This situation may provide economic advantages to retire early and receive retirement benefits, rather than remain employed and risk being let go without an incentive package.

- Policies that permit partial or total pension payments to be received at 55 or 60 years of age after a specified number of years of employment.

- A lowering or elimination of the fixed limit on earnings above which old-age security benefits may not be claimed. This enables an individual to retire with a private pension and still remain eligible to receive old-age security (even if he or she works part-time and earns a salary).

- Threats to raise the mandatory retirement age, which encourage some workers to leave the labour force early.

- A forced horizontal or downward change in jobs, or a reclassification to a lower job category.

- Changing societal norms that make early retirement more socially acceptable.

- Union-management agreements on the maximum number of years of employment (such as 'thirty and out'), and then retirement with full benefits.

- The restructuring, downsizing, or closing of a company, especially if accompanied by an early-retirement incentive plan.

Personal Factors

- Accumulated savings and wealth that are sufficient to support the retiree and partner for an unknown number of years. This is more likely if the person has no mortgage, few dependents, large savings, or a large pension.

- A decline in health, or a disability that cannot be compensated for by a change to a more suitable job.

- A desire to change the way one lives, and having savings, equity in a home, and private pension benefits that will ensure an acceptable standard of living.

- Positive attitudes toward retirement, which is considered to be a satisfying stage in life.

- Support from one's partner and other family members.

- Being single or having few dependents.

- Employment in a physically demanding job where tasks are becoming more difficult.

- Making early and definite plans for retirement.

- Being dissatisfied with one's job while at the same time having some economic security.

A case study of 25 employees in a telecommunications company (Robertson, 2000) found that acceptance of an early retirement incentive plan (ERIP) after an average of 30 to 36 years of employment with the company was influenced by three general factors:

- First, there were personal reasons—'the timing was right', 'the financial package appeared lucrative and too good to refuse'; 'I was ready for a change'; and, 'the ERIP was a better choice than being forced to change job location or type of job', which in some cases is the alternative to an ERIP.

- Secondly, there were major changes occurring in the company—technological advances that necessitated retraining, changes in corporate culture, including a more impersonal and bureaucratic management style and demands for higher productivity.

- The third factor involved changes in the larger industry—the telecom industry was experiencing high levels of competitiveness which required restructuring, mergers, closures of plants, and massive layoffs of workers. Thus, fear of an uncertain employment future influenced the decision to retire early. Interestingly, despite these company and industry factors, most viewed the decision as their choice.

Increasingly, in addition to work place factors, family and health matters are influencing retirement decisions.[6] Some family factors include the work career history and expectations of the partner; whether there are dependent children (as there may be in a late marriage or re-marriage) or grandchildren in the household; whether one or two incomes or pensions are available or needed; the health of each partner; the quality of the marriage, i.e., whether more time together will be more or less enjoyable; and whether aging parents need to be looked after. Being widowed or divorced in mid- or late life usually triggers a decision to work longer. Discussions between the partners about personal wishes influences whether there will be 'joint' or 'out-of-synch' retirements. No longer do these decisions primarily, or only, revolve around retirement decisions by men. It is not unusual for men to retire first and become househusbands while their partner continues to work, perhaps for a number of years if she is much younger or a late entrant to the labour force.

Mandatory versus Voluntary Retirement

Mandatory retirement is often criticized and is periodically challenged in the courts. The main issues are these: Is mandatory retirement a form of age discrimination that denies individuals a choice—to work or not to work? Does it violate constitutional rights to equal treatment? Does it serve a useful social purpose by facilitating the movement of new workers into the labour force?

In the 1990 Supreme Court of Canada decision involving a group of professors and physicians who argued that mandatory retirement violated their rights under the Canadian Charter of Rights, arguments against mandatory retirement included examples of great achievements by gifted and productive older people. After much debate, the court upheld mandatory retirement. Those in favour argued that there was no stigma attached to being retired at age 65, that for those employed in a public institution, such as a university or hospital, any infringement of equal rights is justified under Section 1 of the Charter as a 'reasonable limit' in a democratic society, and that mandatory retirement treats everyone the same over a period of time. In other cases, the courts have relied on stereotypical 'evidence' that older workers are less competent than younger workers. In doing so, they have failed to provide older workers with protection against age-based discrimination (Klassen and Gillin, 1999). Consequently, mandatory retirement is permitted under the Charter, but some provinces and territories have made it illegal.

When retirement is voluntary, people feel that they have more control over the decision. As a result, voluntary retirees, compared with involuntary retirees, often engage in more planning for retirement; have a higher retirement income; report better health and higher levels of satisfaction with retirement; and, in general, have more favourable attitudes toward retirement.

Faced with the two competing alternatives of mandatory and voluntary retirement, the public and private sectors have debated which policy is best. Proponents of a flexible and voluntary retirement policy argue that mandatory retirement

- is a form of age discrimination that violates human rights, especially the freedom to make a choice;

- forces an experienced and skilled worker out of the labour force, whose skill is thus lost to society;

- increases government debt because many of those beyond the mandatory age are supported by social-security payments, especially those with an irregular work history, in particular, women, immigrants, and people with disabilities;

- contributes to alienation, isolation, and dissatisfaction in some older adults; and

- is based on chronological age rather than functional age or work capacity in the later years of life.

Those who support mandatory retirement at a specific chronological age argue that

- reliable tests of competence are not available, and therefore all individuals are treated equally with respect to the timing of their departure from the labour force;

- less competent or less motivated workers are not required to take competence tests that might reveal their weaknesses, and older workers are protected against being forced out of the labour force before the mandatory age;

- mandatory retirement promotes mobility within the labour force, allowing middle-aged workers to be promoted and younger workers to enter the labour force;

- the pension system is more stable because required payments over a number of years can be predicted accurately; and

- mandatory retirement at a specific age ensures public safety and a high level of performance in occupations involving the operation of a vehicle or aircraft.

Adjustment to Retirement

Individual adaptive strategies after retirement involve adjustments to losing the work role and work friends, to a perceived loss of identity and self-worth, to loss of income, to increased free time, to declining health, and to increased time spent with one's partner. If the retirement process involves an unstable exit via a series of 'bridge' jobs or chronic unemployment after a stable career with one company, there can be adverse effects on health (Marshall et al., 2001b; Drentea, 2002). And, if the health of one or both partners declines and caregiving is the major retirement activity, health may decline further and stress is created in the partnership. Similarly, if partners spend more time together following retirement and have few common interests or activities, the relationship may become more stressful than before retirement. Partners can also disagree about where and how they will spend the retirement years and about who should do the housework.

Most research finds that over 70 per cent of repondents have few problems in adjusting to retirement. The transition is easier and more satisfying for those with good health and wealth; for those who have a harmonious marriage and support from a partner and family; for those who continue to participate in social activities; for those with a positive attitude toward leisure; and for those with positive attitudes toward retirement. Those who do not adjust well to retirement either return to the workforce or remain dissatisfied, and often experience a decline in physical or mental health.

Women and the Retirement Process

Just as the study of widowhood for men has been neglected, so too has the effect of retirement on women. As McDonald (2002) noted, because women were invisible in the workplace, they were invisible in the development of legislation and in the early research about retirement.[7] The traditional view held by legislators was that a woman's welfare in later life is tied to her legal male partner or to her children. At first, researchers (mainly men) were concerned primarily with how wives (common-law couples were seldom studied) reacted to their partner's retirement, how retirement affected the marital relationship, and how the adjustment of the husband could be facilitated by his wife! Retirement is no longer a male-only process, and consequently, there is a need to study within-gender retirement issues rather than compare women to men (Price, 2000).

When the work history of women was characterized by discontinuous or random employment, retirement was considered a 'foreign' concept for women. They did not work long enough to accumulate pension rights or to 'talk about' retirement in the traditional sense that applied to men who were in the labour force throughout adulthood. But with higher participation rates by women in the labour force, some for as many years as men, the retirement process for women must be understood, especially given the employment history of baby-boomer women, many of whom will retire late in life after a full career.[8]

Compared with men, women reach retirement 'with fewer financial resources, less preparation for retirement, and a different work and family history' (McDonald and Wanner, 1990: 94). Many women enter and leave the workforce because of the gendered division of family responsibility for child rearing or caring for parents, or to follow a partner whose job required him to move to another city. Moreover, women are less likely to work full-time, they are usually paid less than men, they are more likely to be employed in low-skill service positions, and they are less likely to have a pension.

Some women have less attachment to the workforce and, perhaps, a broader interpretation of the meaning of retirement. They may feel this way because of the discontinuous nature of their work history; their greater involvement in part-time, less career-oriented work; their greater economic dependence on a partner, and their major responsibility for domestic labour, which continues in retirement. If women do return to the labour force full-time in their 40s or 50s, they are more likely to retire early. Indeed, feminist scholars such as Calasanti (1993: 143) argue that women do not 'retire' from the labour force. Rather, they 'merely acquire more freedom to schedule domestic work during normal 'working' hours rather than restricting these responsibilities to evenings and weekends'.

For women, the timing and process of retirement is becoming increasingly diverse. Some studies have found that women are less likely than men to make plans for retirement or to pick a specific time in advance (Marshall, 1995a). The factors influencing both the timing of retirement and women's adjustment to retirement include a change in marital status, i.e., being divorced or widowed, which results in a later retirement; the retirement of a partner, which may lead to an early retirement, as does the unexpected need to care for an elderly parent, an adult child, or grandchildren; and restructuring at the place of employment, which may lead to earlier retirement. Consequently, women often have less choice than men as to when and how they retire. It is much more likely that women retire at the same time as a partner, rather than vice versa, although if a partner is much older, a woman may retire later to fulfill her career ambitions.

Evidence concerning the adjustment of women to retirement is contradictory. Some studies have found that retired older women are less well-adjusted than working older women, although both groups are more satisfied than homemakers who have not worked. Other studies report that there are no gender differences in overall well-being after retirement or in attitudes toward retirement. Some argue that women adapt to retirement more easily because work was not a central role in their life, they are used to living without paid work, and they continue to perform domestic work and fulfill family responsibilities whether they 'work' or not (Bernard et al., 1995). Women may spend 20 or more years in retirement. But they do so, in general, after a much shorter work history involving lower wages and few, if any, pension benefits. Women may require a longer period of adjustment, especially if they hold negative attitudes toward retirement and if they retire involuntarily. As McDonald and Wanner (1990: 116) suggested, women may retire in a more 'disorderly fashion' than men.

Economic Security in Later Life

Introduction

To live independently, with dignity, and at an acceptable or adequate standard of living, individuals and society, jointly, strive to ensure the economic security of all citizens. After retirement, economic security involves being eligible to receive a continuous income that is protected from inflation and that protects a partner (usually women) after the death of the primary wage earner. The meaning or level of economic security varies according to how individuals and governments define 'adequate income', 'poverty', or 'insecurity'. These definitions vary by social status; culture; historical period; geographical region; the state of the economy; and social and demographic phenomena, such as a trend toward early retirement, an increased life expectancy, a decrease in fertility rates, or a shortage of younger workers. Thus, the economic status of older persons, in Canada and globally, ranges from extremely wealthy to very poor. In much of the world, especially developing countries, the economic status of older people is similar to that experienced earlier in life—namely, they continue to live in poverty or near poverty (England, 2001, 2002).

Economic insecurity is created by a uncertainty about one's financial future. A person's standard of living may be lowered by the loss of a job, a divorce, the death of a spouse (particularly for women), the onset of a disability, deteriorating health, or an unexpected retirement. Societal changes such as high inflation, the collapse of a stock market, decreased fertility rates, or a shift in government policies pertaining to pensions, social security[9], or medical care in the later years also have a significant impact on economic status in later life (Brown, 1991: 3–6).

The provision of economic security in later life, which began in the early 1900s, was designed to shift responsibility from the individual to the state. In Canada, the Pension Act of 1918 provided assistance for war veterans only. The first universal pension plan, introduced in 1927 (the Old Age Pension Act), paid $20 a month at age 70 and beyond (at a time when few reached or lived beyond this age). However, this was not a universal plan since a means test determined whether an older person needed the $20. This test was imposed because it was still an expectation that adult children would support their elderly parents, and the financial situation of adult children was included as part of the means test for their parents. It was not until 1952 that a universal Old Age Security (OAS) system was introduced, which paid $40 per month to *all* Canadians over 65 years of age. The OAS system was enhanced in 1966 by the Canada Pension and Quebec Pension Plans (CPP/QPP), in 1967 by the need-based Guaranteed Income Supplement (GIS), and in 1975 by the Spousal Allowance (SPA) for widowed partners (aged 60–4) of OAS recipients.

These programs represented a social contract between the state and all citizens. A contract is also created between generations by which income is redistributed from workers to the retired and from younger to older adults. This redistribution is a 'pay as you go' (PAYG) system in which each generation contributes a portion of its earnings and taxes to support or subsidize members of retired cohorts. As long as there are enough workers employed on a regular basis to meet the projected payments to retirees, the system remains in equilibrium. But, as we have seen in earlier discussions about apocalyptic demography, if unemployment shrinks the labour force, if longevity increases, and if older workers retire before age 65, the PAYG system might run short of funds. Hence, taken to the extreme apocalyptic argument, the economic and social security systems could become bankrupt. However, as we have seen, since CPP contributions have been increased and tax clawbacks instituted, it is highly unlikely that the system will go bankrupt, even when the large baby boom cohort is fully retired. Indeed, as a recent report indicated, the financial reserves in Canada's major retirement programs almost doubled in constant (inflation-adjusted) dollars from to 1990 to 2001 (Statistics Canada, 2003d). In reality, it is private company pension plans that are in more danger today given their stock market losses in the 1998–2003 period. Moreover, some large companies have declared bankruptcy, and both current and former employees have lost their pensions.

The following sections examine Canada's economic retirement system, the economic status of older persons, and issues related to the retirement income of individuals, including the meaning of an 'adequate' income, consumer expenditures, poverty in later life, and the feminization of poverty. Important challenges we will face in the next 20 to 30 years include the following:

- a decrease in the number of workers

- shorter work careers as more years are spent on education and many people take early retirement

- an ever changing mix of philosophy, practice (defined benefits versus defined contributions in private plans, the relative balance of private versus public pensions to provide adequate income), and legislation (should benefits be taxed or not? should RRSP annual contribution limits be increased?) concerning the relative responsibility of the state and the individual to provide an adequate retirement income.

The Retirement-Income System in Canada

Canada's retirement-income system is a dual system in which a basic minimal income is provided by the state through the OAS, GIS, and SPA; and additional income is provided by the state pension system (the CPP/QPP), by private employer pension plans, and by individual savings and investments, including RRSPs. The considerable diversity in economic status among older people is related to education, work history, gender, marital history, consumption and savings patterns over the life course, whether they were renters or homeowners, occupation, and employment status in the retirement years (Highlight 9.7).

At best, income-security systems ensure that most citizens receive an adequate replacement income after they retire so they do not experience economic hardship. Most pension systems are designed to replace between 66 per cent and 80 per cent of a person's pre-retirement income. This level is thought to be sufficient because retirees have lower expenses since they spend less on clothes, they no longer pay union dues, and have less need of transportation; because they no longer contribute to government or employer pension plans or RRSPs; their homes are usually mortgage-free; they receive income- or age-based tax breaks; and they may be eligible for discounts and subsidies, such as free drugs, reduced fares on public transportation, and low-income housing.

An income-security system cannot eliminate income inequality in later life, but it can reduce inequality, at least among some retirees. Less than

Highlight 9.7 The Diversity of Economic Status in Later Life

Mr and Mrs A.

Mr A., now 63, took early retirement at age 61 from his position as vice-president, sales, at a large national food company. A large private pension, CPP benefits, and numerous investments and savings provide Mr and Mrs A. with a combined annual income of over $120,000. Owners of a cottage and a condominium, they winter in the southern United States in an affluent retirement community. Mr A. makes frequent trips back to Canada as a consultant to various food companies.

Mrs B.

Widowed for over 10 years, Mrs B., at age 70, receives small CPP, OAS, and GIS benefits, plus a provincial income supplement. Her deceased husband, who worked for over 40 years as a garage mechanic, never contributed to a private pension plan. Mrs B. worked periodically throughout her life, but spent most of these earnings on mortgage payments or home improvements. While she has some Canada Savings Bonds and owns her home, her annual income seldom exceeds $25,000. With rising property taxes and home-maintenance costs, she may be forced to sell her home, find cheaper housing, and use the proceeds from the sale to survive.

Mr and Mrs C.

Mr C., now 62, was forced to retire at age 58 because of a severe back problem. He receives a disability pension and a much-reduced private pension because of his forced early retirement. Mrs C. earns the minimum wage working as a waitress five evenings a week. Together, their combined income from investments, savings, social security benefits, and earnings is $35,000.

Mr D.

Mr D., a 68-year-old widower, immigrated to Canada 11 years ago to live with his son. Before he was forced to retire last year because of ill health, Mr D. had worked as an unskilled labourer in the construction industry. He is not eligible to receive full OAS benefits because he lived in Canada for only eight years before age 65. His monthly income is less than $500, which he gives to his son in return for housing and care. He has no other source of income and is financially dependent on his son and daughter-in-law.

50 per cent of all paid workers are covered by a private (employer) pension plan, and fewer than 10 per cent over 65 years of age report that a retirement pension or annuity is their major source of income (Cheal and Kampen, 1998). At present, beneficiaries of the CPP can expect, according to assumptions inherent in the system, to receive only about 25 per cent of their average pre-retirement wage. Thus, most retired Canadians are dependent on additional levels of public or personal support. A few studies have shown that the public system helps to 'level out', but not eliminate, income inequality in later life that was created by earlier or life-long economic disadvantages. The primary reason for this convergence in income during retirement is that government benefits (OAS, C/QPP) are more important than wages as a source of income. The system is more generous to those at or near the bottom of the socio-economic scale (Myles, 2000; Prus, 2000,

2003). However, as we will learn later, there are still many older people who live in or near poverty—unattached older women, especially widows; those with less education, who probably had intermittent work histories with low wages; immigrants and Aboriginal people; and those with chronic health problems that reduced their work opportunities or forced them to retire early.

Canada's retirement-support system has three levels, and it represents a mix of government and individual responsibility for ensuring an adequate income in later life (Brown, 1991: 37–53; Oderkirk, 1996a, 1996b, National Council of Welfare, 1999, Denton et al., 2000, Baker et al., 2001, McDonald, 2002). The first two levels, the federal public system, are intended to provide a reasonable, but modest, financial base that individuals must supplement with pri-

vate pensions and savings. As well, some provinces and territories provide income supplements or tax credits to low-income older people.

The first public level includes three programs: Old Age Security (OAS), Guaranteed Income Supplement (GIS), and the Allowance (formerly known as the Spousal Allowance [SPA] before common-law partners, including same-sex partners, were eligible for OAS and CPP benefits). Individuals must apply for these benefits. Currently, about 4 million Canadians receive the OAS benefit (about $460 a month), while an additional 1.5 million receive the GIS (which pays a maximum of about $550 a month). The second public level is the Canada Pension Plan (CPP) or, for residents of Quebec, the Quebec Pension Plan (QPP). Highlight 9.8 presents details about these programs, along with a website that provides cur-

Highlight 9.8 Canada's Retirement Income System[1]

Old Age Security Pension (OAS)

- Paid monthly starting at age 65, but a portion (a 'clawback') is repaid to the government if annual income exceeds a specified threshold, which is linked to inflation (about $58,000 in 2003).

- About 5 per cent of recipients receive reduced OAS pensions, while about 2 per cent lose the entire amount once their net income exceeds $94,000.

- The maximum payable per month is about $500.

- Every Canadian citizen who has maintained a legal residence in Canada for 10 years after age 18 is eligible.

- The amount of the OAS payment is adjusted every three months according to the Consumer Price Index.

- Canadians residing outside Canada are eligible if they lived a minimum of 20 years in Canada.

- Benefits can still be received if a person is employed after age 65.

Guaranteed Income Supplement (GIS)

- Designed to assist low-income elderly people.

- A non-taxable monthly payment based on the income of an individual, plus that of his or her spouse or common-law partner. If combined income exceeds about $32,000 (2003 limit), an individual or couple is ineligible to receive a GIS payment.

continued

Hightlight 9.8 continued

The Allowance

- A monthly, non-taxable allowance paid between the ages of 60 and 64 to low-income spouses or common-law partners of OAS pensioners, and to widowed persons 60–64 if their income does not exceed a set limit (about $24,500 in 2003).

- At age 65, recipients are eligible to receive OAS .

Canada /Quebec Pension Plan (C/QPP)

- A compulsory insurance plan funded equally by contributions from the employer and the employee; self-employed people pay the full amount. Contributions are tax-deductible.

- An insurance plan that provides disability and survivor benefits to a partner and dependent children.

- A 'pay-as-you-go' plan in which current contributions of the employed pay for the pensions of those who are retired.

- Pays a monthly, but reduced, pension to retired people 60–4; a full pension at age 65; or an enhanced pension if payment of the benefit does not begin until 70 years of age.

- Payments are taxable.

- Benefits are indexed every January to reflect the annual cost of living—the maximum payment in 2003 was about $800 a month.

- The C/QPP is designed to replace about 25 per cent of pre-retirement earnings.

- A disability benefit is paid to those under 65 who have CPP credits and who cannot work.

- A lump-sum death benefit is paid to a deceased contributor's estate.

- Drop-out periods (up to 15 per cent of the years between ages 18 and 65), for people with no or low earnings (owing to disability, maternity or child rearing leave, or unemployment), are excluded in the calculation of pensionable earnings.

- Benefits must be shared with a divorced spouse.

Private Pension Plans (RRPs and RRSPs)

- Individual retirement savings plans permit a maximum annual contribution of $14,000, as of 2003, which is tax-deductible.

- After two years of employment, benefits are 'vested' or 'locked in' and can be used only for retirement income.

- Any early withdrawals are taxable.

- At the end of one's sixty-ninth year, RRPs and RRSPs must be converted to an annuity or a Registered Retirement Investment Fund (RRIF), and taxes must be paid on all withdrawals.

- Upon death, pension benefits continue for a designated partner, although not all private pension plans consider a same-sex partner as an eligible beneficiary.

[1]For current payment rates and regulations of Canada's public income security system, see http://www.hrdc-drhc.gc.ca, and click on 'Canada's Retirement Income System'.

rent information about regulations and current payment rates.

To counter apocalyptic fears, and to guarantee sustainability of the OAS and CPP programs, changes were introduced in 1998. These included: an increase in contributions by employees from 5.9 per cent of earnings to 9.9 per cent by 2004; an increase in the reserve fund from the equivalent of two years of total benefits owed to the equivalent of five years of benefits; and a new investment policy to generate higher rates of return on the invested funds.

The third level of the income-security system includes *private* pensions and individual savings and investments. These elements require long-term planning and discipline if they are to ensure a secure financial future. Only about 40 per cent of Canadian workers are covered by a private (employer) pension plan. There are two types of employer pension plans: *defined benefits* (DB), in which a specific, guaranteed monthly benefit is paid upon retirement according to a formula based on average earnings in the last three to five years of employment, plus years of service with the employer; and *defined contributions* (DC), in which the benefit paid after retirement varies by the amount contributed by the individual and the employer, and the investment return on the contributions in the fund. In a DB plan, the risk is assumed by the employer, and all retirees are assured of a specific and known amount of income per month. A DB plan provides long-standing and higher-paid employees with much larger monthly retirement payments. In a DC plan, also known as a money purchase plan, the individual assumes most of the risk. The value of the fund at the time of retirement varies, and for that reason, different people receive pension payments of different amounts, depending on how long they contributed, when they retire, the payment options selected, and the investment success of the plan. In recent years, most new plans and many established plans are created or restructured in the DC format since they are less expensive for employers. The company that man-

ages the DC plan can contribute less than the employee or an equal amount, according to negotiated agreements.

In private plans, where both the employee and the employer make monthly contributions, all accumulated benefits are protected if workers are fired, if they leave the company, or if they retire early. An increasing number of private pension plans are *portable*—contributions can be transferred to a plan in another company. This ensures that retirement benefits are similar to those that would have been paid had the place of employment not changed. Similarly, most plans provide for *vesting*—those who are fired or who quit before they retire receive all or part of the benefits they have earned before leaving the organization, including the employer contributions. Normally, an individual must remain at least two years with an employer before vesting occurs. Most private plans include, as well, *survivor benefits* so that a partner is protected in the event of the employee's death. Increasingly, plans provide *reduced benefits* for those who retire before the age at which a full pension is paid.

The third tier of the system also includes individual savings and investments, such as stocks, bonds, mutual funds, and real estate, some of which can be held in tax-protected RRSPs. Even if a person is self-employed, works for an employer without a pension plan, or is not eligible for an employer's plan, as is the case for most part-time workers, he or she can contribute to a Registered Retirement Savings Plan (RRSP). Individuals can contribute as much as 18 per cent of annual earned income to an RRSP, to a maximum of $73,500. Income from the third tier during retirement is highly dependent on the amount of wealth accumulated. Those with higher levels of education and earnings are generally able to accumulate more wealth for the retirement years. Equity in a home or other property is an important component of personal wealth and economic security in later life. Property can be sold, if necessary, often at a large profit, to generate cash for survival in later life. Capital gains on the principal residence are not taxed. Increasingly, for many recent and future retirees, an inheritance from deceased parents, together with an intergenerational transfer of wealth and property before their death, contributes greatly to retirement wealth.

Pension Issues and Pension Reforms

Periodically, because of changing political or philosophical ideologies, or potential or real economic crises, debate arises concerning the viability of the public retirement system. Most debates are economically driven, and revolve around the appropriate mix of state (public) versus individual (private) responsibility for supporting retired people; how to sustain the system; or how to find revenue for other social problems—poverty among children, high youth unemployment, escalating costs of health care, or the low standard of living of disadvantaged groups, such as Aboriginal people. Specific triggering events for these debates include

- excessive government debts and deficits;
- inflation, which increases the cost of living and requires indexed plans to increase monthly payments;
- a decrease in C/QPP contributions due to an increase in the number of people who retire early, or to high unemployment;
- demographic projections which argue that the C/QPP system will become bankrupt; and
- significant declines in the value of the stock market over an extended period of time.

To maintain or enhance the economic viability of a public pension system, four options are available (McDonald, 1997a):

1. Increase revenues by raising individual and employer C/QPP contributions, levying special taxes, or transferring more general revenue to pension funds.

2. Decrease benefits by changing eligibility requirements, charging penalties or reducing the incentives for early retirement, eliminating partial indexing of pensions, raising the mandatory retirement age which delays payment and shortens the period for which benefits are paid, and eliminating some benefits, such as the death benefit or the Allowance.

3. Shift the burden of financing pensions to individuals or to private pension plans by reducing the tax benefits of RRSPs.

4. Lower the dependency ratio by lowering unemployment rates through job creation and retraining; increasing the labour-force participation rate of older workers to delay or reduce the payment of pension benefits; providing a larger pension for those remaining longer in the labour force; eliminating discrimination in the hiring of, and in the amount of wages paid to, older workers; providing incentives to increase fertility rates so more workers are available in the future; or raising immigration rates among young adults who will work in sectors where workers are needed.

Three major solutions are periodically proposed to make the system sustainable: (1) abolish mandatory retirement in all jurisdictions and employment sectors; (2) retain mandatory retirement, but gradually increase the retirement age to about 70 years, and (3) gradually raise the age of eligibility for benefits (the United States is gradually raising the age to 67). Brown (1991: 111) argued that because of lower mortality rates, the age at retirement should have risen to 67.3 by 1981, to 68.4 by 1991, and to 69.4 by 2001; with further increases to 69.9 in 2011, 70.3 in 2021, and 70.7 in 2031. Similarly, Chen (1994) proposed that for each one-year gain in average life expectancy, normal retirement age should be extended by about nine months. In 1995, the retirement age equal to age 65 in 1940 should have been 70 years and 1 month. If average life expectancy continues to increase as projected, the mandatory retirement age in 2025 and 2060 should be 71 years, 8 months, and 73 years, 1 month, respectively (Chen, 1994). To support this approach to sustainability, Myles (2002: 325) noted that 'a small increase in the average retirement age has a greater impact on retirement costs than large cuts in retirement benefits'.

Others argue that raising the retirement age would have an adverse effect on those with disabilities and in poor health. As well, those at the lower ends of the educational, occupational, and income scales would have a difficult time obtaining jobs or keeping them late in life. On the other side of the argument, enabling older people to work longer would encourage active and healthy aging, would contribute to longer periods of independence for the individual, and would reduce payment burdens for the government (Walker, 2000). Working longer, whether in paid labour or volunteer work, contributes to the productivity of a nation.

The Economic Status of Older Canadians

The financial well-being of retired people is improving because of public and private pension reforms, greater incentives to save and invest, increased in-kind transfers and tax benefits for retirees, and increased participation in private pension plans, especially by women. Three major factors influencing the amount of accumulated wealth and income in later life are education, work history, and marital history.[10] Possible sources of wealth and income for older adults include

- savings and investments (cash, RRSPs, stocks, mutual funds, and bonds);
- private pensions;
- home and other property;
- family transfers (inheritances and gifts);
- social security (OAS and GIS);

- C/QPP payments;
- tax benefits and 'senior' subsidies; and
- earnings from full or part-time work.

The contributions from each source vary by gender, although the gaps are decreasing as more women have a history of regular labour-force participation, increased savings, and greater eligibility for private and C/QPP pension benefits. However, marital status and duration are important factors in the economic status of older women. If women remain married, they have a better chance of financial well-being in retirement (Yabiku, 2000). Being widowed or divorced has a negative effect on retirement financial well-being for both men and women, but especially for women.

Economic status is a vivid example of heterogeneity within the older population, ranging from the very affluent to those living in poverty, including the homeless. The family wealth of households headed by someone 65 years of age and older is increasing. Morissette et al. (2002) found a 56 per cent increase in median wealth ($81,000 to $126,000) and a 51 per cent increase in average wealth ($140,700 to $211,900) from 1984 to 1999. These increases were the result of a combination of factors: large inheritances; greater income from private pensions, C/QPP and OAS payments; more dual-income and two-pension couples; and appreciation in real estate values, including the value of a second, seasonal residence for some older adults. Highlight 9.9 presents some economic 'facts' pertaining to the older population.

It is important when one is assessing the financial situation of older adults to include wealth, not just income. Wealth is the difference between total assets and total debts. While older families have lower average incomes than younger families, few older adults have debt. A report based on 1999 data found that 73 per cent of families headed by a person 65 and over have no debt. For the 610,000 senior families carrying debt, the

Highlight 9.9 Economic Facts about Older Canadians

Savings and Wealth

- About 7 per cent of economic families with the head 65 and older had 'no wealth' in 1999 (Morissette, 2002).

- Home ownership represents a major source of the savings and wealth of older Canadians.

- About 1 million economic family units whose principal wage earner is 45 to 64 years of age, may not be saving enough for retirement (Statistics Canada, 2001).

- Twenty-five per cent of economic family units whose principal wage earner was 45 or older had no private pension assets in 1999 (Statistics Canada, 2001).

Income at Retirement

- The average income of those 65+ is more than $21,000, but there are geographical variations in average income from about $15,000 in Newfoundland to more than $22,000 in Ontario, Alberta and British Columbia (Statistics Canada, 2001).

- The average income of those 65 and over is increasing faster than for those in younger age groups.

- Seventy-five per cent of the total annual income in 2001 for those 65 and over was received from public (OAS, C/QPP) and private (RRSPs, RRPs) income systems; compared to 66 per cent in 1990 (Statistics Canada, 2003).

- The OAS is the largest source of income for older women, whereas an RSP and RRSP is the largest source for retired men (Statistics Canada, 2001).

median value was about $6,500, compared with about $32,000 for younger families. The report also found that more than 50 per cent of seniors own their homes mortgage-free, nearly half are still saving, and only 10 per cent are using investment capital to make ends meet. And, as in most other studies, unattached women aged 65 and over have the lowest income, assets, and net worth.

Many older individuals and couples fear they will experience financial uncertainty as they enter the retirement years. Uncertainty is created by whether they can or will continue to work; how long they will live, and in good health; whether inflation will increase the cost of living, especially if retirement payments are not indexed to inflation; whether there are sufficient survivor benefits for a spouse; and, how long they can live 'rent-free' in the family home. All of these factors influence whether an adequate income in retirement will permit a standard of living that is comparable to the pre-retirement standard.

The definition of an 'adequate' income is based on both objective indicators and subjective perceptions, by an individual and by others. Assessments of adequacy have seldom identified a standard to which 'adequate' can be compared. In comparison with earlier cohorts, current retirees receive more benefits from private pension plans and social-security payments; and greater tax concessions and in-kind benefits. Rising inflation, however, can erase these gains. Poverty can occur if assets, such as stocks, bonds, or real estate, depreciate in value; if pensions or social-security payments lag behind inflation; and if inflation makes it difficult to pay for the essential items, namely, food, utilities, and housing that comprise a large part of a retired person's expenditures.

Within their occupational reference group, older retirees are usually able to maintain their relative position in the income hierarchy and to maintain their relative standard of living in retirement. However, if the income of recent retirees is compared with their pre-retirement incomes, with the income of those in their occupational group who remain in the labour force, or with age peers who continue to work, then their objective economic status is often lower.

Although objective indicators, such as annual income, provide information about the relative economic status of retired cohorts, subjective responses to a lower income must also be assessed, especially when one is considering the relationship between economic status and well-being. Subjective perceptions of financial 'adequacy' by an individual or couple may be more relevant than an evaluation of objective economic indicators by outsiders. Individuals are aware of their own needs and resources, and some are able to accept a satisfactory, albeit lower, standard of living in retirement.

The perceived adequacy of financial resources in retirement is usually based on a comparison with the individual's past lifestyle and with the status of age peers among his or her friends and family circle. Thus, definitions of economic situations in retirement are based more on perceptions about relative deprivation than on actual disposable income. Despite reduced incomes, and even when there are objective indicators of poverty, many retirees report that their economic situation is satisfactory (Hazelrigg and Hardy, 1997). Even in the face of objective evidence that they are close to or below the poverty line, women, especially unattached women, report more positive evaluations of their economic status than do men. It is for this reason that Ballantyne and Marshall (2001) argued that subjective evaluations of income adequacy should not be included in any discussion of social poli-cies for income redistribution. If subjective rather than objective evaluations are used, it is too easy for governments to argue that retirees are satisfied and do not need enhanced economic support.

The most frequent way of managing on a lower income, especially among those who are economically disadvantaged, is to spend less. Many older people report that their basic need for goods and services decreases with age. But changes vary by cohort and gender, and they may involve a more restricted life (moving to a smaller home; spending less on clothing and entertainment; or selling a car) or buying less food or less nutritious food. With a reduced income in later life, older adults must allocate a higher proportion of all their expenditures to food, shelter, and household maintenance. Brown (1991) estimated that over 50 per cent of an older adult's budget is allocated to food and housing expenses.

Older Consumers

With older people making up a large proportion of the population, it is not surprising that the business sector has sought to increase their spending patterns. Each cohort entering retirement has, in general, more discretionary income and more savings than the preceding one. Spending will increase further when the baby boomers retire because they have had a history of being 'spenders' and 'consumers' of products. Not only will they be wealthier, but they will be healthier and have more time, in years, in which to spend money on leisure and consumer goods. An awareness of increased affluence and health among older adults has led to increased advertising and to the marketing of products for the 'maturity' or 'grey' market.[11] For example, in 2002, the average age of a Harley Davidson motorcycle owner was 52!

Older consumers, through focus groups and surveys, are consulted about the design and delivery of goods and services they might purchase, especially with respect to ease of use, taste and nutritional content of food (low in fat, salt, and sugar), and labelling (size of print, clarity of instructions). Advertisements stress active and healthy lifestyles (involving, for example, travel, cycling, tai chi), and they depict active, attractive older role models. Women, especially, demand clothing that is attractive and fashionable and that has buttons and zippers that are easy to use if their flexibility and dexterity decrease. Moreover, older people expect retailers to provide change rooms that have chairs and grab bars and that are accessible to walkers and wheelchairs (Canadian Aging Research Network, 1994). Some companies hire older workers, not only to provide employment for those who need an income or purpose in life, but to demonstrate that they are a 'senior-friendly' company or store.

Older Women: The Feminization of Poverty

As noted earlier, the work histories of most women are intermittent or discontinuous. Women enter and leave the labour force more frequently than men. They also are more likely to work part-time and to retire before they are 65. Moreover, when women are in the labour force many occupy low-prestige, low-income positions; they seldom seek or receive an opportunity to advance to high-status, high-paying positions; and they are less likely to be eligible for private pension plans unless they work full-time for many years. Women are also more likely to convert pension benefits earned early in life into cash when they change jobs or leave the labour force (Hardy and Shuey, 2000). Throughout their working life, women generally earn less than men,[12] save less, invest less, and own less property. Married women earn less than separated, divorced, or widowed women.

The economic situation of older women is improving with each successive cohort that reaches age 65 (Statistics Canada, 2000b). In 1997, women 61 to 69 earned only 61 per cent as much as men (Statistics Canada, 1998), and Old Age Security accounted for 34 per cent of their total income (versus 19 per cent for men). The reverse held for private pensions, where 26 per cent of men's total income, compared to 14 per cent for

women came from this source. C/QPP income represented 20 per cent of men's income and 22 per cent of women's total income. Women 25 to 34 years of age working full-time in the late 1990s were earning about 80 per cent as much as men, and that should translate into improved savings and pension benefits later in life. This improvement is due to higher education, longer periods in full-time jobs, less wage discrimination, increased pension eligibility, greater participation in better-paid professional positions, and more childless and never-married career-oriented women (Rosenthal et al., 2000). At the end of 2001, about 2.5 million female workers belonged to a registered pension plan, compared to 3 million men (Statistics Canada, 2003d).

The economic situation of baby boomer women is better than that of their mothers. However, at present there are large numbers of older women who are at risk of living in poverty for part or all of their later life. This gender gap in later life, labelled the 'feminization of poverty', can apply at earlier stages of life, as well, especially for women who are single parents. Elderly women are poor, not because they created their own poverty, but because society creates gender-based inequalities that have economic consequences. Women reach later life with fewer economic resources because, if married, they are economically tied to their husband's wealth; because they lose economic capital if they are divorced; and because they have not been employed full-time throughout most of their working life. In short, the feminization of poverty in later life is an accumulated economic disadvantage. This occurs because of social responsibilities for child rearing and parent care, the gendered division of labour-force hiring and promotion, wage inequity (unequal pay for equal work), and a dependence on small old-age security payments if they are not eligible for public or private pensions. As Neysmith (1984) summarized, 'older women are like perennial plants—the roots of their poverty develop early in life and come to fruition when they are old.' The cumulative outcomes of gender stratification and discrimination and the lifelong disadvantages that women experience in education, work, and leisure are compounded further the longer a woman lives since scarce resources must be last longer.

Specific subgroups of older women are called the 'hidden' or 'invisible' poor (McDonald, 1997b, 2002). In addition to lifelong systemic factors, some women are disadvantaged because of their ethnic or cultural background, the dissolution of a marriage or common-law relationship, or living alone. Some widows are not eligible for survivor benefits, or, if they remarry they lose accrued benefits from a previous marriage. Older women who were divorced earlier in life are likely to be economically disadvantaged, especially if they were fully responsible for raising children and if they were divorced when pensions were not considered family assets to be shared in a divorce settlement, as they are at present in most jurisdictions. Davies and Denton (2003) found that women who were separated or divorced at age 45 or older were more likely to be poor later in life than either married women, or men who divorced or separated in middle or later life. This poverty is accounted for by gender inequalities in the family, legal, labour force and retirement systems. However, some of these later-life negative economic impacts can be offset by remarriage, by a high level of education, and by labour-force experience before the separation.

Poverty is also more likely among widowed or divorced older women who live alone. They may be 'overhoused' in a family home that is expensive to maintain, or they may not be able to afford housing alternatives because most of their income is derived from OAS and GIS payments (Moore and Rosenberg, 1997; McDonald et al., 2000; Smith et al., 2000). However, never-married women, especially if well-educated, do not fall into this poverty group since they are more likely to have had lifelong employment. These women are less dependent on government transfers and are more likely to have investments and savings, including real estate.

Other groups of highly disadvantaged older women are Aboriginals, recent immigrants, and those living in retirement or nursing homes. Members of these groups are seldom included in research studies about poverty in later life. For example, immigrant women may have no official Canadian labour-force experience and are therefore not eligible for C/QPP pension benefits, or if they arrive in Canada late in life as part of a family reunification plan, they are not eligible for full OAS or GIS benefits. Similarly, if they outlive their husbands, they may not inherit a pension because their husbands may have had a short and irregular work history with low public pension benefits and no private pension. Brotman (1998) found, for example, that poverty rates among black, Chinese, Aboriginal, and Greek women over 65 was at least 5 per cent higher than the national average for older women. And if women from these groups lived alone, they were even more disadvantaged.

Another category of women who may experience poverty in later life are those who remain homemakers throughout their adult life. These women are not eligible to receive public pensions (C/QPP); however, they are eligible, on the basis of need, for OAS and GIS payments. Many argue that the responsibilities of permanent homemakers constitute unpaid labour, and therefore they should be eligible for increased social-security payments in recognition of their labour in the home. It has also been argued that women who spend their adult lives raising children should be eligible for the Canadian Pension Plan because of their contribution to society.[13] Some even argue that increased benefits to married older women should be paid by their husband during his working years, by higher contributions from all workers, or by funds from general tax revenues.

However, others have argued that homemakers should not be eligible for special considerations if this places an economic burden on current workers or if it increases the national debt. Proponents of this view claim that women who remain permanently at home do so voluntarily, often because they feel they do not need to work for economic reasons. Therefore, why should their economic position be any different in retirement? Moreover, women who remain out of the labour force to perform 'work' for their partner should receive retirement benefits from their spouse rather than from society.

Proposals for reducing the feminization of poverty in later life have focused on changing employment and salary conditions early in life so that employed women who take maternity leave or parent-care leave will not lose their jobs, or experience reduced pension benefits or loss of seniority. Increasingly, employers are providing daycare or flexible hours to facilitate child rearing or parent care for women with a full-time career.

In terms of pension reform, some proposed solutions to enhance the benefits for women include the following:

- provisions to allow women to accumulate pension credits when they are absent from the labour force to look after their children or parents

- C/QPP pension eligibility for part-time workers

- a continuation of pension benefits to a surviving spouse, regardless of later marital or economic status

- increased benefits for immigrants who arrive in Canada during middle or late adulthood

- a requirement that private pension plans be offered by all employers, regardless of the size of the company

- unisex tables for the calculation of retirement contributions and benefits

- mandatory coverage in private plans for all permanent part-time employees on a prorated basis.

Clearly, there are many lifelong economic issues that must be addressed to enhance the economic status of the rapidly growing population of older women, especially those who are widowed or divorced and live beyond 80 years of age.

Poverty in Later Life: Fact or Fiction?

Despite economic gains in recent decades, income inequalities persist among older people. Those most vulnerable to economic hardship are those with less education or discontinuous work histories; divorced and widowed women; members of minority and immigrant groups; and those with disabilities and chronic health problems.

What is the poverty line in Canada? Before we can determine who is living near or in poverty, at any age, a commonly accepted measure is needed, because the use of different measures results in different estimates of the number of people living in poverty. Hence, it is difficult to compare individual or family poverty across time or to compare poverty in developed and developing countries across time. As well, different philosophies or policies as to what constitutes poverty makes it difficult to administer welfare programs fairly.

The most common and oldest measure of relative poverty in Canada (it has been in use since 1968) is Statistics Canada's Low Income Cut-Offs (LICOs). This measure, which is adjusted annually according to the Consumer Price Index, is based on patterns of family expenditures. It is not an absolute measure of poverty but rather a *relative* measure of how individuals or subgroups of the population compare at a given time—it identifies those who are less well off than the average for their family size and within their geographical region (Fellegi, 1997). A number of years ago, older people were often the largest group in the low-income category. More recently, lone-parent families headed by women tend to be the largest group. More specifically, LICOs identify the pre-tax or post-tax income below which families or unattached individuals spend 20 per cent more than the average on food, shelter, and clothing. In 2003 it was calculated that Canadians spend an average of 44 per cent of their after-tax incomes on food, shelter, and clothing. Therefore, the LICO drawn by Statistics Canada represents the point where 64 per cent of income is spent on these necessities; and it is then adjusted for family size and geographical region. LICOs, according to Statistics Canada policy, are not to be considered a measure of poverty.

As an absolute measure, the LICO has some limitations. First, it is based on income before taxes and can lead to overestimates of the incidence of poverty.[14] Ruggeri et al. (1994) proposed that when one is assessing the extent of poverty among elderly people, an after-tax measure should be used to assess their 'net purchasing power'. Employing such a measure and 1991 data, they found that only 4.7 per cent of older people were classified as low-income, compared

to 30.6 per cent when the traditional pre-tax LICO measure was used. Others argue that the LICO is misleading because it establishes a very low income for indicating poverty. This means that a large number of people are above the line, and objectively, appear to be in a good financial position, while in reality they are not. It is asked, for example, why a person or couple that is $1 or $10 above the arbitrary LICO line should not be classified as 'poor'? Table 9.2 illustrates the after-tax and before-tax LICOs for 2002 for family units of one to three persons. These cases represent the number of people who normally would be in a retiree household. The average after-tax income of families headed by a person 65 years of age or over who was the main income recipient was $40,400 in 2001. On average, this type of family

Table 9.2 Low-Income Cutoffs (LICOs) for 2002, by Type and Size of Community

Place of Residence	Size of Family Unit	Pre-Tax Level ($)	Post-Tax Level ($)
Rural	1	13,311	10,429
	2	16,639	12,726
	3	20,694	16,096
Population <30,000	1	15,267	12,055
	2	19,083	14,710
	3	23,732	18,604
Population 30,000 to 99,999	1	16,407	13,192
	2	20,508	16,097
	3	25,505	20,360
Population 100,000 to 499,999	1	16,521	13,399
	2	20,651	16,349
	3	25,684	20,679
Population 500,000+	1	19,261	15,907
	2	24,077	19,410
	3	29,944	24,550

Source: Adapted from, and reprinted with permission, of Statistics Canada (2003b).

received $19,900 in government transfers, or 43 per cent of their total income before taxes. The low-income rate for families 65 and over was 3.3 per cent, while for single men over 65 it was 5.1 per cent, and for women over 65, 9.1 per cent (Statistics Canada, 2003c). You might want to compare these levels with your situation as a single student or for your nuclear family.

Another common measure of poverty is the 'low income measure' generated by Statistics Canada since the early 1990s. This is a much simpler measure that draws the low-income line at half the median family or single income in Canada. The median income was $55,016 and $20,213, respectively, in 2000, for families and single people. This absolute measure of poverty, which reflects an inability to pay for groceries, rent, and transit fares, is used to compare year-over-year changes in Canada and to compare Canada with other countries.

Human Resources Development Canada has devised a 'market basket' measure of poverty in which the poverty line is based on the income needed to purchase basic goods and services in the basket. The base measure, calculated for a typical family of four (two parents, a 13-year-old son and a 9-year-old daughter) in 48 geographical areas, can be adjusted to create measures for other family types and sizes. This *absolute* measure of poverty identifies families whose disposable income—i.e., total income minus taxes, payroll deductions, support payments, and child-care and out-of-pocket medical expenses—does not enable them to purchase a basket of basic goods and services, consisting of food, clothing and footwear, shelter, transportation, and other goods and services, including furniture, telephone, and postage stamps. Being able to pay for this basket of goods represents the minimum standard for decent living in Canada. This measure generates a higher reported poverty rate in most communities than the LICO measure. According to the market basket measure, 23.4 per cent of people in Newfoundland and Labrador are poor, and 20

per cent in British Columbia, and 11 per cent in Ontario are poor.

What is the economic status of older people in Canada? Are they an impoverished cohort, as many reports and stereotypes suggest? The answer is: it depends! Poverty is more likely as longevity increases and savings become depleted, especially among widows or divorced women who live into their 80s and beyond. And older widows become more disadvantaged with age if they lose their survivor benefits, if an annuity expires, or if a pension is not indexed to inflation. As well as women, members of immigrant groups, unattached people, and those living in larger urban centres or remote areas are more likely to live at or near the poverty level, however it is defined.

The incomes from 2000 reported in the 2001 census (Statistics Canada, 2003b) show that seniors falling into the low-income category declined from 20 to 17 per cent from 1990 to 2000. However, this still means that over 600,000 individuals 65 and over are classified as low-income. These data indicate that 21 per cent of older women have low incomes, compared to 11 per cent of older men. Most of this difference occurs because of living alone—43 per cent of elderly women who live alone are in the low-income category, compared to 31 per cent of elderly men who live alone. In contrast, only 6 per cent of older people living as a couple fell into this category. The good news is that, compared to 1990, far fewer older women in 2000 fell into the low-income category. This improvement has resulted from increased benefits in the OAS and GIS programs and more women being eligible for C/QPP and private pension plans. For older people in the low-income category, about 85 cents of every dollar of income came from OAS or GIS, compared to about 39 cents of every dollar for older people above the low-income category (Statistics Canada, 2003b).

Factors that reduce the likelihood of poverty in later life include high levels of education, good health, living as a couple, being male, and having a history of full-time employment. To illustrate, Moore and Rosenberg (1997: 45–6) report that women living alone are seven times more susceptible to poverty than men living with spouses; that each year of formal education reduces the likelihood of poverty; and that full-time employment reduces the odds by 70 per cent and part-time employment by 33 per cent, relative to those not in the labour force.

Summary

In the early years of the twenty-first century, the meaning of work and retirement and the economic status of older Canadians continue to change. The pattern of work careers is changing as many older workers have been caught in the middle of a shift from a traditional model of a working life to an emerging model. In the traditional model, a person spent most of his or her career working for the same company and doing much the same type of work. In contrast, the emerging model involves lifelong learning and retraining for many jobs that may be held in a variety of companies or while self-employed. Moreover, new work options that permit more flexibility and more choice as to where and when one works are being introduced.

Among older workers, some wish to continue working beyond the age of mandatory retirement, others wish to retire before 65 years of age. But not all jurisdictions have eliminated mandatory retirement, and therefore many workers do not have a choice. Older workers today have more skills and potential to keep working, and they should not be subject to forced retirement or unemployment on the basis of age. Indeed, given the greying of the labour force as fewer younger workers are available and more older workers opt for early retirement, mechanisms to retain or recruit older workers will be needed before the baby boom is due to be fully retired by about 2030.

Women comprise a larger percentage of the labour force as more gender-equitable opportunities to participate have emerged. Women are acquiring higher levels of education in more diverse fields, and employers are introducing policies that make it easier for women to move in and out of the labour force as family needs dictate.

The definition and timing of retirement are changing for both men and women. Mandatory retirement at age 65 is no longer the only option, as some retire before 65 (voluntarily or involuntarily), while others continue to work for a number of years after 65. Such decisions are influenced by personal work histories, by accumulated savings, by government and employer regulations, and by the relative meaning and importance of work and leisure to an individual. Despite the increased options, few workers engage in much formal retirement planning, and we know very little about the retirement process as experienced by women with a variety of work histories.

It is the responsibility of both the retired individual and the state to ensure that an 'adequate' income is available until death. This income must also protect a partner after the death of the primary or sole wage earner in a marital or common-law partnership. The economic status of older Canadians ranges from extreme affluence to poverty, especially among elderly widows who are not eligible for survivor's benefits in private pension plans. Economic security in later life is more strongly related to education; employment type and history; private pensions; personal savings and investments; and inter-generational transfers; more than to public security systems, i.e. OAS, GIS, and C/QPP. Although the 'feminization of poverty' has been less prevalent in recent years, it is still a reality for many older widowed or divorced women, especially those who were not long-standing members of the workforce earlier in life. To protect more Canadians in the future, pension reforms are periodically debated and introduced, but major changes are slowly or seldom enacted.

For Reflection, Debate, or Action

1. Develop an argument for or against the proposition that women should receive a salary, plus accumulated CPP benefits, for each year they spend out of the labour force looking after their children or parents.

2. If you started your own business in the next few years, what policies would you adopt concerning older workers and such issues as recruitment, retention, remuneration, benefits, and retirement?

3. Write a letter to the editor of a local paper arguing why society should adhere to one of four positions: (1) the mandatory retirement age, with full benefits, should be raised beyond age 65 to some later age; (2) mandatory retirement should be abolished; (3) the mandatory retirement age should be lowered; or (4) mandatory retirement should be occupation- or person-specific.

4. Why might there be gender differences in how men and women view the issue of mandatory retirement?

5. Debate whether the current pension system should be retained or whether it should be totally privatized so that the government does not have any pension responsibility.

6. To ensure that Canada's social-security system is viable and solvent when you and your parents retire, which of the following measures would you implement, and why—raise the eligibility age for benefits; reduce benefits; increase revenues; encourage more private savings; other options?

7. Interview women in the workforce and those who have retired to determine ways in which they have experienced or observed gender differences at work and in retirement.

8. Debate whether the 'feminization of poverty' is primarily a public issue, a private trouble, or both?

Notes

1 From the perspective of a society or an organization, these career changes represent an economic cost or loss in that the investment in training an individual for the career has been lost. To prevent or discourage these organizational losses, some companies improve the work situation by offering their employees new challenges, alternative work patterns, sabbatical leaves, and greater autonomy.

2. Labour-force participation by women is discussed in Gee and Kimball (1987), Nishio and Lank (1987), Parliament (1989), McDonald and Wanner (1990), McDonald and Chen (1994), McDonald (1997a), Connidis (2001), Hughes (2001), Moen and Han (2001), Tremblay (2001), and Davies and Denton (2003).

3. For information about older workers, see Crown (1996), Salthouse and Maurer (1996), Mutran (1997), Walker (2000), Czaja (2001), Marshall et al., (2001a), Marshall (2002), Henretta (2003), www.wane.ca., and http://labour-travail.hrdc-drhc.gc.ca/worklife/aging-workforce-en.cfm. Statistics Canada publishes every month (in print or web format) *Perspectives on Labour and Income* (www.statcan.ca).

4. Retirement as a public policy was first introduced in Germany in 1889 when Bismarck established the first pension act as an 'insurance against invalidity and old age'. German workers were permitted to leave the labour force at 70 years of age with a modest amount of guaranteed economic support. However, since few individuals lived to the age of 70 to reap this benefit, the age criterion was later reduced to 65.

5. For a historical analysis of retirement and retirement policies, see Bryden (1974), Kohli (1987), Myles (1989, 2000, 2002), McDonald and Wanner (1990: 17–38), Snell (1996), and McDonald (2002).

6. For a discussion of decision making see Henkens (1999), Szinovacz and DeVinney (2002), Pienta and Hayward (2002), and Henretta (2003).

7. McDonald (2002) presents a detailed history and analysis of retirement concerning women in Canada.

8. The retirement process for women has been discussed by Arber and Ginn (1995), Bernard et al. (1995), Price (2000), McDonald (2002), Pienta and Hayward (2002).

9. In Canada, social security comprises all subsidized hospital, drug, and medical plans; government subsidies for housing, transportation, and home care; a retirement-income system that includes a basic benefit and a Guaranteed Income Supplement and a Spouse's Allowance (both based on total income), and a public pension plan. See www.canadabenefits.gc.ca.

10. For a discussion of factors influencing income and wealth in later life, see Crown (2001), Kingson and Williamson (2001), Schulz (2001), Morissette (2002), and Statistics Canada (2003e).

11. Most advertising and products directed toward older adults involve leisure and travel; retirement housing; drugs, cosmetics, and health care; clothing; products for easier living; financial services; education; food; and subscriptions for specialized magazines for older people.

12. Statistics Canada reported that in 2000, women aged 15 and over earned 64 cents for every dollar earned by men. This represents only a small increase from 52 cents in 1980 (Statistics Canada, 11 March 2003). Moreover, in 2002 average earnings for women working full-time for a full year were $35,258, compared with $49,250 for men who were employed full-time for a full year.

13. The pension plan operated by the province of Quebec gives special consideration to women during the years they drop out of the labour force to raise children. Quebec family law requires mandatory pension sharing for spouses to recognize the time that women spent out of the labour force. The CPP also provides some credit for women who opt out of the labour force to raise children.

14. As you read media or research articles about LICOs, note carefully whether the annual level is reported in in pre- or post-tax dollars. Those who want to emphasize the extent of poverty usually use the higher pre-tax dollar figures.

References

Anisef, P., and P. Axelrod. 2001. 'Baby Boomers in Transition: Life-Course Experiences of the Class of '73'. Pp. 473–88 in V. Marshall et al. (eds), *Restructuring Work and the Life Course*. Toronto: University of Toronto Press.

Arber, S., and J. Ginn. 1995. 'Choice and Constraint in the Retirement of Older Married Women'. Pp. 69–86 in S. Arber and J. Ginn (eds), *Connecting Gender and Ageing: A Sociological Approach*. Philadelphia: Open University Press.

Baker, M. et al. 2001. *The Retirement Incentive Effects of Canada's Income Security Programs*. SEDAP Research Paper No. 65. Hamilton, Ont.: McMaster University (http://socserv2.mcmaster.ca/sedap).

Ballantyne, P., and V. Marshall. 2001. 'Subjective Income Security of (Middle) Aging and Elderly Canadians', *Canadian Journal on Aging*, 20(2), 151–73.

Bass, S., and M. Oka. 1995. 'An Older-Worker Employment Model: Japan's Silver Human Resource Centers', *The Gerontologist*, 35(5), 679–82.

Bernard, M., et al. 1995. 'Gendered Work, Gendered Retirement'. Pp. 56–68 in S. Arber and J. Ginn (eds), *Connecting Gender and Ageing: A Sociological Approach*. Philadelphia: Open University Press.

Brotman, S. 1998. 'The Incidence of Poverty among Seniors in Canada: Exploring the Impact of Gender, Ethnicity and Race', *Canadian Journal on Aging*, 17(2), 166–85.

Brown, R. 1991. *Economic Security in an Aging Population*. Toronto: Butterworths.

Bryden, K. 1974. *Old-Age Pensions and Policy-Making in Canada*. Montreal: McGill-Queen's University Press.

Calasanti, T. 1993. 'Bringing in Diversity: Toward an Inclusive Theory of Retirement', *Journal of Aging Studies*, 7(2), 133–50.

Canadian Aging Research Network. 1994. *Clothing

Preferences and Problems of Older Adults. Winnipeg: University of Manitoba Centre on Aging.

Chan, D., et al. 2001. 'Linking Technology, Work, and the Life Course: Findings from the Nova Case Study'. Pp. 270–87 in V. Marshall et al. (eds), *Restructuring Work and the Life Course*. Toronto: University of Toronto Press.

Cheal, D., and K. Kampen. 1998. 'Poor and Dependent Seniors in Canada', *Ageing and Society*, 18(2), 147–66.

Chen, Y.-P. 1994. 'Equivalent Retirement Ages and Their Implications for Social Security and Medicare Financing', *The Gerontologist*, 36(6), 731–5.

Connidis, I. 2001. *Family Ties and Aging*. Thousand Oaks, Calif.: Sage.

Crown, W. (ed.). 1996. *Handbook on Employment and the Elderly*. Westport, Conn.: Greenwood Press.

———. 2001. 'Economic Status of the Elderly'. Pp. 352–68 in R. Binstock and L. George (eds), *Handbook of Aging and the Social Sciences*. San Diego, Calif.: Academic Press.

Czaja, S. 2001. 'Technological Change and the Older Worker'. Pp. 547–68 in J. Birren and W. Schaie (eds), *Handbook of the Psychology of Aging*. San Diego, Calif.: Academic Press.

Davies, S. and M. Denton. 2003. 'The Economic Well-Being of Older Women Who Become Divorced or Separated in Mid and Later Life', *Canadian Journal on Aging*, 21(4), 477–93.

Denton, F., et al. (eds). 2000. *Independence and Economic Security in Old Age*. Vancouver: University of British Columbia Press.

Drentea, P. 2002. 'Retirement and Mental Health', *Journal of Aging and Health*, 14(2), 167–94.

Duchesne, D. 2002. 'Seniors at Work', *Perspectives on Labour and Income*, 3(5): 5–16. Statistics Canada Cat. no. 75-001-XIE.

Ekerdt, D., and J. Kay Hackney. 2002. 'Worker's Ignorance of Retirement Benefits', *The Gerontologist*, 42(4), 543–51.

———, et al. 2000. 'The Normative Anticipation of Retirement by Older Workers', *Research on Aging*, 22(1), 3–22.

England, R. 2001. *The Fiscal Challenge of an Aging Industrial World*. Washington, DC: Center for Strategic and International Studies.

———. 2002. *The Macroeconomic Impact of Global Aging: A New Era of Economic Frailty*. Washington, DC: Center for Strategic and International Studies.

Fellegi, I. 1997. *On Poverty and Low Income*. Ottawa: Statistics Canada.

Galarneau, D. 1994. *Female Baby Boomers: A Generation at Work*. Ottawa: Statistics Canada.

Gee, E., and M. Kimball. 1987. *Women and Aging*. Toronto: Butterworths.

Hardy, M., and K. Shuey. 2000. 'Pension Decisions in a Changing Economy: Gender, Structure, and Choice', *Journal of Gerontology: Social Sciences*, 55B(5), S271–7.

Hazelrigg, L., and M. Hardy. 1997. 'Perceived Income Adequacy among Older Adults', *Research on Aging*, 19(1), 69–107.

Heinz, W. 2001. 'Work and the Life Course: A Cosmopolitan-Local Perspective'. Pp. 3–22 in V. Marshall et al. (eds), *Restructuring Work and the Life Course*. Toronto: University of Toronto Press.

Henkens, K. 1999. 'Retirement Intentions and Spousal Support: A Multi-Actor Approach', *Journal of Gerontology: Social Sciences*, 54B(2), S63–73.

Henretta, J. 2001. 'Work and Retirement'. Pp. 255–71 in R. Binstock and L. George (eds), *Handbook of Aging and the Social Sciences*. San Diego, Calif.: Academic Press.

———. 2003. 'The Life Course Perspective on Work and Retirement'. Pp. 85–105 in R. Settersten (ed.). *Invitation to the Life Course: Toward New Understandings of Later Life*. Amityville, NY: Baywood.

Hicks, P. 2003. 'New Policy Research on Population Aging and Life-Course Flexibility', *Horizons*, 6(2), 3–6.

Hughes, K. 2001. 'Restructuring Work, Restructuring Gender: The Movement of Women into Non-Traditional Occupations in Canada'. Pp. 84–106 in V. Marshall et al. (eds), *Restructuring Work and the Life Course*. Toronto: University of Toronto Press.

Karp, D. 1989. 'The Social Construction of Retirement among Professionals 50–60 Years Old', *The Gerontologist*, 29(6), 750–60.

Kingson, E., and J. Williamson. 2001. 'Economic Security Policies'. Pp. 369–86 in R. Binstock and L. George (eds), *Handbook of Aging and the Social Sciences*. San Diego, Calif.: Academic Press.

Klassen, T., and C. Gillin. 1999. 'The Heavy Hand of the Law: The Canadian Supreme Court and Mandatory Retirement', *Canadian Journal on Aging*, 18(2), 259–76.

Kohli, M. 1987. 'Retirement and the Moral Economy: An Historical Interpretation of the German Case', *Journal of Aging Studies*, 1(2), 125–44.

Mackenzie, A., and H. Dryburgh. 2003. 'The Retirement Wave', *Perspectives on Labour and Income*, 4(2): 5–11. Statistics Canada Cat. no. 75-001-XIE.

McDonald, L. 1997a. 'The Link between Social Research and Social Policy Options: Reverse Retirement as a Case in Point', *Canadian Journal on Aging/Canadian Public Policy*, Supplement (Spring), 90–113.

———. 1997b. 'The Invisible Poor: Canada's Retired Widows', *Canadian Journal on Aging*, 16(3), 553–83.

———. 2002. 'The Invisible Retirement of Women'. SEDAP Research Paper No. 69. Hamilton, Ont.: McMaster University (http://socserve2.mcmaster.ca/sedap).

———, and M. Chen. 1994. 'The Youth Freeze and the Retirement Bulge: Older Workers and the Impending Labor Shortage'. Pp. 113–39 in V. Marshall and B. McPherson (eds), *Aging: Canadian Perspectives*. Peterborough, Ont.: Broadview.

———, and R. Wanner. 1987. 'Retirement in a Dual Economy: The Canadian Case'. Pp. 245–61 in V. Marshall (ed.). *Aging in Canada: Social Perspectives*. Markham, ON: Fitzhenry and Whiteside.

———, et al. 2000. 'The Poverty of Retired Widows'. Pp. 328–44 in F. Denton et al. (eds), *Independence and Economic Security in Old Age*. Vancouver: University of British Columbia Press.

———, and R. Wanner. 1990. *Retirement in Canada*. Toronto: Butterworths.

McMullin, J., and V. Marshall. 1999. 'Structure and Agency in the Retirement Process: A Case Study of Montreal Garment Workers'. Pp. 305–38 in C. Ryff and V. Marshall (eds), *The Self and Society in Aging Processes*. New York: Springer.

———. 2001. 'Ageism, Age Relations, and Garment Industry Work in Montreal', *The Gerontologist*, 41(1), 111–22.

Marshall, K. 2003. 'Benefiting from Extended Parental Leave', *Perspectives on Labour and Income*, 15(2). Cat. no. 75-001-XPE). Ottawa: Statistics Canada.

Marshall, V. 1995a. 'Rethinking Retirement: Issues for the Twenty-First Century'. Pp. 31–50 in E. Gee and G. Gutman (eds), *Rethinking Retirement*. Vancouver: Gerontology Research Centre, Simon Fraser University.

———. 1995b. 'The Older Worker in Canadian Society: Is There a Future?' Pp. 51–68 in E. Gee and G. Gutman (eds), *Rethinking Retirement*. Vancouver: Gerontology Research Centre, Simon Fraser University.

———. 2001. 'Canadian Research on Older Workers'. Paper presented at the International Association on Gerontology Congress, July, Vancouver.

———, and P. Clarke. 1996. *Facilitating the Transition from Employment to Retirement*. Ottawa: National Forum on Health.

———., et al. (eds). 2001a. *Restructuring Work and the Life Course*. Toronto: University of Toronto Press.

———., et al. 2001b. 'Instability in the Retirement Transition: Effects on Health and Well-Being in a Canadian Study', *Research on Aging*, 23(4), 379–409.

———, et al. 2002. 'Perspectives on Aging, Work and Retirement'. Paper presented at the Gerontological Society of America Annual Meeting, Boston, November.

Moen, P., and S-K Han. 2001. 'Reframing Careers: Work, Family and Gender'. Pp. 424–45 in V. Marshall et al. (eds), *Restructuring Work and the Life Course*. Toronto: University of Toronto Press.

Moore, E., and M. Rosenberg. 1997. *Growing Old in Canada*. Toronto: Nelson.

Morissette, R. 2002. 'On the Edge: Financially Vulnerable Families', *Canadian Social Trends*, 67 (Winter), 13–17.

———, et al. 2002. 'Are Families Getting Richer', *Canadian Social Trends*, 66 (Autumn), 15–19.

Mutran, E., et al. 1997. 'Self-Esteem and Subjective Responses to Work among Mature Workers: Similarities and Differences by Gender', *Journal of Gerontology: Social Sciences*, 52B(2), S89–96.

Myles, J. 1989. *Old Age in the Welfare State: The Political Economy of Public Pensions*. Lawrence, Kans.: University Press of Kansas.

———. 2000. 'The Maturation of Canada's Retirement Income System: Income Levels, Income Inequality and Low Income Among Older Persons', *Canadian Journal on Aging*, 19(3), 287–316.

———. 2002. 'Back to Bismarck? The Public Policy Implications of Living Longer', *Canadian Journal on Aging*, 21(3), 325–9.

National Council of Welfare. 1999. *A Pension Primer*. Cat. no. 68-49/1999E. Ottawa: Minister of Public Works and Government Services Canada.

Neysmith, S. 1984. 'Poverty in Old Age: Can Pension Reform Meet the Needs of Women?' *Canadian Woman Studies*, 5, 17–21.

Nishio, H., and H. Lank. 1987. 'Patterns of Labor Participation of Older Female Workers'. Pp. 228–44 in

V. Marshall (ed.). *Aging in Canada: Social Perspectives*. Markham, Ont.: Fitzhenry and Whiteside.

Oderkirk, J. 1996a. 'Old Age Security: An Overview', *Canadian Social Trends*, 40 (Spring), 2–7.

———. 1996b. 'Canada and Quebec Pension Plans', *Canadian Social Trends*, 40 (Spring), 8–15.

Parliament, J. 1989. 'Women Employed Outside the Home', *Canadian Social Trends*, 13 (Summer), 2–6.

Phillipson, C. 1998. *Reconstructing Old Age*. Thousand Oaks, Calif.: Sage.

Pienta, A,. et al. 1994. 'Women's Labour Force Participation in Later Life: The Effects of Early Work and Family Experiences', *Journal of Gerontology: Social Sciences*, 49B(5), S231–9.

———, and M. Hayward. 2002. 'Who Expects to Continue Working after Age 62? The Retirement Plans of Couples', *Journal of Gerontology: Social Sciences*, 57B(4), S199–208.

Prager, J. 2002. 'Aging and Productivity: What Do We Know? Pp. 133–89 in D. Cheal (ed.). *Aging and Demographic Change in Canadian Context*. Toronto: University of Toronto Press.

Price, C. 2000. 'Women and Retirement: Relinquishing Professional Identity', *Journal of Aging Studies*, 14(1), 81–101.

Prus, S. 2000. 'Income Inequality as a Canadian Cohort Ages: An Analysis of the Later Life Course', *Research on Aging*, 22(3), 211–37.

———. 2003. 'Changes in Income within a Cohort over the Later Life Course: Evidence for Income Status Convergence', *Canadian Journal on Aging*, 21(4), 475–504.

Quadagno, J., and M. Hardy. 1986. 'Work and Retirement'. Pp. 325–45 in R. Binstock and L. George (eds), *Handbook of Aging and the Social Sciences*. San Diego, Calif.: Academic Press.

Robertson, A. 2000. 'I Saw the Handwriting on the Wall: Shades of Meaning in Reasons for Early Retirement', *Journal of Aging Studies*, 14(1), 63–79.

Rosenthal, C., et al. 2000. 'Changes in Work and Family over the Life Course: Implications for Economic Security of Today's and Tomorrow's Older Women'. Pp. 85–111 in F. Denton et al. (eds), *Independence and Economic Security in Old Age*. Vancouver: University of British Columbia Press.

Ruggeri, G., et al. 1994. 'The Incidence of Low Income among the Elderly', *Canadian Public Policy*, 20(2), 138–51.

Salthouse, T., and T. Maurer. 1996. 'Aging, Job Performance, and Career Development'. Pp. 353–64 in J. Birren and W. Schaie (eds), *Handbook of the Psychology of Aging*. San Diego, Calif.: Academic Press.

Schulz, J. 2001. *The Economics of Aging*. Westport, Conn: Auburn House.

Smith, R., et al. 2000. 'The Independence and Economic Security of Older Women Living Alone'. Pp. 293–327 in F. Denton et al. (eds), *Independence and Economic Security in Old Age*. Vancouver: University of British Columbia Press.

Snell, J. 1996. *The Citizen's Wage: The State and the Elderly in Canada, 1900–1951*. Toronto: University of Toronto Press.

Statistics Canada. 1998. *Labour Force Update: A New Perspective on Wages*. Summer, 2(3). Cat. no. 71-005-XPB. Ottawa: Statistics Canada.

———. 2000a. *Labour Force Historical Review, 1976–2000*. Cat. no. 71F004XCB. Ottawa: Statistics Canada.

———. 2000b. 'Incomes of Younger Retired Women: The Past 30 Years', *The Daily*, 11 December 2000 (www.statcan.ca/daily).

———. 2001. *Seniors in Canada*. Cat. no. 85F0033MIE. Canadian Centre for Justice Statistics Profile Series. Ottawa: Statistics Canada.

———. 2002. *Canada's Aging Population*. Ottawa: Health Canada.

———. 2003a. 'The Changing Profile of Canada's Work Force: Provinces and Territories'. Accessed 6 March 2003 at http://www.12.statcan.ca/English/census01/products/analytic/companion/paid.provs.cfm.

———. 2003b. *Income of Canadian Families*. Cat. no. 96F0030XIE2001014. Ottawa: Statistics Canada.

———. 2003c. 'Family Income of Older Families', *The Daily*, 25 June 2003.

———, 2003d. *Canada's Retirement Income Programs: A Statistical Overview (1990–2000)*. Cat. no. 74-507-XPE. Ottawa: Statistics Canada.

———. 2003e. 'Finances in the Golden Years', *Perspectives on Labour and Income*, 4(11). Cat. no. 75-001-XIE. Ottawa: Statistics Canada.

———. 2004. 'More Seniors at Work', *Perspective on Labour and Income*, 5(2).

Szinovacz, M., and S. DeViney. 2002. 'Marital Characteristics and Retirement Decisions', *Research on Aging*, 22(5), 470–98.

Tremblay, D-G. 2001. 'Polarization of Working Time and

Gender Differences: Reconciling Family and Work by Reducing Working Time of Men and Women'. Pp. 123–41 in V. Marshall et al. (eds), *Restructuring Work and the Life Course*. Toronto: University of Toronto Press.

Underhill, S., et al. 1997. *Options 45+: HRCC Survey Final Report*. Ottawa: One Voice.

Walker, A. 2000. 'Towards Active Ageing in Europe', *Hallym International Journal of Aging*, 2(1), 49–60.

Yabiku, S. 2000. 'Family History and Pensions: The Relationships Between Marriage, Divorce, Children, and Private Pension Coverage', *Journal of Aging Studies*, 14(3), 293–312.

CHAPTER 10

Social Networks and Social Participation in Later Life

Focal Points

- In what way do social networks influence social participation in later life?
- What are the meanings and forms of 'leisure' in later life?
- What is the meaning of time, and how is it used in later life?
- What is the relationship between social participation in later life and a higher quality of life?
- To what extent, and why, are older adults involved in crime, volunteerism, education, tourism, gambling, politics, religion, and the mass media?

Introduction

This chapter examines the everyday social world of older adults. Contrary to popular beliefs, very few older people live in isolation or are lonely. Rather, their social activity resembles that of the earlier years, although the type, location, or intensity of involvement in specific activities may increase or decrease as health, interests, or opportunities change. Social participation occurs inside or outside the home (Table 10.1) through formal or informal activities, alone or with others. Note in Table 10.1 that, for all activities except driving and walking, a higher percentage of women report being involved.

An active social life integrates individuals into a community, helps to create and maintain a social identity, and stimulates cognitive abilities and emotional feelings (Connidis and McMullin, 1992). At the same time, managing daily affairs and being socially active demonstrates self-suffi-

ciency and independence. As Altergott (1988a: 11) noted:

> It is in the domain of daily life, through self-organized activities ranging from self-care to production of goods for others, that older people create independence. It is in the domain of daily life that integration into public and private social worlds is achieved or isolation from others is experienced.

Active engagement with life (Rowe and Kahn, 1998) is important since even with the onset of an illness or some degree of dependence, being socially engaged enhances quality of life and contributes to recovery, coping, and longevity. Indeed, more socially involved older adults have lower morbidity and mortality rates (Lennartsson and Silverstein, 2001).

Table 10.1 Frequently Reported Home and Community Activities for Older Adults (65+)

	Women (%)	Men (%)
Inside the Home		
Watch television	51	49
Listen to radio	49	38
Talk on phone	44	16
Arts and crafts	34	23
Read	66	61
Have family or friends over	49	43
Outside the Home		
Visit relatives or friends	36	31
Shop (not grocery shopping)	32	23
Eat out	21	19
Go for a drive	24	31
Walk	46	52
Clubs, church, community centre	42	36
Library	12	10
Cards, games	27	25

Source: Adapted from Elliott et al (1996: 82–5), based on Health Canada's 1991 Aging and Independence Survey).

Social Engagement in Later Life

Engagement with life involves solitary or group activities, giving and receiving social support, maintaining intimate relationships, and the sharing of self and resources with others. Whether a person is involved in a solitary or group activity, participation provides meaning and purpose in the life of engaged individuals. The possible outcomes of social participation include a perceived higher quality of life; a sense of belonging to a community; better physical and mental health; and an improvement in well-being, especially for people who are widowed, who have little family contact, and for whom illness or declining functional abilities makes social support necessary (Rowe and Kahn, 1998; Bukov et al., 2002;

Silverstein and Parker, 2002). These outcomes are facilitated by social activities that encourage social integration, that offer opportunities to demonstrate competence and independence, and that create a milieu where a person receives cognitive, physical, and emotional stimulation.

Social engagement in later life involves adapting to changing lifestyles across the life course and to social changes. In recent decades, older adults have had to adapt to

- less importance attached to work, with new meanings and greater importance being attached to leisure;
- a shift from a medical and disease-treatment model of health to a health promotion and prevention model, which stresses the impor-

tance of 'active living' or 'active ageing' as the ideal lifestyle (Katz, 2000; Walker, 2000);

- a change in the meaning and use of time as work days and weeks became shorter and vacations longer;

- the promotion of social activities and social involvement as an adaptive strategy to compensate for social, cognitive, and physical losses in later life (Silverstein and Parker, 2002); and

- an increased importance on participating in social networks to enhance health and well-being (Antonucci, 2001).

Activity has become a major feature of retirement lifestyles in recent decades, including obligatory activities like ADLs; social activities; physical and cognitive activities; leisure activities; and productive activities. Being active means living a fulfilling life, and in later life it means living an 'active' life to avoid the stigma of being passive and dependent. Retiring to a rocking chair is no longer the ideal norm or the preferred image for later life. Unfortunately, in efforts to be 'active', some older people engage in activities which merely kill time. These activities provide little personal meaning or satisfaction.

Social engagement and successful aging does not mean being involved only in organized or formal activities. Katz (2000: 142–3) argues that sometimes activity in later life is pursued only to 'manage' or control everyday life or to demonstrate competence and an 'active' image. This over-management, or over-activity, by oneself or by others has inspired resistance on the part of some older persons through anti-activity attitudes or activities! Most retired adults want to be active, but many struggle with the meaning and form of activity. They want to make choices and not have activities imposed on their daily lifestyle. The following comments (Katz, 2000: 144–6) express the views of older people about being 'busy', being 'over-organized', and 'needing to be free' to make choices:

'At first I thought I have to keep going—got to make a contribution—make sure your life is worthwhile. And now I still have to struggle with days when I feel I'm not doing anything. . . . If you live in these places (retirement communities) and don't participate you are pressured into taking part. . . . It isn't that I want to be nonactive, though, it is that I want to choose.'

'You have no idea—exercise—it's just like you were back at school, as if you're such imbeciles you couldn't think of a thing to do yourself. . . . Inside this body, that may look like it's aging to you, is still a fourteen year old screaming to get out.'

'You have to decide what a "senior citizen" is. Do you want to be told what to do, when you should go and play golf, when to join a group, or do you want to do things because you enjoy them? For example, in senior citizen retirement homes, your meals are planned for you and your company is planned for you. You see it right here too, that is, what we could call a senior citizen or active retired "lifestyle". I think some people need this retirement lifestyle, because they are insecure. They want to have their meals planned, they want to be told what to do. This is a good, comfortable way of life, but it's not for everybody.'

In short, active living in later life should provide meaning, should be chosen freely, and should not be 'busy' work. Older people should not be pressured to participate, nor should they be over-organized in socially constructed ideal 'senior' activities.

Most older adults experience events or transitions that restrict or eliminate past activities or types of social involvement. These include retirement, illness, widowhood, loss of mobility, cognitive impairment, caring for a frail spouse, fear of falling, fear of crime, or, a move to a nursing home or long-term care facility (Horgas et al., 1998; Duke et al, 2002; Ice, 2002; Strain et al., 2002; Yardley and Smith, 2002). In all of these situations, a reasonable level of activity and social interaction can continue through the selection of new activities or the adaptation of specific activities to fit with present abilities and needs.[1] For those who live alone or in residential institutions, intervention may be needed to prevent them from doing 'little or nothing' with their expanding time, and to prevent a cycle of sleeping, sitting, or reclining alone in a room while waiting for the next meal. Human agency, program interventions, and the elimination of barriers and constraints facilitate adaptation so that losses in personal confidence, identity, and independence are minimized.

Asocial Behaviour: Older Criminals

Not all behaviour in later life is socially acceptable. The number of criminal offences committed by older people is increasing, although the number of arrests and convictions is quite low.[2] Only about 1 per cent of all persons accused of a Criminal Code offence in 1999 were 65 years of age or over. Of these cases, 40 per cent were for violent offences, including sexual assault; 42 per cent were for property offences, such as thefts; and the remaining 18 per cent were for minor offences such as disturbing the peace or impaired driving. Only 56 per cent of the cases resulted in a conviction since older criminals tend to be treated leniently by the courts—they are placed on probation or receive a fine or reduced sentence unless the crime involved violence or a firearm (Steffensmeir and Motivans, 2000). In Canada's federal prisons, about 12 per cent of the population is over 60 years of age (Finlay, 2000; Simard, 2000), but this includes those who have grown old in prison, repeat offenders, and a few new elderly offenders.

It is unclear whether an increase in crimes by older persons is due to the growth in the size of the older population; to an increase in the num-

ber of habitual criminals who live longer; to an increase in the number of older people who commit their first crime in later life; or to an increase in the number of older persons who are charged by the police if they are apprehended. Accurate statistics about criminal acts by older people are difficult to obtain since victims may not press charges, and the police may not arrest the accused if a crime, such as shoplifting or drunkenness in a public space, is not considered to be serious. Moreover, except for those charged with violent crimes (in 2001, 18 men over 60 years of age were charged with homicide) or drunken driving, representatives of the judicial system are more likely to release than incarcerate older people convicted of crimes. Most offences committed by older men consisted of drunkenness and driving while intoxicated. However, there are an increasing number of sexual assaults by older men and of physical assaults against partners, perhaps owing to the stress of caregiving, alcohol, side effects of drugs, cognitive impairment, or lifelong marital violence. 'Mercy' killings of a frail, impaired partner to relieve him or her from suffering are not uncommon in later life.

Among older women, the most frequent crime is shoplifting—the theft of food, clothing, or other basic necessities. One explanation is economic hardship from living on an ever-decreasing income. For example, an elderly woman caught stealing dog food reported that she did not have a dog. The dog food was cheaper than meat. Similarly, an 82-year-old man, arrested after a string of bank robberies, committed with the aid of stolen bicycles, reported that he needed to supplement his meagre income to survive.

In addition to theft motivated by need, crimes by elderly 'delinquents' also occur. This type of crime is motivated by boredom or by a need for excitement. For example, an 80-year-old bald man was reported to have stolen a hairbrush, and an 82-year-old woman stole birth control pills. Other possible explanations for petty crimes in later life are a reaction to stress associated with transitions and losses in later life; seeking attention because of feelings of marginality or a loss of prestige in society; the side effects of prescription drugs; cognitive impairment; or increased alcohol consumption. Most elderly 'delinquents' receive a warning, are placed on probation, are required to enter an educational program designed to prevent recurrences, or are required to do voluntary work in the community.

Social Networks

Throughout life, social relations occur through a variety of social networks involving individuals, groups, and organizations. Networks include people with whom we maintain personal relations, and they usually involve a relatively permanent core group (the family) and more transitory extended groups (friends, co-workers, neighbours). The transitory component expands and contracts in size and composition as we enter and leave different social worlds across the life course. The network for older people primarily includes close family and friends (Antonucci, 2001). The size and the composition of networks is influenced by our place in the social structure, and it varies by ethnicity, gender, education, income, health, occupation, place of residence (urban versus rural), size and proximity of extended family,

employment status, and marital status. The membership and composition of a network represents those who are potentially available for interaction and support, but does not indicate the sense of obligation, or the content or quality of relationships. Highlight 10.1 illustrates how the presence or absence of a partner in later life influences involvement in a network.

Chronological age has relatively little direct influence on the size or composition of a social network unless we live or work in a totally age-segregated environment. Rather, it is the stage in life and personal changes that alter a social network over the life course. Normally, the size, density (the number of people who know each other), and heterogeneity of our social networks can be represented by a curved line across the life span: the network is small, thin, and homogeneous during infancy and early childhood, when it consists mainly of the family; it grows into a larger, more heterogeneous, and denser network as we move through adolescence and into adulthood (as a result of going to school, working, marrying, and raising children). It decreases to a smaller, less heterogeneous, and less dense network as we move through the later years of life and experience widowhood, retirement, the death of friends, or a decline in health.

Highlight 10.1 Personal Networks and Partner Status

Whether one has a partner or not in later life influences the type and degree of involvement in social networks. All four cases described here involve people from the same class background, of about the same age (mid-70s), and in good health.

Mr and Mrs A.

Married for 55 years, they live in the same home they have owned for 40 years. Many of their friends are also longtime residents of the neighbourhood. Hence, most of their socializing is with neighbours through informal visiting. Mrs A. belongs to a Monday-evening church group and works as a volunteer two mornings a week at an elementary school. Mr A. works part-time as a school crossing guard and plays cards and golf regularly with a group of friends. Mr and Mrs A. belong to

continued

a bridge club at a local seniors' centre, and at least once a month they entertain other couples in their home. Their three children live within 20 miles, and each Sunday they have dinner with one of the children and their family. Mr and Mrs A. have independent social lives and share many couple activities. As a result, they both have a number of high-quality ties that provide emotional support, companionship, and confidants. Even if Mr and Mrs A. were to give up their part-time work and volunteer roles, they would still have a large network of friends, neighbours, and family. Should one of them experience a significant loss of health, a large network of informal support would be available to provide assistance.

Mrs B.

Widowed for five years, Mrs B. never worked outside the home during her adult life, and thus lacks a work-related network of friends. Her only child, a son, lives in another province, and contact with him is limited to random telephone calls and a visit every two or three years. Since the death of her husband, she has lost contact with most of their 'couple' friends, many of whom had worked with her husband. Since she is unable to drive, a volunteer from the church takes her shopping and on errands once or twice a week. Other than casual contact with neighbours in her apartment building and a few phone calls each day, she has little interaction with family, friends, or neighbours. This lifestyle is in sharp contrast to the 'active' social life she led when her husband was alive. Mrs B. lacks daily interaction and close friendships and will encounter difficulties if her health fails because she lacks a support system.

Mr C.

Never married, he has lived in an apartment throughout his adult life. His only relative is an older sister living in a nursing home. He has never been part of a neighbourhood network. Throughout his career he travelled extensively and spent most of his holidays travelling to pursue his major life interest, photography. Now he lacks kin, male and female friends, and neighbours. He has never attended church or belonged to voluntary associations. Not having a large pension, and having spent much of his earnings on travel, he no longer owns a car. Hence, he is spending more and more time in his apartment, and he lacks a network to provide emotional, physical, or social support. In the event of serious health or financial problems, one can only hope that Mr C., or someone on his behalf, can invoke the necessary resources of the formal support system in his local community. Mr C.'s lack of participation in a social network may create hardships in his later years.

Ms D.

One of the few women to graduate from an engineering school in Canada during the 1930s, Ms D. never married, although she has a large network of former colleagues, male and female, whom she visits throughout the year. In addition, she has two older sisters, one widowed and one married, and six nephews and nieces, who have always viewed her as an older sister and a friend. All of her relatives live in the same city, and she has frequent contact with each of them by telephone or face-to-face visits. Seven years ago Ms D. was hospitalized and required a long convalescence. During this period of acute illness, relatives and friends, co-ordinated by a niece, took turns providing care and support. Given this demonstration of support, it is likely that Ms D. will have an extensive network of support should she have a health crisis in the future that requires long-term support or care.

Our social world consists of an expanding and contracting circle of nodes that may include individuals, groups, and formal organizations. These nodes are linked into a network by informal social bonds or by formal relations. Across the life course, these relationships vary in durability, quality, intensity, frequency of interaction, purpose, and reciprocity (that is, they may flow in a one-way or a two-way direction). Throughout the life course, the core group remains relatively stable in size and degree of intimacy, primarily because it consists of relatives and friends. It is this core group, which itself begins to shrink in size or availability, that provides assistance, social support, and social interaction in the later stages of life.

The presence of kin alone does not guarantee that interaction will occur, that support is available, or that all ties will be supportive. Indeed, some relationships within the core become stressful, abusive, or even life-threatening through neglect or abuse. For example, if a close relationship represents a chronic source of stress and strain, it can have negative consequences for psychological and physical functioning (Lachman, 2003). However, in most instances, the network of family, friends, and organizations acts as a 'convoy' (Antonucci, 1990) that surrounds an older person, helping him or her to meet challenges and crises as illness, dependency, and frailty increase. The membership and the nature of relationships in a specific convoy change at different stages in the life course, but many strong intimate bonds persist. Women tend to be more involved in kin networks (as 'kin keepers'), while men are more involved in friend or work-related networks. Not surprisingly, women, especially if employed or active in voluntary organizations, have large and diverse networks and a more permanent, intimate, and confiding convoy; unmarried men have the smallest and least intimate networks and therefore in later life have fewer sources of informal support.

Adults with higher social status generally have larger, more widespread networks consisting of family, friends, and colleagues; whereas those from a lower-class background have smaller networks, mainly involving family and neighbours. Similarly, persons with specific racial, religious, ethnic, or cultural backgrounds, especially if recent immigrants, are linked to a network primarily composed of their family and members of the same religious or cultural group in the neighbourhood, at a place of worship or at an ethnic club (Antonucci, 2001). The density and size of a network also varies by living arrangements, including: the size of the household; whether located in an urban or rural setting; whether age-segregated or age-integrated; and whether one lives in a single-family home, a multi-household building, or a retirement or nursing home.

The structure and importance of a network for an individual is determined by the size, complexity, or number of nodes; by the frequency of contact and the degree and direction of intimacy among members; by the homogeneity of the nodes in terms of socio-demographic characteristics (age, gender, education, religion, and ethnicity); and by the stability of membership over time. The quality of a network experience is measured by the type of social interaction or contact (intimate, casual, or formal), the degree of perceived support, the satisfaction derived from relationships, and whether interactions serve a preventative, rehabilitative, or caretaking function.

Most elderly adults are not isolated, disengaged, alienated, or abandoned. Rather, networks of varying sizes, with relationships of varying strengths and quality, are available for social interaction and social support. These networks provide companionship, knowledge, a confidant,[3] emotional support, help with minor personal or home-care needs, and assistance during acute or chronic illness or crises. While the availability of a social network and the number of ties normally decreases with advancing age, the few ties remaining late in life normally become stronger, although the frequency of interaction may decrease because of declining health and mobility. Not surprisingly, older persons prefer to rely on adult children and friends for interaction and for assistance with basic needs. As dependence increases, the need for more specialized support and caregiving increases. This caregiving network grows to include both informal ties with primary groups (family, friends, and neighbours) and links with formal organizations (social welfare agencies, home-care workers, nursing homes, and respite-care facilities). To provide suitable and adequate assistance, all parts of the support network must be integrated and co-ordinated. This is often difficult to achieve because each node in the network, ranging from the most intimate, usually a spouse or adult child, to the most formal, such as an employee in a long-term-care institution, may have a different opinion about the social, health, and leisure needs of an aging individual. Each person in the network should have different skills or resources to assist and support an older person. Thus, gaps in service or support emerge in a caregiving network if all skills and types of expertise are not available (see Chapter 11).

Leisure and Aging: Conceptual and Methodological Issues

The relative importance of family, work, and leisure in our daily lives changes at different points in the life course. Hence, the way in which time is used for obligatory or discretionary activities varies. Individuals select leisure activities to fit their personal identity (how they define themselves) and their social identity (how they believe they are defined by others). We develop a 'core' of leisure pursuits that persist throughout our lives as part of our usual social life. These might include varying degrees of social interaction (solitary versus group activities), and specific general interests involving the mass media, volunteering, cultural activities, tourism, or sport activities. Then, a balance of activities are pursued to fit the needs or desires of our personal and social identity, and our abilities and interests at specific

stages in life. These latter activities change as roles, self-definitions, occupations, competencies, and opportunities change.

Leisure participation across the life course involves continuity and change according to how we define ourselves and how we wish to be perceived by others in different situations and at different stages (Kelly, 1987, 1993). Like many other aspects of social life, opportunities for leisure vary by income, gender, education, social class, ethnicity, health, employment, and marital status. Hence, as in other domains of our social and working lives, there is inequality in leisure. Structural constraints or lack of personal resources means that some adults are not able to spend their leisure time as they might wish. This can result in a lack of congruence between actual and desired use of leisure time.

Leisure, as an *expressive* rather than an instrumental domain of daily life, has profound meaning for those who do not find their identity in the world of work (Thomas and Venne, 2002; Hendricks and Cutler, 2003). Leisure, as well, is a domain of everyday life that illustrates the importance and potential of personal agency and autonomy and the reality and possibility of shifting priorities and interests over time. In the domains of work and family life, autonomy and free choice are less likely or possible, and structural constraints are more rigid (Hendricks and Cutler, 2003: 123).

With longer lives and changing lifestyles, more leisure time is available across the life course, and new forms of leisure activity are emerging. Moreover, leisure activities are distributed more equitably through one's life, and across the population. There are both individual-level changes over time in agency, abilities and interests; and, at the societal level, in the structure and allocation of leisure opportunities, such as education, facilities, and programs. Accordingly, today we are more likely to observe people from a lower-class background playing golf or enjoying fine art; women engaged in a wider array of leisure activities outside the home; and older adults in their 80s travelling throughout the world and engaging in physical activity.

Increasingly, leisure activities for older people, especially women, take place outside the family in public and private facilities. Shopping malls, coffee shops, restaurants, parks, and recreational facilities are places where older adults engage in a social life and where informal groups can form in safe, public spaces. Often these settings facilitate the creation of informal groups that meet voluntarily and regularly for casual conversation. To illustrate, based on a participant observation study of older adults who regularly met in a fast-food restaurant, Cheang (2002) concludes that older people in this type of setting create non-obligatory, casual friendships involving a form of play and laughter. Serious, personal matters are seldom, if ever, discussed. These group gatherings become an important part of the everyday routine in the lives of older persons. For many of the participants in this study, the setting is more meaningful than a 'senior's centre', which they consider to be a place for 'old folks'.

Defining Leisure

There is no universally accepted definition of leisure, partly because experiences and meanings are extremely personal and diverse. Leisure is defined by the participants, at a point in time, to meet their social, cognitive, and emotional needs; to help define themselves; and perhaps, to provide intrinsic rewards. Many aspects of leisure are similar to those found in work. Both work and leisure have the potential to provide an individual with a sense of worth, identity, prestige and status; with a milieu in which to establish and maintain social interaction; and with an outlet for expressive and instrumental needs. The inability to agree on a definition persists because leisure is a multi-dimensional concept,[4] because activities have a variety of meanings or functions for an individual at different times in the life course,[5] because individuals can engage in more than one leisure activity at a time,[6] and because some activities fall into overlapping categories.[7] Furthermore, leisure can be considered a non-essential, voluntary, not-for-profit activity, or it can be viewed as 'big business' in the professional sport, travel, or entertainment industries.

The meaning of leisure for a given individual or social group is influenced, as well, by cultural or structural norms, values, experiences, and opportunities. Leisure is not found in every culture or for all social groups in many developing countries. In fact, leisure, as a concept, is unknown to members of some cultures. Cultural and structural factors, unique to individuals or groups, sometimes differentiate leisure by age, gender, race, education, ethnicity, socio-economic status, religion, or place of residence. More specifically, the amount, type, or intensity of leisure pursued by individuals is influenced by the demands of a job, marital and family responsibilities, economic status, health, climate, access to transportation, quality of the neighbourhood, and prevailing social values concerning leisure. By way of summary, a definition or conceptualization of leisure may include the following characteristics:

- a social context for establishing and developing primary social relationships
- a state of mind, attitude, or being
- non-work
- freedom of choice in selecting activities
- free or discretionary time
- relaxation and diversion from work and personal maintenance activities
- playfulness or play
- voluntary activity
- expressive activities, in which there is internal satisfaction and an emphasis on the process rather than the end result or product
- instrumental activities, which offer external rewards and which have an end product or outcome as the goal

- spontaneity
- utilitarian and meaningful activities
- active and passive activities
- social (group) or individual (solitary) activities
- expensive or inexpensive activities
- intellectual (that is, cognitive), social, or physical activities
- intrinsic or extrinsic rewards
- creativity
- high culture or mass culture

Although many of these characteristics are viewed as dichotomous scales, in reality they represent continua.[8] Individuals change their type or level of involvement in these dimensions as they age; during different seasons of the year; after moving to a new residence, neighbourhood or region; when there are changes in structural constraints or in cultural or subcultural values or norms; or, as transitions occur in work or family roles. For example, after the completion of formal education and with entrance into the labour force, the type, frequency, and meaning of leisure and social involvement changes owing to such factors as a reduced amount of free time; a new lifestyle because of the demands of a job; and, for many, new responsibilities associated with marriage, career, home ownership, and child rearing.[9] Moreover, since the various characteristics are not mutually exclusive, individuals participate in a variety of quite different activities. Thus, someone can participate equally in a structured, expressive, physical activity, such as a dance class, and in an unstructured, instrumental, passive activity, such as collecting stamps from a specific country.

Increasingly, more emphasis is placed on the *quality* rather than the *quantity* of leisure, in general, and with respect to particular leisure and social activities. The quality or meaning of a specific leisure experience changes as one moves through different parts of the life course. For example, in early adulthood, hiking may be viewed as primarily a physical activity in which one hikes up and down a mountain trail as fast as possible to improve one's fitness. By middle adulthood, hiking may be viewed as a means to escape the urban environment or boredom with one's job. Late in life, hiking up a mountain at a leisurely pace might be pursued to provide a setting for a hobby such as photography. In short, meanings assigned to a specific leisure activity or to leisure and social activities, in general, change across the life course.

The Meaning and Use of Time

Time is a non-renewable resource that, once used or wasted, cannot be replaced. Thus, how we use time and the proportion of time we allocate to specific domains are important decisions that merit both personal reflection and scholarly inquiry. On the basis of time-budget surveys that measure the amount of time allocated to specific activities, we know that members of the lower class, compared with those of the middle and upper classes, are less future-oriented, are less punctual, and adhere less rigidly to time schedules. Yet, those with lower incomes spend fewer hours per week at paid and unpaid work and report having more leisure hours per day, much of which is spent watching television. For example, Williams (2002) found that low- and high-income Canadians spend 132 and 82 minutes a day, respectively, watching television.

Time is a valued commodity and a central element in differentiating contemporary lifestyles. The amount of 'free' time influences whether and when an event will happen; the duration and sequence of events; and when, how, and to what extent we play a variety of social and leisure roles. Over a 24-hour period, daily lives are generally structured into three domains: obligatory activities, social or family activities, and leisure activities (Altergott, 1988b). The amount of time allocated to each domain is influenced by individual values and preferences, the obligatory roles we must perform, social and economic constraints and opportunities, and the demands of others, such as children, partners, employers, and aging parents, for our time. Thus, at different stages in life we perceive and use time in different ways, and we have more or less discretionary time at some stages than at others (Cutler and Hendricks, 1990). As well, differences in time use in later life varies from country to country, with a large portion of time freed up by retirement being reallocated to passive activities (Gauthier and Smeeding, 2003).

When we do not have enough time for obligatory activities, that is, work, family, or household responsibilities, we sacrifice our leisure, sleep, and social activities. Data from the 1998 General Social Survey (Fast et al., 2001) show that leisure activities are occupying a larger share of each day even though, for many, work time has increased. The extra leisure time is captured by spending less time on obligatory personal-care activities such as sleeping, preparing meals, eating, and housework. This survey also confirmed that women have less free time than men and that women spend less time on paid work and more time on unpaid work. To illustrate, the 2001 census reported that 21 per cent of Canadian women but only 8 per cent of men spend 30 hours or more a week on unpaid work. Similarly, 16 per cent of women but only 7 per cent of men devoted 30 hours or more a week to child care; and 20 per cent of women compared to 15 per cent of men were caring for an aging parent.

Retirement, unemployment, living alone, or illness in later life force people to cope with unstructured time after a lifetime in which most of daily life was structured around work and family obligations. In later life there is more discretionary time and less time may be needed for obligatory activities, assuming health and mobility remain constant. As more older adults live alone (about 40 per cent of women and 17 per cent of men 65 and over), more time is spent alone. For those 65 and over, the average number of hours per day spent alone was 6.5 hours for men and 8 hours for women (Clark, 2002).

Contrary to conventional wisdom, the 'problem' of retirement is often not the amount of free time, but rather, an inability to decide how to use that free time. As Zuzanek and Box (1988: 179) stated, 'Having more free time does not automatically translate into greater happiness. Being able to fill this time with activities and to structure it in a meaningful and diversified way does! Acquiring a satisfying lifestyle in retirement presupposes an ability to structure one's time.'

Time is a cultural product that may or may not be viewed as a scarce resource at specific moments or stages in life. The clock and a calendar provide some degree of order, routine, and structure to our lives. However, time is regarded in different ways by different individuals and at different stages in life. Despite the alleged increase in discretionary time due to a shorter work week, some people feel that they never have enough time, and they employ others to clean, cook, or shop for them. Others 'multi-task' by conducting business or social matters during meals; do their telephoning or shaving while driving a car; or reading newspapers or work reports while watching television. In addition, stores are open 24 hours a day and Internet shopping is available to meet the needs of alternative work and leisure lifestyles. For some, time becomes a scarce commodity owing to the demands of increased learning required by an information society, 'moonlighting' at a second job, longer commuting time on congested roads, conflicting schedules of dual-career couples, or caring for an elderly parent or dependent child.

There are generational differences within the same ethnic group in the allocation of time to specific activities, and people with smaller social networks (namely, those who are single, widowed, divorced, retired, or childless) often report having more discretionary time. Moreover, the nature of an activity influences how, when, and whether time is allocated to the activity. For example, consider the ease of watching television or working on a hobby at home compared with reserving a tennis court for a noon-hour game of doubles on a specific day, and then finding three other players of comparable ability to play at the designated time and place.

In the later years of life, some people feel that time passes quickly, others, that it passes slowly. If time is wasted, or if a person is unable to use discretionary time in a meaningful way, time drags and boredom results. Boredom, a self-induced state, occurs when there is an excess of discretionary time or an inability to manage time. Others say that time 'flies' and that they haven't enough of it. In reality, these people do not have less time than others. Rather, they are more socially involved and their daily or weekly calendars are full with meaningful activities.

Social Participation: The Early and Middle Years

The type of activities pursued during leisure time and the meaning and function of these activities vary across the life course. Throughout life's journey we acquire a repertoire of leisure skills and activities that represent a set of meaningful, intrinsically motivated activities that we pursue regularly, such as music, sports, or reading. Activities that remain part of the repertoire across the life course are those in which we display some competence and those that provide meaning or satisfaction in our daily lives.

At different stages in life, individual activities change due to shifts in preferences, individual or societal constraints, abilities, and health. But consistency in the leisure repertoire generally prevails. For example, a lifelong opera fan may attend fewer operas as he or she ages but may spend as much or more time listening to operas on radio or CDs. Likewise, a long-time opera fan is unlikely to become a consumer of country music in later life.

Descriptive studies regularly report the frequency or type of leisure activities at a particular stage in life, at a particular chronological age, or

at a particular point in time. Although some general patterns across the life course can be identified from these cross-sectional studies, longitudinal studies are lacking so it is not possible to explain patterns observed across the life course— are these patterns due to aging, cohort, or period effects? For example, some leisure pursuits, such as skateboarding or specific forms of dance, are fads that influence one age cohort but not others; in other words they are a cohort effect. Or an activity, such as watching 'reality' television shows, may be pursued by those in many age cohorts at the same time but then abandoned later by all age groups, which is a period effect. Other pursuits are abandoned in middle or later life because of normal aging effects such as loss of health, or physical or cognitive changes.

The adoption of a specific leisure or social activity early in life often significantly influences leisure involvement throughout life. For example, those who were pre-adolescents, adolescents, and young adults in the 1980s and 1990s were exposed to the 'fitness boom' and the beginning of the health-promotion movement. Consequently, many adopted some type of daily physical activity. These cohorts will likely engage in higher levels of physical activity than earlier or later cohorts at all subsequent stages in their life course. It is for this reason that many are projecting very 'active' lifestyles among the retired baby boomers.

Although it is not possible to identify a single leisure pattern across the life course, some general patterns can be described. Figure 10.1 illustrates a variety of possible patterns of leisure and social involvement across the life course. The curves represent hypothetical patterns of involvement in sport (A), visiting (B), membership in a political party (C), reading for pleasure (D), travel (E), or home-centred activities (F). These patterns may hold for specific individuals or birth cohorts; they may reflect the pattern for a given activity (reading); or they may apply to six different individuals or six different age cohorts for the same leisure activity. In reality, involvement is not as orderly as these smooth curves suggest. There are peaks and valleys of involvement at various stages in the life course because of institutional, cultural, or individual constraints.

Despite these complex individual differences, there are some general and relatively predictable leisure patterns at different stages in the life course. These patterns are determined by transitions within the family or work careers that require a continuous process of adaptation. During childhood and early adolescence, a variety of leisure experiences are pursued in the family or at school. Many of these are introduced and encouraged by parents, peers, and teachers, and are selected voluntarily by the individual. During middle and late adolescence, the influence of the family decreases while the peer group and the media become more influential in determining leisure lifestyles, particularly for fads and fashions. At this time, if an adolescent enters the labour force part-time, there is often a reduction in discretionary time and an increase in discretionary income.

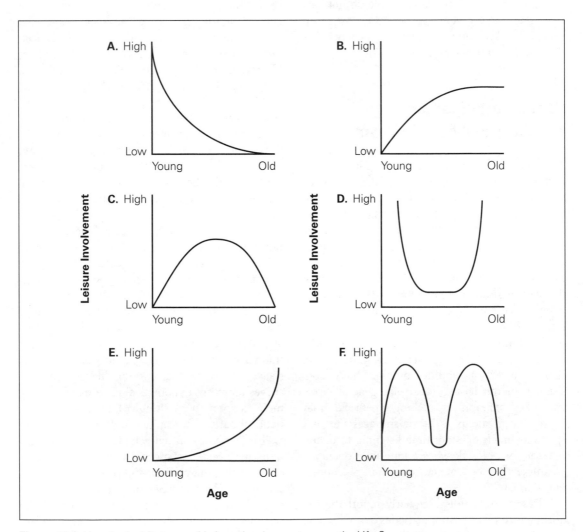

Figure 10.1 Hypothetical Patterns of Leisure Involvement across the Life Course

The next major transition occurs when formal education ends and full-time work begins. Normally, this stage includes, at some point, marriage, home ownership, and the birth of children. Moreover, this stage in life can involve moving to a new neighbourhood or region of the country and the creation of new social networks. The commitment of time to establishing a career and family dramatically restricts or changes leisure and social patterns during the early years of adulthood. During this stage, leisure and social activities are mainly centred in the home and family.

By middle age, careers are established, children leave home, more discretionary time and money may be available, and leisure becomes a more important part of one's identity and lifestyle. However, at this time many women enter or re-enter the labour force, thereby reducing their leisure time. In addition, divorce or the onset of a chronic illness or disability will result in dramatic changes in the type, location, and amount of leisure. During the middle years, couples develop separate or common leisure interests. Generally, the pattern established by the middle years continues into the pre-retirement stage and often into the post-retirement stage. This pattern of continuity suggests that an understanding of social participation and leisure interests and habits during the middle years can help us to predict or plan the use of time, and the type of social participation in the retirement years.

Many patterns of leisure involvement are possible in the early and middle years of adulthood. Individual differences in these patterns are related to social class and type of occupation; to local or regional differences in opportunity and values; to variations in events in an individual family life course; and to variations by gender, race, and ethnicity. For this reason, chronological age is a weak predictor of leisure or social participation patterns across the life course, especially for age-integrated activities. For example, among 24-year-olds, some attend university, others are employed full-time in the labour force, others are unemployed and looking for work; some are members of the upper socio-economic stratum, others are from the lower stratum; some are married, others are not; and some are parents. Similarly, the leisure and social participation patterns of women within any one age category varies depending on social class, marital status, presence and age of children, education, employment status, and past leisure experiences and interests.

Social Participation: Later Life

For most older adults, engaging in leisure activities represents an attempt to use their time in a meaningful way, to find meaning and an identity in daily life, and to facilitate access to social networks. Because of agency and conscious decisions about the meaning of, and identity derived from, leisure, the qualitative (more so than the quantitative) dimensions of leisure are considered more important in later life. This reflects the view that leisure is more than killing time, that new pursuits can be initiated, and that leisure should be a high-quality experience throughout later life, including when older people move into a retirement home or a long-term care facility. Highlight 10.2 illustrates how agency can influence the leisure lifestyles of older adults.

Changing leisure lifestyles reflect the interaction of social structural and historical events with personal biographies or histories. Over time, leisure has become a more significant component of later life, largely because of increased opportunities earlier in life. Leisure experiences earlier in life are cumulative and exert an influence on leisure choices and opportunities in later life. For the most part, there is continuity in individual leisure patterns. But changes in the frequency, type, intensity, and location of leisure are increasingly likely, and possible, in later life. Many older adults renew their participation in activities that have been dormant for years, or begin new activities that were not available earlier in life, or that were heretofore unknown or unaffordable.

Highlight 10.2 Agency in Later Life: We Have Choices

The worst part of aging is internalizing the myth that after 65 you are expected to opt out of life and turn into a vegetable of your choice. The only part of this myth that is salvageable is 'choice'. We do not become a different species at 65, and, in fact, aging can bring freedom to explore and do things for the first time. Examples of new beginnings after 65 abound in everyday life:

- Murray started his third career at the age of 65, and now at 82 he is still going strong as the administrator of a non-profit organization. He walks for over an hour every morning and still lives a life full of zest.

- Ann is an 80-plus retired nurse who recently embarked on a new pursuit as a very successful sculptor. She also finds time to serve as president of a major seniors' organization.

- Al, a retired pharmacist, is fighting hard as a volunteer activist to preserve Canada's medicare system. At the same time, he is the main caregiver for his wife, who suffers from Alzheimer's Disease—a responsibility he never imagined he could cope with, but he does.

- Bernice spent her life as a homemaker looking after her children and husband—and making the best chocolate cookies on the block. At the age of 75, she discovered the Seniors Olympics. Her trophies are the pride of the whole family.

- Bob has come out of retirement at the age of 72 to help his son build his computer programming business. He's happy to be active again and to have the opportunity to apply business skills acquired over 40 years in an earlier career.

- Bertie retired from her seamstress job at 66, after 50 years, to look after her grandson so that her daughter, a single mother, could work. Sharing in the raising of the child, and spending so much time with him, energizes her. She no longer lives alone and is doing what she's always wanted to do—be a homemaker.

- Louis's dream of being a playwright came true for him at the age of 75, when his first script was workshopped and produced by a local seniors' drama group. He is working on his second play, and acting in other productions. A life-long desire that had to be put aside in order to support his parents and then his own family is now being fulfilled.

- Becky was a secretary and political activist until her husband fell ill and she became a full-time caregiver. Since his death, she, now aged 85, has been mentoring immigrant children at school with remedial reading and helps them become integrated into Canadian society.

Source: Adapted from Gleberzon and Cutler (2002). Reprinted by permission of Judy Cutler and Bill Gleberzon, Co-Directors of Advocacy, CARP.

As we enter the early years of the twenty-first century, the lifestyles and leisure pursuits of older adults are dramatically different from those of older people during the early and middle parts of the twentieth century. In the early decades of the 1900s, adults had few leisure opportunities throughout a relatively short life course. The work day was long, many worked on Saturdays, there were few vacations longer than two weeks, there was little discretionary income for leisure, early retirement was unknown, and many worked beyond the normal retirement age of 65 years. Many died soon after retiring. Moreover, most free time was spent in or around the home and with one's family, and women primarily 'worked' in the home and had little leisure beyond that associated with family activities. Two-career couples were unusual, marriages endured (with few divorces), community volunteerism was not common, and later life was passive, sedentary, and home-based for most retirees. Retirement to a 'rocking chair' was considered an ideal goal and a reward for a life of hard work.

Contrast this perspective with the 'freedom 55' image that is promoted today by the insurance, travel, and leisure industries. This message encourages people to retire as early as possible, travel the world, and enjoy 'active' leisure for the rest of their life, which might last as long as 30–40 years. Indeed, in this scenario, some long-living individuals spend more years at 'leisure' than they do at work.

The stereotypical images of leisure pursuits in later life as being sedentary and passive are being cast aside by 'senior' role models, male and female, who volunteer, travel, attend university to earn degrees, and engage in highly competitive sports such as marathon races, hockey, wind surfing, skiing, and weight lifting. These new images fit with the known physical and cognitive capacity and potential of older adults and with the idea that leisure activities, especially outside the home, provide an opportunity for social relations.

Interaction with others in later life is highly correlated with reported well-being, happiness, and life satisfaction. This does not mean that older people do not, or should not, engage in solitary leisure activities, such as reading, stamp collecting, or knitting. But it does imply that a mixture of group and solitary activities creates a balanced life that enhances well-being and both physical and mental health in the later years. There is considerable diversity in the leisure and social pursuits within and among older age cohorts, and this diversity will increase further as the baby boom generation retires, having developed a lifelong leisure-oriented lifestyle.

With partial or full retirement, the amount of unstructured free time increases dramatically. This time can be filled by continuing some form of work, by spending more time on complete daily personal tasks, or by participating in meaningful leisure and social activities. Most studies report continuity between work and retirement leisure lifestyles, although the number of activities and the frequency of involvement may decrease as health or income declines. For many, at least in the early stages, retirement is viewed as a time of increased personal freedom.

During later life a number of individual and societal constraints reduce social involvement or change leisure pursuits. At the *individual* level, such constraints include

- declining health and energy;
- loss of interest in specific activities;
- lack of a partner owing to illness, death, or divorce;
- a decline in financial resources and a loss of discretionary income;
- changes in the leisure interests or health of a spouse; and
- an inability to drive or to use public transportation.

At the *societal* level, constraints are imposed on older adults when

- information about leisure opportunities is not widely disseminated;
- local or regional norms and cultural values discourage the involvement of older adults in specific activities, such as formal education, sports, or drama;
- there are no programs or facilities, such as senior-citizen centres, especially in rural and inner-city areas;
- public transportation is inaccessible or unavailable;
- expensive leisure pursuits are not subsidized;
- a deteriorating and unsafe neighbourhood induces a fear of crime or a fear of falling so that older adults stay at home; and

- myths or negative stereotypes in the media promote the idea that older adults are not capable of or interested in studying and learning, becoming computer literate, becoming physically fit, or dating.

At a stage in life characterized by social and physical changes and losses—the loss of friends and the social milieu at work upon retirement, the deaths of friends and spouse, loss of mobility and independence—leisure and social activities provide an environment and a structure where new social networks can be created. Regardless of the particular activities pursued by older individuals or cohorts, leisure provides a milieu to develop social relationships, and to demonstrate to oneself and to others that he or she is a competent individual with a high sense of self-worth (Kelly, 1987).

To understand more fully the meaning and the use of leisure in later life, we need to examine the ways in which leisure contributes to life satisfaction and to a higher quality of life. Rather than simply determining how many hours per day a person spends watching television, we need to know which programs are watched; with whom, if anyone, they are watched; and what function or meaning the programs have for the viewer. Similarly, it is more informative to determine changes in the meaning of an activity over time rather than whether there has been an hourly, daily, or weekly decrease or increase in participation. Recall the example earlier in this chapter about how hiking can have different meanings and serve different needs at different stages of life.

Volunteerism and Participation in Voluntary Associations

Proponents of apocalyptic demography often hold the view that older people do not make an economic contribution to society. Consequently, they argue, usually without supporting evidence, that older adults are a burden to society. A more positive and realistic view argues that older people represent an untapped resource for society. The contributions of those over 60 years of age are made through voluntary formal involvement in organizations and community groups,[10] or through informal contributions in the form of social support, services, and money to family, friends, or neighbours. Because of this voluntary, unpaid activity, retirees are increasingly viewed by society as productive citizens who can make an economically valuable contribution outside the paid labour force (Robb et al., 1999; Lian et al, 2000; Hendricks and Cutler, 2001; Gottlieb, 2002).

The core elements of voluntary behaviour (Chappell, 2002) are the following:

- Labour is given freely, although involvement may result from peer pressure or a sense of obligation to re-pay society.
- There is a beneficiary, whether it be an individual, group, organization, or the state (caring for dependent relatives is not usually considered as volunteer work, per se).
- There is no financial gain, although some expenses may be reimbursed.

Much of the unpaid help would, if not provided, have to be purchased by others in society or be funded by the state. Some of the contributions provided by older adults include the following: helping or looking after a child or peer; mentoring and counselling; providing leadership in community service; volunteering in political parties or organizations; taking part in not-for-profit associations; and doing a variety of tasks or services related to one's skill and experience (fund raising, doing home repairs, preparing tax returns, tutoring).

There have been various attempts to quantify (by hours or dollars) the contribution of older people to Canadian society. Robb et al. (1999), on the basis of the 1992 Canadian General Social Survey on Time Use, reported the following:

- The average man and woman 55 years of age and older contributed, annually, a value of $2,073 and $1,857, respectively, in unpaid help to others.

- The total market value of unpaid help contributed by those 55 and over in 1992 was about $10.5 billion.

- For those 65 years and older, the total market value of their contribution was $5.5 billion; which was equivalent to about 25 per cent of what they received in public assistance from the OAS and GIS income security programs.

According to 2000 data (Statistics Canada, 2001c), 18 per cent of those 65 and over contributed an average of 269 hours of volunteer time during the year (a decrease from 5 per cent since 1997). Thus, a fewer number of older volunteers are giving even more of their time. Other studies[11] have found that among older adults, more volunteer labour is contributed by married people than single people, by those who are more highly educated, and by those who have had a history of volunteer work.

Membership in voluntary associations tends to be curvilinear[12] across the life course (Curve C in Figure 10.1), with peak involvement occuring within about 10 years of retirement (Cutler and Hendricks, 2000). However, younger age cohorts are demonstrating greater involvement in all forms of volunteer work at earlier ages, and volunteering does not cease for many older adults even after moving into a retirement home. Therefore, many baby boomers are likely to continue volunteer work in later life, and more women will continue to volunteer after they retire because early life involvement as a volunteer continues into later life involvement. And as the state, and educational and work organizations encourage or require more voluntary activity, more citizens will become involved throughout the life course. Highlight 10.3 illustrates how older people contribute to society by volunteering their

services. However, not all volunteer experiences in later life are positive. In a study of 19 not-for-profit agencies using older volunteers to serve older clients, Gottlieb (2002) discovered three issues of concern to older volunteers: (1) clients are becoming more difficult to serve, more demanding, more needy, and more dependent; (2) volunteers are increasingly concerned about their safety and well-being; and (3), which follows from the first two issues, since volunteers do not serve forever, there is high turnover and they are in short supply for this expanding service sector.

Why do people volunteer and what are some of the outcomes for the individual and society? In general, people volunteer their time for these reasons:

- to affiliate with a group
- to be productive and contribute to society
- to share their knowledge, experience, wisdom, and skills
- to advance a personal interest or cause
- to fill time and keep active
- to develop or maintain an identity
- to demonstrate independence
- to acquire new skills
- to play a leadership role
- to interact with others, especially younger people, who have similar interests

Some older (and younger) people who are searching for a full- or part-time job use a volunteer position as a link to future employment. For the active older volunteer, being involved enhances health and well-being, maintains an identity and self-esteem, contributes to productive and active aging, and keeps the person linked and integrated with others (Van Willigen, 2000).

From the perspective of a society or organization, volunteerism builds social responsibility; promotes social cohesion, integration, and assim-

Highlight 10.3 Volunteers in Later Life

Anne

Anne, a 76-year-old volunteer, works a 10-hour shift each weekday at a local hospital. She meets incoming patients scheduled for surgery, takes them to the surgical room, and comforts those who are frightened and alone. At other times she delivers flowers to patients. For the last 10 years she has never missed a day. She volunteers year round and must take two buses to reach the hospital. When winter weather delays the bus, she takes a cab at her own expense in order to arrive on time.[1]

Prue

Since completing a course on peer counselling, Prue has been an active volunteer for 16 years. She spends 15 hours a week as a senior-citizen counsellor in Victoria, BC. Five years into her new career, she recognized the need for a home-delivery service for seniors and the disabled. After approaching grocery stores in the community, she launched Sendial, a program in which volunteers deliver groceries to those who cannot shop at the stores. Prue also helped set up Students/Seniors Work Assistance Program (SWAP). This employment project, run in co-operation with the University of Victoria Employment Centre, enables students to earn money by helping older adults. The students change light bulbs or take older people for car rides.[2]

Bill

A 75-year-old retired businessman, Bill had always wanted to teach. Confined to a wheelchair, he now works two mornings a week at an elementary school, helping students to speak, write, and read in order to improve their literacy. He has also donated $25,000 to the school's literacy program. In addition, Bill has become a friend, counsellor, and storyteller, relating historical events in the community.[3]

[1] 1 Adapted from an article in the *Kitchener-Waterloo Record* (17 February 1997), B1, B2.
[2] Adapted and reprinted with permission from the University of Victoria Centre on Aging *Bulletin*, 5(1) (1997), 6–7.
[3] Adapted and reprinted with permission from *Board's Eye View*, North York Board of Education (June 1990).

ilation (in the case of ethnic associations); builds social capital in a community or organization; creates a sense of community and belonging; provides social services (in the case of service and fraternal groups); and fosters social change (in the case of political activist groups or labour unions). Indeed, many voluntary groups are organized as advisory or advocacy groups to promote the specific interests and needs of older adults or retirees—for example, the National Advisory Council on Aging (NACA) and the Canadian Association of Retired Persons (CARP). Others provide home care or serve as drivers for Meals-on-Wheels programs to help older people remain in their own home for longer when their mobility and independence decline.

A unique age-based type of voluntary organization for older adults is the 'senior citizen' or 'older adult' centre found in many communities. These centres, usually funded by municipal governments or religious organizations, depend heavily on volunteers to offer programs and services. Despite their availability, a majority of older adults do not become involved in these centres, either by choice or because they are not aware of them (Strain, 2001). Those most likely to participate regularly are women; rural residents; those in good health, who live alone, who have easy access to transportation, who have always been 'joiners', who have less formal education, who have a strong identity with the neighbourhood, community or religious sponsor; and those who are not afraid of crime or of falling en route to and from the centre. Non-users say they were unaware of a centre or its programs, are too busy, or are not interested in an 'old folks' club. In many cases those who would benefit the most from attending such a centre, that is, people who are lonely and isolated, do not participate. For older adults who participate regularly in clubs or centres, they provide information, educational services, friendship groups and support networks, and a sense of identity. As well, through programs they foster improved health and safety by providing meals; vision, hearing and dental clinics; counselling; and informal health and safety monitoring by staff and fellow members.

Political Participation

Civic participation in the political process is another form of active and productive aging (Burr, 2002). As the older population has increased in size, and with each cohort that enters later life being better educated, more older adults report being involved as voters, as political candidates, as members of political organizations, and as political activists. While there is a general curvilinear relationship between age and civic activity, especially for voting behaviour, decreased involvement in later life is less pronounced today than it was 20–30 years ago. Much of the increased involvement among older people is accounted for by significant increases in political interest and political activity among women.

Changes in political interest or attitudes across the life course are due to a combination of maturational changes, cohort effects, and period effects. For example, although cross-sectional studies suggest that older people as a group are more conservative than other age cohorts, this does not imply that they become more conservative with age. Rather, they were politically socialized at a period in history when conservatism prevailed. They also appear conservative relative to younger cohorts because of dramatic changes in social values over a 20- or 30-year period characterized by the women's movement, political activism by youth, and new political parties.

Individual priorities attached to specific political issues vary by stage in life. Generally, younger people are more concerned with issues such as rising tuition fees, high unemployment, the environment, women's rights, abortion, and gay rights. Older age cohorts tend to be more concerned with inflation, health care, pension benefits, and increased taxes. Often these different political agendas are reflected in voting behaviour. In short, political interest, orientation, and priorities change with age, particularly on issues related to changing personal situations such as, employment, health, and retirement. Thus, with respect to political behaviour and interest, among older age cohorts there are more differences within this age segment than there are among younger age cohorts (Binstock and Day, 1996). Whether the political views of younger cohorts persist or change across the life course remains to be confirmed by longitudinal studies. Also of influence on age-related differences in political orientations or participation patterns are period effects. A war, a depression, high unemployment, or a political scandal can dramatically change political beliefs, involvement, attitudes, and voting choices for members of specific age cohorts at a specific period in history. Sometimes these period effects persist throughout the life course; at other times they dissipate as history evolves.

There are regional and social-class variations with respect to political matters. For example, the values and lifestyles of those who live in the

Atlantic provinces are traditionally more conservative than those of people living in other provinces such as British Columbia. This regional variation is partly related to prevailing subcultural norms and values, which in turn are related to the geographical distance from the centres of political and economic power in Canada. Regional differences are also related, however, to differences in average ages and levels of educational attainment, and to isolation and rural living, which can restrict access to information. Similarly, members of the lower class in all geographical regions and those in recent immigrant groups, tend to have less access to new ideas, and to adhere to childhood and adolescent political values throughout their lives. They also feel more powerless and are, in general, less interested and influential in the political process.

Political participation, as a form of voluntary behaviour, requires a commitment of time, money, and skills. Beyond voting, involvement includes joining a political party, becoming an activist, attending local meetings, serving on committees, or serving as an elected or appointed public official. Most of this voluntary activity occurs at the local level, at least initially. Most involvement is expressed through voting, and politicians recognize the size of the potential voting bloc of older adults. Consequently, politicians seek to understand why older adults are more involved, and to determine their specific interests, and how they can be mobilized to vote. For example, it is projected that the proportion of all eligible Canadian voters who are over 65 years of age will be 16.5 per cent in 2010, and 25 per cent by 2030.

Generally, participation in voting by older people is high because they have been longtime residents of a community, they have a history and understanding of issues, and they may have a long-standing identification with a particular political party. Increasingly, older adults believe they can avoid becoming marginalized as a group if they participate in demonstrations or present a threat of age-based or block voting on specific

issues, or in general (Binstock and Quadagno, 2001; Turner et al., 2002). There is little evidence, however, that older people vote as a block, primarily because they are a very heterogeneous group. Thus, it is difficult for voters to coalesce and reach consensus on an issue unless, as in the case of reduced pensions or less access to health care, it will have an effect on all, or most, older adults. Nevertheless, by their sheer numbers, they represent an implied electoral force that could swing an election if they voted in concert. But at present, at least beyond local issues, voting behaviour is not strongly related to either 'old-age' policy issues or 'age-based' interests.

People over 60 or 65 are eligible to hold political office. In fact, often older citizens are elected because of their perceived stability and experience, and because they serve as a symbol of wisdom. In both business and politics, a large percentage of leaders are over 60 years of age. In the future, older people are more likely to hold public office because an increasingly larger proportion of the electorate will be their age peers, and because they will enter later life with more understanding and interest in the political process than earlier older age cohorts; this is especially the case for women and members of immigrant groups.

Rather than seeking political office, however, increasing numbers of older citizens who feel marginalized or isolated in the political domain are becoming political activists, either individually or collectively. Highlight 10.4 illustrates the growth of 'grey power' in Canada and describes the mandate of one lobbying group. The creation of age-based interests groups is increasing in Canada but has yet to reach the stage that it has in the Netherlands, where age-based interest groups have evolved into two political parties (the General Senior Citizens Union and Union 55+). In recent elections, these parties have won as many as seven seats in a 150-member parliament.

Age-based interest groups for older adults are created to generate visibility, to pool resources, and to lobby politicians on issues of current con-

Highlight 10.4 Grey Power: A Process of Social Change for Seniors

Political involvement among older adults can be traced back to the 1930s, when the Old Age Pension (OAP) Act was passed. This act created a new social group—pensioners (Gifford, 1990). Despite the OAP, many elderly people still experienced social and economic deprivation because of their age. To draw attention to the inadequacies and unfairness of the OAP regulations, pensioners formed public interest and advocacy groups. One such group was the Old Age Pensioners of British Columbia, founded in 1932. Its aim was:

> to protect the rights and interests of Old Age Pensioners or prospective pensioners over 60; to prevent discrimination, avoid technicalities and undue delay in the consideration of applications for pensions; to endeavour to secure and maintain fair and just legislation and executive action at all times in the best interests of Old Age Pensioners; to preserve their status as citizens, entitled to pensions, as [a] social and legal right, and not by way of relief or charity; and enable them to maintain their dignity and self-respect as pioneer citizens of Canada. (Snell, 1996: 159)

Until the 1970s, the traditional life course pattern of political participation was curvilinear: low involvement beginning in late adolescence, an increase through late middle-age, followed by a decrease in the post-retirement years. Today, older adults actively engage in public dialogue on radio and television, in mail campaigns, and in protest marches and sit-ins to bring their concerns to the public's attention. At first they directed their efforts to such issues as age discrimination, poverty, and inadequate housing. Since the formation of provincial and national lobby or advisory groups (the Canadian Association of Retired Persons, the National Advisory Council on Aging), older adults have been invited to participate in the political decision-making process and are often consulted about issues affecting 'seniors' before decisions are made or actions taken by government agencies.

Where this co-operative mechanism is not used, or where older adults are ignored, radical activist groups may be formed. For example, the Senior Citizens' Coalition, an advocacy group formed to oppose the de-indexing of pensions that was proposed in the 1985 federal budget, collaborated successfully with other interests groups to pressure the government to drop the proposal. At the provincial and local levels, such organizations as the Manitoba Society of Seniors, the United Senior Citizens of Ontario, and the Toronto Association of Jewish Seniors have had modest success as political forces in advocating for the needs, interests, and rights of older adults.

In Canada, many national 'seniors' organizations have been operating independently, often with little effect. In March 2001, 12 seniors' organizations, in conjunction with the Division of Aging and Seniors in Health Canada, created the Congress of National Seniors Organizations (CNSO). The 12 organizations represent more than 2 million older Canadians. They are all not-for-profit organizations and represent all regions of the country. Some, like the Congress of Union Retirees, are umbrella organizations that represent other associations in the provinces and territories. The mandate of CNSO is 'to influence and shape national policies and programs through efficient and effective dialogue between seniors groups and government.' The goal is to influence all levels of government so that necessary policies, programs, and activities are developed and implemented which will ensure that all Canadians age with dignity, in security, and with a high quality of life. Each year the Congress identifies three or four issues that it will focus on for the next year of lobbying. In 2003, the issues were health care reform, following the release of the Romanow Report and other health reform reports; pension reform; ageism; housing; and transportation.

cern, such as health care, housing, pensions, and transportation. Most groups use researchers and marketing experts to develop factual and logical documents, and to prepare effective advertisements or arguments concerning an issue. They also employ skilled lobbyists who create media attention, mobilize seniors as necessary, and meet regularly with politicians and their staff to establish or keep an issue on the public agenda. Increasingly, these groups insist that they be consulted regularly, that they be given the right to contribute to Royal Commissions and other public inquiries, or that they be included on standing or ad hoc committees or as panelists at public meetings.

One recent example of how grey power brought about change at the local level occurred in California in 1999. In order to fight the expansion of an airport beside a retirement community (Leisure World), residents of this community joined with the residents of three nearby assisted-living facilities to create an incorporated city and thereby gain political power and influence. The new municipality, Laguna Woods, is populated almost exclusively by older citizens (Andel and Liebig, 2002). Together with other anti-airport groups, they defeated the proposed airport expansion, and a large park and leisure facility will be constructed on the site.

Participation in Religious Activities

Religious affiliation, spirituality, and degree of religious involvement can influence life satisfaction, the quality of life, and both physical and mental health in later life.[13] Much of this influence is based on the beliefs of a particular religion, and whether these beliefs are valued sufficiently to influence or control the way in which a person lives. Organized religion provides some members of the older population with a sense of meaning and security, a readily available social group, and a possible social role in later life. Spirituality may assist, as well, in helping older people to cope with grief, changing personal situ-

ations, and death. Religion also influences attitudes toward, and beliefs about, the status of older people. For example, in North America, some religious groups, such as Jews, Mennonites, Hutterites, and Amish, believe that high-quality care for older members is an obligation that must be met by the family or the religious community rather than the state. It is interesting to note that members of three of these religious groups usually live in rural settings, often as a subculture outside mainstream society.

For recently arrived elderly immigrants and refugees, religious organizations and institutions can play an important part in their integration into life in Canada. Temples, mosques, synagogues, and churches serve as centres for social, spiritual, and leisure activities, and they provide a range of social-welfare, social-support, health-care, psychological, and financial services that may not be available from mainstream organizations. Sometimes these religious institutions build 'senior' centres or housing for older members of the religious group. This is often done in co-operation with linguistically or culturally related ethnic organizations or with settlement or social-service agencies. The involvement of religious organizations in these types of services may make it easier for elderly newcomers to use social and health services than if they were fully dependent on mainstream agencies.

Religious involvement is a form of voluntary behaviour, and at least four patterns of religious participation, usually measured by attendance, are possible:

1. An increase from childhood to early adulthood, and then remaining stable across the life course.

2. Cyclical, random attendance, often related to stage in family life.[14]

3. A decrease after middle age.

4. Regardless of the pattern earlier in life, an increase in the later years.

Most studies find that attendance at religious services remains stable across the life course, or that there is a temporary or permanent withdrawal in the middle and later years. Religion is an important element in the life of some older adults, and older age cohorts usually report stronger religious beliefs than younger age cohorts (McFadden, 1996). Lindsay (1999) found that 37 per cent of older Canadians reported being engaged in some type of religious activity at least once a week.

Religion is positively related to health, well-being, and social support in later life (McFadden and Levin, 1996; Koenig et al., 1999). Older people who are more involved in, and committed to, their faith tend to enjoy better physical and mental health than those who are not as religious. One explanation is that religious settings create social ties that provide social and emotional support (Krause, 2001). Another explanation is that people who worship together encourage each other to use religious coping responses in times of stress (Pargament, 1997). As well, religious commitment and beliefs may contribute to the avoidance of unhealthy practices, such as smoking, drinking, using recreational drugs, and eating certain types of food, and may lead to optimism and a positive mental attitude (McFadden and Levin, 1996).

As with other forms of social participation, it is important to distinguish between aging, cohort, and period effects with respect to religious activity. It is also essential to differentiate between attitudes, beliefs, and behaviour. Religious attitudes and beliefs, or spirituality, may persist until death, but attendance at religious services (that is, behaviour) may decrease as health or access to transportation declines. Thus, early studies of the religiosity of older adults focused on attendance, and concluded that religiosity decreases with age. More recent studies have adopted a multi-dimensional concept of religious involvement. This model incorporates the degree of public participation in religious services, the strength of reli-gious attitudes and beliefs, and the degree of private participation (for example, watching religious services on television, reading, or praying). Recent longitudinal studies support the finding that religious participation does not end in later life, but that there is a decrease in public participation and a compensating increase in private worship (McFadden, 1996). Moreover, those who are more socially active in general are more active in public, organized religious activities, and older women are more involved in religious activity than men (Levin et al., 1994).

Media Consumption

The media (newspapers, the Internet, radio, and television) are designed to reach a large and diverse audience. As an influential social institution, the media entertain, inform, promote social integration, and perpetuate cultural norms and beliefs. In addition, the media provide indirect contact with the social world, and may help to prevent loneliness and social isolation among older adults.

As people age, they often read fewer books and newspapers. In addition, they attend fewer films because of financial constraints, declining vision, or loss of interest in the content. However, the amount of television viewing increases, especially among women, the less educated, and those with lower incomes. Television is the medium that older adults select most often for entertainment and information.

Although it is still debated whether media consumption is a substitution or a compensation for the lack of face-to-face interpersonal relations, television does provide surrogate companionship for some older people. It also provides a structured daily schedule for older adults, whose meal-times, ADLs and IADLs, and bedtime are regulated or scheduled, to some extent, by the television programs they watch.

The use of television or radio to deliver edu-cational programs for older adults is increasing.

Cable television and pay-TV have the potential to provide learning experiences, intellectual stimulation, and social and commercial services for adults of all ages. In the future, television shopping may serve the needs of more affluent, housebound older people.

Lifelong Learning

As we move toward a knowledge-based economy, lifelong learning is increasingly necessary in the workforce because of rapid technological and social change. But lifelong learning has also become a major leisure activity during adulthood, especially as the level of formal education rises for each new cohort. Moreover, while older cohorts have lower literacy rates than younger age groups, the literacy rate of each cohort that reaches age 65 is higher than that of the preceding cohorts.[15] Today, literacy rates are seldom reported by age cohort in developed countries, because there is so little variation among age groups, although some in each cohort are illiterate. However, in the developing countries the rates vary considerably. In some of those countries, for example, only 10 to 14 per cent of the women aged 60 and over and 34 to 41 per cent of the men of that age can read and write.

Literacy and level of education are related to leisure pursuits and to health practices in that those with low rates tend to watch more television and to read fewer magazines, books, and newspapers. Those with higher levels are exposed to more information and understand more information, including that pertaining to health practices and healthy lifestyles (Roberts and Fawcett, 2003). This greater knowedge often translates into better health (see Chapter 12) through lower mortality rates and better cognitive functioning in later life.

No longer is education completed by late adolescence or early adulthood. In 1997, nearly 100,000 older Canadians were enrolled in some type of educational programs and the number of older households with access to the Internet dou-bled from 1997 to 1999 (Health Canada, 2002). For some older adults, learning is a form of social participation, especially one that fosters age-integrated relationships (Hamil-Luker and Uhlenberg, 2002).

Although it was once thought that older people lacked the ability to learn, recent evidence suggests that, given the opportunity, encouragement, and enough time, an older person can acquire new skills and knowledge through formal and informal educational programs. Education for older adults has not been a high priority of the formal education system, but a shift in values and beliefs about learning in middle and later life, and a recognition that retirees constitute an untapped 'market', has increased the number and type of educational opportunities available in later life. Programs are provided, as well, to enhance knowledge or to increase literacy rates, especially among recent elderly immigrants. Today, many older adults actively seek educational experiences to acquire cultural and intellectual enrichment, to earn a degree, to enhance their social life, or to foster social integration and a higher quality of life. Highlight 10.5 illustrates the later-life educational achievements of an intellectually active retiree.

Changing social norms and new forms of delivery enable adults to pursue higher education in the home by means of audiotapes, radio, television, or the Internet; in off-campus centres in the community; and on college or university campuses. Older students who participate in these programs are more likely to be members of the upper and middle classes, to have completed their early schooling in North America, to be in good health, and to have access to transportation. Highlight 10.6 illustrates educational programs developed for older adults.

Travel and Tourism

With improved health, generally larger discretionary incomes, and a lifetime of pursuing leisure beyond the home, more and more older

Highlight 10.5 A Scholar at 80

Born in the early 1920s, W.T. left high school at 14 years of age during the Depression to help pay taxes on the family farm. He finished high school by correspondence courses while serving in the army from 1942 to 1946. 'In my mind, I had never quit the idea of learning,' he said. 'I can't imagine how dull life would be without it.'

Retiring as a draftsman in 1986 after a 32-year career, he pursued a general BA, graduating in 1993. Then, he continued and earned an honours BA in geography in 1999. He credits his wife with igniting his passion for the environment, and following her death he enrolled in a master's program in environmental studies. At the age of 80, he wrote and successfully defended a 200-page thesis on riverbasin ecosystems to earn his third degree. During his time as a graduate student people would say, 'You'll be 80 years old when you finish.' But he always responded, 'How old will I be if I don't do it?'

During his university career he studied with young students, they borrowed his lecture notes, they went for coffee after class, and they made jokes about his age—'You're 80 and just graduating? You must be a slow learner.' And he, in return, says, 'They helped me more than I helped them. It (university) put me around people who were filled with enthusiasm and life. They're going to make the world better and I assure you they will.' At the age of 82, in September 2003, W.T. began a Ph.D. program in geography. Learning is truly a lifelong pursuit for this older Canadian.

Source: Adapted from B. Aggerholm, 'Never Too Late to Learn', *The Record*, 6 July 2002. Reprinted with permission from The Record of Kitchener, Waterloo, and Cambridge, Ontario.

Highlight 10.6 Education as Leisure in the Later Years

Many older adults are returning to formal or informal education. Some of the educational programs are offered by seniors who volunteer to share a specific skill or type of expertise; others are offered by professors or other professionals through distance education (by means of the Internet, audio-tapes, radio, or television).

Elderhostel (www.elderhostel.org)

Established as a not-for-profit organization in the United States in 1975, and in Canada in 1980, Elderhostel offers an educational experience to over 15,000 older Canadian adults every year. Globally, each year over 200,000 participants register in more than 12,000 programs in over 90 countries. The program offers one- to two-week learning experiences with accommodations that may consist of shared rooms in university residences, single rooms in luxury hotels and conference centres, cabins on trains and ships, mountain chalets, jungle lodges, and cabins in remote regions. Each course normally meets for 90 minutes a day, and classes are scheduled to allow participants (who must be at least 55 years of age) to enrol in up to three courses per session. There are no grades, exams, or homework, and the cost is often under $300 per week for registration, accommodation, meals, classes, and extracurricular activities, including field trips. For those who cannot afford the full tuition, 'hostelships' (scholarships) are available to offset some of the cost.

Most courses are in the humanities and the social sciences, with many programs featuring courses on topics unique to the local culture, geography, or social milieu. For example, Canadian

continued

Hightlight 10.6 continued

offerings have included Cape Breton Gaelic fiddle music, Gaspe Connections, the lives and beliefs of Old Order Mennonites, understanding francophone culture, and photography in the Rockies. In addition, more traditional academic courses are offered, such as computer literacy, astronomy, introductory French, the history of Atlantic Canada, and regional folk music. For the more adventurous and affluent, courses are offered in Africa, Europe, China, India, and South America; and, in recognition of 'active' aging, Elderhostel offers river rafting, cycling, mountain treks, caving, and camping. This innovative learning experience provides intellectual activity for both active and disabled older adults who seek to expand their horizons and develop new interests. Some describe Elderhostel as a global university that offers learning adventures on a worldwide, as well as local, campus.

Universities of the Third Age and Senior Colleges

Universities of the 'Third Age', first established in France in 1973 (United Nations, 1992), and 'Senior Colleges', created in Japan in 1969, offer educational programs designed for older adults. Their purpose is to encourage and support lifelong learning, to improve the quality of life for older citizens, to involve older people in activities that are beneficial to the community, to train volunteer leaders for the community, and to conduct research about aging and older adults. The programs offered include physical activity and health knowledge, cultural and intellectual activities, tourism, the learning and preservation of cultural traditions, and retirement preparation and adjustment.

University and College Programs

Some universities and colleges offer special programs for middle-aged and older people (in addition to credit and non-credit courses). Two examples are the University of Calgary Senior Citizen Program, which offers about 100 events or courses a year, and the McGill Institute for Learning in Retirement, which offers about 30 self-directed study groups a year.

The University of California at Los Angeles offers a program known as the Perpetual Learning and Teaching Organization (PLATO). This society is unique—there are no classes, teachers or exams—only study groups, topic coordinators, and learning for learning's sake. Each member leads a one-week session, usually on a topic not related to his or her life experience or expertise—lawyers lead groups on literature; pharmacists on philosophy; engineers on art. Professors from UCLA are sometimes invited to give a lecture. Informal rules ban any discussion of personal health, wealth, or family matters. But they do allow a few fourth-year honours students from UCLA to attend sessions, thereby fostering intergenerational learning and relationships.

Retirement-Community Programs

In the United States, land developers are building retirement communities near, or on land owned by, universities (see www.kah.kendal.org; www.ithaca.edu/longview; www.hyattclassic.com/paloalto; www.retirement.org/davis). These communities, which have informal and formal links to the campus, appeal to older people who value and pursue lifelong education. They also promote intergenerational contact since students serve as paid or volunteer workers in the retirement community, perform music or plays for the residents, or interact with older residents in their classes. Many of the residents are retired alumni, faculty, and staff. Many links between the community and the campus are fostered, including:

• Residents have access to university classes, cultural events, health care services, and athletic events.

continued

Hightlight 10.6 continued

- Students are employed or volunteer in the retirement dining hall or leisure centre.
- Residents have access to experts and programs in a gerontology centre or program.
- Faculty and students give lectures or musical concerts at the retirement community.
- Residents serve as volunteers or paid part-time workers during university athletic, cultural, or conference events.
- Residents participate in faculty and student research projects.

adults are embracing travel and tourism as forms of social participation in later life. Whether a trip is part of an organized tour or undertaken independently, and whether the purpose is culture, adventure tourism, education (for example, through an Elderhostel program or self-directed learning), camping, photography, or simply pleasure and relaxation (at spas, at beach resorts, and on cruise ships), older adults travel widely. The travel industry organizes tours for older adults, including increased opportunities and accommodations for the older single person who travels alone or as part of a group tour. The frequency and diversity of travel experiences for older adults will increase as well-educated, healthy, and affluent baby boomers, with a history of travelling for work and leisure, enter retirement seeking personal challenges, novelty, education, social relationships, and escape. Already, older travellers, especially women, constitute the fastest growing segment of the travel industry.

Gambling

In 2002, gambling revenue in Canada (net of prizes) from government-operated lotteries, video lottery terminals, and casinos exceeded $11 billion, yielding $6 billion in profit (Muggeridge, 2002; Statistics Canada, 2003). This represented a 6 per cent increase from 2001. Gambling is heavily promoted by governments, which use their share of the revenues to fund health care, the training of elite and Olympic athletics, chari-

ties, and to enhance general revenues. Casinos have become resort-like, with more being constructed as leisure destinations that offer not only gambling, but also concerts and gourmet restaurants. And various forms of gambling are available for older adults on cruise ships and in other public places, such as bars, convenience stores, and grocery stores, depending on local laws.

Whether at bingos or casinos, gambling is a form of public social participation that is increasing among members of the older population (Hope and Havir, 2002; Muggeridge, 2002). O'Brien Cousins et al. (2002) found that about 16 per cent of Albertans 65 years of age and over played bingo regularly because it was less expensive than going to a casino. Most of these participants were women, some of whom had health problems, low incomes, and little education. Many lived alone and played bingo to 'fill time' and enjoy a social outing in a safe place. Although non-smoking sections are available, a social activity like bingo or casino gambling represents a health risk because smoking is permitted, the activity is passive and sedentary, there is little cognitive involvement, and alcohol consumption is encouraged.

For most older adults, gambling is an enjoyable, non-serious leisure activity. It offers social interaction with others, excitement and suspense, and harmless entertainment in a socially acceptable setting. Currently, a visit to any casino in Canada, especially during the day or early evening, illustrates quite dramatically how many retirees are engaged in gambling, whether they are fully mobile or use a cane, a walker, or a wheelchair. Retirees represent big business for the travel industry and casinos. Older adults are delivered, regularly, by bus as part of daily outings organized by tour companies linked to seniors' clubs or residences. Nobody really knows how much older adults spend at casinos—it may range from $25 to hundreds of dollars per visit.

Increasingly, there is evidence that more older people are becoming addicted to gambling, although they are the least likely of all age groups to become addicted and to need counselling or treatment. Nevertheless, staff at telephone call centres for those with gambling problems report more calls are being received from older adults with an apparent gambling problem, or from friends or relatives who worry about gambling by a parent or friend. Most calls express concern about financial losses by someone on a fixed income, or about dramatic changes in social behaviour or relationships. Highlight 10.7 illustrates how a casual, light-hearted pastime became a serious social problem that jeopardized a person's financial security and family relationships.

Highlight 10.7 Hooked on Gambling: A Leisure Problem in Later Life

A Toronto woman who asked to remain anonymous says her 80-year-old mother has lost hundreds of thousands of dollars at the slot machines in the four years since her father died.

Her mother has been heading to the casino four times a week, burning through investments, dipping into annuities that exact stiff tax penalties when broken, and racking up huge credit-card bills, all money her husband had worked to put aside before he died. She has boasted to her daughters about the thousands she was making on the slot machines at Casino Rama and the Woodbine Racetrack in Toronto, never mentioning the tens of thousands she was losing at the same time.

But even with the stockbroker calling to report on her mother's dwindling investment account, the daughter has no rights to protect her mother's money. There is nothing she can do to halt the gambling binge. 'She has done everything she can to get money,' her daughter sighs. 'We're talking major, major bucks. Hundreds and hundreds and hundreds of thousands. It makes me want to be sick when I think about it—that it's now in some slot machine. My father worked too hard for his money for her to do this.'

In one of their mother's rare weak moments, the woman and her sister persuaded her to include her name and photograph on the list of banned addicts collected by the casinos as a gesture to combat problem gambling. But even after her picture was snapped, she has skulked back to the casinos, managing to sneak back to her beloved slot machines without being detected.

Now, her relationship with her two daughters and their families is strained. In her mind, her insensitive daughters are bent on cheating her of the one thrill left in her life. In theirs, she is wrecking her golden years. 'She's destroyed her relationship with her children and her friends. Is this what you want when you're in your 80s, not to even care any more?' her daughter says. 'I've tried everything under the sun to pull this together and get her help. But you can't. It's like someone who's a drug addict or a child with anorexia. I'd rather she buy clothes or jewellery. Just don't give it to a machine and it's gone.' Her mother's story isn't unique, she says. 'There's huge addiction out there for seniors. They're lonely and bored, and they get hooked. It's terrible that our government allows this.'

Source: Adapted and reprinted with permission from the *Globe and Mail*, 22 March 2003, F8.

Summary

To achieve an active, healthy lifestyle, to increase levels of social interaction, and to contribute to society, many older adults are socially active. By engaging in social interaction across a range of diverse activities, people create a leisure lifestyle in later life that provides benefits to both the individual and society. Increasingly, older people are pursuing meaningful leisure experiences that add quality and 'life to years'. An active lifestyle is possible because more activities and opportunities are available outside the home in many social settings. This is especially true for women who are becoming involved in more forms of leisure and in more leisure outside the home. With increases in discretionary income, and as the baby boom generation retires over the next 30 years, a large amount of time and money will be spent on activities that promote and develop the well-being, health, and quality of life of older people. However, being active and busy is not enough to guarantee a higher quality of life. Rather, leisure activities must be freely chosen and must provide personal meaning and satisfaction. The meaning of leisure and of specific activities changes and varies across the life course because of aging, cohort, or period effects. Among the many possible leisure activities that older adults can pursue, involvement is growing especially in volunteering, political organizations, sports, travelling, formal education, and gambling.

For Reflection, Debate, or Action

1. Visit local coffee shops or other public places, such as parks and shopping malls, and observe whether groups of older adults meet regularly at certain times for informal conversation. Note whether there are any common socio-demographic characteristics of the members of the informal group, and whether there are any obvious leaders. Note, as well, how many 'seniors' visit or 'hang out' in the setting on their own.

2. Interview retired men and women in your community who are volunteers, and find out where and how they volunteer, how frequently, and why. Ask them to describe any disadvantages of being a volunteer.

3. To understand better how older people spend their time, select three to five older adults of different ages and ask them to keep a time-use diary for a week, recording every activity they are engaged in for every half hour of a 24-hour day. Assess and analyze how these older adults are socially, cognitively, and physically involved in leisure or work pursuits.

4. On the basis of media coverage in recent months, identify emerging political issues that should be of interest to older Canadians.

5. Develop an argument to support the position that the quality of leisure in later life is more important than the quantity.

6. Interview five older people (men or women) on your campus to determine their views, anxieties, problems, and aspirations about attending classes at your university.

7. Interview some older people you know and ask them when, how, and why their social network changed over the years. Reflect on your own experiences to date, and analyze why and how your network has become larger or smaller.

8. Visit a local seniors' centre to determine the programs and activities that are available. Which activities are the most popular among men and among women? Which activities seem to be age-related, and which are lifelong adult activities?

Notes

1. For activities, programs, and policies, see the journal *Activities, Adaptation and Aging*.

2. Criminal offences by older adults are described in Rothman and Dunlop (2000), Finlay (2000), Simard (2000), Statistics Canada (2001).

3. A confidant is not necessarily a close friend or blood relative. Service or voluntary personnel such as doormen, hairdressers, housekeepers, bartenders, or social workers can play this role so that an older person has at least a some regular social contact with someone with whom they can share concerns, news, or ideas.

4. Some of the common bi-polar dimensions are expressive/instrumental; free choice/constrained involvement; low involvement/high involvement; active/passive; individual/group; home-centred/community-centred; institutionalized/non-institutionalized; inexpensive/expensive; mass culture/high culture; creative/non-creative; spontaneous/planned; structured/unstructured; work/non-work; and physical/non-physical. Each dimension represents a continuum, not a dichotomous 'either/or' scale, and there is overlapping among the dimensions.

5. For example, reading as a leisure activity may be done to improve the mind, to learn a skill, to study for a degree, or to fill free time.

6. For example, listening to music while reading; watching television while visiting someone; or reading a newspaper while watching television.

7. An example of an activity in an overlapping category is television viewing. The activity can be categorized as educational or recreational or as a solitary or group activity, depending on the situation in which it takes place. Similarly, cooking, gardening, or other household activities can be viewed as work or leisure.

8. For example, Gordon and Gaitz (1976: 314) argued that the intensity of expressive involvement in leisure can vary in the cognitive, emotional, and physical dimensions across the following five levels: (1) very high (sexual activity, competitive games, and sports); (2) medium high (creative activities such as music and art); (3) medium (attending cultural events, reading for learning, recreational sport, or exercise); (4) medium-low (watching television, attending spectator sports, working on hobbies, reading for pleasure); and (5) low (solitude, resting, napping, 'killing time').

9. Some events that can change leisure patterns or choices are marriage, the birth of a child, a promotion at work, unemployment, an empty nest, entrance of the partner into the labour force, retirement, death of a partner, looking after an ill partner, divorce, and personal illness.

10. Many terms are used to define this type of voluntary social participation: voluntary activity, volunteerism, volunteer work, voluntary action, voluntary behaviour.

11. Information about volunteer behaviour can be found in Hall et al. (1998); Statistics Canada (1998, 2001b); Chappell (2002); Health Canada (2002); and on websites such as www.voe-reb.org and www.unv.org.

12. The curvilinear pattern may reflect cohort effects rather than aging effects, since older cohorts, at present, are generally less well educated, have had fewer opportunities to join associations, and are more likely to be members of the lower class.

13. For a discussion of religiosity in later life, see Levin et al. (1994); McFadden (1996), Atchley (1997), Thomas (1997), Koenig et al. (1999), and Gatz and Smyer (2001).

14. One pattern for families is a peaking of religious participation when the children are attending Sunday school, and a decline when they leave home; another is shown in a decline from 18 to 35 years of age, and then an increase until the later years, when it decreases again as general social involvement declines because of ill health or difficulty getting around.

15. The International Adult Literacy Survey identifies three dimensions of literacy that should be measured: *prose* (ability to understand and use information from texts); *document* (ability to locate and use information from documents); and *quantitative* (ability to perform everyday arithmetic to balance a chequebook or calculate tips).

References

Altergott, K. 1988a. 'Daily Life in Later Life: Concepts and Methods for Inquiry'. Pp. 11–22 in K. Altergott (ed.). *Daily Life in Later Life: Comparative Perspectives.* Newbury Park, Calif.: Sage.

———. 1988b. *Daily Life in Later Life: Comparative Perspectives.* Newbury Park, Calif.: Sage.

Andel, R., and P. Liebig. 2002. 'The City of Laguna Woods: A Case of Senior Power in Local Politics', *Research on Aging*, 24(1), 87–105.

Antonucci, T. 1990. 'Social Support and Social Relationships'. Pp. 205–26 in R. Binstock and L. George (eds), *Handbook of Aging and the Social Sciences.* New York: Academic Press.

———. 2001. 'Social Relations: An Examination of Social Networks, Social Support, and Sense of Control'. Pp. 427–53 in J. Birren and W. Schaie (eds), *Handbook of The Psychology of Aging.* New York: Academic Press.

Atchley, R. 1997. 'The Subjective Importance of Being Religious and Its Effect on Health and Morale 14 Years Later', *Journal of Aging Studies*, 11(2), 131–42.

Binstock, R., and C. Day. 1996. 'Aging and Politics'. Pp. 362–87 in R. Binstock and L. George (eds), *Handbook of Aging and the Social Sciences.* San Diego, Calif.: Academic Press.

———, and J. Quadagno. 2001. 'Aging and Politics'. Pp. 333–51 in R. Binstock and L. George (eds), *Handbook of Aging and the Social Sciences.* San Diego, Calif.: Academic Press.

Bukov, A., et al. 2002. 'Social Participation in Very Old Age: Cross-Sectional and Longitudinal Findings from BASE', *Journal of Gerontology: Psychological Sciences*, 57B(6), P510–17.

Burr, J., et al. 2002. 'Productive Aging and Civic Participation', *Journal of Aging Studies*, 16(1), 87–105.

Chappell, N. 2002. *Volunteering and Healthy Aging: What We Know.* Ottawa: Health Canada.

Cheang, M. 2002. 'Older Adults' Frequent Visits to a Fast-Food Restaurant: Nonobligatory Social Interaction and the Significance of Play in a 'Third Place'', *Journal of Aging Studies*, 16(3), 303–21.

Clark, W. 2002. 'Time Alone', *Canadian Social Trends*, 66 (Autumn), 2–6.

Connidis, I., and J. McMullin. 1992. 'Getting Out of the House: The Effect of Childlessness on Social Participation and Companionship in Later Life', *Canadian Journal on Aging*, 11(4), 370–86.

Cutler, S., and J. Hendricks. 1990. 'Leisure and Time Use across the Life Course'. Pp. 169–85 in R. Binstock and L. George (eds), *Handbook of Aging and the Social Sciences.* San Diego, Calif.: Academic Press.

———. 2000. 'Age Differences in Voluntary Association Memberships: Fact or Artifact', *Journal of Gerontology: Social Sciences*, 55B(2), S98–S107.

Duke, J., et al. 2002. 'Giving Up and Replacing Activities in Response to Illness', *Journal of Gerontology: Psychological Sciences*, 57B(4), P367–76.

Elliott, G., et al. 1996. *Facts on Aging in Canada.* Hamilton, Ont.: Office of Gerontological Studies, McMaster University.

Fast, J., et al. 2001. 'The Time of Our Lives', *Canadian Social Trends*, (Winter), 20–3.

Finlay, D. 2000. 'Elderly Offenders: Getting By with a Little Help from Their Friends', *Let's Talk: Public Perceptions and Corrections*, 25(2), 5–7.

Gatz, M., and M. Smyer. 2001. 'Mental Health and Aging at the Millennium'. Pp. 523–44 in J. Birren and W. Schaie (eds), *Handbook of The Psychology of Aging.* San Diego, Calif.: Academic Press.

Gauthier, A., and T. Smeeding. 2003. 'Time Use at Older Ages: Cross-National Differences', *Research on Aging*, 25(3), 247–74.

Gleberzon, B., and J. Cutler. 2002. 'Dispelling the Myths of Aging', *Aging, Health and Society: News and Views*, 8(1), 3. Hamilton, Ont.: Program in Gerontology, McMaster University.

Gordon, C., and Gaitz. 1976. 'Leisure and Lives: Personal Expressivity Across the Life Span'. Pp. 310–41 in R. Binstock and E. Shanas (eds), *Handbook of Aging and the Social Sciences.* New York: Van Nostrand Reinhold.

Gottlieb, B. 2002. 'Older Volunteers: A Precious Resource Under Pressure', *Canadian Journal on Aging*, 21(1), 5–9.

Hall, M. et al. 1998. *Caring Canadians, Involved Canadians: Highlights from the 1997 National Survey of Giving, Volunteering and Participating.* Cat. no. 71-542-XPE, August 1998. Ottawa: Statistics Canada.

Hamil-Luker, J., and P. Uhlenberg. 2002. 'Later Life Education in the 1990s: Increasing Involvement and Continuing Disparity', *Journal of Gerontology: Social Sciences*, 57B(6), S324–31.

Health Canada. 2002. *Canada's Aging Population.* Ottawa: Health Canada.

Hendricks, J., and S. Cutler. 2001. 'The Effects of Membership in Church-Related Associations and Labour Unions on Age Differences in Voluntary Association Affiliations', *The Gerontologist*, 41(2), 250–6.

———. 2003. 'Leisure in Life-Course Perspective'. Pp. 107–34 in R. Settersten (ed.). *Invitation to the Life Course: Toward New Understandings of Later Life.* Amityville, NY: Baywood Publishing.

Hope, J., and L. Havir. 2002. 'You Bet They're Having Fun! Older Americans and Casino Gambling', *Journal of Aging Studies*, 16(2), 177–97.

Horgas, A. et al. 1998. 'Daily Life in Very Old Age: Everyday Activities As Expression of Successful Living', *The Gerontologist*, 38(5), 556–68.

Ice, G. 2002. 'Daily Life in a Nursing Home. Has It Changed in 25 Years?', *Journal of Aging Studies*, 16(4), 345–59.

Katz, S. 2000. 'Busy Bodies: Activity, Aging and the Management of Everyday Life', *Journal of Aging Studies*, 14(2), 135–52.

Kelly, J. 1987. *Peoria Winter: Styles and Resources in Later Life.* Lexington, MA: Lexington Books.

———. (ed.) 1993. *Activity and Aging: Staying Involved in Later Life.* Newbury Park, Calif.: Sage.

Koenig, H., et al. 1999. 'Does Religious Attendance Prolong Survival?', *Journal of Gerontology: Medical Sciences*, 54A (6), M370–6.

Krause, N. 2001. 'Social Support'. Pp. 272–94 in R. Binstock and L. George (eds), *Handbook of Aging and the Social Sciences.* San Diego, Calif.: Academic Press.

Lachman, M. 2003. 'Negative Interactions in Close Relationships: Introduction to a Special Section', *Journal of Gerontology: Psychological Sciences*, 58B(2), P69.

Lennartsson, C., and M. Silverstein. 2001. 'Does Engagement with Life Enhance Survival of Elderly People in Sweden? The Role of Social and Leisure Activities', *Journal of Gerontology: Social Sciences*, 56B, (6), S335–S42.

Levin, J., et al. 1994. 'Race and Gender Differences in Religiosity among Older Adults: Findings from Four National Surveys', *Journal of Gerontology: Social Sciences*, 49(3), S137–45.

Lian, J. et al. 2000. 'Unpaid Time Contributions by Seniors in Canada'. pp. 156–80 in F. Denton et al. (eds), *Independence and Economic Security in Old Age.* Vancouver, BC: University of British Columbia Press.

Lindsay, C. 1999. *A Portrait of Seniors in Canada.* Ottawa: Statistics Canada.

McFadden, S. 1996. 'Religion, Spirituality, and Aging'. Pp. 162–77 in J. Birren and W. Schaie (eds), *Handbook of the Psychology of Aging.* San Diego, Calif.: Academic Press.

———, and J. Levin. 1996. 'Religion, Emotions and Health'. Pp. 349–65 in C. Magi and S. McFadden (eds), *Handbook of Emotion, Adult Development, and Aging.* San Diego, Calif.: Academic Press.

Muggeridge, P. 2002. 'Government Greed for Gaming Revenue May Be Hurting Us All', *Fifty Plus* (August), 14–20.

O'Brien Cousins, S. et al. 2002. *High Quality Aging or Gambling With Health? The Lifestyles of Elders Who Play Bingo.* Report for the Alberta Gaming Research Institute, Edmonton, AB: University of Alberta, Faculty of Physical Education and Recreation.

Pargament, K. 1997. *The Psychology of Religion and Coping: Theory, Research and Practice.* New York, NY: Guilford.

Robb, R. et al. 1999. 'Valuation of Unpaid Help by Seniors in Canada: An Empirical Analysis', *Canadian Journal on Aging*, 18(4), 430–46.

Roberts, P., and G. Fawcett. 2003. *At Risk: A Socioeconomic Analysis of Health and Literacy Among Seniors.* Cat. no. 89F010XIE. Ottawa: Statistics Canada.

Rothman, M., and B. Dunlop (eds). 2000. *Elders, Crime and the Criminal Justice System: Myth, Perception and Reality in the 21st Century.* New York: Springer.

Rowe, J., and R. Kahn. 1998. *Successful Aging.* New York: Pantheon.

Silverstein, M., and M. Parker. 2002. 'Leisure Activities and Quality of Life Among the Oldest Old in Sweden', *Research on Aging*, 24(5), 528–47.

Simard, P. 2000. 'Are the Senior Years Really the Golden Years for Offenders?', *Let's Talk: Public Perceptions and Corrections*, 25(2), 4–5.

Statistics Canada. 1998. *National Survey of Giving, Volunteering and Participating (NSGVP), 1997.* Cat. no. 11-001E. Ottawa: Statistics Canada.

———. 2001a. *The 2001 National Survey of Giving, Volunteering and Participating.* Cat. no. 71-542-XPE, Ottawa: Statistics Canada.

———. 2001b. *Seniors in Canada.* Cat. no. 85F0033MIE. Canadian Centre for Justice Statistics Profile Series. Ottawa: Statistics Canada.

———. 2001c. *Caring Canadians, Involved Canadians.* Cat. no. 71-542-XIE. Ottawa: Statistics Canada.

Steffensmeier, D., and M. Motivans. 2000. 'Older Men and Older Women in the Arms of Criminal Law: Offending Patterns and Sentencing Outcomes', *Journal of Gerontology: Social Sciences*, 55B(3), S141–51.

Strain, L. 2001. 'Senior Centres: Who Participates?', *Canadian Journal on Aging*, 20(4), 471–91.

———, et al. 2002. 'Continuing and Ceasing Leisure Activities in Later Life: A Longitudinal Study', *The Gerontologist*, 42(2), 217–23.

Thomas, L. (ed.). 1997. 'Religion, Aging and Spirituality', *Journal of Aging Studies*, 11(2), 97–169.

Thomas, M., and R. Venne. 2002. 'Work and Leisure: A Question of Balance'. Pp. 190–222 in D. Cheal (ed.). *Aging and Demographic Change in Canadian Context*. Toronto: University of Toronto Press.

Turner, M.J., et al. 2002. 'Changes and Continuities in the Determinants of Older Adults' Voter Turnout, 1952–1996', *The Gerontologist*, 41(6), 805–18.

United Nations. 1992. 'The Third Age University', *Bulletin on Ageing*, 3, 5–7.

Van Willigen, M. 2000. 'Differential Benefits of Volunteering Across the Life Course', *Journal of Gerontology: Social Sciences*, 55B(5), S308–18.

Walker, A. 2000. 'Towards Active Aging in Europe', *Hallym International Journal of Aging*, 2(1), 49–60.

Williams, C. 2002. 'Time or Money? How High and Low Income Canadians Spend Their Time', *Canadian Social Trends*, 65 (Summer), 7–11.

Yardley, L., and H. Smith. 2002. 'A Prospective Study of the Relationship Between Feared Consequences of Falling and Avoidance of Activity in Community-Living Older People', *The Gerontologist*, 42(1), 17–23.

Zuzanek, J., and S. Box. 1988. 'Life Course and the Daily Lives of Older Adults in Canada'. Pp. 147–85 in K. Altergott (ed.). *Daily Life in Later Life: Comparative Perspectives*. Newbury Park, Calif.: Sage.

PART 4

Social Interventions and Public Policies for an Aging Population

Support and care for older people is needed within the home and community if a move to an institution is to be delayed or avoided. Public policies concerning home care and community services are essential as more people live longer; as more hospitals perform day surgery, discharge patients earlier after an acute illness or surgery, and offer more outpatient services; and as more women, the traditional providers of home care, are embedded in work careers and otherwise less available to care for their aging relatives.

The last two chapters focus on issues, services, policies, and practices concerning the support and care of older adults who experience physical and cognitive changes because of normal aging, or the onset of acute or chronic diseases that make independent living in their home difficult or impossible. Topics range from self-care to the use of informal and formal support that helps with personal care and the instrumental activities of daily living, as well as offering emotional support. This support involves both caring *about* and caring *for* an older person, it involves volunteer and paid work, and it represents a physical, cognitive, and emotional commitment to an older person.

Chapter 11 examines self-care; the type and amount of informal and formal support provided to older adults; the responsibility, stress, and burden of being an informal and formal caregiver; and intervention and public policy issues facing family caregivers, practitioners, and society. These issues involve the relative caregiving responsibility of the family and the state; the co-ordination of informal and formal support to prevent gaps in needed services; elder abuse; and principles for designing public policies for an aging population.

Chapter 12 discusses individual and population health in later life, including health determinants, health behaviour, health care systems, public health policies, and end-of-life issues (palliative care, power of attorney, advance directives, assisted suicide, and euthanasia). Special attention is directed to the social structural determinants of health, self-perception of health, health promotion in later life, mental health, the costs of health care, and proposed reforms to improve Canada's health care system.

CHAPTER 11

Social Support and Public Policy for an Aging Population

Focal Points

- To what extent should the family or the public sector provide care and assistance to older adults living in the community?

- To what extent, and how, do caregiving responsibilities influence work, family, and leisure life?

- How, and in what ways, can public policy contribute to the co-ordination and integration of informal care and formal community services to enhance the quality of life of older adults living in the community?

- How effective is the co-ordination between informal support and formal support systems?

- Why, and in what form, does elder abuse occur within families, and what are the precipitating factors?

- What criteria should be employed to establish entitlement to support from the state in later life?

Introduction

In an ideal world, an integrated continuum of care and support would enable older people to age in the family home, rather than in institutions or hospitals; to live in their home after being discharged from a hospital; and to receive help with ADLs and IADLs as their strength, mobility, cognitive functioning, or health declines. This continuum consists of

- informal assistance provided to older relatives, friends, or neighbours in the form of shopping, shovelling snow, daily monitoring, and so on;

- informal help with cooking and finances;

- formal care by paid employees who visit or live in the family home to help with meals, bathing, therapy, and mobility;

- 24-hour care in institutions (retirement homes, nursing homes and long-term geriatric care facilities).

Eventually, if only for a short period before death, most older persons need some help with the activities of daily living. To ensure independent living in the community for as long as possible when health and functional abilities begin to decline, a 'partnership' is, ideally, created to provide care and assistance. Or, as Strain and Blandford (2003) stress, a caregiving network needs to be available or created, as necessary, late in life.

Each person's situation is unique, and therefore partnerships involve varying contributions:

- by the individual (through self-care)
- by the family through informal assistance
- by the state through formal home and community services
- by volunteer organizations such as meals-on-wheels
- by the health care system, that is, physicians and hospitals
- by private agencies such as those that supply home care workers or specialized equipment.

The needs of the older person can be so complex and time-consuming that a case manager (such as an adult child or a social worker) is often needed to ensure that full and appropriate assistance and care are available if and when personal needs change.

Changing demographic and social trends—longer life expectancy, lower fertility rates, more childless marriages, higher divorce rates, more single adults, increased geographical mobility of children, more labour-force participation by middle-aged women)—often mean that people are less able to look after or even help their aging relatives directly. Consequently, questions arise that have to be answered: Who should provide care? What type of care and how much should be provided in the family home, and by whom? Who should pay for home care? What interventions are needed to help the care recipients and caregivers? Help with those decisions can be found in various service agencies, and educational programs are available both for older people and for adult children who are their primary caregivers or care managers.[1]

Family Responsibility

For a number of reasons, some adult children are unwilling or unable to look after their elderly parents: family obligations are not considered as important as previously, more middle-aged women are in the labour force, many people live far from their parents. At the same time, more aging adults prefer to remain independent, in as many ways as possible (financial, transportation, home care, health care), for as long as possible and may reject or discourage help from others. But many older people, especially those over 80 years of age, need some help and care as their physical and/or mental health declines.

Family responsibility for caregiving is not a recent issue. Rather, the responsibility of the family for supporting dependent elderly parents was emphasized in the 'filial responsibility' laws of the 1920s and 1930s in a number of provinces. By law, adult children who were capable of doing so were required to support parents who, because of age, disease, or infirmity, were unable to maintain themselves. Any dependent parent could, with the written consent of a crown attorney, summon one or more of their children before a magistrate, who could order support payments of up to $20 weekly, depending on the means and circumstances of the children. Action on the parents' behalf could also be initiated by a designated public official or by the governing body of any government or charitable institution where the dependent person lived (Snell, 1996: 78–9). Before proceeding to court action, officials notified an adult child and appealed to him or her to keep his or her parent off the charity roll, thereby avoiding the stigma of social welfare and poverty for the family. Consequently, the legislation was seldom used to prosecute a family member. In reality, 'there is no evidence that the laws actually increased the level of support for the elderly from their adult children; indeed, there is some evidence to suggest that both intragenerational and intergenerational support, broadly defined, was reduced' (Snell, 1996: 98).

Today, all provinces have laws requiring adult children to assume some responsibility for the support and care of elderly parents. In British Columbia, the Family Relations Act states that 'a child is liable to maintain and support a parent having regard to other responsibilities and liabilities and the reasonable needs of the child.' In Ontario, Newfoundland, and New Brunswick, the legislation states: 'Every child who is not a minor has an obligation to provide support, in accordance with need, for his or her parent who has cared for or provided support for the child, to the extent that the child is capable of doing so.' A child is only liable when the parent is dependent on the child by reason of age, infirmity, or economic circumstances. Section 215 of the Criminal Code of Canada states that 'Everyone is under a legal duty to provide the necessaries of life to a person under his charge, if that person is unable, by reason of detention, age, illness, insanity or other cause to withdraw from that charge, and is unable to provide the necessaries of life.'

Since the early 1980s there have been at least six provincial court cases in which elderly parents have sought payments from children; and at least five cases where adult children have been named as respondents in spousal support proceedings (Parsons and Tindale, 2001). In some of these cases, the courts forced adult children to provide monthly financial support to an elderly parent. But these laws and court rulings apply mainly or only to financial support. They do not require the provision of emotional support or informal care or assistance by a family member.

The amount of support given to an elderly parent or family member is closely related to the sense of obligation and affection built throughout family history. Where intergenerational relations are strong, family assistance is more likely. Mitchell (2003) found that even in families with a strong ethnic identity, and therefore perhaps more obligation to care for parents, the most important predictor of who would share a home with an elderly parent was the *quality* of the adult child's

relationship with his or her mother. However, the type and the quality of assistance, and the degree of perceived responsibility, varies if a caregiver is divorced, is employed, or lives at a distance.

While the family is a major support system for most older adults, the expectations of parents and children regarding the nature of assistance may differ. For example, parents who are over 80 years of age may have adult children in their 60s who need help themselves. In this case, responsibility for the oldest generation may have to be assumed by other relatives or by public or private agencies. And if the parents and the child disagree about what type or level of support is needed, public or private agencies may have to intervene to fill the void left by the lack of adequate family support.

Public Responsibility

As older adults gradually become more dependent, they may have to rely less on family and community support and more on formal support provided by government or private-sector programs. In a welfare state such as Canada, public policies are developed in response to lobbying by interest groups and to perceived public issues or needs. Through this process, programs of assistance are created by different levels of government for the welfare of both the individual and the society. Creating policies inevitably requires that spending choices be made, for example, between universal and need-based services; between building schools and long-term-care facilities; between better roads, health care, social-welfare programs, and economic-security programs.

Public policy is made in a context of either conflict or co-operation among local, regional, provincial, and federal government agencies. Policies are shaped, as well, by the political phil - osophy of the current government and by the existing or anticipated economic climate. Hence, long-term planning is often sacrificed for short-term political gain. Policy making becomes even more complex when public policies must be co-ordinated with those in the private sector, especially in such areas as pensions, housing, and home care for older adults. In these cases it must be determined who is responsible for what actions or programs, and to what extent. Even more important, public policy for an aging population must be integrated with changing family values and family dynamics, especially concerning health and home care. Currently, a debate is emerging about the extent to which elder care is a private trouble or a public issue; and how the responsibility can be shared (Ward-Griffin and Marshall, 2003). Informal and formal care are linked processes, not dichotomous responsibilities, and therefore they require renegotiated responsibilities as the needs of an older person change. Salaried care workers and unpaid family members must work together so that each contributes to ensure that an aging parent receives high-quality care when it is needed.

Social Support

Social support ranges from prevention (a confidant helps the elderly person to cope with stress), to adaptation (a child or a neighbour provides transportation to appointments or social events), to rehabilitation and assistance during convalescence from an acute illness or surgery, to long-term care for the highly dependent older person. Thus, the ideal support system involves a combination of informal and formal components.

The social network for older adults consists primarily of their immediate and extended family, usually a spouse or adult children. Most older adults receive in-home assistance from family members because of intergenerational bonds of attachment, filial piety, and a sense of obligation. While most older men have a wife to provide assistance and care when needed, as many as 20 per cent of women 75 and over have neither a husband nor a child (Connidis, 2003). Indeed, being married appears to protect men. Married men have a 40 per cent chance of living longer

than men who are single, widowed, divorced, or separated in later life (Statistics Canada, 2003).

As we have seen earlier, the alleged 'sandwich generation' is more myth than reality (Rosenthal, 2000), and many adult children, themselves in their 60s, do provide support to aging parents. However, fewer adult children will be available in the future because families are becoming smaller, more people are never marrying or are getting divorced, and more people are not having children. Hence there will be more unattached older persons in the future and, therefore, a greater demand for public- and private-sector programs to meet the needs of aging adults who live alone and do not have a family.

Social support is a major factor in a successful person-environment fit in later life, and providing support can be stressful for many caregivers. Many people over 65 are themselves part of a support system for partners, siblings, friends, or neighbours. Indeed, over 80 per cent of the support received by older persons comes from family members, primarily a spouse or adult children (Connidis, 2001).

On the basis of data in the 2002 General Social Survey (Cranswick, 2003), it can be concluded that there is a move away from 'warehousing' frail older persons in long-term care institutions. The 2001 census found that among those 65 and over, fewer than 10 per cent of women and about 5 per cent of men lived in health-care institutions. But for those 85 and over, the proportion has risen to about 35 per cent for women and 23 per cent for men.

Among those 65 and over who live in the community and receive care because of a long-term health problem, 32 per cent are women and 21 per cent are men. At age 85 and above, the figures rise to 65 per cent for women and 55 per cent for men. Cranswick (2003) found that among people 65 and over, 39 per cent of women and 46 per cent for men received all their care from informal sources. By age 85 and over, however, 20 per cent of women and 30 per cent of men receive only formal care, often because at this stage many are living alone or their spouse is unable to provide the necessary care.

The need for social support becomes most apparent when an older person begins to suffer from memory loss, Alzheimer's disease (AD), or other dementias that lead to functional disabilities, behavioural problems, and increasing dependence on another person, often the spouse. The prevalence of these cognitive impairments and disease states increases with age. It is estimated that Alzheimer's disease and other forms of dementia affect 8 per cent of those 65 and over (almost 400,000 Canadians), and that the proportion rises to 33 per cent for those 85 years and over (Hébert et al., 2003). Almost half live at home with family support, and if this support was not available, the demand for long-term care facilities would increase by 34 per cent (Hébert et al., 2003). Caring for these persons must be addressed because these dementias have a considerable influence on the quality of life for aging persons and for their families and other caregivers.

The sections that follow discuss models of social support, informal social support, and the stress and burden of caregiving. But first, two caveats:

1. Throughout the research literature and journalistic reports, many terms are used to discuss social support, in general. These include: 'assistance', 'caregiving', 'eldercare', 'home care', 'community care', 'monitoring', 'care management', 'case management'. They all represent a form of social support, and often are used interchangeably. However, 'assistance' and 'caregiving' are different. Assistance represents more casual help, including periodic help to others; whereas caregiving involves a regular commitment to help a person with some specific health or personal care need. Assistance may not be requested or required, and the recipient may not even view the help as a 'support' activity. In contrast, caregiving is required and is requested either by the older person or by someone in his or her social world, including a family physician or a family member. Similarly, 'monitoring' is an informal way to keep an eye on an older person's safety, health, and ability to function; whereas 'care or case management' is a formal process carried out regularly by a family member or by professional care workers. Home care and community care, which provide support outside an institution, consist of performing services and tasks in the home or taking an older person to a community-based facility for a program or service.

2. A second caveat is that although many incidents of social support involve assistance and care for those with cognitive impairment or dementias, social support is available in many forms to meet varying degrees of need. Support ranges from spouses helping each other with household or personal activities, to regular visits to the home by professional care workers who provide therapy, bathing, nursing care, counselling, or do home repairs. Support, which can be informal or formal, is an important component of successful aging (Krause, 2001). Social support is an essential emotional resource during stress or crises in later life, whether due to an acute illness, a chronic physical or cognitive health problem, or the normal frailties that make daily living more difficult for some older adults.

Theories and Models of Social Support

Throughout life, social support and the exchange of gifts, help, and money usually flow in two directions between aging individuals and others in their social network. Most exchange occurs in the extended family, but neighbours and friends also exchange help and assistance in the course of daily living. Late in life this network provides subtle or direct forms of assistance and monitoring as older people experience financial difficulties or a decline in health or functional abilities. This help may not be noticed or requested by the older person until it becomes regular and more pervasive. Often the assistance begins at a time of acute illness or hospitalization, after the death of a spouse, or during the winter when walking or driving is difficult for many older people.

Most social relationships, especially within the kinship system, are based on the principles of reciprocity and mutual obligation. Within the family, physical, emotional, economic, and social resources are exchanged, depending on the needs and the stage in life. Serial, or one-way, exchanges of resources are most common, and they generally involve a downward flow of assistance from the older generation to a younger generation because of a sense of responsibility and affection (see the discussion of intergenerational transfers in Chapter 6).

Reciprocal exchange, or a two-way flow, is most common between the members of the middle and oldest generations. This process of exchange usually involves services, such as baby-sitting, giving advice, shopping, and household maintenance; gifts of money or goods; or companionship through visits, telephone calls, or while helping an older person with an ADL or IADL. Reciprocity continues in later life as children spend more time helping and monitoring their parents. For many, but not all, children, this support to aging parents is a privilege, an obligation, and a right. These feelings vary by the personal history of a specific relationship, i.e., whether or not it has been rewarding; and by cultural beliefs based on ethnicity, class, race, or gender. There also tends to be more support if more time has been spent on shared activities with the parents and if the parents have provided financial support to adult children (Silverstein et al., 2002).

Because relationships among family and intimate friends are strong and persist over time, exchange is viewed as a basic principle of the informal support system for older people (Uhlenberg, 1996; Connidis, 2001). The amount and type of support given and received is influenced by physical and mental health, skills and knowledge, opportunities, and love and motivation on the part of both the giver and the receiver. Thus, each exchange relationship is unique (Uhlenberg, 1996).

For some older adults, a child's offer of assistance is interpreted as a disruption of the balance of exchange, even though most, if not all, exchange relationships are imbalanced because one gives more than the other. If an older person's resources are diminished or devalued, dependence is perceived in the exchange relationship. If reciprocity is not possible, this can lower the self-esteem and morale of the older person, who may refuse to accept help from members of the informal network. This is more likely to happen in relationships with friends and neighbours than in kinship relations. Even in the later years, parent-child relationships are based on reciprocity, with emotional and financial support being the most common type of exchange, and older parents still trying to give something in return (Keefe and Fancey, 2002).

In a study of 400 older adults (65 and over) in London, Ontario, 63 per cent of the parents reported that they gave and received support in a variety of areas, and only 15 per cent stated that they received but did not give any assistance (Connidis, 2001: 132). Parents reported a high level of satisfaction; 95 per cent believed their children gave them about the right amount of help, and 92 per cent believed they in turn gave their children the right amount of help. The respondents in this study were relatively healthy, community-dwelling older adults. However, when there is a health crisis, the balance of power and obligation can shift suddenly to an adult child, especially if an older parent is widowed. Eventually, a frail older parent loses control and independence, often being unable to provide advice or emotional support to the adult child, who becomes their primary caregiver.

Faced with changing health or economic status, or with difficulties in performing ADLs or IADLs, older people have three choices: (1) continue to live as always, refusing assistance and failing to make adaptive changes in their daily lives; (2) recognize the need for adaptation and take action alone; or (3) seek help from informal and formal sources of support available in their social network and community. To help explain the process of seeking support, four general models of social support have been proposed. There has not been a great deal of research on any of these models (Chappell, 1992: 61–7). However, the conceptual schemes provide us with a way to think about policies and programs that would help older adults and enable them to remain in a familiar environment.

The **hierarchical-compensatory** model (Cantor and Little, 1985) argued that privacy, intimacy, and personal responsibility are crucial factors in the choice of support; that caregivers from the kinship network are preferred over non-kin; and that informal sources are preferred before formal resources, which are selected only as a last resort. Cantor and Little (1985: 748) describe the social support system for older people as a series of concentric rings, with the older person in the middle. The innermost circle consists of spouse and children; the next circle, moving outward from the centre, includes friends and neighbours; and the third circle consists of volunteers and employees of religious and ethnic groups and voluntary associations serving the needs of older adults. All of these individuals and groups are capable of providing informal support to aging adults. The family, along with extended kin and close friends, provides the first level of assistance and support. Indeed, the relatively small percentage of older people living in long-term-care facilities (fewer than 9 per cent) shows that a large amount of assistance and care is provided in the home by family, friends, and neighbours. For older couples, a partner is the first choice, followed in order by an adult child, a sibling, and a niece or nephew. If the first choice is not available or is unable or unwilling to assist, then the next level of intimacy is selected. Similarly, for unattached older adults without children, ties are developed with siblings and

friends (fictive kin) who serve as companions, confidants, and a source of assistance.

The **task-specificity** model (Litwak, 1985) proposed that the type of assistance needed dictates who in the support network becomes involved. This model assumes that a diverse network with diverse resources and skills is available, and that the tasks required rather than the social relationships are more important when decisions are made. The model also assumes that decisions by or for older adults about assistance are objective, rational, and utilitarian, and that there is a willingness to seek and accept help from formal support services if needed.

The **help-seeking** model (Corin, 1987) focused on the process of decision making to enhance person-environment fit. This model argued that personal needs and the ability to function in a given environment changes later in life and that social resources must be obtained to maintain and enhance well-being and functional ability. Corin argued that the help-seeking process involves making decisions about four possible sources of support: oneself and one's own resources; informal resources; formal resources, alone or in addition to informal resources; or a combination of support involving oneself and informal and formal resources. Each person tends to use one strategy for seeking help. The choice of one style or another depends on

- the availability of social relations in the personal network;

- the availability and knowledge of formal resources;

- the type and seriousness of the situation, the length of time it has lasted, and whether there are other problems;

- the lifelong personal style of relating to others, i.e, reserved or sociable, independent or dependent; and

- attitudes about seeking and accepting help, which vary according to class, gender, ethnicity, and whether one lives in an urban or a rural environment.[2]

The **convoy** model of support (Antonucci, 1990; Antonucci and Akiyama, 1995; Haines and Henderson, 2002) is a dynamic, life-course model. Throughout our lives we develop and cultivate, consciously or unconsciously, a network of supportive people through the giving and receiving of emotions, goods, and services. At different stages of life, the balance and type of exchange varies, and members enter and leave the convoy. That is, new friends are made; some friendships disappear while others endure; relatives are gained and lost through birth, death, marriage, divorce, or personal feuds. Thus, later in life, if assistance and care are needed, members of a person's convoy may or may not be available or willing to provide support depending on the size of the convoy at that point, and the history of interpersonal relationships and exchanges with specific members. Usually it is assumed that those with strong affective ties to the older person provide the support when needed. But not all strong, intimate ties are supportive owing to distance or an inability or an unwillingness to accept caregiving responsibility. In contrast, relatively weak ties (i.e. with friends or neighbours) can provide instrumental assistance and monitoring, especially in a crisis (Haines and Henderson, 2002).

Elements of all four models are present and complement each other when support is needed by a specific individual in a specific situation. When support responsibilities become too demanding for those in the informal network, the formal system is called on. The formal care system compensates for the absence of a spouse or child, and it supplements the informal support system provided by a spouse or child (Denton, 1997). Where it exists, the informal system never disappears completely. Even when a person enters an institution, a spouse or child monitors the formal care and helps with caregiving during visits (Dawson and Rosenthal, 1996; Ross et al., 1997).

Informal Social Support

Informal support is provided in the home or community by family, friends, neighbours, or volunteers. Even when elderly persons have no family, fictive or quasi-kin often substitute for blood relatives (MacRae, 1992). For elderly women living alone, these fictive kin play instrumental and emotional roles in later life that would normally be played by family members. These activities and services help to maintain independence, self-esteem, and an acceptable quality of life. Such assistance may involve companionship; providing information; helping with housework, transportation, and shopping; or helping with moderate levels of personal care (dressing, bathing, or feeding) during recuperation from an acute illness or surgery, or as health and functional ability fluctuates or deteriorates. Informal support may also involve monitoring the quality of care and assisting with personal care in a long-term-care institution. In these facilities, family members, through shared experiences, frequent contact, and the building of trust, form relationships with the staff who care for their dependent parent. Gladstone and Wexler (2002) identified five types of relationships that evolve between a family member and resident staff: collegial, professional, friendship, distant, and tense. Most support is a family matter,[3] and it is only in difficult personal situations that a formal support system is invoked. An estimated 70 to 80 per cent of care provided to older adults in private households is delivered by informal caregivers (Hébert et al., 2001; Carrière et al., 2002). Of these caregivers, more than 50 per cent are adult children (Health Canada, 2002). Cranswick (2003) found that in 2002 over 2 million people were providing informal care to a family member or friend over 65 years of age. About 6 per cent of these 2 million caregivers were 75 or over themselves. Thus, older adults give as well as receive care.

Informal support has a subjective and an objective component (Chappell, 1992). The *subjective* component involves the quality (access to people one can trust, share intimacies with, and confide in), meaning (the importance or value of contact with kin and friends for well-being), and satisfaction with the support that is received. The *objective* component refers to the quantity of relationships (number of available kin, friends, and neighbours), the availability of assistance when needed; and the degree to which the available support is used (the amount, frequency, and intensity of interaction).

Friends and neighbours are a significant source of informal support for older adults through visiting, shopping, performing chores, taking non-drivers to appointments, and telephone conversations (Stewart et al., 2001), and by general monitoring in the absence of children. These helping relationships are based on mutual choice and need, rather than on lifelong family obligations. However, the non-family support network becomes smaller once declining health reduces the amount and frequency of social interaction and mobility outside the home, and when more intimate care is needed. A network is also reduced when friends die or move away, or experience declining health themselves.

Sources of Informal Support: The Caregivers

Although family support is evident throughout adult life, as parents reach their later years, their children begin to monitor them more closely, and to show more concern about a parent's health, safety, and ability to complete ADLs and IADLs in the family home. In most cases, when we speak of 'family' we usually mean a daughter or daughter-in-law. Even where a married man says he provides support, it may be that the help he is reporting is actually provided by his wife (Keating et al., 1999; Connidis, 2001; Matthews, 2002). Daughters generally monitor their parents more closely and frequently than do sons, and they travel farther and more often to help their aging parents (Hallman and Joseph, 1999). This is espe-

cially true if a daughter is unmarried. Thus, much informal support is a gendered process.

Throughout life, daughters or daughters-in-law tend to be the primary caregivers, and elderly women, especially widows and divorcees, tend to be the recipients of more social support than men. These patterns evolve because:

- women are more likely to be comfortable with both giving and receiving in expressive, nurturing relationships;

- mother-daughter relationships are stronger and more intimate; and

- women are more likely to live close to members of the family and therefore to visit often.

However, as more women join the labour force, the level and type of available support changes. Increasingly, working women become case managers, and in addition to providing some direct help, such as shopping, home care, emotional support, and transportation, they purchase other home and personal-care services from home-care and nursing agencies. Although daughters who are not in the labour force contribute more tangible services than their employed sisters when a parent's health deteriorates, employed sisters are expected to contribute during the evenings and weekends (Matthews, 2002). These 'secondary' caregivers provide indirect support, and are an important element in the caregiving system, especially if respite-care services are not available.

The gendered nature of caregiving, where it exists,[4] is due to gender role expectations and to the preference of care recipients, especially women, to be helped by a daughter because of the personal nature of care. Among couples, men report that they 'expect' to receive care from their partner, whereas women 'feel guilty' when their partner has to take care of them (Davidson et al., 2000). There are also gender differences among siblings in how and what care should be provided to parents. Whereas daughters are more likely to take the initiative in providing care and provide more services, sons wait to be asked for assistance, and then tend to provide financial assistance to buy services (Matthews, 2002). Women are also more likely to be the primary or sole caregiver to a parent, whereas sons may be part of a team if there are other siblings, or a son may 'manage' a team of informal and formal caregivers. Grandchildren, as young adults, often serve as a secondary level of support to help with the care and monitoring of a grandparent.

As we enter the twenty-first century, more men are involved as primary caregivers[5] (Harris, 1998; Russell, 2001; Matthews, 2002). This occurs because gender roles are changing, more women are employed full-time and less available as full-time caregivers, and married men are living longer and assuming a caregiving role for their partner. Older men caring for a frail spouse must learn new household tasks. And, like any caregiver, their social life decreases, and they experience decreased psychological and physical well-being due to loss of sleep and the physically and emotionally exhausting care work (Kramer and Lambert, 1999). Sons are increasingly more involved as caregivers if they are an only child or the nearest child, and because there is a growing cultural expectations that men should accept some of the family responsibilities formerly borne by women.

Employment status is an increasingly important factor in who provides care and in what type and frequency of care that is provided. People who work part-time, who are in a supervisory position, or who are in a full-time position where there is job flexibility, a higher income, or parental-care-support programs are more likely to assume the role of caregiver (Guberman and Maheu, 1999; Matthews, 2002). Where one lives also has an influence on caregiving. Those who live in rural communities generally receive more help from community members, perhaps more so than from relatives who live far away. Thus, rural caregivers, who generally have fewer formal support services to call on, provide more informal care and report more stress than urban caregivers (Keating et al., 2001; Skinner and Rosenberg, 2002).

The giving (and receiving) of social support in the later years is influenced as well by the cultural beliefs, practices, and values of a specific ethnic, religious, or racial group (Dilworth-Anderson et al., 2002; Wu and Hart, 2002; Brotman, 2003). More assistance is offered within a cultural group where older people are highly respected and valued, where assistance and care are believed to be private family matters, and where elderly people are ineligible for government assistance. Family assistance is greater when the older person doesn't speak English and therefore can't use formal support systems or understand diagnoses or medical instructions; when the older person has been economically disadvantaged throughout life; and when the older members of an ethnic group have not been culturally or structurally assimilated into mainstream society. Moreover, members of small ethnic-minority groups are less likely to have access to interpreters or culturally sensitive services (Brotman, 2003). The high levels of help given to older relatives among ethnic groups is partly due, as well, to the fact that many immigrants live with their adult children for financial reasons (Keefe et al., 2000).

Among Canada's Aboriginal people, older adults are highly dependent on the economic and emotional support of the extended family (Bienvenue and Havens, 1986; Wister and Moore, 1997). The provision of informal support is a traditional part of the respect for elders and is usually provided by wives or non-resident daughters who return to the community. Many older people in these communities need a great deal of care because of chronic health problems, poor nutrition, and substance abuse. Because they tend to live in small or isolated communities, few formal services are available, and that increases the pressure on their relatives to provide high levels of support (Buchignani and Armstrong-Esther, 1999). Even when government support services and medical services exist, Aboriginal people tend to make less use of them because of cultural beliefs or past practices.

Outcomes of Informal Support

For older people, an informal support network has the potential to prevent or alleviate stress and to help them make decisions, live independently, and recuperate from an acute illness or adapt to a chronic illness. Supportive family, friends, and neighbours can enhance or maintain physical or mental health and contribute to higher levels of well-being and life satisfaction. Among older adults who live alone, isolation and loneliness can be alleviated by an informal network of supportive friends and acquaintances.

The presence of a spouse, adult child, other relative, friend, or neighbour does not guarantee that assistance will be provided, or that it will be of high quality. Rather, the social and physical environment of the elderly person, and the personal characteristics of both the potential caregivers and recipients must be considered when one is assessing the resources of an informal support network. Of particular importance are the degree of frailty or dependency of the elderly person, the proximity of the caregiver, and his or her social, ethnic, health, and employment background, especially if the caregiver is not a member of the immediate family. It is also important that a caregiver have or acquire sufficient knowledge to be effective as a caregiver, especially for older people with cognitive impairments or severe dementia.

However, not all assistance is beneficial. Although the caregiver may have the best intentions, the recipient may see things quite differently. For example, an older person may resent the loss of privacy that results from increasing levels of personal care—they may feel they are being overprotected and losing personal control, and may resent the demeaning, childlike treatment

they receive. If different formal care workers visit the home, an older person may not trust them, may regard them as unwanted strangers in their home, or may view their work as unnecessary or shoddy (Aronson, 2002). Moreover, if the level of interaction with caregivers fails to meet needs or expectations, or if a primary caregiver experiences a crucial life transition (a job promotion, failing health), an older person may feel neglected, deprived, and isolated. In extreme cases, he or she may become the victim of neglect or of physical, psychological, or financial abuse (see below).

The Cost of Caregiving

The emotional, psychological, and financial costs of informal caregiving are difficult to estimate (Fast et al., 1997; Zukewich, 2003). The financial costs for a caregiver are subtle but considerable, especially if the parent lacks the necessary funds and must be supported by his or her children. The costs include loss of wages for time away from work, transportation to and from the recipient's home, long-distance telephone calls, home renovations, drugs and other medical supplies, and food. The cost of caregiving can create financial hardship for a caregiver who strives to keep a parent out of a residential institution.

Informal care also has a non-financial cost. First, a caregiver may lose the freedom to enjoy leisure time with his or her family and friends. Second, after a period of time, his or her health suffers through loss of sleep, anxiety, feelings of guilt, and a general failure to pay attention to nutrition and good health practices owing to the demands of caregiving and a lack of time (Pearlin et al., 2001). Some caregivers provide 40 to 60 hours a month, or more, of informal assistance. Third, the time that women spend out of the labour force because of caregiving leads to lost career opportunities, lower salaries, and smaller pensions (Gottlieb et al., 1994; Martin Matthews and Campbell, 1995; Gignac et al., 1996; Keating et al., 1999). Fourth, if caregivers are employed, the employer loses money from absenteeism; loss of productivity owing to phone calls from the parents, worry, early departure or late arrival, job turnover, and greater use of employee assistance programs that provide information and counselling to employees experiencing stress. Finally, when someone leaves paid employment to care for an aging parent, the government loses income-tax revenue, as well as sales taxes due to reduced spending.

Caregiver Stress and Burden

Adult children and others, when asked, report many benefits of being a caregiver—the satisfaction of helping others, repaying a debt for past assistance and support, preventing their parent from having to live in a retirement or nursing home or at least postponing the time when that becomes necessary, greater empathy for older adults, helping to prepare themselves for later life, increased knowledge about themselves, and increased intimacy with a parent (Keating et al., 1999; Chappell and Reid, 2002).

As volunteers, however, many caregivers feel the burden as the length of time in the role grows, as the amount of care required increases, and as the parent's behaviour becomes more aberrant and he or she becomes more dependent (Chappell, 1992: 41–4; Pearlin et al., 1996; Joseph and Hallman, 1996; Connidis, 2001: 141–6). The most burdensome cases involve caring for a person with dementia because of behavioural problems such as wandering, sleep disturbances, agitation, verbal or physical attacks on the caregiver, incontinence, and paranoia (Hawranik, 2002). The burden is greater if the caregiver lives with the older person 24 hours a day. Even among formal home-care workers there is considerable stress created by shift work, pain, injuries from lifting or being attacked by a client, verbal harassment, and long hours with low pay (Denton et al., 1999).

Most studies find that fewer than 10 per cent of caregivers say they are experiencing a significant burden. However, there is likely underreporting, especially by family members; the more serious cases may have been transferred to a long-term care facility; and in many cases, the burden is random and cyclical rather than constant. Nevertheless, caregiving stress and burden is an important social issue that must be addressed by making help available, when needed, to adult children and others who take the responsibility of caregiving.

Caregiving can conflict with other responsibilities—as a parent, employee, employer, partner, and friend. Although this conflict is felt mainly by women because most primary caregivers are women, when men play the primary role, similar conflicts are reported. The highest levels are generally reported by women who continue working full-time (Kemp and Rosenthal, 2000).

Caregiving stress involves fatigue, anxiety, and guilt as to whether the person is being properly cared for; low morale and perhaps depression; and a sense of being alone, helpless, and isolated while providing care. These feelings and reactions are sometimes called the *subjective* components of burden (Keating et al., 1999). The *objective* components of burden, which are more visible, include

- changes in lifestyle;

- loss of sleep;

- changing employment status, such as quitting work or beginning to work part-time;

- financial difficulties as a result of increased expenses and loss of income;

- physical health problems, such as sore knees or back from lifting, increased alcohol consumption;

- loss of friends and leisure time as a result of having no vacations or days off; and

- a deteriorating personal relationship with the older person (Keating et al., 1999).

In these situations, caregivers become hidden victims in the social support system if they do not receive education and assistance from the formal support system. To assess the objective and objective levels of stress that a caregiver may be experiencing, the 13 Item Caregiver Strain Index (Thornton and Travis, 2003) provides a check list to sensitize informal caregivers to issues, and to assess how they are coping. In extreme cases, primary caregivers simultaneously play the role of nurse, homemaker, social worker, psychologist, and chauffeur—often in addition to their 'normal' responsibilities at work and at home. To assist primary caregivers, social intervention services and programs are being introduced in some communities (see 'Assisting Caregivers' below).

Caregiving is especially stressful when an elderly person is caring for a cognitively impaired spouse. These difficulties are compounded by the emotional loss of a partner; by physical difficulties in coping with some of the necessary tasks; by anxiety about financial matters; by a deterioration of one's own physical health; and by depression or loneliness. There is often, at least initially, little, if any, use of formal services by the caregiving spouse who wishes to be seen as competent, loving, and ready to accept this new marital responsibility (O'Connor, 1999). A caregiving spouse lives on a rigid, fixed schedule, and all personal time is devoted to the spouse, especially if formal support services are ignored or not available. Often spousal care is not adequate, compared with that available in an institution. But sometimes a decision to transfer a dependent spouse is not made, even if he or she no longer wishes to be a burden to the spouse or family. Highlight 11.1 describes case studies about the burden of caring for a spouse.

The level of stress and burden experienced by an adult child caring for a parent is related to the unique interaction of a number of factors:

- the type and degree of impairment in terms of functional ability and behavioural problems
- the personality and self-perceived ability of the caregiver to play the role

Highlight 11.1 The Burden of Spousal Care

Case 1

Suzy, at age 72, cares for her husband, who is 74. They have no children and are financially well off. Besides having Parkinson's disease, John has suffered a 'cerebrovascular accident' and two heart attacks. He can barely speak, and spends his time either in bed or in a wheelchair. Suzy tells of an intense love between them throughout the years, signs of which are still clearly evident today: 'We shared everything. We were always together. Always! Our relations were simply perfect. We had a good time together. Every minute was a delight. Even today it's great when he feels a little better and manages to sit next to me.'

John remains in their bedroom in front of the loud television set. 'That's how John likes to watch TV,' Suzy says, even though he appears to be asleep and oblivious of what is going on around him. Although he eats little, Suzy still cooks and bakes his favourite dishes. She often smiles at him, strokes him, and touches him. Suzy makes a habit of speaking to John about day-to-day things, even though he does not respond. She frequently turns to him with questions, and when no answer is given, she answers for him. When her gaze rests upon him, she comments, 'He's tired' or 'He's cold, we should close the window.' When she 'feels' he is cold, she covers him, and when she 'feels' he is hungry, she feeds him.

continued

Hightlight 11.1 continued

Suzy does not leave John at home alone even for a few minutes. When she can leave the house, she does so only to run errands, and even then it is a race against time. She sleeps lightly, for fear she might not hear something John says. She devotes all her time to him, having adapted her way of life to his needs. Each activity in her daily routine is meticulously fixed: every morning she shaves her husband, bathes him, prepares his food, and so on. She says her mind is constantly preoccupied with planning: how to move John, what to cook for him.

Ignoring her own personal needs, Suzy has completely abandoned all her previous friends and pastimes. When asked whether she is well, she answers in the affirmative, but then recalls that she has angina pectoris and tachycardia. In response to other questions, she reports about exhaustion and a sense of slowly losing her mind. However, when John's name is mentioned, she becomes focused again: 'Now he must be given the best care possible.' And with genuine indignation she adds, 'These idiots come along and say to me, "Why don't you put him in an institution?" We've always been together and both of us can't bear the idea of separation. We just can't. I think it's because of the bond between us.'

Case 2

Robert is 68 years old and takes care of Fran, who is 66. The couple have a son, and their financial situation is adequate. Fran has cancer and is bedridden. She had a colostomy, and also suffers from asthma, from severe swelling in her legs, and from pains. Before Fran's illness, the couple followed a tranquil routine. 'All that belongs to the past,' Robert recalls sadly, 'Fran was always at home. She was a good housewife. When I came home from work, I would always find that dinner was ready and the apartment was clean and tidy. In the evenings we watched TV together. I can hardly remember any arguments between us.' Despite Fran's presence, Robert often speaks for her. When she does try to say something, he interrupts her and completes the sentence. Fran sighs a lot; each time Robert goes over to change her position. At night he sleeps lightly, since Fran constantly needs his assistance, and even a small sigh is enough to get him out of bed.

Robert is now responsible for all family and domestic needs. He does the shopping, cleans, and prepares light meals. Insisting on a fixed schedule, he attempts to devote himself utterly to help Fran: 'The entire day revolves around her medication and walking her to the toilet.' Even when he leaves the house, only to go on errands, his mind is troubled, and he is quick to return. He no longer sees his friends, and says his state of mind is deteriorating: 'It's nerve-wracking to be together all the time and not see other faces. I want to go out but I can't leave her. Like in a prison, I'm with her and she's with me all the time.'

Yet, although Robert sometimes complains about Fran—'She makes me nervous,' 'She irritates me'—he is quick to add: 'Everything is painful to her, everything bothers her. But still, she's a good woman, poor soul.' He feels helpless, but says he has no regrets about devoting himself to his wife. 'She is unfortunate, I can't let her suffer,' Robert says, 'I have to help her. Who else will come and help her, God?' When reminded about the option of institutionalization, he rejects the idea outright: 'Never. Even at home she suffers more than enough. She doesn't deserve having more troubles. No. I couldn't do it.'

Sources: Adapted from Navon and Weinblatt (1996). Reprinted by permission of the *Journal of Aging Studies*, (JAI Press)

- the availability and use of educational and training programs and self-help groups

- the availability of social support from both outside and within the family

- the personality and demands of the older person

- the quality of the lifelong relationship between the adult child and elderly parent

- the presence of competing demands or problems in the caregiver's life, such as a career, children, his or her health, alcoholism, or unemployment.

Highlight 11.2 illustrates some of the difficulties that face adult children who care for an aging parent.

Sometimes the stress and the continuing physical, mental, and emotional burden leads to elder abuse (see below). Some incidents of abuse can be avoided through social support and interventions such as educational programs regarding the specific disease state, respite care, self-help support groups, and financial assistance to caregivers through tax deductions or payment for services to replace income lost owing to caregiving.

Formal Social Support

Formal support is provided to dependent and frail adults by public and private agencies, in the home or in an institution, by trained volunteers or professional health- and social-care workers. Programs created by the state result from laws, policies, or regulations created by different levels of government. Private sector programs fill a service gap when public policies are inequitable, dysfunctional, or non-existent; or when the elderly person's children are unable to meet the needs of aging parents. It was noted earlier that the support system can be described as a series of concentric circles surrounding an older person at the core. While the elements of the informal system are generally more intimate and accessible, the formal system is more impersonal and bureaucratic and may be difficult to use, even if it is available.

Formal support includes a range of health-care and social services provided by government agencies, not-for-profit voluntary organizations, or private businesses. The aim is to provide a safety net through such services as community-based and in-home programs, adult day-care centres, retirement homes, nursing homes, and long-term chronic-care institutions. Ideally, formal support should constitute a co-ordinated system so that all needs are met and so that no one is neglected or overlooked. Historically,[6] public funds have been allocated to pensions and health care, including long-term institutional housing. As a result, a system evolved that encouraged the 'warehousing' or 'over-institutionalization' of the frail elderly in long-term-care facilities (Forbes et al., 1987). (Institutionalized care, part of the continuum of formal care services in later life, is discussed in Chapter 7.) In this section the emphasis is on formal support provided through home care and community-based programs. This section builds on earlier discussions of later-life living arrangements, family ties, social networks and economic security.

Since the 1970s, there has been a gradual social movement toward de-institutionalizing all special groups—physically and mentally disabled people of all ages, elderly people, criminals. Not surprisingly, the rising cost[7] of caring for an expanding aging population has forced the state to shift more responsibility for the care of frail and dependent older adults to individuals and families or to the private sector. However, to help families assume more responsibility, governments and employers have introduced services for caregivers, as well as for elderly care recipients. These programs are designed to support and complement the services provided by informal family caregivers. Highlight 11.3 lists formal services provided in some communities, while Highlight 11.4 describes contrasting experiences with community-based services.

Highlight 11.2 The Burden of Parent Care

The following statements and situations, as reported in the media or to case workers and social scientists, vividly depict the extent to which stress, fear, guilt, and bizarre behaviour can occur in a caregiving relationship:

- I was talking on the telephone, trying to rearrange my schedule for the day, when my mother attacked me from behind with a pot because I wasn't paying attention to her. Never in my life had I seen her utter a violent word or action.

- In the last six months since my mother moved into the house, I have experienced both mental and physical fatigue and have started drinking again. My teenage son is having emotional and scholastic problems at school and I feel helpless since I just do not have enough time for him in the evening.

- He is not the father I knew. If he asks for something to eat, he later asks why I served him lunch. Now he is confined to bed and I need help to lift him. I cannot meet his ever-increasing demands and I feel guilty.

- Her mental condition has deteriorated rapidly. She is verbally abusive toward me, my family, and visitors. My own health has deteriorated over the past two years and I must now seriously consider placing my mother in a nursing home.

- When it became apparent that my mother could no longer live by herself, two choices were available: move her to a nursing home, wherever and whenever a bed became available, or move her into our home. My daughter had just left for college, I was tired of my job, so I decided to care for her in my home. I thought it would work. I was unprepared to meet her need for medical care. Her emotional outbursts and demands made me feel like a child again, and my husband grew more distant as I was consumed by the demands of caregiving. In about three years it became a question of my marriage and sanity versus institutionalized care for my mother. The decision wasn't easy, but it had to be made. It has taken me a long time to resolve the guilt of this decision, especially when I visit and see her empty life. The full responsibility and 'wear and tear' have fallen on me. My sister who lives 10 miles away contributes nothing but telephone calls to me, to see how 'her' mother is doing. She never asks how I am doing or if she can help in any way.

Formal and Informal Support: Toward an Interactive Care System

Whereas it used to be relatively easy to distinguish between informal (home-based) support and formal support (in an institution), today the distinctions are blurred. A shift to a continuum of support and care has evolved through the creation of less expensive support in the form of home and community-care services, and through increased assistance to the family by community agencies (McCarthy, 2002; Stephenson and Sawyer, 2002). Indeed, family care is the most essential component, with 80 to 90 per cent of the assistance being provided by informal caregivers and as little as 10 to 15 per cent by formal care workers (Denton, 1997: 31).

Community-based services are designed to facilitate independent living in the community and to prevent premature admission to, or a long-term stay in, an acute- or chronic-care hospital. Ideally, agencies should:

Highlight 11.3 Formal Support Services for an Aging Population

Home-Based

- Visiting (companions) and monitoring those who live alone
- Meals-on-Wheels
- Daily or 24-hour telephone contact
- Home-care workers—for personal care, cleaning, meal preparation
- Counselling
- Home maintenance and renovation
- Palliative care
- Equipment and supplies (walkers, canes, bedpoles, raised chairs)
- Professional visits—nurses, therapists, social workers

Community-Based

- Information and referral services and assessments
- Outreach programs to locate elderly people at risk in their home
- Training and educating caregivers
- Self-help support groups (e.g., for those caring for a parent with Alzheimer's disease or Parkinson's disease)
- Day care
- Respite care
- Transportation (subsidized dial-a-bus or taxi services for appointments

Employer-Based

- Parental leave policies
- Employee-assistance programs, including advice and support for employees caring for an aging parent
- Flextime

- provide co-ordinated, unduplicated services through 'one-stop access' or a 'single entry point' to a variety of services;
- disseminate information about services available in the community;
- assess services needed by a specific individual;
- provide treatment or assistance; and
- relieve burdens on the family.

Highlight 11.4 Contrasting Experiences with Community-Based Services

A Negative Experience

An elderly woman is referred to the social services department by a neighbour or family member without being consulted. They feel she is becoming too great a burden for them. The case is passed to a social worker, who summons the elderly person, together with family, to an assessment meeting. Upon arrival, the elderly person and family wait in a drafty waiting room before being ushered into an office. Professionals sit on one side of the table behind their files; the visitors sit across the table, but the elderly person is given a low easy chair from which she can hardly see across the table; 'you'll be more comfortable there, Alice dear,' referring to her by her Christian name as though she were a child. The professionals introduce themselves in a mumbling way; the visitors are unsure who they are, what they do; they are ignorant of the form of the meeting or of the services to be offered.

The professionals have a very clear idea of the agenda. Rapidly the needs and attributes of the elderly person are listed in their own terminology; together they place her in a well-defined category for which an inappropriate package is available—home help, meals on wheels—designed to be cost-effective and to meet local availability. Interjections by the visitors are brushed aside; their ignorance is demonstrated by their incorrect designation of services. The elderly person begins to feel that she is not going to get what she really wants, but before she can collect her thoughts, the discussion has moved on. The professionals, clearly accustomed to meeting together in this way, conduct their business and visibly demonstrate control as they write in their files. When one of the visitors asks if more services could not be provided, she is reminded that 'there are many more elderly people out there whose needs are much greater', thus eliciting feelings of guilt. Thus, in control over information and agenda, in their definition of the problem, and through speech and body language, the assessment team induces in their clients a sense of complete lack of control, yet a gratitude that they have been given as much as they have. To protest might well mean being branded as a troublemaker with consequent loss of services.

A Positive Experience

An elderly woman has decided that the time has come for her to have some external help. She has armed herself with a package of leaflets and booklets from her local Age Concern office and has discussed them (and the quality of the local delivery of such services) with others at her club. A meeting is arranged at her home; she makes tea for her visitors before describing her problems in her own words. Those present—social worker, health-care worker, voluntary agency helper, daughter, friend, and neighbour—offer possible services. The result may fall short of expectations, but the process has at least demonstrated the control exercised by the elderly person. It might be argued here that many an elderly person will already have become so frail as to be unable to exercise such control; here an advocate—a daughter or friend but not a professional—could assume the central role. The experience of control is enhanced both by a belief that the statutory services are received as a right (and therefore to be demanded) rather than as 'charity' and by the introduction of reciprocity into informal caring relationships (small gift exchanges, token payments, a service rendered in return).

Sources: Adapted from Lloyd (1991: 133–4). Reprinted with permission of JAI Press.

A long-standing policy debate has centred on whether the formal system should be a substitute for, or a complement to, informal support. The *substitution* hypothesis argues that a formal safety net must be provided by the public sector when families are unavailable, unable, or unwilling to help; when older adults are isolated or abandoned; or when informal caregivers can no longer provide adequate support. In contrast, the *complementarity* hypothesis argues that a co-ordinated system of informal support (by the family) and formal support (by government or the private sector) is essential to enhance the quality of life of both older people and their caregivers (Denton, 1997; Ward-Griffin, 2002; Ward-Griffin and Marshall, 2003). Evidence suggests that the ideal and most successful formal system is complementary and provides a continuum of assistance and care to meet the diverse and ever-changing needs of an elderly person and his or her caregivers.

Even when elderly parents are hospitalized for an acute or chronic illness, or when they are living in a retirement home or long-term-care facility, they receive help from adult children. This help may include companionship or personal care such as feeding, shaving, and bathing. In effect, a family member provides assistance, and serves as a case manager to provide a link between the informal and the formal systems on behalf of an elderly parent. This latter process involves serving as a facilitator, mediator, advocate, and adviser and acting as a buffer against the formal bureaucracy of a government or institution (Rosenthal and Martin-Matthews, 1999). This intervention can, however, lead to conflict between a caregiver and care recipient as the demands or expectations of the recipient increase, or as an older person loses independence and the power to make decisions.

A major weakness in the informal and formal continuum of support is the lack of co-ordination between the two levels in many jurisdictions. This occurs because potential users lack information about a service. In other situations, the two systems compete for the right to provide a similar service, or the demand for formal services far exceeds the capacity of the system.

A variety of mechanisms have been proposed to integrate the two levels of support. These include using professional case work managers, training a family member to be a case manager, and creating a single agency in each community to serve as a source of information and as a single entry point into the formal support system (the 'one-stop' or 'single-entry' concept). Such an agency has responsibility for

- assessing the needs of recipients and their caregivers;
- lobbying for additional services and facilities in the community;
- assessing the quality of the public or private facilities and services;
- monitoring the quality of care provided by informal caregivers; and
- co-ordinating information about the availability of, and access to, the range of services provided by various levels of government and the private sector.

The Use of Formal Services

The use of formal services by older adults is quite low, the main users being frail couples living in their home; those who live alone, especially women; those over 75 years of age with poor self-reported health; and those who have used home care previously (Hall and Coyte, 2001). There are several possible reasons that community services are often not used:

- a lack of knowledge about the availability of formal services, or how to use them;
- a desire to remain independent or dependent on a spouse, child, or friend;
- a denial that services are needed;

- subtle discrimination against elderly members of ethnic groups who only speak and read their own language;

- user fees, which may be too expensive for some older people;

- lack of services in rural or remote communities;

- a cultural tradition of seeking help only from family caregivers;

- a shortage of personnel with proper certification and training; and high staff turnover due to stress and low wages;

- cognitive or behavioural problems that are beyond the service level available;

- a shortage of volunteers to deliver services (such as telephone companions or drivers for meals-on-wheels programs);

- bureaucratic barriers, such as eligibility tests for need; and

- lack of need when a person is being looked after satisfactorily by the family or can afford private care services.

Levels of use are determined, as well, by the rules and regulations of a given program or agency. Are services available to all citizens who reach a certain age, therefore representing a universal program (such as health care)? Or is access limited to those who can demonstrate need, such as the unavailability of children or poverty? It is argued, increasingly, that formal support policies should be based on need rather than age. This would reduce the total cost of such services to the public, but it might place more pressure on families to contribute to the caregiving of elderly parents. A question that remains to be resolved is how to define and measure need in the social-service domain.

Home-Care Services

The home-care or community-care system was established in Canada in the early 1990s to relieve overburdened hospitals and long-term care facilities, as well as overburdened or untrained informal caregivers. If people who were ill, disabled, or dying could be cared for at home, governments would save money, more beds would be available in hospitals for the treatment of acute illness, and older people could live at home in a more familiar and comfortable environment. The demand for home-care programs has increased in recent years as hospitals are closed or downsized, especially in small and rural communities. In 2000, 44 per cent of Canadians reported that at least one member of their extended family used home care, with women between the ages of 65 and 69 most likely to use these services (CARP, 2001: 4, 68).

Health Canada defines home care as 'an array of services enabling Canadians, incapacitated with a disability or a chronic health problem, in whole or in part, to live at home, often with the effect of preventing, delaying or substituting for long-term care or acute care alternatives.' Home care is provided by professional care workers, including nurses, social workers, and therapists, who provide services in the home or in the community, and the provision of programs both for the care recipient (stimulation and activity programs for people with Alzheimer's disease or exercise programs for people who have had a stroke); and for the caregiver—adult day care programs or long-term respite care. Each situation is unique, and therefore home-care programs must first assess the functional capacity and health of the older person, the safety of the home, what informal support is available, and how to co-ordinate the delivery of needed support.

The programs offered consist of a blend of health, social, and non-medical support services to the client and his or her caregiver (Keefe, 2002; Shapiro, 2002). From the perspective of the individual, there are both *therapeutic* and *compensatory* goals. The therapeutic goal may be to help the older person recover from an accidents or illness and prevent further deterioration from a medical or disease condition. The *compensatory* goals may be to promote comfortable and meaningful daily living despite the onset of dependence created by disabilities or frailties (Feldman, 1999b). From the perspective of society, the goals include efficiency, cost effectiveness, and equity in access. (See Highlight 11.5.)

Home care is usually successful and cost-effective if it is combined with appropriate levels of informal support. Some care services are provided by the public sector, with or without a user fee; others, such as 24-hour nursing or companionship and monitoring, are provided by private

Highlight 11.5 Home Care Goals: A Dual Perspective

Individual Goals

1. Improve or maintain health.
2. Maximize function; improve or slow the deterioration of functional abilities.
3. Enhance psychological and social well-being.
4. Meet needs for care and assistance.
5. Promote comfort and freedom from pain.
6. Promote meaningful lives.
7. Maximize consumer independence, autonomy, and choice.
8. Improve consumer knowledge and self-care abilities.
9. Assure safety.
10. Allow the consumer to remain at home.

Societal Goals

1. Promote access to services by the greatest number of those with needs.
2. Target those most in need.
3. Provide comprehensive services that address the full range of identified needs.
4. Provide an adequate level and appropriate mix of services to meet needs.
5. Promote a fair and equitable distribution of services.
6. Maximize individual choice.
7. Tailor services to individuals.
8. Ensure acceptable quality of services.
9. Integrate and coordinate services.
10. Keep services affordable for consumers and government.
11. Promote the efficient production of cost-effective services.
12. Strengthen and promote informal systems of family provided care.
13. Maximize individual responsibility for long-term care.

Sources: Reprinted with permission from Feldman (1999). Copyright © 1999. Reprinted by permission of Sage Publications.

agencies. Private services, which are very expensive (up to $1,500 a week depending on the services provided), have emerged to fill a demand that the public sector cannot meet. In addition to home-care workers, some of these businesses provide a geriatric care manager for an older person whose relatives live at a distance. The managers or their staff become surrogate family members who monitor, visit, perform household tasks, and provide transportation for shopping, medical visits, and social outings. They report regularly to the family and serve as a resource for the older person to call if he or she needs help. For a relative living far away, this arrangement, if it can be afforded, is preferable to moving a parent into a nursing home.

Because home care is an effective and necessary part of the health-care system, advocates argue that a national home-care system should be included in the Canada Health Act (CAG, 1999; NACA, 2000; CARP, 2001; Shapiro, 2002). CARP (2001: 8) reported that 85 per cent of Canadians want home care covered in the Canada Health Act, and 61 per cent prefer that a home care program be established before a pharmacare program. At present, home care is a provincial, regional, or municipal service, and consequently there is considerable variation in cost, availability, content, quality, accessibility, and eligibility. Some jurisdictions charge user fees; have residence requirements (how long one has lived in the province, region, or municipality); set limits on the number of service hours per week or on the maximum amount that can be spent on one individual; or require some services to be delivered by the private sector (Shapiro, 2002). Hence, both CARP (2001) and Shapiro (2002) argued strongly for a universal national home care program that is provided by both the federal and the provincial and territorial governments. Similarly, the Commission on the Future of Health Care in Canada argued that home care should be 'the next essential service' included in the Canada Health Act (Romanow, 2002: 171–82; Shapiro, 2003).

In their assessment of home care in Canada, CARP (2001) gave the present system a failing 'report card'. Specifically, they concluded that:

- Federal and provincial governments are not providing sufficient guidance or leadership to the home-care system; i.e., the system is fragmented.

- Programs are underfunded, even though funding has increased.

- Home-care wages are low, the working conditions are poor, and the workers do not receive enough training. For these reasons, it is difficult to recruit and retain home care workers (there is high staff turnover).

- Service delivery is hindered by user fees, co-payments, and defining the complexity or level of care that is needed.

- The system does not provide adequate training, education, or assistance to informal caregivers, especially elderly spouses.

- The system does not provide economic incentives for employers to give caregiver leave, nor does it replace lost income or offset CPP losses when someone leaves a job to care for an elderly parent.

Highlight 11.6 illustrates one problem with the current system—a shortage of trained support workers.

Social Intervention Strategies and Issues

Strategies must be developed to ensure a minimum level of care, equal access to home care, and assistance for informal caregivers. In some communities, home care is available to everyone; in others it is available only if need can be demonstrated; in others, such as rural areas, few, if any, services are available. Furthermore, some services

Highlight 11.6 Cracks in the Home-Care System

Case A

M. and J. retired to a small Cape Breton, NS, community in 1986 to enjoy their retirement. In 1997, their lifestyle was interrupted when J. was diagnosed with vascular dementia, and M. took on the task of caring for him. It was just around the time home care was starting in Nova Scotia and no one really had an idea of what they were getting into.

What followed was not a pleasant period in her life. 'The whole thing was a bad experience, from start to finish,' M. says, pausing uncomfortably at the memory of it. 'No one is facing up to the fact that there's far too much stress being placed on the informal caregiver. Under the current system, the lot of the informal caregiver is one of total frustration.'

The problem lies in the fact that home care isn't nine to five, Monday to Friday. It's a job that demands being constantly on call. In M.'s case, a nurse coming in for a few minutes to take J.'s blood pressure or a home care support worker visiting once a week wasn't enough. More help was needed but funding and staffing shortages made it impossible for Home Care Nova Scotia to respond.

M.'s cry for support cuts to the heart of one of the greatest issues in home care. In each province it seems that the informal caregiver has slipped through the healthcare safety net, ignored by the system. For M., there were many other areas where she could have used a helping hand but what she needed most was a break. Though it might seem harsh, it's the brutal reality of caring for someone day after day without any break. 'As J.'s faculties diminished, he needed stimulation from someone other than me.' Plus she needed time on her own. However, they lived in a rural area where no geriatric daycare services were available; any respite she could garner, she had to pay for from her own pocket. 'The wealthy can look after themselves and the poor get government assistance,' she says. 'But for the working poor and middle-class informal caregiver, it's a disaster of unimagined proportions.'

Worn down by constantly caring for her husband without help, M.'s own health failed when she developed a thyroid problem. It became clear that for her sake, J. needed to be placed in a long-term care facility. After researching all her available options, M. found a good set up for J. at a home in Ontario, where the couple had lived for much of their lives. Then came the final blow. The federal government didn't react kindly when she tried to claim through income tax the costs of moving her husband to Toronto, attendant expenses, and the cost of long-term care. In fact, for three years, the revenue department chased after her, trying to recoup the income tax claims she'd made. 'All I was looking for was 17 cents on the dollar, to recover my out-of-pocket medical expenses,' she says, referring to the maximum amount she could claim through income tax. 'But the tax system doesn't do the caregiver any favours—in fact, it's punitive.'

Case B

J. vividly recalls the day when he and his wife became casualties of Canada's home care system. It was a Tuesday and he had planned a few hours off—get a haircut, renew his driver's licence and stop by the local coffee shop to read the paper.

Most days, the retired school teacher from Hamilton, Ont., is tied to his home. He's primary caregiver to his wife, M., who suffers from Alzheimer's-related dementia—one of the wide range of ailments that nowadays are taken care of at home. He values his Tuesdays when, for a few hours, respite comes in the form of a home care support worker who cleans up the house, prepares a meal and looks after M. Though he paid for these services, J. needed a break.

continued

Hightlight 11.6 continued

But that Tuesday, he was chagrined to find that the home care support worker wasn't coming. 'M's illness had caused her to become very aggressive and agitated,' says J. 'And M. began directing this anger toward her home care worker.' In the end, the home care worker grew weary of the abuse and quit. Her replacement soon caught wind of M.'s difficult behaviour, and she, too, declined the assignment. After that, there weren't any support workers available.

Without a replacement, J.'s much-anticipated day went up in smoke. 'I'm not blaming anyone,' he says. 'I just needed a break, but the community care system couldn't provide me with one.' Staff shortages forced J. to put in another long, unpaid and stressful day, without much chance of relief.

Source: Reproduced with permission from the CARP *Report Card on Home Care in Canada 2000* (CARP, 2001).

are provided at no cost; others require the recipient or the caregiver to pay some or all of the costs. The number and the variety of services available in any given community depends on the tax revenues available, the quality of leadership, and the priorities of politicians and city or regional staff. This section introduces intervention strategies, as well as some issues related to intervention approaches.

Assisting Caregivers

The pool of primary caregivers is shrinking because of the falling birth rate, rising divorce rates, increased geographical mobility by children, and more labour-force participation by women. Moreover, as the size of the older population increases because of greater life expectancy, the age of potential caregivers is rising. For those reasons, the private sector, government agencies, and voluntary associations are developing intervention strategies to assist caregivers of the frail elderly. These strategies must ensure, wherever possible, that the care recipient has some choice in deciding who provides the care, and where. And, regardless of whether caregivers are paid or not, a caring relationship involving trust, respect, and some affection must evolve between care recipients and caregivers.

There is considerable debate about whether and how family caregivers should be assisted. One approach argues that a family should assume full responsibility for the care of aging parents and that the government should only assist those who have no living relatives. Extreme proponents of this view argue that if family members are unable to cope with caring for a frail parent, they must reimburse the government for the cost of institutionalization. Another approach assumes that while most families do as much as they can to care for frail parents, caregivers become overburdened at some point. Hence, formal assistance is needed so that a family can avoid, for as long as possible, moving a parent to a long-term care facility. Adherents of this approach argue that the government has a responsibility to assist the primary caregivers of frail adults.

The quality of home-care service provided by family members, volunteers, or salaried home-care workers varies greatly. Those caring for a frail elderly person, especially one with a dementia, may work in isolation, lack training and information about the disease or its behavioural manifestations, get little or no time off, have round-the-clock responsibility, and not receive any feedback. Moreover, for many paid home-care workers, wages are low, the training is inadequate, there is little opportunity for career advancement, and they often serve several clients a day, in many parts of a city or region. The working conditions for home-care workers are seldom considered in the design or implementation of policies.

There are three general methods of helping both older people and their primary caregivers. First, to relieve the stress of the caregiver and improve the quality of care for the recipient, programs provide educational, emotional, and social support for the caregiver (Hébert et al., 2003). These programs include: individual or group education or counselling about the specific disease state, or about palliative care; skills training so that health and personal-care needs can be met in the home; and the formation of mutual-help support groups (e.g., for caregivers of Alzheimer's patients).

A second type of assistance consists of financial incentives or reimbursements for the caregiver through tax credits or a subsidy to offset lost income or to purchase needed services. Working women would probably use this financial assistance to purchase daytime personal care for an elderly parent (Quebec offers $600 a year for respite services). Sometimes payments are provided directly to the care recipient, who purchases whatever services are needed, and from whomever they wish. Whether such financial assistance should go to the older person or to the primary caregiver, and who should decide, continues to be a policy debate. In Nova Scotia, the Home Life Support program compensates family caregivers of frail elderly people. Recipients of this compensation tend to be younger women who live in non-urban areas and who live with the care recipient. Because of regulations in this policy about maximum earned income, caregivers must have a family income that is under or near the poverty line to be eligible for this compensation program. Keefe and Fancey (1997) found that paid caregivers in Nova Scotia spend 31 to 40 hours a week on care and receive an average compensation of only $88 a week (much less than the minimum wage). There are some who argue that payments to caregivers may increase the incidence of elder abuse (see below).

A third source of assistance consists of formal care or assistance provided within or outside the home either by the public sector (with or without a user fee) or by the private sector. Some of these programs include the provision of assistive devices or home maintenance services, such as installing monitoring devices; transportation; congregate or communal housing; or personal in-home health care, such as bathing, nursing, and therapy. Adult day programs provide older people with social and physical stimulation and their caregivers with respite. These programs offer a variety of social and therapeutic programs, usually for at least three days a week. Sometimes these programs take place in a nursing home, and that, unfortunately, may create a stigma about being old and, therefore, discourage people from using these programs (Weeks and Roberto, 2002).

Respite care provides temporary supervision or care by professionals so that a primary caregiver receives a daily, weekend, or vacation break from the routine, responsibility, and burden of caregiving. The older person either remains in his or her home and a companion moves in; or is moved to a retirement or nursing home as a short-term visitor, to an adult day care centre, or to a day hospital as an outpatient.

Ideally, respite care is used before there is a family crisis. Respite care is underused because people may not know it exists, and if they do, they may be worried about the quality of care; it may be too difficult to transport a parent to the respite site; or the parent's emotional and behavioural problems prevent him or her from attending. For caregivers, the temporary relief gives them an opportunity to look after other responsibilities or take care of themselves; to get in touch with friends and others in similar situations (through support groups); to have a complete physical and mental break from caregiving and the care recipient; to do some reading, take part in a hobby, or get some exercise; and to be happy and free of worry (Chappell et al., 2001).

Co-ordination of Services: An Integrated Continuum of Care

Assistance for older people and their caregivers is also available from employers and voluntary associations. The volunteer sector includes programs such as home nursing offered by the Victorian Order of Nurses; widow-to-widow support networks; adult recreation centres; and self-help or mutual-support groups that provide direct or indirect assistance to primary caregivers. Some employers offer flextime or family leave for an employee who is the primary caregiver for an elderly person. However, family leave for parental care is not universally available because a number of issues remain to be resolved: is the leave paid or unpaid? If a paid leave, who is responsible for payment, the government or the employer? Who is eligible, and for how long? These cost-related issues are an obstacle to innovative programs through which employers could provide support to primary caregivers. Thus, most assistance of this type is informal and ad hoc, and occurs because of a personal relationship between a sympathetic employer or supervisor and a burdened employee who may be considering withdrawing from the labour force.

At one time, the level and location of care for older people was determined mainly by physicians or hospital staff. Community agencies provided assistance only if requested by an older adult, or if a person needed assistance after being discharged from an acute-care hospital. Frequently, acute-care hospitals kept older patients long after they needed primary medical care because there was no suitable housing for them while they convalesced. Or an older patient might be transferred to a nursing home, often before he or she needed that level of care, because it was the only housing available for those without family, home care, or community assistance.

Since the 1970s, many provinces and some communities have created integrated, case management systems. Under the leadership of a case manager, community and social-service agencies provide information and participate in decision-making about the ideal type, location, and level of care needed by an older person. The caregiving model has shifted from medical-care management after an acute illness to on-going assessment and case management of personal competencies and of the living environment, preferably before a crisis occurs. This system has a single entry point, which is initiated through an in-home or in-hospital assessment by a multi-disciplinary team consisting of a social worker, a nurse, a homemaker, and a doctor. Then, after the assessment and a discussion with the older person and his or her family caregivers, recommendations are made about the best location and sources of care. Once an initial decision has been made about needs and care, the team performs regular assessments.

A continuum-of-care model, designed to meet the changing needs of older adults, integrates home, community, and residential care services so that a person can be transferred seamlessly, as needed, from one level to the next (Hollander, 2002). Once a person is in this system, premature admission to a nursing home, which should be the last option on the continuum, is less likely. The Senior Citizens Department of the Niagara Region in Ontario defined a continuum of care as:

> a range of planned, organized, financed and co-ordinated support programs and living options, which are based on careful assessment of individual needs such as preventive health, life enrichment, health promotion and wellness that promote overall well-being and independence as long as possible. As well, it should include support programs and living options that enhance the quality of life and support the independence and needs of the community-based older person and family caregivers. A range of institutional settings recognizes that there are varying degrees of physical and mental frailty (CMHC, 1990: 19).

Figure 11.1 illustrates the components of an ideal continuum of care system, while Highlight 11.6 illustrates two contrasting ways in which an older person can enter such a system.

The Niagara continuum-of-care system has five main elements:

- a single point of entry and a single administration for record keeping;

- an initial and ongoing social, functional, cognitive, and medical assessment by a multidisciplinary team;

- a range of service options once an older adult is 'in the system';

- regular communication, under the direction of a case manager, among staff, volunteers, and the individual and his or her family, about changing needs; and

- regional coverage in which service is delivered by homes for the aged, community support offices, and day program or resource centres, each of which serves a specific geographic region so that older people remain close to their home, friends, and families.

Figure 11.1 A Continuum of Care

Well Elderly	Frail Elderly	Functionally Disabled Elderly		Ill Elderly
		Living in the Community	*Living in Institutions*	
• Self-care/Mutual aid	• Informal care	• Home care/ continuing care	• Nursing homes	• Acute-care hospitals
• Health promotion	• Congregate meals		• Chronic-care facilities	• Out-patient clinics
• Information referral	• Transportation services	• Adult day care	• Rehabilitative care facilities	• Community health clinics
• Education	• Home maintenance services	• Respite care		• Physicians/health professionals
• Counselling		• Meals on wheels		
• Senior clubs	• Community support programs	• Homebound learning		
• Senior centres	• Community health centres	• Alzheimer resource centre		
• Advocacy		• Public trustee		
• Travel	• Aids to independent living	• Day hospital		
• Job bureaus		• Geriatric assessment units		
• Fitness programs	• Emergency response systems			
• Victim services	• Elder abuse resource centres			
• Legal services				

Source: Havens (1995). Previously published in *Canadian Journal on Aging/La Revue canadienne du vieillissement*, 14 (2), 245–62. Reprinted by permission of the publisher, University of Toronto Press Incorporated (www.utpjournals.com). Copyright © 1995.

Highlight 11.7 Entrance to a Continuum of Care System: Two Examples

Mrs S.

Mrs S. initially contacted the Senior Citizens Department six months after her husband's death. She said that she found yard work and other home maintenance chores very difficult. She thought she would have to sell her house and move to an apartment. A Community Worker from the Senior Citizens Department arranged for a Home Help worker to assist Mrs S. with the chores she was unable to do.

A year later, Mrs S. suffered a stroke. After her hospitalization, she moved to the home of her daughter. Her daughter and son-in-law both worked outside the home full-time and Mrs S. found herself lonely and lacking the stimulation to be as physically active as her doctor recommended. She called the Community Worker, who suggested participation in a Day Program. The Community Worker referred Mrs S. to the Admissions Counsellor, who facilitated her admission to the Day Program in the Home for the Aged nearest to where Mrs S. lives. She has attended the program twice a week for eighteen months.

When her daughter and son-in-law were planning a vacation, they requested that Mrs S. be admitted to vacation/respite care. Mrs S. chose instead to increase her attendance at the Day Program to five days a week. Mrs S. is aware that her attendance at the Day Program provides her with priority for admission to the Home, but she has told the Day Program Supervisor 'it's not time yet.'

Mrs T.

Mrs T. was admitted to the residential care area of a Home for the Aged, directly from hospital. She had been in hospital for several months, having been in a weakened physical condition due to poor nutrition and inadequate management of her diabetic condition.

Although Mrs T. found it difficult at first to adjust to the Home, in time she grew accustomed to the group living situation. With proper attention to her nutritional and medical needs, her physical and emotional condition improved. Mrs T. then expressed a desire to move back to the community.

The Home's Social Worker, Admissions Counsellor, and Director of Care worked together to assist her to make arrangements for community living. The Admissions Counsellor contacted the Housing Authority and helped Mrs T. make arrangements for an apartment and for attending the Day Program two days a week. The Director of Care assessed her care needs and worked with the doctor to make a referral to Home Care. The Social Worker counselled Mrs T. regarding her short- and long-term options and plans. The Director of Care and Social Worker met with Mrs T. and her son to review plans and assure them of priority readmission to the Home for the Aged if that became necessary. Following discharge, the Social Worker kept in touch with Mrs T. regarding services and her transition back into the community.

Mrs T. lived safely in her apartment for two years. Further medical difficulties arose, so she applied for readmission to the Home. She was readmitted to the first appropriate bed and is now very content in the Home, having enjoyed two additional years in the community.

Highlight 11.8 decribes some of the programs and services offered through the integrated system in the Niagara Region.

Elder Abuse and Neglect: A Hidden Problem

Elder abuse was first exposed in the late 1980s when the media reported incidents of 'granny bashing' and gerontologists began to study the prevalence and causes of abuse and neglect.[8] Like child and spousal abuse, abuse and neglect of older people is difficult to identify and confirm. Non-reporting and under-reporting by victims occurs if they are unaware that certain behaviour is abusive; if they fear reprisal or loss of care from caregivers or abusers, or if they do not know where to report the abuse. Others fear that disclosing abuse will be seen as a sign of incompetence and frailty. In most cases, abused and abusive people are family members. Thus, abuse occurs behind closed doors and is viewed as a family matter, even though some forms of abuse are crimes. Usually there is an unwillingness by suspecting neighbours to intervene in family troubles, or by formal care workers to build a case to support their observations.

Older dependent adults are potentially vulnerable to abuse and neglect in institutions. However, regulations and laws have reduced these risks and provided increased protection for residents. To prevent abuse there is more supervi-

---

Highlight 11.8 Integrated Programs to Provide Home, Community, and Institutional Care

The Regional Municipality of Niagara provides an integrated program of community- and institutionally-based services for older adults. The Senior Citizens department has a mandate to develop and deliver services; to develop programs, and then let other groups (such as charitable organizations or seniors' groups) operate the programs; to serve as an advocate for the needs and rights of older adults; and to provide information and assistance. In short, the department serves as the major agency for the leadership and coordination of policies and services for older people in the region. As a result, conflict between different agencies has been eliminated and 'cracks' in the care system are identified and resolved. Some of the services include the following:

Accommodation Options

- *Home-Sharing program*: A senior lives with a homeowner in the community who is seeking companionship, has extra space, or needs to supplement his or her income. Or a senior takes in one or more 'home mates' who pay a low rent or who are willing to do household chores in return for housing.

- *Satellite Homes*: Older people who are unable to live independently live in community-based congregate housing. They are encouraged to help with chores around the house, but meals and laundry are provided. Each home is affiliated with a home for the aged, which provides temporary housing when needed.

- *Homes for the Aged*: These facilities offer residential care (requiring less than 1.5 hours of nursing care per day) and extended care (more than 1.5 hours of nursing care per day is required). Admissions are made only after the resources and options of other community-based services are exhausted.

continued

Hightlight 11.8 continued

Community Support and Life Enrichment Programs

- *Integrated Home Help*: Includes meal preparation, meals-on-wheels, personal care, housekeeping, lawn mowing, snow shovelling, home repairs, and so forth. These services are provided free of charge by volunteers or at a low hourly rate.

- *Postal Alert Security System*: Letter carriers 'watch' seniors who may be at risk.

- *Adult Day Care and Vacation Care Respite Services*: To relieve some of the burden for caregivers, a few beds in the satellite homes and homes for the aged are designed for short-term stays at a per diem rate, for a maximum stay of four weeks.

- *Senior Volunteers*: Seniors help other seniors in their homes, or in the homes for the aged.

- *Communication Programs*: The Talk-a-Bit program provides daily calls from volunteers to seniors; the Pen Pals program encourages communication with age peers outside the region; and the Friendly Visiting program offers friendship and support to alleviate boredom and loneliness.

- *Senior-Citizen Centres*: A variety of social and leisure programs are available.

- *Home Nursing/Therapy Program*: Services are provided in the home so that an older adult with limited mobility does not have to go to a clinic or a hospital.

- *Family Education and Support Groups*: Professionals volunteer to provide education about the aging process, community resources, and products related to the care of older people. Information, counselling, support groups, and training are provided to caregivers of cognitively impaired older adults.

- *Transportation*: Volunteer drivers for those without cars and a formal system for seniors in wheelchairs are available.

- *Adopt-a-Grandparent*: An intergenerational program that brings children of the community together with older residents in the regional homes.

- *Foster Grandparent*: Encourages seniors to create a one-to-one relationship with children who have special needs.

sion and training of employees, there is mandatory reporting of suspected cases of mistreatment by staff; and guardianship and adult-protection laws concerning the use of restraints and the rights of residents have been passed.[9] Moreover, most jurisdictions employ an ombudsperson to investigate complaints of abuse in nursing homes or long-term- care institutions.

Definitions of Abuse and Neglect

Behaviour defined as abusive or neglectful in one jurisdiction may not be considered as such in another jurisdiction. Similarly, what is considered

abusive in one family may be considered normal in another family because of past practices, or cultural or religious traditions.

In general, three types of instruments have been used to measure or identify abuse or neglect: interviews with older people by professional care workers to identify victims; classification schemes to indicate types of abuse (Wilber and McNeilly, 2001); and survey instruments with lists of abusive behaviour to identify incidents of abuse, or attitudes as to whether such behaviour is abusive or not, and if so, how severe (Stones and Bédard, 2003: Appendix). The Elder Abuse Survey Tool

(EAST), designed by Stones and Bédard, lists 96 behaviours that constitute mistreatment in a situation where a person lives with, or is supervised by, a person in a position of trust; and 15 that might take place when older people live in an institution.

Elder abuse occurs in situations where a frail, dependent person is assisted or cared for by a person in a position of trust such as a relative, friend, or employee of an institution where the person lives. Abuse represents a conscious or unconscious act that violates the trust and moral obligation to care for and protect a vulnerable, dependent person. Acts of abuse include varying degrees of:

- physical abuse—the use of physical force, punishment, physical restraint, coercion, personal attacks, or rough handling that leads to physical pain, bruises, abrasions, dislocations, fractures, burns, or, in extreme cases, death;

- sexual abuse—non-consensual sexual contact of any kind

- emotional or psychological abuse—yelling, verbal threats, insults, or humiliation; blackmail; lack of attention or withholding of affection; isolation by confinement to a chair, bed, or room;

- medical abuse—withholding food or medicine; not seeking medical assistance; over- or under-administering prescribed drugs;

- financial or material abuse—stealing money or possessions; cashing and keeping pension cheques; fraud; dishonest use of an elderly person's money or property;

- legal abuse—any violation of human rights and freedoms, forced changes in a will, or denying access to public services such as home-care, nursing, or therapeutic services;

- abandonment—desertion by a person who had legal, physical custody or a moral responsibility to care for an older person.

Elder neglect, which may be intentional or unintentional, is the failure or refusal to perform necessary caregiving or monitoring responsibilities for an older adult, especially one who is cognitively or physically impaired. Lack of knowledge about how to care for an Alzheimer's patient or about community support services can lead to unintentional neglect that has serious consequences for the dependent elderly person. Neglect on the part of a caregiver to meet the physical, psychological, or emotional needs of an older person is often a precursor to abandonment. An interesting legal issue involves who, among potential primary caregivers, might be considered negligent or neglectful in their responsibilities to an elderly parent who, in turn, is considered a legally independent adult. Highlight 11.9 illustrates some tragic case histories of elder abuse and neglect.

Older adults, themselves, may engage in self-neglect or self-abuse that threatens their own safety and health. Self-neglect is the failure to provide oneself with the necessities to ensure physical and mental health and a safe environment—food, clean clothing, regular bathing, shelter, medication, social interaction. Self-neglect involves self-abuse, such as malnutrition or drug or alcohol abuse, which may result in physical or mental injury. For some, self-abuse is a continuation of behaviour exhibited in early and middle adulthood, especially if the person is socially isolated. For others, this behaviour begins after they retire, are widowed, or are diagnosed with a chronic or terminal illness and become depressed or isolated. Self-neglect does not include a situation where a mentally competent person makes a conscious and voluntary decision, fully understanding the consequences, to engage in behaviour that, sooner or later, may be life-threatening.

In addition to abuse and neglect, older adults are often victims of fraud—telephone sales, donations to charities (real or fabricated), unneeded home repairs, and Internet scams.[10] Fraud is often under-reported because of embarrassment and lack of information about who committed the fraud.

Highlight 11.9 Elder Abuse and Neglect: Tragic Family Scenarios

Financial Abuse, Alcoholism, and Neglect

An alcoholic in his 50s, Fred moved in with his elderly mother after he lost his job. She receives a large pension and has other sources of income, but is physically and cognitively impaired. Fred cashed her cheques and went on drinking binges, often leaving her alone for days. During one of these bouts, a concerned neighbour found Fred's mother lying on the living-room floor in a disoriented, malnourished, dehydrated, and unclean state.

Marital Discord and Spousal Abuse

After a long and tension-filled marriage, John became bedridden and incontinent. His wife, obliged to care for him 24 hours a day, began to withhold drugs and food, and slapped him and screamed at him whenever he demanded attention and care. When he was unexpectedly visited at home by a physician, bruises were discovered on his face and arms and he was moved to a long-term-care institution.

Psychological Abuse

An elderly woman, no longer able to maintain the family home yet unwilling to move, invited a single niece to share her home in return for help with the housekeeping. For two years the relationship appeared to be mutually beneficial, but increasingly the niece began to insult her aunt and threatened that she would leave if she did not receive large sums of money on a regular basis. The niece began to assume that it was her home—she decided which television programs were watched, when they went to bed and ate meals, when and if they went out, and how the aunt's money was spent. Moreover, the niece only talked to the aunt when it was essential, withdrew all signs of affection, and encouraged the aunt to spend more and more time in her bedroom. In reality, the aunt had become a prisoner in her own home with no meaningful social interaction.

Frustration and Stress

Charged with the killing of his 84-year-old wife, the defendant argued that he was no longer able to care for his mentally and physically frail wife, whose sight, hearing, and cognitive abilities had deteriorated rapidly. He stated that he could no longer tolerate her suffering, his own stress, or the frustration of dealing with the social-welfare system. Despite repeated calls to the local social-service office for assistance, he reported that 'no one wanted to look after us. We were condemned to die like two dogs.' After receiving a suspended sentence, he was admitted to a nursing home, which is what he had wanted for his wife all along.

The Prevalence of Abuse

Prevalence statistics are derived from cross-sectional studies that identify the proportion of incidents or cases of abuse that have been experienced or observed by members of a particular age group (in this case 65 and over), gender, or residential (retirement home) group. They identify the approximate extent of the problem by type (nationally, regionally, or locally), and by gender of the victim and perpetrator.

It is difficult to determine the number and type of elder abuse cases in a given community or setting. Most studies lack a control group and are often based on small and non-representative samples (since the respondents are volunteers) or on case studies of a few abused elders. Studies are weak, as well, because different definitions of abuse are used; respondents may not be able to remember or be willing to report incidents; and reported cases can not be confirmed. As Kozak et al. (1995: 134) stated, 'the only conclusion one can derive from these findings is that abuse and neglect of seniors exists throughout Canada, with some regional variation. No information can be discerned regarding the extent of the existing problem (prevalence) nor can anything be said about the number of new cases (incidence).'

The 1999 General Social Survey (2000; Dauvergne, 2003) included questions about emotional and financial abuse; and about physical and sexual assaults by children, paid or unpaid caregivers in the home, and spouses (current and formal marital and common-law partners). Only 1 per cent of older Canadians living in private dwellings reported that they had been physically or sexually assaulted by a spouse, adult child, or caregiver in the five years preceding the GSS survey. However, 7 per cent of older adults reported experiencing some form of emotional or financial abuse, most of it committed by an adult child, caregiver, or spouse in the previous five years. Nine per cent of older men and 6 per cent of older women had been victims of emotional or financial abuse. Overall, emotional abuse was reported more often (7 per cent) than financial abuse (1 per cent). The most common forms of emotional abuse reported by older adults were being 'put down' or 'called names' (3 per cent) and 'having contact with family or friends limited by others' (2 per cent). About 70 per cent of family violence against older adults was committed by a spouse or an adult child.

Explanations for Abuse
Most abuse and neglect occurs in family settings by someone in a position of trust who is known to the victim. The most vulnerable older people are women; those who are frail, cognitively impaired, or physically disabled; and those who live with the perpetrator. To explain why abuse occurs, early explanations were based on a situational-stress model where it was argued that caring for a dependent elderly person, especially one who is cognitively impaired and prone to behavioural problems, leads to significant stress for the caregiver, who reacts by engaging in abuse or negligence. Today, this model has little support. Rather, the focus is more on family relations, personal characteristics, and lifestyle factors unique to the relationship between the caregiver and the care recipient. For example, abuse and violence can occur in both directions, especially if an older person is cognitively impaired, or there has been a history of conflict between two people. Thus, where a care recipient threatens, attacks, or is verbally abusive toward the caregiver, the caregiver may react by also being abusive.

Abuse and neglect also result from cultural beliefs about child and spousal relationships. In some cultures the use of physical force is considered normal—child and spousal beatings or verbal abuse are common throughout life and are never questioned or discussed. Often the father or husband is considered to have a 'right' to engage in such behaviour. Some incidents of spousal elder abuse are a continuation of lifelong spousal abuse. In other cases, an adult child 'pays back' an abusive parent and uses physical force or verbal abuse to control the parent. Finally, abuse may be due to cognitive, emotional, or behavioural problems, such as substance abuse or mental health disorders, on the part of the abuser. The abusive person may be dependent on the victim, financially or for shelter.

Preventing Abuse
A variety of intervention strategies have been proposed for protecting victims of elder abuse.[11] These may include the education and training of health care professionals, members of the legal

and law enforcement communities, older adults, family members, and the public; crisis shelters for abused older adults, especially women; assessment, screening, and intervention programs; legal advice; and peer counselling and support groups[12]. Different types of abuse and different situations require different interventions. Intervention involves identifying high-risk elders and caregivers, and providing social assistance; educating seniors about abuse, neglect, and fraud; protecting the rights of elderly people; enforcing and prosecuting violations of criminal and civil law; developing and delivering education and counselling programs to family caregivers and professional health and social care workers; and requiring professionals to report any suspected cases of abuse or neglect (Gordon, 1995). Some specific policies or programs include:

- providing social, financial, and health resources directly to an elderly person, who then purchases services from whomever they choose;

- establishing self-help counselling or support groups for caregivers;

- offering financial support to caregivers, who purchase services such as nursing care and transportation from trained professionals, thereby alleviating some of the burden;

- providing professional case managers to make decisions about who should be the primary caregiver, and how total care should be managed;

- training police officers in each community to deal exclusively with the problem of elder abuse, fraud, or neglect; and

- establishing a Senior's Abuse telephone line (Au Coin, 2003: 27). In Manitoba, such a service was established in 1999, and in the period from April 1999 to March 2002 over 300 calls were received from seniors. The majority of these calls concerned emotional or financial abuse.

Barriers to Intervention

Conflicting ethics in a profession can prevent identification and intervention (McDonald et al., 1995). For example, there may be disagreement about what information can be revealed, and to whom, as well as about who should or can be the target of intervention (the abuser or the victim?). Moreover, legislation varies between different jurisdictions as to how abuse is defined; what investigative powers are given to the authorities (such as whether they can enter a person's home and whether a physician may examine an alleged victim); whether a person who reports an abusive situation is protected from identification and retaliation; and whether and to what extent due process and legal representation are assured for the victims.

These uncertainties have lead, at least partially, to recent political action by one member of Parliament. On 28 May 2003, Bill C-439, the Older Adult Justice Act, was introduced in the House of Commons. This Act would ensure that older adults are officially protected under Canadian law and that they have an advocate to address their needs. Whether this Act will be passed into law remains to be seen, but if it is, it would help protect older adults from abuse, neglect, exploitation, and fraud. The Act would:

- establish an ombudsperson responsible for the protection of older adult rights;

- establish the Canadian Older Adult Justice Agency to coordinate and implement older adult justice policies and programs; and

- amend the Criminal Code in two ways— expand the category of victims to include an offender's mother or father, or any person for whom the offender is providing care; and make it an offence to knowingly target an older adult for a criminal purpose.

Traditional intervention strategies are less successful in multicultural settings where cultural or ethnic differences in values, traditions, beliefs, and language make it difficult for an outside professional worker to intervene. Both the victim and the abuser may not understand that the abusive behaviour violates the values or laws of mainstream Canadian society. Where power and control is based on a patriarchal system, elderly women may consider verbal, physical, or material abuse by a spouse or son to be normal. As well, abuse is more likely to continue if members of an ethnic group make little use of social and health-care services because they don't know about the service or how to use it, because they don't speak English, or because the service is too expensive.

Public Policy For an Aging Population

The Public Policy Context in Canada

Public policies represent distant forces that can have a positive or negative impact on individual lives, especially in the inter-connected domains of education, work, family, economic security, and health care across the life course (Settersten, 2003). They have the potential to facilitate or constrain human development and independence across the life course. For most of the twentieth century, public policies were designed for a young society, and policies for older people were a secondary consideration, except for economic security. This approach illustrates how a 'cultural or structural lag' exists in policy making. Today, population aging and changing social values require that public policies meet the needs of *all* citizens in an aging society,[13] regardless of age, and hence, the proposal to introduce Bill C-439 as described in the previous section.

In a welfare state like Canada, fully funded or subsidized government programs are designed to enhance well-being, to provide a safety net for citizens, and to ensure financial security, health care, and social assistance for all citizens. These programs aim to enhance the welfare of both the individual and the state. **Public policy** consists of a set of laws, regulations, services, support systems, and programs that result from the decisions made by one or more of the federal, provincial, regional, or local governments. Some programs, such as the Canada Pension Plan, are designed and delivered at the federal level only. Some, such as the health system under the Canada Health Act and federal and provincial regulations, are co-ordinated (hopefully!) and delivered across two levels. Many are addressed by several levels of government in different but often uncoordinated ways, as is the case with home care, transportation, and housing. And some programs, such as education, are funded at one level and delivered at another.

The issue of who is responsible for the welfare of older adults is complicated by the multi-level structure of government in Canada (federal, provincial, regional, and local). The British North America Act (1867) gave the federal government jurisdiction over social matters and economic security, that is, public pensions, but left other, related responsibilities to the provinces. However, the provinces could not afford to offer all necessary services and became dependent on the federal government for transfer payments to pay for health care, education, social welfare, and transportation. Recently, with the growth of the federal debt and deficits, transfer payments to the provinces have been reduced or eliminated. One outcome of reduced transfer payments has been a deterioration in the quality of, and accessibility to, health care, higher education, and community social services.

Seldom, if ever, is one agency responsible for the needs of older adults. Uncertainty over jurisdictional responsibility fosters a lack of coordination between agencies, an inefficient use of scarce resources, and gaps in the ideal continuum of services. Moreover, there may be conflict over how funds are to be spent, for example, on health promotion to prevent disease and disability or on diagnosis and treatment of acute and chronic illness. As well, the needs of specific groups may be neglected because one level believes that another level of government should be responsible; or services may be duplicated or uncoordinated. For example, ideological conflict can occur between a health ministry, which seeks to cure and care for elderly people (often in hospitals or long-term-care institutions), and a social-service ministry, which seeks to provide services that will keep elderly people living in the community.

Public policy is a shared responsibility of the state, the individual and family, and the private sector. At present, as in the past, Canada lacks an integrated, comprehensive, and effective public policy for older people. As early as 1991, the National Advisory Council on Aging (NACA, 1991) argued for a national aging policy in which all levels of government work with the private sector to coordinate, harmonize, and standardize services for aging Canadians. This same argument is made today in the lobbying efforts to enhance health care, home care (a 'hot' policy issue), and drug benefits for older adults.

Developing policies inevitably involves making choices—who is responsible? Who is eligible, and for how long? Which policy domain is most urgent? Who will deliver the programs? The process occurs in a context of conflict and co-operation among different levels of government; in the presence of disagreements about whether programs should be universal or need-based programs; and about which need (e.g., a school or a long-term-care facility) is greater; and with many competing demands from different interest groups. As well, policies are shaped, or not introduced at all, by the political ideology of the party in power, and by the existing or anticipated economic climate. Thus, while few, in principle, argue against a national home-care policy, the question remains whether we can afford such a program, and whether it is compatible with the ideology of the ruling political party, which may be different at the federal and provincial level?

The process of government policy-making becomes even more complex when programs have to be coordinated with the private sector for either funding or delivery of the service. This process is particularly difficult with such issues as: minimal levels of economic security, housing subsidies, the provision of home-care services, and private diagnostic or health-care services. There are many perennial questions in these domains: Who is responsible for ensuring an 'adequate' income after retirement—the government, the employer, or the individual? What is an 'adequate' income, and 'adequate' for whom? Who should ensure safe and secure housing and home care for older Canadians—the public sector, the private sector, the family, or if all three, in what proportion? And who should pay, and to what extent, for prescription drugs for older people?

Policy Issues for an Aging Population

Reactive versus Proactive Policies

Many policies are adopted in response to a problem, such as poverty, isolation, or lack of access to appropriate care. However, policies must also try to delay or prevent the problems from arising. For example, home-renovation subsidies can prevent falls and institutionalization, and spousal benefits can protect common-law and same-sex partners. In the past, many public policies were based on the assumption that elderly people became dependent on others in society. It was alleged that this dependence occurred because of inevitable, deteriorating biological or cognitive changes, and because of financial dependence following retirement. Moreover, since the older population was assumed to be homogeneous, eligibility for assistance was determined by age rather than by need. More recent policies are designed to provide a variety of services to a heterogeneous older population. Thus, both elderly people who live in the community and more dependent elderly people who live in an extended-care institution are eligible to receive assistance.

Equity in Delivery

Services and programs provided under a policy should not create or perpetuate social inequality, nor give some eligible recipients an advantage over others. Policies must accommodate gender, marital, ethnic, regional, class, urban-rural and other personal differences among both the recipients and those who provide care and services. Women are most likely to be both the recipients and providers of care, and they are more likely to live longer and to need both economic and social support for a longer time. Given the sex ratio of the older population, social policies must not ignore the special needs of older women, especially those who live alone (Brewer, 2001). Yet, many policies disadvantage women, both as care providers and care recipients, and ignore the considerable amount of free labour that women contribute to the economic and social support systems. Similarly, members of some religious or ethnic groups are ignored in health, social, or economic policies.

Inequality and neglect are introduced when policy-makers erroneously assume that all older Canadians have the same social characteristics, employment history, language ability, number of years as a resident in Canada, and knowledge of health-care and social-service agencies. Policies should address the needs of older people who are most at risk because of their personal circumstances. What is needed are 'inclusive' policies that take into account a variety of risk factors that are often related (such as being a divorced women and poverty); emerging situations (such as benefits for gay and lesbian partners); and diverse geographical settings where older people may live (rural as opposed to urban or an Aboriginal community in a remote northern region) (Settersten, 2003).

Fiscal Responsibility and Entitlement
The apocalyptic view of public policy is that population aging means we can no longer finance all health, social, and economic benefits that older adults need. Thus, public policies are often shaped by the desire to reduce public expenditures rather than to meet individual needs: taxes are increased; user fees are introduced; benefits like OAS and GIS are 'clawed back' from those

with higher incomes; and programs with universal entitlements are converted to need-based programs. As Gee (1995: 17) critically noted, 'demographic change has become wedded to economic troubles in the last part of the twentieth century.' Consequently, the social contract between the government and older Canadians is being revised. Less often, and in more policies, universal benefits, or an automatic entitlement, are not provided to all older adults who attain a specified age (usually 65). Rather, policies include a mix of universal and need-based benefits, social insurance, and increased individual responsibility (Hudson, 1997; Béland and Shapiro, 1995; Feldman, 2003).

In the income security domain, McDonald (1997) labelled this new approach the residual model of social welfare, which emphasizes a shift from full entitlement to 'social insurance' (adequate and continuous income for everyone during retirement) to partial 'social assistance' (subsistence income is provided only to 'needy' retirees). On the other hand, Settersten (2003) argues that an age-based entitlement to benefits stigmatizes older adults and increases the possibility of ageism and intergenerational conflict. Yet, at the same time he notes how difficult it is to measure and define need, as we learned in Chapter 9 with respect to defining poverty and eligibility for economic assistance.

Proponents of universal systems of support argue that they promote equity and enhance the dignity of all citizens because no one has to undergo a means test for eligibility. Universal eligibility also means that programs can be administered more efficiently and that the difficulty of objectively measuring need is eliminated. In contrast, proponents of need-based support argue that not all older adults need assistance from the government, and that such programs become considerably less expensive when the size of the eligible group is limited to those who demonstrate need.

Regardless of whether need or universality prevails, past contributions to society must be repaid; some minimal standard of living must be attained; equal access to needed services must be guaranteed; and there must be equity in sharing the costs of needed services or facilities. There is also a continuing debate as to whether expensive health-care services, such as heart and hip replacements, MRI diagnosis, pacemakers, and kidney dialysis, should be rationed or restricted on the basis of age rather than need.

Who is Responsible for Support?

Underlying the development of public policies for an aging population is the long-standing debate about whether the needs of older people should be viewed as a 'private trouble' of the individual or a 'public issue'. This debate is fuelled when the following questions about economic and social security are raised:

- Should the public provide universal and complete pensions, or should individuals, through the private sector, be responsible for building their own pension benefits?

- Should the family or the state be responsible for the care and welfare of older citizens?

- Do older adults have the right, because of their past contributions, to be cared for in the later years?

- Should scarce resources be reallocated to the elderly in the interest of social justice? For example, should we reduce public financial support for schools and universities to provide more universal programs and facilities for baby-boom retirees?

Rather than an 'either-or' solution, ideally there would be programs and services that meet needs along a continuum from 'individualism' (personal responsibility) to 'collectivism' (public responsibility). Moreover public policies for older adults should integrate the responsibilities and contributions of individuals and families with those of the public and private sectors, especially with respect to housing, health care, and home care. Because there are many diverse family structures, public policies must serve older people and their caregivers who live within all types of family structures and living arrangements.

Privatization of Services

An emerging issue in health and home care is whether services that were previously the responsibility of the public sector should be privatized. Since most older adults do not need or use most public services, the advocates of privatization of services argue that it is would ease the public financial burden. In this process, some or all of the responsibility for health and social services would be transferred to the charities, private foundations, and religious or ethnic groups or to the for-profit sector. Privatization of services for older adults involves nursing homes, personal and home-care services, and expensive diagnostic and health-care procedures, some of which are elective. For governments, privatization is a way to reduce deficits and demonstrate fiscal restraint to the voting public. However, the public is asking whether private services are more efficient, whether access to services will be restricted to those who can afford them (a two-tiered system), and whether a lower quality of care may result if public services are discontinued, or if the required standards of care are unenforceable or are reduced in order to generate a profit by a private entrepreneur.

Principles of Public Policy-Making to Serve an Aging Population

In order to enhance well-being and independence, to ensure comprehensive coverage and full access to the benefits provided by policies, to contain costs, and to meet the diverse needs of an aging population, policy-makers need to be guided by fundamental principles and core values. Those values and principles help to eliminate discriminatory practices against older people; and ensure the autonomy, independence, safety, security, dignity, self-esteem, privacy, and right to choose of older adults. Policies and programs for older adults are often most effective if they are:

- Inclusive and provide equitable benefits to all—ask who is included and excluded? Are the needs of the frail elderly and special groups, such as Aboriginal people, recent immigrants, and the homeless, being met?

- Based on sharing through user fees—costs can be covered through full or partial subsidies and by co-payments from the private and public sectors and the individual.

- Client-centred—direct or indirect payments can be paid to the client or the caregiver.

- Coordinated and integrated so that there are no gaps between the informal and formal support systems—has jurisdictional responsibility been established or negotiated to prevent gaps in the system?

- Based on a comprehensive, ongoing, fair and objective assessment of needs.

- Based on collaboration and co-operation between ministries or agencies concerned with social housing and health, and including organizations in both the public and private sectors.

- Protective of legal and human rights, whether an older person is living in the community or in an institution.

- Designed to ensure that a minimum standard of living is maintained throughout later life for all older citizens—policies and programs must serve the needs of aging persons more than those of the state.

- Sensitive to the potential human and financial cost to a society of *not* adopting a particular policy.

- Subject to change—a schedule is established for reviewing and, if necessary, rescinding the policy if it is not meeting its objectives.

- Flexible—allowing for access to benefits on a temporary or permanent basis; and providing minimum or maximum amounts of support as needs change.

Summary

Most individuals, regardless of age, are never totally isolated from others. Rather, a social world evolves around an individual to provide informal or formal assistance and support. This network consists of the individual, his or her family, friends, neighbours, and ultimately formal care workers. Informal support, provided mainly by the family, especially daughters, is available to most older adults who have lived in an extended family system. This system involves reciprocal exchange relationships in which older adults are helped in later life by adult children who have been supported and assisted by their parents throughout their lives.

For family caregivers, there are hidden financial, emotional, and health costs that add to the burden of caring for a frail or demented parent over a long period of time. Sometimes caregiving leads to elder abuse or neglect in the family; although in some cases abuse is due to cultural traditions or lifelong habits. Some of the burden borne by caregivers can be relieved by respite care and education programs, such as an Alzheimer's support group. Eventually, in most cases, informal support is supplemented or replaced by services in the formal support system, such as home-care workers provided by the public or private sector.

Public policies to support older adults are necessary but difficult to design because of the heterogeneous needs of older adults. Key policy areas that require attention in an aging society include the assurance of economic security and health care in later life; the elimination of age discrimination; the provision of high-quality and effective home care and long-term care; and the preservation of the dignity and human rights of older people, including the right to full social participation in their social world. These policies must protect the human rights of older people and ensure that there is equity in the delivery of services, that all responsible jurisdictions co-ordinate their services to eliminate gaps in the system, and that the family, the state, and the private sector have a shared responsibility for the assistance and care of older people.

For Reflection, Debate, or Action

1. If an older member of your family needed assistance and regular help, who would be available, and why? If nobody is likely to be available, explain why, and how you as a case manager would ensure that the person received complete assistance and care.

2. To what extent, and in what ways, does reciprocal and serial exchange occur in your family?

3. Should the support of older relatives in later life be a private or a public responsibility? How would you allocate, and in what areas, proportionate responsibility?

4. What are the differences, and why, in the type of support provided to aging parents by daughters and sons? Will these differences remain when you and your siblings reach middle age and are needed to provide assistance to your parents? If not, what will have changed, and why, over the next 20 years?

5. Interview a caregiver in your family or in the community to identify sources of stress and the burdens associated with caring for an older adult.

6. Interview doctors, social workers, and/or lawyers to determine whether and to what extent, they have encountered elder abuse or neglect in their practice. What are their major concerns about the abuse and neglect they have observed? What are their interpretations of why abuse or neglect occurs, and can they suggest how it could be eliminated?

7. In your neighbourhood, you meet a 69-year-old widow who has recently moved to Canada from Jamaica to live with her daughter. She reports that she is lonely, feels useless, and receives little social or emotional support at home. What local services would enable this woman to expand her social network and become involved with age peers in the community?

8. On the basis of your reading, social philosophy, and political views, debate with a friend the following contrasting views about the intent or content of public policies designed for older people. Should programs be

   - need-based or universal?

   - based on user-pay, or fully or partially subsidized?

   - the responsibility of the local, regional, provincial, or federal government?

   - funded by a subsidy or grant to the older person so that he or she can buy services, or by a grant to a volunteer caregiver for the purchase of services or as compensation for lost income?

Notes

1. See Mindszenthy and Gordon (2002), Government of Canada (2003), and the following websites:

   - www.canada.gc.ca
   - www.servicecanada.gc.ca
   - www.caregiver.on.ca
   - www.howtocare.com
   - www.ccc-ccan.ca
   - www.cdnhomecare.on.ca
   - www.caregiving.com
   - www.caregiver.org
   - www.caremanager.org
   - www.hecol.ualberta.ca/rapp
   - www.ec-online.net

2. Corin (1987: 390) suggests that a 'norm of privacy' prevails in rural areas. This norm could act as a defence against the invasion of private space. Such a norm may partially explain the tendency of rural elderly people to rely almost exclusively on the nuclear family, especially the spouse, for expressive and instrumental support. However, this may be a 'chicken-egg' situation since there are also, in general, fewer formal sources of support and care in rural communities.

3. Informal social support by family members is discussed in Angus et al. (1995), Chappell and Kuehne (1998), Keating et al. (1999), Martin-Matthews (2000), Connidis (2001), Henderson (2002), Matthews (2002), and Mindszenthy and Gordon (2002).

4. Gender differences in caregiving are discussed in Harris and Long (1999), Kramer and Lambert (1999), Campbell and Martin Matthews (2000), Connidis (2001: 137–40), Dupuis and Norris (2001), Matthews (2002), and Ward-Griffin and Marshall (2003).

5. Gender differences in the quality and quantity of support disappear as the aging parent becomes more frail and dependent. As health status deteriorates, sons and daughters become more involved in decisions that must be made.

6. Chappell et al. (1986: 90–5) describe the development of the formal care system in Canada and the United States; Forbes et al. (1987: 2–14) chronicle the history of institutional care from early Christian and medieval periods to the present era; Gee and Boyce (1988) and Montigny (1997) discuss how legislation (from before 1918 to the 1980s) contributed directly and indirectly to the development of health and social services for older Canadians; Snell (1990, 1996) examines the history of filial responsibility laws in Canada; Keating et al. (1999) analyze the context, content, and consequences of eldercare in the late 1990s; CARP (2001) presents a 'Report Card' on homecare services in Canada, and Alexander (2002) describes the history of long-term care in Canada.

7. The estimated savings to the public budget are somewhere between $5,000 and $10,000 per person, per year, if an older person can be provided with informal and formal care services, and remain in his or her home, even at the palliative-care stage, that is, within one to six months of a projected death from a terminal illness.

8. For information about elder abuse, see Hudson and Johnson (1986), Brillon (1987: 69–86), Podnieks et al. (1990), McDonald et al. (1991), Decalmer and Glendenning (1993), Maclean (1995), McDonald and Wigdor (1995), Carp (2000), McDonald and Collins (2000), Wilber and McNeilly (2001), World Health Organization (2002), Dauvergne (2003), Stones and Bédard (2003), Au Coin (2003), and the *Journal of Elder Abuse and Neglect*.

9. There are three kinds of adult protective legislation in Canada. In the Atlantic provinces, personnel are assigned to investigate suspected cases of abuse. The legislation has the legal power to investigate and intervene, and may require the mandatory reporting of suspected cases of senior abuse. The second kind, found in Ontario, includes adult-protection provisions in legislation pertaining to adult guardianship. Allegations that an older person is unable to manage his or her property or personal care, is being abused, or is in danger of being abusedmust be investigated, but no services are provided to the victim. The third kind of legislation, found in British Columbia, provides for intervention in cases of abuse, neglect, or self-neglect and provides community-based service networks to help seniors (Au Coin, 2003: 28).

10. In Ontario, fraud is the number-one crime against older adults. In 1999, seniors lost $3.5 million to

telephone fraud, and the Ontario Provincial Police report that 85 per cent of consumers who have lost more than $5,000 to fraud are seniors (Au Coin, 2003: 27). Consequently, each year the government distributes the Fraud Free Calendar for Seniors, which illustrates how to avoid becoming a victim.

11. The National Film Board of Canada has produced two films in its The Elderly at Risk series: *Mr Nobody*, which is concerned with self-neglect, and *A House Divided*, which examines caregiver stress and elder abuse.

12. Health Canada (1999), in *A Directory of Services and Programs Addressing the Needs of Older Adult Victims of Violence in Canada*, lists services and programs for seniors in each province and territory.

13. For discussions of public policy for aging societies, see *The Public Policy and Aging Report* (published by the Gerontological Society of America); the *Canadian Journal on Aging; Canadian Public Policy*; Canadian Policy Research Networks (www.cprn.ca); the Seniors Policies and Programs Database (www.sppd.gc.ca); *Horizons* (published by the Policy Research Initiative—www.policyresearch.gc.ca); *A Quebec for All Ages* (published by the Government of Quebec, 2002); Estes et al. (2001); and Settersten (2003).

References

Alexander, T. 2002. 'The History and Evolution of Long-Term Care in Canada'. Pp. 1–55 in M. Stephenson and E. Sawyer (eds), *Continuing the Care: The Issues and Challenges for Long-Term Care*. Ottawa: CHA Press.

Angus, D., et al. 1995. *Sustainable Health Care for Canada*. Ottawa: University of Ottawa Economic Projects.

Antonucci, T. 1990. 'Social Supports and Social Relationships'. Pp. 186–204 in R. Binstock and L. George (eds), *Handbook of Aging and the Social Sciences*. San Diego, Calif.: Academic Press.

———, and H. Akiyama. 1995. 'Convoys of Social Relations: Family and Friendship within a Life Span Context'. Pp. 355–72 in R. Blieszner and V. Hilkevitch Bedford (eds), *Handbook of Aging and the Family*. Westport, Conn.: Greenwood Press.

Aronson, J. 2002. 'Frail and Disabled Users of Home Care: Confident Consumers or Disentitled Citizens', *Canadian Journal on Aging* 21(1), 11–25.

Au Coin, K. 2003. 'Family Violence against Older Adults'. Pp. 21–32 in H. Johnson and K. Au Coin (eds), *Family Violence in Canada: A Statistical Profile*, 2003. Cat. no. 85-224-XIE. Ottawa: Statistics Canada.

Béland, F., and E. Shapiro (eds), 1995. 'Policy Issues in Care for the Elderly in Canada', *Canadian Journal on Aging*, 14(2), 153–8.

Bienvenue, R., and B. Havens. 1986. 'Structural Inequalities, Informal Networks: A Comparison of Native and Non-Native Elderly', *Canadian Journal on Aging*, 5(4), 241–8.

Binstock, R. 2002. 'Declaration of the Rights of Older Persons', *The Gerontologist*, 42(2), 152–3.

Brewer, L. 2001. 'Gender Socialization and the Cultural Construction of Elder Caregivers', *Journal of Aging Studies*, 15(3), 217–35.

Brillon, Y. 1987. *Victimization and Fear of Crime among the Elderly*. Toronto: Butterworths.

Brotman, S. 2003. 'The Limits of Multiculturalism in Elder Care Services', *Journal of Aging Studies*, 17(2), 209–29.

Buchignani, N., and C. Armstrong-Esther. (1999. 'Informal Care and Older Native Canadians', *Ageing and Society*, 19(1), 3–32.

CAG. 1999. 'Canadian Association on Gerontology Policy Statement on Home Care in Canada', *Canadian Journal on Aging*, 18(3), i–vii.

Campbell, L., and A. Martin-Matthews. 2000. 'Caring Sons: Exploring Men's Involvement in Filial Care', *Canadian Journal on Aging*, 19(1), 57–79.

Cantor, M., and V. Little. (1985. 'Aging and Social Care'. Pp. 745–81 in R. Binstock and E. Shanas (eds), *Handbook of Aging and the Social Sciences*. New York: Van Nostrand Reinhold.

Carp, F. 2000. *Elder Abuse in the Family: An Interdisciplinary Model for Research*. New York: Springer.

CARP. 2001. *CARP's Report Card on Home Care in Canada, 2000*. Toronto: Canadian Association for Retired Persons.

Carrière, Y., et al. 2002. 'Changing Demographic Trends and Use of Home Care Services'. Pp. 137–59 in *Report on the Demographic Situation in Canada*. Cat. no. 91-209-XPE. Ottawa: Statistics Canada.

Chappell, N. 1992. *Social Support and Aging*. Toronto: Butterworths.

———, and V. Kuehne 1998. 'Congruence Among Husband and Wife Caregivers', *Journal of Aging Studies*, 12(3), 239–54.

———, and R. Reid. 2002. 'Burden and Well-Being among Caregivers: Examining the Distinction', *The Gerontologist*, 42(6), 772–80.

———, et al. 1986. *Health and Aging: A Social Perspective*. Toronto: Holt, Rinehart and Winston.

———, et al. 2001. 'Respite Reconsidered: A Typology of Meanings Based on the Caregiver's Point of View', *Journal of Aging Studies*, 15(2), 201–16.

CMHC. 1990. *The Senior Citizens' Department of the Regional Municipality of Niagara, Ontario, and Its Continuum of Care Model: A Case Study*. Ottawa: Canada Mortgage and Housing Corporation.

Connidis, I. 2001. *Family Ties and Aging*. Thousand Oaks, Calif.: Sage.

———. 2003. 'The Impact of Demographic and Social Trends on Informal Support for Older Persons'. Pp. 105–32 in D. Cheal (ed.), *Aging and Demographic Change in Canadian Context*. Toronto: University of Toronto Press.

Corin, E. 1987. 'The Relationship between Formal and Informal Social Support Networks in Rural and Urban Contexts'. Pp. 367–94 in V. Marshall (ed.), *Aging in Canada: Social Perspectives*. Markham, Ont.: Fitzhenry and Whiteside.

Cranswick, K. 2003. *General Social Survey Cycle 16: Caring for an Aging Society*. Cat. no. 89-582-XIE. Ottawa: Statistics Canada.

Dauvergne, M. 2003. 'Family Violence against Seniors', *Canadian Social Trends*, 68 (Spring), 10–14.

Davidson, K., et al. 2000. 'Gendered Meanings of Care Work within Late Life Marital Relationships', *Canadian Journal on Aging*, 19(4), 536–53.

Dawson, P., and C. Rosenthal. 1996. 'Wives of Institutionalized Elderly Men: What Influences Satisfaction with Care?' *Canadian Journal on Aging*, 15(2), 245–63.

Decalmer, P., and F. Glendenning (eds), 1993. *The Mistreatment of Elderly People*. Newbury Park, Calif.: Sage.

Denton, M. 1997. 'The Linkages between Informal and Formal Care of the Elderly', *Canadian Journal on Aging*, 16(1), 30–50.

———, et al. 1999. 'Occupational Health Issues among Employees of Home Care Agencies', *Canadian Journal on Aging*, 18(2), 154–81.

Dilworth-Anderson, P., et al. 2002. 'Issues of Race, Ethnicity, and Culture in Caregiving Research: A 20-Year Review (1980–2000)', *The Gerontologist*, 42(2), 237–72.

Dupuis, S., and J. Norris. 2001. 'The Roles of Adult Daughters in Long-Term Care Facilities: Alternative Role Manifestations', *Journal of Aging Studies*, 15(1), 27–54.

Estes, C., et al. 2001. *Social Policy and Aging: A Critical Perspective*. Thousand Oaks, Calif.: Sage.

Fast, J., et al. 1997. *Conceptualizing and Operationalizing the Costs of Informal Elder Care*. Edmonton: Department of Human Ecology, University of Alberta.

Feldman, P. 1999. 'Doing More with Less: Advancing the Conceptual Underpinnings of Home-Based Care', *Journal of Aging and Health*, 11(3), 261–76.

———. (ed.). 2003. 'Special Issue: From Philosophy to Practice: Selected Issues in Financing and Co-ordinating Long-Term Care', *Journal of Aging and Health*, 15(1), 5–291.

Forbes, W., et al. 1987. *Institutionalization of the Elderly in Canada*. Toronto: Butterworths.

Gee, E. 1995. 'Population Aging: A Contested Terrain of Social Policy'. Pp.13–29 in E. Gee and G. Gutman (eds), *Rethinking Retirement*. Vancouver: Simon Fraser University, Gerontology Research Centre.

———, and M. Boyce. 1988. 'Veterans and Veterans Legislation in Canada: An Historical Overview', *Canadian Journal on Aging*, 7(3), 204–17.

Gignac, M., et al. 1996. 'The Impact of Caregiving on Employment: A Mediational Model of Work-Family Conflict', *Canadian Journal on Aging*, 15(4), 525–42.

Gladstone, J., and E. Wexler. 2002. 'Exploring the Relationships between Families and Staff Caring for Residents in Long-Term Care Facilities: Family Member's Perspectives', *Canadian Journal on Aging*, 21(1), 39–46.

Gordon, R. 1995. 'Adult Guardianship and Adult Protection Legislation in Canada: Recent Reforms and Future Problems', *Canadian Journal on Aging*, 14 (Supplement 2), 89–102.

Gottlieb, B., et al. 1994. 'Aspects of Eldercare That Place Employees at Risk', *The Gerontologist*, 34(6), 815–21.

Government of Canada. 2003. *Services for Seniors*.

Ottawa Ont.: Minister of Public Works (www.canada.gc.ca).

Government of Quebec. 2002. *A Quebec for All Ages*. Quebec City: Province of Quebec (www.bnquebec.ca).

Guberman, N., and P. Maheu. 1999. 'Combining Employment and Caregiving: An Intricate Juggling Act', *Canadian Journal on Aging*, 18(1), 84–106.

Haines, V., and L. Henderson. 2002. 'Targeting Social Support: A Network Assessment of the Convoy Model of Social Support', *Canadian Journal on Aging*, 21(2), 243–56.

Hall, R., and P. Coyte. 2001. 'Determinants of Home Care Utilization: Who Uses Home Care in Ontario?', *Canadian Journal on Aging*, 20(2), 175–92.

Hallman, B., and A. Joseph. 1999. 'Getting There: Mapping the Gendered Geography of Caregiving to Elderly Relatives', *Canadian Journal on Aging*, 18(4), 397–414.

Harris, P. 1998. 'Listening to Caregiving Sons: Misunderstood Realities', *The Gerontologist*, 38(3), 342–52.

———, and S. Long. 1999. 'Husbands and Sons in the United States and Japan: Cultural Expectations and Caregiving Experiences', *Journal of Aging Studies*, 13(3), 241–67.

Havens, B. 1995. 'Long-Term Care Diversity within the Care Continuum', *Canadian Journal on Aging*, 14(2), 245–62.

Hawranik, P. 2002. 'Inhome Service Use by Caregivers and Their Elders: Does Cognitive Status Make a Difference?', *Canadian Journal on Aging*, 21(2), 257–71.

Health Canada. 1999. *A Directory of Services and Programs Addressing the Needs of Older Adult Victims of Violence in Canada*. Ottawa: National Clearinghouse on Family Violence.

———. 2002. *Canada's Aging Population*. Ottawa: Health Canada.

Hébert, R., et al. 2001. 'Resources and Costs Associated with Disabilities of Elderly People Living at Home and in Institutions', *Canadian Journal on Aging*, 20(1), 1–21.

———, et al. 2003. 'Efficacy of a Psychoeducative Group Program for Caregivers of Demented Persons Living at Home: A Randomized Controlled Trial', *Journal of Gerontology: Social Sciences*, 58B(1), S58–67.

Henderson, K. 2002. 'Informal Caregivers'. Pp. 267–90 in J. Stephenson and E. Sawyer (eds), *Continuing the Care: The Issues and Challenges for Long-Term Care*. Ottawa: CHA Press.

Hollander, M. 2002. 'The Continuum of Care: An Integrated System of Service Delivery'. Pp. 57–70 in M. Stephenson and E. Sawyer (eds), *Continuing The Care: The Issues and Challenges for Long-Term Care*. Ottawa: CHA Press.

Hudson, M., and T. Johnson. 1986. 'Elder Neglect and Abuse: A Review of the Literature'. Pp. 81–134 in C. Eisdorfer (ed.), *Annual Review of Gerontology and Geriatrics*, Vol. 6. New York: Springer.

Hudson, R. 1997. *The Future of Age-Based Public Policy*. Baltimore, Md: Johns Hopkins University Press.

Joseph, A., and B. Hallman. 1996. 'Caught in the Triangle: The Influence of Home, Work and Elder Location on Work-Family Balance', *Canadian Journal on Aging*, 15(3), 393–412.

Keating, N., et al. 1997. 'Bridging Policy and Research in Eldercare', *Canadian Journal on Aging*, 16 (Supplement), 22–41.

———. 1999. *Eldercare in Canada: Context, Content and Consequences*. Ottawa: Statistics Canada.

———. 2001. 'A Good Place to Grow Old? Rural Communities and Support to Seniors'. Pp. 263–77 in R. Epp and D. Whitson (eds), *Writing Off the Rural West: Globalization, Governments and the Transformation of Rural Communities*. Edmonton: University of Alberta Press.

Keefe, J. 2002. 'Home and Community Care'. Pp. 109–40 in M. Stephenson and E. Sawyer (eds), *Continuing the Care: The Issues and Challenges for Long-Term Care*. Ottawa: CHA Press (www.cha.ca).

———, and P. Fancey. 2002. 1997. 'Financial Compensation or Home Help Service: Examining Differences among Program Recipients', *Canadian Journal on Aging*, 16(2), 254–78.

———. 'Work and Eldercare: Reciprocity between Older Mothers and Their Employed Daughters', *Canadian Journal on Aging*, 21(2), 229–41.

———, et al. 2000. 'The Impact of Ethnicity on Helping Older Relatives: Findings from a Sample of Employed Canadians', *Canadian Journal on Aging*, 19(3), 317–42.

Kemp, C., and C. Rosenthal. 2000. 'The Consequences of Caregiving: Does Employment Make a Difference?'. SEDAP Research Paper No. 36. Hamilton, Ont.: McMaster University (http://socserv2.mcmaster.ca/sedap).

Kozak, J., et al. 1995. 'Epidemiological Perspectives on the Abuse and Neglect of Seniors: A Review of the National and International Research Literature'. Pp. 129–41 in M. Maclean (ed.), *Abuse and Neglect of Older Canadians: Strategies for Change*. Toronto: Thompson Educational.

Kramer, B., and J. Lambert. 1999. 'Caregiving as a Life Course Transition among Older Husbands: A Prospective Study', *The Gerontologist*, 39(6), 658–67.

Krause, N. 2001. 'Social Support'. Pp. 272–94 in R. Binstock and L. George (eds), *Handbook of Aging and the Social Sciences*. San Diego, Calif.: Academic Press.

Litwak, E. 1985. *Helping the Elderly: The Complementary Roles of Informal Networks and Formal Systems*. New York: Guilford Press.

Lloyd, P. 1991. 'The Empowerment of Elderly People', *Journal of Aging Studies*, 5(2), 125–35.

McCarthy, J. 2002. 'Formal Caregivers'. Pp. 237–66 in M. Stephenson and E. Sawyer (eds), *Continuing the Care: The Issues and Challenges for Long-Term Care*. Ottawa: CHA Press.

McDonald, L. 1997. 'The Link between Social Research and Social Policy Options: Reverse Retirement as a Case in Point', *Canadian Journal on Aging/Canadian Public Policy*, Supplement (Spring), 90–113.

———, and A. Collins. 2000. *Abuse and Neglect of Older Adults: A Discussion Paper*. Ottawa: Health Canada, Family Violence Prevention Unit.

———, and B. Wigdor (eds). 1995. 'Elder Abuse Research in Canada', *Canadian Journal on Aging*, 14 (Supplement 2), 1–140.

———, et al. 1991. *Elder Abuse and Neglect in Canada*. Toronto: Butterworths.

———, et al. 1995. 'Issues in Practice with Respect to Mistreatment of Older People' Pp. 5–16 in M. Maclean (ed.), *Abuse and Neglect of Older Canadians: Strategies for Change*. Toronto: Thompson Educational.

Maclean, M. (ed.). 1995. *Abuse and Neglect of Older Canadians: Strategies for Change*. Toronto: Thompson Educational.

MacRae, H. 1992. 'Fictive Kin as a Component of the Social Networks of Older People', *Research on Aging*, 14(2), 226–47.

Martin Matthews, A., and L. Campbell. 1995. 'Gender Roles, Employment and Informal Care'. Pp. 129–43 in S. Arber and J. Ginn (eds), *Connecting Gender and Ageing*. Philadelphia: Open University Press.

Martin-Matthews, A. 2000. 'Intergenerational Caregiving: How Apocalyptic and Dominant Demographies Frame the Questions and Shape the Answers'. Pp. 64–79 in E. Gee and G. Gutman (eds), *The Overselling of Population Aging*. Don Mills, Ont.: Oxford.

Matthews, S. 2002. *Sisters and Brothers/Daughters and Sons: Meeting the Needs of Old Parents*. Bloomington, Ind.: Unlimited.

Mindszenthy, B., and M. Gordon. 2002. *Parenting Your Parents: Support Strategies for Meeting the Challenge of Aging in the Family*. Toronto, Ont.: Dundurn Press.

Mitchell, B. 2003. 'Would I Share a Home with an Elderly Parent? Explaining Ethnocultural Diversity and Intergenerational Support Relations during Adulthood', *Canadian Journal on Aging*, 22(1), 69–82.

Montigny, E-A. 1997. *Foisted upon the Government? State Responsibilities, Family Obligations and the Care of the Elderly in Late-Nineteenth Century Ontario*. Montreal: McGill-Queen's University Press.

NACA. 1991. *Intergovernmental Relations and the Aging of the Population*. Ottawa: National Advisory Council on Aging.

———. 2000. *The NACA Position on Home Care*. Ottawa: National Advisory Council on Aging.

Navon, L., and N. Weinblatt. 1996. 'The Show Must Go On: Behind the Scenes of Elderly Spousal Caregiving', *Journal of Aging Studies*, 10(4), 329–42.

O'Connor, D. 1999. 'Living With a Memory-Impaired Spouse: (Re)cognizing the Experience', *Canadian Journal on Aging*, 18(2), 211–35.

Parsons, J., and J. Tindale. 2001. 'Parents Who Sue Their Adult Children for Support: An Examination of Decisions by Canadian Court Judges', *Canadian Journal on Aging*, 20(4), 451–70.

Pearlin, L., et al. 1996. 'Caregiving and Its Social Support'. Pp. 283–302 in R. Binstock and L. George (eds), *Handbook of Aging and the Social Sciences*. San Diego, Calif.: Academic Press.

———, et al. 2001. 'Caregiving by Adult Children: Involvement, Role Disruption, and Health'. Pp. 238–54 in R. Binstock and L. George (eds), *Handbook of Aging and the Social Sciences*. San Diego, Calif.: Academic Press.

Podnieks. E., et al. 1990. *National Survey of Abuse of the Elderly in Canada*. Toronto: Ryerson Polytechnical University.

Pruchno, R., and N. Resch. 1989. 'Aberrant Behaviors and Alzheimer's Disease: Mental Health Effects on Spouse Caregivers', *Journal of Gerontology: Social Sciences*, 44(5), S177–82.

Romanow Commission. *See* Royal Commission on the Future of Health Care in Canada.

Rosenthal, C. 2000. 'Aging Families: Have Current Changes and Challenges Been "Oversold"?' Pp. 45–63 in E. Gee and G. Gutman (eds), *The Overselling of Population Aging*. Don Mills, Ont.: Oxford University Press.

————, and A. Martin-Matthews. 1999. 'Families as Care-Providers versus Care-Managers? Gender and Type of Care in a Sample of Employed Canadians.' SEDAP Research Report No. 4. Hamilton, Ont.: McMaster University (http://socserv2.mcmaster.ca/sedap).

Ross, M., et al. 1997. 'Spousal Caregiving in the Institutional Setting: Task Performance', *Canadian Journal on Aging*, 16(1), 51–69.

Royal Commission on the Future of Health Care in Canada. 2002. *Building on Values: The Future of Health Care in Canada*. Ottawa: The Commission.

Russell, R. 2001. 'In Sickness and in Health: A Qualitative Study of Elderly Men Who Care for Wives with Dementia', *Journal of Aging Studies*, 15(4), 351–67.

Settersten, R. 2003. 'Rethinking Social Policy: Lessons of a Life-Course Perspective'. Pp. 191–222 in R. Settersten (ed.), *Invitation to the Life Course: Toward New Understandings of Later Life*. Amityville, NY: Baywood.

Shapiro, E. 2002. 'Home Care'. Health Transition Fund Synthesis Series. Ottawa: Health Canada (www.hc-sc.gc.ca).

————. 2003. 'The Romanow Commission Report and Home Care', *Canadian Journal on Aging*, 22(1), 13–17.

Silverstein, M., et al. 2002. 'Reciprocity in Parent-Child Relations over the Adult Life Course', *Journal of Gerontology: Social Services*, 57B(1), S3–13.

Skinner, M., and M. Rosenberg. 2002. 'Health Care in Rural Communities: Exploring the Development of Informal and Voluntary Care'. SEDAP Research Paper No. 79. Hamilton, Ont.: McMaster University (http://socserv2.mcmaster.ca/sedap).

Snell, J. 1990. 'Filial Responsibility Laws in Canada: A Historical Study', *Canadian Journal on Aging*, 9(3), 268–77.

————. 1996. *The Citizen's Wage: The State and the Elderly in Canada, 1900–1951*. Toronto: University of Toronto Press.

Statistics Canada. 2001. *Seniors in Canada*. Ottawa: Ministry of Industry.

————. 2003. 'Social Support and Mortality among Seniors', *Health Reports*, 14(3).

Stephenson, M., and E. Sawyer (eds), 2002. *Continuing the Care: The Issues and Challenges for Long-Term Care*. Ottawa: CHA Press (www.cha.ca).

Stewart, M. et al. 2001. 'Telephone Support Groups for Seniors with Disabilities', *Canadian Journal on Aging*, 20(1), 47–72.

Stones, M., and M. Bédard. 2003. 'Higher Thresholds for Elder Abuse with Age and Rural Residence', *Canadian Journal on Aging*, 21(4), 577–86.

Strain, L., and A. Blandford. 2003. 'Caregiving Networks in Later Life: Does Cognitive Status Make a Difference?' *Canadian Journal on Aging*, 22(3), 261–73.

Thornton, M., and S. Travis. 2003. 'Analysis of the Reliability of the Modified Caregiver Strain Index', *Journal of Gerontology: Social Sciences*, 58B(2), S127–32.

Uhlenberg, P. 1996. 'The Burden of Aging: A Theoretical Framework for Understanding the Shifting Balance of Caregiving and Care Receiving as Cohorts Age', *The Gerontologist*, 36(6), 761–7.

Ward-Griffin, C. 2002. 'Boundaries and Connections between Formal and Informal Caregivers', *Canadian Journal on Aging*, 21(2), 205–16.

————, and V. Marshall. 2003. 'Reconceptualizing the Relationship Between 'Public' and 'Private' Eldercare', *Journal of Aging Studies*, 17(2), 189–208.

Weeks, L., and K. Roberto. 2002. 'Comparison of Adult Day Services in Atlantic Canada, Maine and Vermont', *Canadian Journal on Aging*, 21(2), 273–82.

Wilber, K., and D. McNeilly. 2001. 'Elder Abuse and Victimization'. Pp. 569–92 in J. Birren and W. Schaie (eds), *Handbook of the Psychology of Aging*. New York: Academic Press.

Wister, A., and C. Moore. 1997. 'First Nations Elders in Canada: Issues, Problems and Successes in Health Care Policy'. Pp. 83–104 in A. Wister and G. Gutman (eds), *Health Systems and Aging in Selected Pacific Rim Countries: Ethnic Diversity and Change*. Vancouver: Gerontology Research Centre, Simon Fraser University.

World Health Organization. 2002. *Missing Voices: Views of Older Persons on Elder Abuse*. Geneva: World Health Organization.

Wu, Z., and R. Hart. 2002. 'Social and Health Factors Associated with Support among Elderly Immigrants in Canada', *Research on Aging*, 24(4), 391–412.

Zukewich, N. 2003. 'Unpaid Informal Caregiving', *Canadian Social Trends* (Autumn), 14–18.

CHAPTER 12

Individual and Population Health in Later Life

Focal Points

- How do chronic diseases in later life lower one's quality of life and increase dependence on others?

- How are health and health behaviour influenced by cultural, lifestyle, and social structural factors?

- Why are self-perceptions of health a predictor of illness and death?

- Is sexuality expressed in later life?

- How, and why, does an inability to cope with change and stress in later life, including a decline in physical health, lead to mental health problems?

- Who decides, and when, if there should be a transition from 'cure' to 'care' during the late stages of a chronic or terminal illness?

- How well does our health-care system serve older Canadians?

- With increasing costs, should health care for older persons be rationed?

- How do we, as individuals and as a society, ensure a 'good' death with dignity and choice?

Introduction

Defining 'health' is much like defining 'love'. There are many individual meanings and interpretations, and often they are not very precise or consistent across time. What is clear is that health is a multi-dimensional concept involving

- individual physical, biological, psychological, and social dimensions;

- the social and physical environment;

- lifestyles (health habits and behaviour);

- the health-care system (medical care by physicians and in hospitals); and

- health promotion (education, self-care, behaviour modification).

It is beyond the scope of this chapter to address the multi-dimensional meanings and measurements of health as a concept. However, there are many excellent discussions of the meaning and measurement of health and its various components, and of the health-care system itself.[1]

The World Health Organization defines good health as the absence of symptoms of illness or signs of disease; the presence of well-being and a sense of being healthy (or not ill or sick); and, the capacity to perform activities of daily living and to function with some degree of independence. Illness, a subjective experience or feeling, is based on personal perceptions of symptoms such as swelling, pain, nausea, weakness, or dizziness. These feelings and experiences may or may not be revealed to others, including physicians. However, when revealed to a physician, and after diagnostic tests and assessments, an illness can be labelled as acute or chronic.

Subjective feelings and experiences are important when reporting self-perceptions of health in social surveys ('Do you rate your health as excellent, good, fair, or poor?'), and when deciding how to react and cope with an apparent change in one's health. Do we treat the symptoms ourselves with rest, home remedies, or over-the-counter drugs? Do we seek advice from family and friends? Do we visit a health-care specialist—physician, pharmacist, therapist, psychologist, psychiatrist, or psycho-geriatrician? Do we visit a health-care clinic or the emergency department of a hospital? Or do we decide to change our health behaviour through exercise, diet, or decreased smoking or drinking?

Health and illness are processes that have consequences over the life course, especially in later life. Stability and change in a person's health is not just a biological or medical process. Rather, health is a significant social process that involves the interaction of human agency (decisions made or not made about health and lifestyle matters), personal history (heredity, personality, and lifestyles), and social conditions (our place in the social structure, environmental factors, where we live, and our social networks and social relations) (George, 2003).

Health and health behaviours change as people move from the middle to later years of life. Chronic health problems and disabilities, if they become severe during the later working years, often lead to absenteeism, loss of productivity, or early retirement. Most older adults are living longer and healthier lives, although the longer they live the greater the risk of experiencing chronic diseases and physical or cognitive impairments. In later life there is variation in the incidence and progression of diseases and disability states such as: arthritis, rheumatism, hypertension, strokes, cancers, cardiovascular disease, diabetes, osteoporosis, Parkinson's disease, and Alzheimer's disease. At some point, these conditions, especially if there is co-morbidity (more than one condition at the same time), *may* lead to decreased functional capacity and independence; to decreased well-being; to isolation; to being stigmatized as frail, sick, dependent, or disabled; and to moving from one's home to a residential-care facility.

For many years, especially when life expectancy was shorter and disability rates among older adults were higher, health was considered a medical problem. This *medical* model of health care focused on the incidence, causes, and treatment of disease. Thus, the emphasis was on treating or curing health problems with surgery, drugs, bed rest, or for elderly patients, moving them to a facility offering 24-hour nursing care. One outcome of this medical model was the perpetuation of negative images of aging—that later life is a time of decay, inactivity, frailty, dependence and incompetence. Yet, as Highlight 12.1 illustrates, 'you can not judge a book by its cover'—the appearance of older people can be deceiving.

As a result of government reports (Lalonde, 1974; Epp, 1986; Romanow Commission, 2002) and the research of many health scholars in Canada, there has been a gradual shift to a *social* model of health care. This model considers the social determinants of health, human agency in health decisions, self-care, health promotion to change behaviours and beliefs, and a definition of health care beyond that provided by physicians and hospitals. Thus, there is less dependence on drugs, surgery, and hospital stays. This model also includes a continuum of care in which health care and social services are provided in homes, the community, and residential facilities so that the 'right services, in the right place, at the right

Highlight 12.1 Changing Impressions about the Health of Older Adults

The following story, told by a registered nurse, illustrates how her impressions and expectations of a 'decrepit' and 'stooped' 101-year-old resident in a nursing home led her to a completely erroneous conclusion about the man's health status and lifestyle:

> So I'm taking care of this little gentleman who's 101 years old. Well I had never met any-body over 80 in that state. Even today, I think 101 would really impress me. But this little fellow is sitting on the bed this morning and he says: 'I certainly would like to get on with this day.' And I'm saying (to myself): 'Okay.' Now this guy is in fairly good health, but I come to find out he was going on a trip, he tells me, to southern California. He looks out of the window and says: 'See over there in the parking lot. There's that little truck with a camper on it. That's mine and I've got to get out of here because I've got to be in L.A. by the end of the week to meet so and so because we're going to such and such a place.' And I'm going to myself: 'Oh, sure, uh-huh, yeah. How many other confused patients will I have today (laughs). This little guy is senile. Sure there's a truck outside but he's telling me sto-ries . . .' But (it turned out that) his story was absolutely true. So here is this 101 year old that I took as a very decrepit old man with stooped shoulders and off he went in his little truck to southern California. (Fineman, 1994: 267)

time' are delivered to older people as their needs change (Stephenson and Sawyer, 2002: 3). Increasing attention is being directed to ensuring that a safety net prevents older people from 'falling through the cracks' where a fragmented system of service delivery may exist.

The continuum of care model was intro-duced in Chapter 7 (which discussed housing options) and Chapter 11 (which discussed home and community support). In this chapter, the focus is on a continuum of care in the health domain. The information in this chapter is based on the assumption, espoused by Moore and Rosenberg (1997: 156), that the overwhelming majority of those under 80 years of age enjoy good health and pursue active lives with little dependence on external agencies for health care or social support. It is at more advanced ages that the incidence of severe functional limitations rises substantially.

The older population is as heterogeneous with respect to physical and mental health as it is with respect to wealth, mobility, and social involvement. Many older adults live independ-ently in their own homes, with few debilitating health problems until 6–18 months before their death. Others, especially women, live a long life and gradually experience frailty and cognitive impairment that requires them to move to a resi-dential facility. Still others, especially if chronic conditions begin in mid-life, experience multiple chronic and acute conditions, and spend much of their later life in hospitals or long-term-care facil-ities. So that we can better understand health issues in later life, this chapter addresses the physical and mental health of older adults; the interaction of older people with Canada's health-care system, and reforms to the health-care sys-tem that are being considered; and the issues sur-rounding the end of life and dying.

Physical Health

The incidence of acute and chronic illness in later life and in individual reactions to illness, frailty and death varies greatly among older adults.

Some older people experience chronic health problems in their 60s; others not until well into their 80s (Martin-Matthews, 2002). Nevertheless, health, illness, and health care are a common concern of older Canadians and their families because of increasing life expectancy (Riley, 2001). As well, there is increasing evidence that there is a 'compression of morbidity',[2] in later life (Hubert et al., 2002). If a cure or a drastic elimination in the incidence of the cancers and the cardiovascular diseases could be realized, morbidity rates would decline even more dramatically. As well, older people are experiencing more years of disability-free life expectancy. Estimates suggest that only 18 per cent of 65- to 79-year-olds, 22 per cent of 80- to 84-year-olds, and 40 per cent of those over 85 years of age have activity limitations caused by chronic health conditions (Moore and Rosenberg, 1997: 117).

Health status influences both the quality and quantity of life. How an individual reacts and adapts to declining health, including a major disability or a terminal illness, may have more influence on the quality of life than the illness per se. For this reason it is important to understand all the factors associated with morbidity, and with the reaction to an illness in later life: the *cultural factors* (ethnic health and medical beliefs and practices); the *personal factors* (adaptation to stress and pain and coping strategies); the *social factors*, that is, the support system; and the *structural factors* (gender, age, class, and ethnicity). Highlight 12.2 illustrates how a social encounter dramatically altered pain management and improved the quality of life for an older woman.

Acute and Chronic Conditions[3]

The health of older people, on average, is improving in most industrialized societies because of advances in nutrition, environmental and housing conditions, health promotion, and health care. Acute conditions, many of which are treatable by drugs, therapy, or surgery, occur less frequently among older adults than do chronic conditions. But, when acute conditions do emerge among older adults, compared to younger people, they often require a longer period of recovery and, when combined with a chronic illness, deplete the physical or mental capacity of an older person to adapt or function. An apparently minor acute illness can subsequently have major consequences for the long-term health, adaptation, and well-being of an older person.

Many older people report having symptoms of a chronic illness, and many report the presence of more than one chronic health problem (co-morbidity)[4]. The most prevalent chronic conditions influencing the physical health of older people are arthritis and rheumatism, hypertension and strokes, heart problems, respiratory diseases, diabetes, and cancers. The major causes of death are coronary heart disease, cancer, strokes, and respiratory-system diseases. An increasing number of older adults, especially men who live beyond 80, experience the slowly debilitating ravages of Parkinson's disease.

In later life, pain from arthritis, osteoporosis, diabetes, angina, cancer, or muscular and joint trauma restricts social, physical, or mental activities. Many older adults consider pain a 'normal' part of aging and suffer without reporting the symptoms or seeking treatment (see Highlight 12.2). Pain and drugs taken to reduce pain can disturb sleep, suppress appetite, and cause depression, drowsiness, and unclear thinking. Above all, pain influences mobility, social interaction, well-being, and quality of life.

Health Status and Activity Limitation

The impact of a disease or illness on an older person varies greatly, depending on the severity and duration of the illness, the coping mechanisms of the individual, and the availability and use of social support and adaptive devices. Most acute illnesses involve only temporary restrictions or changes in lifestyle. However, chronic conditions, which range from minor aches and pains to long-term physical or mental disability, eventually

Highlight 12.2 Enhanced Pain Management through Communication and Interaction

Jane is 73. She and her husband Ray, age 72, have always enjoyed an active life. They are general-ly in good health, but in the last few years, Jane has felt some pain and stiffness, especially in her knees. It's beginning to cramp Jane's style—she still attends social events, but if an activity involves a lot of walking, she sometimes stays home. After an active day, her knees ache, making for a rest-less night's sleep. Jane prides herself on being self-reliant—she's not one to complain—so she doesn't mention this, even to Ray. The pain seems to be getting worse, but she dismisses it as just part of getting older. When she does visit her physician, she ignores or downplays her suffering, so the doctor takes no action.

One day her friend Barbara mentions that she is enjoying outings with the birding club much more now that her arthritis pain is under control. Jane is surprised—she didn't even know Barbara had arthritis. Barbara explains that her doctor prescribed a new anti-inflammatory drug—one that doesn't bother her stomach as much. This conversation makes Jane realize she might be suffering needlessly.

Jane makes an appointment with her doctor and prepares for the visit by writing down what she wants to talk about: a description of her aches and stiffness and how long she's had them; the fact that pain occurs mainly in the morning, after sitting for a while, or if she's been very active that day; and the medication she is taking. After listening to Jane's story, an anti-inflammatory drug is prescribed, along with physiotherapy to strengthen her muscles and increase her flexibility. The doc-tor suggests that a hot bath could also help her on mornings when stiffness is a problem. Also, after an active day of birding or gardening, she should place a cold pack or a bag of frozen peas on her knees while she relaxes with a book. The anti-inflammatories take a couple of weeks to help, but they give Jane significant relief. The physiotherapy takes a little longer, but after two months, Jane can do much more than she used to. She no longer avoids activities involving long walks, and even if she overdoes it a bit, the frozen peas and a hot bath the next morning give her enough relief to keep going. Jane is sleeping better—and she's glad the topic of Barbara's arthritis came up that day!

Source: *Expression* 15(3), Division of Aging and Seniors, Health Canada, 2002. Adapted and reproduced with the permission of the Minister of Public Works and Government Services of Canada, 2004.

restrict social interaction, mobility, the ability to care for oneself, and the fulfilling of family responsibilities. Highlight 12.3 illustrates some of the health challenges facing older adults.

A medical diagnosis of a chronic condition or a terminal illness dramatically alters lifestyles in the later years, for both the older person and his or her spouse, relatives, and caregivers. A positive reac-tion to a medical diagnosis involves a determina-tion to engage in treatment or rehabilitation and to prevent the chronic condition from changing one's lifestyle to any appreciable degree. A negative response leads to giving up the fight to live because the person cannot tolerate treatment or pain; can-not accept a change in self-image; or is unwilling to

be dependent on others or to cope with the physi-cal and mental stresses associated with the illness.

Activity limitation in later life, which is one consequence of illness or disease, can be labelled as an impairment or a disability (Moore and Rosenberg, 1997). An *impairment* represents the loss, to some degree, of physical capacity, such as hearing, vision, or use of the legs, or of mental capacity. If sufficiently severe, an impairment becomes a *disability* that prevents the person, par-tially or totally, from performing an activity relat-ed to work, leisure, or personal care. Older peo-ple may under-report impairments or disabilities to maintain an image of independence or to avoid decisions about a change in housing or employ-

Highlight 12.3 Health Challenges in Later Life

Vignette 1

A 64-year-old woman had a major stroke eight months ago, causing paralysis of her right side. She is unable to get out of bed and into her wheelchair or onto the toilet without physical assistance. Her 71-year-old husband, who has some minor health problems, finds it very difficult to help her and is only just managing. Also, he is obviously having trouble coping emotionally with seeing his wife in such a weak condition. Their only source of income is the government old-age pension, so they are unable to afford private help.

Vignette 2

An 81-year-old widow was managing well on her own despite arthritis in her hips that limited her mobility. Four months ago she fell and broke her left hip, which required an operation. She was sent to a convalescent hospital where she received physiotherapy. Despite recovering quite well, she has not been able to regain her previous level of function. The staff at the hospital is considering discharging her, but they are uncertain whether she will be able to cope unassisted in her own apartment. She is unable to afford a private nursing home and the waiting time for a publicly- funded facility is at least six months. She cannot stay in the hospital that long so other arrangements must be made.

Vignette 3

A 76-year-old man has had Alzheimer's disease for the last four years. He presently lives with his wife in an apartment where a community nurse visits him every week. Besides poor memory, his major problem is that he has no understanding of his illness. He gets quite upset, and at times aggressive, when anyone tries to get him to do something against his will. He tends to get more agitated at night and has trouble sleeping. He has reached the stage where he requires supervision for most activities and so cannot safely be left alone for any length of time.

His wife, who is 72 years old, is in reasonable physical health but is becoming exhausted because of the demands of having to take care of her husband. She is unable to get a good night's sleep and cannot rest during the day because she is afraid her husband will get into trouble.

Source: Wolfson et al. (1993). Reprinted by permission of The Gerontological Society of America.

ment. Consequently, in a clinical or care-management setting, personal reports about impairments should be supplemented with direct measurements of memory, hearing or vision to determine the degree of any limitation, and whether the person should, for example, be forbidden to drive at night, or whether he or she needs an adaptive device such as a cane or hearing aid.

Self-Perceptions of Health

The prevalence of serious, chronic health problems increases with age, and between 60 and 80 per cent of adults 65 years of age and over report having at least one chronic health problem, an activity limitation, or a mobility limitation. Yet, numerous surveys throughout the 1990s found that older people say that they are 'well', or that their health is 'good' or 'excellent' (Statistics Canada, 1993; Wilkins and Cott, 1994; Idler, 1998; Clarke et al., 2000). These favourable subjective assessments of personal health, even by a person experiencing losses in physical health, are generally made more often by those with higher levels of social involvement and education, positive attitudes about life, and positive personality characteristics; by those who are married; and by those who receive social support from family and friends. Just as age, per se, is socially defined, so too is health. Thus, some older people define their health as good or excellent so as to be perceived as independent and autonomous. Some others may define their health as poor, perhaps to seek attention or more support.

As long as symptoms, such as pain, less sleep, or less mobility, do not reduce functional ability, especially in daily and social life, most people report their health status as 'good' or 'excellent'. This assessment is influenced by the 'relative' rather than the 'absolute' level of health. That is, older people compare themselves and their situation with age peers or with common images of the expected health of someone their age, rather than with their own health 10, 15, or 20 years ago. Perceptions are influenced, as well, by others who comment on their appearance, ability, or accomplishments, often in comparison with others they know of about the same age. Where self-perceptions are low, and health is rated as 'not good' or 'poor', there is some evidence that subjective measures are a predictor of impending death. Menec et al. (1999) reported that those who rate their health as 'bad/poor' or 'fair' were more than twice as likely to die within three to three and a half years following the survey than those who perceived their health as 'excellent'. There is no clear explanation for this relationship, but it may be that personal feelings are more insightful about health than some objective measures. Or those with low perceptions may fail to take action to improve the situation; that is, they may not seek treatment or try to live more healthily. Or with perceived poor health, they finally seek treatment and a full diagnosis, but it is too late for them to be cured.

Social Structural Determinants of Health

Health in later life is determined not only by biology or genetic factors, but also by

- lifestyle choices and behaviour;
- our place in the social structure;

- our physical environment, including pollution, living conditions, and safety;
- our social environment, including family violence and social support; and
- our work environment, such as exposure to stress, unemployment, pollutions, or accidents.

These factors operate across the life course and can have cumulative effects on health in later life. There are also cohort differences in health that are due to advances in health promotion, self-care, health-care technology, social support, and health practices. But health inequalities emerge *within* each cohort because of social structural inequities related to social class, that is, income and education; gender; ethnicity; and geographical location.

Just as structural inequalities create different life chances, experiences, and lifestyles across the life course because of differential access to social resources, so too are there health inequities throughout life and in later life (Armstrong and Armstrong, 2003). To illustrate, lower health status is associated with having less education and income, having smaller social networks, being female, living in rural or remote locations, and being a member of an ethnic group. These structural barriers influence who has more access to health knowledge and beliefs, better access to health care, higher-quality diets, better living and working conditions, and a predisposition to specific disease states. Individuals with fewer of these health-related resources are victims of a social structure, and should not be blamed or held responsible for being in poor health in later life. Just as structural inequalities (see Chapter 6) influence income, power, education, and lifestyle, so too do they influence health and health practices throughout the life course.

Social Class

Older Canadians with higher incomes, wealth, and education have lower rates of morbidity and mortality (Cairney, 2000). Individuals in the upper-middle and upper income levels of Canadian society are more likely to report and enjoy good to excellent health for a longer period of time. Health and social status are strongly related for both the incidence of specific diseases and for morbidity and mortality in general. People with more social capital generally exhibit better health, perhaps because they have more knowledge power (from education), more purchasing power (from income), and more employment power (from prestige and access to networks) (Veenstra, 2001). These individuals are also less likely to engage in risky health behaviours.

Money and education influence lifestyle, and it may be one's relative position in the social structure rather than the absolute amount of wealth, income, or education that matters. From a global perspective 'we know that the longest life expectancies are found not in the wealthiest countries (USA) but in those countries (Japan) with the smallest spread of incomes and the smallest proportion of the population in relative poverty' (Martin-Matthews, 2002: 21). It may be that higher education makes people better able to understand health risks, educational material, and health-care instructions by physicians. Moreover, good literacy skills enable older people to assimilate health information from the media, books, and the Internet. Some indirect evidence that education is an important element comes from findings which show that, in later life, those with less education experience health problems sooner (Roberts and Fawcett, 1998; Cairney, 2000).

Gender

There are gender differences in both subjective (perceived) and objective (diagnosed) health status. As Gee and Kimball (1987: 31) noted, 'Women get sick but men die.' Women are more likely to report a greater number of health problems than men. Women live longer, but they live alone and experience more years with some disability, with non-fatal chronic diseases, with more symptoms of illness, and with more stress and anxiety, especially after they are widowed (Maxwell and Oakley,

1998; Clarke, 2000; Segall and Chappell, 2000). Moreover, women are more frequent users of health-care services, drugs, and residential-care facilities. As well, they experience more days of restricted activity, have more days of bed confinement, and make more visits to physicians.

Women engage in more self-care than men by paying attention to nutrition and treating symptoms arising from a cold or flu. Older women are more likely than men to have chronic conditions, such as arthritis, cataracts, and high blood pressure, and physical limitations, such as deafness and difficulty in walking; and older women are twice as likely as older men to require help with one or more daily activities, such as cooking, housework, and personal care. In addition, women have more skin allergies, migraine headaches, falls with hip fractures, adverse reactions to drugs, sleep disorders, memory loss, pain, anxiety, and depression (Maxwell and Oakley, 1998). Throughout the life course, women, on average, smoke more than men, exercise less, and have fewer economic resources, especially if they are divorced or widowed.

Ethnicity

Life expectancy and general health are higher for immigrants than for persons born in Canada, and non-European immigrants have higher life expectancies than European immigrants (D'Arcy, 1998; Perez, 2002; Gee et al., 2003). This difference between immigrants and those born in Canada is known as the 'healthy-immigrant effect'. The effect is strongest among recent immigrants because healthier people are more likely to emigrate, and because health requirements in the Immigration Act screen out people with serious medical conditions (Gee et al., 2003).

The longer immigrants live in Canada, the more their self-reported health resembles that of the rest of the population (Clarke, 2000: 131–2). Both Perez (2002) and Ali (2002), when examining the physical and mental health of immigrants over time, found that the longer the residence in Canada, the more the immigrants' health status approached the Canadian norm, even when socio-economic and lifestyle factors were controlled. Recently the 'healthy-immigrant' effect was tested for both middle-aged (45–64) and older people (65 and over) (Gee et al., 2003). They found that middle-aged male immigrants who had arrived within the last 10 years had better functional and self-rated health than those who had immigrated 10 or more years before. The health of the latter group was similar to that of Canadian-born age peers. However, older, recent immigrants, especially the women, had poorer health than longer-term immigrants and Canadian-born age peers.

Why is there a change in the reported health status of immigrants over time? Ethnicity is related to class, and recent immigrants and members of some groups have incomes that are significantly below average. Thus, we might expect to find poorer health over time in immigrant ethnic groups because of poverty, poor living and working conditions, change of diet, discrimination, and ineligibility for some health services. As well, studies have indicated that immigrants make less use of health services, especially mental and preventive health services, than the Canadian-born population. For example, Chinese immigrants, like Aboriginal people,[5] often adhere to their traditional medical practices and beliefs. Other reasons for less frequent use of health services are that immigrants find the services to be inadequate (because of language difficulties or the 'foreign' diets provided in hospitals), or they they just don't know about them, especially home care. Some immigrants do not understand English, especially in a stressful hospital setting, or in conversations involving medical terminology or instructions (Mutran and Sudha, 2000; Sudha and Mutran, 2001). In a multicultural society, health policies must address the need for different health services to serve older recent immigrants, especially if family reunification is to be encouraged.

Rural and Remote Living

Geographical location is a determinant of health (Gesler et al., 1998). Most surveys indicate that residents of rural and remote communities have poorer health than people who live in urban centres, and the farther a community is from a large urban centre, the poorer the health of the residents. Because many rural and remote communities have a shrinking population base, it is difficult to develop an efficient health-care system.

Rural communities are relatively homogeneous with respect to socio-demographic characteristics, and many older residents have lived in the same community for years. When communities with different socio-demographic profiles are compared, rural and remote living accounts for 25 to 55 per cent of any variation in the health status of residents in communities (Statistics Canada, 2002). For example, the 2000–1 Canadian Community Health Survey found that rural regions had average life expectancies that were lower than the Canadian average; higher disability and accident rates; and rates of smoking, obesity, and heavy alcohol consumption that were above the Canadian average. This suggests that unhealthy lifelong habits are more prevalent in rural areas, which is reflected in a lower health status in later life.

Although more than 20 per cent of older Canadians live in rural areas, public policies neglect this sector in the allocation of health-care resources (Keating et al., 2001). This situation has become worse in recent years with the fragmentation of services, the closing of small rural hospitals, the restructuring and regionalization of health services, and the continued difficulty that rural communities have in attracting and retaining physicians and other health-care and social-service workers.

In rural and remote areas where the young people have moved away from the community, where distances to urban centres are great, and where fewer services are available, older people experience inequities in access to health services. Acute-care services may be located in another town, and the region, in general, may lack mental- or physical-therapy services, rehabilitative or palliative care, mental-health services, and home- and community-care services that are needed for continuing care. Even if private services could fill the void, many rural residents with limited incomes could not afford them. Moreover, rural communities seldom offer many, if any, alternative housing options for older people who can no longer live in their home. An older person who cannot drive is even more disadvantaged. Thus, rural residents throughout adulthood, and especially late in life, are disadvantaged in terms of both health status and in access to health and social services that are necessary to maintain an independent life. Some of these disadvantages are offset by self-care and by strong community support from family and friends. But as more children migrate to urban areas, increasingly a community of older people tries to survive by helping and supporting each other. At some point, if health or home care is not readily available, people are forced to move to a city or larger town late in life.

Rural and remote communities are diverse in size, in location, and in the age and social composition of residents. This makes it very difficult to develop one policy that meets the needs of all individuals in all communities. This challenge, recognized by the Romanow Commission on the Future of Health Care (2002: 159-69), recommended the creation of a Rural and Remote Access Fund. This fund would be used to attract and retain health-care providers, to expand tele- health services, and to develop innovative ways for delivering health-care services in smaller communities so as to reduce the rural-urban disparities in health and health services. Telehealth involves the use of the Internet and satellite services by physicians and other health-care workers for the diagnosis and treatment of illnesses, for consultations with specialists, for the transfer of health information (records), and for educating patients about disease or healthy lifestyles.

Health Behaviours in Later Life

Health and health behaviours in later life are influenced by habits acquired over a lifetime. Health behaviour is the way people perceive, understand, and respond to illness, disease, stress, and accidents; and the steps they take to promote wellness and prevent disease and disabilities.

Self-Care

Older people are encouraged to engage in self- care in order to improve or maintain their health, to prevent illness or disease, and in response to illness and frailty (Gottlieb, 2000; Penning and Keating, 2000; Morrongiello and Gottlieb, 2000). Self-care is a major component of health behaviour. It includes seeking health information, examining oneself for symptoms of disease, adopting healthier habits, and treating oneself for minor ailments, such as colds, flu, fevers, sprains, headaches, or rashes, with rest, over-the-counter medications, or a visit to a physician. Self-care also includes attending programs on topics such as fall preventions, medication management, dental health, weight loss, and physical activity, and joining self-help groups to acquire mutual aid, social support, or coping skills, for example, for widows and widowers, people with alcohol or gambling problems, or caregivers to Alzheimer's patients. By engaging in self-care, older individuals demonstrate independence and empowerment, lower the cost of community and health care, and improve their quality of life. While as few as 2 to 4 per cent of seniors join self-help groups (NACA, 1999), 80 to 95 per cent engage in self-care before seeking medical advice (Morrongiello and Gottlieb, 2000).

When symptoms of illness or pain appear, some individuals decide either to do nothing or to practise some form of self-care, such as exercising, dieting, taking over-the-counter drugs, or using alternative therapies. With increasing levels of health knowledge, self-care has become an integral part of the health-care and social-support continuum-of-care model. Consequently, primary health-care resources, that is, clinics, hospitals, and doctors are used less often, at least in the initial stages of an illness.

The coping strategies we learn throughout our lives for dealing with pain and minor acute illnesses carry over when chronic health problems or disabilities emerge in later life. We also learn about and, hopefully, adopt healthy habits that reduce health risks across the life course. The onset and severity of many chronic diseases, such as cardiovascular disease, cancer, diabetes, and osteoarthritis, is influenced by lifestyle choices concerning sleep, diet, exercise, and the use of tobacco, alcohol, and drugs across the life course. Even in later life, health and well-being can be maintained and improved by adhering to healthy habits or adopting better habits. Such habits could involve self-screening, more sleep, stop smoking, better nutrition, more exercise, and safe living habits (Deeg et al., 1996; Leventhal et al., 2001). These changes are more likely if a physician is active in health promotion and teaches and encourages self-care.

Sexuality

Sexuality involves expressing feelings of passion, intimacy, and affection for another person through various forms of sexual activity, and the subjective meaning and quality of the experience for both partners. This topic is an ideal example of the interdisciplinarity of research about aging since it requires a biological, medical, sociological, and psychological perspective for a full understanding.[6] Sexuality could have been discussed in Chapter 3 when physical, cognitive, and emotional changes that take place with age were examined; in Chapter 8 in the discussion of intimate family relationships, although sexuality is expressed, as well, outside family or marital bonds; or in Chapter 10 as a form of leisure and social participation. Here, sexuality is discussed as a form of healthy aging that contributes to physical and emotional health across the life course, including in later life, although the frequency, meaning, and form of sexual expression may change.[7]

Sexuality can be a significant component of the intimate relationships that are needed in later life by many men and women. Contrary to popular beliefs, lack of interest in sex by older adults is no longer the norm. Rather, in contrast to ageist and sexist images about losses or inabilities concerning

sex that were portrayed 10 to 15 years ago, with the recent interest in male impotence and the wonder drug Viagra, sexual activity is being sold and promoted as part of healthy aging, especially for men. An image of sexual decline, lack of interest, and dysfunction has been replaced by one promoting active sexuality as an essential part of one's identity in later life and of successful aging (Katz and Marshall, 2003). The marketing of *life-long* sex is similar to that for lifelong learning—use it or lose it; it is never too late to teach an old dog new tricks; do it for enjoyment and health. Much of this marketing is directed primarily to men. Ironically, and somewhat comically, a vicious cycle can result from this marketing, as noted in the following quotation from a letter to the *New England Journal of Medicine*. The letter, written to draw attention to an increase in vaginal irritation by middle-aged women who were partners of men using erection-enhancing drugs, stated:

> The man's pill makes the woman need a lubricant. The woman's lubricant makes the man need a penile sensory enhancer. The man's sensory enhancer makes the woman need a desire additive. The woman's desire additive makes a man need an energy stimulant. The man's energy stimulant makes him need anti-anxiety medication. And so on. (Tiefer, 2001: 90).

Sexual desire and the ability and need to engage in sex are, of course, highly dependent on biological and psychological functioning (such as the ability to express feelings of passion and affection in an intimate way). Hormonal changes in women and the general neuro-muscular slowing with age among men are normal outcomes of the aging process; hence it may take longer to become aroused, there may be less stamina, and it may take longer to reach satisfaction. Thus, while sexual desire and behaviour decrease as men and women age, the decline is not as fast nor does it reach as low a level as early research and popular belief would have us believe (DeLamater and Sill, 2003). Both hetero- and homosexual intimacy are possible well into the later years, although sexual intercourse is not always possible or necessary to express feelings. However, physical and emotional changes, chronic illness (diabetes, heart disease, arthritis) and some prescription drugs reduce or eliminate sexual desire and behaviour among older adults. Rather than biological deficiencies, however, the more likely explanations for reduced sexual activity in later life are psychological or social problems (fear of sexual inadequacy or anxiety about dating); the side effects of drugs; negative attitudes of adult children, physicians, friends, or staff in retirement or nursing homes; and lack of opportunity, that is, having no partner or no privacy. Stones and Stones (1996: 1), after interviewing over 100 middle-aged and older adults, concluded, 'sex isn't wasted on the old as most people can continue to enjoy their sexuality throughout their lives'.

Sexuality is socially constructed and varies across cultures and age cohorts. Thus, some religious subcultures believe sex is only for reproduction; some cultures encourage and promote sex at a very early age; others discourage sex at later ages. Sexuality is influenced by ageism and sexism in a society, especially where advertising images only include attractive young men and women. Whether one is interested in or engaged in sexual behaviour in later life is greatly influenced by attitudes toward and knowledge about sex, by past practices and experiences, and by whether one has an interested partner (DeLameter and Sill, 2003). It is for this reason that we observe cohort differences in expressed attitudes and behaviour about intimacy and sexuality with each new generation of older adults.[8] Many people now entering later life were part of the sexual revolution and the women's liberation movement of the 1960s and 1970s. They have always had more freedom to express sexual desires, and some have been involved in serial relationships, both inside and outside marriage. Many of the baby boomers, who will be elderly in the next 30 years, have experienced serial common-law or marital relationships, some have never married, and there are more gay and lesbian partnerships. Thus, the definition and parameters of sexuality for aging boomers will be different than that observed among earlier cohorts of older adults.

Despite the increased number of surveys, it is still difficult to determine accurately how many older adults engage in heterosexual or homosexual behaviour, with what meaning, and how frequently. Many older adults refuse to discuss the topic, and intimate questions about sexual behaviour are seldom included in surveys. Nevertheless, cultural norms and attitudes are changing, and the number of older people who report that they are sexually active, or willing to be active, is increasing. This increase reflects a cohort effect (that is, people are healthier and have more positive attitudes toward sex), and also an increased honesty in response to questions about sexuality. The most sexually active older people are those in good physical health, who have a high self-esteem, who have an interested partner, who have continued a high level of sexual activity throughout adulthood, and who live in their own home. A dilemma faced by nursing-home personnel is how to provide for the sexual needs of older residents, married or unmarried. The lack of privacy and the segregation of men and women, including married couples, is a major obstacle to sexual expression, and in some homes policies and practices prevent or discourage sexual intimacy.

Oral Health

Often ignored, and certainly under-researched, oral health is an essential component of health maintenance in later life (Payne 1994; Gift et al., 1997). Oral infections, gum disease, and poorly fitting dentures cause pain and discomfort, interfere with chewing and swallowing, and lead to loss of appetite and inadequate nutrition. Uncomfortable dentures (about 50 per cent of older people wear dentures) influence an older person's self-esteem and well-being since ill-fitting dentures alter one's facial appearance and create difficulties in speaking or eating. This discomfort, in turn, leads a person to refrain from eating in public or from interaction with others because of slurred speech. And in turn, the reduced social interaction detracts from the quality of a person's life.

For some older people, dental treatment is too expensive, especially if they do not belong to a dental plan. For others, poor oral health is due to lack of knowledge (oral health should be covered in health-promotion programs), inadequate lifelong dental care, or cognitive impairment (forgetting to brush or floss). And once a person is in a residential care facility, oral health is seldom a priority of the staff.

Health Promotion in Later Life

Healthy living across the life course can postpone and reduce disease and disabilities (Hubert, 2002), thereby contributing to a compression of morbidity. It is never too late to initiate health promotion and prevent disease (Morley and Flaherty, 2002; Wister, 2003). Consequently, health-promotion programs must target older adults, including those who are frail and chronically ill (McWilliam, 2001). Health promotion is a process by which, through education and motivation, people take control and improve their health through such activities as

- increasing the amount of physical and mental activity;
- accepting responsibility for personal health;
- maintaining a healthy well-balanced, low-cholesterol diet;
- ceasing to smoke;
- reducing alcohol consumption; and
- reducing stress and boredom.

An important part of health promotion is disease and injury prevention through flu shots; self-care; self-screening for acute and chronic diseases, such as prostate and breast cancer, depression,

and diabetes; and preventing falls and other accidents by ensuring one's home is safe.

To increase the level of health literacy among older people, Health Canada, with input and management by the Canadian Association on Gerontology, operates a 'Seniors' section on the Canadian Health Network (www.canadian health- network.ca). Similarly, to increase communication between older patients and their physicians, a 'Passport to Aging Successfully' lists health practices and behaviours that adults should discuss with their physician (www.thedoctorwillseeyounow.com).

Nutrition

Food provides the essential energy and nutrients to maintain health, well-being, and functional ability, and to fight illness and disease. Our energy expenditure through physical and cognitive activity determines the level of energy intake that is needed to function effectively. Given the active lifestyles pursued by many older adults, some nutritionists argue that the 'recommended' daily caloric intake is too low.

Although many lifelong dietary choices and habits persist in later life, changes in appetite and in dietary preferences do occur in the later years. These changes may result from poorly fitting dentures, a diminished sense of taste or smell, depression and cognitive impairment, difficulties in preparing and cooking food, the increasing cost of some foods, problems in chewing or digesting certain types of food, or the use of multiple medications that changes the taste or smell of some foods. In addition, retirement, widowhood, being unable to shop, or having a low income can change the diet of an elderly person, leading to potential health or social problems. For example, a person who lives alone may not enjoy mealtimes and may skip meals and not eat properly, perhaps suffering eventually from malnutrition. Older adults are also more susceptible to fad diets or miracle foods that are advertised as nutritious and essential for health. Many older adults, unknowingly, generate a dysfunctional cycle of poor eating habits; malnutrition, loss of weight, strength and energy; and then a further loss of appetite.

Changes in eating habits result in lower energy reserves and increased susceptibility to illness. Consequently, community service agencies and families should monitor the nutritional status of older people, especially those who live alone. Interventions to change and improve nutritional habits include prescribed and over-the-counter nutritional supplements, as well as education about selecting and preparing foods. One of the most successful programs that ensures adequate nutrition is 'meals-on-wheels', a service in which a volunteer delivers at least one hot meal per day to an older person's home. In addition, the volunteer may remain for a visit while the meal is eaten, thereby making meal time a social event.

Physical Activity and Sport Participation

Since the early 1990s, health-promotion programs have stressed the importance of an active, healthy life to increase disability-free years, increase the quality of life, and enhance longevity. Consequently, an increasing number of middle-aged and older adults include daily or weekly physical activity in their routine. Popular phrases encouraging active lifestyles include: 'those who do not find time for exercise will have to find time for illness'; and 'add life to years, rather than just years to life'.

Exercise and physical activity provides a number of benefits for aging adults[9]:

- increased life satisfaction, confidence, and self-worth

- reduced morbidity and mortality

- reduced risk of cognitive impairment

- improved physical health and functional ability, especially in flexibility, balance, strength, and endurance

- less stress and less depression

- a higher self-reported quality of life.

Regular physical activity involving, at a minimum, brisk walking for about 30 minutes a day is considered sufficient to induce needed health outcomes. Clearly, being involved in regular physical activity is a necessary part of healthy aging.

Yet, as many studies have found, physical activity declines with age. Often, this pattern begins during adolescence or early adulthood, before physical activity is integrated into one's leisure style. This pattern of decreasing involvement is more pronounced among the less educated, women, those with lower incomes, those who live in rural areas and small towns, and those employed in manual occupations. Again, structural inequalities intervene to make it less likely that some adults will have an opportunity or desire to participate in regular physical activity during their leisure time.

The erroneous but prevailing myth that it is 'dangerous' for older people to be physically active discourages both personal involvement and the provision of physical activity programs and facilities for older adults. Because of age grading and age criteria for participation, facilities and programs for older adults are seldom provided by communities or the private sector. 'Acting one's age' used to mean that participation in sport or physical activity in the later years was not socially acceptable. These age norms interacted with gender-based norms to create even greater social barriers for older women. Moreover, if physically active older role models were not visible in the community, ageism concerning the need for, and right to, physical activity in later life was further entrenched.

In recent years there are greater numbers of physically active adults at *all* ages, including those over 70 years of age, who are demanding activity opportunities. These visible, active older adults are helping to remove restrictive age norms that discourage involvement in physical activity by older men and women. Moreover, scientific evidence has demonstrated that moderate to high levels of physical activity are possible at all ages and that regular activity enhances physical and mental health. 'Master', 'Veteran', or 'Senior' sport competitions, including marathon runs, are organized for older adults, by age group. This change to a more active lifestyle for older adults has occurred for a number of reasons:

- increased knowledge about the benefits of lifelong physical activity
- new definitions of aging lifestyles
- changing values and norms regarding exercise and activity, especially for women
- effective health-promotion programs in which physical activity is a key component
- an increase in the number and quality of public and private facilities where adults can be physically active.

Periodically, the media report the accomplishments of older men and women in their 60s, 70s, and 80s who, for example, cycle almost 9,000 kilometres from Victoria to St John's, Newfoundland; who swim across a lake or channel; who complete a marathon in times ranging from 5 to 11 hours; who high-jump, pole-vault, hang-glide, water-ski, snow board, lift weights, or who accomplish some other feat remarkable for their age or sex. Clearly, these are unique individuals and they are exceptions to the norm. But such people help to refute the myth that older adults should spend the later years in a rocking chair. Moreover, extreme achievements confirm that, with proper training and supervision, and the right genes, older people can attain performances and goals far beyond what they or others expected.

Drug Use, Misuse, and Abuse

The use of drugs to maintain or enhance the health behaviour and mobility of older adults has become more prevalent, although accurate statistics on the use of both prescription drugs and over-the-counter medications are difficult to obtain. Most studies find that the number and frequency of medications increase with age, and that many older adults take more than one drug per day (this practice is known as polypharmacy).

In later life, drugs are prescribed for chronic conditions, such as arthritis, heart disease, memory loss, Alzheimer's disease, insomnia, depression, anxiety, and Parkinson's disease. Drugs can alleviate symptoms, such as pain, hand tremors, or agitation, but most do not cure the underlying condition. In general, women take more drugs than men, partly because they consult doctors more often and because they live longer. In contrast, members of some cultural groups (such as Chinese-Canadians who prefer traditional Chinese medicine) use fewer drugs than their age peers because of their cultural beliefs and practices about illness and healing (Tjam and Hirdes, 2002).

Medication management is a form of self-care. Increased self- or prescribed-medication use among older adults has raised a number of issues pertaining to the cost of drugs; the need for more rigorous research and testing of new drugs to ensure that they are safe and effective for older adults; and the need for education about medication management (Tamblyn, 2000; Tamblyn and Perreault, 2000, Maddigan et al., 2003). Unsuitable medications can alter the way older people think, move, or express their feelings. Some drugs, especially if taken in conjunction with other drugs, caffeine, or alcohol, can cause drowsiness, falls, accidents, nausea, convulsions, or even death.

These interactive conditions are more likely to occur if a person is engaging in over-medication by taking more than one drug, if drugs prescribed for someone else are shared, or if over-the-counter drugs are taken without the knowledge of a physician. Over-medication also results when an older person gets a prescription from more than one physician or has his or her prescriptions filled at more than one pharmacy. This occurs most often with sedative drugs that treat anxiety and insomnia or the pain of musculoskeletal problems like osteoarthritis. Over-medication results, as well, from drug plans that cover most costs and that therefore indirectly foster increased use of drugs; from increased advertising of 'wonder' drugs in publications targeted to older adults; and from an increase in the availability of over-the-counter drugs for a variety of ailments or illnesses.

In addition to the overuse of medication, intentional or unintentional non-compliance with a prescribed drug regimen (such as forgetting when or how to take the pills) creates similar outcomes. Tamblyn (2000) reports that the rates of adherence to prescribed medication among elderly adults varies from 16 to 73 per cent. This non-compliance may be due to forgetfulness or confusion, the complexity of the instructions for taking the medication, difficulty opening the bottles, or an inability to read and understand instructions. Older people are also more likely to hoard or share drugs, or to use drugs beyond the expiry date. Under-use occurs when older adults stop taking a prescribed drug because of side effects or cost, and do not inform their physician.

With increasing age, there are changes in the rate of drug absorption by the body. As a result, older people are more sensitive to some drugs than younger people and may experience more side effects. This requires that the dosage be reduced, or that the drug not be prescribed for older adults. Some drugs should not be prescribed if an older person is already taking another drug for a co-existing disease or condition. These prescribing errors, along with polypharmacy, which happens when physicians over-prescribe, account for 19 to 36 per cent of drug-related hospital admissions (Tamblyn, 2000).

The cost of drugs has become a major issue for consumers, governments, and the insurance companies that fund drug plans for employees. At present, Canada does not have a national pharmacare program, and many lobbyists, on behalf of senior citizens, argue that such a program should be included in the Canada Health Act. Coverage for prescription drugs in Canada involves a mix of private and public coverage, and there is considerable variation between the drug plans of the provinces. There are differences in who is covered, what drugs are covered, whether there is a co-payment, how large the deductible is, and whether there is a maximum amount of coverage per year. There is very little interprovincial portability in drug plans, and that often necessitates a three-month wait for coverage after a person moves to another province.

In total, about $12.3 billion was spent in 2001 on prescription drugs by all Canadians, regardless of age. This represents about 6 per cent of the total spending on health care in the country (Romanow Commission, 2002: 196–7). In 1999, 22 per cent of prescription drug costs were paid by individuals, 44 per cent by public insurance plans, and 34 per cent by private insurance plans (CIHI, 2002a). People 65 years of age and over, who make up only about 12 per cent of the population, receive an estimated 28 to 40 per cent of all prescription drugs (Tamblyn and Perreault, 2000). As drug costs escalate and pharmacare coverage decreases due to rising costs and increased prescribing, some older people are having to reduce or quit their medication because they can no longer afford the cost. This is one driving force behind the attempt to introduce a national pharmacare plan; although such a plan was not recommended by the Romanow Commission on the Future of Health Care (Romanow Commission, 2002: 189–210). However, Romanow did recommend the creation of a 'catastrophic drug transfer' plan to protect people who have excessively high drug costs owing to the critical nature of their illness. This insurance plan would reduce disparities in the level of reimbursement across Canada. The Commission also recommended the creation of a National Drug Agency to evaluate and approve new prescription drugs, evaluate existing drugs, negotiate and contain drug prices, and provide comprehensive and accurate information about prescription drugs and drug usage to the public and to health-care providers.

To ensure safe and effective use of necessary prescription drugs, older adults need more education about their use and compliance; physicians and pharmacists need to communicate with each other about drugs prescribed for and purchased by a specific patient; and the possibility of over-prescribing should be considered if a person makes repeated visits to a physician or pharmacist. As well, relatives and care workers need to monitor drug-taking and general behaviour, and alert the physician about possible adverse effects of a drug or the interaction of two or more drugs, over-prescribing, non-compliance, or possible drug sharing with others.

Use of Health-Care Services

Health care at one time referred to treatment by a doctor in an office or by other health-care workers in an acute-care hospital. Today, there are three interacting levels of service: self-care (described earlier), community and home care (described in Chapter 11), and formal medical care. Our health-care system was designed to be highly accessible to most Canadians, except those living in rural or remote areas, where fewer services were available. Since the mid-1990s, however, regardless of the size of their community, Canadians have been complaining about waiting lists for services and waiting times for elective surgery, appointments with specialists, diagnostic tests, and for a bed on a ward, rather than a stretcher in an emergency department (Chen et al., 2002). To illustrate the level of unmet need for health services, Statistics Canada (*The Daily*, July 15, 2002) reported the results of their Health Services Access Survey: four million Canadians reported a difficulty obtaining routine care, health information, or immediate care for a minor health problem; while 1.4 million encountered a problem getting a diagnostic test, seeing a specialist, or having elective surgery. Among the 1.4 million, 5 per cent said they waited, on average, 26 or more weeks to be assessed by a specialist or to have a sophisticated diagnostic test.

While it is a commonly held belief that aging increases the consumption of all types of health care, this is not supported by statistics. Moore and Rosenberg (1997: 127–34) reported that only 10 per cent of men and women 70 and over and only 12 per cent of women 80 and older spent more than seven days in a hospital in the previous year. Hospital usage is less for those with social support (Penning, 1995), and greater for those who live alone, especially older women. There is also considerable variation in the amount, regularity, and continuity of health care for older adults. Some older people (acute-care patients) have a high amount of use for a short time; some (out-patients) have a low amount of use but for a long period of time; and still others (chronic-care patients) have a high amount of use for a long period of time.

The rate of health-care use by older people is influenced by a variety of factors:

- predisposing, or structural factors (age, gender, beliefs, attitudes, ethnicity)
- enabling factors (presence or absence of a spouse or family, rural or urban place of residence, availability of health-care personnel or facilities)
- need factors (subjective perceptions and objective diagnoses).

Barriers to access include lack of transportation, language and cognitive deficits, and cultural differences (Chipperfield, 1993). Members of some ethnic groups do not seek medical care because of differing cultural beliefs about health care, a lack of knowledge about the availability of services, or the presence of language barriers when they do seek assistance. In addition, health-care personnel may not understand the unique cultural norms, beliefs and values that ethnic groups bring to a health-care centre (see Highlight 12.4). Similarly, elderly people living in remote or rural communities may not seek medical care if they have to travel a long distance to a hospital in another community. Thus, even though universal access to health care is a right and an expectation, some Canadians who are

Highlight 12.4 Multicultural Diversity in Access to and Use of Health-Care Services

In 1988 an in-depth report was produced by the Ontario Advisory Council on Senior Citizens entitled, *Aging Together: An Exploration of Attitudes toward Aging in Multicultural Ontario.* Interviewers learned about the importance of culture in shaping desires and perceptions about health care. The ideas and concerns expressed in this report are magnified even further today because of the large influx of immigrants over the past 15 years from even more diverse cultures. Note that most of the concerns are expressed about doctor-patient relationships.

Barriers are created by a lack of awareness and understanding of their needs among members of the health professions. An Italian woman said that seniors from her community need 'doctors who understand the family situation,' adding that most physicians do not understand 'the special needs of Italian seniors.' Another said that doctors 'don't understand how people of different cultures experience pain.' A South Asian senior said doctors 'don't understand illness with a tropical background.' The discomfort felt by Chinese seniors when asked to disrobe in a physician's office was also noted.

Because physicians are frequently unaware of cultural preferences and norms which contradict western medical practices, older adults from certain ethnic backgrounds are reluctant to consult a North American–trained physician. Many do not understand Ontario's health-care system and the place of physicians in it. Also, many do not fully understand the nature of physician-patient relationships. They should be given a full explanation *in a language they understand.*

Older people from many ethnic groups typically place a great deal of trust in their physicians, whether or not they understand them. One individual said that many Italian seniors 'just say "yes" to an English-speaking doctor because they don't understand.'

When visiting physicians or hospitals, ethnic seniors have difficulty in obtaining both language and cultural interpreters. Family members are often unsuitable, simply because of the personal nature of medical visits. This is especially true when seniors require psychogeriatric services.

One health-care professional said, 'We can't expect ethnocultural seniors to accept North American-trained health-care professionals until they feel we value their ideas, views and traditions and will listen to them.' It is for this reason that many hospitals, primarily in large urban areas, have trained staff available as translators to meet the needs of an increasingly diverse mix of emergency room patients.

Source: Adapted from Ontario Gerontology Association (1989).

most in need are not served adequately or fully by the health-care system.

Mental Health

In later life some loss in the ability to remember and make decisions is normal. These changes, in themselves, are challenging and require coping strategies and social support from others. If, significant or rapid declines in cognitive, behavioural, or emotional functioning occur, they are often the result of disease processes or stressors in daily living. Stressors can be triggered by the loss of physical health, the death of a partner, moving out of the family home, financial difficulties, social isolation and loneliness, or the loss of social support. Or stressors can be long-standing chronic strains, for example, in one's health, finances, or marriage, which become major stressors in later life. Our ability to cope with stress decreases as our strength, energy, and cognitive functioning decline, and when more than one of these events happens at the same time.

An inability to cope with change and stress in later life can lead to mental-health problems. In Canada, the most commonly cited definition of **mental health** states:

> mental health is the capacity of the individual, the group and the environment to interact with one another in ways that promote subjective well-being, the optimal development and use of mental abilities (cognitive, affective, relational), the achievement of individual and collective goals consistent with justice, and the attainment and preservation of conditions of fundamental equality (Health and Welfare Canada, 1988: 7).

A simpler definition is that mental health represents a sense of well-being and control over one's life, and the absence of mental-health problems (mood disorders, anxiety, depression) or medical disorders, including psychiatric symptoms.

A mental-health *problem* is a 'disruption in the interactions between the individual, the group, and the environment and may result from factors associated with the individual (physical or mental illness, inadequate coping skills), or from external factors (unsafe or difficult environment, relationship difficulties with family or friends, structural inequities)' (Health and Welfare Canada, 1988: 7). In contrast, a mental *disorder* is a medically diagnosed illness that 'results in significant impairment of an individual's cognitive, affective and relational abilities' (Health and Welfare Canada, 1988: 8). Mental-health problems and disorders may co-exist, and are often co-morbid with physical health problems.

Public-health policies, personal medical care, and research focus primarily on issues related to the treatment of mental-health problems and disorders. Until recently, little attention has been paid to the promotion of mental health or to the prevention and early detection of mental illness. Yet, there is much that the older person and his or her caregivers can do to encourage and facilitate mental health in later life. Some of these include:

- Engaging in social, physical, and intellectual activities to maintain competence.

- Being connected to others in social networks for social interaction and social support. Social isolation is a risk factor for decreased mental health.

- Maintaining independence and control over one's life through empowerment and decision-making.

- Attending educational programs to learn coping and adapting strategies for normal aging losses and changes.

- Ensuring that older people live in a safe, secure, and familiar environment.

- Providing financial assistance to low-income older people to relieve some uncertainty and stress in daily living.

- Screening periodically for declines in cognitive function.[10]

- Providing support at times of stress and loss—retirement, death of a partner, an acute illness or injury, or moving from the family home.

- Monitoring existing lifelong physical or mental problems that may become more pronounced as normal aging progresses.

- Encouraging older people who present symptoms of mental illness to use mental-health services. Many will not refer themselves because of the stigma associated with mental illness, and many family physicians do not notice signs or symptoms of mental illness during brief visits for physical problems.

Mental health contributes to the quality of life of older people and their caregivers. A failure to prevent, detect early enough, or treat mental health problems or disorders often leads to premature institutionalization. Therefore, strategies to promote mental health among older adults are needed, including through home-care services.[11]

Mental Health Disorders

Most older adults do not experience severe mental disorders, although from 10 to 40 per cent of the older population may have mild to severe cognitive impairment (MacCourt et al., 2002). The most common age-related mental health disorders among the older population are depression, dementia and anxiety, delirium, and delusional disorders. Women tend to have higher rates of mental illness than men, especially depression and the dementias.

Depression

Depression, found in 10 to 20 per cent of the older population, especially after the mid-80s, is a frequent cause of emotional suffering and a decreased quality of life. Symptoms may include a depressed mood and a lack of interest in people and things, feelings of worthlessness, unreasonable feelings of guilt, inability to concentrate or make decisions, fatigue, sleep deprivation, agitation, significant changes in appetite (either a decrease or increase), visible sadness, withdrawal, or reduced energy (Blazer, 2003).

Depression is triggered by multiple concurrent personal losses; lack of social support; living alone; drug interactions; pain; physical illnesses, such as Parkinson's disease, strokes, or cancer; a dementia; the strain of caring for a frail spouse; or the diagnosis of a terminal illness. Outcomes include withdrawal from social interaction, loss of physical and/or cognitive functioning, increased dependence, and suicide (if severe and prolonged, especially among men). If social support and professional care are available and used, depression can be treated, controlled, or eliminated.

Delirium

This common, but reversible, cognitive disorder involves fluctuation in consciousness, an inability to focus, hallucinations, periods of disorientation, and bizarre behaviour at random moments. Among older people delusions about theft and about the infidelity of a partner are common.

Delirium is related to insomnia, the onset and progression of chronic diseases, the onset of either sensory deprivation or sensory overload, bereavement, relocation to a new residence, or drug interactions.

Dementia

Dementia, an organic brain disorder of later life, impairs memory, thinking, and behaviour. It is characterized, as it progresses, by the following severe losses in more than one aspect of the cognitive, emotional, or social abilities:

- cognitive abilities: impairment of short-term memory, comprehension, language, and reasoning

- emotional abilities: unable to express emotions, aggressiveness and shouting

- social abilities: cannot start a conversation, difficulty in planning and making decisions, aggressive or inappropriate or repetitive behaviour, wandering.

These losses interfere with daily functioning and reduce independence and one's quality of life (Burke et al., 2000; Tierney and Charles, 2002). Dementia occurs in 'clear consciousness'—the person is awake and alert. Differentiating between depression and dementia is difficult since a common symptom is memory impairment (Holstein, 1997). Yet, a correct diagnosis is essential to prevent incorrect labelling and to ensure that appropriate treatment is provided.

The most common type of dementia is Alzheimer's disease (AD), a degenerative disease of the brain that begins with the loss of short-term memory and progressively destroys most cognitive functioning.[12] Age-related memory impairment and cognitive impairment are often precursors to AD. But loss of memory capacity alone does not constitute a diagnosis of AD. The rate of progression is unpredictable, and various levels and types of care are required, depending on the symptoms. We must not label all those with memory problems as AD patients, unless the other symptoms emerge and progress. There are no simple tests to confirm a diagnosis of AD. Rather, the only sure diagnosis is by a brain autopsy after death; although expensive magnetic resonance imaging (MRI) of the brain over a period of time can demonstrate changes in the brain structure.

As AD progresses, it may involve personality changes, disorientation (both temporal and spatial), wandering, added confusion at sundown, agitation, hostility, and the loss of self and a core identity (see Case B in Highlight 12.5). This disease destroys the mind of the afflicted person; devastates the family members, especially a primary caregiver (see Case A in Highlight 12.5); and results in increasing and significant demands on the health- and social-care systems. Case A is described by a caregiving son, who also expresses his own frustration and anguish; Case B is seen through the eyes of a partner.[13]

Whereas we celebrate increasing longevity and improvements in treating cancer and heart disease, relatively little progress is being made in the prevention, early detection, or treatment of AD. The disease may not be increasing in frequency, per se, but because more people are living beyond 80 years of age, more people are being diagnosed with AD, and more people are living longer with the symptoms. The actual prevalence of AD is difficult to estimate since only sophisticated technological diagnostic procedures or an autopsy of the brain after death can confirm a diagnosis. It is known that the prevalence is greater among women, and that it increases with age. Estimates of its prevalence range from 5 to 10 per cent of those over 65 years of age and from 20 to 40 per cent for those over 80 (Vinters, 2001). Some projections indicate that the number of older people in Canada with any type of dementia might reach 600,000 by 2021 (Tierney and Charles, 2002).

Highlight 12.5 The Ravages of Alzheimer's Disease

Case A[1]

She lives alone in the family home in a small town where she has lived all her life. She is unable to perform jobs that have sequential tasks associated with them such as meal preparation, house maintenance, and finances. Her short-term memory is very poor. By that I mean she cannot remember things said in the same hour that they're said. She is unable to retain or understand a schedule of visits. She does not know that her meals will be prepared for her or that she'll be visited. The significance is that she doesn't anticipate visits. She will cannibalize frozen foods for whatever is in them that's edible. She doesn't realize that this is strange behaviour. She has a recent history of a cat problem. Currently she has two cats. Last summer one cat bit a neighbor's child. The health department came in, and we were in court. Since then we've taken out about two dozen cats. She's currently under a local court order. She cannot have more than two cats on the premises.

She's very resentful of my brother's, my sister's, and my assumption of responsibility for her. Depending on her mood, she gets angry, yells. We end up having to leave. She's ambulatory—all her physical limbs are fine. Outwardly, she looks okay. She appears to maintain minimal hygiene. If we don't visit her on a regular basis, our experience has been that refuse will build up—just be left lying around. Her medical evaluation stated that she should not be left alone for more than an hour. The stove has been turned off. A microwave is used by caregivers in preparing meals. She does not wander outside the house. Her nocturnal activities are a subject of concern. My sister has spent the night, and there was activity during the night.

continued

Hightlight 12.5 continued

After she was discharged from the hospital a few months ago, we set up a schedule among the three children, plus a local caregiver. She does not like to talk about going to a nursing home. Those two topics, money and where she'll live, create a bad relationship between us. I go to an Alzheimer's support group. That helps. And I have a wonderful wife. Mom resents that I have title to her home, a result of a tax debt seven years ago that she could not satisfy. I emptied the house of all her paperwork, unbeknownst to her. I went through it all, organized it. I saw she no longer had any money. She bounced checks in the summer. She spent a $10,000 gift from her sister over six or seven years. The house was a mess. I began visiting her twice a week and contrived to get her into the hospital. The theme of this whole thing has been deception. I have to lie about what we've done. It does not please me to have to use deception. I feel very sorry for her.

Case B[2]

At age 65, Mr Tom X. retired from a successful careeer as a journalist. Tom hoped to 'sit tight' after years of travel and write a book of reminiscences of his journalistic exploits. For the next six years he enjoyed his retirement and sprinkled his leisure time with an assortment of freelance writing assignments as well as working on his book. However, his wife began to notice slight changes in his personality—her husband whose 'bread and butter' had been a keen memory and tremendous initiative seemed to her to be having difficulty in remembering where he put things, with whom he had spoken and what time it was. He began to make mistakes when paying their bills and making change in stores. He couldn't find the right words for objects. He took longer to do routine things. Gradually he grew worse.

Tom had frequently said, 'I don't want to live a long life if my mind goes.' Cognizant of some of the changes that were taking place, he became at times anxious and at times depressed. He recognized that the considerable body of knowledge he had accumulated and his imagination in which he took pride were crumbling away, but he did his best to fabricate an outer facade to conceal from others the advancing decay beneath.

As his condition worsened, he became less and less aware of what was happening. He became hostile, even assaultive, when his wife tried to feed or dress him. He would wander outside if she did not keep a watchful eye on him. His wife and companion of 40 years, herself suffering from crippling arthritis, was unable to care for him at home any longer, so, with a mixture of shame and regret, admitted him to a nursing home, putting her own financial security at risk. There, he deteriorated rapidly. Incontinent and often reverting to speaking the Norwegian language of his childhood, he eventually could not even recognize himself in the mirror. In the near-final phase he became a 'screamer' and was hopelessly confused. The end stage was coma.

The death certificate read, 'Cause of death, aspiration pneumonia.' But what first killed his mind and then his body was senile dementia of the Alzheimer's type.

[1]Adapted and reproduced with permission of the author from Matthews (2002: 42–4; ISBN 1–58832–067–7). Acquired from Unlimited Publishing LLC, March 2004.
[2]Reproduced with permission from Butler (2003: 2)

Ultimately, 24-hour care may be required, and AD may become the major factor in a decision to move an older person into a residential-care facility. This relocation is necessary for their care and safety, and for the relief of family caregivers who can no longer cope with behavioural problems, such as agitation, verbal or physical aggressiveness, wandering, repetitive behaviour, and incontinence. Some studies report that more than 50 per cent of the residents of long-term care facilities have AD.

Interventions for dementia involve self-care, providing home care, using drugs to calm the person and to slow the process, employing recreational therapy programs at home or in the community, and constantly reassuring the person that they are safe. For caregivers, interventions involve learning about the disease, joining a support group, using respite care, and being trained in nursing and home care skills unique to the care of a person with a dementia (Grossberg and Desai, 2003).

Suicide in Later Life

In most countries, suicide rates increase with age, with males 85 and older being the highest group at risk. In Canada, in 1998, 21 men per 100,000 in the 60–74 age group, 25 per 100,000 in the 75–84 age group, and 31 per 100,000 in the 85 and over group committed suicide. For women the incidence was 5 per 100,000 in all age groups (Langlois and Morrison, 2002). Moreover, men who attempt suicide are more likely to be successful while women are more likely to be unsuccessful and to be hospitalized. Suicide is one outcome of severe depression that is not diagnosed soon enough or treated successfully.

Suicide is not the leading cause of death among older people, but rates are rising as longevity increases. Prevention includes monitoring those who live alone and have recently suffered multiple losses, providing social support, making sure someone is in regular contact by phone or a visit, and encouraging a person who appears depressed to seek professional help. Among the risk factors for suicide are a history of suicide or dysfunction in the family; distressing life events, such as the death of a partner; a feeling of uselessness; an inability to satisfy basic needs to belong or feel safe (Legris and Préville, 2003); alcoholism; living alone and feeling isolated; the availability of a firearm or drugs in the

home; and having a life-threatening or debilitating disease.

Barriers to Mental Health Care

Older adults with mental health problems or disorders are vulnerable people with unique, but often neglected or ignored health-care needs. They present a difficult challenge to society and to their family, especially if they cannot leave the home for treatment. Possible sources of help or service include self-help, peer and family support, home-care services, and the formal primary health-care system. Early screening and diagnosis is essential but this seldom happens. Rather, cognitive difficulties in remembering are attributed to normal aging processes, which they may be, at least initially.

There are a number of barriers to mental health care (Administration on Aging, 2001; Conn, 2002):

- a failure of individuals, partners, or family to refer a person to a mental-health clinic

- inadequate funding for mental-health care versus physical care

- a shortage of trained personnel for geriatric mental-health services

- a shortage of mental-health clinics in a community, especially ones that encourage attendance by older people and that are staffed by psycho-geriatricians

- lack of co-ordination between the primary-care system (physicians and acute-care hospitals) and mental-health and aging service personnel in the community

- a lack of support groups or peer counselling programs for mental illnesses, such as depression and AD

- inadequate treatment for mental-health problems in long-term care facilities

- lack of outreach programs in the community for screening, diagnosis, and intervention

- mis- or over-prescribing of psychotropic drugs, and inadequate monitoring for drug interactions

- a lack of mental-health promotion and prevention

- lack of training and education about mental health for home-care workers and family caregivers

- lack of trained personnel to cope with diverse cultural and ethnic beliefs and practices concerning health care, in general, and mental health care, in particular.

Canada's Health-Care System: Serving Older Adults

The Medicare System

The federal government, which created medicare through the Canada Health Act of 1984, is responsible for health protection, disease prevention, and health promotion; and for health-service delivery to specific groups, namely, veterans, inmates of federal prisons, Aboriginal people living on reserves, and military personnel (Health Canada, 1999b). The management and delivery of health services to all other Canadians is the responsibility of each province and territory.

To be eligible for federal funding, provincial and territorial health-insurance plans must adhere to five criteria (known as 'the principles'). These principles state that health services must be:

- publically administered, on a non-profit basis.

- comprehensive—All 'medically necessary' services provided by hospitals and physicians must be insured, including drugs, supplies, and diagnostic procedures within a hospital; some out-patient services; and chronic-care services, if accommodation

costs are shared by the resident. However, there is considerable provincial and territory variation in access, cost sharing, and the quality of long-term care facilities.

- universal—All eligible residents are insured equally.

- accessible—No additional charges can be applied for insured services, and there must be no discrimination on the basis of age, income, health status, gender, or ethnicity.

- portable—Residents are insured fully when they travel within Canada, and to some extent when they travel abroad; and are fully insured when they move to another province.

Medicare is based extensively on primary-care physicians (general practitioners), who, except for emergency care or walk-in clinics, serve as the primary contact or entry point to the system. Physicians provide access to specialists, prescribed drug therapy, hospital admissions (unless an individual visits an emergency care department of a hospital), and diagnostic testing; and make referrals to other allied health providers. Hospitals, most of which are private, not-for-profit organizations, are managed by community boards, voluntary organizations like charities and religious groups, or local or regional municipal governments. In addition to the insured hospital and physician services, the provinces and territories provide varying levels of supplementary health benefits, including prescription drugs, vision care, assistive devices, and the services of podiatrists and chiropractors for specified groups, such as people 65 and over, children, and welfare recipients. Most supplementary health benefits for the general population are paid for by the individual or by private or employer-sponsored insurance (often with a deductible or a co-payment).

Health care in Canada is a shared responsibility involving the individual, the community, and different levels of government. The key principle is that all Canadians have equal access regardless of their ability to pay. However, since this access is to 'medically necessary' hospital and physician services, the emphasis is on curing acute rather than chronic illnesses, and on treatment rather than on disease prevention, health promotion, community care, or long-term care in later life. Thus, medicare is no longer considered to be a 'health' model. Rather, it is based on a 'medical' model controlled by physicians; it is institution-based versus community-based; and it is a shared federal-provincial-territorial responsibility. This multi-level responsibility can create disputes, as well as the duplication of services and facilities. Moreover, as costs have escalated and budgets have been reduced, the system has become inefficient, with more downloading of responsibilities for care to the individual and family (usually daughters and daughters-in-law).

Another concern is the fragmentation of services in the health-care system. This is seen in the separation of acute care from health promotion; and in a failure to integrate services in the ideal continuum of care from acute hospital and physician care to community social and health care to long-term care. Fragmentation is most evident when the system is serving those who suffer cognitive decline and chronic illnesses in later life. Some of these later life health problems could be addressed through an integrated system of self-care, health promotion, home care, and community care so that a person could be served by the right level of care across the continuum of care, as needed. In the current system, cognitive impairments and mental illnesses tend to receive less attention than physical diseases, especially in the early stages. Fragmentation is seen, as well, when health-care workers in one part of the system do not communicate with other workers in related areas. For example, a hospital discharge planner may not notify the community home-care workers that an older patient is being sent home to recuperate.

Older People in the Health-Care System

How well does the health-care system serve older Canadians? Although constituting about 12 per cent of the population in 2000, persons over 65 accounted for over 50 per cent of the patient days in acute-care hospitals. In general, more older men than women are admitted to hospitals because of their higher incident of heart disease and stroke. The average stay for those 65 and over is 17 days compared to 10 days for the rest of the population. By age 65, a person is 33 per cent more likely to spend time in a hospital than a person 45-64 years of age. And at age 75 and over, the likelihood is 70 per cent higher. People who rate their own health as 'poor' or 'low' visit physicians more often, undergo more medical tests, and are more likely to be hospitalized. Thus, self-rated health is a fairly reliable predictor of health-care use in later life (Menec and Chipperfield, 2001).

Older people experience a form of double jeopardy in health status since *both* physical and mental disabilities and disease are more prevalent in later life. These changes with age have a considerable effect on daily functioning, although losses can be delayed with healthy living at *all* stages of life, and with the provision of a supportive, safe environment. Most studies find that older people do not misuse or make unreasonable use of the health-care system (Rosenberg and James, 2000).

In spite of their growing numbers, there has been a decrease in acute hospital stays among older people in recent years. This may be due to faster recoveries through a greater use of drug and other non-surgical kinds of treatment, more self-care, more day surgery, and an increase in the availability of home care or private care during convalescence. And, during acute-care stays, these patients have to wait longer for help with using the toilet, getting in and out of bed, and eating, and that may encourage patients to return home earlier (Pringle, 1998; Saunders et al., 2001). Moreover, acute-care patients of all ages are being discharged from hospitals much earlier than in the past to create beds for waiting patients. Unfortunately, for older patients an early discharge, especially to the family home without adequate assistance, can increase the risks of falls, malnutrition, and self-medication problems that may lead to a cycle of readmission and eventually longer average stays. This issue illustrates the need for a coordinated and integrated system that provides suitable treatment at the right time; suit-able placement in rehabilitation hospitals, in the home, or in long-term care facilities; and assurance that the necessary informal family and formal community support is available if a patient is discharged to his or her home. Highlight 12.6 describes the inadequacies of equitable, but unsuitable treatment in a hospital. The tragic outcome of this case was due to rationing and rationalization of services and an unreasonable and rigid classification system for prioritizing care.

Highlight 12.6 Inadequate Treatment in a Bureaucratic System

Our health-care system is deteriorating. It is too late for my husband—he died because he did not receive adequate care in the hospital.

My husband went into hospital last January with viral pneumonia. He had many things wrong and it wasn't a lack of specialists looking at him. Rather than looking at the whole person, they just focused on the parts. And they missed the most important part, his pneumonia. His kidneys had stopped and he had a poor heart condition since his angioplasty a year earlier.

We wanted him in the intensive care unit because of his heart and kidney problems. Three years previously, at another hospital, he had been in ICU [the intensive care unit] with a serious bout of pneumonia. My husband had been a doctor there so we knew the staff and we got the care he needed and he recovered. It seems to me that you have to know someone to get adequate care. Unfortunately, we did not know people at the hospital where he died.

The hospital told me that he did not qualify for intensive care according to their new classification system. They have some new tri-level treatment scheme where level 1 patients receive intensive care. My husband was assessed as 'level 2' and placed on a general medical ward. These new standards seem like a way to justify cuts. He was judged not sick enough even though he had a history of heart problems and the kidney specialists were considering dialysis. They told me that my husband did not need intensive care because they had enough staff on the wards. Yet, I saw how understaffed they were. On the night my husband died there were only three nurses for 37 patients, which was not enough.

Over the last two days of his life, his pneumonia worsened. He was really panting for breath. I knew this would strain his heart so I asked if he could not be considered for intensive care and they said no because he didn't 'qualify'. There were only two ICU beds with the kind of life support he needed—one was for cardiac arrest and one was for surgical patients.

They focussed on treating his kidney; but all the while he was panting for breath. The kidney specialists wanted to start my husband on dialysis but the doctor in charge told me that it would be difficult to gain access to dialysis once my husband came home. However, we agreed to that treatment feeling that we would meet the problem of scarcity of dialysis on an outpatient basis when it arrived. He did receive dialysis on the last day of his life.

On the fifth day in the hospital my husband was really in distress, hallucinating for most of the afternoon. That night, the nurses' chart reported that my husband was crying out for help and he

continued

Hightlight 12.6 continued

had pulled off his oxygen mask. They did not monitor him closely. My husband had a cardiac arrest in the middle of the night. When the nurses found him they put out a code blue to get him on resuscitation and life support. Another code blue had been called at the same time and my husband lost the draw. It seems that the hospital could only handle one code blue at a time. I thought that a cardiac arrest victim would have a greater chance of survival in a hospital—not my husband. By the time he was finally placed on life support he was clinically brain dead.

Wouldn't you know it. Now that my husband was clinically brain dead he 'qualified' for the expensive intensive care unit. It wouldn't do him any good but he was in intensive care. It is a really sad commentary on the state of the health-care system that a live patient like my husband in desperate need of life support systems is refused entry into ICU. But once he had the cardiac arrest, even though officially recorded as brain dead and beyond the need of further help, he was readily admitted to ICU. A nurse told me that they had beds available in the surgical intensive care unit in the week leading up to his death but my husband didn't qualify.

My husband was a doctor. We trusted the doctors and administration and I believe our trust was very much misplaced. The two-tiered health-care system is here already. Since my husband's death, I've heard about other people hiring private-duty nurses to watch over people in the hospital because they are so understaffed. Had I received some straight information about my husband's condition I would gladly have paid for a private-duty nurse or had my family come in to sit with him in shifts because there was not enough staff and he was not monitored closely enough.

After my husband's death we were told by the staff that in five years they will have a multi-system intensive care unit and then people like my husband would be able to receive the proper care (all the extra monitoring and life support systems) that he was denied. This was little consolation.

I think they wrote my husband off because he had a number of health problems. With adequate care he beat those problems with his previous illness. This time he simply wasn't given the chance. He died at 68.

Source: Abridged and reprinted with permission from Armstrong and Armstrong (2003: 160–1).

The Cost of Health Care

Health care is financed primarily through federal, provincial, and corporate taxes and individual employees' contributions to insurance plans that provide supplementary health benefits. However, in some provinces, sales taxes, health-care premiums, and lottery sales supplement the revenue generated by taxation. The federal government's contribution to the provinces is transferred, under the Canada Health and Social Transfer (CHST) agreement of 1997, as a combination of cash contributions and tax credits. Figure 12.1 illustrates this complex funding structure.[14]

In 2002 the total expenditure for health care in Canada was an estimated $108 billion (about $3,300 per citizen), of which about 73 per cent (about $2,400 per citizen) was derived from government sources and about 27 per cent from individuals (www.cihi.ca). For the 2001–2 fiscal year, through the CHST agreement, $34.2 billion was transferred to the provinces and territories by the federal government in the form of tax credits and cash contributions. Of the total cost for health care, the federal government contributes about 14 per cent (down from an estimated 40 to 50 per cent in 1977), while the provinces contribute about 86 per cent (www.cihi.ca). About 45 per cent of the current total expenditure of $108 billion is allocated to hospitals, 15 per cent to drug prescriptions, 14 per cent to physician payments, and 5 per cent to home care.

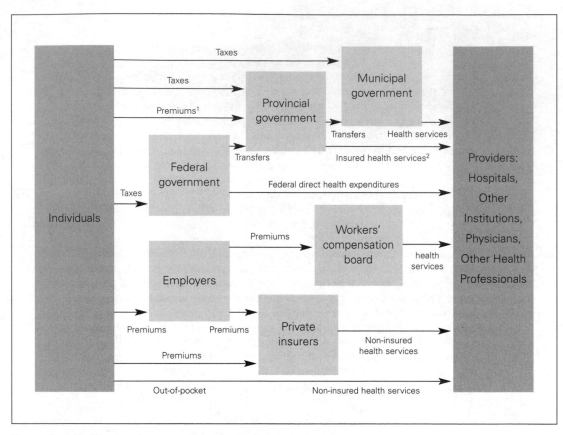

Figure 12.1 The Funding Structure of the Health System in Canada

[1]Two provinces, British Columbia and Alberta, levy health premiums. [2]Medically necessary hospital and physican services

Reprinted with permission from Health Canada (1999b).

Given the rapidly rising costs and recent severe cutbacks in spending and services by hospitals, Canadians are seeking reform and improved services, especially in light of population aging and the expected demand on the system in the near future. At all ages, people who need hospital care, diagnostic tests, or elective surgery are experiencing long waits or postponement of services. Thus it is being asked whether the health-care system is sustainable and whether it will become bankrupt. Those fears have been allayed, and alternative measures have been proposed for coping with the needs of an increasing older population (Carrière, 2000; Evans et al., 2001). Armstrong and Armstrong (2003: 157) state, 'Canadian public spending on health care is not significantly out of line with that of other countries, not out of control, and not disproportionately concentrated in acute-care facilities . . . what is growing disproportionately is drug expenditures.' An interesting statistic is that, in 2002, spending for drugs (15 per cent) exceeded that for doctors (14 per cent). Elderly people should not be viewed as the enemy—after all, we all reach that stage! Rather, elderly people constitute a large, special group with unique needs at a particular point in the life course. Given their increasing numbers, however, over the next 30 to 40 years, they will put extra pressure on the health-care system.

Those who say that health-care costs can be contained and that the system will remain sustainable, argue that we have time to change the system before the baby boomers reach their later years. Moreover, they argue that the boomers will be healthier than previous generations in the early years of later life, and thus a crisis, if it occurs, will be concentrated into a few years when most of the boomers are over 80 years of age—beginning in about 2030. They argue, as well, that on a per capita cost, older people do not create higher health-care costs (Evans et al., 2001). Rather, the costs are rising because of expensive drug therapy and high-tech diagnostic procedures, as well as excessive use of acute-care hospitals to house elderly people with severe chronic illnesses, many of whom are near death. Thus, new policies and practices are needed to reduce drug, diagnostic, and caring costs. Finally, more efficiencies in assessing older people and in centralized record keeping are needed to ensure the needs of the entire person are known and addressed by the many health-care personnel who see the same patient. Some possible reforms are discussed in the next section.

Health-Care Reform and Renewal: Toward a Better Future

Since 2001, inquiries and commissions at both the provincial level of government   (such as the Fyke Commission in Saskatchewan and the Clair Commission in Quebec) and the federal level (Kirby, 2002; Romanow Commission, 2002) have critiqued and analyzed the health-care system and recommended improvements to it. These reports deal with the future health-care needs of all Canadians, but if their recommendations are enacted, they will have a major impact on future cohorts of older Canadians. The impetus for reform stems from a range of issues and problems:

- accountability and the spiralling cost of primary health care and the need to decentralize services and responsibilities away from hospitals;

- an emphasis on quality of life to the end of life, including empowerment, choice, and dignity for the patient;

- reduced accessibility of primary-care services, owing to waiting times for emergency care, for transfer from an emergency ward to an acute-care bed (sometimes as long as three or four days), for surgery, and for personal assistance in hospital;

- too much emphasis on primary health care (the use of doctors and hospital care) and too little on disease prevention, health promotion, and home and community care;

- a shortage of, and high turnover among health-care personnel, including family doctors and specialists; and a shortage of modern diagnostic tools and treatment facilities in many communities;

- a need to fairly, effectively, and efficiently serve all members of the diverse Canadian society, especially Aboriginal people, immigrants, residents of rural and remote regions, and those with lower levels of income and education;

- whether health care is a public or a private responsibility, and in what proportion. The merits, if any, of privatizing health-care[15] services and of imposing user fees must be determined;

- questions about about 'scope of practice' , that is, who should perform which tasks—general practitioners or specialists, doctors or nurse practitioners, nurses or nurse's aids or home-care workers;

- federal-provincial-regional disputes over cost sharing and the devolving of jurisdictional responsibilities;

- whether the Canada Health Act should be expanded beyond the 'medically necessary' criterion to include post-acute and chronic illness care, home care, palliative care, pharmacare, rehabilitation services, counselling for mental illness, and more benefits for those in long-term-care facilities;

- the inflationary cost of drug research and the need to protect against catastrophic (poverty-inducing) prescription drug expenses for individuals. Some individuals may have drug expenses in excess of $5000 a month.

Radical reform threatens doctors and hospital administrators who oppose change. Thus, an evolutionary process is required that will 'build on values' (Romanow Commission, 2002) and result in a new, efficient, and effective system that meets the needs of all Canadians, equitably and promptly. With enhanced health promotion and the adoption of healthy lifestyles, older adults should require fewer health-care services in later life. This can be facilitated by more self-screening and self-care, which is based on increased knowledge, much of which can be obtained on the Internet.[16]

New methods of prevention, cure, and care are needed so that stays in acute care can be shortened for more older people and entry to long-term-care facilities can be delayed. For older people who are having difficulty living in their home, a single access point, such as One Stop Access or a Community Care Access Centre, enables case workers to make a full and co-ordinated assessment of their medical, cognitive, and physical needs, and of home safety and environment issues. Such an assessment ensures that the right kind of assistance is provided at the right time, by the right people. The Romanow Commission (2002: 50–2) recommended that Canadians adopt a health covenant that would:

- state the objectives of a health-care system for the public, patients and health- care providers

- inform, educate and support better decision making within the health-care system

- serve as a common foundation for collaboration among governments, the public and health-care providers and managers.

Over the next five to ten years there will be many debates about health reform. As concerned citizens, you must become involved in these debates. Your future quality of life is at stake, as well as that of your parents and other members of your current or future extended family.

End of the Life Course: Dying Well, with Dignity

Our last chapter in the life course is concerned with facing and coping with death, and managing the process of dying with dignity and with as little pain and suffering as possible. Very few people die suddenly from a stroke, heart attack, or accident. Rather, most older people die over a period of time that may range from a few months to a few years. Dying, like birth, marriage, or retirement, is a life-course transition where cultural values and practices, and interactions with others, are important elements. This final transition in the life course is a biological, psychological, and social process that takes place in a cultural context as health and quality of life begin to decline, often quite rapidly.

Just as the quality of life in later life is important, so too is the quality of dying. As more older people suffer from a degenerative chronic illness or live longer with frailty, more older adults are being kept alive through the use of technology and medication. Presented with a severe chronic illness, frailty, and the accompanying failure of major body organs or systems, the health-care system has the capacity and the mission to prolong life. Or, from another perspective, it also has the capacity to prolong the process of dying. Consequently, at some point, individuals and their family may question whether they are 'living a good life' or 'dying a bad death' and whether the focus should shift from 'curing' to 'caring'. Living and dying well requires open communication about death, emotional support, informed choice about treatment, as much personal control as possible, and the maintenance of personal dignity (Fisher et al., 2000).

Dying is primarily a later-life event: people 65 and over account for about 80 per cent of all the deaths in Canada every year. Some deaths take place fairly quickly, but many are slow and often include prolonged physical, cognitive, and emotional pain and suffering. In addition to concerns about the quality of care, and how to provide care as death approaches, the following questions are being debated:

- Where should end-of-life care be provided— in a hospital, at home, or in special facilities?

- When should there be a transition from 'cure' (living well) to 'care' (dying well), and who should make such decisions, and on what basis?

- Do individuals have the right to die when, how, and where they choose?

- Who has a legal and moral responsibility to make decisions for an incapacitated dying person to ensure a good death?

- Should euthanasia and assisted suicide be permitted?

- How can the last chapter in the life course be completed with dignity and as much personal control as possible?

- For those on total life-support systems, when does death occur?[17]

The Social Context of Death and Dying

Unless death is sudden, as in an accident, stroke, or heart attack, most people die over a period of time, in a social setting. This setting involves interactions, positive and negative, with family, friends, and health and social-service workers. Just as many older people prefer to age in place at home, many also prefer to die at home.

In reality, however, most older people end their life journey in a hospital or long-term-care facility, a process that is a very expensive for the state, and often for the individual and the family. Many hospital beds are occupied by older people who are dying. Wilson (2002: 391) estimated that if 71 per cent of the expected 225,000 deaths in 2002 took place in an acute-care hospital after an average stay of 21 days or longer, then every hospital bed in Canada would be used at least one month a year for end-of-life care. Statistics like those are used to argue for more end-of-life care at home or in long-term-care facilities. Consequently, new models and practices for end-of-life care are being proposed. The proposals include palliative care in other than primary health-care facilities, support systems or groups for family and paid care givers, and sensitivity in the type of care provided to account for cultural and religious diversity associated with dying and death among Canadians. These practices try to account for diversity in the meaning and alleviation of pain; in who has the right to make health-care decisions; in dietary requirements; and in practices such as the withdrawal or withholding of treatment.

Dying, as a social process, involves the individual, who is striving for a good exit and a dignified death; professional health and social care workers; and family and friends who provide support, make decisions, and begin to mourn the impending loss of a loved one. Dying and death, for most, is a family experience. Family members are involved in caregiving; in making decisions about health care, financial matters, and the care and support of the other parent; and in arranging a funeral. Such responsibilities have the potential to create either conflict or harmony among siblings (Matthews, 2002), and to bring economic hardship to one or more generations if a death is long and expensive (Wilkinson and Lynn, 2001).

Today, more than in the past, more older adults understand, and are ready to talk about, the process of dying. They express concerns about pain, losing self-control, becoming a burden to others and to society, and wanting to control when and how they die. With increased longevity and more chronic illness, many people fear that they will spend their last days, months, or years living in a totally dependent, painful, confused, or comatose state. If this happens, communication and social relationships cease, and the social value of continuing to live is questioned. These concerns are magnified if dying is prolonged through the use of medical technology, and when options for a quicker death are known, and perhaps available.

Regardless of whether an individual dies in an institution or at home, an increasing number of older adults express a wish to experience a 'good exit' for themselves and their survivors, especially a spouse. They do not want to be neglected or abandoned, yet they do not want to become a burden to others. Consequently, an increasing number of people state, through advance directives, how they would like to die, and more people are planning their own funerals and how they wish to be remembered and honoured after they die. This planning consists of organizing their personal matters, reflecting on their life and perhaps writing their own obituary, and discussing what kind of medical care they want when they are dying and whether they want to die at home or in an institution. Highlight 12.7 presents the reflections of an 82-year-old man who spent his last days, not regretting or fearing death, but reviewing his life so that he could pass on wisdom that might make life better for others.

Advance Directives: Protecting Dependent Older People

A major issue in end-of-life care is the need to protect the legal rights of older people who are

---

Highlight 12.7 If I Had My Life to Live Over . . .

An 82-year-old man expressed the following thoughts as he neared, and accepted death.

If I had my life to live over . . .

I'd try to make more mistakes next time. I would relax, I would limber up. I would be crazier than I've been this trip. I know very few things I'd take seriously anymore. I would take more chances, I would take more trips. I would scale more mountains, I would swim more rivers. And I would watch more sunsets. I would eat more ice cream and fewer beans. I would have more actual troubles and fewer imaginary ones. You see . . . I was one of those people who lived prophylactically and sensibly and sanely, hour after hour and day after day. Oh, I've had my moments, and if I had it to do all over again, I'd have many more of them. In fact, I'd try not to have anything else, just moments, one after another, instead of living so many years ahead of my day. I've been one of those people who never went anywhere without a thermometer, a hot water bottle, a gargle, a raincoat and a parachute. If I had to do it all over again, I'd travel lighter, much lighter than I have. I would start barefoot earlier in the spring, and stay that way later in the fall. And I would ride more merry-go-rounds, and catch more gold rings, and greet more people, and pick more flowers, and dance more often. . . . If I had it to do all over again, but you see, I don't.

Source: Reprinted from a submission in 1999 to http://seniors-site.com.

unable to make decisions about living or dying.[18] The ability to prolong life, along with changing social values about death and dying, means that more people are seeking to protect their autonomy and right to choose. They express their preferences, in advance, about treatments, such as the use of life-support systems, tube feeding and resuscitation, and about how and when to die. Without a written document expressing the wishes of an individual, who can make such decisions becomes a legal and ethical issue. These decisions are particularly complex if a person is comatose or mentally incapacitated, and his or her wishes were not previously known. While a verbal expression of personal wishes might provide a clue, it has no legal status.

Advance directives written by lawyers, duly witnessed, and signed by an individual are legal documents about preferences for medical and personal care if, at any time in the future, they cannot speak for themselves. Thus, they enable incapacitated people to control their destiny. These documents can be amended or revoked at any time as long as the person remains mentally competent. Family doctors should have a copy in the patient's file because adult children may not be present or able to make a decision, if needed.

The subject of advance directives is usually introduced by a lawyer at the time a will is prepared or revised. Seldom are adult children involved in such discussions, and even a partner may not know his or her partner's wishes (Rosnick and Reynolds, 2003). People most likely to prepare an advance directive are those who have higher levels of income and education; who are taking more prescription drugs and are therefore more aware of their declining health; and who have experienced such events as the prolonged death of a friend or relative (Rosnick and Reynolds, 2003).

A Living Will

This document expresses, in writing, personal wishes about medical treatment to be provided or withdrawn in the event of a terminal illness or an accident where they are comatose or mentally incompetent. Organ donations can be authorized, as well, if the person dies in a hospital. A major problem with living wills is that they are usually not available in an emergency, and therefore they cannot be invoked until they are produced by a member of the family. Moreover, doctors are free to ignore the document in the interest of saving a life.

Power of Attorney

Older adults are protected better by assigning power of attorney to someone they trust who can make decisions on their behalf, if the need arises. A 'durable' power of attorney authorizes an agent (usually the spouse or one or more children) to act on behalf of an individual with regard to property, such as selling a home, or financial matters. A 'medical' or 'health-care' power of attorney authorizes an agent to make decisions about medical care for a person who is incapable of making such decisions. These decisions in later life usually involve whether or not to resuscitate, whether to move a person to a long-term-care facility, or whether a high-risk medical procedure should be undertaken.

A power of attorney allows more decisions by someone else than is possible with a living will. For example, a living will is of little use in determining where a severely impaired AD patient should live, whether an investment portfolio should be restructured or sold, what doctors should be visited, or what treatments should be attempted. A medical power of attorney gives an agent the legal authority to deal with all those matters, and more, as needed. Thus, ideally, an older person and his or her designated power of attorney should have a detailed discussion about his or her wishes about life support, major surgery, tube feeding, do-not-resuscitate orders, dialysis, and tolerance of pain. Questionnaires are available that can help to ensure that most situations that may arise have been included in the power of attorney.[19]

Guardianship

In Chapter 11 we learned about guardianship in cases of neglect and abuse. In the absence of living wills or 'durable' or 'medical' powers of attorney, a court order assigning guardianship to one or more people (inside or outside the family or the Public Guardian) may be necessary if an older person without relatives is unable to make decisions about personal care or financial matters. Or guardianship may be necessary if a family member with power of attorney is accused by others of not acting in the best interest of an individual.

The Right-to-Die: Euthanasia and Assisted Suicide

In primitive societies, communities often had formal or informal customs about when and how older members died if they were ill or no longer able to contribute or keep up as a nomadic tribe moved forward. Older people might be abandoned or killed, or they might leave the group on their own to enter the next world. Today, end-of-life issues are being raised by those who argue that health-care resources should be rationed and not 'wasted' on older people; by enlightened older adults who seek the right to die with dignity at a time and place of their choosing; and by advocacy groups on behalf of frail elderly people. Euthanasia and assisted suicide are hotly debated topics, and many complex legal, ethical, medical, religious, or philosophical arguments have been made for or against such procedures.[20] In Canada, euthanasia and assisted suicide are illegal,[21] but they have been legalized in other places, notably Oregon and the Netherlands.

In ancient Greece, euthanasia meant a 'good' death. Today, people are discussing the merits and advantages of a 'good' versus a 'bad' death, and whether an individual, or his or her delegate, has the right to choose the time and manner of death. Such a decision is taken to improve the quality of death when quality of life is lost because of pain or from being bed-ridden, comatose, or mentally incapacitated. *Passive* euthanasia allows death to occur by withdrawing treatment, such as drugs or life support, while providing medication to relieve pain. Or the family or health-care workers may ignore a patient's refusal to eat or take medication. *Active* euthanasia causes death by refusing to continue treatment, by requesting a discharge from a hospital to die at home, or by taking an overdose of drugs.

Assisted suicide is active euthanasia with the assistance of a physician who provides a lethal injection, or provides medication, knowing it will be used to cause death. Labelled as either a compassionate act or legalized murder, depending on one's views, euthanasia has been legally possible in Oregon since the passage of the Death with Dignity Act in 1997. The Act contains rigid guidelines for all parties involved in the decision and act. After the passage of this Act, the Supreme Court of the United States ruled that physician-assisted suicide for terminally ill patients is not a constitutional right. Since then, there have been test cases in other states every few years. Opponents argue that there is an important difference between refusing life-sustaining medical treatment and obtaining a lethal dose of medication. They argue that if the right is upheld, patients could lose the right to refuse treatment, and refusing treatment is not the same as hastening death with a lethal dose of medication (a physician-assisted suicide). Other opponents argue that dying patients are not receiving the care they need, and if good palliative care were available, physician-assisted suicide would no longer be necessary.

In the Netherlands, there were over 3,000 cases of euthanasia each year for over 20 years, all illegal but without sanctions. However, in April 2001 euthanasia was legalized in the Netherlands, as long as the person or their delegate consults at least two physicians, with both attesting that no reasonable alternatives are available to improve the quality of life. Many residents of the Netherlands carry 'euthanasia' passports, which request assistance with suicide if specified medical conditions arise.

The practice of euthanasia raises many difficult moral and ethical questions: Should euthanasia or assisted suicide be available to anyone at any time or only for those in certain age groups? Should it be available only for a terminal illness and only when the quality of life deteriorates beyond a defined point? Should it be used only for physical but not for mental illnesses? Who should be involved in the decision to end a life—the individual, the family, a guardian, a physician, a religious figure? These complex issues must be resolved before the practice is likely to be debated or legalized in Canada. Highlight 12.8 presents a compelling argument against making too hasty a decision to end a person's life.

Palliative Care

Palliative care, sometimes called hospice care, is designed for those with a terminal illness who need relief from pain and other symptoms such as loss of appetite, nausea, incontinence, and

---

Highlight 12.8 The Right to Die . . . Slowly

About three years ago, my mother began her journey to death; she completed it just over three weeks ago. Along the way there was occasional pain, increasing dependence, and frequent frustration. Some bad falls broke bones, toxins briefly but periodically robbed her of her mind and her muscles, and for the last few months we lived in a state of perpetual crisis.

This may not sound like quality of life, but the details I've just given, only a fraction of what she endured, were most emphatically not what stood out during these past three years. These facts did not determine how she—or we—saw her life. She chose to gauge the quality of her existence by the joy she found every day in her interaction with others. With a few well-chosen words, she could dissolve my teenaged daughter into giggles; on Christmas mornings she was the most delightful kid in the house as she ripped the paper off her presents, or smiled impishly as we opened the surprises she had engineered for each of us. She spent three years dying as she had always lived, with a zest for life that filled all around her with wonder that such a frail shell could house a spirit so blithely defiant of the very idea of surrender.

At a robust 70, Mom had been plunged into her three-year death with a sudden coma brought on by inexplicable liver failure. Some medical staff suggested that the kindest response to this crisis would be to do nothing, allowing the coma to become her final sleep. Luckily her wonderful family doctor knew that she was as feisty an old lady as she was a sick one, and he persuaded others to give her a chance with 48 hours of concentrated but fairly simple treatment. When her worsening condition made even that compromise seem a waste, she was left to draw her last breath. Three days later she woke up cracking jokes, and laughed her way into the hearts of all who encountered her for the next three years.

The miracle of that recovery (recorded as such on her medical chart) led to a three-year celebration of life in the shadow of death; as various scientific tests chronicled the gradual cessation of crucial parts of my mother's system, she continued to laugh and shop. Even being in the hospital for the last few weeks of her life could not prevent her from living her death just as she had her life.

She teased her doctors about their good looks, joked with her student nurses about taking them on a cruise, and was as interested in the hairdresser who came to her bedside as in the medical staff trying futilely to find a viable vein for a transfusion.

She entered what seemed final unconsciousness on a Wednesday afternoon. Nearly 12 hours later, with every laboured breath still expected to be the last, her minister began his final prayers for

continued

Hightlight 12.8 continued

her. In the still of the night, my mother's little voice suddenly joined his, apparently an unconscious reflex, but as he made the sign of the cross on her forehead, she bolted upright and asked me urgently, 'Am I dying? I knew I was sick, but I didn't think I was that sick! I'm not going.'

Overcoming my astonishment, I tried to speak to her honestly but reassuringly, admitting that she was indeed very sick, but agreeing that she had surprised the doctors before. That Thursday morning, from 1 a.m. until 5 a.m., she talked with my sister and me, determinedly repeating things like, 'I've been this sick before and I fought it, and I'm going to fight it again. I know it's going to be tougher this time—I can feel that—but I've got the boxing gloves on and I'm not going to give in. Now, girls, I'll need your help just like before, and I'll need the help of my doctor, and especially of the good Lord above, but I'm going to do it.'

After four hours of talking and singing along with tapes playing softly in the background, Mom asked me for a light sedative that would not, in her words, be 'so heavy that I can't fight my way back from it.' Part of her was obviously fighting the medication even as she wanted its relief, because she did not fall asleep until almost 9 o'clock on Thursday morning.

For the next 33 hours Mom was once again comatose. Her dedicated doctor checked her as usual about 4:30 p.m. Friday, careful to take his leave of her 'until tomorrow'. A few minutes later, the end came, but not with my mother's collusion. Without any change of expression, a little tear welled out of one eye, and we knew that she was fully conscious of being at the end of her journey. We then saw the effort of love focus her eyes as she looked at us and grieved that she would have to leave. Then that incredible little face screwed itself up into the determined boxing-glove look we knew so well: slowly and deliberately she told my sister to get the doctor as she had in so many past crises. My sister ran to fetch him, despite the obvious futility. As I stroked Mom's face and soothed her, the pulse in her neck made one final little leap of protest, and the light went out of her eyes.

Every one of us is an individual, and every death will be individual, too. Ever since my mother's initial illness I have been sensitive to what seems to me to be a dominant note in the 'right to die with dignity' debate. I believe that all patients should be free to make choices about the treatment they wish to receive or reject, but I also worry that some members of the medical staff and the general public interpret this as meaning that all dying is undignified and should be concluded as swiftly as possible.

Whether that decision is based on a compassionate wish to end suffering or on an economic judgement to conserve resources, we have no right to choose the pace of another's death. My mother lived her death for nearly three years, and in that time her love of life never faltered. Her experiences were heart-rending for those around her, but none of us have the right to try to lessen our pain by speeding another along the final path. Mom died slowly, but she died well; she made the choice not to 'go gently into that good night.'

Our society must be careful not to assume that everyone means a quick, quiet death when they speak of 'dying with dignity'.

Source: Adapted from 'A Celebration to the End' (*Globe and Mail*, 16 July, 1997). Written by Professor Diana Austin, University of New Brunswick, dedicated to her mother, Madeline Austin, and reprinted with the permission of Professor Austin.

breathing difficulties. The goal is to improve the *quality* not the quantity of life through physical, social, emotional, and spiritual support, and through education and training of caregivers. This care is available in a limited number of beds in acute-care hospitals, in nursing homes, in the person's home, or in hospices, which are separate buildings used only for this purpose.[22] To date, most palliative care facilities are dedicated to those dying of cancer or AIDS, and there is little space for or attention to older people with dementias or chronic degenerative disease.

The hospice movement was founded in 1967 in London, England, by Dame Cicely Saunders. Saunders established St Christopher's Hospice as a care centre for those dying from a terminal illness, as a research centre about caring for dying patients, and as a source of education and support for families during the dying and bereavement stages. The first hospice in Canada was established in 1975 at the Royal Victoria Hospital in Montreal, but at present, there are few hospices in Canada.

The hospice movement is a philosophy as much as it is a facility. It represents a 'death with dignity' approach to caring and provides an array of services when further hospital treatment is no longer possible for those with a terminal illness. Services and education are provided to the dying person's family. No aggressive life-saving devices or procedures are used, but efforts are made to alleviate the patient's pain. Volunteers provide help with nursing, homemaking chores, and emotional support. They also provide information and understanding through discussions about death with both the dying person and his or her immediate family. Often the hospice program is linked with widow-to-widow support programs that help women adapt to life without a spouse.

A major difficulty with palliative care is that it is unclear who should cover the cost of medication, care workers, and medical supplies and equipment if care is provided *outside* a hospital. In long-term-care settings, only some of these costs are fully absorbed by the facility. In some provinces, the costs of palliative care at home are reimbursed through the provincial health plan as part of home care or as a separate program. For example, in February 2001, the British Columbia Ministry of Health introduced the Palliative Care Benefits program. A doctor, in consultation with the patient and family, decides whether a hospital or home is the right place to live when life expectancy is six months or less. A palliative performance scale is used by physicians to assess patients. Anyone with a score of 50 or less (on a scale of 100) qualifies for prescription and non-prescription drugs, supplies, and equipment that helps to improve the quality of life of those who choose to end their life at home. At the federal level, the Romanow Commission (2002) recommended that the Canada Health Act be expanded to include palliative home-care services in the last six months of life.

Death, Bereavement, and Cultural Rituals

Death is a biological state. But the meaning of death is socially constructed in different cultural contexts, as is the coping by family and friends through bereavement, and the rituals associated with burial, and with honouring and remembering deceased relatives and friends.

Death

Social values, beliefs and practices concerning death and dying are changing. There is more open discussion about, and acceptance of, death; more advance directives are written; more palliative care is provided; more decisions are being made not to delay or impede death; there is more emphasis on managing a 'good and dignified death'; there is increasing support for the right to die through euthanasia or assisted suicide; death ceremonies and rituals are viewed more as a celebration of life; and more bodies are cremated.

The rituals, meanings, attitudes, fears, denials, unknowns, realities, and processes associated with death and dying are complex and diverse,[23] and it is beyond the scope of this book to discuss them in detail. Most universities and colleges offer courses, or sections within courses, on death and dying from a particular disciplinary perspective, or using an inter-disciplinary approach.[24]

Just as there are individual differences in the way people live, so too are there differences in beliefs and practices concerning death. First, individual differences in personality and cognitive abilities influence how a person approaches and copes with dying. There are individual differences in coping skills, cognitive competence, understanding and acceptance of death, in the will to live, and in pain tolerance. Second, the type and amount of emotional support given to a dying person by his or her family influences whether he or she dies well and with dignity. And third, there are socio-cultural differences in how members of social groups manage the dying process, and in how they honour deceased persons. Death rituals change as new ways of thinking about death are introduced into a society, subculture, or religion. Often, religious and cultural beliefs and practices interact or co-exist, as in the case of Catholicism and Hispanic culture. Such interactions have a direct influence on bereavement practices; on whether and how end-of-life decisions are made, or not made (Braun et al., 2001; Leichtententritt and Rettig, 2001); and on the type of ceremony to honour and bury a relative.

Bereavement: Mourning and Grief Management

No one is ever fully prepared for the death of a partner, parent, or sibling, whether death is sudden or has been a long-term process. Bereavement is the objective state of having lost a significant other and of coping with a death. Consequently, the days following a death involve grief, an emotional reaction, which can be expressed through shock, numbness, vulnerability, and depression. A grief response involves expressing feelings for a deceased person, as well as a recognition of the social loss and vacuum created by his or her death. A partner is left alone; and a son or daughter becomes an orphan when the last parent dies. The death of the last parent makes adult children realize they will be the next generation to die. The grief period raises thoughts and questions about the reality of death and the meaning of life, and it offers a period in which to reflect and to learn about oneself and others.

The mourning period, during which grief is expressed, involves short-term decisions about religious and cultural rituals—a public or private service; a funeral or a memorial service; internment in a casket or cremation; flowers or charitable donations; a small reception or a wake; and about personal behaviour—such as what to wear for a service, the amount of social interaction and with whom. Mourning is both an individual and a cultural matter. This period is somewhat easier if the deceased openly discussed his or her wishes with partners and family, and if pre-planned funeral arrangements were made, including: payment for a plot, and a casket or urn; the format of the service; and even the writing of an obituary.

Grief management is a longer process for survivors, especially for an intimate elderly partner. Even if a partner was severely ill for months or years, and some anticipatory grieving occurred before the death, the grieving process often endures for six to twelve months or more after the death of a loved one. A surviving spouse may experience loneliness, depression, and an inability to function, and some are at risk for suicide in the grieving period and beyond.

The grieving process involves three stages (Morgan, 1994). The initial stage includes feelings such as shock, disbelief, guilt, depression, denial, loneliness, sleeplessness, and anxiety about the future. The second stage can involve emotional instability, such as anger or loss of motivation; health problems; social withdrawal; and an inability to make decisions. The third stage includes a period of resolution and acceptance, and involvement in new activities and relationships. Throughout these stages, and depending on the form and severity of grieving, social support, counselling, and medication may be needed, especially during the first six months, which are the most difficult. Bereavement support groups, for example hospice volunteers and widow-to-widow volunteers, create a sense of community and support with others who understand or who have experienced a similar loss of a loved one. Support groups prevent isolation and loneliness from becoming a way of life, they monitor physical and mental health, and they help a widowed person adjust to life as a single person.

Death Rituals and Ceremonies

Death rituals and ceremonies are managed by the funeral home industry.[25] Regardless of the type of funeral selected, a funeral home must be involved in the burial of human remains. The cost of a funeral for the service, an administration fee and a casket or urn, plus a burial plot, can range from about $3,000 to over $20,000. If a death is sudden, and services and a plot have not already been arranged for, survivors who are emotionally vulnerable may not make rational decisions about the purchase of funeral services. If a public funeral service is held, those who cannot attend often can participate in the ceremony through an online web broadcast (see www.benjamins.ca).

To honour a deceased person, a death announcement, or obituary, is placed in newspapers or on the web. Obituaries range from serious, short, factual statements about the person and his or her survivors to lengthy narratives about lifetime achievements and interests. Sometimes humour is included to express the deceased person's personality, foibles, or zest for life. Obituaries are part of the grieving process and help to define the individual and his or her place in the world.[26] Long obituaries may be written as a kind of public eulogy. Highlight 12.9 illustrates that some dying people write their own obituary as a final public statement to their family, friends, and colleagues.

Highlight 12.9 A Self-Written Obituary

John Ross Cuthbert (August 29, 1952 – November 24, 1999)

My Friends

Forgive me for leaving the party early. I have chosen not to have a standard funeral or a formal viewing because these would not be happy events—and I insist on leaving this world the same way I have tried to live in it—with smiles, joy and goodwill.

My death is sad but not tragic because I have had a rich life. I have laughed, cried, loved and been loved, enjoyed the company of friends and lived life to the fullest extent that I could. I have lived longer than expected and survived against the odds to find romance, love, and above all, to witness the birth and development of my two little miracles—Brittany and Yardley. Who would have believed it possible 30 years ago?

I have treasured the many and varied friends I have had at my side throughout my journey. There are no words to express my gratitude, to repay you for all the love and comradeship, the support given so freely—no words to even say a proper 'thanks' just for being a friend. I will miss you. But I have had yet another gift lately—the time to visit, call or talk to as many of my friends and family as possible. Let these happy contacts serve as my goodbyes to you all.

My family will be saying goodbye to me privately on the Scarborough Bluffs—one of our favourite places to be together, to walk and find peace. Please remember me in a similar fashion. Remember the good times, the laughs we had, the special times we all shared. No greater tribute could I request.

I leave asking but one last favour. Cathy, Brittany and Yardley will be beyond my protection and I will be unable to supply the hugs and kisses that they all need. Please remember them and love them as you would your own family—they will need good friends at every step of their life's journey.

My love to you all—may you walk life's journey in good health, with friends at your side and a smile on your face.

Ross Cuthbert

November 1999

Source: The *Globe and Mail*, November 1999.

Eulogies, delivered at funerals and memorial services by a friend or relative, are a public expression of how much, and in what way, a deceased person has meant to those who knew the person well, and to the world. Increasingly, these oral statements at funeral services are being expanded into published statements shared with a wider public who never knew the deceased person. Through newspaper columns, such as 'Lives Lived' in the *Globe and Mail* and statements published on funeral home websites, friends and relatives honour the person by expressing, in public, their love and respect for the deceased person. Highlight 12.10 describes poignantly a daughter's love for her deceased father.

Although less common today, with more people being cremated and remembered by a small plaque in the ground, gravestones can record permanent

---

Highlight 12.10 Yellow Pencils and a Daughter's Love

He was young, slim, fleet-footed, cheerful and to my nine-year-old eyes and sensibilities, the handsomest, smartest and best of all fathers.

He never raised his voice to me and he never scolded me. He sneaked Hershey bars and quarters into my hand when my mother wasn't looking and gave me one of his lamb chops when I had finished mine. Ignoring my mother's protestations, he bought me an oversized doll house with electric lamps and tiny oriental rugs as well as the dolls to go with it. He told me the entire world would always be mine and said I was one in a million. His was the last kiss each night.

He changed jobs and travelled three weeks out of each month, selling fancy dining and bath linens to stores hundreds of kilometres away. We didn't have a phone. Communication was by letters to my mother and funny greeting cards to me, addressed to 'My one-in-a-million girl.'

I languished during those first three weeks with my mother, a woman of solemn nature. The house was stagnant. His return brought exuberance and laughter into my life once more. But then he would be gone again.

In the top drawer of my mother's bureau was a shoe box filled with yellow pencils, some sharpened, others not. There must have been more than 50 of them. I don't know why. After my father drove off on his trips, I took the shoe box out of the drawer and emptied the pencils onto the floor. I lined them up side by side in two columns and whispered to them that they were to march or halt or turn around. I changed and reversed the order several times. I repeated this ritual only on the mornings when he left for a trip. I couldn't control reality so I created my own.

At 13, I was madly in love with him. He was Tyrone Power, Alan Ladd and Robert Taylor rolled into one being. The churning within me was not overtly sexual; it was simply bliss to be in this man's presence; and yes, his looks and physique did thrill me. He had a habit of not wearing a shirt or undershirt in the house. I loved his smooth hairless chest and arms and would reach out to touch him. One day, he pushed me away and gave me a stern look. Once I leaned my head on his bare chest and again he pushed me away. There were no words.

At 14, I was summoned to the school office and learned that my father had been in an automobile accident. I was to meet my mother at the hospital. On the bus, I told myself that he had been just slightly bruised and that it wasn't serious. I was wrong. His body was bloody and broken and he was unconscious. My screams reverberated through the hospital's walls. Two weeks later, a subdued and seemingly older man returned home to us.

He was still gregarious, but now had a short temper. I would be admonished by him almost daily. Soon I began to keep my distance from him and dislike him intensely. A strained and distant

continued

Hightlight 12.10 continued

relationship prevailed over the years, eroding into perfunctory long-distance phone calls when I married and moved away.

Before my wedding he told my husband-to-be to take good care of me because I was 'one in a million'. It had been several years since he had said those words. I realized how much I had missed hearing them.

When my mother was dying of cancer, I marvelled over his care for her: He had arranged for a paid leave from work so he could spend each full day with her in her hospital room, taking over many of the nurses' duties including cleaning her colostomy bag. He told the nurses that I was one in a million. I kept my arm around his shoulders at her funeral.

A year later he brought his new wife to us. He appeared to be happy and I didn't begrudge him his new life, partly because now I could discard the guilt I carried about not inviting him to live with us.

He made a fuss over my sons and they loved him but he ridiculed them about their Beatles hair cut. Nothing I could say would put an end to his assaults. I was grateful that we lived in separate parts of the country, preventing him from experiencing my eldest son's Tiny Tim phase.

After my divorce, the boys and I visited my father and his wife, making the mistake of staying in their apartment. Dinners out were at 4:30 p.m. and by the end of each meal, he had found a reason to tell the waiter to go to hell; he had also attacked my sons' taste in music, the way they dressed, the food they ordered, my failure at marriage and my lifestyle. There were no subsequent visits. We spoke a couple of times a month by phone, neither having much to communicate; it was usually just a check-in call.

One day his wife called and said he was in the hospital dying. I flew to him. What I saw was the remnants of a man. His mouth was a hollow cave whose dentures had been lost and he had a terrifying stare. He turned to me and whispered, 'Miss, why are those people up there above me? They might fall on me.' I answered, 'Daddy, it's me.' He said, 'Miss, please help me. Who are they?' I asked him what they were doing. He said they were dancing. I said, 'Yes, they are and they will not fall on you. Watch them dance. Look how beautiful the ladies' dresses are. Listen to how lovely the waltz music is. They are dancing just for you. Let's watch them together.' I sat on the bed, held his hand, hummed *The Merry Widow Waltz* and we watched until he was gone.

On the ceiling I saw a lonely and very sad little girl emptying a shoe box filled with yellow pencils onto the floor.

Source: Reprinted with permission of the author (Ginger Howard Friedman) and the *Globe and Mail*, 28 July 1998, A22.

thoughts of the deceased, or their loved ones, that express values, and the uniqueness of a person beyond basic chronological facts. A walk through a cemetery, especially those with markers from earlier centuries, reveals such thoughts and reflections. To illustrate, a grave marker in the original cemetery in Aspen, Colorado, offered this reflective thought by a deceased person: To enter the highlands of the mind, into the mountains I must go.

Summary

Physical and mental health, and issues pertaining to death and dying, are major concerns as people move into the later years. Health in early and middle life is related to health and functional independence in later life. Clearly, health is determined by more than biology and heredity. Our place in the social structure influences the onset of both acute and chronic illnesses. Chronic illnesses and mental health disorders are major factors influencing the quality of life in later life. Mental health disorders are the hidden enemy in the health of many older adults. They are often undiagnosed or misdiagnosed, especially depression, and older people are seldom referred to mental-health professionals and seldom actively seek such help. The dementias, especially Alzheimer's disease, are not well understood or treated, their prevalence is growing, and they are devastating for individuals and family caregivers.

Our health-care system is not broken, but it is under severe stress, not because of population aging, but because of financial cutbacks and rapid inflation in the cost of producing and prescribing drugs. Recent provincial and federal health inquiries and commissions have recommended reforms in the Canada Health Act to cover more than 'medical' treatments. Some needed additions are a national home-care program; a national pharmacare program; eligibility of palliative care costs for a dying person; increased mental-health services; and increased facilities and services for rural and remote areas. If Canadians of all ages are to have equitable and timely access to health-care services, regardless of age, economic status, or place of residence, changes must be made in the health-care system.

As we enter the twenty-first century, there is more open discussion and acceptance of death among older people, and more individuals are expressing their wishes about health care and death through living wills and powers of attorney. There is more emphasis on 'dying a good death' with as little pain and suffering as possible, and with less burden on family members. Palliative care in non-hospital settings is increasing, but more facilities and trained personnel are needed.

For Reflection, Debate, or Action

1. Examine your own health habits and consider how they might be improved to enhance your quality of life across the life course.

2. What policies and programs might reduce inequalities in health across the life course?

3. Consult some of the websites listed in Endnote 16 and collect health statistics for your home community.

4. Assess whether there is a continuum of care in your home community, and identify major gaps in the current system.

5. Identify a health-related policy or issue pertaining to aging or older adults that is of personal concern to you, and write a letter to a local politician arguing why changes are needed, and offering some creative solutions for consideration.

6. Visit a nursing home, a palliative-care facility, and a funeral home to observe and learn about emerging thoughts and practices concerning dying and death.

7. Develop an argument, pro or con, as to why governments should or should not legalize assisted suicide. In your argument, address the questions raised in the last paragraph of the section on euthanasia and assisted suicide. Should this legislation, if approved, apply only to people of a certain age?

8. Debate whether health care and home care for older people should or should not be rationed. If you believe they should be rationed, who should make the decision about an individual, and what criteria should be employed to make a fair and objective decision?

9. The cost of health care in Canada is a major component of government budgets. Debate whether those who damage their health by improper or poor eating habits, not exercising, drinking to excess, smoking, not wearing seatbelts, etc., should be required to pay a supplementary health user fee, or to go to the end of a queue if there is a waiting list for services.

Notes

1. For a discussion of health concepts, definitions, and the health-care system, see Coburn et al. (1998); J. Clarke (2000); Segall and Chappell (2000); Armstrong et al. (2001); Alexander (2002); Statistics Canada (2002); and Armstrong and Armstrong (2003); issues of the *Journal of Aging and Health*, the *Canadian Journal on Aging*, *The Gerontologist*, the *Journal of Aging Studies*, *Research on Aging*, and the *Journals of Gerontology*; and major government reports such as Lalonde (1974), Epp (1986), and the Romanow Commission (2002).

2. The compression-of-morbidity thesis argues that most chronic and severe health problems experienced by older adults are compressed into the last few months or years of their lives because of improvements in health promotion, health prevention, and health care.

3. Acute conditions are of a limited duration; they include flu, colds, and minor or major surgery. Chronic conditions persist over time, even though they may begin with an acute condition, such as a heart attack or hip fracture. They are treated to reduce symptoms, pain or trauma, but are less likely to be cured. Examples are heart disease, cancer, diabetes, and arthritis.

4. Sources of current information concerning health statistics and health status include *Health Reports*, published quarterly by Statistics Canada (Cat. # 82-003-XPE), Health Canada (1999a), CIHI (2002b, 2003), and www.cihi.ca.

5. The health of Aboriginal people is discussed in Chapter 2 under 'Indigenous Subcultures: The Aboriginal People of Canada', and in Improving the Health of Canadians (CIHI, 2004).

6. Biologists, psychologists, sociologists, social workers, and medical personnel have studied such topics as sexuality and aging; sexual identity in the later years; the physiology of sex and age; sex and institutionalized elderly people; love in later life; and male and female sexual needs, interests, activity and problems in later life.

7. For discussions about sexuality in later life, see Neugebauer-Visano (1995), Gatz et al. (1996), Minichiello et al. (1996), Stones and Stones (1996), Gray et al. (2000), Connidis (2001), Gatz and Smyer (2001), MacCourt et al. (2002), DeLamater and Sill (2003), and Katz and Marshall (2003).

8. Some of the highlights in earlier chapters are concerned with love and intimacy in later life.

9. See the *Journal of Aging and Physical Activity* (www.hkusa.com/products/journals/journal.cfm?id=JAPA) for many articles on the social, physiological and psychological benefits of engaging in regular physical activity throughout the middle and later years; Wister (2003); Canada's *Physical Activity Guide for Older Adults* (www.paguide.com); and, First Step to Active Health (www.firststeptoactivehealth.com).

10. The most common screening tool is the Mini Mental State Examination, which consists of 30 items for assessing cognitive functioning. A score of 24 or less generally indicates a significant problem.

11. The Canadian Mental Health Association (www.cmha.ca) published two useful guides in 2002: *Supporting Seniors' Mental Health through Home Care: A Guide*; and *Supporting Seniors' Mental Health: A Guide for Home Care Staff*. Another source of information is the Canadian Coalition for Senior's Mental Health (www.ccsmh.ca).

12. The other major, but less prevalent, type is vascular dementia, which is caused by arteriosclerosis, which is a hardening of the cerebral arteries. Vascular dementia deprives the brain cells of nutrients and oxygen and leads to the atrophy and destruction of brain tissue.

13. A poignant and courageous *personal* account of the onset and progression of Alzheimer's disease is chronicled in a book by DeBaggio (2003).

14. Feder et al. (2001) describe the different funding system for health care found in the United States.

15. Privatization of health care, as it is available in the United States, is a contentious issue in Canada (Romanow Commission, 2002: 6–9). It raises the possibility of a two-tier system where the wealthy receive better care; it could mean inaccessibility and inequality, and a greater burden on families who cannot afford private services; and it could

lead to costly competition to generate a profit. On the other hand, privatization could reduce waiting times, reduce public expenditures, provide higher-quality diagnostic and treatment procedures, and offer more free choice as to where to obtain treatment. Reflecting this diversity of opinion, the Kirby (2002) report recommended that private care be permitted; whereas the Romanow Commission (2002) did not make a recommendation and discouraged any developments in this direction.

16. The following are useful websites pertaining to health knowledge, policy, and statistics: www.cihi.ca (Canadian Institute for Health Information); www.hc-sc.gc.ca/seniors-aines (Diversity of Aging and Seniors, Health Canada); www.cmha.ca (Canadian Mental Health Association); www.canadian-healthcare.org (Canadian Healthcare Association); www.statcan.ca (Statistics Canada); www.cwhn.ca (Canadian Women's Health Network); www.cihr-usc.gc.ca (Canadian Institutes on Health Research); www.cihr.usc.gc.ca/institutes/ia/ (CIHR Institute on Aging); www.canadian-health-network.ca (Canadian Health Network); and www.chsrf.ca (Canadian Health Services Research Foundation); and www.ccsmh.ca (Canadian Coalition for Senior's Mental Health).

17. For discussions about death and dying see Morgan (1996), Albom (1997), Johnson (1999), Auger (2000), Kaufman (1998, 2000), Lawton (2000, 2001), Northcott and Wilson (2001), Buckwalter (2002), Kuhl (2002), Wilson (2002), and Bryant (2003).

18. Most of this debate, and possible actions, beyond the philosophical, moral and ethical aspects, centres on government legislation and laws. Books and articles which discuss legal matters and aging in Canada (NACA, 2001) and the United States (Kapp, 2001) should be consulted for a more detailed discussion than is possible in this section. Laws and legislation change, and they often vary across federal and provincial jurisdictions, especially in Quebec, where the Civil Code prevails. In Quebec the principles of powers of attorney are called 'mandates'.

19. A useful book, which provides such a questionnaire, is *Let Me Decide* (Molloy et al., 1996).

20. Right-to-Die issues, pro and con, are discussed by Weir (1997), Braun et al. (2000), Brogden (2001), Snyder and Caplan (2001), Foley and Hendin (2002), Fisher et al. (2000); while Yahnke (2003a, 2003b) reviewed videos and films about end-of-life issues and decisions.

21. In Canada, aiding and abetting a suicide is a crime under the Criminal Code, and carries a maximum prison term of 14 years if convicted.

22. Information about palliative care can be found at: www.lastacts.org; www.nho.org; www.pccchealth.org/pced/index.html; www.chpca.ca; www.ontariopalliativecare.org; www.hospice.on.ca; www.nursing.ualberta.ca/endoflife; and http://sen.parl.gc.ca/scarstairs/new-index-e.htm.

23. Dimensions of death have been studied and taught by scholars in anthropology, biology, chemistry, economics, business, health studies, nursing, medicine, sociology, psychology, philosophy, ethics, law, history, and religious studies, social work, and education.

24. Institutions of higher education prepare students for life, and they should help students to understand death (Ross et al., 2002).

25. Websites about the funeral home industry include www.funeralnet.com, and www.drkloss.com. Many funeral homes have websites where they announce deaths, provide information about death and dying, and give friends of the deceased an opportunity to express condolences to the family through 'electronic sympathy cards'.

26. Changes in obituaries over the years are captured in *Goodbye! The Journal of Contemporary Obituaries*, on www.obitpage.com, and in anthologies of obituaries that are available in public libraries.

References

Administration on Aging. 2001. *Older Adults and Mental Health: Issues and Opportunities*. Washington, DC: Department of Health and Human Services, Administration on Aging.

Albom, M. 1997. *Tuesdays with Morrie: An Old Man, A Young Man, and Life's Greatest Lesson*. New York: Doubleday.

Alexander, T. 2002. 'The History and Evolution of Long-Term Care in Canada'. Pp. 1–55 in M. Stephenson and E. Sawyer (eds), *Continuing the Care: The Issues and Challenges for Long-Term Care*. Ottawa: CHA Press (www.cha.ca).

Ali, J. 2002. 'Mental Health of Canada's Immigrants', *Health Reports*, 13. Cat. no. 82- 003. Ottawa: Statistics Canada.

Armstrong, P., and H. Armstrong. 2003. *Wasting Away: The Undermining of Canadian Health Care*. Don Mills, Ont.: Oxford University Press.

———, et al., (eds). 2001. *Unhealthy Times: Political Economy Perspectives on Health and Care in Canada*. Don Mills, Ont.: Oxford University Press.

Auger, J. 2000. *Social Perspectives on Death and Dying*. Halifax: Fernwood.

Blazer, D. 2003. 'Depression in Late Life: Review and Commentary', *Journal of Gerontology: Medical Sciences*, 58A(3), M249–65.

Braun, K., et al. (eds). 2000. *Cultural Issues in End-of-Life Decision Making*. Thousand Oaks, Calif.: Sage.

———. 2001. 'Support for Physician-Assisted Suicide: Exploring the Impact of Ethnicity and Attitudes toward Planning for Death', *The Gerontologist*, 41(1), 51–60.

Brogden, M. 2001. *Geronticide: Killing the Elderly*. Philadelphia: Jessica Kingsley.

Bryant, C. (ed.). 2003. *Handbook of Death and Dying*. Thousand Oaks, Calif.: Sage.

Buckwalter, K. (ed.). 2002. 'End of Life Research: Focus on Older Populations', *The Gerontologist*, 42 (Special Issue III), 4–131.

Burke, M., et al. 1997. 'Dementia among Seniors', *Canadian Social Trends*, 45 (Summer), 24–7.

Butler, R. 2003. 'Senility: The Epidemic of the Twenty-First Century of Longevity', Unpublished essay in the Imagining Longevity Series. New York: International Longevity Center (www.ilcusa.org).

Cairney, J. 2000. 'Socio-economic Status and Self-Rated Health among Older Canadians', *Canadian Journal on Aging*, 19(4), 456–78.

Carrière, Y. 2000. 'The Impact of Population Aging and Hospital Days'. Pp. 26–44 in E. Gee and G. Gutman, (eds), *The Overselling of Population Aging: Apocalyptic Demography, Intergenerational Challenges, and Social Policy*. Don Mills, Ont.: Oxford University Press.

Chen, J., et al. 2002. 'Unmet Health Care Needs', *Canadian Social Trends*, 67 (Winter), 18–22.

Chipperfield, J. 1993. 'Perceived Barriers in Coping with Health Problems', *Journal of Aging and Health*, 5(1), 123–39.

CIHI. 2002a. *Drug Expenditure in Canada, 1985–2001*. Ottawa: Canadian Institute for Health Information.

———. 2002b. *Health Care in Canada*. Ottawa: Canadian Institute for Health Information (www.cihi.ca).

———. 2003. *How Healthy Are Canadians, 2002?* Ottawa: Canadian Institute for Health Information (www.cihi.ca).

———. 2004. *Improving the Health of Canadians*. Ottawa: Canadian Institute for Health Information (www.cihi.ca).

Clarke, J. 2000. *Health, Illness, and Medicine in Canada*. Don Mills, Ont.: Oxford University Press.

Clarke, P., et al. 2000. 'Well-Being in Canadian Seniors: Findings from the Canadian Study of Health and Aging', *Canadian Journal on Aging*, 19(2), 139–59.

Coburn, D., et al. (eds). 1998. *Health and Canadian Society: Sociological Perspectives*. Toronto: University of Toronto Press.

Commission on the Future of Health Care in Canada. 2002. *Building On Values: The Future of Health Care in Canada*. Ottawa: The Commission.

Conn, D. 2002. 'Mental Health Services and Long-Term Care'. Pp. 143–61 in M. Stephenson and E. Sawyer (eds), *Continuing the Care: The Issues and Challenges for Long-Term Care*. Ottawa: CHA Press.

Connidis, I. 2001. *Family Ties and Aging*. Thousand Oaks, Calif.: Sage.

D'Arcy, C. 1998. 'Health Status of Canadians'. Pp. 43–68 in D. Coburn et al. (eds), *Health and Canadian Society: Sociological Perspectives*. Toronto: University of Toronto Press.

DeBaggio, T. 2003. *Losing My Mind: An Intimate Look at Life with Alzheimer's*. New York: Free Press.

Deeg, D., et al. 1996. 'Health, Behaviour, and Aging'. Pp. 129–49 in J. Birren and W. Schaie (eds), *Handbook of the Psychology of Aging*. San Diego, Calif.: Academic Press.

DeLamater, J., and M. Sill. 2003. 'Sexual Desire in Later Life', Center for Demography and Ecology Working Paper No. 2003-05. Madison, Wis.: Center for Demography and Ecology, University of Wisconsin.

Epp, J. 1986. *Achieving Health for All: A Framework for Health Promotion*. Ottawa: Minister of National Health and Welfare.

Evans, R., et al. 2001. 'Apocalypse NO: Population Aging and the Future of Health Care Systems', *Canadian Journal on Aging*, 20 (Supp. 1), 160–91.

Feder, J., et al. 2001. 'The Financing and Organization of Health Care'. Pp. 387–405 in R. Binstock and L. George (eds), *Handbook of Aging and the Social Sciences*. San Diego, Calif.: Academic Press.

Fineman, N. 1994. 'Health Care Providers' Subjective Understanding of Old Age: Implications for Threatened Status in Later Life', *Journal of Aging Studies*, 8(3), 255–70.

Fisher, R., et al. (eds). 2000. *A Guide to End-of-Life Care for Seniors*. Ottawa: Population Health Directorate, Health Canada (www.rgp.Toronto.on.ca/iddg).

Foley, K., and H. Hendin. (eds). 2002. *The Case against Assisted Suicide: For the Right to End-of-Life Care*. Baltimore, Md: Johns Hopkins University Press.

Gatz, M., and M. Smyer. 2001. 'Mental Health and Aging at the Outset of the Twenty-First Century'. Pp. 523–44 in J. Birren and W. Schaie (eds), *Handbook of the Psychology of Aging*. San Diego, Calif.: Academic Press.

———, et al. 1996. 'Aging and Mental Disorders'. Pp. 365–82 in J. Birren and W. Schaie (eds), *Handbook of the Psychology of Aging*. San Diego, Calif.: Academic Press.

Gee, E., and M. Kimball 1987. *Women and Aging*. Toronto: Butterworths.

———, et al. 2003. 'Examining the 'Healthy Immigrant Effect' in *Later Life: Findings from the Canadian Community Health Survey*. Hamilton, Ont.: McMaster University, SEDAP Research Paper No. 98 (http://soc-serv2.mcmaster.ca/sedap).

George, L. 2003. 'What Life-Course Perspectives Offer the Study of Aging and Health'. Pp. 161–88 in R. Settersten (ed.), *Invitation to the Life Course: Toward New Understandings of Later Life*. Amityville, NY: Baywood.

Gesler, W., et al. (eds.). 1998. *Rural Health and Aging Research: Theory, Methods and Practical Applications*. Amityville, NY: Baywood.

Gift, H., et al. 1997. 'Conceptualizing Oral Health and Quality of Life', *Social Science and Medicine*, 44(5), 601–8.

Gottlieb, B. 2000. 'Self-Help, Mutual Aid and Support Groups among Older Adults', *Canadian Journal on Aging*, 19 (Supp. 1), 58–74.

Gray, J., et al. 2000. *Canadian Mental Health Law and Policy*. Toronto: Butterworths.

Grossberg, G., and A. Desai. 2003. 'Management of Alzheimer's Disease', *Journal of Gerontology: Medical Sciences*, 58A(4), 331–53.

Health and Welfare Canada. 1988. *Mental Health for Canadians: Striking a Balance*. Ottawa: Supply and Services Canada.

Health Canada. 1999a. *Toward a Healthy Future: Second Report on the Health of Canadians*. Ottawa: Health Canada.

———. 1999b. *Canada's Health Care System*. Ottawa: Health Canada (www.hc.sc.gc.ca/medicare/).

Holstein, M. 1997. 'Alzheimer's Disease and Senile Dementia, 1885–1920: An Interpretive History of Disease Negotiation', *Journal of Aging Studies*, 11(1), 1–13.

Hubert, H., et al. 2002. 'Lifestyle Habits and Compression of Morbidity', *Journal of Gerontology: Medical Sciences*, 57A(6), M347–51.

Idler, E. (ed.). 1999. 'Self-Assessments of Health: The Next Stage of Studies', *Research on Aging*, 21(3), 387–505.

Johnson, T. (ed.). 1999. *Handbook on Ethical Issues in Aging*. Westport, Conn.: Greenwood Press.

Kapp, M. 2001. *Lessons in Law and Aging*. New York: Springer.

Katz,, S. and B. Marshall. 2003. 'New Sex for Old: Lifestyle, Consumerism, and the Ethics of Aging Well', *Journal of Aging Studies*, 17(1), 3–16.

Kaufman, S. 1998. 'Intensive Care, Old Age, and the Problem of Death in America', *The Gerontologist*, 38(6), 715–25.

———. 2000. 'Senescence, Decline, and the Quest for a Good Death: Contemporary Dilemmas and Historical Antecedents', *Journal of Aging Studies*, 14(1), 1–23.

Keating, N., et al. 2001. 'A Good Place to Grow Old? Rural Communities and Support to Seniors'. Pp. 263–77 in R. Epp and D. Whitson (eds), *Writing Off the Rural West: Globalization, Governments and the Transformation of Rural Communities*. Edmonton: University of Alberta Press.

Kirby, M. 2002. *The Health of Canadians: The Federal Role*. Ottawa: The Senate (www.parl.gc.ca).

Kuhl, D. 2002. *What Dying People Want*. Toronto: Doubleday Canada.

Lalonde, M. 1974. *A New Perspective on the Health of*

Canadians. Ottawa: Information Canada.

Langlois, S., and P. Morrison. 2002. 'Suicide Deaths and Attempts', *Canadian Social Trends*, 66 (Autumn), 20–5.

Lawton, P. (ed.). 2000. 'Focus on the End of Life: Scientific and Social Issues', *Annual Review of Gerontology and Geriatrics*, 20, 1–320.

———. 2001. 'Quality of Life and the End of Life'. Pp. 593–616 in J. Birren and W. Schaie (eds), *Handbook of the Psychology of Aging*. New York: Academic Press.

Legris, L., and M. Préville. 2003. 'Les Motifs du suicide gériatrique: une étude explorative', *Canadian Journal on Aging*, 22(2), 197–205.

Leichtentritt, R., and K. Rettig. 2001. 'The Construction of the Good Death: A Dramaturgy Approach', *Journal of Aging Studies*, 15(1), 85–103.

Leventhal, H., et al. 2001. 'Health Risk Behaviors and Aging'. Pp. 186–214 in J. Birren and W. Schaie (eds), *Handbook of the Psychology of Aging*. San Diego, Calif.: Academic Press.

MacCourt, P., et al. 2002. 'CAG Policy Statement on Issues in the Delivery of Mental Health Services to Older Adults', *Canadian Journal on Aging*, 21(2), 165–74.

McWilliam, C. 2001. 'Canadian Association on Gerontology Policy Statement on Health Promotion for Individual Seniors', *Canadian Journal on Aging*, 20(2), i–iv.

Maddigan, S., et al. 2003. 'Predictors of Older Adults' Capacity for Medication Management in a Self-Medication Program', *Journal of Aging and Health*, 15(2), 332–52.

Martin-Matthews, A. 2002. *Seniors' Health*. Ottawa: Health Canada Synthesis Series (www.hc-sc.gc.ca/htf-fass).

Matthews, S. 2002. *Sisters and Brothers/Daughters and Sons: Meeting the Needs of Old Parents*. Bloomington, Ind.: Unlimited (www.unlimitedpublishing.com).

Maxwell, C. and K. Oakley. 1998. 'Editorial: Older Women's Health Issues', *Canadian Journal on Aging*, 17(2), i–ix.

Menec, V., and J. Chipperfield. 2001. 'A Prospective Analysis of the Relation between Self-Rated Health and Health Care Use Among Elderly Canadians', *Canadian Journal on Aging*, 20(3), 293–306.

———, et al. 1999. 'Self-Perceptions of Health: A Prospective Analysis of Mortality, Control and Health', *Journal of Gerontology: Psychological Science*, 54B(2), P85–93.

Minichiello, V., et al. 1996. 'Sexuality and Older People: Social Issues'. Pp. 93–111 in V. Minichiello et al. (eds), *Sociology of Aging: International Perspectives*. Melbourne,

Australia: THOTH Design and Promotion.

Molloy, D., et al. 1996. *Let Me Decide*. Toronto: Penguin Books.

Moore, E., and M. Rosenberg. 1997. *Growing Old in Canada*. Toronto: Nelson.

Morgan, J. 1994. 'Bereavement in Older Adults', *Journal of Mental Health Counselling*, 16(3), 318–26.

———. 1996. *Ethical Issues in the Care of the Dying and Bereaved Aged*. Amityville, NY: Baywood.

Morley, J., and J. Flaherty. 2002. 'It's Never Too Late: Health Promotion and Illness Prevention in Older Persons', *Journal of Gerontology: Medical Sciences*, 57A(6), M338–42.

Morrongiello, B., and B. Gottlieb. 2000. 'Self-Care among Older Adults', *Canadian Journal on Aging*, 19 (Supplement 1), 32–57.

Mutran, E., and S. Sudha (eds). 2000. 'Age and Health in a Multiethnic Society, I: Patterns and Methods', *Research on Aging*, 22(6), 589–795.

NACA. 1999. 'Self-Help Groups', *Expression*, 12(4), 1–8. A Division of Aging and Seniors, Health Canada.

———. 2001. 'Seniors and the Law', *Expression*, 14(3), 1–8. A Division of Aging and Seniors, Health Canada.

———. 2002. *Mental Health and Aging*. Writings in Gerontology Series No. 18. Ottawa: National Advisory Council on Aging.

Neugebauer-Visano, R. (ed.) 1995. *Seniors and Sexuality: Experiencing Intimacy in Later Life*. Toronto: Canadian Scholars' Press.

Northcott, H., and D. Wilson. 2001. *Dying and Death in Canada*. Aurora, Ont.: Garamond Press.

Ontario Gerontology Association. 1989. 'Aging Together: An Exploration of Attitudes toward Aging in Multicultural Ontario', *OGA Bulletin/Newsletter*, September.

Payne, B. 1994. 'Exploring the Social and Psychological Determinants of Health, Illness and Disease in Older Adults: Oral Health as a Model'. Doctoral dissertation, University of Toronto.

Penning, M. 1995. 'Health Care, Social Support, and the Utilization of Health Services Among Older Adults', *Journal of Gerontology: Social Sciences*, 50B(5), S330–39.

———, and N. Keating. 2000. 'Self-, Informal and Formal Care: Partnerships in Community-Based and Residential Long-Term Care Settings', *Canadian Journal on Aging*, 19 (Supp. 1), 75–100.

Perez, C. 2002. 'Health Status and Health Behaviour Among Immigrants', *Health Reports*, 13. Cat. no. 82-003. Ottawa: Statistics Canada.

Pringle, D. 1998. *Aging and the Health Care System: Am I in the Right Queue?* Forum Collection. Ottawa: National Advisory Council on Aging.

Riley, J. 2001. *Rising Life Expectancy: A Global History*. New York: Cambridge University Press.

Roberts, P., and G. Fawcett. 1998. *At Risk: Socio-Economic Analysis of Health and Literacy among Seniors*. Cat. no. 89-552-MPE, no. 5. Ottawa: Statistics Canada.

Romanow Commission. 2002. *See* Commission on the Future of Health Care in Canada.

Rosenberg, M. and A. James. 2000. 'Medical Services Utilization Patterns by Seniors', *Canadian Journal on Aging*, 19 (Supp. 1), 125–42.

Rosnick, C. and S. Reynolds. 2003. 'Thinking Ahead: Factors Associated With Executing Advance Directives', *Journal of Aging and Health*, 15(2), 409–29.

Ross, M. et al. 2002. 'End-of-Life Care for Seniors: Public and Professional Awareness', *Educational Gerontology*, 28(5), 353–66.

Saunders, L., et al. 2001. 'Trends in the Utilization of Health Services by Seniors in Alberta', *Canadian Journal on Aging*, 20(4), 493–516.

Segall, A., and N. Chappell. 2000. *Health and Health Care in Canada*. Toronto: Prentice Hall.

Snyder, L., and A. Caplan (eds). 2001. *Assisted Suicide: Finding Common Ground*. Indianapolis, Ind.: Indiana University Press.

Statistics Canada. 1993. *Survey on Aging and Independence: Overview of a National Survey*. Cat. no. H88-3/13-1993E. Ottawa: Statistics Canada.

————. 2002. *How Healthy are Canadians? A Summary 2002 Annual Report* Cat. # 82-003-SIE. Ottawa: Statistics Canada.

Stephenson, M., and E. Sawyer (eds). 2002. *Continuing the Care: The Issues and Challenges for Long-Term Care*. Ottawa: Canadian Healthcare Association Press.

Stones, L., and M. Stones. 1996. *Sex May Be Wasted on the Young*. North York, Ont.: Captus Press.

Sudha, S., and E. Mutran (eds). 2001. 'Age and Health in a Multiethnic Society, II: Health Care Issues', *Research on Aging*, 23(1), 3–126.

Tamblyn, R. 2000. 'Editorial: Canadian Association on Gerontology Policy Statement: Seniors and Prescription Drugs', *Canadian Journal on Aging*, 19(1), vii–xiv.

————, and R. Perreault. 2000. 'Prescription Drug Use and Seniors', *Canadian Journal on Aging*, 19 (Supp. 1), 143–75.

Tiefer, L. 2001. 'A New View of Women's Sexual Problems: Why New? Why Now?', *Journal of Sex Research*, 38(2), 89–96.

Tierney, M., and J. Charles. 2002. 'The Care and Treatment of People with Dementia and Cognitive Impairment'. Pp. 97–113 in NACA, *Mental Health and Aging*. Ottawa: National Advisory Council on Aging (www.naca.ca).

Tjam, E., and J. Hirdes. 2002. 'Health, Psycho-Social and Cultural Determinants of Medication Use by Chinese-Canadian Older Persons', *Canadian Journal on Aging*, 21(1), 63–173.

Veenstra, G. 2001. 'Social Capital and Health', *Isuma*, 2(1), 72–81.

Vinters, H. 2001. 'Aging and the Human Nervous System'. Pp. 135–60 in J. Birren and W. Schaie (eds), *Handbook of the Psychology of Aging*. San Diego, Calif.: Academic Press.

Weir, R. (ed.) 1997. *Physician-Assisted Suicide*. Indianapolis, Ind.: Indiana University Press.

Wilkins, S., and C. Cott. 1994. 'Aging, Chronic Illness and Disability'. Pp. 363–77 in M. Nagler (ed.). *Perspectives on Disability*. Palo Alto, Calif.: Health Markets Research.

Wilkinson, A., and J. Lynn. 2001. 'The End of Life'. Pp. 444–61 in R. Binstock and L. George (eds), *Handbook of Aging and the Social Sciences*. San Diego, Calif.: Academic Press.

Wilson, D. 2002. 'End-of-Life Issues'. Pp. 387–420 in M. Stephenson and E. Sawyer (eds), *Continuing the Care: The Issues and Challenges for Long-Term Care*. Ottawa: CHA Press.

Wister, A. 2003. 'It's Never Too Late: Healthy Lifestyles and Aging', *Canadian Journal on Aging*, 22(2), 149–50.

Wolfson, C., et al. 1993. Adult Children's Perceptions of Their Responsibility to Provide Care for Dependent Elderly Parents', *The Gerontologist*, 33 (3) , 315–23.

Yahnke, R. (ed.). 2003a. 'End-of-Life Decisions, Part 1', *The Gerontologist*, 43(1), 140–3.

———— (ed.). 2003b. 'End-of-Life Decisions, Part II', *The Gerontologist*, 43(2), 285–8.

GLOSSARY

Aboriginal People The original or indigenous inhabitants of Canada, which normally includes three general categories of people, as defined by the government of Canada: Status Indians, Métis, and Inuit.

Acculturation A process in which individuals from one cultural group, through contact with another cultural group, learn and internalize the cultural traits of the other group.

Active life expectancy The number of years an individual can expect to live free of serious disability.

ADLs Basic personal and necessary activities of daily living, such as getting in and out of bed or a chair, dressing, grooming, toileting, and eating.

Age grading The process in which age determines social location, roles, norms, and interpersonal relationships.

Age Discrimination The unequal treatment of someone because of their age. This can be preferential, but differential treatment, by age, or exclusion from some right on the basis of one's age. It often arises where ageism is present. In some jurisdictions, age discrimination, such as mandatory retirement at age 65, is prohibited by law

Ageism Discriminatory attitudes or actions toward others on the basis of negative perceptions or beliefs about the actual or perceived chronological age of an individual or group.

Agency A process in which individuals construct and shape their biographies across the life course and determine their personal experience of aging (within a unique class, race, or gender structure) by acting or choosing, as opposed to letting events or situations happen to them without being proactive or reactive.

Age strata Age groups used in a classification system in which individuals are grouped according to chronological age (for example, 10–19, 20–39, 40–59, 60–69, 70–79, 80+).

Anticipatory socialization The learning and acceptance of beliefs, values, norms, language, or dress of a status position to which an individual aspires to belong, or to which he or she will belong.

Assimilation A process by which an individual or group becomes more like the dominant group in such cultural elements as language, dress, values, and identity.

Beliefs Socially constructed and shared views that influence the perceptions and behaviour of people.

Cautiousness A generalized tendency to respond slowly or not at all to a stimulus or task, perhaps out of fear of making a mistake or in order to complete the task as successfully as possible.

Centenarians Persons aged 100 years or over.

Chronological age norms Expected patterns of behaviour that are based on the chronological age of individuals in a particular society or subculture. These rights and/or responsibilities are assigned or earned by reaching a specific age or stage in life.

Cohort A group of individuals born in the same year (for example, 1990), or within the same period of time (for example, a five- or ten-year period).

Cohort analysis A comparative analysis of specific birth cohorts.

Cohort flow A process in which a series of birth cohorts, varying in size and composition, succeed one another over time.

Competence Adaptive behaviour that is demonstrated to varying degrees in a specific situation.

Concept An abstract, generalized idea about an object or a phenomenon that provides a common meaning.

Creativity The quantitative and qualitative productivity of an individual that is evaluated by others.

Crude birth rate The number of births per 1,000 people during a one-year period.

Crude death rate The number of deaths per 1,000 people during a one-year period.

Crystallized intelligence Based on education, experience, and acculturation, this type of intelligence involves vocabulary, verbal comprehension, and a numerical ability to solve problems.

Culture A set of shared symbols and their meanings that are passed on to subsequent generations within a society. Some cultural elements are language, dress, art, literature, music, laws, folklore, ceremonies, rituals, sports, and games.

Demographic transition A gradual process in which a society moves from having high rates of fertility *and* mortality to low rates of fertility and mortality. Populations begin to age when fertility declines and adult mortality rates decline.

Demography A field of study that examines changes

in the fertility, mortality, and migration rates of a society, and that makes projections pertaining to the future size and composition of the population.

Dependency ratio The number of non-workers who are supported directly or indirectly by members of the labour force.

Dependent variable The outcome or consequent variable in a hypothesized relationship between two variables.

Disability A physical or mental condition or a health problem in which an individual is restricted, partially or totally, in the ability to perform a physical, social, or cognitive activity in the manner or within the range considered normal for a human being.

Elder abuse A conscious or unconscious physical, psychological or fraudulent act against a frail or dependent older person. This action may result in physical, psychological, or financial trauma for the older person.

Elder neglect The failure or refusal on the part of a caregiver to meet the physical or psychological needs of an older adult.

Empty nest A state experienced by parents once the last child has moved out of the family home, thereby signalling the end of child rearing.

Environment The sum of the various personal, group, social, and physical components that influence behaviour and life chances throughout the life cycle.

Epidemiological transition A process by which the *health* of a nation improves as nutrition, personal health care, and public sanitation improve. During the transition, the leading causes of death shift from infectious, parasitic, acute and epidemic illnesses to chronic and degenerative diseases, especially as the population ages.

Ethics An objective and reflective way of thinking about how we should debate and resolve moral or social issues, taking into account the best interests of all involved in the decision or its outcome.

Ethnic subculture A subgroup within a larger society in which members have a common ancestry and an identifiable culture, including customs, beliefs, language, dress, foods, or religion (for example, Cubans, Aboriginal people, East Indians, Italians, Portuguese).

Ethnocentrism A tendency for individuals or groups to consider their own culture as superior to others and as the ideal standard when evaluating the worth of those from other cultures, societies, or groups.

Euthanasia An active or passive action which is taken to end a life.

Family A kinship group where members are determined by blood or marriage ties.

Fictive kin Informal, family-like relationships with a friend or neighbour in which the person is viewed almost as a blood relative. They often are a core part of the informal social network of older persons who lack legal kin, or who do not have legal kin available for support and assistance.

Filial piety A felt need, duty, or moral obligation to honour and care for one's parents in their middle and later years.

Fluid intelligence Based on the functioning of the nervous system, this type of intelligence involves incidental learning that is necessary for reasoning and problem solving.

Formal social support The provision of assistance and care by formal or voluntary associations in the private sector and by formal agencies in the public sector.

Frailty A disease state that is most common late in life. It is characterized by muscular weakness, fatigue and low energy, weight loss, slow or unsteady gait, and decreased physical and social activity.

Gender The cultural definition of what it means to be male and female. Gender-related behaviour and attributes are linked to the social roles of men and women, and to the cultural definitions of masculinity and femininity, which are learned and perpetuated within a culture or a subculture.

Gender relations The interaction of men and women based on the changing definitions and roles of what it means to be male or female in a particular social group.

Generation A unique group of people (for example, baby boomers), born during the same period, who have experienced and reacted similarly to significant social, political, or historical events that emerged at particular points in their life. These special events or factors have led members of the cohort to think and behave in ways that make them different from other generations.

Generational analysis A comparison of age cohorts outside the family structure.

Generational equity The perceived or actual fairness in the distribution of publicly funded resources and obligations across age groups and generations.

Generational unit Within a generation, a subgroup whose members demonstrate unique styles of thought, dress, and behaviour at a particular point in their life (for example, hippies, skinheads, rappers).

Generativity A process in mid-life in which individuals become less concerned with the self and more concerned and involved with mentoring others and with contributing to various groups, organizations, or communities.

Gentrification The gradual resettlement and reconstruction of inner-city neighbourhoods by young to middle-aged affluent adults. As a result of this process, the elderly and other low-income groups are usually displaced.

Guardian A person lawfully invested by a court with the power to make some or all personal-care decisions on behalf of a person who is mentally incapable of personal care.

Handicap A condition that results from impairment and disability and prevents a person from performing a role that is normal.

Health According to the World Health Organization, a state of complete physical, mental, and social well-being, and not merely the absence of disease.

Hierarchical-compensatory model A system of social support in which the kinship network provides assistance first, followed in order by other informal sources and then by formal sources. Within the kinship system, the spouse is selected as the preferred caregiver, followed in order by an adult child, a close relative such as a sibling, and then by other relatives.

Hospice movement A philosophy that promotes 'death with dignity' by providing care centres to assist those who are dying from a terminal illness, and to provide support to relatives and friends of the person who is dying.

Hypothesis A prediction about the relationship between two or more variables.

IADLs Instrumental activities of daily living that demonstrate competence and independence, such as preparing meals, shopping, banking and managing finances, cleaning and maintaining a home, driving a car.

Impairment The loss of some physical or mental function.

Incidence The frequency of new occurrences during a specific period of time, usually one year.

Independent variable The antecedent variable that is hypothesized to explain the outcome of a relationship between two or more variables.

Individual aging The structural, physical, sensory, motor, cognitive, and behavioural changes *within* an individual over a period of years.

Inflation A large increase in the price of consumer goods and services that results in a loss of purchasing power, especially for those whose income remains fixed or whose income rises slower than inflation. Inflation is often measured by the size and the rate of increase in the Consumer Price Index.

Informal social support The provision of care and assistance by members of the extended family, neighbours, and friends. This process may or may not involve an exchange of resources.

Intelligence An ability to think logically, to conceptualize, and to reason.

Interpretive perspective A sociological view of the world in which individuals negotiate, define, interpret, and control their involvement in institutionalized social roles, thereby creating and controlling the social order.

Kin keeper A member of the extended family who takes responsibility for informing the family about others and for organizing and perpetuating family rituals.

Leisure Involvement in freely selected activities during the time not required for work or for mandatory personal or domestic responsibilities.

Lineage effects A comparison of generations within extended families.

Life chances Variation in educational, occupational, and leisure opportunities in early and mid-life that are influenced by social structural attributes such as gender, social class, religion, race, ethnicity, and place of residence.

Life course A social construct that reflects our personal biography across the time we live.

Life-course perspective A perspective that considers the timing and order of major life events, and the dialectical interplay between biographies and population aging, as well as the interplay among the individual, age cohorts, and a changing social structure.

Life expectancy The average number of years of life remaining at a given age (for example, at birth, at age 65).

Life span The theoretical maximum number of years an individual can live.

Lifestyle Patterns of thought, behaviour, dress, and leisure pursuits that represent personal or group expressions of values and norms.

Mental health The ability to think, feel, and interact with others as we encounter challenges in daily life.

Mental illness A disorder of thinking, feeling, and acting that can range from a stressful disorder to an organic brain disease with severe disorientation and memory impairment. The causes of mental illness may be social, psychological, or physical.

Migration Movement by an individual or group from one geographic region to another.

Migration stream A group of migrants who, individually, leave the same area of origin and arrive at a common receiving area (for example, a stream from Newfoundland to Ontario).

Minority group A group having subordinate status in the social, political, or economic sense rather than in the numerical sense. These groups are blocked from full and equal participation in some or all phases of social life because of their age, gender, ethnicity, or race.

Modernization A shift from an agricultural to an industrialized economy, or from a 'traditional' primitive, rural social system to a 'modern' industrialized, urban social system.

Morbidity A state of disease or chronic illness.

Mortality The incidence of death in a population during a period of time.

Norm A commonly accepted formal or informal rule about how an individual or group is expected to act in a specific social situation.

Normative perspective A sociological view of the world in which it is assumed that individuals learn, internalize, and accept social rules and roles without question, thereby having little control over their lives.

Old-age dependency ratio The number of retired people supported by those in the labour force who are between 18 and 64 years of age.

Operational definition A statement of the precise procedures used to measure a variable.

Palliative care A type of care that seeks to improve the quality of life for a dying person by relieving his or her physical pain and psychosocial discomfort.

Personality The characteristic style of thought, feeling, and behaviour of an individual, as measured by multi-dimensional traits.

Personality trait A distinguishing characteristic or quality of the human personality (for example, passive, aggressive, extraverted, egocentric, emotional).

Personality type A characteristic way of thinking and behaving that tends to prevail in most or all social settings.

Population aging A demographic phenomenon in which, because of decreased fertility and longer life expectancy, an increasing percentage of the population is made up of older people

Population displosion A process in which the composition of a population within a geographic region becomes more heterogeneous (for example, in terms of age, wealth, power, education).

Population explosion A demographic process that results in a large increase in the size of a population over a relatively short time (for example, the baby boom from the late-1940s to the mid-1960s).

Population implosion A demographic process in which the population becomes concentrated in urban areas.

Power of attorney A written document that gives someone the power to act on another's behalf in financial matters.

Presbycusis A progressive inability to hear higher-frequency sounds in music and speech.

Presbyopia A progressive loss of flexibility in the lens of the eye that decreases the ability to focus on objects at varying distances..

Prevalence The number of cases of a phenomenon in a population at a specified point in time, such as the number of cases of elder abuse per 1,000 older persons.

Public policy The outcome of a decision-making process that leads to laws, procedures, regulations, or programs that help individuals and society to cope with current issues or problems.

Racial subculture A subgroup within a larger society in which biological physical appearances, along with cultural commonalities, combine to define the boundaries of membership (for example, African Canadians, Aboriginal people).

Reaction time The period of time from the perception of a stimulus (such as a red light) and the initiation of an appropriate reaction (such as moving the foot from the accelerator to the brake).

Resocialization The process of learning and adopting new expectations, values, beliefs, and types of behaviour associated with a new status (for example, from being married to being a widow).

Respite care A service available to caregivers that gives them relief from daily caregiving demands through a daily, weekly, or vacation break. Respite provides brief periods of temporary emotional, psychological and social normality in a caregiver's life.

Retirement The process of withdrawal from the labour force, normally at or around 65 years of age.

Role A social definition of the behavioural patterns, rights, and responsibilities expected from those occupying a specific status position. These normative expectations serve as guidelines for behaviour in specific situations.

Self-abuse The outcome of a lifestyle in which an individual consumes excessive amounts of alcohol or drugs or ignores normal safety or nutrition practices, thereby placing himself or herself at risk.

Self-care The actions and decisions that an individual takes to maintain and improve health; to prevent, diagnose, and treat personal ill health; and to use both informal support systems and formal medical services.

Self-neglect The failure of a person to provide him- or herself with the necessities for physical and mental health, including a safe environment.

Sex The reproductive, physiological, and sexual characteristics that differentiate females from males and influence some aspects of behaviour that are determined by genetic differences in abilities and capacities (for example, strength, speed).

Social institution A cultural product that persists across generations to provide values, norms, beliefs, traditions, and a social structure.

Socialization A complex developmental process by which individuals learn and internalize (adopt) the norms, roles, language, beliefs, and values of a society or subgroup.

Social differentiation The separation and ranking of positions based on ascribed attributes (for example, age, gender, class, ethnicity, race) or achieved roles (for example, spouse, parent, employee).

Social network A set of formal and informal relationships that include a core group (the family) and a more transitory extended group (friends, co-workers, neighbours). The number and availability of members in the network varies at different stages across the life course.

Social phenomenon An observable fact or occurrence that appears in social life on a regular or patterned basis. Most social phenomena stem from the influence of one or more persons on another person or group. They represent patterns of behaviour, thoughts, or events that comprise the basic data and knowledge of sociology.

Social stratification The differential ranking or evaluation of persons in a society or group based on social attributes that are either *ascribed* (for example, age, gender, class, race, ethnicity) or *achieved* (for example, social class, education).

Social structure Patterned relationships that differentially rank or distribute individuals according to socially evaluated characteristics (for example, age, race, gender, social class, ethnicity, education, wealth).

Status A culturally defined position in a society or a group that reflects ideas about what rights, responsibilities, and obligations are accorded to specific individuals. The status may be acquired (for example, by means of education or wealth) or ascribed (because of race, sex, age).

Structural lag A period of social change in which social norms and social institutions fail to keep pace with changes in the lives of individuals.

Subculture A set of unique and distinctive beliefs, norms, values, symbols, and ideologies that guide the thinking, behaviour, and lifestyles of a subset of the larger population.

Symbolic interactionism A sociological view of the world in which individuals are active participants in defining both the social situation and the self according to how they interpret and define a situation.

Technoplosion A rapid growth in the discovery and adoption of technological developments, which, in turn, has a significant impact on the work and leisure lifestyles of the population.

Theoretical definition A statement of the standard, general meaning of a concept.

Theory A set of interrelated propositions that presents a tentative explanation of a phenomenon.

Values Cultural or subcultural ideas about the desirable goals and behaviour for members of a group. These internalized criteria are employed to judge the appropriateness or inappropriateness of individual and group actions.

Variable A concept (such as age) that has more than one value and to which numbers can be assigned to measure variation from one situation, individual, or group to another situation, individual, or group.

Wisdom An accumulated ability based on experience that enables an individual to adapt to changing situations and to make appropriate decisions.

How to Read a Statistical Table or Figure

Throughout this book, and particularly in journal articles, information is often presented graphically in tables or figures. You should learn to read and interpret this information, so that you gain a more thorough understanding of the relationships or trends being discussed. A thorough analysis of a table or figure involves three main stages: (1) reading to acquire an overview of the information presented; (2) analyzing the numbers in the body of the table; and (3) interpreting the information. *Statistics: Power from Data!*, is a free electronic resource for students that will help you understand all aspects of statistics from the data collection to the analysis stage (www.statcan.ca → Learning Resources → Students).

An Overview

Read the title of the table or figure, which should tell you the specific topic and content of the material; what information is included; whether the information is presented by subcategories such as age, gender, or region; and how the information is presented (in raw numbers, means, percentages, correlations, or ratios). It should also indicate whether the information is purely descriptive (percentages), or whether it illustrates a relationship between variables (a cross-classification of variables or a correlation matrix for a number of variables).

Next, read the labels above each vertical column and beside each horizontal row to determine what data appear in a table. Similarly, in a graph or figure read the labels on the vertical and horizontal axes. Examine any footnotes to determine the source of the data (the year, the country, or region), the definitions of variables, and whether data are missing.

An Analysis of the Numbers or Plots

Determine the size and type of units that are used (raw numbers or percentages, hundreds or millions, inches or centimeters, etc.). Next, look at the overall totals, and at the highest, lowest, and average figures. Compare these with other data in the table, and note trends and deviations. In a table the figures in the lower right-hand corner usually give the overall total or average for the entire population in the study. If the percentages total 100 in the columns, then the table should be read across the rows to determine group differences or patterns.

A third step is to determine the range or variability of the information (ages 20 to 60; income $5,000 to $50,000, etc.). Next, look at the totals, averages, or percentages for each subgroup, or examine the patterns exhibited by subgroups in a figure where the data are plotted. Is the pattern linear (as height increases, weight increases) or curvilinear (strength increases with age to a maximum and then declines with age)? Does the pattern increase, decrease, remain stable, or fluctuate in any observable pattern with age or over time? Finally, look for unexpected irregularities or findings (for example, males over 65 reporting higher income than 55-year-olds), and think about explanations and interpretations for atypical or unusual patterns.

Interpreting the Information

In many cases the author will present an interpretation in the text. However, it is possible that there might be an equally valid alternative interpretation. In addition to becoming more familiar with the data from which conclusions are drawn, this search for alternative explanations is a reason for you to analyze and interpret graphic information carefully and thoroughly. Do not automatically accept the author's interpretation as the only one.

In order to interpret the data, begin by attempting to explain patterns and irregularities in the data and decide whether this explanation agrees with previous information cited in other sources. If it does not, question the explanation by considering whether the interpretation is spurious—that is, whether the relationship is due solely to the fact that a variable happens to be associated with another variable. For example, an observed relationship between a large number of storks in a certain area and a high birth rate could be interpreted to mean that storks deliver babies. However, this interpretation is spurious, since a greater number of storks inhabit rural areas, and the rural birth rate is higher than the urban birth rate. Tables and graphs must be analyzed carefully to fully understand the evidence on which a conclusion is based, and to determine if a misleading or unlikely explanation has been presented. Finally, remember to note whether different patterns or results occur by social categories such as age, gender, race, class, education, nationality, religion, ethnicity, geographical region, or place of residence.

APPENDIX B

Study Resources

Books, Reports, Monographs, Dictionaries, Encyclopedias

American Association of Retired Persons. 2002. *Thesaurus of Aging Terminology*. Washington, DC: American Association of Retired Persons.

Association of Gerontology in Higher Education. 1997–. 'Brief Annotated Bibliography Series' (www.aghe.org/aghe).

Binstock, R., and L. George (eds). 2001. *Handbook of Aging and the Social Sciences*. San Diego, Calif.: Academic Press.

Birren, J. (ed.). 1996. *Encyclopedia of Gerontology*. San Diego, Calif.: Academic Press.

Birren, J., and W. Schaie (eds). 2001. *Handbook of Aging and Psychology*. San Diego, Calif.: Academic Press.

Butterworth's Monograph Series on Individual and Population Aging

    McDaniel, S. 1986. *Canada's Aging Population*.

    Brillon, Y. 1987. *Victimization and Fear of Crime among the Elderly*.

    Driedger, L., and N. Chappell. 1987. *Aging and Ethnicity: Toward an Interface*.

    Forbes, W., J. Jackson, and A. Kraus. 1987. *Institutionalization of the Elderly in Canada*.

    Gee, E., and M. Kimball 1987. *Women and Aging*.

    Northcott, H. 1988. *Changing Residence: The Geographic Mobility of Elderly Canadians*.

    McDonald, L., and R. Wanner. 1990. *Retirement in Canada*.

    Brown, R. 1991. *Economic Security in an Aging Population*.

    Keating, N. 1991. *Aging in Rural Canada*.

    McDonald, L., et al. 1991. *Elder Abuse and Neglect in Canada*.

    Martin Matthews, A. 1991. *Widowhood in Later Life*.

    Chappell, N. 1992. *Social Support and Aging*.

Cole, T. and M. Winkler (eds). 1994. *The Oxford Book of Aging: Reflections on the Journey of Life*. New York: Oxford University Press.

Connidis, I. 2001. *Family Ties and Aging*. Thousand Oaks, Calif.: Sage.

Ekerdt, D. (ed.). 2002. *Encyclopedia of Aging*. New York: Macmillan.

Folts, W., et al. 1995. *Aging Well: A Selected, Annotated Bibliography*. Westport, Conn: Greenwood Press.

Harris, D. (ed.). 1988. *Dictionary of Gerontology*. New York: Greenwood Press.

Maddox, G. (ed.). 1995. *The Encyclopedia of Aging*. 2nd ed. New York: Springer.

National Advisory Council on Aging (NACA)

    The NACA Position on . . .—a series of policy papers with opinions and recommendations relating to older adults and an aging population.

    Writings in Gerontology—periodic reports that examine current aging issues in depth.

    The Forum Collection—a periodic information report to create public awareness and discussion.

    Expression—a newsletter with facts and opinions.

United Nations. 2002. *World Population Ageing, 1950–2050*. New York: United Nations.

Journals

Abstracts in Social Gerontology
Annual Review of Gerontology and Geriatrics
Canadian Journal on Aging
The Gerontologist
Journal of Gerontology: Social and Psychological Sciences
Canadian Population Studies
Canadian Public Policy
Death Studies
Health Reports
Canadian Journal of Public Health
Contemporary Long Term Care
Canadian Journal of Policy Research—Isuma
Canadian Social Trends

Ethics, Law and Aging Review
Journal of Palliative Care
Journal of Aging and Identity
Journal of Gerontology: Biological and Medical Sciences
Research on Aging
Journal of Aging Studies
Journal of Aging and Health
Journal of Aging and Identity
Journal of Applied Gerontology
Journal of Aging and Social Policy
Journal of Women and Aging
Journal of Cross-Cultural Gerontology
Journal of Elder Abuse and Neglect
Journal of Gerontological Social Work
Aging and Mental Health
The Public Policy and Aging Report
International Journal of Technology and Aging
Journal of Housing for the Elderly
Journal of Aging and Physical Activity
Contemporary Gerontology: A Journal of Reviews and Critical Discourse
Educational Gerontology
Journal of Educational Gerontology
Journal of Mental Health and Aging

Abstracts, Citation Indexes

Current Contents: Social and Behavioral Sciences
Gerontological Abstracts
Psychological Abstracts
Quarterly Index to Periodical Literature on Aging
Social Sciences Citation Index
Sociological Abstracts

Internet, World Wide Web, CD-Rom Sources

Note: Website addresses change. Those listed were correct as of early 2004. If an address is not accessible, consult with your instructor or use a search engine to locate the current address. In addition to the sites listed below, other sites are listed in the endnotes to many chapters.
- American Association of Retired Persons, http://www.aarp.org/
- Alzheimer's Information

www.alzheimer.ca
www.alzheimersresearchexchange.ca
- AARP Ageline Database, http://research.aarp.org/ageline
- Association for Gerontology in Higher Education, http://www.aghe.org/aghe
- United Nations, www.un.org
- Active Living, http://www.activeliving.ca/activeliving/index.html
- Canadian Association on Gerontology, http://www.cagacg.ca
- Canadian Association of Retired Persons, http://www.fifty-plus.net
- Caregiver Network, www.caregiver.com
- Canadian Hospice Palliative Care Association, www.chpca.net
- Ontario Palliative Care Association, www.ontariopalliativecare.org
- Canadian Home Care Association, www.cdnhomecare.on.ca
- Elderhostel, http://www.elderhostel.org/welcome/home.asp
- Gerontological Society of America, http://www.geron.org
- Geroweb Virtual Library on Aging http://www.iog.wayne.edu/GeroWebd/GeroWeb.html
- Health Canada, Division of Aging and Seniors, http://www.hc-sc.gc.ca/seniors-aines/
- National Advisory Council on Aging, www.hc.sc.gc.ca/seniors-aines/seniors/english/naca/naca.htm
- Statistics Canada, http://www.statcan.ca
- University of Manitoba Centre on Aging, http://www.umanitoba.ca/centres/aging
- Simon Fraser University Gerontology Research Centre http://www.harbour.sfu.ca/gero/info_services.html (for over 150 journals on aging topics)
- University of Waterloo, http://www.uwaterloo.ca/canu/index.html
- University of North Carolina Institute on Aging, http://www.aging.unc.edu (go to agelib, click on 'Find' for over 300 websites)
- Canadian Seniors Policies and Programs Database, http://www.sppd.gc.ca
- Canadian Mental Health Association, www.cmha.ca; wws.seniorsmentalhealth.ca
- Canadian Coalition for Seniors Mental Health, www.cccsmh.ca
- Canadian Health Services Research Foundation,

www.chsrf.ca
- Canadian Network for Third Age Learning, http://prometheus.ca.uregina.ca/catalist
- SeniorNet, www.seniornet.org/php/
- SeniorsCan, www.seniorscan.ca
- Older Volunteers, www.civicventures.org/index.html
- Canadian Social Research Links, www.canadiansocialresearch.net
- Global Demographic Statistics, www.census.gov./ftp/pub/ipc/www/
- McGraw-Hill Internet Guide to Sociology, www.mhhe.com/socscience/sociology/guide
- World Bank, www.worldbank.org/publications
- US Administration on Aging Elder Page, www.aoa.dhhs.gov/elderpage.html
- University of California, Electronic Library on Aging http://garnet.berkeley.edu/~aging/Electronic_library.html
- Guide to Internet Resources Related to Aging, www.aarp.org/cyber/guide1.htm
- Current Awareness in Aging Research—Weekly Report www.ssc.wisc.edu/cdha/caar/caar-index.htm
- Careers and Graduate Programs in Gerontology www.cagacg.ca (click on 'Education') www.gradschools.com/listings/menus/gerontology_menu.html www.careersinaging.com
- Religion and Aging, http://www.hrmoody.com/art3.html
- International Longevity Center—USA, www.ilcusa.org (click on 'Links')
- US National Institute on Aging, www.nih.gov.nia
- World Health Organization, www.who.int/en
- Veteran Affairs Canada Caregivers Resource, www.vac-acc.gc.ca/providers
- Government of Canada—Seniors Canada On-Line, www.seniors.gc.ca/index.jsp
- Canadian Policy Research Network, http://policyresearch.gc.ca
- Canada Mortgage and Housing Corporation, www.cmhc-schl.gc.ca/en/index.cfm
- Human Resources Development Canada www.hrdc-drhc.gc.ca http://labour-travail.hrdc-drhc.gc.ca/aging-workforce-en.cfm http://labour-travail.hrdc-drhc.gc.ca/work-life-balance-en.cfm
- McMaster University, Social and Economic Dimensions of an Aging Population (SEDAP), http://socserv.socsci.mcmaster.ca/sedap
- University of Alberta, Research on Aging, Policies and Praxis (RAPP) www.hecol.ualberta.ca/RAPP
- University of Western Ontario, Aging and Information Technology in the Workplace, www.wane.ca
- International Association of Gerontology, www.sfu.ca/iag/
- Canadian Institutes of Health Research, Institute of Aging www.cihr-irsc.gc.ca/institutes/ia/index_e.shtml
- Canadian Health Network—Seniors, www.canadian-health- network.ca/1seniors.html
- Canadian Institute for Health Information, http://secure.cihi.ca/cihiweb/splash.html

Audiovisual Sources

- National Film Board of Canada—films about aging and older adults
- University of Florida, http://aging.ufl.edu/apadiv20/cinema.htm
- University of Minnesota, www.gen.umn.edu/faculty-staff/yahnke/aging/intergen.htm
- *The Gerontologist*—each issue includes reviews of films and videos which include aging themes and topics
- The AV section of public and university libraries

Sources of Data

Centre on Aging 1996. *Manitoba Fact Book on Aging*. Winnipeg: Centre on Aging, University of Manitoba.

Elliott, G., et al. 1996. *Facts on Aging in Canada*. Hamilton, Ont.: Office of Gerontological Studies, McMaster University.

Gutman, G., et al. 2000. *Fact Book on Aging in British Columbia*. 3rd edn. Vancouver: Gerontology Research Centre, Simon Fraser University.

International Demographic Statistics http://www.

libraries.colorado.edu.gov/for/fordemo.html

Kinsella, K., and V. Velkoff. 2001. *An Aging World: 2001.* Washington, DC: US Government Printing Office.

McDaniel, S. 1987. *Canada's Aging Population.* Toronto: Butterworths.

Martin, L., and S. Preston (eds). 1994. *Demography of Aging.* Washington, DC: National Academy Press.

Moore, E., and M. Rosenberg 1997. *Growing Old in Canada.* Scarborough, Ont.: ITP Nelson.

National Archive of Computerized Data on Aging (NACDA) http://www.icpsr.umich.edu/NACDA.

Norland, J. 1994. *Profile of Canada's Seniors.* Ottawa: Statistics Canada.

Northcott, H. 1997. *Aging in Alberta.* 2nd ed. Calgary: Detselig Enterprises Ltd.

Statistics Canada (http://www.statcan.ca)
   Canadian Social Trends—a quarterly journal
   Report on the Demographic Situation in Canada (an annual report)
   The Daily, www.statcan.ca/english/dai-quo/
   2001 Census of Canada, http://www12.statcan.ca/english/census01/home/Index.cfm

INDEX